JDBC™ API Tutorial and Reference, Third Edition

JDBC™ API Tutorial and Reference, Third Edition

Maydene Fisher
Jon Ellis
Jonathan Bruce

✦✦ Addison-Wesley

Boston • San Francisco • New York • Toronto • Montreal
London • Munich • Paris • Madrid
Capetown • Sydney • Tokyo • Singapore • Mexico City

Library of Congress Cataloging-in-Publication Data
Fisher, Maydene.
 JDBC API tutorial and reference / Maydene Fisher, Jon Ellis, Jonathan Bruce.—3rd ed.
   p. cm.
 ISBN 0-321-17384-8 (alk. paper)
  1. Internet programming. 2. Database management. 3. Java (Computer program language) I. Ellis, Jonathan. II. Bruce, Jonathan. III. Title.

QA76.625.F57 2003
 005.75'6—dc21

                                                          2003050236

ISBN 0-321-17384-8
Text printed on recycled paper
1 2 3 4 5 6 7 8 9 10—CRS—0706050403
First printing, June 2003

Acknowledgments

THIS book is the result of many people's efforts. The specification for the JDBC 3.0 API is largely the work of Jon Ellis. Seth White and Mark Hapner wrote the specification for the JDBC 2.0 API, and Graham Hamilton and Rick Cattell wrote the specification for the JDBC 1.0 API. Maydene Fisher expanded the JDBC 1.0 specification into the first edition of this book, *JDBC*™ *Database Access with Java*™: *A Tutorial and Annotated Reference*. Working with Seth White, she expanded the JDBC 2.0 specification into the book *JDBC*™ *API Tutorial and Reference, Second Edition: Universal Data Access for the Java*™ *2 Platform*. Finally, working with Jon Ellis and Jonathan Bruce, she expanded the JDBC 3.0 specification into the current edition.

Many developers supplied input to the JDBC specifications and thereby contributed to their development, for which we are very grateful. We are also indebted to our reviewers, whose insightful comments were a great help. Peter den Haan deserves special mention for the quality and thoroughness of his comments.

A huge thank you goes to Alison Huml, who created and fine tuned the icons used throughout the book. Jon Ellis gets credit for the concept used in the cover design.

As always, many thanks are due to Lisa Friendly, the series editor, who makes the hard decisions and keeps things on track. Many people at Addison-Wesley helped with the book, and we especially want to thank Tyrrell Albaugh and Ann Sellers.

And, of course, none of this could have come to be without the loving and generous support of our families and friends.

We will be grateful to readers who alert us to errors by sending e-mail to

jdbc-book@sun.com

Errata for this book and information on other books in the Addison-Wesley Java Series will be posted at

http://java.sun.com/Series

Contents

Part Two

Part One

Part One contains material that introduces JDBC technology. The first chapter, "Introduction," briefly explains what JDBC technology is and presents overviews of the Java programming language and relational databases. The four tutorial chapters demonstrate how to use the JDBC API. "Basic Tutorial" walks you through the basic API, "Advanced Tutorial" shows how to use the functionality introduced in the JDBC 2.0 API and in the JDBC 3.0 API. "Metadata Tutorial" explains how to use the metadata API, and "Rowset Tutorial" demonstrates what you can do with rowsets.

CHAPTER 1

Introduction

THIS book covers all of the JDBC™ API, the application programming interface that provides universal data access for the Java™ programming language. The first edition covered the JDBC 1.0 API, which provides the basic functionality for data access. The second edition added the JDBC 2.0 API, which supplements the basic API with more advanced features. The 2.0 API provides a standard way to access the latest object-relational features being supported by today's relational database management systems. In addition, it includes features such as scrollable and updatable result sets and improved performance. Further, it extends JDBC technology beyond the client to the server with connection pooling and distributed transactions.

This third edition covers the complete JDBC 3.0 API. The specification for the JDBC 3.0 API combines all previous specifications, including the JDBC Optional Package specification, into one comprehensive document. It also adds new functionality, such as savepoints, auto-generated keys, and parameter metadata, plus enhancements to existing functionality. Beginning with the release of the Java™ 2 Platform, Standard Edition (J2SE™), version 1.4, the complete JDBC 3.0 API is bundled as part of the J2SE download. Previously, the JDBC Optional Package had to be downloaded separately.

A summary and complete list of the features added in the JDBC 2.0 API and JDBC 3.0 API can be found in Appendix B, starting on page 1121. An application will run successfully only if the driver and DBMS support all of the functionality it uses.

1.1   What the JDBC 3.0 API Includes

The JDBC 3.0 API includes all of the API in the `java.sql` package (sometimes called the core API) and the `javax.sql` package (the Optional Package API, formerly called the Standard Extension API).

The following list defines terms as they are used in this book.

- JDBC 3.0 API—the incorporation of all previous JDBC specifications plus the addition of new functionality.

- JDBC 2.0 API—the complete JDBC 2.0 API, including both the `java.sql` package (the JDBC 2.1 core API) and the `javax.sql` package (the JDBC Optional Package API).

- JDBC 2.0 core API—the JDBC 2.0 `java.sql` package. Some of the features introduced in this package are scrollable result sets, batch updates, programmatic updates, and support for the new SQL99 data types. For changes between JDBC 2.0 core API and JDBC 2.1 core API, see "Overview of JDBC 2.0 Core API Changes," on page 1132. In this book, "JDBC 2.0 core API" is a generic term that includes the JDBC 2.1 core API.

- JDBC Optional Package API—the package `javax.sql`. This package makes it easier to build server-side applications using the Java platform by providing an open architecture that supports connection pooling and distributed transactions that span multiple database servers. The `DataSource` API plays an integral part in these capabilities and also works with the Java™ Naming and Directory Interface™ (JNDI) to improve portability and make code maintenance easier. The `javax.sql` package also provides the `RowSet` API, which makes it easy to handle data sets from virtually any data source as JavaBeans™ components.

- `java.sql` package—the core JDBC API, including the JDBC 1.0, JDBC 1.1, JDBC 2.0, JDBC2.1, and JDBC 3.0 API.

- `javax.sql` package—the JDBC Optional Package API

The earliest book about the JDBC API in the Java Series, *JDBC™ Database Access with Java™*, covered only the JDBC 1.0 API. The second book, *JDBC™ API Tutorial and Reference, Second Edition,* built on the earlier one, updating the original material where necessary and adding a great deal of new material. In similar fashion, this book, *JDBC™ API Tutorial and Reference, Third Edition*, builds on the second edition, adding new material and revising existing material where necessary.

In keeping with the policy of maintaining backward compatibility, applications written using the JDBC 1.0 API will continue to run with both the Java 2 SDK, Standard Edition, and the Java 2 SDK, Enterprise Edition, just as they have always run. Having been well designed from the beginning, the JDBC 1.0 API is essentially unchanged. Applications using features added in the JDBC 2.0 API or 3.0 API will, of course, need to be run using a driver that supports those features.

1.2   Conventions Used in This Book

This book uses various conventions as aids to understanding or as a means of reducing repetition.

1.2.1   Fonts to Indicate Function

Different fonts indicate that text is being used in a special way.

FONT	USED FOR
`Lucida sans Typewriter`	code, which includes what would be typed in a source code file or at the command line; URLs; file names; keywords; name of a class, interface, exception, constructor, method, or field
italic code font	a variable used in text or in a method explanation
italic	a new term being introduced; emphasis
➥	the output of executing JDBC code

1.2.2   Icons to Indicate New Material

Some readers will be using drivers and data sources that do not yet implement the new features in the JDBC 3.0 API. Some will be using drivers that do not implement the JDBC 2.0 API. To make it easy to see what has been added to the JDBC 1.0 API, new material is marked with an icon to indicate when it was added.

New features in the JDBC 3.0 core API are marked with the 3.0 icon:

Features added in the JDBC 2.0 core API are marked with the 2.0 icon:

The JDBC Optional Package features are marked with the `javax.sql` icon:

Note that the `javax.sql` icon indicates API that was added in the 2.0 time frame. As of the JDBC 3.0 API specification, both the JDBC 2.0 core API and the JDBC Optional Package API are part of the JDBC 3.0 API. The icons indicate when the API was added.

If an entire reference chapter is new, it will have an icon to the right of the chapter title to indicate when it was introduced. New chapters also have an icon in the outer margin by the class or interface definition heading to indicate that all the API listed is new. For convenience, all explanations of new methods, constructors, and fields are individually marked with an icon so that someone looking up only a method or field can see whether it is new in the JDBC 2.0 API or the JDBC 3.0 API without checking for an icon at the beginning of the section.

In chapters where only some material is new, an icon will appear in the margin to indicate what is new. If an entire section is new, the icon will appear next to the section heading; an icon next to a paragraph indicates that part of the section, starting at the icon, is new. In the class or interface definition section and in the sections explaining constructors, methods, exceptions, or fields, an icon marks the API that is new.

Appendix B, "Summary of Changes," starting on page 1121, summarizes all of the new features and gives a complete list of what has been added to the JDBC API. The summary is divided into three sections: one for new features in the JDBC 3.0 API, one for the features added in the JDBC 2.0 core API, and another section for the Optional Package API.

1.2.3   Special Page Designations in the Index

The index uses "T" after a page number to indicate that material is in a tutorial. The designation "tb" after a page number means that the information is in a table.

1.2.4   SQLException **Is Implied in Method Explanations**

In Part Two, every method whose signature includes "throws SQLException", which is nearly every method in the JDBC API, may throw an SQLException. In the overwhelming majority of cases, this exception is thrown because there has been an error in attempting to access data. Access errors can be caused by a locking conflict, a deadlock, a permission violation, a key constraint (trying to insert a duplicate key, for instance), and so on.

To conserve space, one explanation of SQLException is given here rather than being repeated in nearly every method explanation throughout the reference section. In other words, the fact that a method throws an SQLException when there is an access error is implied for each and every method whose signature includes "throws SQLException." The Throws section in a method explanation is implied and not included when the only reason for throwing the SQLException is an access error. If an SQLException is thrown for any other reason, a Throws section gives the exception and the conditions that cause it to be thrown. Other exceptions that a method can throw are always listed and explained.

1.2.5   **Some Method Explanations Are Combined**

In order to avoid unnecessary repetition, the method explanations for some methods are combined.

- The getter methods and the updater methods in the ResultSet interface all have two basic versions, one that takes a column index as a parameter and one that takes a column name as a parameter. The explanations for both versions are combined into one entry. This also applies to the getter methods in the CallableStatement interface.

- Every getter and updater method in the ResultSet interface takes a column parameter. This parameter (a column index or a column name) is explained only once, at the beginning of the section "ResultSet Methods," on page 730. The explanation is implied for every ResultSet getter method and for every ResultSet updater method rather than being repeated for each method.

- The three versions of the `DriverManager.getConnection` method are combined into one entry.

1.3   Contents of the Book

As was true with the previous editions, this book is really two books in one: a tutorial and the definitive reference manual for the JDBC API. The goal is to be useful to a wide range of readers, from database novices to database experts. Therefore, we have arranged the book so that information needed only by experts is separate from the basic material. We hope that driver developers and application server developers as well as application programmers and MIS administrators will find what they need. Because different sections are aimed at different audiences, we do not expect that everyone will necessarily read every page. We have sometimes duplicated explanations in an effort to make reading easier for those who do not read all sections.

1.3.1   Part One

Part One includes five chapters, an introduction and four tutorial chapters. Part Two, the reference manual, has a chapter for each class or interface, a chapter on the DISTINCT data type, a chapter on how SQL and Java types are mapped to each other, two appendices, a glossary, and an index.

Chapter 1, "Introduction," outlines the contents of the book and gives overviews of the Java programming language and SQL. The overview of the Java programming language summarizes many concepts and is not intended to be complete. We suggest that anyone who is unfamiliar with the language refer to one of the many excellent books available. The overview of relational databases and SQL likewise covers only the highlights and presents only basic terminology and concepts.

Chapter 2, "Basic Tutorial," walks the reader through how to use the basic JDBC API, giving many examples along the way. The emphasis is on showing how to execute the more common tasks rather than on giving exhaustive examples of every possible feature.

Chapter 3, "Advanced Tutorial," starting on page 113, covers the new features added to the `java.sql` package in the JDBC 3.0 API and the JDBC 2.0 core API and also some of the features from the `javax.sql` package. Although the data types and new functionality can be considered advanced in relation to the material in the basic tutorial, one does not need to be an advanced programmer to learn how to use them. On the contrary, one of the strengths of the new JDBC API is that it makes using the new features easy and convenient.

Chapter 4, "Metadata Tutorial," shows how to use the JDBC metadata API, which is used to get information about result sets, databases, and the parameters to PreparedStatement objects. It will be of most interest to those who need to write applications that adapt themselves to the specific capabilities of several database systems or to the content of any database.

Chapter 5, "Rowset Tutorial," gives examples of how to use rowsets and summarizes the RowSet reference implementations that are being developed to serve as standards for further implementations.

1.3.2 Part Two

Part Two is the definitive reference manual for the complete JDBC 3.0 API. Thus it covers both the core JDBC API (the java.sql package) and the Optional Package JDBC API (the javax.sql package).

Chapters 6 through 50, which are arranged alphabetically for easy reference, cover all of the JDBC classes and interfaces. The only chapter that does not refer to a class or interface is Chapter 19 on the JDBC type DISTINCT; this data type maps to a built-in type rather than to a JDBC class or interface.

Chapter overviews generally show how to create an instance of the class or interface and how that instance is commonly used. Overviews also present a summary of what the class or interface contains and explanatory material as needed.

The class and interface definitions list the constructors, methods, and fields, grouping them in logical order (as opposed to the alphabetical order used in the sections that explain them).

Sections for explanations of each constructor, method, and field follow the class or interface definition. The explanations in these sections are in alphabetical order to facilitate looking them up quickly.

Chapter 50, "Mapping SQL and Java Types," which explains the standard mapping of Java and SQL types, includes tables showing the various mappings.

Appendix A, "For Driver Writers," contains information for driver writers, including requirements, allowed variations, and notes on security.

Appendix B, "Summary of Changes," summarizes the new features in the JDBC 3.0 API and the JDBC 2.0 API. It presents a complete list of every new interface, class, exception, constructor, method, and field. The summary for the JDBC 3.0 API comes first, followed by summaries of the JDBC 2.0 core API and the JDBC Optional Package API. This is followed by a list of the API that has been deprecated, which includes the API to use in place of the deprecated API, where applicable. The last part of Appendix B gives a brief history of API changes, going back to the beginning, and also explains various early design decisions. This section should answer some questions about how JDBC got to its present form.

Completing the book are a glossary and a comprehensive index, which we hope readers find helpful and easy to use.

A Quick Reference Card can be found inside the back cover. It includes the most commonly used methods and SQL/Java type mappings.

1.3.3   Suggested Order for Reading Chapters

This section suggests an order in which to read chapters for the person learning how to use the JDBC API. There is no right or wrong way, and some may find another order better for them. For example, some people may find it more helpful to read relevant reference chapters before they look at the tutorials. Some may prefer to read only the tutorials. The only firm suggestions are that beginners should read Chapters 1 and 2 first and that everyone should read the section "Conventions Used in This Book," on page 5. The following is one suggested order for reading chapters:

1. Chapter 1, Introduction

2. Chapter 2, Basic Tutorial
   - ResultSet
   - Chapters on SQL statements
     - Statement
     - PreparedStatement
     - CallableStatement
   - Connection
   - Chapters on establishing a connection
     - DriverManager
     - DataSource

3. Chapter 3, Advanced Tutorial

- Mapping SQL and Java Types

- SQL99 Types

  - Clob
  - Blob
  - Array
  - Struct
  - Ref

- Exceptions

  - SQLException
  - BatchUpdateException
  - SQLWarning
  - DataTruncation

4. Chapter 5, Rowset Tutorial

- Rowset

5. Chapter 4, Metadata Tutorial

- ResultSetMetaData

- DatabaseMetaData

- ParameterMetaData

1.3.4 Where to Find Information by Topic

This section groups chapters together by topic to make it easier to find information about a particular topic. Each topic gives the chapter to read for an overall explanation, the tutorial in which the topic is illustrated, and a list of related chapters. The Index is the place to look for more specific topics.

Executing SQL statements
  - Overall explanation: Statement
  - Tutorial: Basic Tutorial
  - Related chapters: PreparedStatement, CallableStatement

Batch updates
  - Overall explanation: Statement

- Tutorial: Advanced Tutorial
- Related chapters: PreparedStatement, CallableStatement, BatchUpdate-Exception

Custom mapping
- Overall explanation: Struct, SQLData
- Tutorial: Advanced Tutorial
- Related chapters: SQLInput, SQLOutput
- Explanation of type maps: Connection

Rowsets
- Overall explanation: RowSet
- Tutorial: Rowset Tutorial
- Related chapters: RowSetEvent, RowSetListener, RowSetInternal, RowSetMetaData, RowSetReader, RowSetWriter

Connection pooling
- Overall explanation: PooledConnection
- Tutorial: Advanced Tutorial
- Related chapters: ConnectionPoolDataSource, ConnectionEvent, Connection Event Listener, DataSource

Transactions
- Overall explanation: Connection
- Tutorial: Basic Tutorial

Distributed transactions
- Overall explanation: XAConnection
- Tutorial: Advanced Tutorial, Rowset Tutorial
- Related chapter: DataSource, XADataSource

Date-related types
- Overall explanation: Date
- Related chapters: Time, Timestamp

User-defined types
- Overall explanation: Struct, Distinct
- Tutorial: Advanced Tutorial
- Related chapters: See custom mapping chapters

1.3.5   Resources on the Web

This section lists the URLs for getting information about the JDBC API and related technologies.

- JDBC 3.0 specification, JDBC 1.0 API specification, JDBC 2.1 Core API specification, and JDBC 2.0 Optional Package API specification

  `http://java.sun.com/products/jdbc`

- Java Transaction API (JTA)

  `http://java.sun.com/products/jta`

- Java Transaction Service (JTS)

  `http://java.sun.com/products/jts`

- Java Naming and Directory Interface (JNDI)

  `http://java.sun.com/products/jndi`

- Enterprise JavaBeans (EJB)

  `http://java.sun.com/products/ejb`

1.4   What Is the JDBC API?

The JDBC API is a Java API for accessing virtually any kind of tabular data. (As a point of interest, JDBC is a trademarked name and is not an acronym; nevertheless, JDBC is often thought of as standing for "Java Database Connectivity." Originally, JDBC was the only trademarked name for the data source access API, but more recently, Java™ DataBase Connectivity has been added as a second trademarked name.) The JDBC API consists of a set of classes and interfaces written in the Java programming language that provide a standard API for tool/database developers and makes it possible to write industrial-strength database applications entirely in the Java programming language.

The JDBC API makes it easy to send SQL statements to relational database systems and supports all dialects of SQL. But the JDBC API goes beyond SQL, also making it possible to interact with other kinds of data sources, such as files containing tabular data.

The value of the JDBC API is that an application can access virtually any data source and run on any platform with a Java Virtual Machine. In other words, with the JDBC API, it isn't necessary to write one program to access a Sybase database, another program to access an Oracle database, another program to access an

IBM DB2 database, and so on. One can write a single program using the JDBC API, and the program will be able to send SQL or other statements to the appropriate data source. And, with an application written in the Java programming language, one doesn't have to worry about writing different applications to run on different platforms. The combination of the Java platform and the JDBC API lets a programmer "write once and run anywhere™." We explain more about this later.

The Java programming language, being robust, secure, easy to use, easy to understand, and automatically downloadable on a network, is an excellent language basis for database applications. What is needed is a way for Java applications to talk to a variety of different data sources. The JDBC API provides the mechanism for doing this.

The JDBC API extends what can be done with the Java platform. For example, the JDBC API makes it possible to publish a web page containing an applet that uses information obtained from a remote data source. Or, an enterprise can use the JDBC API to connect all its employees (even if they are using a conglomeration of Windows, Macintosh, and UNIX machines) to one or more internal databases via an intranet. With more and more programmers using the Java programming language, the need for easy and universal data access from the Java programming language continues to grow.

MIS managers like the combination of the Java platform and JDBC technology because it makes disseminating information easy and economical. Businesses can continue to use their installed databases and access information easily even if it is stored on different database management systems or other data sources. Development time for new applications is short. Installation and version control are greatly simplified. A programmer can write an application or an update once, put it on the server, and then everybody has access to the latest version. And for businesses selling information services, the combination of the Java and JDBC technologies offers a better way of distributing information updates to external customers.

We will discuss various ways to use the JDBC API in more detail later.

1.4.1   What Does the JDBC API Do?

In simplest terms, a JDBC technology-based driver ("JDBC driver") makes it possible to do three things:

1. Establish a connection with a data source

2. Send queries and update statements to the data source

3. Process the results

The following code fragment gives a simple example of these three steps:

```
Connection con = DriverManager.getConnection(
                    "jdbc:myDriver:wombat", "myLogin", "myPassword");
Statement stmt = con.createStatement();
ResultSet rs = stmt.executeQuery("SELECT a, b, c FROM Table1");
while (rs.next()) {
    int x = rs.getInt("a");
    String s = rs.getString("b");
    float f = rs.getFloat("c");
}
```

1.4.2   A Base for Other APIs

The JDBC API is used to invoke (or "call") SQL commands directly. It works very well in this capacity and is easier to use than other database connectivity APIs, but it was also designed to be a base upon which to build alternate interfaces and tools. An alternate interface tries to be "user-friendly" by using a more understandable or more convenient API that is translated behind the scenes into the JDBC API. Because the JDBC API is complete and powerful enough to be used as a base, it has had various kinds of alternate APIs developed on top of it, including the following:

1. An embedded SQL for Java
   A consortium including Oracle, IBM, Sun, and others has defined the SQLJ specification to provide an embedded SQL for the Java programming language. JDBC technology requires that SQL statements basically be passed as uninterpreted strings to Java methods. An embedded SQL preprocessor provides compile-time type checking and allows a programmer to intermix SQL statements with Java programming language statements. For example, a Java variable can be used in an SQL statement to receive or provide SQL values. The SQLJ preprocessor effectively translates this Java/SQL mix into the Java programming language with JDBC calls.

   The SQLJ specification is currently evolving to support JDBC 3.0 features such as savepoints, multiple open ResultSet objects, and the DATALINK data type.

2. Technologies for persisting Java objects

Two Java technologies provide the ability to map Java objects to relational databases: Java™ Data Objects (JDO) API, developed through the Java Community Process as JSR 12, and Enterprise JavaBeans™ (EJB™) technologies (Container Managed Persistence (CMP) and Bean Managed Persistence (BMP)). With these technologies, data in a data store can be mapped to Java objects, and Java objects can be stored persistently in a data store.

For example, some of the the most popular JDO implementations use JDBC to map from Java classes to relational database tables. Each row of the table represents an instance of the class, and each column represents a field of that instance. The JDO specification provides a standard API to access the rows and columns of relational databases as if they were native Java objects stored in the database.

The JDO API provides transparent database access, letting a programmer write code in the Java programming language that accesses an underlying data store without using any database-specific code, such as SQL. To make this possible, a JDO implementation might use SQL and the JDBC API behind the scenes to access data in a relational database. The JDO API also provides a query language, JDOQL, that allows a user to write a query using Java boolean predicates to select persistent instances from the data store. When a relational database is being accessed, these queries are mapped under the covers directly to SQL queries and executed via the JDBC API. EJB technology also provides its own query language, the Enterprise JavaBeans Query Language (EJBQL).

JDO technology provides a way to persist plain old Java objects. As such , it complements rather than competes with JDBC technology. JDO technology also complements the CMP and BMP technologies, offering an alternative way to persist objects. The difference is that EJB technology uses entity beans to persist business components, whereas JDO technology persists general Java objects. Both can use the JDBC API "under the covers" in their implementations.

For more information on the JDO API, see

```
http://java.sun.com/products/jdo
```

The JDO user community can be reached at

> `http://JDOCentral.com`

Information about EJB technology is available at

> `http://java.sun.com/products/ejb`

3. Tools making it easier to use the JDBC API

    As interest in JDBC technology has grown, various tools based on the JDBC API have been developed to make building programs easier. For example, an application might present a menu of database tasks from which to choose. After a task is selected, the application presents prompts and blanks for filling in information needed to carry out the selected task. With the requested input typed in, the application then automatically invokes the necessary JDBC commands. With the help of such a tool, users can perform database tasks even when they have little or no knowledge of SQL syntax.

1.4.3 The JDBC API versus ODBC

Prior to the development of the JDBC API, Microsoft's ODBC (Open DataBase Connectivity) API was the most widely used programming interface for accessing relational databases. It offers the ability to connect to almost all databases on almost all platforms. So why not just use ODBC from the Java programming language?

The answer is that you can use ODBC from the Java programming language, but this is best done with the help of the JDBC API by using the JDBC–ODBC Bridge, which we will cover shortly. The question now becomes, "Why do you need the JDBC API?" There are several answers to this question.

1. ODBC is not appropriate for direct use from the Java programming language because it uses a C interface. Calls from Java to native C code have a number of drawbacks in the security, implementation, robustness, and automatic portability of applications.

2. A literal translation of the ODBC C API into a Java API would not be desirable. For example, Java has no pointers (address variables), and ODBC makes copious use of them, including the notoriously error-prone generic pointervoid *. You can think of JDBC as ODBC translated into a high-level

object-oriented interface that is natural for programmers using the Java programming language.

3. ODBC is hard to learn. It mixes simple and advanced features together, and it has complex options even for simple queries. The JDBC API, on the other hand, was designed to keep simple things simple while allowing more advanced capabilities where required. The JDBC API is also easier to use simply because it is a Java API, which means that a programmer does not need to worry about either memory management or data byte alignment.

4. A Java API like JDBC is needed in order to enable a "pure Java" solution, that is, a solution that uses only Java API. When ODBC is used, the ODBC driver manager and drivers must be manually installed on every client machine. When the JDBC driver is written completely in Java, however, JDBC code is automatically installable, portable, and secure on all Java platforms, from network computers to mainframes.

5. The JDBC 3.0 API includes functionality that is not available with ODBC. For example, ODBC does not support SQL99 data types, auto-generated keys, or savepoints.

In summary, the JDBC API is a natural Java interface for working with SQL. It builds on ODBC rather than starting from scratch, so programmers familiar with ODBC will find it very easy to learn. The JDBC API retains some of the basic design features of ODBC; in fact, both interfaces are based on the Open Group (formerly X/Open) SQL CLI (Call Level Interface). The big difference is that the JDBC API builds on and reinforces the style and virtues of the Java programming language, and it goes beyond just sending SQL statements to a relational database management system.

Microsoft has introduced new APIs beyond ODBC such as OLE DB, ADO (ActiveX Data Objects), and ADO.NET. In many ways these APIs move in the same direction as the JDBC API. For example, they are also object-oriented interfaces to databases that can be used to execute SQL statements. However, OLE DB is a low-level interface designed for tools rather than developers. ADO and ADO.NET are newer and more like the JDBC API and the RowSet interface, but they are not pure Java and therefore do not provide portable implementations.

1.4.4   Two-tier and Three-tier Models

The JDBC API supports both two-tier and three-tier models for database access. Figure 1.1 illustrates a two-tier architecture for data access.

Figure 1.1: Two-tier Model

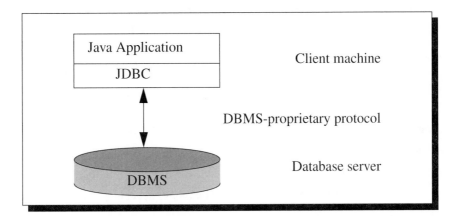

In the two-tier model, a Java applet or application talks directly to the data source. This requires a JDBC driver that can communicate with the particular data source being accessed. A user's commands are delivered to the database or other data source, and the results of those statements are sent back to the user. The data source may be located on another machine to which the user is connected via a network. This is referred to as a *client/server* configuration, with the user's machine as the client and the machine housing the data source as the server. The network can be an intranet, which, for example, connects employees within a corporation, or it can be the Internet.

In the three-tier model, commands are sent to a "middle tier" of services, which then sends the commands to the data source. The data source processes the commands and sends the results back to the middle tier, which then sends them to the user. MIS directors find the three-tier model very attractive because the middle tier makes it possible to maintain control over access and the kinds of updates that can be made to corporate data. Another advantage is that it simplifies the deployment of applications. Finally, in many cases, the three-tier architecture can provide performance advantages.

Figure 1.2 illustrates a three-tier architecture for database access.

Figure 1.2:   JDBC Three-tier Model

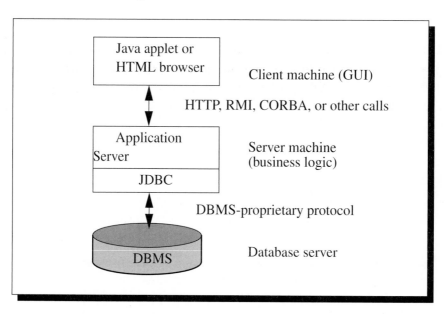

At one time, the middle tier was typically written in languages such as C or C++, which offer fast performance. However, with the introduction of optimizing compilers that translate Java bytecode into efficient machine-specific code and the widespread adoption and success of the J2EE platform, the Java platform has become the standard for middle-tier development. This lets developers take advantage of the robustness, multithreading, and security features that the Java programming language offers plus features such as enhanced security, connection pooling, and distributed transactions available with the J2EE platform.

Thus, the JDBC API plays an essential role in both two-tier and three-tier architectures. With enterprises using the Java programming language for writing server code, the JDBC API is being used extensively in the middle tier of a three-tier architecture. Some of the features that make JDBC a server technology are its support for connection pooling, distributed transactions, and disconnected rowsets, all of which are explained later in the book. And, of course, the JDBC API is what allows access to a data source from a middle tier written in the Java programming language.

1.4.5   SQL Conformance

SQL is the standard language for accessing relational databases. Unfortunately, SQL is not yet as standard as one would like.

One area of difficulty is that data types used by different DBMSs (DataBase Management Systems) sometimes vary, and the variations can be significant. JDBC deals with this by defining a set of generic SQL type identifiers in the class `java.sql.Types`. Note that, as used in this book, the terms "JDBC SQL type," "JDBC type," and "SQL type" are interchangeable and refer to the generic SQL type identifiers defined in `java.sql.Types`. There is a more complete discussion of data type conformance in "Mapping SQL and Java Types," starting on page 1065. The section "JDBC Types Mapped to Database-specific SQL Types," on page 1093, shows vendor-specific data types.

Another area of difficulty with SQL conformance is that although most DBMSs use a standard form of SQL for basic functionality, they do not conform to the more recently defined standard SQL syntax or semantics for more advanced functionality. For example, not all databases support stored procedures or outer joins, and those that do are not always consistent with each other. Also, support for SQL99 features and data types varies greatly. It is hoped that the portion of SQL that is truly standard will expand to include more and more functionality. In the meantime, however, the JDBC API must support SQL as it is.

One way the JDBC API deals with this problem is to allow any query string to be passed through to an underlying DBMS driver. This means that an application is free to use as much SQL functionality as desired, but it runs the risk of receiving an error on some DBMSs. In fact, an application query may be something other than SQL, or it may be a specialized derivative of SQL designed for specific DBMSs (for document or image queries, for example).

A second way JDBC deals with problems of SQL conformance is to provide ODBC-style escape clauses, which are discussed in "SQL Escape Syntax in Statements," on page 958. The escape syntax provides a standard JDBC syntax for several of the more common areas of SQL divergence. For example, there are escapes for date literals and for stored procedure calls.

For complex applications, JDBC deals with SQL conformance in a third way. It provides descriptive information about the DBMS by means of the interface `DatabaseMetaData` so that applications can adapt to the requirements and capabilities of each DBMS. Typical end users need not worry about metadata, but experts may want to refer to Chapter 15, "DatabaseMetaData," starting on page 449.

Because the JDBC API is used as a base API for developing database access tools and other APIs, it also has to address the problem of conformance for anything built on it. A JDBC driver must support at least ANSI SQL92 Entry Level. (ANSI SQL92 refers to the standards adopted by the American National Standards Institute in 1992. Entry Level refers to a specific list of SQL capabilities.) Note, however, that although the JDBC 2.0 API includes support for SQL99 and SQLJ, JDBC drivers are not required to support them.

Given the wide acceptance of the JDBC API by database vendors, connectivity vendors, Internet service vendors, and application writers, it has become the standard for data access from the Java programming language.

1.4.6   Products Based on JDBC Technology

The JDBC API is a natural choice for developers using the Java platform because it offers easy database access for Java applications and applets.

JDBC technology has gathered significant momentum since its introduction, and many products based on JDBC technology have been developed. You can monitor the status of these products by consulting the JDBC web site for the latest information. It can be found at the following URL:

```
http://java.sun.com/products/jdbc
```

1.4.7   JDBC Product Framework

Sun Microsystems provides a framework of JDBC product components:

- the JDBC driver manager (included as part of the Java 2 Platform)

- the JDBC–ODBC bridge (included in the Solaris and Windows versions of the Java 2 Platform)

- The JDBC API Test Suite (available from the JDBC web site)

The JDBC `DriverManager` class has traditionally been the backbone of the JDBC architecture. It is quite small and simple; its primary function is to connect Java applications to the correct JDBC driver and then get out of the way. With the availability of the `javax.naming` and `javax.sql` packages, it is now also possible to use a `DataSource` object registered with a Java Naming and Directory Interface (JNDI) naming service to establish a connection with a data source. Both means of getting a connection can be still used, but using a `DataSource` object is recommended whenever possible.

The JDBC–ODBC bridge driver allows ODBC drivers to be used as JDBC drivers. It was implemented as a way to get JDBC technology off the ground quickly, providing a way to access some of the data sources for which there were no JDBC drivers. Currently, however, there are a large number of JDBC drivers available, which greatly reduces the need for the JDBC–ODBC bridge driver.

Even though the JDBC–ODBC bridge driver has been updated to include some of the more advanced features of the JDBC API, it is not intended for use developing products. It is intended to be used only for prototyping or when no JDBC driver is available.

A further component in the framework is the JDBC API driver test suite, which is aimed at driver developers. It comes in two versions: the JDBC API Test Suite v1.2.1 and the JDBC API Test Suite v.1.3.1. These test suites cover J2EE compatibility and indicate whether a driver is compatible with other products that conform to the J2EE specification. More complete information, including download information, can be found in the section "JDBC Test Suite," on page 1116.

1.4.8   JDBC Driver Types

The JDBC drivers that we are aware of at this time generally fit into one of four categories:

1. *JDBC–ODBC bridge driver plus ODBC driver:* The Sun Microsystems bridge product provides JDBC access via ODBC drivers. Note that ODBC binary code, and in many cases database client code, must be loaded on each client machine that uses this driver. As a result, this kind of driver is most appropriate on a corporate network where client installations are not a major problem or for application server code written in Java in a three-tier architecture.

2. *Native-API partly Java driver:* This kind of driver converts JDBC calls into calls on the client API for Oracle, Sybase, Informix, IBM DB2, or other DBMSs. Note that, like the bridge driver, this style of driver requires that some operating system-specific binary code be loaded on each client machine.

3. *JDBC-Net pure Java driver:* This driver translates JDBC calls into a DBMS-independent net protocol, which is then translated to a DBMS protocol by a server. This net server middleware is able to connect its pure Java clients to many different databases. The specific protocol used depends on the vendor.

In general, this is the most flexible JDBC alternative. It is likely that all vendors of this solution will provide products suitable for intranet use. In order for these products to support Internet access as well, they must handle the additional requirements for security, access through firewalls, and so forth, that the Web imposes.

4. *Native-protocol pure Java driver:* This kind of driver converts JDBC calls directly into the network protocol used by DBMSs. This allows a direct call from the client machine to the DBMS server and is an excellent solution for intranet access. Several that are now available include Oracle, Sybase, IBM DB2, Borland InterBase, and Microsoft SQL Server.

Figure 1.3 illustrates various types of driver implementations.

Figure 1.3: JDBC Driver Implementations

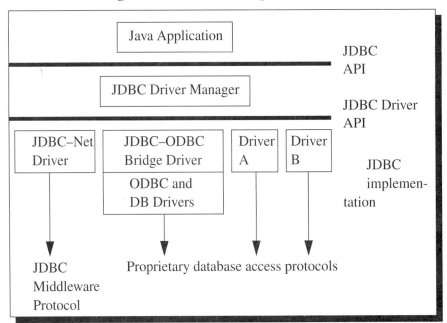

Driver categories 3 and 4 are the preferred way to access databases using the JDBC API. Driver categories 1 and 2 are interim solutions where direct pure Java drivers are not yet available. There are possible variations on categories 1 and 2 (not shown in the table "Driver Categories," on page 25) that require middleware, but these are generally less desirable solutions. Categories 3 and 4 offer all the advantages of Java technology, including automatic installation (for example, downloading the JDBC driver with an applet that uses it).

Table 1.1 shows the four categories and their properties. The table uses the following definitions for types of network connections:

- Direct—a connection that a JDBC client makes directly to the DBMS server, which may be remote

- Indirect—a connection that a JDBC client makes to a middleware process that acts as a bridge to the DBMS server

Table 1.1: Driver Categories

Driver Category	All Java	Network Connection
1. JDBC–ODBC Bridge	No	Direct
2. Native API as basis	No	Direct
3. JDBC-Net	client, Yes server, Maybe	Indirect
4. Native protocol as basis	Yes	Direct

1.4.9   Obtaining JDBC Drivers

The web site for the JDBC API maintains a database with information about JDBC drivers, including what type they are and what functionality they support. There are currently over 200 drivers in this database, which you can search to find a driver that fits your needs. To get the latest information, check the web site at

```
http://industry.java.sun.com/products/jdbc/drivers
```

1.4.10 Java-relational DBMSs

A new generation of DBMSs that are Java-aware has been emerging. These new DBMSs, called Java-relational DBMSs, include new data types that allow an object in the Java programming language to be used as a column value in a database table. The JDBC 2.0 and 3.0 features support this new generation of DBMSs, and several database vendors are creating products with Java-relational capabilities. It should be noted, however, that the 2.0 and 3.0 mechanisms are optional. If a DBMS does not support a particular feature, a JDBC driver is not required to implement it.

1.4.11 Other Products

Various application development tools using JDBC technology are under way. Watch the `java.sun.com/products/jdbc` web pages for updates.

1.5   The JDBC API and the Java Platforms

The JDBC API has become increasingly important to all three Java Platforms: the Java™ 2 Platform, Standard Edition (J2SE™); the Java™ 2 Platform, Enterprise Edition (J2EE™); and the Java™ 2 Platform, Micro Edition (J2ME™).

1.5.1   The JDBC API and the J2SE Platform

Database applications have long played an important role in business, scientific, government, and many other kinds of computer programs. The importance of the ability to store and retrieve data reliably cannot be overstated. In fact, database access is the foundation for the bulk of applications written today. As a result, JDBC is one of the essential APIs for J2SE, reflected by the fact that beginning with J2SE, version 1.4, the complete JDBC 3.0 API is bundled with the J2SE download. The core JDBC API has always been part of the J2SE platform, and now the JDBC Optional Package is also included.

1.5.2   The JDBC API and the J2EE Platform

Enterprise applications almost always depend on retrieving data from a DBMS. Furthermore, they often need to get data from more than one database server and handle an increasingly large volume of transactions. The `javax.sql` package provides the ability to pool database connections, thereby reducing the amount of resources needed and increasing performance. Added to that, it also provides the ability to use distributed transactions, which has become increasingly necessary, especially with the growth of Web services.

The J2EE platform simplifies the development of complex distributed applications by providing the "plumbing" for services such as security, distributed transactions, and connection pooling. A J2EE application server works with

JDBC `DataSource` implementations to supply the infrastructure required for distributed transactions and connection pooling.

The need for a J2EE application server to connect with a JDBC driver is so great that the JDBC team has been developing a component called the JDBC Connector. The JDBC Connector, based on the Connector 1.0 and Connector 1.5 specifications, allows any JDBC driver to be plugged in to any J2EE application server that adheres to the Connector specification requirements. As of this writing, the JDBC Connector is available as an early access release from the Java Developer Connection web site. Information is available at

```
http://java.sun.com/products/jdbc/related.html
```

The download includes documentation explaining how the JDBC Connector works and how to use it to plug a JDBC driver in to a J2EE application server. Driver vendors should check the section "Connectors," on page 1117.

1.5.3   The JDBC API and the J2ME Platform

The Java programming language is ideal for the burgeoning market of small devices. To make database access possible from the Java programming language for small devices, a community of experts is developing a subset of the JDBC API to achieve a smaller footprint while still providing useful database operations. These experts are developing this pared-down JDBC API through the Java Community Process[SM] as JSR (Java Specification Request) 169.

The remainder of this chapter gives a brief overview of the Java programming language and of SQL, a language for defining, accessing, and manipulating data in a relational database. Readers familiar with the Java programming language can skip "Java Overview," starting on page 27; readers familiar with SQL can skip "Relational Database Overview," starting on page 38.

1.6   Java Overview

The Java programming language is a powerful but lean object-oriented programming language. It originally generated a lot of excitement because it makes it possible to program for the Internet by creating applets, programs that can be embedded in a web page. The content of an applet is limited only by one's imagination. For example, an applet can be an animation with sound, an interactive game (that could include various animations with sound), or a ticker tape with constantly updated stock prices. Applets can be just little decorations to liven up a web page, or they can be serious applications such as word processors or spreadsheets.

But Java technology is far more than a programming language for writing applets. It has become one of the standard languages for general-purpose and business programming. With the development of the Java 2 SDK, Enterprise Edition, and its "industrial strength" capabilities, Java technology has become more and more pervasive in the enterprise arena. There are many buzzwords associated with the Java platform, but because of its spectacular growth in popularity, one buzzword has taken hold: *ubiquitous*. Indeed, all indications are that it will soon be everywhere.

Java builds on the strengths of C++. It has taken the best features of C++ and discarded the more problematic and error-prone parts. To this lean core it has added garbage collection (automatic memory management), multithreading (the capacity for one program to do more than one thing at a time), and security capabilities. The result is that Java is simple, elegant, powerful, and easy to use.

Java is actually a platform consisting of three components: (1) the Java programming language, (2) the Java library of classes and interfaces, and (3) the Java Virtual Machine. The following sections will say more about these components.

1.6.1 Java Is Portable

One of the biggest advantages Java technology offers is that it is portable. An application written in the Java programming language will run on all of the major platforms. Any computer with a Java-based browser can run applets written in the Java programming language. A programmer no longer has to write one program to run on a Macintosh, another program to run on a Windows machine, still another to run on a Solaris or Linux machine, and so on. In other words, with Java technology, developers write their programs only once.

The Java Virtual Machine is what gives the Java programming language its cross-platform capabilities. Rather than being compiled into a machine language, which is different for each operating system and computer architecture, Java code is compiled into bytecodes. This makes Java applications bytecode portable.

With other languages, program code is compiled into a language that the computer can understand. The problem is that other computers with different machine instruction sets cannot understand that language. Java code, on the other hand, is compiled into bytecodes rather than a machine language. These bytecodes go to the Java Virtual Machine, which executes them directly or translates them into the language that is understood by the machine running it.

In summary, with the JDBC API extending Java technology, a programmer writing Java code can access virtually any data source on any platform that supports the Java Virtual Machine.

1.6.2   Java Is Object-oriented

The Java programming language is object-oriented, which makes program design focus on *what* is being dealt with rather than on *how* to do something. This makes it more useful for programming in sophisticated projects because one can break things down into understandable components. A big benefit is that these components can then be reused.

Object-oriented languages use the paradigm of classes. In simplest terms, a class includes both data and the functions to operate on that data. You can create an *instance* of a class, also called an *object*, which will have all the data members and functionality of its class. Because of this, you can think of a class as being like a template, with each object being a specific instance of a particular type of class. For example, suppose you have a very simple class called Person, which has three *fields* (a data member is called a *field* in Java) and one *method* (a function is called a *method* in Java). The following code illustrates creating a simplified class. Don't worry if you don't understand everything in this example; just try to get a general idea. The first thing inside the beginning brace ({) is a constructor, a special kind of method that creates an instance of a class and sets its fields with their initial values.

```
public class Person {
    public Person(String n, int a, String oc) {
        name = n;
        age = a;
        occupation = oc;
    }
    public void identifySelf() {
        System.out.print("I am " + name + ", a " + age);
        System.out.println("-year-old " + occupation + ".");
    }
    protected String name;     // three attributes of Person
    protected int age;
```

```
        protected String occupation;
    }
```

The last three items are *fields*, which are attributes of a `Person` object. They are given the access specifier `protected`, which means that these fields can be used by subclasses of `Person` but not by any other classes. (We will explain subclasses later in this section.) If the access specifier had been `private`, only the class `Person` could access these fields. The access specifier `public` allows access by all classes.

The following code creates an instance of `Person` and stores it in the variable *p*. This means that *p* is of type `Person`—a new class is a new type. This newly created instance of `Person`, *p*, is given the name, age, and occupation that were supplied to the constructor for `Person`. Note that the method `new` is used with a constructor to create a new instance of a class.

```
Person p = new Person("Adela", 37, "astronomer");
```

The following line of code causes *p* to identify herself. The results follow. (Note that the curved arrow signifies a line of output and is not part of the actual output.)

```
p.identifySelf();
```

➥ I am Adela, a 37-year-old astronomer.

The following code creates a second instance of `Person` and invokes the method `identifySelf`:

```
Person q = new Person("Hakim", 22, "student");
q.identifySelf();
```

➥ I am Hakim, a 22-year-old student.

The class paradigm allows one to *encapsulate* data so that specific data values or function implementations cannot be seen by those using the class. In the class `Person`, the fields `name`, `age`, and `occupation` are all given the access modifier `protected`, which signifies that these fields can be assigned values only by using methods in the class that defines them or in its subclasses—in this case, class `Person` or a subclass of `Person`.

In other words, the only way a user can change the value of private or protected fields in a class is to use the methods supplied by the class. In our example, the `Person` class does not provide any methods other than the constructor for assigning values, so in this case, a user cannot modify the name, age, or occupation of an instance of `Person` after its creation. Also, given the way `Person` is defined here, there is only one way a user can find out the values for `name`, `age`, and `occupation`: to invoke the method `identifySelf`.

To allow a user to modify, say, the field `occupation`, one could write a method such as the following:

```
public void setOccupation(String oc) {
    occupation = oc;
}
```

The following code defines methods that will return the current values of `name` and `occupation`, respectively:

```
public String getName() {
    return name;
}
```

```
public String getOccupation() {
    return occupation;
}
```

Using `Person` *p* in our example, the following code fragment sets the field `occupation` to a new value and verifies its current value.

```
p.setOccupation("orthodontist");
String newOccupation = p.getOccupation();
System.out.print(p.getName() + "'s new occupation is ");
System.out.println(newOccupation + ".");
```

➥ `Adela's new occupation is orthodontist.`

Encapsulation makes it possible to make changes in code without breaking other programs that use that code. If, for example, the implementation of a function is changed, the change is invisible to another programmer who invokes that function, and it doesn't affect his/her program, except, hopefully, to improve it.

The Java programming language includes *inheritance*, or the ability to derive new classes from existing classes. The *derived* class, also called a *subclass*, inherits all the data and functions of the existing class, referred to as the *parent* class or *superclass*. A subclass can add new data members to those inherited from the parent class. As far as methods are concerned, the subclass can reuse the inherited methods as they are, change them, and/or add its own new methods. For example, the subclass VerbosePerson could be derived from the class Person, with the difference between instances of the Person class and instances of the VerbosePerson class being the way they identify themselves. The following code creates the subclass VerbosePerson and changes only the implementation of the method identifySelf:

```
public class VerbosePerson extends Person {
    public VerbosePerson(String n, int a, String oc) {
        super(n, a, oc);  // this calls the constructor for Person
    }

    // modifies the method identifySelf in class Person

    public void identifySelf() {
        System.out.println("Hi there! How are you doing today?");
        System.out.println("I go by the name of " + name + ".");
        System.out.print("I am " + age + " years old, and my ");
        System.out.println("occupation is " + occupation + ".");
    }
}
```

An instance of VerbosePerson will inherit the three protected data members that Person has, and it will have the method identifySelf but with a different implementation. The following code fragment creates an instance of the class VerbosePerson:

```
VerbosePerson happyPerson = new VerbosePerson(
                                "Buster Brown", 45, "comedian");
```

A call to the method identifySelf will produce the following results:

```
happyPerson.identifySelf();
```

```
➥ Hi there! How are you doing today?
➥ I go by the name of Buster Brown.
➥ I am 45 years old, and my occupation is comedian.
```

1.6.3   Java Makes It Easy to Write Correct Code

In addition to being portable and object-oriented, Java facilitates writing correct code. Programmers spend less time writing Java code and a lot less time debugging it. In fact, many developers have reported slashing development time by as much as two-thirds. The following is a list of some of the features that make it easier to write correct code in the Java programming language:

- **Garbage collection** automatically takes care of deallocating unused memory. If an object is no longer being used (has no references to it), then it is automatically removed from memory, or "garbage collected." Programmers don't have to keep track of what has been allocated and deallocated themselves, which makes their job a lot easier, but, more importantly, it stops memory leaks.

- **No pointers** eliminates a big source of errors. By using object references instead of memory pointers, problems with pointer arithmetic are eliminated, and problems with inadvertently accessing the wrong memory address are greatly reduced.

- **Strong typing** cuts down on run-time errors. Because of strong type checking, many errors are caught when code is compiled. Dynamic binding is possible and often very useful, but static binding with strict type checking is used when possible.

- **Exception handling** provides a safe mechanism for error recovery, which facilitates writing correct code.

- **Simplicity** makes the Java programming language easier to learn and use correctly. The Java programming language keeps it simple by having just one way to do something instead of having several alternatives, as in some languages. Java also stays lean by not including multiple inheritance, which eliminates the errors and ambiguity that arise when you create a subclass that inherits from two or more classes. To replace the capabilities that multiple inheritance provides, the Java programming language lets you add functionality to a class through the use of interfaces. See the next section for a brief explanation of interfaces.

1.6.4   Java Includes a Library of Classes and Interfaces

The Java platform includes an extensive class library so that programmers can use already-existing classes as is, create subclasses to modify existing classes, or implement interfaces to augment the capabilities of classes.

Both classes and interfaces contain data members (fields) and functions (methods), but there are major differences. In a class, fields may be either variable or constant, and methods are fully implemented. In an interface, fields must be constants, and methods are just prototypes with no implementations. The prototypes give the method signature (the return type, the function name, and the number of parameters with the type for each parameter), but the programmer must supply implementations. To use an interface, a programmer defines a class, declares that it implements the interface, and then implements all of the methods in that interface as part of the class.

These methods are implemented in a way that is appropriate for the class in which the methods are being used. For example, suppose a programmer has created a class Person and wants to use an interface called Sortable, which contains various methods for sorting objects. If the programmer wanted to be able to sort instances of the Person class, she would declare the class to implement Sortable and write an implementation for each method in the Sortable interface so that instances of Person would be sorted by the criteria the she supplies. For instance, Person objects could be sorted by age, by name, or by occupation, and the order could be ascending or descending. Interfaces let a programmer add functionality to a class and give a great deal of flexibility in doing it. In other words, interfaces provide most of the advantages of multiple inheritance without its disadvantages.

A *package* is a collection of related classes and interfaces. The following list, though not complete, gives examples of some Java packages and what they cover.

- java.lang—the basic classes. This package is so basic that it is automatically included in any Java program. It includes classes dealing with numerics, strings, objects, run time, security, and threads.

- java.io—classes that manage reading data from input streams and writing data to output streams

- java.util—miscellaneous utility classes, including generic data structures, bit sets, time, date, string manipulation, random number generation, system properties, notification, and enumeration of data structures

- java.net—classes for network support

- `java.swing`—a set of graphical user interface (GUI) components that allow for portable graphical applications between Java enabled platforms. GUI components include user interface components such as windows, dialog boxes, buttons, checkboxes, lists, menus, scrollbars, and text fields.

- `java.applet`—the `Applet` class, which provides the ability to write applets; this package also includes several interfaces that connect an applet to its document and to resources for playing audio

- `java.sql`—the JDBC core API, which has classes and interfaces for accessing data sources

- `java.beans`—classes for creating reusable components (known as Java-Beans™ components, or Beans), which are typically, though not necessarily, graphical user interface components

- `java.rmi`—the package that lets Java applications make remote method invocations on Java objects

- `java.security`—the security framework for applications written in the Java programming language

- `org.omg.CORBA`—the main package for Java IDL, which allows Java applications to call remote CORBA objects

- `javax.naming`—a unified interface to multiple naming and directory services in the enterprise

- `javax.sql`—the package that provides server-side database capabilities such as connection pooling and distributed transactions

1.6.5   Java Is Extensible

A big plus for the Java programming language is the fact that it can be extended. It was purposely written to be lean with the emphasis on doing what it does very well; instead of trying to do everything from the beginning, it was written so that extending it is easy. Programmers can modify existing classes or write their own new classes. They can also write whole new packages or expand existing ones. For example, the JDBC 2.0 API greatly expanded the `java.sql` package and added an entirely new package, the `javax.sql` package. The JDBC 3.0 API added two new interfaces and many new methods to existing interfaces.

In addition to extensions, there are also many tools being developed to make existing capabilities easier to use. For example, a variety of tools greatly simplify creating and laying out graphical user interfaces, such as menus, dialog boxes, buttons, and so on.

1.6.6   Java Is Secure

It is important that a programmer not be able to write subversive code for applications or applets. This is especially true with the Internet being used more and more extensively for Web services and the electronic distribution of software and multimedia content.

The Java platform builds in security in four ways:

- **The way memory is allocated and laid out.** In Java technology, an object's location in memory is not determined until run time, as opposed to C and C++, where the compiler makes memory layout decisions. As a result, a programmer cannot look at a class definition and figure out how it might be laid out in memory. Also, since the Java programming language has no pointers, a programmer cannot forge pointers to memory.

- **The way incoming code is checked.** The Java Virtual Machine does not trust any incoming code and subjects it to what is called bytecode verification. The bytecode verifier, part of the Virtual Machine, checks that (1) the format of incoming code is correct, (2) incoming code doesn't forge pointers, (3) it doesn't violate access restrictions, and (4) it accesses objects as what they are (for example, an InputStream object is used only as an InputStream object).

- **The way classes are loaded.** The Java bytecode loader, another part of the Virtual Machine, checks whether classes loaded during program execution are local or from across a network. Imported classes cannot be substituted for built-in classes, and built-in classes cannot accidentally reference classes brought in over a network.

- **The way access is restricted for untrusted code.** The Java security manager allows users to restrict untrusted Java applets so that they cannot access the local network, local files, and other resources.

1.6.7 Java Performs Well

Java's performance is better than one might expect. Java's many advantages, such as having built-in security and being interpreted as well as compiled, do have a cost attached to them. However, various optimizations have been built in, and the byte-code interpreter can run very fast because it does not have to do any checking. As a result, code written in the Java programming language has done quite respectably in performance tests. Its performance numbers for interpreted bytecodes are usually more than adequate to run interactive graphical end-user applications. For situations that require unusually high performance, bytecodes can be translated on the fly, generating the final machine code for the particular CPU on which the application is running, at run time.

High-level interpreted scripting languages generally offer great portability and fast prototyping but poor performance. Low-level compiled languages such as C and C++ offer great performance but require large amounts of time for writing and debugging code because of problems with areas such as memory management, pointers, and multiple inheritance. Java offers good performance with the advantages of high-level languages but without the disadvantages of C and C++. In the world of design trade-offs, and with its performance being continually upgraded, the Java programming language provides a very attractive alternative.

1.6.8 Java Scales Well

The Java platform is designed to scale well, from portable consumer electronic devices (PDAs) to powerful desktop and server machines. The Java Virtual Machine takes a small footprint, and Java bytecode is optimized to be small and compact. As a result, the Java platform accommodates the need for both low storage and low bandwidth transmission over the Internet.

1.6.9 Java Is Multithreaded

Multithreading is simply the ability of a program to do more than one thing at a time. For example, an application could be faxing a document at the same time it is printing another document. Or, a program could process new inventory figures while it maintains a feed of current prices. Multithreading is particularly important in multimedia, where a program might often be running a movie, running an audio track, and displaying text all at the same time.

1.7   Relational Database Overview

A database is a means of storing information in such a way that information can be retrieved from it. In simplest terms, a *relational* database is one that presents information in tables with rows and columns. A table is referred to as a *relation* in the sense that it is a collection of objects of the same type (rows). Data in a table can be related according to common keys or concepts, and the ability to retrieve related data from a table is the basis for the term *relational database*. A Database Management System (DBMS) handles the way data is stored, maintained, and retrieved. In the case of a relational database, a Relational Database Management System (RDBMS) performs these tasks. DBMS as used in this book is a general term that includes RDBMS.

1.7.1   Integrity Rules

Relational tables follow certain integrity rules to ensure that the data they contain stay accurate and are always accessible. First, the rows in a relational table should all be distinct. If there are duplicate rows, there can be problems resolving which of two possible selections is the correct one. For most DBMSs, the user can specify that duplicate rows are not allowed, and if that is done, the DBMS will prevent the addition of any rows that duplicate an existing row.

A second integrity rule of the traditional relational model is that column values must not be repeating groups or arrays. A third aspect of data integrity involves the concept of a *null* value. A database takes care of situations where data may not be available by using a null value to indicate that a value is missing. It does not equate to a blank or zero. A blank is considered equal to another blank, a zero is equal to another zero, but two null values are not considered equal.

When each row in a table is different, it is possible to use one or more columns to identify a particular row. This unique column or group of columns is called a *primary key*. Any column that is part of a primary key cannot be null; if it were, the primary key containing it would no longer be a complete identifier. This rule is referred to as *entity integrity*. (The rule for *referential integrity* is discussed in the section "Joins," on page 42.)

Table 1.2 illustrates some of these relational database concepts. It has five columns and six rows, with each row representing a different employee.

Table 1.2: Employees

Employee_ Number	First_Name	Last_Name	Date_of_Birth	Car_ Number
10001	Axel	Washington	28-AUG-43	5
10083	Arvid	Sharma	24-NOV-54	null
10120	Jonas	Ginsburg	01-JAN-69	null
10005	Florence	Wojokowski	04-JUL-71	12
10099	Sean	Washington	21-SEP-66	null
10035	Elizabeth	Yamaguchi	24-DEC-59	null

The primary key for this table would generally be the employee number because each one is guaranteed to be different. (A number is also more efficient than a string for making comparisons.) It would also be possible to use First_Name and Last_Name because the combination of the two also identifies just one row in our sample database. Using the last name alone would not work because there are two employees with the last name of "Washington." In this particular case the first names are all different, so one could conceivably use that column as a primary key, but it is best to avoid using a column where duplicates could occur. If Elizabeth Taylor gets a job at this company and the primary key is First_Name, the RDBMS will not allow her name to be added (if it has been specified that no duplicates are permitted). Because there is already an Elizabeth in the table, adding a second one would make the primary key useless as a way of identifying just one row. Note that although using First_Name and Last_Name is a unique composite key for this example, it might not be unique in a larger database. Note also that Table 1.2 assumes that there can be only one car per employee.

1.7.2   SELECT Statements

SQL is a language designed to be used with relational databases. There is a set of basic SQL commands that is considered standard and is used by all RDBMSs. For example, all RDBMSs use the SELECT statement.

A SELECT statement, also called a *query*, is used to get information from a table. It specifies one or more column headings, one or more tables from which to select, and some criteria for selection. The RDBMS returns rows of the column entries that satisfy the stated requirements. A SELECT statement such as the following will fetch the first and last names of employees who have company cars:

```
SELECT First_Name, Last_Name
FROM Employees
WHERE Car_Number IS NOT NULL
```

The result set (the set of rows that satisfy the requirement of not having null in the Car_Number column) follows. The first name and last name are printed for each row that satisfies the requirement because the SELECT statement (the first line) specifies the columns First_Name and Last_Name. The FROM clause (the second line) gives the table from which the columns will be selected.

```
FIRST_NAME              LAST_NAME

----------              -----------

Axel                    Washington
Florence                Wojokowski
```

The following code produces a result set that includes the whole table because it asks for all of the columns in the table Employees with no restrictions (no WHERE clause). Note that "SELECT *" means "SELECT all columns."

```
SELECT *
FROM Employees
```

1.7.3   WHERE Clauses

The WHERE clause in a SELECT statement provides the criteria for selecting values. For example, in the following code fragment, values will be selected only if they occur in a row in which the column Last_Name begins with the string 'Washington'.

```
SELECT First_Name, Last_Name
FROM Employees
WHERE Last_Name LIKE 'Washington%'
```

The keyword LIKE is used to compare strings, and it offers the feature that patterns containing wildcards can be used. For example, in the code fragment above, there is a percent sign (%) at the end of 'Washington', which signifies that any value containing the string `'Washington'` plus zero or more additional characters will satisfy this selection criterion. So `'Washington'` or `'Washingtonian'` would be matches, but `'Washing'` would not be. The other wildcard used in LIKE clauses is an underbar (_), which stands for any one character. For example,

```
WHERE Last_Name LIKE 'Ba_man'
```

would match `'Batman'`, `'Barman'`, `'Badman'`, `'Balman'`, `'Bagman'`, `'Bamman'`, and so on.

The code fragment below has a WHERE clause that uses the equal sign (=) to compare numbers. It selects the first and last name of the employee who is assigned car 12.

```
SELECT First_Name, Last_Name
FROM Employees
WHERE Car_Number = 12
```

The next code fragment selects the first and last names of employees whose employee number is greater than 10005:

```
SELECT First_Name, Last_Name
FROM Employees
WHERE Employee_Number > 10005
```

WHERE clauses can get rather elaborate, with multiple conditions and, in some DBMSs, nested conditions. This overview will not cover complicated WHERE clauses, but the following code fragment has a WHERE clause with two conditions; this query selects the first and last names of employees whose employee number is less than 10100 and who do not have a company car.

```
SELECT First_Name, Last_Name
FROM Employees
WHERE Employee_Number < 10100 and Car_Number IS NULL
```

A special type of WHERE clause involves a join, which is explained in the next section.

1.7.4   Joins

A distinguishing feature of relational databases is that it is possible to get data from more than one table in what is called a *join*. Suppose that after retrieving the names of employees who have company cars, one wanted to find out who has which car, including the make, model, and year of car. This information is stored in another table, `Cars`, shown in Table 1.3.

Table 1.3: Cars

Car Number	Make	Model	Year
5	Honda	Civic DX	1996
12	Toyota	Corolla	1999

There must be one column that appears in both tables in order to relate them to each other. This column, which must be the primary key in one table, is called the *foreign key* in the other table. In this case, the column that appears in two tables is `Car_Number`, which is the primary key for the table `Cars` and the foreign key in the table `Employees`. If the 1996 Honda Civic were wrecked and deleted from the `Cars` table, then `Car_Number` 5 would also have to be removed from the `Employees` table in order to maintain what is called *referential integrity*. Otherwise, the foreign key column (`Car_Number`) in `Employees` would contain an entry that did not refer to anything in `Cars`. A foreign key must either be `null` or equal to an existing primary key value of the table to which it refers. This is different from a primary key, which may not be `null`. There are several `null` values in the `Car_Number` column in the table `Employees` because it is possible for an employee not to have a company car.

The following code asks for the first and last names of employees who have company cars and for the make, model, and year of those cars. Note that the `FROM` clause lists both `Employees` and `Cars` because the requested data is contained in both tables. Using the table name and a dot (.) before the column name indicates which table contains the column.

```
SELECT Employees.First_Name, Employees.Last_Name, Cars.Make,
        Cars.Model, Cars.Year
FROM Employees, Cars
WHERE Employees.Car_Number = Cars.Car_Number
```

This returns a result set that will look similar to the following:

FIRST_NAME	LAST_NAME	MAKE	MODEL	YEAR
Axel	Washington	Honda	CivicDX	1996
Florence	Wojokowski	Toyota	Corolla	1999

1.7.5   Common SQL Commands

SQL commands are divided into categories, the two main ones being Data Manipulation Language (DML) commands and Data Definition Language (DDL) commands. DML commands deal with data, either retrieving it or modifying it to keep it up-to-date. DDL commands create or change tables and other database objects such as views and indexes.

A list of the more common DML commands follows:

- SELECT—used to query and display data from a database. The SELECT statement specifies which columns to include in the result set. The vast majority of the SQL commands used in applications are SELECT statements.

- INSERT—adds new rows to a table. INSERT is used to populate a newly created table or to add a new row (or rows) to an already-existing table.

- DELETE—removes a specified row or set of rows from a table

- UPDATE—changes an existing value in a column or group of columns in a table

The more common DDL commands follow:

- CREATE TABLE—creates a table with the column names the user provides. The user also needs to specify a type for the data in each column. Data types vary from one RDBMS to another, so a user might need to use metadata to establish the data types used by a particular database. (See "Metadata," on page 46, for a definition of metadata. Also, the table "JDBC

Types Mapped to Database-specific SQL Types," on page 1093, shows the type names used by some leading DBMSs.) CREATE TABLE is normally used less often than the data manipulation commands because a table is created only once, whereas adding or deleting rows or changing individual values generally occurs more frequently.

- DROP TABLE—deletes all rows and removes the table definition from the database. A JDBC API implementation is required to support the DROP TABLE command as specified by SQL92, Transitional Level. However, support for the CASCADE and RESTRICT options of DROP TABLE is optional. In addition, the behavior of DROP TABLE is implementation-defined when there are views or integrity constraints defined that reference the table being dropped.

- ALTER TABLE—adds or removes a column from a table; also adds or drops table constraints and alters column attributes

1.7.6   Result Sets and Cursors

The rows that satisfy the conditions of a query are called the *result set*. The number of rows returned in a result set can be zero, one, or many. A user can access the data in a result set one row at a time, and a *cursor* provides the means to do that. A cursor can be thought of as a pointer into a file that contains the rows of the result set, and that pointer has the ability to keep track of which row is currently being accessed. A cursor allows a user to process each row of a result set from top to bottom and consequently may be used for iterative processing. Most DBMSs create a cursor automatically when a result set is generated.

The JDBC 2.0 API added new capabilities for a result set's cursor, allowing it to move both forward and backward and also allowing it to move to a specified row or to a row whose position is relative to another row.

1.7.7   Transactions

When one user is accessing data in a database, another user may be accessing the same data at the same time. If, for instance, the first user is updating some columns in a table at the same time the second user is selecting columns from that same table, it is possible for the second user to get partly old data and partly updated data. For this reason, DBMSs use *transactions* to maintain data in a consistent state (*data consistency*) while allowing more than one user to access a database at the same time (*data concurrency*).

A transaction is a set of one or more SQL statements that make up a logical unit of work. A transaction ends with either a *commit* or a *rollback*, depending on whether there are any problems with data consistency or data concurrency. The `commit` statement makes permanent the changes resulting from the SQL statements in the transaction, and the `rollback` statement undoes all changes resulting from the SQL statements in the transaction.

A *lock* is a mechanism that prohibits two transactions from manipulating the same data at the same time. For example, a table lock prevents a table from being dropped if there is an uncommitted transaction on that table. In some DBMSs, a table lock also locks all of the rows in a table. A row lock prevents two transactions from modifying the same row, or it prevents one transaction from selecting a row while another transaction is still modifying it.

Chapter 11, "Connection," has more information about transactions. See especially the sections "Transactions," on page 392, and "Transaction Isolation Levels," on page 393.

1.7.8   Stored Procedures

A *stored procedure* is a group of SQL statements that can be called by name. In other words, it is executable code, a mini-program, that performs a particular task that can be invoked the same way one can call a function or method. Traditionally, stored procedures have been written in a DBMS-specific programming language. The latest generation of database products allows stored procedures to be written using the Java programming language and the JDBC API. Stored procedures written in the Java programming language are bytecode portable between DBMSs. Once a stored procedure is written, it can be used and reused because a DBMS that supports stored procedures will, as its name implies, store it in the database.

The following code is an example of how to create a very simple stored procedure using the Java programming language. Note that the stored procedure is just a static Java method that contains normal JDBC code. It accepts two input parameters and uses them to change an employee's car number.

Do not worry if you do not understand the example at this point; it is presented only to illustrate what a stored procedure looks like. You will learn how to write the code in this example in the tutorials that follow. Specifically, the sections "SQL Statements for Creating a Stored Procedure," "Calling a Stored Procedure

Using the JDBC API," and "Stored Procedures Using SQLJ and the JDBC API," all in Chapter 2, "Basic Tutorial," explain more about writing stored procedures.

```java
import java.sql.*;

public class UpdateCar {

    public static void UpdateCarNum(int carNo, int empNo)
                                              throws SQLException {
        Connection con = null;
        PreparedStatement pstmt = null;

        try {
          con = DriverManager.getConnection("jdbc:default:connection");

            pstmt = con.prepareStatement(
                        "UPDATE EMPLOYEES SET CAR_NUMBER = ? " +
                        "WHERE EMPLOYEE_NUMBER = ?");
            pstmt.setInt(1, carNo);
            pstmt.setInt(2, empNo);
            pstmt.executeUpdate();
        }
        finally {
            if (pstmt != null) pstmt.close();
        }
    }
}
```

1.7.9   Metadata

Databases store user data, and they also store information about the database itself. Most DBMSs have a set of system tables, which list tables in the database, column names in each table, primary keys, foreign keys, stored procedures, and so forth. Each DBMS has its own functions for getting information about table layouts and database features. JDBC provides the interface `DatabaseMetaData`, which a driver writer must implement so that its methods return information about the driver and/or DBMS for which the driver is written. For example, a large number of methods return whether or not the driver supports a particular functionality. This interface gives users and tools a standardized way to get metadata. See "DatabaseMetaData Overview," on page 449, and "ResultSetMetaData Overview," on page 783, for more information. In general, developers writing tools and drivers are the ones most likely to be concerned with metadata.

CHAPTER 2

Basic Tutorial

J DBC technology was designed to keep simple things simple. This means that the JDBC API makes everyday database tasks, such as simple SELECT statements, very easy. This chapter will walk you through examples of using the JDBC API to execute common SQL statements, letting you see for yourself how easy it is to use the basic JDBC API.

By the end of this chapter, you will know how to use the JDBC API to do the following:

- create tables

- insert values into tables

- query the tables

- retrieve the results of the queries

- update tables

In this process, you will learn how to use simple statements and prepared statements, and you will see an example of a stored procedure. You will also learn how to perform transactions and how to catch exceptions and warnings. Finally, you will see how to create an applet.

Chapter 3, "Advanced Tutorial," shows you how to use the functionality and data types introduced in the JDBC 2.0 and 3.0 API. This includes new features in the java.sql package and also the functionality in the javax.sql package. Chapter 4, "MetaData Tutorial," shows how to use the metadata API, which is used in more sophisticated programs, such as applications that must dynamically discover and present the table structure of a target database. Chapter 5, "Rowset Tutorial," explains rowsets and gives examples of using two different kinds of rowsets. One example uses a rowset in the context of an Enterprise JavaBeans (EJB) component.

2.1   Getting Started

The first thing you need to do is check that you are set up properly, which involves the following steps:

1. Install the Java platform, which includes the JDBC API.

   To install both Java and JDBC, simply follow the instructions for downloading the Java 2 SDK, Standard Edition. The download for version 1.4 includes the entire JDBC 3.0 API, which includes the packages `java.sql` and `javax.sql`. You can find the latest release of the Java 2 Platform at the following URL:

   ```
   http://java.sun.com/products/JDK/CurrentRelease
   ```

   The sample code used in "Basic Tutorial" was written for JDK™ 1.1 and will run with JDK1.1 or the Java 2 Platform. The sample code in "Advanced Tutorial" must be run with the Java 2 Platform and a driver that supports the JDBC 2.0 API or the JDBC 3.0 API, depending on when a feature was introduced into the JDBC API.

2. Install a driver.

   Your driver should include instructions for installing it. For JDBC drivers written for specific DBMSs, these instructions should be very easy; there is no special configuration needed.

   The JDBC–ODBC Bridge driver is not quite as easy to set up. If you download either the Solaris or Windows versions of the Java 2 SDK, Standard Edition or Enterprise Edition, you will automatically get the JDBC–ODBC Bridge driver, which does not itself require any special configuration. ODBC, however, does. If you do not already have ODBC on your machine, you will need to read your ODBC driver documentation for information on installation and configuration.

3. Install your DBMS if needed.

If you do not already have a DBMS installed, you will need to follow the vendor's instructions for installation. Most users will have a DBMS installed and will be working with an established database.

2.2   Setting Up a Database

We will assume that the database COFFEEBREAK already exists. (Creating a database is not at all difficult, but it requires special permissions and is normally done by a database administrator.) When you create the tables used as examples in this tutorial, they will be in the default database. We purposely kept the size and number of tables small to keep things manageable.

Suppose that our sample database is being used by the proprietor of a small coffee house, The Coffee Break, where coffee beans are sold by the pound and brewed coffee is sold by the cup. To keep things simple, also suppose that the proprietor needs only two tables, one for types of coffee and one for coffee suppliers.

First we will show you how to open a connection with your DBMS, and then, because the JDBC API sends SQL statements to a DBMS, we will demonstrate some SQL statements. After that, we will show you how easy it is to use the JDBC API to pass these SQL statements to your DBMS and process the results that are returned.

For your convenience, the JDBC code used in this chapter can be downloaded from our web site:

```
http://www.java.sun.com/products/jdbc/book.html
```

This code has been tested on most of the major DBMS products. However, you may encounter some compatibility problems using it with older ODBC drivers with the JDBC–ODBC Bridge.

2.3   Establishing a Connection

The first thing you need to do is establish a connection with the data source you want to use. This chapter shows you how to use the DriverManager facility for making a connection to a DBMS; the next chapter will show you how to use a Data-

Source object to establish a connection. Using the `DriverManager` class to make a connection involves two steps: (1) loading the driver and (2) making the connection.

2.3.1   Loading Drivers

Loading the driver or drivers you want to use is very simple and involves just one line of code. If, for example, you want to use the JDBC–ODBC Bridge driver, the following code will load it:

```
Class.forName("sun.jdbc.odbc.JdbcOdbcDriver");
```

Your driver documentation will give you the class name to use. For instance, if the class name is `jdbc.DriverXYZ`, you would load the driver with the following line of code:

```
Class.forName("jdbc.DriverXYZ");
```

You do not need to create an instance of a driver and register it with the `DriverManager` because calling the method `Class.forName` will do that for you automatically. If you were to create your own instance, you would be creating an unnecessary duplicate.

When you have loaded a driver, it is available for making a connection with a DBMS.

2.3.2   Making the Connection

The second step in establishing a connection is to have the appropriate driver connect to the DBMS. The following line of code illustrates the general idea:

```
Connection con = DriverManager.getConnection(
                                 url, "myLogin", "myPassword");
```

This step is also simple, the hardest part being what to supply for *url*. If you are using the JDBC–ODBC Bridge driver, the JDBC URL will start with `jdbc:odbc:`. The rest of the URL is generally your data source name or database system. So, if you are using ODBC to access an ODBC data source called "Fred", for example, your JDBC URL could be `jdbc:odbc:Fred`. In place of "myLogin" you put the name you use to log in to the DBMS; in place of "myPassword" you put your password for the DBMS. So if you log in to your DBMS with a login name of "Fernanda" and a password of "J8", just these two lines of code will establish a connection:

```
String url = "jdbc:odbc:Fred";
Connection con = DriverManager.getConnection(url, "Fernanda", "J8");
```

If you are using a JDBC driver, the documentation will tell you what subprotocol to use, that is, what to put after `jdbc:` in the JDBC URL. For example, if the driver developer has registered the name *acme* as the subprotocol, the first and second parts of the JDBC URL will be `jdbc:acme:`. The driver documentation will also give you guidelines for the rest of the JDBC URL. This last part of the JDBC URL supplies information for identifying the data source.

If one of the drivers you loaded recognizes the JDBC URL supplied to the method `DriverManager.getConnection`, that driver will establish a connection to the DBMS specified in the JDBC URL. The `DriverManager` class, true to its name, manages all of the details of establishing the connection for you behind the scenes. Unless you are writing a driver, you will probably never use any of the methods in the interface `Driver`, and the only `DriverManager` method you really need to know is `DriverManager.getConnection`.

The connection returned by the method `DriverManager.getConnection` is an open connection you can use to create JDBC statements that pass your SQL statements to the DBMS. In the previous example, *con* is an open connection, and we will use it in the examples that follow.

NOTE: The JDBC Optional Package API adds the `DataSource` interface for making a connection. A `DataSource` object uses the Java™ Naming and Directory Interface™ (JNDI), which means that you can make a connection without having to hardcode the driver name. When it is possible, using a `DataSource` object is the preferred alternative to using the `DriverManager`. Using a `DataSource` object to get a connection is explained in the section "Using a `DataSource` Object to Get a Connection," starting on page 168.

2.4   Setting Up Tables

2.4.1   Creating a Table

First, we will create one of the tables in our example database. This table, COFFEES, contains the essential information about the coffees sold at The Coffee Break, including the coffee names, their prices, the number of pounds sold during the current week, and the number of pounds sold to date. The table COFFEES, which we describe in more detail later, is shown in Table 2.1.

Table 2.1: Coffees

COF_NAME	SUP_ID	PRICE	SALES	TOTAL
Colombian	101	7.99	0	0
French_Roast	49	8.99	0	0
Espresso	150	9.99	0	0
Colombian_Decaf	101	8.99	0	0
French_Roast_Decaf	49	9.99	0	0

The column storing the coffee name is COF_NAME, which holds values with an SQL type of VARCHAR and a maximum length of 32 characters. Since we will use different names for each type of coffee sold, the name will uniquely identify a particular coffee and can therefore serve as the primary key. The second column, named SUP_ID, will hold a number that identifies the coffee supplier; this number will be of SQL type INTEGER. The third column, called PRICE, stores values with an SQL type of FLOAT because it needs to hold values with decimal points. (Note that money values would normally be stored in an SQL type DECIMAL or NUMERIC, but because of differences among DBMSs and to avoid incompatibility with older versions of JDBC, we are using the more standard type FLOAT for this tutorial.) The column named SALES stores values of SQL type INTEGER and indicates the number of pounds of coffee sold during the current week. The final column, TOTAL, contains an SQL INTEGER and gives the total number of pounds of coffee sold to date.

SUPPLIERS, the second table in our database, gives information about each of the suppliers. It is shown in Table 2.2.

The tables COFFEES and SUPPLIERS both contain the column SUP_ID, which means that these two tables can be used in SELECT statements to get data based on the information in both tables. The column SUP_ID is the primary key in the table SUPPLIERS, and as such, it uniquely identifies each of the coffee suppliers. In the table COFFEES, SUP_ID is called a foreign key. (You can think of a foreign key as being foreign in the sense that it is imported from another table.)

Table 2.2: Suppliers

SUP_ID	SUP_NAME	STREET	CITY	STATE	ZIP
101	Acme, Inc.	99 Market Street	Groundsville	CA	95199
49	Superior Coffee	1 Party Place	Mendocino	CA	95460
150	The High Ground	100 Coffee Lane	Meadows	CA	93966

Note that each SUP_ID number appears only once in the SUPPLIERS table; this is required for it to be a primary key. In the COFFEES table, where it is a foreign key, however, it is perfectly all right for there to be duplicate SUP_ID numbers because one supplier may sell many types of coffee. Later in this chapter, you will see an example of how to use primary and foreign keys in a SELECT statement. Such a statement, called a *join*, was explained in "Joins," on page 42.

The following SQL statement creates the table COFFEES. The entries within the outer pair of parentheses consist of the name of a column followed by a space and the SQL type to be stored in that column. A comma separates the entry for one column (consisting of column name and SQL type) from the next one. The type VARCHAR is created with a maximum length, so it takes a parameter indicating that maximum length. The parameter must be in parentheses following the type. The SQL statement shown here, for example, specifies that the name in column COF_NAME may be up to 32 characters long.

```
CREATE TABLE COFFEES
(COF_NAME VARCHAR(32),
 SUP_ID INTEGER,
 PRICE FLOAT,
 SALES INTEGER,
 TOTAL INTEGER)
```

This code does not end with a DBMS statement terminator, which can vary from DBMS to DBMS. For example, some DBMSs use a semicolon (;) to indicate the end of a statement, whereas another one uses the word go as a statement terminator. The driver you are using will automatically supply the appropriate statement terminator, and you will not need to include it in your JDBC code.

Another thing we should point out about SQL statements is their form. In the CREATE TABLE statement, key words are printed in all capital letters, and each item is on a separate line. SQL does not require either; these conventions simply make statements easier to read. The standard in SQL is that key words are not case sensitive, so, for example, the following SELECT statement (from the relational database overview in Chapter 1) can be written various ways. As an example, the following two versions are equivalent as far as SQL is concerned.

```
SELECT First_Name, Last_Name
FROM Employees
WHERE Last_Name = 'Washington'

select First_Name, Last_Name from Employees where
Last_Name = 'Washington'
```

Quoted material, however, is case sensitive; in the name "Washington", "W" must be capitalized, and the rest of the letters must be lowercase.

Requirements can vary from one DBMS to another when it comes to identifier names. For example, some DBMSs require that column and table names be given exactly as they were created in the CREATE TABLE statement, while others do not. You can find more information in the section "String Patterns as Arguments," on page 451. To be safe, we will use all uppercase for identifiers such as COFFEES and SUPPLIERS because that is how we defined them.

So far we have written the SQL statement that creates the table COFFEES. Now let's put quotation marks around it (making it a string) and assign that string to the variable *createTableCoffees* so that we can use the variable in our JDBC code later. As just shown, the DBMS does not care about where lines are divided, but the Java compiler will not compile a String object that extends beyond one line. Consequently, when you are giving strings in the Java programming language, you need to enclose each line in quotation marks and use a plus sign (+) to concatenate them.

```
String createTableCoffees = "CREATE TABLE COFFEES " +
    "(COF_NAME VARCHAR(32), SUP_ID INTEGER, PRICE FLOAT, " +
    "SALES INTEGER, TOTAL INTEGER)";
```

The type names we used in our CREATE TABLE statement are the generic SQL type names (also called JDBC type names). Type codes for the JDBC type names are defined in the class java.sql.Types. DBMSs generally use these standard type names, so when the time comes to try out some JDBC applications, you can just use the application CreateCoffees.java, which uses the CREATE TABLE statement. If your DBMS uses its own local type names, we supply another application for you, which we will explain fully later.

Before running any applications, however, we are going to walk you through the basics of the JDBC API.

2.4.2   Creating JDBC Statements

A `Statement` object is what sends your SQL statement to the DBMS. You simply create a `Statement` object and then execute it, supplying the SQL statement you want to send to the appropriate `execute` method. For a `SELECT` statement, the method to use is `executeQuery`. For statements that create or modify tables, the method to use is `executeUpdate`.

It takes an instance of an active connection to create a `Statement` object. In the following example, we use our `Connection` object *con* to create the `Statement` object *stmt*:

```
Statement stmt = con.createStatement();
```

At this point *stmt* exists, but it does not have an SQL statement to pass on to the DBMS. We need to supply that to the method we use to execute *stmt*. For example, in the following code fragment, we supply `executeUpdate` with the SQL statement from the previous example:

```
stmt.executeUpdate("CREATE TABLE COFFEES " +
    "(COF_NAME VARCHAR(32), SUP_ID INTEGER, PRICE FLOAT, " +
    "SALES INTEGER, TOTAL INTEGER)");
```

Since we made a string out of the SQL statement and assigned it to the variable *createTableCoffees*, we could have written the code in this alternate form:

```
stmt.executeUpdate(createTableCoffees);
```

2.4.3   Executing Statements

We used the method `executeUpdate` because the SQL statement contained in *createTableCoffees* is a DDL (data definition language) statement. Statements that create a table, alter a table, or drop a table are all examples of DDL statements and are executed with the method `executeUpdate`. As you might expect from its name, the method `executeUpdate` is also used to execute SQL statements that update a table. In practice, executeUpdate is used far more often to update tables than it is to create them because a table is created once but may be updated many times.

The method used most often for executing SQL statements is executeQuery. This method is used to execute SELECT statements, which comprise the vast majority of SQL statements. You will see how to use this method shortly.

2.4.4   Entering Data into a Table

We have shown how to create the table COFFEES by specifying the names of the columns and the data types to be stored in those columns, but this only sets up the structure of the table. The table does not yet contain any data. We will enter our data into the table one row at a time, supplying the information to be stored in each column of that row. The values to be inserted into the columns are listed in the same order that the columns were declared when the table was created, which is the order that an INSERT statement expects by default. Note, however, that the order in which columns are actually stored in a table depends on how a particular database is implemented.

The following code inserts one row of data, with Colombian in the column COF_NAME, 101 in SUP_ID, 7.99 in PRICE, 0 in SALES, and 0 in TOTAL. (Since The Coffee Break has just started out, the amount sold during the week and the total to date are zero for all the coffees.) Just as we did in the code that created the table COFFEES, we will create a Statement object and then execute it using the method executeUpdate.

```
Statement stmt = con.createStatement();
stmt.executeUpdate("INSERT INTO COFFEES " +
                   "VALUES ('Colombian', 101, 7.99, 0, 0)");
```

Because the SQL statement will not quite fit on one line on the page, we have split it into two strings concatenated by a plus sign (+) so that it will compile. Pay special attention to the need for a space between COFFEES and VALUES. This space must be within the quotation marks and may be after COFFEES or before VALUES; without a space, the SQL statement will erroneously be read as "INSERT INTO COFFEESVALUES . . ." and the DBMS will look for the table COFFEESVALUES. Also note that we use single quotation marks around the coffee name to indicate a character literal, which is the standard SQL syntax for indicating a literal value. Double quotation marks indicate a String value being sent to the DBMS.

The code that follows inserts a second row into the table COFFEES. Note that we can just reuse the Statement object *stmt* rather than having to create a new one for each execution.

```
stmt.executeUpdate("INSERT INTO COFFEES " +
            "VALUES ('French_Roast', 49, 8.99, 0, 0)");
```

Values for the remaining rows can be inserted as follows:

```
stmt.executeUpdate("INSERT INTO COFFEES " +
            "VALUES ('Espresso', 150, 9.99, 0, 0)");
```

```
stmt.executeUpdate("INSERT INTO COFFEES " +
            "VALUES ('Colombian_Decaf', 101, 8.99, 0, 0)");
```

```
stmt.executeUpdate("INSERT INTO COFFEES " +
            "VALUES ('French_Roast_Decaf', 49, 9.99, 0, 0)");
```

2.5 Getting Data from a Table

Now that the table COFFEES has values in it, we can write a SELECT statement to access those values. The star (*) in the following SQL statement indicates that all columns should be selected. Since there is no WHERE clause to narrow down the rows from which to select, the following SQL statement selects the whole table.

```
SELECT *
FROM COFFEES
```

The result, which is the entire table, will look similar to the following. Note that some DBMSs might show the rows in a different order.

COF_NAME	SUP_ID	PRICE	SALES	TOTAL
Colombian	101	7.99	0	0
French_Roast	49	8.99	0	0
Espresso	150	9.99	0	0
Colombian_Decaf	101	8.99	0	0
French_Roast_Decaf	49	9.99	0	0

The result above is what you would see on your terminal if you entered the SQL query directly to the database system. When we access a database through a Java application, as we will be doing shortly, we will need to retrieve the results so that we can use them. You will see how to do this in the next section.

Here is another example of a SELECT statement; this one will get a list of coffees and their respective prices per pound.

```
SELECT COF_NAME, PRICE
FROM COFFEES
```

The results of this query will look something like this:

```
COF_NAME                PRICE
------------------      -----
Colombian               7.99
French_Roast            8.99
Espresso                9.99
Colombian_Decaf         8.99
French_Roast_Decaf      9.99
```

The SELECT statement above generates the names and prices of all of the coffees in the table. The following SQL statement limits the coffees selected to just those that cost less than $9.00 per pound:

```
SELECT COF_NAME, PRICE
FROM COFFEES
WHERE PRICE < 9.00
```

The results would look similar to this:

```
COF_NAME                PRICE
----------------        -----
Colombian               7.99
French_Roast            8.99
Colombian_Decaf         8.99
```

2.6   Retrieving Values from Result Sets

You will now see how to send the previous SELECT statements to a database from a Java program and get the results we showed.

The JDBC API returns results in a ResultSet object, so we need to declare an instance of the class ResultSet to hold our results. The following code demonstrates declaring the ResultSet object *rs* and assigning the results of our earlier query to it.

```
ResultSet rs = stmt.executeQuery(
                     "SELECT COF_NAME, PRICE FROM COFFEES");
```

2.6.1   Using the Method next

The variable *rs*, which is an instance of ResultSet, contains the rows of coffees and prices shown in the result set example above. In order to access the names and prices, we will go to each row and retrieve the values according to their types. The method next moves what is called a *cursor* to the next row and makes that row (called the *current row*) the one upon which we can operate. Since the cursor is initially positioned just above the first row of a ResultSet object, the first call to the method next moves the cursor to the first row and makes it the current row. Successive invocations of the method next move the cursor forward one row at a time from the first row to the last row. This method can be used in a while statement because it returns true as long as the cursor is on a valid row. When the cursor goes beyond the last row, the method next returns false, thereby terminating the while loop.

2.6.2   Retrieving Column Values

We use a getter method (for example, getInt, getString, getDouble, and so on) of the appropriate type to retrieve the value in each column. For example, the first column in each row of *rs* is COF_NAME, which stores a value of SQL type VARCHAR. The method for retrieving a value of SQL type VARCHAR is getString. The second column in each row stores a value of SQL type FLOAT, and the method for retrieving values of that type is getFloat. The following code accesses the values stored in the current row of *rs* and prints a line with the name followed by three spaces and the price. Each time the method next is invoked, the next row becomes the current row, and the loop continues until there are no more rows in *rs*.

```
String query = "SELECT COF_NAME, PRICE FROM COFFEES";
ResultSet rs = stmt.executeQuery(query);

while (rs.next()) {
    String s = rs.getString("COF_NAME");
    float n = rs.getFloat("PRICE");
    System.out.println(s + "     " + n);
}
```

The output will look something like this:

➥ Colombian   7.99
➥ French_Roast   8.99
➥ Espresso   9.99
➥ Colombian_Decaf   8.99
➥ French_Roast_Decaf   9.99

Note that we use a curved arrow to identify output from JDBC code; it is not part of the output. The arrow is not used for results in a result set, so its use distinguishes between what is contained in a result set and what is printed as the output of an application.

Let's look a little more closely at how the getter methods work by examining the two getter methods in this code. First let's examine getString.

```
String s = rs.getString("COF_NAME");
```

The method getString is invoked on the ResultSet object *rs*, so getString will retrieve (*get*) the value stored in the column COF_NAME in the current row of *rs*. The value that getString retrieves has been converted from an SQL VARCHAR to a Java String, and it is assigned to the String object *s*. Note that we used the variable *s* in the println expression above (println(s + "   " + n)).

The situation is similar with the method getFloat except that it retrieves the value stored in the column PRICE, which is an SQL FLOAT, and converts it to a Java float before assigning it to the variable *n*.

The JDBC API offers two ways to identify the column from which a getter method gets a value. One way is to give the column name, as was done in the example above. The second way is to give the column *index* (number of the column), with 1 signifying the first column, 2 , the second, and so on. You might use the column number instead of the column name when your query has the form SELECT * FROM TABLE_NAME, as shown in the following code fragment.

```
ResultSet rs = stmt.executeQuery("SELECT * FROM COFFEES");
rs.next();
String s = rs.getString(1);
float n = rs.getFloat(2);
// ... and so on for all the columns in COFFEES
```

The first line of code gets the value in the first column of the current row of *rs* (column COF_NAME), converts it to a Java String object, and assigns it to *s*. The second line of code gets the value stored in the second column of the current row of *rs*, converts it to a Java float, and assigns it to *n*. Note that the column number refers to the column number in the result set, not in the original table.

In summary, JDBC allows you to use either the column name or the column number as the argument to a getter method. Using the column number is slightly more efficient, and there are some cases where the column number is required. In general, though, supplying the column name is essentially equivalent to supplying the column number.

JDBC allows a lot of latitude as far as which getter methods you can use to retrieve the different SQL types. For example, the method getInt can be used to retrieve any of the numeric or character types. The data it retrieves will be converted to an int, so if you use the method getInt to retrieve a value whose SQL type is VARCHAR, the driver will attempt to parse an int out of the VARCHAR. The method getInt is recommended for retrieving only SQL INTEGER types, however.

Table 50.6, "Use of getter Methods to Retrieve JDBC Data Types," on page 1092, shows the conversions that can be made by the getter methods in the ResultSet interface. Thus, it shows which methods can legally be used to retrieve SQL types and, more important, which methods are recommended for retrieving the various SQL types. Note that this table uses the term "JDBC type" in place of "SQL type." Both terms refer to the generic SQL types whose type codes are defined in the class java.sql.Types, and they are interchangeable.

2.6.3   Using the Method getString

Although the method getString is recommended for retrieving the SQL types CHAR and VARCHAR, it is possible to retrieve any of the JDBC 1.0 JDBC types with it (all types except the SQL99 types and JAVA_OBJECT). Getting values with getString can be very useful, but it also has its limitations. For instance, if it is used to retrieve a numeric type, getString will convert the numeric value to a Java String object, and the value will have to be converted back to a numeric type before it can be operated on as a number. In cases where the value will be treated as a string anyway, there is no drawback. If, however, you want an application to be able to retrieve values of any SQL type, including SQL99 data types and JAVA_OBJECT, the method to use is getObject, which is explained later.

2.7   Updating Tables

Suppose that after a successful first week, the proprietor of The Coffee Break wants to update the SALES column in the table COFFEES by entering the number of pounds sold for each type of coffee. The SQL statement to update one row might look like this:

```
String updateString = "UPDATE COFFEES " +
                      "SET SALES = 75 " +
                      "WHERE COF_NAME = 'Colombian'";
```

Using the Statement object *stmt*, the following line of JDBC code executes the SQL statement contained in *updateString*.

```
stmt.executeUpdate(updateString);
```

The table COFFEES will now look like this:

COF_NAME	SUP_ID	PRICE	SALES	TOTAL
Colombian	101	7.99	75	0
French_Roast	49	8.99	0	0
Espresso	150	9.99	0	0
Colombian_Decaf	101	8.99	0	0
French_Roast_Decaf	49	9.99	0	0

Note that we have not yet updated the column TOTAL, so it still has the value 0.

Now let's select the row we updated, retrieve the values in the columns COF_NAME and SALES, and print out those values:

```
String query = "SELECT COF_NAME, SALES FROM COFFEES " +
               "WHERE COF_NAME = 'Colombian'";
ResultSet rs = stmt.executeQuery(query);
```

```
while (rs.next()) {
    String s = rs.getString("COF_NAME");
    int n = rs.getInt("SALES");
    System.out.println(n + " pounds of " + s + " sold this week.");
}
```

This will print the following:

➥ 75 pounds of Colombian sold this week.

Since the WHERE clause limited the selection to only one row, there was just one row in the ResultSet *rs* and one line printed as output. Accordingly, it is possible to write the code without a while loop:

```
rs.next();
String s = rs.getString(1);
int n = rs.getInt(2);
System.out.println(n + " pounds of " + s + " sold this week.");
```

Even when there is only one row in a result set, you need to use the method next to access it. A ResultSet object is created with a cursor pointing above the first row. The first call to the next method positions the cursor on the first (and in this case, only) row of *rs*. In this code, next is called only once, so if there happened to be another row, it would never be accessed.

Now let's update the TOTAL column by adding the weekly amount sold to the existing total, and then let's print out the number of pounds sold to date:

```
String updateString = "UPDATE COFFEES " +
                      "SET TOTAL = TOTAL + 75 " +
                        "WHERE COF_NAME = 'Colombian'";
stmt.executeUpdate(updateString);

String query = "SELECT COF_NAME, TOTAL FROM COFFEES " +
               "WHERE COF_NAME = 'Colombian'";
ResultSet rs = stmt.executeQuery(query);
while (rs.next()) {
    String s = rs.getString(1);
    int n = rs.getInt(2);
```

```
        System.out.println(n + " pounds of " + s + " sold to date.");
    }
```

Note that in this example, we used the column index instead of the column name, supplying the index 1 to getString (the first column of the result set is COF_NAME) and the index 2 to getInt (the second column of the result set is TOTAL). It is important to distinguish between a column's index in the database table as opposed to its index in the result set table. For example, TOTAL is the fifth column in the table COFFEES but the second column in the result set generated by the query in the preceding example.

2.8   Milestone: The Basics of JDBC

You have just reached a milestone.

With what we have done so far, you have learned the basics of using the JDBC API. You have seen how to create a table, insert values into it, query the table, retrieve results, and update the table. These are the nuts and bolts of using a database, and you can now utilize them in a Java program using the JDBC API. We have used only very simple queries in our examples so far, but as long as the driver and DBMS support them, you can send very complicated SQL queries using only the basic JDBC we have covered so far. The rest of this chapter looks at how to use features that are a little more advanced: prepared statements, stored procedures, and transactions. It also illustrates warnings and exceptions and gives an example of how to convert a JDBC application into an applet. The final part of this chapter is sample code that you can run yourself.

2.9   Using Prepared Statements

Sometimes it is more convenient or more efficient to use a PreparedStatement object for sending SQL statements to the database. This special type of statement is derived from the more general class, Statement, that you already know.

2.9.1   When to Use a PreparedStatement Object

If you want to execute a Statement object many times, it will normally reduce execution time to use a PreparedStatement object instead.

The main feature of a PreparedStatement object is that, unlike a Statement object, it is given an SQL statement when it is created. The advantage to this is that, in most cases, this SQL statement will be sent to the DBMS right away, where it will be compiled. As a result, the PreparedStatement object contains not just an SQL statement, but an SQL statement that has been precompiled. This means that when the PreparedStatement is executed, the DBMS can just run the PreparedStatement's SQL statement without having to compile it first.

Although PreparedStatement objects can be used for SQL statements with no parameters, you will probably use them most often for SQL statements that take parameters. The advantage of using SQL statements that take parameters is that you can use the same statement and supply it with different values each time you execute it. You will see an example of this in the following sections.

2.9.2   Creating a PreparedStatement Object

As with Statement objects, you create PreparedStatement objects with a Connection method. Using our open connection *con* from previous examples, you might write code such as the following to create a PreparedStatement object that takes two input parameters.

```
PreparedStatement updateSales = con.prepareStatement(
    "UPDATE COFFEES SET SALES = ? WHERE COF_NAME = ?");
```

The variable *updateSales* now contains the SQL statement, "UPDATE COFFEES SET SALES = ? WHERE COF_NAME = ?", which has also, in most cases, been sent to the DBMS and been precompiled.

2.9.3   Supplying Values for PreparedStatement Parameters

You will need to supply values to be used in place of the question mark placeholders, if there are any, before you can execute a PreparedStatement object. You do this by calling one of the setter methods defined in the interface PreparedStatement. If the value you want to substitute for a question mark is a Java int, you call the method setInt. If the value you want to substitute for a question mark is a Java String, you call the method setString, and so on. The methods you can use to set parameter values are listed in the section "PreparedStatement Methods," starting on page 657. In general, there is a setter method for each Java type.

Using the PreparedStatement object *updateSales* from the previous example, the following line of code sets the first question mark placeholder to a Java int with a value of 75:

```
updateSales.setInt(1, 75);
```

As you might surmise from the example, the first argument given to a setter method indicates which question mark placeholder is to be set, and the second argument indicates the value to which it is to be set. The next example sets the second placeholder parameter to the string "Colombian":

```
updateSales.setString(2, "Colombian");
```

After these values have been set for its two input parameters, the SQL statement in *updateSales* will be equivalent to the SQL statement in the String object *updateString* that we used in the previous update example. Therefore, the following two code fragments accomplish the same thing.

Code Fragment 1:

```
String updateString = "UPDATE COFFEES SET SALES = 75 " +
                      "WHERE COF_NAME = 'Colombian'";
stmt.executeUpdate(updateString);
```

Code Fragment 2:

```
PreparedStatement updateSales = con.prepareStatement(
        "UPDATE COFFEES SET SALES = ? WHERE COF_NAME = ?");
updateSales.setInt(1, 75);
updateSales.setString(2, "Colombian");
updateSales.executeUpdate();
```

We used the method executeUpdate to execute both the Statement *stmt* and the PreparedStatement *updateSales*. Notice, however, that no argument is supplied to executeUpdate when it is used to execute *updateSales*. This is true because *updateSales* already contains the SQL statement to be executed.

Looking at these examples, you might wonder why you would choose to use a PreparedStatement object with parameters instead of just a simple statement, since the simple statement involves fewer steps. If you were going to update the

SALES column only once or twice, then there would be no need to use an SQL statement with input parameters. If you will be updating often, on the other hand, it might be much easier to use a PreparedStatement object, especially in situations where you can use a for loop or while loop to set a parameter to a succession of values. You will see an example of this later in this section.

Once a parameter has been set with a value, it will retain that value until it is reset to another value or the method clearParameters is called. Using the Prepared-Statement object *updateSales*, the following code fragment illustrates reusing a prepared statement after resetting the value of one of its parameters and leaving the other one the same.

```
updateSales.setInt(1, 100);
updateSales.setString(2, "French_Roast");
updateSales.executeUpdate();
// changes SALES column of French Roast row to 100

updateSales.setString(2, "Espresso");
updateSales.executeUpdate();
// changes SALES column of Espresso row to 100 (the first parameter
// stayed 100, and the second parameter was reset to "Espresso")
```

2.9.4   Using a Loop to Set Values

You can often make coding easier by using a for loop or a while loop to set values for input parameters.

The code fragment that follows demonstrates using a for loop to set values for parameters in the PreparedStatement object *updateSales*. The array *sales-ForWeek* holds the weekly sales amounts. These sales amounts correspond to the coffee names listed in the array *coffees*, so that the first amount in *salesForWeek* (175) applies to the first coffee name in *coffees* ("Colombian"), the second amount in *salesForWeek* (150) applies to the second coffee name in *coffees* ("French_Roast"), and so on. The following code fragment demonstrates updating the SALES column for all the coffees in the table COFFEES.

```
PreparedStatement updateSales;
String updateString = "update COFFEES " +
                 "set SALES = ? where COF_NAME = ?";
updateSales = con.prepareStatement(updateString);
int [] salesForWeek = {175, 150, 60, 155, 90};
```

```
String [] coffees = {"Colombian", "French_Roast", "Espresso",
                     "Colombian_Decaf", "French_Roast_Decaf"};
int len = coffees.length;
for(int i = 0; i < len; i++) {
    updateSales.setInt(1, salesForWeek[i]);
    updateSales.setString(2, coffees[i]);
    updateSales.executeUpdate();
}
```

When the proprietor wants to update the sales amounts for the next week, he can use this same code as a template. All he has to do is enter the new sales amounts in the proper order in the array *salesForWeek*. The coffee names in the array *coffees* remain constant, so they do not need to be changed. (In a real application, the values would probably be input from the user rather than from an initialized Java array.)

2.9.5   Return Values for the Method `executeUpdate`

Whereas executeQuery returns a ResultSet object containing the results of the query sent to the DBMS, the return value for executeUpdate is an int that indicates how many rows of a table were updated. For instance, the following code shows the return value of executeUpdate being assigned to the variable *n*:

```
updateSales.setInt(1, 50);
updateSales.setString(2, "Espresso");
int n = updateSales.executeUpdate();
// n = 1 because one row had a change in it
```

The table COFFEES was updated by having the value 50 replace the value in the column SALES in the row for Espresso. That update affected one row in the table, so *n* is equal to 1.

When the method executeUpdate is used to execute a DDL statement, such as in creating a table, it returns the int 0. Thus, in the following code fragment, which executes the DDL statement used to create the table COFFEES, *n* will be assigned a value of 0.

```
int n = stmt.executeUpdate(createTableCoffees); // n = 0
```

Note that when the return value for `executeUpdate` is 0, it can mean one of two things: (1) the statement executed was an update statement that affected zero rows, or (2) the statement executed was a DDL statement.

2.10 Using Joins

Sometimes you need to use two or more tables to get the data you want. For example, suppose the proprietor of The Coffee Break wants a list of the coffees he buys from Acme, Inc. This involves information in the COFFEES table as well as the yet-to-be-created SUPPLIERS table. This is a case where a *join* is needed. A join is a database operation that relates two or more tables by means of values that they share in common. In our example database, the tables COFFEES and SUPPLIERS both have the column SUP_ID, which can be used to join them.

Before we go any further, we need to create the table SUPPLIERS and populate it with values. The following code creates the table SUPPLIERS.

```
String createSUPPLIERS = "create table SUPPLIERS (SUP_ID INTEGER, " +
    "SUP_NAME VARCHAR(40), STREET VARCHAR(40), CITY VARCHAR(20), " +
    "STATE CHAR(2), ZIP CHAR(5))";
stmt.executeUpdate(createSUPPLIERS);
```

The following code inserts rows for three suppliers into the table SUPPLIERS.

```
stmt.executeUpdate("insert into SUPPLIERS values (101, " +
    "'Acme, Inc.', '99 Market Street', 'Groundsville', " +
    "'CA', '95199')");

stmt.executeUpdate("insert into SUPPLIERS values (49, " +
    "'Superior Coffee', '1 Party Place', 'Mendocino', 'CA', " +
    "'95460')");

stmt.executeUpdate("insert into SUPPLIERS values (150, " +
    "'The High Ground', '100 Coffee Lane', 'Meadows', 'CA', " +
    "'93966')");
```

The following line of code selects the whole table and lets us see what the table SUPPLIERS looks like.

```
ResultSet rs = stmt.executeQuery("select * from SUPPLIERS");
```

The result set will look similar to this.

SUP_ID	SUP_NAME	STREET	CITY	STATE	ZIP
101	Acme, Inc.	99 Market Street	Groundsville	CA	95199
49	Superior Coffee	1 Party Place	Mendocino	CA	95460
150	The High Ground	100 Coffee Lane	Meadows	CA	93966

Now that we have the tables COFFEES and SUPPLIERS, we can proceed with the scenario where the owner wants to get a list of the coffees he buys from a particular supplier. The names of the suppliers are in the table SUPPLIERS, and the names of the coffees are in the table COFFEES. Since both tables have the column SUP_ID, this column can be used in a join. It follows that you need some way to distinguish which SUP_ID column you are referring to. This is done by preceding the column name with the table name, as in "COFFEES.SUP_ID" to indicate that you mean the column SUP_ID in the table COFFEES. The following code, in which *stmt* is a Statement object, selects the coffees bought from Acme, Inc.

```
String query = "SELECT COFFEES.COF_NAME " +
               "FROM COFFEES, SUPPLIERS " +
               "WHERE SUPPLIERS.SUP_NAME = 'Acme, Inc.' and " +
               "SUPPLIERS.SUP_ID = COFFEES.SUP_ID";

ResultSet rs = stmt.executeQuery(query);
System.out.println("Coffees bought from Acme, Inc.: ");
while (rs.next()) {
    String coffeeName = rs.getString("COF_NAME");
    System.out.println("     " + coffeeName);
}
```

This will produce the following output:

```
➥ Coffees bought from Acme, Inc.:
➥     Colombian
➥     Colombian_Decaf
```

2.11 Using Transactions

There are times when you do not want one statement to take effect unless another one also succeeds. For example, when the proprietor of The Coffee Break updates the amount of coffee sold each week, he will also want to update the total amount sold to date. However, he will not want to update one without also updating the other; otherwise, the data will be inconsistent. The way to be sure that either both actions occur or neither action occurs is to use a *transaction*. A transaction is a set of one or more statements that are executed together as a unit, so either all of the statements are executed or none of them are executed.

2.11.1 Disabling Auto-commit Mode

When a connection is created, it is in auto-commit mode. This means that each individual SQL statement is treated as a transaction and will be automatically committed right after it is executed. (To be more precise, the default is for an SQL statement to be committed when it is *completed*, not when it is *executed*. A statement is completed when all of its result sets and update counts have been retrieved. In almost all cases, however, a statement is completed, and therefore committed, right after it is executed.)

The way to allow two or more statements to be grouped into a transaction is to disable auto-commit mode. This is demonstrated in the following line of code, where *con* is an active connection:

```
con.setAutoCommit(false);
```

2.11.2 Committing a Transaction

Once auto-commit mode is disabled, no SQL statements will be committed until you call the method `commit` explicitly. All statements executed after the previous call to the method `commit` will be included in the current transaction and will be committed together as a unit. The following code, in which *con* is an active connection, illustrates a transaction:

```
con.setAutoCommit(false);
PreparedStatement updateSales = con.prepareStatement(
        "UPDATE COFFEES SET SALES = ? WHERE COF_NAME = ?");
updateSales.setInt(1, 50);
updateSales.setString(2, "Colombian");
updateSales.executeUpdate();
PreparedStatement updateTotal = con.prepareStatement(
    "UPDATE COFFEES SET TOTAL = TOTAL + ? WHERE COF_NAME = ?");
updateTotal.setInt(1, 50);
updateTotal.setString(2, "Colombian");
updateTotal.executeUpdate();
con.commit();
con.setAutoCommit(true);
```

In this example, auto-commit mode is disabled for the connection *con*, which means that the two prepared statements *updateSales* and *updateTotal* will be committed together when the method `commit` is called. Whenever the `commit` method is called (either automatically when auto-commit mode is enabled or explicitly when it is disabled), all changes resulting from statements in the transaction will be made permanent. In this case, the SALES and TOTAL columns for Colombian coffee have been changed to 50 (if TOTAL had been 0 previously) and will retain this value until they are changed with another update statement. "Sample Code 6," on page 96, illustrates a similar kind of transaction but uses a `for` loop to supply values to the setter methods for *updateSales* and *updateTotal*.

The final line of the previous example enables auto-commit mode, which means that each statement will once again be committed automatically when it is completed. You will then be back to the default state where you do not have to call the method `commit` yourself.

There are pros and cons to disabling auto-commit mode. Obviously, you will disable it when you want more than one statement in a transaction. But if performance is your concern, the situation is not so simple. Disabling auto-commit mode may improve performance by cutting down on the number of commits and thereby cutting down on the input/output overhead associated with them. In cases where there may be conflicts with other users, however, enabling auto-commit mode may mean better performance because database locks are not unnecessarily held for multiple statements, which increases the likelihood of conflicts.

2.11.3 Using Transactions to Preserve Data Integrity

In addition to grouping statements together for execution as a unit, transactions can help to preserve the integrity of the data in a table. For instance, suppose that an employee was supposed to enter new coffee prices in the table COFFEES but delayed doing it for a few days. In the meantime, prices rose, and today the owner is in the process of entering the higher prices. The employee finally gets around to entering the now outdated prices at the same time that the owner is trying to update the table. After inserting the outdated prices, the employee realizes that they are no longer valid and calls the Connection method rollback to undo their effects. (The method rollback aborts a transaction and restores values to what they were before the attempted update.) At the same time, the owner is executing a SELECT statement and printing out the new prices. In this situation, it is possible that the owner will print a price that was later rolled back to its previous value, making the printed price incorrect.

This kind of situation can be avoided by using transactions. If a DBMS supports transactions, and almost all of them do, it will provide some level of protection against conflicts that can arise when two users access data at the same time. To avoid conflicts during a transaction, a DBMS will use *locks*, mechanisms for blocking access by others to the data that is being accessed by the transaction. (Note that in auto-commit mode, where each statement is a transaction, locks are held for only one statement.)

How locks are set is determined by what is called a *transaction isolation level*, which can range from not supporting transactions at all to supporting transactions that enforce very strict access rules. One example of a transaction isolation level is TRANSACTION_READ_COMMITTED, which will not allow a value to be accessed until after it has been committed. The interface Connection includes five constants, which represent the transaction isolation levels you can use in JDBC applications. These are defined in the section "Connection Fields," starting on page 428.

For example, if all transactions are using the transaction isolation level of TRANSACTION_READ_COMMITTED, a DBMS will lock a row of a table until updates to it have been committed. The effect of this lock is to prevent a user from getting a *dirty read*, that is, reading a value before it is made permanent. Accessing an updated value that has not been committed is considered a dirty read because it is possible for that value to be rolled back to its previous value. If you read a value that is later rolled back, you will have read an invalid value.

Normally, you do not need to do anything about the transaction isolation level; you can just use the default one for your DBMS. The JDBC API allows you to find out what transaction isolation level your DBMS is set to (using the `Connection` method `getTransactionIsolation`) and also allows you to set it to another level (using the `Connection` method `setTransactionIsolation`). Keep in mind, however, that even though the JDBC API allows you to set a transaction isolation level, doing so will have no effect unless the driver you are using supports it. For those who need more information, "`Connection` Overview," starting on page 385, explains transactions and transaction isolation levels in more detail.

2.11.4 When to Roll Back a Transaction

As mentioned earlier, calling the method `rollback` aborts a transaction and returns any values that were modified to the values they had at the beginning of the transaction. If you are trying to execute one or more statements in a transaction and get an `SQLException`, you should call the method `rollback` to abort the transaction and start the transaction over again. That is the only way to be sure of what has been committed and what has not been committed. Catching an `SQLException` tells you that something is wrong, but it does not tell you what was or was not committed. Since you cannot count on the fact that nothing was committed, calling the method `rollback` is the only way to be sure.

"Sample Code 6," on page 96, demonstrates a transaction and includes a `catch` block that invokes the method `rollback`. In this particular situation, it is not really necessary to call `rollback`, and we do it mainly to illustrate how it is done. If the application continued and used the results of the transaction, however, it would be necessary to include a call to `rollback` in the `catch` block in order to protect against using possibly incorrect data.

A rollback can occur without your invoking the method `rollback`. This can happen, for example, when your computer crashes or your program terminates unexpectedly.

| 3.0 | Savepoints, which mark intermediate points within a transaction, are new in the JDBC 3.0 API. They let you roll back a transaction to a point you have set rather than having to roll back the entire transaction. You will find an explanation of savepoints with a complete code example in "Using Savepoints," on page 182.

2.12 Stored Procedures

A stored procedure is a group of SQL statements that form a logical unit and perform a particular task. Stored procedures are used to encapsulate a set of operations or queries to execute on a database server. For example, operations on an employee database (hire, fire, promote, lookup) could be coded as stored procedures executed by application code. Stored procedures can be compiled and executed with different parameters and results, and they may have any combination of input, output, and input/output parameters.

Stored procedures are supported by most DBMSs, but there is a fair amount of variation in their syntax and capabilities. For this reason, we will show you a simple example of what a stored procedure looks like and how it is invoked from a Java application, but this sample is not intended to be run. It simply exemplifies a proprietary stored procedure, that is, a stored procedure whose syntax is specific to one DBMS or selected DBMSs and consequently works with only those DBMSs. We will also show you a stored procedure written in the Java programming language that will work for any DBMS that implements the SQLJ specification for stored procedures. First, let's look at an example of a proprietary stored procedure.

2.12.1 SQL Statements for Creating a Stored Procedure

This section looks at a very simple proprietary stored procedure that has no parameters. Even though most stored procedures do something more complex than this example, it serves to illustrate some basic points about them. As previously stated, the syntax for defining a stored procedure is different for each DBMS. For example, some use begin . . . end or other keywords to indicate the beginning and ending of the procedure definition. In some DBMSs, the following SQL statement creates a stored procedure.

```
create procedure SHOW_SUPPLIERS
as
select SUPPLIERS.SUP_NAME, COFFEES.COF_NAME
from SUPPLIERS, COFFEES
where SUPPLIERS.SUP_ID = COFFEES.SUP_ID
```

The following code puts the SQL statement into a string and assigns it to the variable *createProcedure*, which we will use later.

```
String createProcedure = "create procedure SHOW_SUPPLIERS " +
              "as " +
              "select SUPPLIERS.SUP_NAME, COFFEES.COF_NAME " +
              "from SUPPLIERS, COFFEES " +
              "where SUPPLIERS.SUP_ID = COFFEES.SUP_ID ";
```

The following code fragment uses the Connection object *con* to create a Statement object, which is used to send the SQL statement creating the stored procedure to the database.

```
Statement stmt = con.createStatement();
stmt.executeUpdate(createProcedure);
```

The procedure SHOW_SUPPLIERS will be compiled and then stored in the database as a database object that can be called, similar to the way you would call a method.

2.12.2   Calling a Stored Procedure Using the JDBC API

The JDBC API allows you to call a database stored procedure from a Java program. The first step is to create a CallableStatement object. As with Statement and PreparedStatement objects, this is done with an open Connection object. A CallableStatement object contains a *call* to a stored procedure; it does not contain the stored procedure itself. The first line of code below creates a call to the stored procedure SHOW_SUPPLIERS using the connection *con*. The part that is enclosed in curly braces is the escape syntax for stored procedures. When the driver encounters "{call SHOW_SUPPLIERS}", it will translate this escape syntax into the native SQL used by the database to call the stored procedure named SHOW_SUPPLIERS.

```
CallableStatement cs = con.prepareCall("{call SHOW_SUPPLIERS}");
ResultSet rs = cs.executeQuery();
```

The ResultSet *rs* will be similar to the following:

```
SUP_NAME                COF_NAME
----------------        -----------------------
Acme, Inc.              Colombian
Acme, Inc.              Colombian_Decaf
Superior Coffee         French_Roast
```

```
SUP_NAME              COF_NAME, continued
----------------      -----------------------
Superior Coffee   French_Roast_Decaf
The High Ground   Espresso
```

Note that the method used to execute *cs* is executeQuery because *cs* calls a stored procedure that contains one query and thus produces one result set. If the procedure had contained one update or one DDL statement, the method execute-Update would have been the one to use. It is sometimes the case, however, that a stored procedure contains more than one SQL statement, in which case it will produce more than one result set, more than one update count, or some combination of result sets and update counts. In this case, where there are multiple results, the method execute should be used to execute the CallableStatement. The section "Executing Special Kinds of Statements," on page 965, explains how to use this method and retrieve all results.

The class CallableStatement is a subclass of PreparedStatement, so a CallableStatement object can take input parameters just as a PreparedStatement object can. In addition, a CallableStatement object can take output parameters or parameters that are for both input and output. Check "CallableStatement Overview," starting on page 321, and the section "SQL Statement with INOUT Parameters," on page 1081, for examples and more detailed information.

Later in this chapter, after you have learned how to write a complete, runnable program, you will see how to write this same stored procedure in the Java programming language. The section "Stored Procedures Using SQLJ and the JDBC API," on page 107, gives code samples and explains why you will probably prefer this way of writing stored procedures.

2.13   Creating Complete JDBC Applications

Up to this point you have seen only code fragments. Later in this chapter you will see sample programs that are complete applications you can run.

The first sample code creates the table COFFEES; the second one inserts values into the table and prints the results of a query. The third application creates the table SUPPLIERS, and the fourth populates it with values. After you have run this code, you can try a query that is a join between the tables COFFEES and SUPPLIERS, as in the fifth code example. The sixth code sample demonstrates a transaction and also shows how to set placeholder parameters in a `PreparedStatement` object using a `for` loop.

Because they are complete applications, they include some elements of the Java programming language we have not shown before in the code fragments. We will explain these elements briefly here, but if you need more explanation, you should refer to one of the many books on the Java programming language. We especially recommend *The Java™ Tutorial*, by Mary Campione and Kathy Walrath, and *The Java™ Language Specification,* by James Gosling, Bill Joy, and Guy Steele. Both books are published by Addison-Wesley.

2.13.1   Putting Code in a Class Definition

In the Java programming language, any code you want to execute must be inside a class definition. You type the class definition in a file and give the file the name of the class with `.java` appended to it. So if you have a class named `MySQLStatement`, its definition should be in a file named `MySQLStatement.java`.

2.13.2   Importing Classes to Make Them Visible

The first thing to do is to import the packages or classes you will be using in the new class. The classes in our examples all use the `java.sql` package (the JDBC core API), which is made available when the following line of code precedes the class definition:

```
import java.sql.*;
```

The star (*) indicates that all of the classes in the package `java.sql` are to be imported. Importing a class makes it visible and means that you do not have to write out the fully qualified name when you use a method or field from that class. If you do not include "`import java.sql.*;`" in your code, you will have to write "`java.sql.`" plus the class name in front of all the JDBC fields or methods you use every time you use them. Note that you can import individual classes selectively rather than an entire package. Java does not require that you import classes or packages, but doing so makes writing code a lot more convenient.

Any lines importing classes appear at the top of all the code samples, as they must if they are going to make the imported classes visible to the class being defined. The actual class definition follows any lines that import classes.

2.13.3 Using the `main` Method

If a class is to be executed, it must contain a `static public main` method. This method comes right after the line declaring the class and invokes the other methods in the class. The keyword `static` indicates that this method operates on a class level rather than on individual instances of a class. The keyword `public` means that members of any class can access this `main` method. Since we are not just defining classes to be used by other classes but instead want to run them, the example applications in this chapter all include a `main` method. Chapter 3 has an example of a class that is used by another class rather than running by itself; this class, in "Sample Code 10 and 11," on page 199, does not have a `main` method.

2.13.4 Using `try` and `catch` Blocks

Something else that all the sample applications include is `try` and `catch` blocks. These are the Java programming language's mechanism for handling exceptions. Java requires that when a method throws an exception, there be some mechanism to handle it. Generally a `catch` block will catch the exception and specify what happens, which you may choose to be nothing. In the sample code, we use two `try` blocks and two `catch` blocks. The first `try` block contains the method `Class.for-Name`, from the `java.lang` package. This method throws a `ClassNotFoundException`, so the `catch` block immediately following it handles that exception. The second `try` block contains JDBC methods, all of which throw an `SQLException`, so one `catch` block at the end of the application can handle all of the rest of the exceptions that might be thrown because they will all be `SQLException` objects.

2.13.5 Retrieving Exceptions

The JDBC API lets you see the warnings and exceptions generated by your DBMS and by the Java Virtual Machine. To see exceptions, you can have a `catch` block print them out. For example, the following two `catch` blocks from the sample code print out a message explaining the exception.

```
try {
    Class.forName("myDriverClassName");
} catch(java.lang.ClassNotFoundException e) {
    System.err.print("ClassNotFoundException: ");
    System.err.println(e.getMessage());
}
```

```
try {
    // Code that could generate an exception goes here.
    // If an exception is generated, the catch block below
    // will print out information about it.
} catch(SQLException ex) {
    System.err.println("SQLException: " + ex.getMessage());
}
```

If you were to run CreateCOFFEES.java twice, you would get an error message similar to this:

```
SQLException: There is already an object named 'COFFEES' in the da-
tabase.
Severity 16, State 1, Line 1
```

This example illustrates printing out the message component of an SQLException object, which is sufficient for most situations.

There are actually three components, however, and to be complete, you can print them all out. The following code fragment shows a catch block that is complete in two ways. First, it prints out all three parts of an SQLException object: the message (a string that describes the error), the SQL state (a string identifying the error according to the X/Open SQLState conventions), and the vendor error code (a number that is the driver vendor's error code number). The SQLException object ex is caught, and its three components are accessed with the methods getMessage, getSQLState, and getErrorCode.

The second way the following catch block is complete is that it gets all of the exceptions that might have been thrown. If there is a second exception, it will be chained to ex, so ex.getNextException is called to see if there is another exception. If there is, the while loop continues and prints out the next exception's message, SQLState, and vendor error code. This continues until there are no more exceptions.

```
try {
    // Code that could generate an exception goes here.
    // If an exception is generated, the catch block below
    // will print out information about it.
} catch(SQLException ex) {
    System.out.println("\n--- SQLException caught ---\n");
```

```
        while (ex != null) {
            System.out.println("Message:     " + ex.getMessage ());
            System.out.println("SQLState:    " + ex.getSQLState ());
            System.out.println("ErrorCode:   " + ex.getErrorCode ());
            ex = ex.getNextException();
            System.out.println("");
        }
    }
```

If you were to substitute the catch block above into Sample Code 1 (Create-Coffees) and run it after the table COFFEES had already been created, your printout would be similar to the following:

```
➡
➡ --- SQLException caught ---
➡
➡ Message:  There is already an object named 'COFFEES' in the
➡ database.
➡ Severity 16, State 1, Line 1
➡ SQLState: 42501
➡ ErrorCode:   2714
➡
```

SQLState is a code defined in X/Open and ANSI–92 that identifies the exception. Two examples of SQLState code numbers and their meanings follow:

```
08001 – No suitable driver
HY011 – Operation invalid at this time
```

The vendor error code is specific to each driver, so you need to check your driver documentation for a list of error codes and what they mean.

2.13.6 Retrieving Warnings

SQLWarning objects are a subclass of SQLException that deal with database access warnings. Warnings do not stop the execution of an application, as exceptions do; they simply alert the user that something did not happen as planned. For example, a warning might let you know that a privilege you attempted to revoke was not revoked, or a warning might tell you that an error occurred during a requested disconnection.

A warning can be reported on a `Connection` object, a `Statement` object (including `PreparedStatement` and `CallableStatement` objects), or a `ResultSet` object. Each of these interfaces has a `getWarnings` method, which you must invoke in order to see the first warning reported on the calling object. If `getWarning` returns a warning, you can call the `SQLWarning` method `getNextWarning` on it to get any additional warnings. Executing a statement automatically clears the warnings from a previous statement, so they do not build up. This means, however, that if you want to retrieve warnings reported on a statement, you must do so before you execute another statement. You can get more information on warnings in Chapter 42, "SQLWarning," starting on page 945.

The following code fragment illustrates how to get complete information about any warnings reported on the `Statement` object *stmt* and also on the `ResultSet` object *rs*.

```
Statement stmt = con.createStatement();
ResultSet rs = stmt.executeQuery("select COF_NAME from COFFEES");

SQLWarning warning = stmt.getWarnings();
if (warning != null) {
    System.out.println("\n---Warning---\n");
    while (warning != null) {
        System.out.println("Message: " + warning.getMessage());
        System.out.println("SQLState: " + warning.getSQLState());
        System.out.print("Vendor error code: ");
        System.out.println(warning.getErrorCode());
        System.out.println("");
        warning = warning.getNextWarning();
    }
}

while (rs.next()) {
    String coffeeName = rs.getString("COF_NAME");
    System.out.println("Coffees available at the Coffee Break:   ");
    System.out.println("    " + coffeeName);
    SQLWarning warn = rs.getWarnings();
    if (warn != null) {
        System.out.println("\n---Warning---\n");
        while (warn != null) {
            System.out.println("Message: " + warn.getMessage());
```

```
                System.out.println("SQLState: " + warn.getSQLState());
                System.out.print("Vendor error code: ");
                System.out.println(warn.getErrorCode());
                System.out.println("");
                warn = warn.getNextWarning();
            }
        }
    }
```

Warnings are actually rather uncommon. Of those that are reported, by far the most common warning is a DataTruncation warning, a subclass of SQLWarning. All DataTruncation objects have an SQLState of 01004, indicating that there was a problem with reading or writing data. DataTruncation methods let you find out in which column or parameter data was truncated, whether the truncation was on a read or write operation, how many bytes should have been transferred, and how many bytes were actually transferred. See Chapter 17, "DataTruncation," starting on page 581, if you want more information.

2.14 Running the Sample Applications

You are now ready to actually try out some sample code. The file book.html links to complete, runnable applications that illustrate concepts presented in this chapter and the next. You can download this sample code from the JDBC web site located at:

    http://www.java.sun.com/products/jdbc/book.html

Before you can run one of these applications, you will need to edit the file by substituting the appropriate information for the following variables:

- *url*—the JDBC URL; parts one and two are supplied by your driver, and the third part specifies your data source

- *myLogin*—your login name or user name

- *myPassword*—your password for the DBMS

- *myDriver.ClassName*—the class name supplied with your driver

The first example application is the class `CreateCoffees`, which is in a file named `CreateCoffees.java`. Below are instructions for running `CreateCoffees.java` on the three major platforms.

The first line in the instructions below compiles the code in the file `CreateCoffees.java`. If the compilation is successful, it will produce a file named `CreateCoffees.class`, which contains the bytecodes translated from the file `CreateCoffees.java`. These bytecodes will be interpreted by the Java Virtual Machine, which is what makes it possible for Java code to run on any machine with a Java Virtual Machine installed on it.

The second line of code is what actually makes the code run. Note that you use the name of the class, `CreateCoffees`, *not* the name of the file, `CreateCoffees.class`.

UNIX or Microsoft Windows

```
javac CreateCoffees.java
java CreateCoffees
```

MacOS

Drag the `CreateCoffees.java` file icon onto the Java Compiler icon
Double-click the `CreateCoffees.class` file icon

2.15   Sample Code

As stated previously, you will find the `.java` files for these applications on the JDBC web page at the following URL:

```
http://java.sun.com/products/jdbc/book.html
```

Much of this code should look familiar because the code samples incorporate JDBC code fragments used in earlier examples.

2.15.1 Sample Code 1 and 2

Sample Code 1 is `CreateCoffees.java`, and Sample Code 2 is `InsertCoffees.java`. After you have created the table COFFEES with Sample Code 1, you can use Sample Code 2 to populate it with values.

You create the table COFFEES by simply running the application `CreateCoffees.java` (the first sample code shown later in this section), following the steps previously described in "Running the Sample Applications," on page 85. `CreateCoffees.java` uses standard SQL data types and will work for most DBMSs.

It is possible that your DBMS uses nonstandard names for data types or that it uses its own types that are specific to it. Because of this possibility, we have provided an application, called `CreateNewTable.java`, that will discover the local type names for you and then use them to create your table. You will find this application and its explanation starting on page 233, but do not feel that you need to understand it before you can run it. Even though it contains some features that are not explained until later, running it is quite easy, as you will see.

Before running `CreateNewTable.java`, you will need to modify it by substituting the appropriate URL, login name, password, and driver class name, as is true with all of the sample code. Then, on Solaris and Windows platforms, run the application by typing the following two lines at the command line:

```
javac CreateNewTable.java
java CreateNewTable
```

On a Macintosh platform, you drag the `CreateNewTable.java` icon onto the Java compiler icon and then double-click the `CreateNewTable.class` file icon.

The application will prompt you for the table name, column names, and column types. You just type the following after the appropriate prompts:

```
COFFEES
COF_NAME
VARCHAR
32
SUP_ID
INTEGER
PRICE
FLOAT
SALES
INTEGER
```

```
            TOTAL
            INTEGER
```

The output from `CreateNewTable` is printed after the application. This output shows what you will see on the screen when you run the application, and it also includes the responses you need to type (the responses just listed) in order to create the table we use in later applications.

After you have created the table `COFFEES`, you are ready to run `InsertCof-fees.java`, which inserts values into `COFFEES`, sends a `select` statement, retrieves the results of the query, and prints out the results. If you ran `CreateCoffees.java` and got no results after running `InsertCoffees.java`, your DBMS probably did not create the table `COFFEES`. Try creating the table again by running `Create-NewTable.java` and then run `InsertCoffees.java` again.

The file `CreateCoffees.java` follows:

```
import java.sql.*;

public class CreateCoffees {

    public static void main(String args[]) {

        String url = "jdbc:mySubprotocol:myDataSource";
        Connection con;
        String createString;
        createString = "create table COFFEES " +
                        "(COF_NAME VARCHAR(32), " +
                        "SUP_ID INTEGER, " +
                        "PRICE FLOAT, " +
                        "SALES INTEGER, " +
                        "TOTAL INTEGER)";
        Statement stmt;

        try {
            Class.forName("myDriver.ClassName");

        } catch(java.lang.ClassNotFoundException e) {
            System.err.print("ClassNotFoundException: ");
```

```
                System.err.println(e.getMessage());
        }

        try {
            con = DriverManager.getConnection(url,
                                "myLogin", "myPassword");

            stmt = con.createStatement();
            stmt.executeUpdate(createString);

            stmt.close();
            con.close();

        } catch(SQLException ex) {
            System.err.println("SQLException: " + ex.getMessage());
        }
    }
}
```

The file `InsertCoffees.java` follows:

```
import java.sql.*;

public class InsertCoffees {

    public static void main(String args[]) {

        String url = "jdbc:mySubprotocol:myDataSource";
        Connection con;
        Statement stmt;
        String query = "select COF_NAME, PRICE from COFFEES";
        try {
            Class.forName("myDriver.ClassName");
            } catch(java.lang.ClassNotFoundException e) {
            System.err.print("ClassNotFoundException: ");
            System.err.println(e.getMessage());
        }
```

```java
    try {
        con = DriverManager.getConnection(url,
                          "myLogin", "myPassword");

        stmt = con.createStatement();

        stmt.executeUpdate("insert into COFFEES " +
            "values('Colombian', 101, 7.99, 0, 0)");

        stmt.executeUpdate("insert into COFFEES " +
            "values('French_Roast', 49, 8.99, 0, 0)");

        stmt.executeUpdate("insert into COFFEES " +
            "values('Espresso', 150, 9.99, 0, 0)");

        stmt.executeUpdate("insert into COFFEES " +
             "values('Colombian_Decaf', 101, 8.99, 0, 0)");

        stmt.executeUpdate("insert into COFFEES " +
            "values('French_Roast_Decaf', 49, 9.99, 0, 0)");

        ResultSet rs = stmt.executeQuery(query);

        System.out.println("Coffee Break Coffees and Prices:");
        while (rs.next()) {
            String s = rs.getString("COF_NAME");
            float f = rs.getFloat("PRICE");
            System.out.println(s + "     " + f);
        }

        stmt.close();
        con.close();
    } catch(SQLException ex) {
        System.err.println("SQLException: " + ex.getMessage());
    }
  }
}
```

The printout for InsertCoffees.java looks like this:

➡ Coffee Break Coffees and Prices:
➡ Colombian   7.99
➡ French_Roast   8.99
➡ Espresso   9.99
➡ Colombian_Decaf   8.99
➡ French_Roast_Decaf   9.99

2.15.2 Sample Code 3 and 4

Sample Code 3 is CreateSuppliers.java, and Sample Code 4 is InsertSuppliers.java. These applications are similar to Sample Code 1 and 2 except that CreateSuppliers.java creates the table SUPPLIERS, and InsertSuppliers.java populates the table SUPPLIERS.

If you needed to use the generic application CreateNewTable to create the table COFFEES, you will also need to use it to create the table SUPPLIERS. Follow the same directions, using the following responses:

```
SUPPLIERS
SUP_NAME
VARCHAR
40
STREET
VARCHAR
40
CITY
VARCHAR
20
STATE
CHAR
2
ZIP
CHAR
5
```

Here is the file CreateSuppliers.java:

```java
import java.sql.*;

public class CreateSuppliers {

    public static void main(String args[]) {

        String url = "jdbc:mySubprotocol:myDataSource";
        Connection con;
        String createString;
        createString = "create table SUPPLIERS " +
                    "(SUP_ID INTEGER, " +
                    "SUP_NAME VARCHAR(40), " +
                    "STREET VARCHAR(40), " +
                    "CITY VARCHAR(20), " +
                    "STATE CHAR(2), ZIP CHAR(5))";

        Statement stmt;

        try {
            Class.forName("myDriver.ClassName");

        } catch(java.lang.ClassNotFoundException e) {
            System.err.print("ClassNotFoundException: ");
            System.err.println(e.getMessage());
        }

        try {
            con = DriverManager.getConnection(url,
                                "myLogin", "myPassword");

            stmt = con.createStatement();
            stmt.executeUpdate(createString);

            stmt.close();
            con.close();
```

```
        } catch(SQLException ex) {
            System.err.println("SQLException: " + ex.getMessage());
        }
    }
}
```

The following code, found in the file `InsertSuppliers.java`, inserts values into the table SUPPLIERS, queries for the name and supplier identification number for each of the suppliers, and prints out the results.

```java
import java.sql.*;

public class InsertSuppliers {

    public static void main(String args[]) {

        String url = "jdbc:mySubprotocol:myDataSource";
        Connection con;
        Statement stmt;
        String query = "select SUP_NAME, SUP_ID from SUPPLIERS";

        try {
            Class.forName("myDriver.ClassName");
        } catch(java.lang.ClassNotFoundException e) {
            System.err.print("ClassNotFoundException: ");
            System.err.println(e.getMessage());
        }

        try {
            con = DriverManager.getConnection(url,
                                "myLogin", "myPassword");

            stmt = con.createStatement();

            stmt.executeUpdate("insert into SUPPLIERS " +
                "values(49, 'Superior Coffee', '1 Party Place', " +
                "'Mendocino', 'CA', '95460')");
```

```
        stmt.executeUpdate("insert into SUPPLIERS " +
            "values(101, 'Acme, Inc.', '99 Market Street', " +
            "'Groundsville', 'CA', '95199')");

        stmt.executeUpdate("insert into SUPPLIERS " +
             "values(150, 'The High Ground', '100 Coffee Lane', " +
            "'Meadows', 'CA', '93966')");

        ResultSet rs = stmt.executeQuery(query);
            System.out.println("Suppliers and their ID Numbers:");
        while (rs.next()) {
            String s = rs.getString("SUP_NAME");
            int n = rs.getInt("SUP_ID");
            System.out.println(s + "    " + n);
        }

        stmt.close();
        con.close();

    } catch(SQLException ex) {
        System.err.println("SQLException: " + ex.getMessage());
    }
  }
}
```

The printout for `InsertSuppliers.java` follows:

```
➥ Suppliers and their ID Numbers:
➥ Superior Coffee    49
➥
➥ Acme, Inc.    101
➥ The High Ground    150
```

2.15.3 Sample Code 5

Sample Code 5 is the file `Join.java`. This application does a simple join between the tables COFFEES and SUPPLIERS. It should look familiar because it incorporates an example used previously into a runnable program. Here is the file `Join.java`:

```java
import java.sql.*;

public class Join {

    public static void main(String args[]) {

        String url = "jdbc:mySubprotocol:myDataSource";
        Connection con;
        String query = "select SUPPLIERS.SUP_NAME, COFFEES.COF_NAME " +
                        "from COFFEES, SUPPLIERS " +
                        "where SUPPLIERS.SUP_NAME = 'Acme, Inc.' and " +
                        "SUPPLIERS.SUP_ID = COFFEES.SUP_ID";
        Statement stmt;

        try {
            Class.forName("myDriver.ClassName");

        } catch(java.lang.ClassNotFoundException e) {
            System.err.print("ClassNotFoundException: ");
            System.err.println(e.getMessage());
        }

        try {
            con = DriverManager.getConnection (url,
                                "myLogin", "myPassword");

            stmt = con.createStatement();

            ResultSet rs = stmt.executeQuery(query);
            System.out.println("Supplier, Coffee:");
            while (rs.next()) {
                String supName = rs.getString(1);
                String cofName = rs.getString(2);
                System.out.println("    " + supName + ", " + cofName);
            }

            stmt.close();
            con.close();
```

```
        } catch(SQLException ex) {
            System.err.print("SQLException: ");
            System.err.println(ex.getMessage());
        }
    }
}
```

The output of Join.java looks like this:

```
➥ Supplier, Coffee:
➥     Acme, Inc., Colombian
➥     Acme, Inc., Colombian_Decaf
```

2.15.4   Sample Code 6

Sample Code 6 is the file TransactionPairs.java. This application uses two PreparedStatement objects, one to update the SALES column and one to update the TOTAL column. The values for the input parameters are set using a for loop that iterates through an array. Refer back to "Using a Loop to Set Values," on page 69, for a more thorough explanation.

In TransactionPairs.java there are five transactions, each occurring in one iteration through the for loop. In each iteration, the values for the input parameters are set, the two prepared statements are executed, and the method commit is called. Thus, each iteration constitutes a transaction, ensuring that neither *updateTotal* nor *updateSales* will be committed unless the other is committed.

This code invokes the method con.rollback in a catch block, which is explained in the section "When to Roll Back a Transaction," on page 76. Because of that, we initialized the Connection object *con* to null. Then in the catch block, we tested to see if *con* is still null. If it is, a connection was never even established, and the exception being caught is a result of that failure. In other words, *con* was not assigned a value in the following statement: con = DriverManager.getConnection(url, "myLogin", "myPassword"). Consequently, it is not necessary to call the method rollback because nothing was committed. If *con* had not originally been set to null, the Java compiler would have complained that *con* might not have been initialized.

Here is TransactionPairs.java:

```java
import java.sql.*;

public class TransactionPairs {

    public static void main(String args[]) {

        String url = "jdbc:mySubprotocol:myDataSource";
        Connection con = null;
        Statement stmt;
        PreparedStatement updateSales;
        PreparedStatement updateTotal;
        String updateString = "update COFFEES " +
                    "set SALES = ? where COF_NAME = ?";

        String updateStatement = "update COFFEES " +
                "set TOTAL = TOTAL + ? where COF_NAME = ?";
        String query = "select COF_NAME, SALES, TOTAL from COFFEES";

        try {
            Class.forName("myDriver.ClassName");

        } catch(java.lang.ClassNotFoundException e) {
            System.err.print("ClassNotFoundException: ");
            System.err.println(e.getMessage());
        }
        try {

            con = DriverManager.getConnection(url,
                            "myLogin", "myPassword");

            updateSales = con.prepareStatement(updateString);
            updateTotal = con.prepareStatement(updateStatement);
            int [] salesForWeek = {175, 150, 60, 155, 90};
            String [] coffees = {"Colombian", "French_Roast",
                        "Espresso", "Colombian_Decaf",
                        "French_Roast_Decaf"};
            int len = coffees.length;
            con.setAutoCommit(false);
```

```java
        for (int i = 0; i < len; i++) {
            updateSales.setInt(1, salesForWeek[i]);
            updateSales.setString(2, coffees[i]);
            updateSales.executeUpdate();

            updateTotal.setInt(1, salesForWeek[i]);
            updateTotal.setString(2, coffees[i]);
            updateTotal.executeUpdate();
            con.commit();
        }

        con.setAutoCommit(true);

        updateSales.close();
        updateTotal.close();

        stmt = con.createStatement();
        ResultSet rs = stmt.executeQuery(query);

        while (rs.next()) {
            String c = rs.getString("COF_NAME");
            int s = rs.getInt("SALES");
            int t = rs.getInt("TOTAL");
            System.out.println(c + "      " + s + "      " + t);
        }

        stmt.close();
        con.close();

    } catch(SQLException ex) {
        System.err.println("SQLException: " + ex.getMessage());
        if (con != null) {
            try {
                System.err.print("Transaction is being ");
                System.err.println("rolled back");
                con.rollback();
            } catch(SQLException excep) {
                System.err.print("SQLException: ");
                System.err.println(excep.getMessage());
```

```
                }
            }
        }
    }
}
```

When the initial values for SALES and TOTAL are 0, the output looks like this:

```
➥ Colombian       175      175
➥ French_Roast        150       150
➥ Espresso      60     60
➥ Colombian_Decaf       155      155
➥ French_Roast_Decaf      90      90
```

If you were to run TransactionPairs a second time, the printout would be:

```
➥ Colombian       175      350
➥ French_Roast        150       300
➥ Espresso      60     120
➥ Colombian_Decaf       155      310
➥ French_Roast_Decaf      90      180
```

2.16 Creating an Applet from an Application

Suppose that the owner of The Coffee Break wants to display his current coffee prices in an applet on his web page. He can be sure of always displaying the most current price by having the applet get the price directly from his database.

In order to do this, he needs to create two files of code, one with applet code and one with HTML code. The applet code contains the JDBC code that would appear in a regular application plus additional code for running the applet and displaying the results of the database query. In our example, the applet code is in the file OutputApplet.java. To display our applet in an HTML page, the file OutputApplet.html tells the browser what to display and where to display it.

The rest of this section will tell you about various elements found in applet code that are not present in standalone application code. Some of these elements involve advanced aspects of the Java programming language. We will give you some rationale and some basic explanation, but explaining them fully is beyond the scope of this book. For purposes of this sample applet, you need to grasp only the general idea, so don't worry if you don't understand everything. You can simply use the applet code as a template, substituting your own queries for the one in the applet.

2.16.1 Writing Applet Code

To begin with, applets will import classes not used by standalone applications. Our applet imports two classes that are special to applets: the class `Applet`, which is part of the `java.applet` package, and the class `Graphics`, which is part of the `java.awt` package. This applet also imports the general-purpose class `java.util.Vector` so that we have access to an array-like container whose size can be modified. This code uses `Vector` objects to store query results so that they can be displayed later.

All applets extend the `Applet` class; that is, they are subclasses of `Applet`. Therefore, every applet definition must contain the words `extends Applet`, as shown here:

```
public class MyAppletName extends Applet {
  . . .
}
```

In our applet example, this line also includes the words `implements Runnable`, so it looks like this:

```
public class OutputApplet extends Applet implements Runnable {
  . . .
}
```

`Runnable` is an interface that makes it possible to run more than one *thread* at a time. A thread is a sequential flow of control, and it is possible for a program to be multithreaded, that is, to have many threads doing different things concurrently. (We introduced this concept in "Java Is Multithreaded," on page 37.) The class `OutputApplet` implements `Runnable` by defining the method `run`, `Runnable`'s only method. In our example the `run` method contains the JDBC code for opening a connection, executing a query, and getting the results from the result set. Since database connections can be slow, sometimes taking several seconds, it is generally a good idea to structure an applet so that it can handle the database work in a separate thread.

Similar to a standalone application, which must have a `main` method, an applet must implement at least one `init`, `start`, or `paint` method. Our example applet defines a `start` method and a `paint` method. Every time `start` is invoked, it creates a new thread (named *worker*) to reevaluate the database query. Every time `paint` is invoked, it displays either the query results or a string describing the current status of the applet.

As stated previously, the `run` method defined in `OutputApplet` contains the JDBC code. When the thread *worker* invokes the method `start`, the `run` method is called automatically, and it executes the JDBC code in the thread *worker*. The code in `run` is similar to the code you have seen in our other sample code with three exceptions. First, it uses the class `Vector` to store the results of the query. Second, it does not print out the results but rather adds them to the `Vector` *results* for display later. Third, it likewise does not print out exceptions but instead records error messages for later display.

Applets have various ways of drawing, or displaying, their content. This applet, a very simple one that has only text, uses the method `drawString` (part of the `Graphics` class) to display its text. The method `drawString` takes three arguments: (1) the string to be displayed, (2) the x coordinate, indicating the horizontal starting point for displaying the string, and (3) the y coordinate, indicating the vertical starting point for displaying the string (which is below the text).

The method `paint` is what actually displays something on the screen, and in `OutputApplet.java`, it is defined to contain calls to the method `drawString`. The main thing `drawString` displays is the contents of the `Vector` *results* (the stored query results). When there are no query results to display, `drawString` will display the current contents of the `String` *message*. This string will be "Initializing" to begin with. It gets set to "Connecting to database" when the method `start` is called, and the method `setError` sets it to an error message when an exception is caught. Thus, if the database connection takes much time, the person viewing this applet will see the message "Connecting to database" because that will be the contents of *message* at that time. (The method `paint` is called by AWT when it wants the applet to display its current state on the screen.)

The last two methods defined in the class `OutputApplet`, `setError` and `setResults`, are private, which means that they can be used only by `OutputApplet`. These methods both invoke the method `repaint`, which clears the screen and calls `paint`. So if `setResults` calls `repaint`, the query results will be displayed, and if `setError` calls `repaint`, an error message will be displayed.

A final point to be made is that all the methods defined in `OutputApplet` except `run` are *synchronized*. The key word `synchronized` indicates that while a method is accessing an object, other `synchronized` methods are blocked from accessing that object. The method `run` is not declared `synchronized` so that the applet can still paint itself on the screen while the database connection is in progress. If the database access methods were `synchronized`, they would prevent the applet from being repainted while they are executing, and that could result in delays with no accompanying status message.

To summarize, in an applet, it is good programming practice to do some things you would not need to do in a standalone application:

1. Put your JDBC code in a separate thread.

2. Display status messages on the screen during any delays, such as when a database connection is taking a long time.

3. Display error messages on the screen instead of printing them to `System.out` or `System.err`.

2.16.2   Running an Applet

Before running our sample applet, you need to compile the file `OutputApplet.java`. This creates the file `OutputApplet.class`, which is referenced by the file `OutputApplet.html`.

The easiest way to run an applet is to use the appletviewer, which is included as part of the Java 2 Platform. Simply follow the instructions below for your platform to compile and run `OutputApplet.java`:

UNIX and Microsoft Windows

```
javac OutputApplet.java
appletviewer OutputApplet.html
```

MacOS

Drag the `OutputApplet.java` file icon onto the Java Compiler icon.
Drag the `OutputApplet.html` file icon onto the appletviewer icon.

Applets loaded over the network are subject to various security restrictions. Although this can seem bothersome at times, it is absolutely necessary for network security, and security is one of the major advantages of programming with Java. An applet cannot make network connections except to the host it came from unless the browser allows it. Whether one is able to treat locally installed applets as "trusted" also depends on the security restrictions imposed by the browser. An applet cannot ordinarily read or write files on the host that is executing it, and it cannot load libraries or define native methods.

Applets can usually make network connections to the host they came from, so they can work very well on intranets.

The JDBC–ODBC Bridge driver is a somewhat special case. It can be used quite successfully for intranet access, but it requires that ODBC, the bridge, the bridge native library, and the JDBC API be installed on every client. With this configuration, intranet access works from Java applications and from trusted applets. However, since the bridge requires special client configuration, it is not practical to run applets on the Internet with the JDBC–ODBC Bridge driver. Note that this is a limitation of the JDBC–ODBC Bridge, not of JDBC. With a pure Java JDBC driver, you do not need any special configuration to run applets on the Internet.

2.16.3 Sample Code 7 and 8

Sample Code 7 is `OutputApplet.java`, and Sample Code 8 is `OutputApplet.html`. The sample code in this section is a demonstration JDBC applet. It displays some simple standard output from the table `COFFEES`.

The contents of `OutputApplet.java` are printed first, and the contents of the file `OutputApplet.html` follow.

Here is `OutputApplet.java`:

```java
import java.applet.Applet;
import java.awt.Graphics;
import java.util.Vector;
import java.sql.*;

public class OutputApplet extends Applet implements Runnable {
    private Thread worker;
    private Vector queryResults;
    private String message = "Initializing";
    public synchronized void start() {
```

```java
    // Every time "start" is called, we create a worker thread to
    // reevaluate the database query.

    if (worker == null) {
        message = "Connecting to database";
        worker = new Thread(this);
        worker.start();
    }

    public void run() {
        String url = "jdbc:mySubprotocol:myDataSource";
        String query = "select COF_NAME, PRICE from COFFEES";

        try {
         Class.forName("myDriver.ClassName");
        } catch(Exception ex) {
         setError("Can't find Database driver class: " + ex);
         return;
        }

        try {
            Vector results = new Vector();
            Connection con = DriverManager.getConnection(url,
                          "myLogin", "myPassword");
            Statement stmt = con.createStatement();
            ResultSet rs = stmt.executeQuery(query);
            while (rs.next()) {
               String s = rs.getString("COF_NAME");
               float f = rs.getFloat("PRICE");
               String text = s + "      " + f;
                  results.addElement(text);
            }

        stmt.close();
        con.close();

        setResults(results);

      } catch(SQLException ex) {
```

```
            setError("SQLException: " + ex);
        }
    }


    public synchronized void paint(Graphics g) {
    // If there are no results available, display the current message.
        if (queryResults == null) {
            g.drawString(message, 5, 50);
            return;
        }
        // Display the results.
        g.drawString("Prices of coffee per pound:  ", 5, 10);
        int y = 30;
        java.util.Enumeration enum = queryResults.elements();
        while (enum.hasMoreElements()) {
            String text = (String)enum.nextElement();
            g.drawString(text, 5, y);
            y = y + 15;
        }
    }


    private synchronized void setError(String mess) {
        queryResults = null;
        message = mess;
        worker = null;
        // And ask AWT to repaint this applet.
        repaint();
    }


    private synchronized void setResults(Vector results) {
        queryResults = results;
        worker = null;
        // And ask AWT to repaint this applet.
        repaint();
    }
}
```

What follows is the html file that places our applet on the HTML page.

```
<HTML>
<HEAD>
<TITLE> Query Output </TITLE>
</HEAD>
<BODY>
<CENTER>
Output from query select NAME, PRICE from COFFEES
<BR>
<APPLET CODEBASE=. CODE="OutputApplet.class"
    WIDTH=350 HEIGHT=200>
</CENTER>
</APPLET>
</BODY>
</HTML>
```

Our applet is very simple. It runs the file OutputApplet.class that is in the current directory and displays it in a window with a width of 350 and a height of 200 with no graphics or sound. If the applet were more complex, involving many files for graphics and sound, we would have used a JAR (Java ARchive) file to bundle all the files together and compress them. Using a JAR file, the applet and its requisite components (.class files, images, and sounds) can be downloaded to a browser much more quickly. This is true because everything is in one compressed file and can be downloaded in a single HTTP transaction rather than using a new connection for each piece. Another advantage to using a JAR file is that individual entries in a JAR file may be digitally signed by the applet author to authenticate their origin.

To use a JAR file in an applet, you modify the applet tag in the HTML file by adding the ARCHIVE parameter. The value you supply to this parameter is the name of the JAR file, with the directory location of the file being relative to the location of the HTML page. For example, the following code fragment indicates that the JAR file, coffees.jar, is in the subdirectory jars relative to the HTML file.

```
<APPLET CODEBASE=. CODE="OutputApplet.class"
ARCHIVE="jars/coffees.jar"
WIDTH=350 HEIGHT=200>
</APPLET>
```

2.17   Stored Procedures Using SQLJ and the JDBC API

With the introduction of SQLJ, a series of specifications for ways to use the Java programming language with SQL, it is now possible to write a stored procedure that will work with any DBMS that conforms to the relevant SQLJ specification.

2.17.1   Creating a Stored Procedure

The following code sample creates a stored procedure that does the same thing as SHOW_SUPPLIERS, the stored procedure created in the section "SQL Statements for Creating a Stored Procedure," on page 77. The difference is that this stored procedure is written in the Java programming language using the JDBC API, and because it conforms to the SQLJ standard, it can be run on any DBMS that adheres to the SQLJ specification for writing stored procedures in the Java programming language.

In the Java programming language, stored procedures are written as static methods. These methods will always be declared public static void, similar to a main method. In our example, the class SuppliersProcs contains the static method showSuppliers, which performs a join to select the coffees from each supplier. The method showSuppliers takes one parameter, which is an array of ResultSet objects that contains one element. It will return one ResultSet object, which it assigns to the one element in the array, rs[0]. Had showSuppliers taken more parameters, there could have been a result set returned for each.

Note that the DBMS does many things for you behind the scenes. For example, it automatically creates the ResultSet array *rs* before invoking showSuppliers and takes care of closing rs[0] after the stored procedure call finishes.

Another thing the DBMS does for you is keep track of the connections you used to call a stored procedure. The method showSuppliers uses this default connection in order to create a Statement object. Because the JDBC URL supplied to the method getConnection is jdbc:default:connection, the DriverManager knows that it should return a Java object that references the current default connection rather than creating a new connection.

Here is the code for SuppliersProcs.java:

```
import java.sql.*;

public class SuppliersProcs {
```

```
      public static void showSuppliers(ResultSet[] rs )
                                              throws SQLException {
         String query = "select SUPPLIERS.SUP_NAME, COFFEES.COF_NAME " +
                        "from SUPPLIERS, COFFEES " +
                        "where SUPPLIERS.SUP_ID = COFFEES.SUP_ID";

         Connection con = DriverManager.getConnection(
                                    "jdbc:default:connection");

         Statement stmt = con.createStatement();

         rs[0] = stmt.executeQuery(query);
      }
   }
```

2.17.2 Installing a Stored Procedure

The previous code example is a class that defines what a stored procedure does. The next sample code creates a stored procedure for `SuppliersProcs` and installs it in the DBMS as a JAR file. A stored procedure written in the Java programming language is packaged as a JAR file so that it can be deployed on the DBMS. The code should look familiar except for the two statements it sends to the DBMS. One calls a SQLJ built-in procedure to install the JAR file, and one creates the stored procedure. We will examine these two statements in detail.

The sample code assumes that the DBMS already stores the built-in SQLJ procedure `sqlj.install_jar`, which loads a set of classes written in the Java programming language in an SQL system. To be precise, the JAR file stores the `.class` files that are produced by compiling `.java` files. The following `String` object uses the standard JDBC stored procedure escape syntax for calling the procedure `sqlj.install_jar`.

```
"{call sqlj.install_jar(" +
        "'file:/myDir/SQLRoutines.jar', 'routines_jar', 0)}"
```

This procedure takes three parameters. The first is the URL giving the location of the JAR file that contains the stored procedure you want to install. The second parameter is the SQL name that you want to give to the JAR file. The third parameter gives instructions to the DBMS and will be either 1 or 0. For this example, you may ignore the third parameter.

2.17.3   Declaring a Stored Procedure in SQL

Once the JAR file is installed in the DBMS, you need to give an SQL declaration for the stored procedures it contains. The following String command contains the SQL declaration for our stored procedure. In essence, it specifies that the SQL name for the method in SuppliersProcs is showSuppliers. This establishes a correspondence between the two names so that when an SQL client (including a client using the JDBC API) invokes show_suppliers, the DBMS will map this to an invocation of the showSuppliers method.

```
"create procedure show_suppliers " +
    "reads sql data " +
    "dynamic result sets 1 " +
    "external name 'routines_jar:SuppliersProcs.showSuppliers' " +
    "language java parameter style java"
```

The first line specifies that the name of the stored procedure is show_suppliers, which is the name to use in a CallableStatement object when you want to call this stored procedure. For example, the following line of code calls the stored procedure show_suppliers.

```
CallableStatement cstmt = con.prepareCall("{call show_suppliers}");
```

The next line tells the DBMS that this stored procedure reads SQL data but does not write it, which is true because the stored procedure contains a query but no update statements that would write to the database. The third line tells the DBMS that the stored procedure produces one result set. The fourth line gives the name of the stored procedure and what it contains in a three-part format. The first part, preceding the colon, is the SQL name that you have given to the JAR file. The second and third parts, which are in the format className.methodName, give the Java name of a class in the JAR file and a method that it contains. The last line tells the DBMS that the Java programming language is being used and that the parameter style is that of the Java programming language.

The class `InstallProcs`, which follows, creates a connection, creates a `Statement` object, and then uses it to execute the two statements we have just examined. Here is what `InstallProcs.java` looks like:

```java
import java.sql.*;

class InstallProcs {

    static void main(String[] args) {
        String url = "jdbc:mySubprotocol:myDataSource";
        Connection con;
        String installJar;
        String createProc;
        installJar = "{call sqlj.install_jar(" +
                "'file:/myDir/SQLRoutines.jar', 'routines_jar', 0)}";
        createProc = "create procedure show_suppliers " +
         "reads sql data " +
         "dynamic result sets 1 " +
         "external name 'routines_jar:SuppliersProcs.showSuppliers' " +
         "language java parameter style java";

        Statement stmt;

        try {
            Class.forName("myDriver.ClassName");
        } catch(java.lang.ClassNotFoundException e) {
            System.err.print("ClassNotFoundException: ");
            System.err.println(e.getMessage());
        }

        try {
            con = DriverManager.getConnection(url,
                            "myLogin", "myPassword");

            stmt = con.createStatement();

            stmt.executeUpdate(installJar);
            stmt.executeUpdate(createProc);
```

```
        stmt.close();
        con.close();

    } catch(SQLException ex) {
        System.err.println("SQLException: " + ex.getMessage());
    }
  }
}
```

After you have run InstallProcs, you can call the static method Supplier-
Procs.showSuppliers as the SQL stored procedure show_suppliers using the
JDBC API or some other language. The following code fragment creates the call
to show_suppliers, executes it, and then retrieves and prints out the values in the
ResultSet object that show_suppliers returns. Note that this code is just like what
we have used before to call a stored procedure written in another language.

```
CallableStatement cstmt = con.prepareCall("{call show_suppliers}");
ResultSet [] rs = cstmt.executeQuery();

while (rs[0].next()) {
    String supName = rs[0].getString(1);
    String cofName = rs[0].getString(2);
    System.out.println(supplierName + " supplies " + cofName);
}
```

CHAPTER 3

Advanced Tutorial

THE "Basic Tutorial" chapter covered the JDBC 1.0 API. This chapter covers the features added in the JDBC 2.0 API and the JDBC 3.0 API. Although the features described in this chapter are more advanced than those in the "Basic Tutorial" chapter, you do not have to be an advanced programmer to go through this chapter.

In this chapter you will learn to do the following:

JDBC 2.0 features

- Scroll forward and backward in a result set or move to a specific row
- Make updates to database tables using methods in the Java programming language (instead of using SQL commands)
- Send multiple SQL update statements to the database as a unit, or batch
- Use the new SQL99 data types as column values
- Create new SQL user-defined types (UDTs)
- Map an SQL UDT to a class in the Java programming language
- Make a connection that participates in connection pooling
- Make a connection that can be used for a distributed transaction

JDBC 3.0 features

- Use savepoints in a transaction
- Retrieve automatically generated keys

Note that JDBC 3.0 changes involving metadata are covered in Chapter 4, "MetaData Tutorial," starting on page 193. There you will see how to use the new ParameterMetaData interface and the new methods in the DatabaseMetaData interface.

Also, you will find examples showing how to use new methods added to various interfaces in the reference chapters for those interfaces. For example, the chapters "Blob" and "Clob" have examples showing how to make internal updates to the data in Blob and Clob objects. And, in the chapter "Ref," you will see how to use the new JDBC 3.0 API to retrieve the SQL structured type instance that a Ref object represents.

3.1   Getting Set Up to Use the JDBC 2.0 and 3.0 API

This section describes what you need to do in order to write or run code that uses features introduced in the JDBC 2.0 API and the JDBC 3.0 API.

3.1.1   Setting Up to Run Code

In order to run code that uses JDBC 2.0 API features, you need a DBMS and driver that implement those features; likewise, to use JDBC 3.0 API features, your DBMS and driver must implement those features. To write or run code that employs features introduced in the JDBC 2.0 API or JDBC 3.0 API, you will need to do the following:

1. Download the Java 2 SDK, Standard Edition, following the download instructions. For JDBC 2.0 API features, you need version 1.2 or later. For JDBC 3.0 API features, you need version 1.4 or later.

2. Install a JDBC driver that implements the JDBC 2.0 and 3.0 features used in the code. Not all drivers implement all features, so you need to check your driver documentation. Also, at the following web page you can use various search criteria to find drivers that support certain features:

   http://industry.java.sun.com/products/jdbc/drivers

3. Access a DBMS that works with your driver.

Note that when you download J2SE, version 1.4 or later, you will get all of the JDBC API, including both the `java.sql` and `javax.sql` packages. Previous versions of the J2SE did not include the `javax.sql` package, otherwise known as the JDBC Optional Package API. Consequently, if your driver vendor did not bundle the Optional Package with its driver product, you had to download it yourself.

NOTE: If you write server-side code, you will want to download the Java 2 Platform, Enterprise Edition (J2EE). The Enterprise Edition has the advantage of including the packages `javax.naming`, `javax.transaction`, and other extension packages needed for enterprise operations such as distributed transactions. If you are not writing server-side code, however, you will probably want to stick with downloading only the Standard Edition.

3.1.2   Using Code Examples

You can download example code from

```
http://java.sun.com/products/jdbc/book.html
```

The code examples for SQL99 functionality are written following the SQL99 standard. As of this writing, no one driver implements all of the functionality provided by the JDBC 2.0 API or JDBC 3.0 API. Also, some DBMSs use a slightly different syntax for certain operations. For example, the syntax for creating a new data type can vary. At the appropriate point in the tutorial, we show you how to change the generic code we provide for creating a new data type so that it conforms to the syntax your DBMS requires.

Therefore, before you try to run any of the code, check the documentation provided with your driver and DBMS to see what functionality they support and what syntax is expected for the operations they perform. Even if it turns out that you cannot run all of the example code with your driver, you can still learn from the examples.

NOTE: Even though the preferred way to obtain a connection is to use a Data-Source object, the example code uses the `DriverManager` class for creating connections. This is done because a `DataSource` object must be registered with a naming service before it can be used, which means that using a `DataSource` object is not practical for many readers.

2.0

3.2   Moving the Cursor in Scrollable Result Sets

One of the features introduced in the JDBC 2.0 API is the ability to move a result set's cursor backward as well as forward. There are also methods that move the cursor to a particular row and that check the position of the cursor. Scrollable result sets make it easy to create a graphical interface for browsing result set data, which will probably be one of the main uses for this feature. Another important use is moving the cursor to a row so that you can make updates to that row.

2.0

3.2.1   Creating a Scrollable Result Set

Before you can take advantage of these features, however, you need to create a `ResultSet` object that is scrollable. Keep in mind that scrollable result sets involve overhead, so you should create them only when your application uses scrolling. The following code fragment creates a scrollable `ResultSet` object.

```
Statement stmt = con.createStatement(
    ResultSet.TYPE_SCROLL_INSENSITIVE, ResultSet.CONCUR_READ_ONLY);
ResultSet srs = stmt.executeQuery("SELECT COF_NAME, PRICE
                          FROM COFFEES");
```

This code is similar to what you have used earlier except that it adds two arguments to the method `createStatement`. The first new argument must be one of the three constants added to the `ResultSet` interface to indicate the type of a `ResultSet` object. These constants are `TYPE_FORWARD_ONLY`, `TYPE_SCROLL_INSENSITIVE`, and `TYPE_SCROLL_SENSITIVE`. The second new argument must be one of the two `ResultSet` constants for specifying whether a result set is read-only or updatable: `CONCUR_READ_ONLY` or `CONCUR_UPDATABLE`. The point to remember is that if you specify a result set type, you must also specify whether the result set is read-only or updatable. Also, the order is important. You must specify the type first, and because both parameters are of type `int`, the compiler will not complain if you switch the order.

Specifying the constant `TYPE_FORWARD_ONLY` creates a nonscrollable result set, that is, one in which the cursor moves only forward. If you do not specify any constants for the type and updatability, you will automatically get the default, which is a `ResultSet` object that is `TYPE_FORWARD_ONLY` and `CONCUR_READ_ONLY` (as has always been the case).

To get a scrollable `ResultSet` object, you must specify one of the following `ResultSet` constants: `TYPE_SCROLL_INSENSITIVE` or `TYPE_SCROLL_SENSITIVE`. In some instances, however, specifying one of these constants does not necessarily mean that you will get a scrollable result set. If your driver does not support them, you will get a result set in which the cursor moves forward only. A driver may provide scrollable result sets even if the underlying DBMS does not support them; however, a driver is not required to provide scrolling when the DBMS does not do so. In the end, it is the way your driver is implemented that determines whether you can get a scrollable result set.

The following line of code checks whether the `ResultSet` object *rs* is scrollable.

```
int type = rs.getType();
```

The variable *type* will be one of the following:

1003 to indicate `ResultSet.TYPE_FORWARD_ONLY`

1004 to indicate `ResultSet.TYPE_SCROLL_INSENSITIVE`

1005 to indicate `ResultSet.TYPE_SCROLL_SENSITIVE`

For a larger code example, see "Getting Other Information," on page 207.

The difference between result sets that are `TYPE_SCROLL_INSENSITIVE` and those that are `TYPE_SCROLL_SENSITIVE` has to do with whether they reflect changes that are made to them while they are open and whether certain methods can be called to detect those changes. Generally speaking, a result set that is `TYPE_SCROLL_INSENSITIVE` does not reflect changes made while it is still open, and one that is `TYPE_SCROLL_SENSITIVE` does. All three types of result sets will make changes visible if they are closed and then reopened. At this stage, you do not need to worry about the finer points of a ResultSet object's capabilities; we will go into more detail about ResultSet objects later.

3.2.2   Moving the Cursor Forward and Backward

Once you have a scrollable ResultSet object, *srs* in the example in the previous section, you can use it to move the cursor around in the result set. Remember that when you created a new ResultSet object in the previous chapter, it had a cursor positioned before the first row. Even when a result set is scrollable, the cursor is still initially positioned before the first row. In the JDBC 1.0 API, the only way to move the cursor was to call the method next. This is still the appropriate method to call when you want to access each row, going from the first row to the last row, but the JDBC 2.0 API adds many other ways to move the cursor.

The counterpart to the method next, which moves the cursor forward one row (toward the end of the result set), is the new method previous, which moves the cursor backward (one row toward the beginning of the result set). Both methods return false when the cursor goes beyond the result set (to the position after the last row or before the first row), which makes it possible to use them in a while loop. In the basic tutorial you used the method next in a while loop, but to refresh your memory, here is an example in which the cursor moves to the first row and then to the next row each time it goes through the while loop. The loop ends when the cursor has gone after the last row, causing the method next to return false. The following code fragment prints out the values in each row of *srs*, with five spaces between the name and price:

```
Statement stmt = con.createStatement(
                            ResultSet.TYPE_SCROLL_INSENSITIVE,
                            ResultSet.CONCUR_READ_ONLY);
ResultSet srs = stmt.executeQuery(
                        "SELECT COF_NAME, PRICE FROM COFFEES");
while (srs.next()) {
    String name = srs.getString("COF_NAME");
    float price = srs.getFloat("PRICE");
    System.out.println(name + "     " + price);
}
```

The printout will look something like this:

➡ Colombian   7.99
➡ French_Roast   8.99
➡ Espresso   9.99
➡ Colombian_Decaf   8.99
➡ French_Roast_Decaf   9.99

As in the following code fragment, you can process all of the rows in *srs* going backward, but to do this, the cursor must start out being after the last row. You can move the cursor explicitly to the position after the last row with the method `afterLast`. From this position, the method `previous` moves the cursor to the last row, and then with each iteration through the `while` loop, it moves the cursor to the previous row. The loop ends when the cursor reaches the position before the first row, where the method `previous` returns `false`.

```
Statement stmt = con.createStatement(
    ResultSet.TYPE_SCROLL_INSENSITIVE, ResultSet.CONCUR_READ_ONLY);
ResultSet srs = stmt.executeQuery(
                        "SELECT COF_NAME, PRICE FROM COFFEES");
srs.afterLast();
while (srs.previous()) {
    String name = srs.getString("COF_NAME");
    float price = srs.getFloat("PRICE");
    System.out.println(name + "    " + price);
}
```

The printout will look similar to this:

➡ French_Roast_Decaf   9.99
➡ Colombian_Decaf   8.99
➡ Espresso   9.99
➡ French_Roast   8.99
➡ Colombian   7.99

As you can see, the printout for each has the same values, but the rows are in the opposite order. For simplicity, we will assume that the DBMS always returns rows in the same order for our sample query.

3.2.3   Moving the Cursor to a Designated Row

You can move the cursor to a particular row in a `ResultSet` object. The methods `first`, `last`, `beforeFirst`, and `afterLast` move the cursor to the position that their names indicate. The method `absolute` will move the cursor to the row number indicated in the argument passed to it. If the number is positive, the cursor moves the given number from the beginning, so calling `absolute(1)` puts the cursor on the first row. If the number is negative, the cursor moves the given number from the end, so calling `absolute(-1)` puts the cursor on the last row. The following line of code moves the cursor to the fourth row of *srs*:

```
srs.absolute(4);
```

If *srs* has 500 rows, the following line of code will move the cursor to row 497:

```
srs.absolute(-4);
```

Three methods move the cursor to a position relative to its current position. As you have seen, the method `next` moves the cursor forward one row, and the method `previous` moves the cursor backward one row. With the method `relative`, you can specify how many rows to move from the current row and also the direction in which to move. A positive number moves the cursor forward the given number of rows; a negative number moves the cursor backward the given number of rows. For example, in the following code fragment, the cursor moves to the fourth row, then to the first row, and finally to the third row:

```
srs.absolute(4); // cursor is on the fourth row
    .   .   .
srs.relative(-3); // cursor is on the first row
    .   .   .
srs.relative(2); // cursor is on the third row
```

3.2.4   Getting the Cursor Position

Several methods give you information about the cursor's position.

The method `getRow` lets you check the number of the row where the cursor is currently positioned. For example, you can use `getRow` to verify the position of the cursor in the previous example, as follows:

```
srs.absolute(4);
int rowNum = srs.getRow(); // rowNum should be 4
srs.relative(-3);
rowNum = srs.getRow(); // rowNum should be 1
srs.relative(2);
rowNum = srs.getRow(); // rowNum should be 3
```

Four additional methods let you verify whether the cursor is at a particular position. The position is stated in the method names: isFirst, isLast, isBefore-First, isAfterLast. These methods all return a boolean and can therefore be used in a conditional statement.

For example, suppose you have iterated through some rows in a result set and want to print two columns from the current row. To be sure that the cursor has not gone beyond the last row, you could use code such as the following, in which *srs* is a scrollable ResultSet object.

```
if (!srs.isAfterLast()) {
    String name = srs.getString("COF_NAME");
    float price = srs.getFloat("PRICE");
    System.out.println(name + "      " + price);
}
```

The preceding code fragment performs as expected because we know that the ResultSet object *srs* is not empty. The method isAfterLast returns false when the cursor is not after the last row and also when the result set is empty, so this code fragment would not have worked correctly if the result set had been empty.

In the next section, you will see how to use the two remaining ResultSet methods for moving the cursor, moveToInsertRow and moveToCurrentRow. You will also see examples illustrating why you might want to move the cursor to certain positions.

3.3   Making Updates to Updatable Result Sets

2.0

Another feature introduced in the JDBC 2.0 API makes JDBC programming easier. This feature is the ability to update rows in a result set using methods in the Java programming language rather than SQL commands.

3.3.1   Creating an Updatable Result Set

Before you can make updates to a ResultSet object, you need to create one that is updatable. In order to do this, you supply the ResultSet constant CONCUR_UPDATABLE to the createStatement method. The Statement object that is created will produce an updatable ResultSet object each time it executes a query. The following code fragment illustrates creating the updatable ResultSet object *uprs*. Note that the code also makes *uprs* scrollable. An updatable ResultSet object does not necessarily have to be scrollable, but when you are making changes to a result set, you generally want to be able to move around in it. This would be true if, for example, you were editing a form using a graphical user interface (GUI).

```
Connection con = DriverManager.getConnection(
                            "jdbc:mySubprotocol:mySubName");
Statement stmt = con.createStatement(
    ResultSet.TYPE_SCROLL_SENSITIVE, ResultSet.CONCUR_UPDATABLE);
ResultSet uprs = stmt.executeQuery(
                "SELECT COF_NAME, PRICE FROM COFFEES");
```

The ResultSet object *uprs* might look something like this:

```
COF_NAME              PRICE
------------------    -----
Colombian             7.99
French_Roast          8.99
Espresso              9.99
Colombian_Decaf       8.99
French_Roast_Decaf    9.99
```

We can now use JDBC 2.0 methods in the ResultSet interface to insert a new row into *uprs*, delete one of its existing rows, or modify one of its column values.

You might note that just specifying that a result set be updatable does not guarantee that the result set you get is updatable. If a driver does not support updatable result sets, it will return one that is read only. The query you send can also make a difference. In order to get an updatable result set, the query must generally specify the primary key as one of the columns selected, and it should select columns from only one table.

The following line of code checks whether the ResultSet object *uprs* is updatable.

```
int concurrency = uprs.getConcurrency();
```

The variable *concurrency* will be one of the following:

1007 to indicate ResultSet.CONCUR_READ_ONLY

1008 to indicate ResultSet.CONCUR_UPDATABLE

For a larger code example, see "Getting Other Information," on page 207.

3.3.2   Updating a Result Set Programmatically

An update is the modification of a column value in the current row. Suppose that we want to raise the price of French Roast Decaf coffee to 10.99. Using the JDBC 1.0 API, the update would look something like this:

```
stmt.executeUpdate("UPDATE COFFEES SET PRICE = 10.99 " +
                   "WHERE COF_NAME = 'French_Roast_Decaf'");
```

The following code fragment uses the JDBC 2.0 core API to accomplish the same update made in the previous example. In this example, *uprs* is the updatable result set generated in the previous section.

```
uprs.last();
uprs.updateFloat("PRICE", 10.99f);
```

Update operations in the JDBC 2.0 API affect column values in the row where the cursor is positioned, so in the first line, the ResultSet *uprs* calls the method last to move its cursor to the last row (the row where the column COF_NAME has the value 'French_Roast_Decaf'). Once the cursor is on the last row, all of the update methods you call will operate on that row until you move the cursor to another row. The second line changes the value in the PRICE column to 10.99 by calling the method updateFloat. This method is used because the column value we want to update is a float in the Java programming language.

Note that there is an f following the float values (as in 10.99f) to indicate to the Java compiler that the number is a float. If the f were not there, the compiler would interpret the number as a double and issue an error message. This does not apply to the SQL statements sent to the DBMS, which all of our previous updates have been, because they are not compiled by the Java compiler.

The `ResultSet` updater methods generally take two parameters: the column to update and the new value to put in that column. As with the `ResultSet` getter methods, the parameter designating the column may be either the column name or the column number. There is a different updater method for updating each data type (`updateString`, `updateBigDecimal`, `updateInt`, and so on) just as there are different getter methods for retrieving different data types.

At this point, the price in *uprs* for French Roast Decaf will be 10.99, but the price in the table COFFEES in the database will still be 9.99. To make the update take effect in the database, we must call the `ResultSet` method updateRow. Here is what the code should look like to update both *uprs* and COFFEES:

```
uprs.last();
uprs.updateFloat("PRICE", 10.99f);
uprs.updateRow();
```

Note that you must call the method updateRow before moving the cursor. If you move the cursor to another row before calling updateRow, the updates are lost, that is, the row will revert to its previous column values.

Suppose that you realize that the update you made is incorrect. You can restore the previous value by calling the cancelRowUpdates method if you call it before you have called the method updateRow. Once you have called updateRow, the method cancelRowUpdates will no longer work. The following code fragment makes an update and then cancels it.

```
uprs.last();
uprs.updateFloat("PRICE", 10.99f);
. . .
uprs.cancelRowUpdates();
```

Now the price is once again 9.99 in both the result set and the database because the value in the database was never changed.

Changes always affect the current row, so if you want to update the price for Colombian_Decaf, you have to move the cursor to the row containing that variety of coffee. Because the row for Colombian_Decaf immediately precedes the row for French_Roast_Decaf, you can call the method previous to position the cursor on the row for Colombian_Decaf. The following code fragment changes the price in that row to 9.79 in both the result set and the underlying table in the database.

```
uprs.previous();
uprs.updateFloat("PRICE", 9.79f);
uprs.updateRow();
```

All cursor movements refer to rows in a `ResultSet` object, not rows in the underlying database. If a query selects five rows from a database table, there will be five rows in the result set, with the first row being row 1, the second row being row 2, and so on. The ordering of the rows in the result set has nothing at all to do with the order of the rows in the base table. In fact, the order of the rows in a database table is indeterminate. The driver keeps track of which rows were selected, and it makes updates to the proper rows, but they may be located anywhere in the table. When a row is inserted, for example, there is no way to know where in the table it has been inserted.

3.3.3   Inserting and Deleting Rows Programmatically

In the previous section, you saw how to modify a column value using methods in the JDBC API rather than having to use SQL commands. You can also insert a new row into a table or delete an existing row programmatically.

Let's suppose that The Coffee Break is getting a new variety from one of its suppliers and the proprietor wants to add the new coffee to his database. Using the JDBC 1.0 API, he would write code that passes an SQL `INSERT` statement to the DBMS. The following code fragment, in which *stmt* is a `Statement` object, shows this approach.

```
stmt.executeUpdate("INSERT INTO COFFEES " +
                        "VALUES ('Kona', 150, 10.99, 0, 0)");
```

You can do the same thing without using any SQL commands by using `ResultSet` methods added to the JDBC 2.0 API. For example, after you generate a `ResultSet` object containing results from the table `COFFEES`, you can build a new row and then insert it into both the result set and the table `COFFEES` in one step. Every `ResultSet` object has a row called the *insert row*, a special row in which you can build a new row. This row is not part of the result set returned by a query execution; it is more like a separate buffer in which to compose a new row.

The first step is to move the cursor to the insert row, which you do by invoking the method `moveToInsertRow`. The next step is to set a value for each column in the row. You do this by calling the appropriate updater method for each value.

Note that these are the same updater methods you used in the previous section for changing a column value. Finally, you call the method `insertRow` to insert the row you have just populated with values into the result set. This one method simultaneously inserts the row into both the `ResultSet` object and the database table from which the result set was selected.

The following code fragment creates the scrollable and updatable `ResultSet` object *uprs*, which contains all of the rows and columns in the table COFFEES.

```
Connection con = DriverManager.getConnection(
                            "jdbc:mySubprotocol:mySubName");
Statement stmt = con.createStatement(
    ResultSet.TYPE_SCROLL_SENSITIVE, ResultSet.CONCUR_UPDATABLE);
ResultSet uprs = stmt.executeQuery("SELECT * FROM COFFEES");
```

The next code fragment uses the `ResultSet` object *uprs* to insert the row for Kona coffee, shown in the previous SQL code example. It moves the cursor to the insert row, sets the five column values, and inserts the new row into *uprs* and COFFEES.

```
uprs.moveToInsertRow();

uprs.updateString("COF_NAME", "Kona");
uprs.updateInt("SUP_ID", 150);
uprs.updateFloat("PRICE", 10.99f);
uprs.updateInt("SALES", 0);
uprs.updateInt("TOTAL", 0);

uprs.insertRow();
```

Because you can use either the column name or the column number to indicate the column to be set, your code for setting the column values could also have looked like this:

```
uprs.updateString(1, "Kona");
uprs.updateInt(2, 150);
uprs.updateFloat(3, 10.99f);
uprs.updateInt(4, 0);
uprs.updateInt(5, 0);
```

You might be wondering why the updater methods seem to behave differently here from the way they behaved in the update examples. In those examples, the value set with an updater method immediately replaced the column value in the result set. That was true because the cursor was on a row in the result set. When the cursor is on the insert row, the value set with an updater method is likewise immediately set, but it is set in the insert row rather than in the result set itself. In both updates and insertions, calling an updater method does not affect the underlying database table. The method updateRow must be called to have updates occur in the database. For insertions, the method insertRow inserts the new row into the result set and the database at the same time.

You might also wonder what happens if you insert a row without supplying a value for every column in the row. If a column has a default value or accepts SQL NULL values, you can get by with not supplying a value. If a column does not accept NULL values and does not have a default value, you will get an SQLException if you fail to set a value for it. You will also get an SQLException if a required table column is missing in your ResultSet object. In the example above, the query was SELECT * FROM COFFEES, which produced a result set with all the columns of all the rows. When you want to insert one or more rows, your query does not have to select all rows, but you should generally select all columns. You will normally want to use a WHERE clause to limit the number of rows returned by your SELECT statement, especially if your table has hundreds or thousands of rows.

After you have called the method insertRow, you can start building another row to be inserted, or you can move the cursor back to a result set row. Note that you can move the cursor to another row at any time, but if you move the cursor from the insert row before calling the method insertRow, you will lose all of the values you have added to the insert row.

To move the cursor from the insert row back to the result set, you can invoke any of the following methods: first, last, beforeFirst, afterLast, absolute, previous, relative, or moveToCurrentRow. When you call the method moveToInsertRow, the result set keeps track of which row the cursor is sitting on, which is, by definition, the current row. As a consequence, the method moveToCurrentRow, which you can invoke only when the cursor is on the insert row, moves the cursor from the insert row back to the row that was previously the current row. This also explains why you can use the methods previous and relative, which require movement relative to the current row.

3.3.4   Sample Code 20

The following code sample shows how to insert a row. It is a complete program that you can run if you have a driver that implements scrollable and updatable result sets. Here are some things you might notice about the code:

1. The ResultSet object *uprs* is updatable, scrollable, and sensitive to changes made by itself and others. Even though it is TYPE_SCROLL_SENSITIVE, it is possible that the getter methods called after the insertions will not retrieve values for the newly-inserted rows. There are methods in the DatabaseMetaData interface that will tell you what is visible and what is detected in the different types of result sets for your driver and DBMS. (These methods are discussed in detail in Chapter 4, "Metadata Tutorial.") In this code sample, we wanted to demonstrate cursor movement in the same ResultSet object, so after moving to the insert row and inserting two rows, the code moves the cursor back to the result set, going to the position before the first row. This puts the cursor in position to iterate through the entire result set using the method next in a while loop. To be absolutely sure that the getter methods include the inserted row values no matter what driver and DBMS is used, you can close the result set and create another one, reusing the Statement object *stmt* with the same query (SELECT * FROM COFFEES). A result set opened after a table has been changed will always reflect those changes.

2. After all the values for a row have been set with updater methods, the code inserts the row into the result set and the database with the method insertRow. Then, still staying on the insert row, it sets the values for another row.

```
import java.sql.*;

public class InsertRows {

    public static void main(String args[]) {

        String url = "jdbc:mySubprotocol:myDataSource";
        Connection con;
        Statement stmt;
        try {
            Class.forName("myDriver.ClassName");
```

```java
  } catch(java.lang.ClassNotFoundException e) {
     System.err.print("ClassNotFoundException: ");
     System.err.println(e.getMessage());
  }

  try {

     con = DriverManager.getConnection(url,
                         "myLogin", "myPassword");

     stmt = con.createStatement(ResultSet.TYPE_SCROLL_SENSITIVE,
                            ResultSet.CONCUR_UPDATABLE);
     ResultSet uprs = stmt.executeQuery("SELECT * FROM COFFEES");

     uprs.moveToInsertRow();

     uprs.updateString("COF_NAME", "Kona");
     uprs.updateInt("SUP_ID", 150);
     uprs.updateFloat("PRICE", 10.99f);
     uprs.updateInt("SALES", 0);
     uprs.updateInt("TOTAL", 0);

     uprs.insertRow();

     uprs.updateString("COF_NAME", "Kona_Decaf");
     uprs.updateInt("SUP_ID", 150);
     uprs.updateFloat("PRICE", 11.99f);
     uprs.updateInt("SALES", 0);
     uprs.updateInt("TOTAL", 0);

     uprs.insertRow();

     uprs.beforeFirst();

     System.out.println("Table COFFEES after insertion:");
     while (uprs.next()) {
        String name = uprs.getString("COF_NAME");
        int id = uprs.getInt("SUP_ID");
        float price = uprs.getFloat("PRICE");
```

```
                int sales = uprs.getInt("SALES");
                int total = uprs.getInt("TOTAL");
                System.out.print(name + "    " + id + "    " + price);
                System.out.println("    " + sales + "    " + total);
            }

            uprs.close();
            stmt.close();
            con.close();

        } catch(SQLException ex) {
            System.err.println("SQLException: " + ex.getMessage());
        }
    }
}
```

2.0   3.3.5   Deleting a Row Programmatically

So far, you have seen how to update a column value and how to insert a new row.
Deleting a row is the third way to modify a ResultSet object, and it is the simplest.
You simply move the cursor to the row you want to delete and then call the
method deleteRow. For example, if you want to delete the fourth row in the Result-
Set *uprs*, your code will look like this:

```
    uprs.absolute(4);
    uprs.deleteRow();
```

These two lines of code remove the fourth row from *uprs* and also from the database.

The only issue about deletions is what the ResultSet object actually does
when it deletes a row. With some JDBC drivers, a deleted row is removed and is
no longer visible in a result set. Some JDBC drivers use a blank row as a placeholder (a "hole") where the deleted row used to be. If there is a blank row in place
of the deleted row, you can use the method absolute with the original row positions to move the cursor because the row numbers in the result set are not changed
by the deletion.

In any case, you should remember that JDBC drivers handle deletions differently. You can use methods in the `DatabaseMetaData` interface to discover the exact behavior of your driver.

3.3.6   Seeing Changes in Result Sets

Result sets vary greatly in their ability to reflect changes made in their underlying data. If you modify data in a `ResultSet` object, the change will always be visible if you close it and then reopen it during a transaction. In other words, if you re-execute the same query after changes have been made, you will produce a new result set based on the new data in the target table. This new result set will naturally reflect changes you made earlier. You will also see changes made by others when you reopen a result set if your transaction isolation level makes them visible.

So when can you see visible changes that you or others made while the `ResultSet` object is still open? (Generally, you will be most interested in the changes made by others because you know what changes you made yourself.) The answer depends on the type of `ResultSet` object you have.

With a `ResultSet` object that is `TYPE_SCROLL_SENSITIVE`, you can always see visible updates made to existing column values. You may see inserted and deleted rows, but the only way to be sure is to use `DatabaseMetaData` methods that return this information. ("Features Added in the JDBC 2.0 Core API," on page 453, explains how to ascertain the visibility of changes.)

You can, to some extent, regulate what changes are visible by raising or lowering the transaction isolation level for your connection with the database. For example, the following line of code, where *con* is an active `Connection` object, sets the connection's isolation level to `TRANSACTION_READ_COMMITTED`:

```
con.setTransactionIsolation(
                Connection.TRANSACTION_READ_COMMITTED);
```

With this isolation level, a `TYPE_SCROLL_SENSITIVE` result set will not show any changes before they are committed, but it can show changes that may have other consistency problems. To allow fewer data inconsistencies, you could raise the transaction isolation level to `TRANSACTION_REPEATABLE_READ`. The problem is that, in most cases, the higher the isolation level, the poorer the performance is likely to be. And, as is always true of JDBC drivers, you are limited to the levels your driver actually provides. Many programmers find that the best choice is generally to use their database's default transaction isolation level. You can get the default with the following line of code, where *con* is a newly created connection:

```
int level = con.getTransactionIsolation();
```

The section "Connection Fields," beginning on page 428, gives the transaction isolation levels and their meanings. If you want more information about the visibility of changes and transaction isolation levels, see "What Is Visible to Transactions," on page 715.

In a ResultSet object that is TYPE_SCROLL_INSENSITIVE, you cannot see changes made to it by others while it is still open, but you may be able to see your own changes with some implementations. This is the type of ResultSet object to use if you want a consistent view of data and do not want to see changes made by others.

3.3.7   Getting the Most Recent Data

Another feature added in the JDBC 2.0 API is the ability to get the most recent data. You can do this using the method refreshRow, which gets the latest values for a row straight from the database. This method can be relatively expensive, especially if the DBMS returns multiple rows each time you call refreshRow. Nevertheless, its use can be valuable if it is critical to have the latest data. Even when a result set is sensitive and changes are visible, an application may not always see the very latest changes that have been made to a row if the driver retrieves several rows at a time and caches them. Thus, using the method refreshRow is the only way to be sure that you are seeing the most up-to-date data.

The following code sample illustrates how an application might use the method refreshRow when it is absolutely critical to see the most current values. Note that the result set should be sensitive; if you use the method refreshRow with a ResultSet object that is TYPE_SCROLL_INSENSITIVE, refreshRow does nothing. (The urgency for getting the latest data is a bit improbable for the table COFFEES, but a commodities trader's fortunes could depend on knowing the latest prices in a wildly fluctuating coffee market. Or, for example, you would probably want the airline reservation clerk to check that the seat you are reserving is really still available.)

```
Statement stmt = con.createStatement(
                    ResultSet.TYPE_SCROLL_SENSITIVE,
                    ResultSet.CONCUR_READ_ONLY);
```

```
ResultSet srs = stmt.executeQuery("SELECT COF_NAME, PRICE
                                        FROM COFFEES");

srs.absolute(4);
float price1 = srs.getFloat("PRICE");
// do something. . .
srs.absolute(4);
srs.refreshRow();
float price2 = srs.getFloat("PRICE");
if (price2 > price1) {
    // do something. . .
}
```

3.4   Making Batch Updates

A batch update is a set of multiple update statements that is submitted to the database for processing as a batch. Sending batch updates can, in some situations, be much more efficient than sending update statements separately. This ability to send updates as a unit, referred to as the batch update facility, is one of the features provided with the JDBC 2.0 API.

3.4.1   Using `Statement` Objects for Batch Updates

In the JDBC 1.0 API, `Statement` objects submit updates to the database individually with the method `executeUpdate`. Multiple `executeUpdate` statements can be sent in the same transaction, but even though they are committed or rolled back as a unit, they are still processed individually. The interfaces derived from `Statement`— `PreparedStatement` and `CallableStatement`—have the same capabilities, using their own versions of `executeUpdate`.

With the JDBC 2.0 core API, `Statement`, `PreparedStatement` and `CallableStatement` objects maintain all of their old functionality and have as an additional feature a list of commands associated with them. This list may contain statements for updating, inserting, or deleting a row; and it may also contain DDL statements such as `CREATE TABLE` and `DROP TABLE`. It cannot, however, contain a statement that would produce a `ResultSet` object, such as a `SELECT` statement. In other words, the list can contain only statements that produce an update count.

The list, which is associated with a `Statement` object at its creation, is initially empty. You can add SQL commands to this list with the method `addBatch` and empty it with the method `clearBatch`. When you have finished adding statements to the list, you call the method `executeBatch` to send them all to the database to be executed as a unit, or batch. Now let's see how these methods work.

Let's suppose that our coffeehouse proprietor wants to start carrying flavored coffees. He has determined that his best source is one of his current suppliers, Superior Coffee, and he wants to add four new coffees to the table COFFEES. Because he is inserting only four new rows, a batch update may not improve performance significantly, but this is a good opportunity to demonstrate how to make batch updates. Remember that the table COFFEES has five columns: column COF_NAME is type VARCHAR(32), column SUP_ID is type INTEGER, column PRICE is type FLOAT, column SALES is type INTEGER, and column TOTAL is type INTEGER. Each row the proprietor inserts must have values for the five columns in order. The code for inserting the new rows as a batch might look like this:

```
con.setAutoCommit(false);
Statement stmt = con.createStatement();

stmt.addBatch("INSERT INTO COFFEES " +
              "VALUES('Amaretto', 49, 9.99, 0, 0)");
stmt.addBatch("INSERT INTO COFFEES " +
              "VALUES('Hazelnut', 49, 9.99, 0, 0)");
stmt.addBatch("INSERT INTO COFFEES " +
              "VALUES('Amaretto_decaf', 49, 10.99, 0, 0)");
stmt.addBatch("INSERT INTO COFFEES " +
              "VALUES('Hazelnut_decaf', 49, 10.99, 0, 0)");

int [] updateCounts = stmt.executeBatch();
con.commit();
con.setAutoCommit(true);
```

Now let's examine the code line by line.

```
con.setAutoCommit(false);
```

This line disables auto-commit mode for the Connection object *con* so that the transaction will not be automatically committed or rolled back when the method `executeBatch` is called. (If you do not recall what a transaction is, you should review the section "Transactions," on page 392.) To allow for correct error handling, you should always disable auto-commit mode before beginning a batch update.

```
Statement stmt = con.createStatement();
```

This line of code creates the Statement object *stmt*. As is true of all newly created Statement objects, *stmt* has an initially empty list of commands associated with it.

```
stmt.addBatch("INSERT INTO COFFEES " +
            "VALUES('Amaretto', 49, 9.99, 0, 0)");
stmt.addBatch("INSERT INTO COFFEES " +
            "VALUES('Hazelnut', 49, 9.99, 0, 0)");
stmt.addBatch("INSERT INTO COFFEES " +
            "VALUES('Amaretto_decaf', 49, 10.99, 0, 0)");
stmt.addBatch("INSERT INTO COFFEES " +
          "VALUES('Hazelnut_decaf', 49, 10.99, 0, 0)");
```

Each of these lines of code adds a command to the list of commands associated with *stmt*. These commands are all INSERT INTO statements, each one adding a row consisting of five column values. The values for the columns COF_NAME and PRICE are self-explanatory. The second value in each row is 49 because that is the identification number for the supplier, Superior Coffee. The last two values, the entries for the columns SALES and TOTAL, all start out being zero because there have been no sales yet. (SALES is the number of pounds of this row's coffee sold in the current week; TOTAL is the total of all the cumulative sales of this coffee.)

```
int [] updateCounts = stmt.executeBatch();
```

In this line, *stmt* sends the four SQL commands that were added to its list of commands off to the database to be executed as a batch. Note that *stmt* uses the method executeBatch to send the batch of insertions, not the method executeUpdate, which sends only one command and returns a single update count. The DBMS will execute the commands in the order in which they were added to the list of commands, so it will first add the row of values for Amaretto, then add the row for Hazelnut, then Amaretto decaf, and finally Hazelnut decaf. If all four commands execute successfully, the DBMS will return an update count for each command in the order in which it was executed. The update counts, int values indicating how many rows were affected by each command, are stored in the array *updateCounts*.

If all four of the commands in the batch were executed successfully, *update-Counts* will contain four values, all of which are 1 because an insertion affects one row. The list of commands associated with *stmt* will now be empty because the four commands added previously were sent to the database when *stmt* called the method executeBatch. You can at any time explicitly empty this list of commands with the method clearBatch.

```
con.commit();
```

The Connection.commit method makes the batch of updates to the COFFEES table permanent. This method needs to be called explicitly because the auto-commit mode for this connection was disabled previously.

```
con.setAutoCommit(true);
```

This line of code enables auto-commit mode for the Connection *con*, which is the default. Now each statement will automatically be committed after it is executed, and an application no longer needs to invoke the method commit.

The previous code fragment exemplifies a static batch update. It is also possible to have a parameterized batch update, as shown in the following code fragment where *con* is a Connection object.

```
con.setAutoCommit(false);
PreparedStatement pstmt = con.prepareStatement(
                "INSERT INTO COFFEES VALUES(?, ?, ?, ?, ?)");
pstmt.setString(1, "Amaretto");
pstmt.setInt(2, 49);
pstmt.setFloat(3, 9.99);
pstmt.setInt(4, 0);
pstmt.setInt(5, 0);
pstmt.addBatch();

pstmt.setString(1, "Hazelnut");
pstmt.setInt(2, 49);
pstmt.setFloat(3, 9.99);
pstmt.setInt(4, 0);
```

```
pstmt.setInt(5, 0);
pstmt.addBatch();

// ... and so on for each new type of coffee

int [] updateCounts = pstmt.executeBatch();
con.commit();
con.setAutoCommit(true);
```

3.4.2   Batch Update Exceptions

You will get a `BatchUpdateException` when you call the method `executeBatch` if (1) one of the SQL statements you added to the batch produces a result set (usually a query) or (2) one of the SQL statements in the batch does not execute successfully for some other reason.

You should not add a query (a `SELECT` statement) to a batch of SQL commands because the method `executeBatch`, which returns an array of update counts, expects an update count from each SQL command that executes successfully. This means that only commands that return an update count (commands such as `INSERT INTO`, `UPDATE`, `DELETE`) or that return 0 (such as `CREATE TABLE`, `DROP TABLE`, `ALTER TABLE`) can be successfully executed as a batch with the `executeBatch` method.

A `BatchUpdateException` contains an array of update counts that is similar to the array returned by the method `executeBatch`. In both cases, the update counts are in the same order as the commands that produced them. This tells you how many commands in the batch executed successfully and which ones they are. For example, if five commands executed successfully, the array will contain five numbers: the first one being the update count for the first command, the second one being the update count for the second command, and so on.

`BatchUpdateException` is derived from `SQLException`. This means that you can use all of the methods available to an `SQLException` object with it. The following code fragment prints all of the `SQLException` information plus the update counts contained in a `BatchUpdateException` object. Because `BatchUpdateException.getUpdateCounts` returns an array of `int`, the code uses a `for` loop to print each of the update counts.

```
try {
// make some updates
} catch(BatchUpdateException b) {
    System.err.println("----BatchUpdateException----");
```

```
        System.err.println("SQLState:   " + b.getSQLState());
        System.err.println("Message:    " + b.getMessage());
        System.err.println("Vendor:    " + b.getErrorCode());
        System.err.print("Update counts:   ");
        int [] updateCounts = b.getUpdateCounts();
        for (int i = 0; i < updateCounts.length; i++) {
            System.err.print(updateCounts[i] + "    ");
        }

        System.err.println("");
    }
```

2.0 3.4.3   Sample Code 21

The following code puts together the code fragments from previous sections to
make a complete program illustrating a batch update. One thing you might notice is
that there are two catch blocks at the end of the application. If there is a BatchUpdateException object, the first catch block will catch it. The second one will catch an
SQLException object that is not a BatchUpdateException object. (All methods will
throw an SQLException if there is an error accessing data.)

```
import java.sql.*;

public class BatchUpdate {

    public static void main(String args[]) {

        String url = "jdbc:mySubprotocol:myDataSource";
        Connection con;
        Statement stmt;
        try {
            Class.forName("myDriver.ClassName");

        } catch(java.lang.ClassNotFoundException e) {
            System.err.print("ClassNotFoundException: ");
            System.err.println(e.getMessage());
        }
```

```java
    try {

        con = DriverManager.getConnection(url,
                                "myLogin", "myPassword");

        con.setAutoCommit(false);
        stmt = con.createStatement();
        stmt.addBatch("INSERT INTO COFFEES " +
            "VALUES('Amaretto', 49, 9.99, 0, 0)");
          stmt.addBatch("INSERT INTO COFFEES " +
            "VALUES('Hazelnut', 49, 9.99, 0, 0)");
          stmt.addBatch("INSERT INTO COFFEES " +
            "VALUES('Amaretto_decaf', 49, 10.99, 0, 0)");
          stmt.addBatch("INSERT INTO COFFEES " +
            "VALUES('Hazelnut_decaf', 49, 10.99, 0, 0)");

        int [] updateCounts = stmt.executeBatch();
        con.commit();
        con.setAutoCommit(true);

        ResultSet rs = stmt.executeQuery("SELECT * FROM COFFEES");

        System.out.println("Table COFFEES after insertion:");
        while (rs.next()) {
            String name = rs.getString("COF_NAME");
            int id = rs.getInt("SUP_ID");
            float price = rs.getFloat("PRICE");
            int sales = rs.getInt("SALES");
            int total = rs.getInt("TOTAL");
            System.out.print(name + "    " + id + "    " + price);
            System.out.println("    " + sales + "    " + total);
        }

        rs.close();
        stmt.close();
        con.close();

    } catch(BatchUpdateException b) {
        System.err.println("----BatchUpdateException----");
```

```
            System.err.println("SQLState:   " + b.getSQLState());
            System.err.println("Message:    " + b.getMessage());
            System.err.println("Vendor:     " + b.getErrorCode());
            System.err.print("Update counts:   ");
            int [] updateCounts = b.getUpdateCounts();
            for (int i = 0; i < updateCounts.length; i++) {
                System.err.print(updateCounts[i] + "   ");
            }
            System.err.println("");

        } catch(SQLException ex) {
            System.err.println("----SQLException----");
            System.err.println("SQLState:   " + ex.getSQLState());
            System.err.println("Message:    " + ex.getMessage());
            System.err.println("Vendor:     " + ex.getErrorCode());
        }
    }
}
```

2.0   3.5   SQL99 Data Types

The data types commonly referred to as SQL99 types are the new data types being adopted in the next version of the ANSI/ISO SQL standard. The JDBC 2.0 API provides interfaces that represent the mapping of these SQL99 data types into the Java programming language. With these new interfaces, you can work with SQL99 data types the same way you do other data types.

The new SQL99 data types give a relational database more flexibility in what can be used as a value for a table column. For example, a column may now be used to store the new type BLOB (Binary Large Object), which can store very large amounts of data as raw bytes. A column may also be of type CLOB (Character Large Object), which is capable of storing very large amounts of data in character format. The new type ARRAY makes it possible to use an array as a column value. Even the new SQL user-defined types (UDTs), structured types and distinct types, can now be stored as column values.

The following list gives the JDBC 2.0 interfaces that map SQL99 types. We will discuss them in more detail later.

- A Blob instance maps an SQL BLOB value.

- A Clob instance maps an SQL CLOB value.

- An Array instance maps an SQL ARRAY value.

- A Struct instance maps an SQL structured type value.

- A Ref instance maps an SQL REF value.

3.5.1   DISTINCT Type

2.0

There is one more SQL99 data type, the DISTINCT type. We consider it separately because it behaves differently from the other SQL99 data types. Being a user-defined type that is based on one of the already existing built-in types, it has no interface as its mapping in the Java programming language. Instead, the standard mapping for a DISTINCT type is the Java type to which its underlying SQL type maps.

To illustrate, we will create a DISTINCT type and then see how to retrieve, set, or update it. Suppose you always use a two-letter abbreviation for a state and want to create a DISTINCT type to be used for these abbreviations. You could define your new DISTINCT type with the following SQL statement:

```
CREATE TYPE STATE AS CHAR(2);
```

Some DBMSs use an alternate syntax for creating a DISTINCT type, which is shown in the following line of code:

```
CREATE DISTINCT TYPE STATE AS CHAR(2);
```

If one syntax does not work, you can try the other. Or, you can check the documentation for your driver to see the exact syntax it expects.

These statements create a new data type, STATE, which can be used as a column value or as the value for an attribute of an SQL structured type. Because a value of type STATE is in reality a value that is two CHARs, you use the same method to retrieve it that you would use to retrieve a CHAR value, that is, getString. For example, assuming that the fourth column of ResultSet *rs* stores values of type STATE, the following line of code retrieves its value.

```
String state = rs.getString(4);
```

Similarly, you would use the method setString to store a STATE value in the database and the method updateString to modify its value.

3.5.2   Using SQL99 Data Types

You retrieve, store, and update SQL99 data types the same way you do other data types. You use getter methods in either the ResultSet or CallableStatement interface to retrieve them, setter methods in the PreparedStatement interface to store them, and update methods in the ResultSet interface to update them. Probably 90 percent of the operations performed on SQL99 types involve using getter, setter, and updater methods. Table 3.1 shows which methods to use.

Table 3.1: Methods for SQL99 Data Types

SQL99 type	getter method	setter method	updater method
BLOB	getBlob	setBlob	updateBlob*
CLOB	getClob	setClob	updateClob*
ARRAY	getArray	setArray	updateArray*
Structured type	getObject	setObject	updateObject
REF(structured type)	getRef	setRef	updateRef*

* The methods updateArray, updateBlob, updateClob, and updateRef were added to the JDBC 3.0 API. If you are not sure whether your DBMS supports these updater methods, you can use the method updateObject, which works for all types.

For example, the following code fragment retrieves an SQL ARRAY value. For this example, suppose that the column SCORES in the table STUDENTS contains values of type ARRAY. The variable *stmt* is a Statement object.

```
ResultSet rs = stmt.executeQuery(
                "SELECT SCORES FROM STUDENTS WHERE ID = 002238");
rs.next();
Array scores = rs.getArray("SCORES");
```

The variable *scores* is a logical pointer to the SQL ARRAY object stored in the table STUDENTS in the row for student 002238.

If you want to store a value in the database, you use the appropriate setter method. For example, the following code fragment, in which *rs* is a ResultSet object, stores a Clob object:

```
Clob notes = rs.getClob("NOTES");
PreparedStatement pstmt = con.prepareStatement(
          "UPDATE MARKETS SET COMMENTS = ? WHERE SALES < 1000000");
pstmt.setClob(1, notes);
pstmt.executeUpdate();
```

This code sets *notes* as the first parameter in the update statement being sent to the database. The CLOB value designated by *notes* will be stored in the table MARKETS in column COMMENTS in every row where the value in the column SALES is less than one million.

3.5.3   Blob, Clob, and Array Objects

An important feature of Blob, Clob, and Array objects is that you can manipulate them without having to bring all of their data from the database server to your client machine. An instance of any of these types is actually a locator (logical pointer) to the object in the database that the instance represents. Because an SQL BLOB, CLOB, or ARRAY object may be very large, this feature can make performance significantly faster.

If you want to bring the data of an SQL BLOB, CLOB, or ARRAY value to the client, you can use methods in the Blob, Clob, and Array interfaces that are provided for this purpose. Blob and Clob objects materialize the data of the objects they represent as a stream or as a Java array, whereas an Array object materializes the SQL ARRAY it represents as either a result set or a Java array. For example, after retrieving the SQL ARRAY value in the column ZIPS as a java.sql.Array object, the following code fragment materializes the ARRAY value on the client. It then iterates through *zips*, the Java array that contains the elements of the SQL ARRAY value, to check that each zip code is valid. This code assumes that the class ZipCode has been defined previously with the method isValid returning true if the given zip code matches one of the zip codes in a master list of valid zip codes.

```
ResultSet rs = stmt.executeQuery("SELECT ZIPS FROM REGIONS");
while (rs.next()) {
   Array z = rs.getArray("ZIPS");
```

```
        String[] zips = (String[])z.getArray();
        for (int i = 0; i < zips.length; i++) {
            if (!ZipCode.isValid(zips[i])) {
                . . . // code to display warning
            }
        }
    }
```

The preceding example brings out some of the fine points of the `Array` interface. In the following line, the `ResultSet` method `getArray` returns the value stored in the column ZIPS of the current row as the `java.sql.Array` object *z*.

```
        Array z = rs.getArray("ZIPS");
```

The variable *z* contains a locator, which means that it is a logical pointer to the SQL ARRAY on the server; it does not contain the elements of the ARRAY itself. Being a logical pointer, *z* can be used to manipulate the array on the server.

In the following line, `getArray` is the `Array.getArray` method, not the `ResultSet.getArray` method used in the previous line. Because `Array.getArray` returns an `Object` in the Java programming language and because each zip code is a `String` object, the result is cast to an array of `String` objects before being assigned to the variable *zips*.

```
        String[] zips = (String[])z.getArray();
```

The `Array.getArray` method materializes the SQL ARRAY elements on the client as an array of `String` objects. Because, in effect, the variable *zips* contains the elements of the array, it is possible to iterate through *zips* in a `for` loop, looking for zip codes that are not valid.

2.0   3.5.4   Creating an SQL Structured Type

SQL structured types and DISTINCT types are the two data types that a user can define in SQL. They are often referred to as UDTs (user-defined types), and you create them with an SQL CREATE TYPE statement.

Getting back to our example of The Coffee Break, let's suppose that the proprietor has been successful beyond all expectations and has been expanding with new branches. He has decided to add a STORES table to his database containing information about each establishment. STORES will have four columns: STORE_NO for each store's identification number, LOCATION for its address, COF_TYPES for the coffees it sells, and MGR for its manager. The proprietor, now an entrepreneur, opts to make use of the SQL99 data types. Accordingly, he makes the column LOCATION be an SQL structured type, the column COF_TYPES an SQL ARRAY, and the column MGR a REF(MANAGER), with MANAGER being an SQL structured type.

The first thing our entrepreneur needs to do is define the new structured types for the address and the manager. An SQL structured type is similar to structured types in the Java programming language in that it has members, called *attributes*, that may be any data type. The entrepreneur writes the following SQL statement to create the new data type ADDRESS:

```
CREATE TYPE ADDRESS
(
NUM INTEGER,
STREET VARCHAR(40),
CITY VARCHAR(40),
STATE CHAR(2),
ZIP CHAR(5)
);
```

In this definition, the new type ADDRESS has five attributes, which are analogous to fields in a Java class. The attribute NUM is an INTEGER, the attribute STREET is a VARCHAR(40), the attribute CITY is a VARCHAR(40), the attribute STATE is a CHAR(2), and the attribute ZIP is a CHAR(5).

The following code fragment, in which *con* is a valid Connection object, sends the definition of ADDRESS to the DBMS:

```
String createAddress =  "CREATE TYPE ADDRESS " +
         "(NUM INTEGER, STREET VARCHAR(40), CITY VARCHAR(40), " +
         "STATE CHAR(2), ZIP CHAR(5))";
Statement stmt = con.createStatement();
stmt.executeUpdate(createAddress);
```

Now ADDRESS is registered with the database as a data type, and our entrepreneur can use it as the data type for a table column or an attribute of a structured type.

3.5.5   Creating a DISTINCT Type

One of the attributes our coffee entrepreneur plans to include in the new structured type MANAGER is the manager's phone number. Because he will always list the phone number as a ten-digit number (to be sure it includes the area code) and will never manipulate it as a number, he decides to define a new type called PHONE_NO that consists of ten characters. The SQL definition of this new DISTINCT type, which can be thought of as a structured type with only one attribute, looks like this:

```
CREATE TYPE PHONE_NO AS CHAR(10);
```

Or, as noted earlier, for some drivers the syntax might look like this:

```
CREATE DISTINCT TYPE PHONE_NO AS CHAR(10);
```

A DISTINCT type is always based on another data type, which must be a predefined type. In other words, a DISTINCT type cannot be based on a UDT. To retrieve or set a value that is a DISTINCT type, you use the appropriate method for the underlying type (the type on which it is based). For example, to retrieve an instance of PHONE_NO, which is based on a CHAR, you would use the method getString because that is the method for retrieving a CHAR.

Assuming that a value of type PHONE_NO is in the fourth column of the current row of the ResultSet object *rs*, the following line of code retrieves it.

```
String phoneNumber = rs.getString(4);
```

Similarly, the following line of code sets an input parameter that has type PHONE_NO for a prepared statement being sent to the database.

```
pstmt.setString(1, phoneNumber);
```

Adding to the previous code fragment, the definition of PHONE_NO will be sent to the database with the following line of code:

```
stmt.executeUpdate("CREATE TYPE PHONE_NO AS CHAR(10)");
```

After registering the type PHONE_NO with the database, our entrepreneur can use it as a column type in a table or, as he wants to do, as the data type for an attribute in a structured type. The definition of MANAGER in the following SQL statement uses PHONE_NO as the data type for the attribute PHONE.

```
CREATE TYPE MANAGER
(
 MGR_ID INTEGER,
 LAST_NAME VARCHAR(40),
 FIRST_NAME VARCHAR(40),
 PHONE PHONE_NO
);
```

Reusing *stmt*, defined previously, the following code fragment sends the definition of the structured type MANAGER to the database.

```
String createManager = "CREATE TYPE MANAGER " +
                "(MGR_ID INTEGER, LAST_NAME VARCHAR(40), " +
                "FIRST_NAME VARCHAR(40), PHONE PHONE_NO)";
stmt.executeUpdate(createManager);
```

3.5.6   Sample Code 22

The following JDBC code, CreateUDTs.java, sends the definitions for ADDRESS, MANAGER, and PHONE_NO to the database. If your DBMS uses type names that are different from the data types used in these definitions, you will need to run the program CreateNewType.java to create the new types, which is explained immediately following the code for CreateUDTs.java. If your driver does not implement DISTINCT types, you will need to use CHAR(10) as the type for the column PHONE and delete the line that creates the type PHONE_NO as CHAR(10).

```
import java.sql.*;

public class CreateUDTs {
    public static void main(String args[]) {

        String url = "jdbc:mySubprotocol:myDataSource";
        Connection con;
        Statement stmt;
        String createAddress = "CREATE TYPE ADDRESS (NUM INTEGER, " +
```

```
                          "STREET VARCHAR(40), CITY VARCHAR(40), " +
                          "STATE CHAR(2), ZIP CHAR(5))";

        String createManager = "CREATE TYPE MANAGER (MGR_ID INTEGER, " +
                "LAST_NAME VARCHAR(40), FIRST_NAME VARCHAR(40), " +
                "PHONE PHONE_NO)";

        try {
            Class.forName("myDriver.ClassName");
        } catch(java.lang.ClassNotFoundException e) {
            System.err.print("ClassNotFoundException: ");
            System.err.println(e.getMessage());
        }

        try {

            con = DriverManager.getConnection(url,
                    "myLogin", "myPassword");
            stmt = con.createStatement();

            stmt.executeUpdate(createAddress);
            stmt.executeUpdate("CREATE TYPE PHONE_NO AS CHAR(10))");
            stmt.executeUpdate(createManager);

            stmt.close();
            con.close();

        } catch(SQLException ex) {
            System.err.println("-----SQLException-----");
            System.err.println("SQLState:  " + ex.getSQLState());
            System.err.println("Message:  " + ex.getMessage());
            System.err.println("Vendor:  " + ex.getErrorCode());
        }
    }
}
```

If your DBMS uses its own DBMS-specific data types, using CreateUDTs may not work because it does not use the specific local type names that your DBMS requires. In this case, you can run the code provided in "Sample Code 19," on page 244, to create each UDT individually. This code, `CreateNewType.java`, is very similar to `CreateNewTable.java`, which you probably used to create the tables in the basic tutorial. Instructions for use follow the code.

3.5.7   Using References to Structured Types

Our coffee entrepreneur has created three new data types that he can now use as column types or attribute types in his database: the structured types `LOCATION` and `MANAGER`, and the `DISTINCT` type `PHONE_NO`. He has already used `PHONE_NO` as the type for the attribute `PHONE` in the new type `MANAGER`, and he plans to use `ADDRESS` as the data type for the column `LOCATION` in the table `STORES`. He can use `MANAGER` as the type for the column `MGR`, but he prefers to use the type `REF(MANAGER)` because he often has one person manage two or three stores. By using `REF(MANAGER)` as a column type, he avoids repeating all the data for `MANAGER` when one person manages more than one store.

With the structured type `MANAGER` already created, our entrepreneur can now create a table containing instances of `MANAGER` that can be referenced. A reference to an instance of `MANAGER` will have the type `REF(MANAGER)`. An SQL `REF` is nothing more than a logical pointer to a structured type, so an instance of `REF(MANAGER)` serves as a logical pointer to an instance of `MANAGER`.

Because an SQL `REF` value needs to be permanently associated with the instance of the structured type that it references, it is stored in a special table together with its associated instance. A programmer does not create `REF` types directly but rather creates the table that will store instances of a particular structured type that are to be referenced. Every structured type whose instances are to be referenced will have its own table. When you insert an instance of the structured type into the table, the DBMS automatically creates a `REF` instance. For example, to hold instances of `MANAGER`, our entrepreneur created the following special table using SQL:

```
CREATE TABLE MANAGERS OF MANAGER (OID IS REF(MANAGER)
                                  SYSTEM GENERATED);
```

This statement creates a table with the special column `OID`, which stores values of type `REF(MANAGER)`. Each time an instance of `MANAGER` is inserted into the table, the DBMS will generate an instance of `REF(MANAGER)` and store it in the column `OID`. Implicitly, an additional column stores each attribute of `MANAGER` that has been inserted into the table, as well. For example, the following code fragment shows how our entrepreneur created three instances of MANAGER to represent three of his managers:

```
INSERT INTO MANAGERS (MGR_ID, LAST_NAME, FIRST_NAME, PHONE) VALUES
(
    000001,
    'MONTOYA',
    'ALFREDO',
    '8317225600'
);

INSERT INTO MANAGERS (MGR_ID, LAST_NAME, FIRST_NAME, PHONE) VALUES
(
    000002,
    'HASKINS',
    'MARGARET',
    '4084355600'
);

INSERT INTO MANAGERS (MGR_ID, LAST_NAME, FIRST_NAME, PHONE) VALUES
(
    000003,
    'CHEN',
    'HELEN',
    '4153785600'
);
```

The table MANAGERS will now have three rows, one row for each manager inserted so far. The column OID will contain three unique object identifiers of type REF(MANAGER), one for each instance of MANAGER. These object identifiers were generated automatically by the DBMS and will be permanently stored in the table MANAGERS. Implicitly an additional column stores each attribute of MANAGER. For example, in the table MANAGERS, one row contains a REF(MANAGER) that references Alfredo Montoya, another row contains a REF(MANAGER) that references Margaret Haskins, and a third row contains a REF(MANAGER) that references Helen Chen.

To access a REF(MANAGER) instance, you select it from its table. For example, our entrepreneur retrieved the reference to Alfredo Montoya, whose ID number is 000001, with the following code fragment:

```
String selectMgr = "SELECT OID FROM MANAGERS WHERE MGR_ID = 000001";
ResultSet rs = stmt.executeQuery(selectMgr);
rs.next();
Ref manager = rs.getRef("OID");
```

Now he can use the variable *manager* as a column value that references Alfredo Montoya.

3.5.8   Sample Code 23

2.0

The following code example illustrates creating an SQL REF value. It creates the table MANAGERS, a table of instances of the structured type MANAGER, and inserts three instances of MANAGER into the table. The column OID in this table will store instances of REF(MANAGER). After this code is executed, MANAGERS will have a row for each of the three MANAGER objects inserted, and the value in the OID column will be the REF(MANAGER) that identifies the instance of MANAGER stored in that row.

```
import java.sql.*;

public class CreateRef {

    public static void main(String args[]) {

        String url = "jdbc:mySubprotocol:myDataSource";

        Connection con;
        Statement stmt;
        try {
            Class.forName("myDriver.ClassName");

        } catch(java.lang.ClassNotFoundException e) {
            System.err.print("ClassNotFoundException: ");

            System.err.println(e.getMessage());
        }

        try {
            String createManagers = "CREATE TABLE MANAGERS OF MANAGER " +
```

```
                        "(OID IS REF(MANAGER) SYSTEM GENERATED)";

        String insertManager1 = "INSERT INTO MANAGERS " +
                "(MGR_ID, LAST_NAME, FIRST_NAME, PHONE) VALUES " +
                "(000001, 'MONTOYA', 'ALFREDO', '8317225600')";

        String insertManager2 = "INSERT INTO MANAGERS " +
                "(MGR_ID, LAST_NAME, FIRST_NAME, PHONE) VALUES " +
                "(000002, 'HASKINS', 'MARGARET', '4084355600')";

        String insertManager3 = "INSERT INTO MANAGERS " +
                "(MGR_ID, LAST_NAME, FIRST_NAME, PHONE) VALUES " +
                "(000003, 'CHEN', 'HELEN', '4153785600')";

        con = DriverManager.getConnection(url,
                            "myLogin", "myPassword");

        stmt = con.createStatement();
        stmt.executeUpdate(createManagers);
        con.setAutoCommit(false);

        stmt.addBatch(insertManager1);
        stmt.addBatch(insertManager2);
        stmt.addBatch(insertManager3);
        int [] updateCounts = stmt.executeBatch();

        con.commit();

        System.out.println("Update count for:  ");
        for (int i = 0; i < updateCounts.length; i++) {
            System.out.print("    command " + (i + 1) + " = ");
            System.out.println(updateCounts[i]);
        }

        stmt.close();
        con.close();

    } catch(BatchUpdateException b) {
        System.err.println("-----BatchUpdateException-----");
```

```
            System.err.println("Message:   " + b.getMessage());
            System.err.println("SQLState:   " + b.getSQLState());
            System.err.println("Vendor:   " + b.getErrorCode());
            System.err.print("Update counts for successful commands:  ");
            int [] rowsUpdated = b.getUpdateCounts();
            for (int i = 0; i < rowsUpdated.length; i++) {
                System.err.print(rowsUpdated[i] + "   ");
            }
            System.err.println("");
        } catch(SQLException ex) {
            System.err.println("------SQLException------");
            System.err.println("Error message:  " + ex.getMessage());
            System.err.println("SQLState:   " + ex.getSQLState());
            System.err.println("Vendor:   " + ex.getErrorCode());
        }
    }
}
```

NOTE: At the time of this writing, not all drivers fully support the APIs used in this sample code. Consequently, the code has been compiled but not executed. It is included as an aid to understanding how the API can be used. In addition, SQL syntax and dialects may differ between DBMS implementations. It is therefore highly recommended that you consult your DBMS documentation to see the exact syntax you should use.

3.5.9   Using SQL99 Types as Column Values

Our entrepreneur now has the UDTs he needs to create the table STORES. He will use the new data types as column types so that he can store instances of the new types in STORES. He will use the structured type ADDRESS as the type for the column LOCATION and the type REF(MANAGER) as the type for the column MGR.

He will also use the SQL99 predefined type ARRAY as a column type. The following line of code creates the type COF_ARRAY as an ARRAY value with ten elements. The base type of COF_ARRAY is VARCHAR(40).

```
CREATE TYPE COF_ARRAY AS ARRAY(10) OF VARCHAR(40);
```

With the new data types defined, the following SQL command creates the
table STORES.

```
CREATE TABLE STORES
(
    STORE_NO INTEGER,
    LOCATION ADDRESS,
    COF_TYPES COF_ARRAY,
    MGR REF(MANAGER)
);
```

3.5.10 Sample Code 24

The class CreateStores demonstrates using SQL99 types. The type names to use in
your JDBC code for creating STORES may be different from those used in the preceding CREATE TABLE statement, depending on the type names used by your DBMS. If
you know that your DBMS uses the same type names, you can simply run the program CreateStores.java, shown here. If not, refer to the instructions immediately
following CreateStores.java.

```
import java.sql.*;

public class CreateStores {

    public static void main(String args[]) {

        String url = "jdbc:mySubprotocol:myDataSource";
        Connection con;
        String createTable;
        String createArray;
        createArray = "CREATE TYPE COF_ARRAY AS ARRAY(10) " +
                                    "OF VARCHAR(40)";
        createTable = "CREATE TABLE STORES ( " +
                    "STORE_NO INTEGER, LOCATION ADDRESS, " +
                    "COF_TYPES COF_ARRAY, MGR REF(MANAGER))";
        Statement stmt;
```

```
        try {
            Class.forName("myDriver.ClassName");

        } catch(java.lang.ClassNotFoundException e) {
            System.err.print("ClassNotFoundException: ");
            System.err.println(e.getMessage());
        }

        try {
            con = DriverManager.getConnection(url,
                            "myLogin", "myPassword");

            stmt = con.createStatement();
            stmt.executeUpdate(createArray);
            stmt.executeUpdate(createTable);

            stmt.close();
            con.close();
        } catch(SQLException ex) {
            System.err.println("SQLException: " + ex.getMessage());
        }
    }
}
```

NOTE: At the time of this writing, not all drivers fully support the APIs used in this sample code. Consequently, the code has been compiled but not executed. It is included as an aid to understanding how the API can be used. In addition, SQL syntax and dialects may differ between DBMS implementations. It is therefore highly recommended that you consult your DBMS documentation to see the exact syntax you should use.

If you needed to run CreateNewTable.java to create the tables COFFEES and SUPPLIERS, you should run it to create the table STORES as well. As you might recall, this program first prompts you to supply the name and data type for each column in the table. Then it queries the database about the names it uses for each of the data types you supplied and builds a CREATE TABLE statement using those type names. You can see the code and an explanation of it in the section "Generic Applications," on page 233. Note that in CreateStores, the type for the column MGR is REF(MANAGER), which is the standard format for an SQL REF type. Some drivers, however, may require that the code use the format REF MANAGER instead.

The following list gives the responses you should type if you run the program CreateNewTable.java. Note that the first response is the name of the table. Subsequent responses give the name of a column and then the data type for that column.

```
STORES
STORE_NO
INTEGER
LOCATION
ADDRESS
COF_TYPES
COF_ARRAY
MGR
REF(MANAGER)
```

3.5.11 Inserting SQL99 Types into a Table

The following code fragment inserts one row into the STORES table, supplying values for the columns STORE_NO, LOCATION, COF_TYPES, and MGR, in that order.

```
INSERT INTO STORES VALUES
(
   100001,
   ADDRESS(888, 'Main_Street', 'Rancho_Alegre', 'CA', '94049'),

   COF_ARRAY('Colombian', 'French_Roast', 'Espresso',
                  'Colombian_Decaf','French_Roast_Decaf'),
   SELECT OID FROM MANAGERS WHERE MGR_ID = 000001
);
```

Now let's walk through each column and the value inserted into it.

```
STORE_NO: 100001
```

This column is type INTEGER, and the number 100001 is simply an INTEGER, similar to entries we have made before in the tables COFFEES and SUPPLIERS.

```
LOCATION: ADDRESS(888, 'Main_Street', 'Rancho_Alegre', 'CA',
                                                       '94049')
```

The type for this column is the structured type ADDRESS, and this value is the constructor for an instance of ADDRESS. When we sent our definition of ADDRESS to the DBMS, one of the things it did was to create a constructor for the new type. The comma-separated values in parentheses are the initialization values for the attributes of ADDRESS, and they must appear in the same order in which the attributes were listed in the definition of ADDRESS. 888 is the value for the attribute NUM, which is an INTEGER. "Main_Street" is the value for STREET, and "Rancho_Alegre" is the value for CITY, with both attributes being type VARCHAR(40). The value for the attribute STATE is "CA", which is a CHAR(2), and the value for the attribute ZIP is "94049", which is a CHAR(5).

```
COF_TYPES: COF_ARRAY('Colombian', 'French_Roast', 'Espresso',
               'Colombian_Decaf','French_Roast_Decaf'),
```

The column COF_TYPES is type COF_ARRAY with a base type of VARCHAR(40), and the comma-separated values between parentheses are the String objects that are the array elements. Our entrepreneur defined the type COF_ARRAY as having a maximum of ten elements. This array has five elements because he supplied only five String objects for it.

```
MGR: SELECT OID FROM MANAGERS WHERE MGR_ID = 000001
```

The column MGR is type REF(MANAGER), which means that a value in this column must be a reference to the structured type MANAGER. All of the instances of MANAGER are stored in the table MANAGERS. All of the instances of REF(MANAGER) are also stored in this table, in the column OID. The manager for the store described in this row of our table is Alfredo Montoya, and his information is stored in the instance of MANAGER that has 100001 for the attribute MGR_ID. To get the REF(MANAGER) instance associated with the MANAGER object for Alfredo Montoya, we select the column OID that is in the row where MGR_ID is 100001 in the table MANAGERS. The value that will be stored in the MGR column of STORES (the REF(MANAGER) value) is the value the DBMS generated to uniquely identify this instance of MANAGER.

We can send the preceding SQL statement to the database with the following code fragment:

```
String insertMgr = "INSERT INTO STORES VALUES (100001, " +
    "ADDRESS(888, 'Main_Street', 'Rancho_Alegre', 'CA', '94049'), " +
    "COF_ARRAY('Colombian', 'French_Roast', 'Espresso', " +
                "'Colombian_Decaf', 'French_Roast_Decaf'), " +
    "SELECT OID FROM MANAGERS WHERE MGR_ID = 000001)";


stmt.executeUpdate(insertMgr);
```

However, because we are going to send several INSERT INTO statements, it will be more efficient to send them all together as a batch update, as in Sample Code 25, which follows.

3.5.12 Sample Code 25

InsertStores.java uses a batch update to insert four stores into the table STORES, and then it prints out the information for the stores that were inserted.

```
import java.sql.*;

public class InsertStores {

    public static void main(String args[]) {

        String url = "jdbc:mySubprotocol:myDataSource";
        Connection con;
        Statement stmt;
        try {

            Class.forName("myDriver.ClassName");

        } catch(java.lang.ClassNotFoundException e) {
            System.err.print("ClassNotFoundException: ");
            System.err.println(e.getMessage());
        }
```

```
try {

    con = DriverManager.getConnection(url,
                        "myLogin", "myPassword");
    stmt = con.createStatement();
    con.setAutoCommit(false);

    String insertStore1 = "INSERT INTO STORES VALUES (" +
        "100001, " +
        "ADDRESS(888, 'Main_Street', 'Rancho_Alegre', " +
            "'CA', '94049'), " +
        "COF_ARRAY('Colombian', 'French_Roast', 'Espresso', " +
            "'Colombian_Decaf', 'French_Roast_Decaf'), " +
        "(SELECT OID FROM MANAGERS WHERE MGR_ID = 000001))";

    stmt.addBatch(insertStore1);
    String insertStore2 = "INSERT INTO STORES VALUES (" +
        "100002, " +
        "ADDRESS(1560, 'Alder', 'Ochos_Pinos', " +
            "'CA', '94049'), " +
        "COF_ARRAY('Colombian', 'French_Roast', 'Espresso', " +
            "'Colombian_Decaf', 'French_Roast_Decaf', " +
            "'Kona', 'Kona_Decaf'), " +
        "(SELECT OID FROM MANAGERS WHERE MGR_ID = 000001))";

    stmt.addBatch(insertStore2);

    String insertStore3 = "INSERT INTO STORES VALUES (" +
        "100003, " +
        "ADDRESS(4344, 'First_Street', 'Verona', " +
            "'CA', '94545'), " +
        "COF_ARRAY('Colombian', 'French_Roast', 'Espresso', " +
            "'Colombian_Decaf', 'French_Roast_Decaf', " +
            "'Kona', 'Kona_Decaf'), " +
        "(SELECT OID FROM MANAGERS WHERE MGR_ID = 000002))";

    stmt.addBatch(insertStore3);
```

```java
        String insertStore4 = "INSERT INTO STORES VALUES (" +
          "100004, " +
          "ADDRESS(321, 'Sandy_Way', 'La_Playa', " +
             "'CA', '94544'), " +
          "COF_ARRAY('Colombian', 'French_Roast', 'Espresso', " +
             "'Colombian_Decaf', 'French_Roast_Decaf', " +
             "'Kona', 'Kona_Decaf'), " +
          "(SELECT OID FROM MANAGERS WHERE MGR_ID = 000002))";

        stmt.addBatch(insertStore4);

        String insertStore5 = "INSERT INTO STORES VALUES (" +
          "100005, " +
          "ADDRESS(1000, 'Clover_Road', 'Happyville', " +
             "'CA', '90566'), " +
          "COF_ARRAY('Colombian', 'French_Roast', 'Espresso', " +
             "'Colombian_Decaf', 'French_Roast_Decaf'), " +
          "(SELECT OID FROM MANAGERS WHERE MGR_ID = 000003))";

        stmt.addBatch(insertStore5);

        int [] updateCounts = stmt.executeBatch();

        ResultSet rs = stmt.executeQuery("SELECT * FROM STORES");

        System.out.println("Table STORES after insertion:");
        System.out.println("STORE_NO    LOCATION    COF_TYPE    MGR");

        while (rs.next()) {
            int storeNo = rs.getInt("STORE_NO");
            Struct location = (Struct)rs.getObject("LOCATION");
            Object[] locAttrs = location.getAttributes();
            Array coffeeTypes = rs.getArray("COF_TYPE");
            String[] cofTypes = (String[])coffeeTypes.getArray();

            Ref managerRef = rs.getRef("MGR");
            PreparedStatement pstmt = con.prepareStatement(
                "SELECT MANAGER FROM MANAGERS WHERE OID = ?");
            pstmt.setRef(1, managerRef);
```

```java
            ResultSet rs2 = pstmt.executeQuery();
            rs2.next();
            Struct manager = (Struct)rs2.getObject("MANAGER");
            Object[] manAttrs = manager.getAttributes();

            System.out.print(storeNo + "    ");
            System.out.print(locAttrs[0] + " " + locAttrs[1] + " " +
                locAttrs[2] + ", " + locAttrs[3] + "   " +
                locAttrs[4] + " ");
            for (int i = 0; i < cofTypes.length; i++)
                System.out.print(cofTypes[i] + " ");
            System.out.println(manAttrs[1] + ", " + manAttrs[2]);

            rs2.close();
            pstmt.close();
        }

        rs.close();
        stmt.close();
        con.close();

    } catch(BatchUpdateException b) {
        System.err.println("-----BatchUpdateException-----");
        System.err.println("SQLState: " + b.getSQLState());
        System.err.println("Message:  " + b.getMessage());
        System.err.println("Vendor:   " + b.getErrorCode());
        System.err.print("Update counts:  ");
        int [] updateCounts = b.getUpdateCounts();
        for (int i = 0; i < updateCounts.length; i++) {
            System.err.print(updateCounts[i] + "    ");
        }
        System.err.println("");

    } catch(SQLException ex) {
        System.err.println("SQLException: " + ex.getMessage());
        System.err.println("SQLState:  " + ex.getSQLState());
        System.err.println("Message:   " + ex.getMessage());
        System.err.println("Vendor:    " + ex.getErrorCode());
    }
```

```
    }
}
```

NOTE: At the time of this writing, not all drivers fully support the APIs used in this sample code. Consequently, the code has been compiled but not executed. It is included as an aid to understanding how the API can be used. In addition, SQL syntax and dialects may differ between DBMS implementations. It is therefore highly recommended that you consult your DBMS documentation to see the exact syntax you should use.

3.6   Using Custom Mapping

With business booming, our entrepreneur has found that he is regularly adding new stores and making changes to his database. To make his life a little easier, he has decided to use a custom mapping for the structured type ADDRESS so that he can simply make changes to the Java class that maps ADDRESS. The Java class will have a field for each attribute of ADDRESS, and he can name the class and the fields whatever he wants.

3.6.1   Implementing SQLData

The first thing required for a custom mapping is to create a class that implements the interface SQLData. You will not normally have to do this yourself because tools are being developed to do it. Just so you know what is involved, we will show you what a tool might do. If you want a complete discussion of custom mapping and how it works, see "Creating a Custom Mapping," on page 896.

The SQL definition of the structured type ADDRESS looked like this:

```
CREATE TYPE ADDRESS
(
   NUM INTEGER,
   STREET VARCHAR(40),
```

```
    CITY VARCHAR(40),
    STATE CHAR(2),
    ZIP CHAR(5)
);
```

A class generated by a tool to implement SQLData for the custom mapping of ADDRESS might look like this:

```
public class Address implements SQLData {
    public int num;
    public String street;
    public String city;
    public String state;
    public String zip;

    private String sql_type;
    public String getSQLTypeName() {
        return sql_type;
    }

    public void readSQL(SQLInput stream, String type)
                                        throws SQLException {
        sql_type = type;
        num = stream.readInt();
        street = stream.readString();
        city = stream.readString();

        state = stream.readString();
        zip = stream.readString();
    }

    public void writeSQL(SQLOutput stream) throws SQLException {
        stream.writeInt(num);
        stream.writeString(street);
        stream.writeString(city);
        stream.writeString(state);
        stream.writeString(zip);
    }
}
```

3.6.2   Using a Connection's Type Map

After writing a class that implements the interface SQLData, the only other thing you have to do to set up a custom mapping is to make an entry in a type map. For our example, this means entering the fully qualified SQL name for ADDRESS and the Class object for the class Address. A type map, an instance of java.util.Map, is associated with every new connection when it is created, so we can just use that one. Assuming that *con* is our active connection, the following code fragment adds an entry for the UDT ADDRESS to the type map associated with *con*.

```
java.util.Map map = con.getTypeMap();
map.put("SchemaName.ADDRESS", Address.class);
```

Whenever we call the getObject method to retrieve an instance of ADDRESS, the driver will check the type map associated with the connection and see that it has an entry for ADDRESS. The driver will note the Class object for Address, create an instance of it, and do many other things behind the scenes to map ADDRESS to Address. The nice thing is that you do not have to do anything more than generate the class for the mapping and then make an entry in a type map to let the driver know that there is a custom mapping. The driver will do all the rest.

Note that there are two ways to indicate the Class object:

- using the method Class.forName("ClassName")
- using ClassName.class

The sample code in the tutorials uses the method Class.forName to indicate the Class object for the driver because a driver is supposed to be implemented so that it creates an instance of the driver class and loads it when this method is called. However, for indicating the Class object to be included in a type map, we use ClassName.class. The reason is that errors are reported at compile time if there is a problem. With the method Class.forName, errors are not reported until the code is run.

The situation for storing a structured type that has a custom mapping is similar to that for retrieving one. When you call the method setObject, the driver will check to see if the value to be set is an instance of a class that implements the interface SQLData. If it is (meaning that there is a custom mapping), the driver will use the custom mapping to convert the value to its SQL counterpart before returning it to the database. Again, the driver does the custom mapping behind the scenes; all you need to do is supply the method `setObject` with a parameter that has a custom mapping. You will see an example of this later in this section.

Now let's look at the difference between working with the standard mapping, a `Struct` object, and the custom mapping, a class in the Java programming language. The following code fragment shows the standard mapping to a `Struct` object, which is the mapping the driver uses when there is no entry in the connection's type map.

```
ResultSet rs = stmt.executeQuery(
              "SELECT LOCATION WHERE STORE_NO = 100003");
rs.next();
Struct address = (Struct)rs.getObject("LOCATION");
```

The variable *address* contains the following attribute values: 4344, "First_Street", "Verona", "CA", "94545".

The following code fragment shows what happens when there is an entry for the structured type ADDRESS in the connection's type map. Remember that the column LOCATION stores values of type ADDRESS.

```
ResultSet rs = stmt.executeQuery(
              "SELECT LOCATION WHERE STORE_NO = 100003");
rs.next();
Address store_3 = (Address)rs.getObject("LOCATION");
```

The variable *store_3* is now an instance of the class `Address`, with each attribute value being the current value of one of the fields of `Address`. Note that you need to remember to convert the object retrieved by `getObject` to an `Address` object before assigning it to *store_3*. Note also that *store_3* must be an `Address` object.

Now let's compare working with the `Struct` object to working with the instance of `Address`. Suppose the store moved to a better location in the neighboring town and we need to update our database. With the custom mapping, we simply need to reset the fields of *store_3*, as in the following code fragment.

```
ResultSet rs = stmt.executeQuery(
              "SELECT LOCATION WHERE STORE_NO = 100003");
rs.next();
Address store_3 = (Address)rs.getObject("LOCATION");
store_3.num = 1800;
store_3.street = "Artsy_Alley";
```

```
store_3.city = "Arden";
store_3.state = "CA";
store_3.zip = "94546";
PreparedStatement pstmt = con.prepareStatement(
        "UPDATE STORES SET LOCATION = ? WHERE STORE_NO = 100003");
pstmt.setObject(1, store_3);
pstmt.executeUpdate();
```

Values in the column LOCATION are instances of ADDRESS. The driver checks the connection's type map and sees that there is an entry linking ADDRESS with the class Address and consequently uses the custom mapping indicated in Address. When the code calls setObject with the variable *store_3* as the second parameter, the driver checks and sees that *store_3* represents an instance of the class Address, which implements SQLData for the structured type ADDRESS, and again automatically uses the custom mapping.

Without a custom mapping for ADDRESS, the update would look more like this:

```
PreparedStatement pstmt = con.prepareStatement(
        "UPDATE STORES SET LOCATION.NUM = 1800, " +
        "LOCATION.STREET = 'Artsy_Alley', " +
        "LOCATION.CITY = 'Arden', " +
        "LOCATION.STATE = 'CA', " +
        "LOCATION.ZIP = '94546' " +
        "WHERE STORE_NO = 100003");
pstmt.executeUpdate;
```

3.6.3   Using Your Own Type Map

Up to this point, we have used only the type map associated with a connection for custom mapping. Normally, that is the only type map most programmers will use. However, it is also possible to create a type map and pass it to certain methods so that the driver will use that type map instead of the one associated with the connection. This allows two different mappings for the same UDT. In fact, it is possible to have multiple custom mappings for the same UDT as long as each mapping is set up with a class implementing SQLData and an entry in a type map. If you do not pass a type map to a method that can accept one, the driver will by default use the type map associated with the connection.

Very few situations call for using a type map other than the type map associated with a connection. It could be necessary to supply a method with a type map if, for instance, several programmers working on a JDBC application brought their components together and were using the same connection. If two or more programmers had created their own custom mappings for the same SQL UDT, each would need to supply his/her own type map, thus overriding the connection's type map.

3.7 Using a DataSource Object

2.0

This section covers DataSource objects, which are the preferred means of getting a connection to a data source. In addition to their other advantages, which will be explained later, DataSource objects can provide connection pooling and distributed transactions. The DataSource interface, along with its related interfaces and classes, was introduced in the JDBC 2.0 Optional Package API. Note that with the introduction of the JDBC 3.0 API, this API is included in the J2SE 1.4 download, making it is easier to use a DataSource object to get a connection to a data source. In addition to being the preferred means of getting a connection, the DataSource API is essential for enterprise database computing. In particular, it is integral to Enterprise JavaBeans (EJB) technology.

Using the DataSource API is not difficult from the programmer's point of view because, in the spirit of EJB, most of the heavy lifting is done for you behind the scenes. This section will show you how to get a connection using the DataSource interface and how to make use of distributed transactions and connection pooling. Both of these involve very little change in coding on the part of the application programmer.

The work performed to deploy the classes that make these operations possible, which a system administrator usually does with a tool, varies with the type of DataSource object that is being deployed. As a result, most of this section is devoted to showing how a system administrator sets up the environment so that programmers can use a DataSource object to get connections. The other major set of functionality in the JDBC Optional Package API, rowsets, is covered in the chapter, "Rowset Tutorial," starting on page 255. It explains rowsets and gives examples of what you can do with them.

3.7.1   Using a `DataSource` Object to Get a Connection

In the chapter "Basic Tutorial" you learned how to get a connection using the `DriverManager` class. This section will show you how to use a `DataSource` object to get a connection to your data source, which is the preferred way. You will see why it is better as you go through the rest of this chapter.

A `DataSource` object represents a particular DBMS or some other data source, such as a file. If a company uses more than one data source, it will deploy a separate `DataSource` object for each of them. A `DataSource` object may be implemented in three different ways:

1. **A basic `DataSource` implementation**

   A basic implementation produces standard `Connection` objects that are not pooled or used in a distributed transaction.

2. **A `DataSource` implementation that supports connection pooling**

   An implementation that supports connection pooling produces Connection objects that participate in connection pooling, that is, connections that can be recycled.

3. **A `DataSource` implementation that supports distributed transactions**

   An implementation that supports distributed transactions produces `Connection` objects that can be used in a distributed transaction, that is, a transaction that accesses two or more DBMS servers.

A driver that supports the JDBC 2.0 API should include at least a basic `DataSource` implementation. A `DataSource` class that supports distributed transactions typically also implements support for connection pooling. For example, a `DataSource` class provided by an EJB vendor will almost always support both connection pooling and distributed transactions.

Let's assume that the owner of the thriving chain of The Coffee Break shops, from our previous examples, has decided to expand further by selling coffee over the Internet. With the amount of traffic he expects, he will definitely need connection pooling. Opening and closing connections involves a great deal of overhead, and he anticipates that his online ordering system will necessitate a sizable number of queries and updates. With connection pooling, a pool of connections can be used over and over again, avoiding the expense of creating a new connection for every database access. In addition, he now has a second DBMS that contains data for the coffee roasting company he has just acquired. This means that he will want to be able to write distributed transactions that use both his old DBMS server and the new one.

Our entrepreneur has reconfigured his computer system to serve his new, larger customer base. He has bought a JDBC driver that supports all of the JDBC 2.0 API. He has also bought an EJB application server that works with the JDBC 2.0 API to be able to use distributed transactions and get the increased performance that comes with connection pooling. Because of the JDBC 2.0 API, he can choose from a variety of JDBC drivers that are compatible with the EJB server he has purchased. He now has a three-tier architecture, with his new EJB application server and JDBC driver in the middle tier and the two DBMS servers as the third tier. Client machines making requests are the first tier.

Now he needs to have his system administrator, SoLan, deploy the `Data-Source` objects so that he and his programmers can start using them. Deploying a `DataSource` object consists of three tasks:

1. Creating an instance of the `DataSource` class

2. Setting its properties

3. Registering it with a naming service that uses the Java Naming and Directory Interface (JNDI) API

The next section will walk you through these steps.

3.7.2 Deploying a Basic **DataSource** Object

First, let's consider the most basic case, which is to use a basic implementation of the `DataSource` interface, that is, one that does not support connection pooling or distributed transactions. In this case there is only one `DataSource` object that needs to be deployed. A basic implementation of `DataSource` produces the same kind of connections that the `DriverManager` produces.

Suppose a company that wants only a basic implementation of `DataSource` has bought a JDBC driver from the vendor DB Access, Inc., that includes the class `com.dbaccess.BasicDataSource`. Now let's look at some code that creates an instance of the class `BasicDataSource` and sets its properties. After the instance of `BasicDataSource` is deployed, a programmer can call the method `Data-Source.getConnection` on it to get a connection to the company's database, `CUSTOMER_ACCOUNTS`. First, the system administrator creates the `BasicDataSource` object *ds* using the default constructor; then she sets three properties. Note that the code shown here is code that will typically be executed by a tool.

```
com.dbaccess.BasicDataSource ds =
                            new com.dbaccess.BasicDataSource();
ds.setServerName("grinder");
ds.setDatabaseName("CUSTOMER_ACCOUNTS");
ds.setDescription("Customer accounts database for billing");
```

The variable *ds* now represents the database CUSTOMER_ACCOUNTS installed on the server grinder. Any connection produced by *ds* will be a connection to the database CUSTOMER_ACCOUNTS. With the properties set, the system administrator can register the BasicDataSource object with a JNDI naming service. The particular naming service that is used is usually determined by a system property, which is not shown here. Let's look at the code that registers the BasicDataSource object, binding it with the logical name jdbc/billingDB.

```
Context ctx = new InitialContext();
ctx.bind("jdbc/billingDB", ds);
```

This code uses the JNDI API. The first line creates an InitialContext object, which serves as the starting point for a name, similar to root in a directory file system. The second line associates, or binds, the BasicDataSource object *ds* to the logical name jdbc/billingDB. Later you will see that you can give the naming service this logical name, and it will return the BasicDataSource object. The logical name can be almost anything you want. In this case, the company decided to use the name billingDB as the logical name for the CUSTOMER_ACCOUNTS database.

In this example, jdbc is a subcontext under the initial context, just as a directory under the root directory is a subdirectory. You can think of jdbc/billingDB as being like a path name, where the last item in the path is analogous to a file name. In our case, billingDB is the logical name we want to give to *ds*. The subcontext jdbc is reserved for logical names to be bound to DataSource objects, so jdbc will always be the first part of a logical name for a data source.

After a basic DataSource implementation is deployed by a system administrator, it is ready for a programmer to use. This means that a programmer can give the logical data source name that was bound to an instance of a DataSource class, and the JNDI naming service will return an instance of that DataSource class. The method getConnection can then be called on that DataSource object to get a connection to the data source it represents. For example, a developer might write the following two lines of code to get a DataSource object that will produce a connection to the database CUSTOMER_ACCOUNTS.

```
Context ctx = new InitialContext();
DataSource ds = (DataSource)ctx.lookup("jdbc/billingDB");
```

The first line of code gets an initial context as the starting point for retrieving a DataSource object. When we supply the logical name jdbc/billingDB to the method lookup, it returns the DataSource object that the system administrator bound to jdbc/billingDB at deployment time. Because the return value of the method lookup is a Java Object, we need to cast it to the more specific Data-Source type before assigning it to the variable *ds*.

The variable *ds* is an instance of the class com.dbaccess.BasicDataSource that implements the DataSource interface. Calling the method getConnection on *ds* will produce a connection to CUSTOMER_ACCOUNTS.

```
Connection con = ds.getConnection("fernanda", "brewed");
```

Only the user name and password need to be passed to the getConnection method because *ds* has the rest of the information necessary for establishing a connection with CUSTOMER_ACCOUNTS, such as the database name and location, in its properties.

Because of its properties, a DataSource object is a better alternative than the DriverManager facility for getting a connection. For one thing, programmers no longer have to hard code the driver name or JDBC URL in their applications, which makes them more portable. Also, DataSource properties make maintaining code much simpler. If there is a change, the system administrator can simply update the data source's properties, and you don't have to worry about changing every application that makes a connection to the data source. For example, if the data source was moved to a different server, all the system administrator would need to do is set the serverName property to the new server name.

Aside from portability and ease of maintenance, using a DataSource object to get connections can offer other advantages. When a DataSource class is implemented to work with a ConnectionPoolDataSource implementation, all of the connections produced by instances of that DataSource class will automatically be pooled connections. Similarly, when a DataSource class is implemented to work with an XADataSource class, all of the connections it produces will automatically be connections that can be used in a distributed transaction. The next section shows how to deploy these types of DataSource implementations.

3.7.3   Deploying Other DataSource Implementations

A system administrator or another person working in that capacity can deploy a DataSource object so that the connections it produces are pooled connections. To do this, he/she first deploys a ConnectionPoolDataSource object and then deploys a DataSource object implemented to work with it. The properties of the Connection-PoolDataSource object are set so that it represents the data source to which connections will be produced. After the ConnectionPoolDataSource object has been registered with a JNDI naming service, the DataSource object is deployed. Generally only two properties need to be set for the DataSource object: description and dataSourceName. The value given to the dataSourceName property is the logical name identifying the ConnectionPoolDataSource object previously deployed, which is the object containing the properties needed to make the connection.

If you are interested in what happens internally, you can refer to Chapter 14, "ConnectionPoolDataSource," starting on page 439. Basically, with the ConnectionPoolDataSource and DataSource objects deployed, you can call the method DataSource.getConnection on the DataSource object and get a pooled connection. This connection will be to the data source specified in the ConnectionPoolDataSource object's properties.

Let's look at how a system administrator would deploy a DataSource object implemented to provide pooled connections. The system administrator would typically use a deployment tool, so the code fragments shown in this section are the code that a deployment tool would execute.

Let's go back to our entrepreneur to make things more concrete. To get better performance, The Coffee Break has bought a driver from DB Access, Inc., that includes the class com.dbaccess.ConnectionPoolDS, which implements the ConnectionPoolDataSource interface. SoLan, the system administrator, will create an instance of this class, set its properties, and register it with a JNDI naming service. The Coffee Break has bought its DataSource class, com.applogic.PooledDataSource, from its EJB server vendor, Application Logic, Inc. The class com.applogic.PooledDataSource implements connection pooling by using the underlying support provided by classes that implement the interface ConnectionPoolDataSource, such as com.dbaccess.ConnectionPoolDS. Table 3.2 illustrates example class names for implementations of the ConnectionPoolDataSource and DataSource interfaces.

Table 3.2: Examples of Implementation Classes

Interface	Class
ConnectionPoolDataSource	com.dbaccess.ConnectionPoolDS
DataSource	com.applogic.PooledDataSource

The `ConnectionPoolDataSource` object needs to be deployed first. Here is the code to create an instance of `com.dbaccess.ConnectionPoolDS` and set its properties.

```
com.dbaccess.ConnectionPoolDS cpds =
                          new com.dbaccess.ConnectionPoolDS();
cpds.setServerName("creamer");
cpds.setDatabaseName("COFFEEBREAK");
cpds.setPortNumber(9040);
cpds.setDescription("Connection pooling for COFFEEBREAK DBMS");
```

After the `ConnectionPoolDataSource` object has been deployed, SoLan will deploy the `DataSource` object. Here is the code for registering the `com.dbaccess.ConnectionPoolDS` object *cpds* with a JNDI naming service. Note that the logical name being associated with cpds has the subcontext `pool` added under the subcontext `jdbc`, which is similar to adding a subdirectory to another subdirectory in a hierarchical file system. The logical name of any instance of the class `com.dbaccess.ConnectionPoolDS` will always begin with `jdbc/pool`. We recommend putting all `ConnectionPoolDataSource` objects under the subcontext `jdbc/pool`.

```
Context ctx = new InitialContext();
ctx.bind("jdbc/pool/fastCoffeeDB", cpds);
```

Now it is time to deploy the `DataSource` class that is implemented to interact with *cpds*, an object that implements `ConnectionPoolDataSource`. Here is the code for creating an instance and setting its properties. Note that only two properties are set for this instance of `com.applogic.PooledDataSource`. The `description` property is set because it is always required. The other property that is set, `dataSourceName`, gives the logical JNDI name for *cpds*. In this case, the logical name is `"jdbc/pool/fastCoffeeDB"`, which was bound to *cpds* in the preceding code fragment. Being an instance of the class `com.dbaccess.ConnectionPoolDS`, *cpds* represents the `ConnectionPoolDataSource` object that will implement connection pooling for our `DataSource` object.

The following code fragment, which would probably be executed by a deployment tool, creates a `PooledDataSource` object, sets its properties, and binds it to the logical name `jdbc/fastCoffeeDB`.

```
com.applogic.PooledDataSource ds =
                          new com.applogic.PooledDataSource();
ds.setDescription("produces pooled connections to COFFEEBREAK");
ds.setDataSourceName("jdbc/pool/fastCoffeeDB");

Context ctx = new InitialContext();
ctx.bind("jdbc/fastCoffeeDB", ds);
```

We now have a `DataSource` object deployed that an application can use to get pooled connections to the database COFFEEBREAK.

3.7.4   Getting and Using a Pooled Connection

Now that these `DataSource` and `ConnectionPoolDataSource` objects are deployed, an application programmer can use the `DataSource` object to get a pooled connection. The code for getting a pooled connection is just like the code for getting a nonpooled connection, as shown in the following two lines.

```
ctx = new InitialContext();
ds = (DataSource)ctx.lookup("jdbc/fastCoffeeDB");
```

The variable *ds* represents a `DataSource` object that will produce a pooled connection to the database COFFEEBREAK. We need to retrieve this `DataSource` object only once because we can use it to produce as many pooled connections as we need. Calling the method `getConnection` on *ds* will automatically produce a pooled connection because the `DataSource` object that *ds* represents was configured to produce pooled connections.

As explained in "Application Code for Connection Pooling," on page 637, connection pooling is generally transparent to the application programmer. There are only two things you need to do when you are using pooled connections:

1. Use a `DataSource` object rather than the `DriverManager` class to get a connection. In the following line of code, *ds* is a `DataSource` object implemented and deployed so that it will create pooled connections.

```
Connection con = ds.getConnection("myLogin", "myPassword");
```

2. Use a `finally` statement to close a pooled connection. The following `finally` statement would appear after the `try/catch` block that applies to the code in which the pooled connection was used.

```
Connection con = null;
try {
    con = ds.getConnection("myLogin", "myPassword");

    // . . . code to use the pooled connection con

} catch (Exception ex {
    // . . . code to handle exceptions
} finally {
    if(con != null) con.close();
}
```

Otherwise, an application using a pooled connection is identical to an application using a regular connection. The only other thing an application programmer might notice when connection pooling is being done is that performance is better.

You will soon see some sample code (Sample Code 25) that gets a `DataSource` object that produces connections to the database `COFFEEBREAK` and uses it to update a price in the table `COFFEES`. The connection obtained in this code sample participates in connection pooling because the following are true:

- An instance of a class implementing `ConnectionPoolDataSource` has been deployed.
- An instance of a class implementing `DataSource` has been deployed, and the value set for its `dataSourceName` property is the logical name that was bound to the previously deployed `ConnectionPoolDataSource` object.

Note that the code will be very similar to code you have seen before; however, it is different in the following ways:

- It imports the `javax.sql`, `javax.ejb`, and `javax.naming` packages in addition to the `java.sql` package.

  The `DataSource` and `ConnectionPoolDataSource` interfaces are in the `javax.sql` package, and the JNDI constructor `InitialContext` and method `Context.lookup` are part of the `javax.naming` package. This particular example code is in the form of an EJB component (an enterprise Bean) that uses API from the `javax.ejb` package. The purpose of this example is to show that you use a pooled connection the same way you use a non-pooled connection, so you need not worry about understanding the EJB API.

- It uses a `DataSource` object to get a connection instead of using the `Driver-Manager` facility.

- It uses a `finally` statement to be sure that the connection is closed.

3.7.5   Sample Code 26

Here is the code example we have been talking about. It obtains and uses a pooled connection, which is used in exactly the same way a regular connection is used. Note that this code sample is not runnable because, as an EJB component, it is not complete in itself.

```
import java.sql.*;
import javax.sql.*;
import javax.ejb.*;
import javax.naming.*;

public class ConnectionPoolingBean implements SessionBean {

    // . . .

    public void ejbCreate () throws CreateException {
        ctx = new InitialContext();
        ds = (DataSource)ctx.lookup("jdbc/fastCoffeeDB");
    }

    public void updatePrice(float price, String cofName)
                                        throws SQLException{
```

```
        Connection con;
        PreparedStatement pstmt;
        try {
            con = ds.getConnection("webLogin", "webPassword");
            con.setAutoCommit(false);
            pstmt = con.prepareStatement("UPDATE COFFEES " +
                "SET PRICE = ? WHERE COF_NAME = ?");
            pstmt.setFloat(1, price);
            pstmt.setString(2, cofName);
            pstmt.executeUpdate();

            con.commit();

            pstmt.close();

        } finally {
            if (con != null) con.close();
        }
    }
    private DataSource ds = null;
    private Context ctx = null;
}
```

NOTE: At the time of this writing, not all drivers fully support the APIs used in this sample code. Consequently, the code has been compiled but not executed. It is included as an aid to understanding how the API can be used. In addition, SQL syntax and dialects may differ between DBMS implementations. It is therefore highly recommended that you consult your DBMS documentation to see the exact syntax you should use.

So far you have seen that an application programmer can get a pooled connection without doing anything different. When someone acting as a system administrator has deployed a `ConnectionPoolDataSource` object and a `DataSource` object properly, an application simply uses that `DataSource` object to get a pooled connection. You have also seen that using a pooled connection is just like using a regular connection. An application should, however, use a `finally` clause to close the pooled connection. For simplicity in the preceding code example, we used a `finally` block but no `catch` block. If an exception is thrown by a method in the `try` block, it will be thrown by default, and the `finally` clause will be executed in any case.

3.7.6   Deployment for Distributed Transactions

This section shows how to deploy `DataSource` objects for getting connections that can be used in distributed transactions. As with connection pooling, two different class instances must be deployed: an `XADataSource` object and a `DataSource` object that is implemented to work with it.

Suppose that the EJB server that our entrepreneur bought includes the `Data-Source` class `com.applogic.TransactionalDS`, which works with an `XAData-Source` class such as `com.dbaccess.XATransactionalDS`. The fact that it works with any `XADataSource` class makes the EJB server portable across JDBC drivers. When the `DataSource` and `XADataSource` objects are deployed, the connections produced will be able to participate in distributed transactions. In this case, the class `com.applogic.TransactionalDS` is implemented so that the connections produced are also pooled connections, which will usually be the case for `DataSource` classes provided as part of an EJB server implementation.

The `XADataSource` object needs to be deployed first. Here is the code to create an instance of `com.dbaccess.XATransactionalDS` and set its properties.

```
com.dbaccess.XATransactionalDS xads =
                           new com.dbaccess.XATransactionalDS();
xads.setServerName("creamer");
xads.setDatabaseName("COFFEEBREAK");
xads.setPortNumber(9040);
xads.setDescription(
        "Distributed transactions for COFFEEBREAK DBMS");
```

Here is the code for registering the `com.dbaccess.XATransactionalDS` object *xads* with a JNDI naming service. Note that the logical name being associated with *xads* has the subcontext `xa` added under `jdbc`. We recommend that the logical name of any instance of the class `com.dbaccess.XATransactionalDS` always begin with `jdbc/xa`.

```
Context ctx = new InitialContext();
ctx.bind("jdbc/xa/distCoffeeDB", xads);
```

Now it is time to deploy the DataSource object that is implemented to interact with *xads* and other XADataSource objects. Note that our DataSource class, com.applogic.TransactionalDS, can work with an XADataSource class from any JDBC driver vendor. Deploying the DataSource object involves creating an instance of com.applogic.TransactionalDS and setting its properties. The dataSourceName property is set to jdbc/xa/distCoffeeDB, the logical name associated with com.dbaccess.XATransactionalDS. This is the XADataSource class that implements the distributed transaction capability for our DataSource class. The following code fragment deploys an instance of our DataSource class.

```
com.applogic.TransactionalDS ds =
                         new com.applogic.TransactionalDS();
ds.setDescription(
    "Produces distributed transaction connections to COFFEEBREAK");
ds.setDataSourceName("jdbc/xa/distCoffeeDB");

Context ctx = new InitialContext();
ctx.bind("jdbc/distCoffeeDB", ds);
```

Now that we have deployed instances of the classes com.applogic.TransactionalDS and com.dbaccess.XATransactionalDS, an application can call the method getConnection on instances of TransactionalDS to get a connection to the COFFEEBREAK database that can be used in distributed transactions.

3.7.7   Using Connections for Distributed Transactions

To get a connection that can be used for distributed transactions, you need to use a DataSource object that has been properly implemented and deployed, as shown in the preceding section. With such a DataSource object, you simply call the method getConnection on it. Once you have the connection, you use it just as you would use any other connection. Because "jdbc/distCoffeesDB" has been associated with an XADataSource object in a JNDI naming service, the following code fragment produces a Connection object that can be used in distributed transactions.

```
Context ctx = new InitialContext();
DataSource ds = (DataSource)ctx.lookup("jdbc/distCoffeesDB");
Connection con = ds.getConnection();
```

There are some minor but important restrictions on how this connection is used while it is part of a distributed transaction, however. A transaction manager controls when a distributed transaction begins and when it is committed or rolled back; therefore, application code should never call the methods `Connection.commit` or `Connection.rollback`. An application should likewise never call `Connection.setAutoCommit(true)`, which enables auto-commit mode, because that would also interfere with the transaction manager's control of the transaction boundaries. This explains why a new connection that is created in the scope of a distributed transaction has its auto-commit mode disabled by default. Note that these restrictions apply only when a connection is participating in a distributed transaction; there are no restrictions while the connection is not part of a distributed transaction.

For the following example (Sample Code 26), suppose that an order of coffee has been shipped, which triggers updates to two tables that reside on different DBMS servers. The first table is a new INVENTORY table, and the second is the COFFEES table. Because these tables are on different DBMS servers, a transaction that involves both of them will be a distributed transaction. The code in the following example, which obtains a connection, updates the COFFEES table, and closes the connection, is the second part of a distributed transaction.

Note that the code does not explicitly commit or rollback the updates because the scope of the distributed transaction is being controlled by the middle-tier server's underlying system infrastructure. Also, assuming that the connection used for the distributed transaction is a pooled connection, the application uses a `finally` clause to close the connection. This guarantees that a valid connection will be closed even if an exception is thrown, thereby ensuring that the connection is recycled.

3.7.8   Sample Code 27

This code sample illustrates an enterprise Bean, a class that implements the methods that can be called by a client. The purpose of this example is to demonstrate that application code for a distributed transaction is no different from other code except that it does not call the `Connection` methods `commit`, `rollback`, or `setAutoCommit(true)`. Therefore, you do not need to worry about understanding the EJB API that is used. If you are interested, the section "Distributed Transactions and EJB," on page 1050, describes the scope of transactions in EJB applications. "Overview of an EJB Application," on page 270, explains the parts of an EJB application. Note that this code sample is not complete in itself and therefore is not runnable.

```java
import java.sql.*;
import javax.sql.*;
import javax.ejb.*;
import javax.naming.*;

public class DistributedTransactionBean implements SessionBean {

    // . . .

    public void ejbCreate () throws CreateException {
        ctx = new InitialContext();
        ds = (DataSource)ctx.lookup("jdbc/distCoffeesDB");
    }

    public void updateTotal(int incr, String cofName)
                                        throws SQLException {
        Connection con;
        PreparedStatement pstmt;
        try {
            con = ds.getConnection("webLogin", "webPassword");
            pstmt = con.prepareStatement("UPDATE COFFEES " +
                "SET TOTAL = TOTAL + ? WHERE COF_NAME = ?");
            pstmt.setInt(1, incr);
            pstmt.setString(2, cofName);
            pstmt.executeUpdate();
            stmt.close();

        } finally {
            if (con != null) con.close();
        }
    }
    private DataSource ds = null;
```

```
        private Context ctx = null;
}
```

NOTE: At the time of this writing, not all drivers fully support the APIs used in this sample code. Consequently, the code has been compiled but not executed. It is included as an aid to understanding how the API can be used. In addition, SQL syntax and dialects may differ between DBMS implementations. It is therefore highly recommended that you consult your DBMS documentation to see the exact syntax you should use.

Congratulations! You have completed your walk through the new functionality added in the JDBC 2.0 core API (the java.sql package), and you have also learned how to use the javax.sql package API for getting a connection from a DataSource object. You can now create scrollable and updatable result sets, move the cursor many different ways, make updates programmatically, send batch updates, create UDTs, use SQL99 types, and do custom mapping of UDTs. In addition, you know how to write code that uses connection pooling and distributed transactions.

The remainder of this chapter covers the main functionality added to the JDBC 3.0 API.

3.8   JDBC 3.0 Functionality

The JDBC 3.0 API includes new functionality and enhancements to round out a maturing technology. This section shows you how to use savepoints and also how to use keys that a DBMS generates automatically when a new row is inserted into a table.

3.8.1   Using Savepoints

Savepoints, introduced in the JDBC 3.0 API, mark an intermediate point within a transaction. If you want to roll back only part of a transaction, you can roll it back to a savepoint that you have set. Everything before the savepoint will be saved, and everything after the savepoint will be rolled back to the values that existed at the beginning of the transaction.

The following line of code is an example of how to set a Savepoint object. The variable *con* is a Connection object.

```
Savepoint save = con.setSavepoint();
```

Note that because transactions take place in the context of a connection, you use a Connection method to create and set a Savepoint object. You also use a Connection method to remove one.

```
con.releaseSavepoint(save);
```

Also, you use a Connection method to roll back a transaction to a Savepoint object. Any operations after the Savepoint object will be removed from the transaction.

```
con.rollback(save);
```

3.8.2   Sample Code 28

Let's look at an example of using a Savepoint object. Suppose our coffee entrepreneur wants to set the prices for some of his coffees based on their popularity. The more popular the coffee, the more he will charge for it, up to a limit. If the prices get too high for certain coffees, he will roll back the most recent price increase. If the code includes two rounds of price increases, he can set savepoints before the first one and before the second one, thus being able to roll back increases that go over a specified limit.

Sample code 28 illustrates one way of doing this. We will examine the code in more detail following the example.

```
import java.sql.*;
public class SetSavepoint {

    public static void main(String args[]) {

        try {
```

```java
        Class.forName("myDriver.className");

    } catch(java.lang.ClassNotFoundException e) {
        System.err.print("ClassNotFoundException: ");
        System.err.println(e.getMessage());
    }

try {

    Connection con = DriverManager.getConnection(
        "jdbc:mySubprotocol:myDataSource:" +
        "User=myLogin;Password=myPassword;SID=demo");

    con.setAutoCommit(false);

    String query = "SELECT COF_NAME, PRICE FROM COFFEES " +
                                "WHERE TOTAL > ?";
    String update = "UPDATE COFFEES SET PRICE = ? " +
                                "WHERE COF_NAME = ?";
    PreparedStatement getPrice = con.prepareStatement(query);
    PreparedStatement updatePrice = con.prepareStatement(
                                                update);

    getPrice.setInt(1, 7000);
    ResultSet rs = getPrice.executeQuery();

    Savepoint save1 = con.setSavepoint();

    while (rs.next())  {
        String cof = rs.getString("COF_NAME");
        float oldPrice = rs.getFloat("PRICE");
        float newPrice = oldPrice + (oldPrice * .05f);
        updatePrice.setFloat(1, newPrice);
        updatePrice.setString(2, cof);
        updatePrice.executeUpdate();
        System.out.println("New price of " + cof + " is " +
                                                newPrice);
        if (newPrice > 11.99) {
            con.rollback(save1);
```

```
        }
    }

    getPrice = con.prepareStatement(query);
    updatePrice = con.prepareStatement(update);

    getPrice.setInt(1, 8000);

    rs = getPrice.executeQuery();
    System.out.println();

    Savepoint save2 = con.setSavepoint();

    while (rs.next())  {
        String cof = rs.getString("COF_NAME");
        float oldPrice = rs.getFloat("PRICE");
        float newPrice = oldPrice + (oldPrice * .05f);
        updatePrice.setFloat(1, newPrice);
        updatePrice.setString(2, cof);
        updatePrice.executeUpdate();
        System.out.println("New price of " + cof + " is " +
                                            newPrice);

        if (newPrice > 11.99) {
            con.rollback(save2);
        }
    }

    con.commit();
    Statement stmt = con.createStatement();
    rs = stmt.executeQuery("SELECT COF_NAME, " +
            "PRICE FROM COFFEES");

    System.out.println();
    while (rs.next()) {
        String name = rs.getString("COF_NAME");
        float price = rs.getFloat("PRICE");
        System.out.println("Current price of " + name +
                        " is " + price);
    }
```

```
            rs.close();
            stmt.close();
            con.close();

        } catch (Exception e) {
            e.printStackTrace();
        }
    }
}
```

The first part of the code creates the Connection object *con*. Because we do not want each execution of a statement to be a transaction, the code turns off auto-commit mode for *con* with the following line of code.

```
con.setAutoCommit(false);
```

Next, the code creates two PreparedStatement objects, *getPrice* and *update-Price*. The SQL statement for *getPrice* retrieves coffee names and prices for coffees with total sales greater than a specified total. This statement has one parameter placeholder for setting the total. The SQL statement for *updatePrice* has two parameter placeholders, one for the price to be set and one for the name of the coffee.

The parameter for *getPrice* is set to 7000 and then executed, producing the ResultSet object *rs*. *rs* contains the names and prices of the coffees that have total sales greater than 7000 pounds of coffee. The prices for these coffees will be increased by five percent in the first while loop.

The first Savepoint object, *save1*, is set just before the first while loop, which means that this is the point to which the transaction will be rolled back if the method rollback is called with *save1* as the argument. Within the while loop, the code retrieves the name and price for each row in *rs*, increases the price by five percent, and prints the new prices. The last thing in the while loop is an if clause saying that the method rollback(save1) will be called if a new price exceeds 11.99.

A second Savepoint object, *save2*, is set just before a second ResultSet object, *rs*, is generated. This time, *rs* contains the names and prices of the coffees with total sales greater than 8000 pounds instead of 7000, as in the first ResultSet object. The while loop for retrieving and increasing the prices is essentially identical to the previous one, the only differences being that the ResultSet object contains one less row and the rollback method takes *save2* as its argument instead of *save1*. So if a price exceeds 11.99 in the second round of increases, the increases executed in the first round will be retained while the increases in the second round will be rolled back.

If the application SetSavepoint is run multiple times, a price will eventually get to be greater than 11.99 and trigger the invocation of the rollback method. When 11.99 is exceeded depends, of course, on what the values were originally. The following printout shows the results of running SetSavepoint multiple times for one DBMS and driver starting with the following values.

First, here are the coffees and their prices before SetSavepoint is run:

```
Colombian  7.99
French_Roast  8.99
Espresso  9.99
Colombian_Decaf  8.99
French_Roast_Decaf  9.99
```

Here are the coffees and their total sales before SetSavepoint is run:

```
Colombian  10000
French_Roast  8500
Espresso  7500
Colombian_Decaf  3500
French_Roast_Decaf  3000
```

When SetSavepoint is run the first time, the printout is as follows. Note that the first three coffees are the ones retrieved from the ResultSet object in the first while loop, in which prices are increased for coffees that have sold more than 7000 pounds. The decaf coffees are not included because they sold less than 7000 pounds. The next two coffees are retrieved in the second while loop, in which prices are increased for coffees that have sold more than 8000 pounds. Espresso was included in the first set but is not included in this set because its total sales are 7500. The third set shows the prices for all of the coffees as they appear in the database at that point. The prices for Colombian and French_Roast were increased five percent in both while loops, so the current prices are those from the second set of prices. Espresso was increased only once, and the decaf coffee prices were not changed.

```
➥ New price of Colombian is 8.3895
➥ New price of French_Roast is 9.4395
➥ New price of Espresso is 10.4895
➥
➥ New price of Colombian is 8.808974
➥ New price of French_Roast is 9.911475
➥
➥ Current price of Colombian is 8.808974
➥ Current price of French_Roast is 9.911475
➥ Current price of Espresso is 10.4895
➥ Current price of Colombian_Decaf is 8.99
➥ Current price of French_Roast_Decaf is 9.99
```

Here are the results of running SetSavepoint a second time.

```
➥ New price of Colombian is 9.249423
➥ New price of French_Roast is 10.407049
➥ New price of Espresso is 11.013975
➥
➥ New price of Colombian is 9.711894
➥ New price of French_Roast is 10.927402
➥
➥ Current price of Colombian is 9.711894
➥ Current price of French_Roast is 10.927402
➥ Current price of Espresso is 11.013975
➥ Current price of Colombian_Decaf is 8.99
➥ Current price of French_Roast_Decaf is 9.99
```

The third time SetSavepoint is run, the price of French_Roast goes over
11.99 in the second round of price increases (the second while loop). This causes
con.rollback(save2) to be called, so the prices in the second round of increases
are rolled back, leaving the increases in the first round intact. The current price
listing, which shows the prices in the database, reflects the rollback to *save2*.

```
➥ New price of Colombian is 10.197489
➥ New price of French_Roast is 11.473772
➥ New price of Espresso is 11.564674
➥
➥ New price of Colombian is 10.707363
➥ New price of French_Roast is 12.047461
➥
➥ Current price of Colombian is 10.197489
➥ Current price of French_Roast is 11.473772
➥ Current price of Espresso is 11.564674
```

➥ Current price of Colombian_Decaf is 8.99
➥ Current price of French_Roast_Decaf is 9.99

Running SetSavepoint again will cause French_Roast to exceed 11.99 in the first while loop and thus trigger the invocation of con.rollback(save1). Once the method rollback has been called on a transaction, however, any Savepoint objects in it become invalid. As a result, the call to con.rollback(save1) will throw an exception.

➥ New price of Colombian is 10.707363
➥ New price of French_Roast is 12.047461
➥ New price of Espresso is 12.142908
➥ java.sql.SQLException: The specified Savepoint is invalid.
➥ at SetSavepoint.main(SetSavepoint.java:48)

Note that for simplicity's sake, the error message has been edited. Line 48 in SetSavepoint.java is "con.rollback(save1);".

3.8.3   Using Automatically Generated Keys

Some DBMSs automatically generate a key for a row that is inserted into a table. For example, one DBMS creates a unique identifier and puts it in the pseudo column ROWID. If you later want to update that row, you can use this key to identify the row instead of using a primary key.

You can find out whether your driver supports automatically generated keys with the following lines of code.

```
DatabaseMetaData dbmd = con.getMetaData();
boolean b = dbmd.supportsGetGeneratedKeys();
```

If your driver supports them and you want to use them, you need to instruct the driver to make automatically generated keys available for retrieval with the constant Statement.RETURN_GENERATED_KEYS. For a Statement object, you pass this constant to the executeUpdate method, as in the following line of code. The String object *sqlString* is an SQL INSERT statement.

```
stmt.executeUpdate(sqlString, Statement.RETURN_GENERATED_KEYS);
```

For a PreparedStatement object, you supply the constant when you create the PreparedStatement object.

```
pstmt = con.prepareStatement(sqlString,
                        Statement.RETURN_GENERATED_KEYS);
```

After executing the statement, you retrieve any generated keys with the following line of code.

```
ResultSet keys = stmt.getGeneratedKeys();
```

Each key will be a row in the ResultSet object that is returned. It is possible for a key to be more than one column, so in that case, the row will have as many columns as are in the key.

You retrieve the key from the ResultSet object the same way you retrieve any other value from a ResultSet object. In the example code that follows, the programmer knows that the key is contained in one column and that the column name is KEY. Therefore, he simply calls the method next on the ResultSet object *keys*. If the key were more than one column, he would need to call the method next in a while loop to be sure of getting all of the columns in the key.

Another way to signal the driver that it should prepare for returning generated keys is to pass it an array with either the column names or column indexes of the key. If the programmer had chosen to use this alternative, the code would have looked like this:

```
String [] keyArray = {"KEY"};
stmt.executeUpdate(sqlString, keyArray);
```

3.8.4   Sample Code 29

This code example shows how to use an automatically generated key. It uses the PreparedStatement object *pstmt* to insert a new row and then to update that row. After retrieving the automatically generated key from *keys*, which it stores in the variable *key*, it sets *key* as the value for the second parameter in the String *update*. In this case, it is known that the key is only one column and that it is an int.

```
pstmt.setInt(2, key);
```

Here is an example of using an automatically generated key to indicate the row to be updated.

```
import java.sql.*;

public class AutoGenKeys {

    public static void main(String args[]) {

        String url = "jdbc:mySubprotocol:myDataSource";
        Connection con = null;
        PreparedStatement pstmt;
        String insert = "INSERT INTO COFFEES VALUES ('HYPER_BLEND', " +
                                        "101, 10.99, 0, 0)";
        String update = "UPDATE COFFEES SET PRICE = ? WHERE KEY = ?";

        try {
            Class.forName("myDriver.ClassName");

        } catch(java.lang.ClassNotFoundException e) {
            System.err.print("ClassNotFoundException: ");
            System.err.println(e.getMessage());
        }

        try {

            con = DriverManager.getConnection(url,
                                        "myLogin", "myPassword");
            pstmt = con.prepareStatement(insert,
                            Statement.RETURN_GENERATED_KEYS);

            pstmt.executeUpdate();
            ResultSet keys = pstmt.getGeneratedKeys();

            keys.next();
            int key = keys.getInt(1);

            pstmt = con.prepareStatement(update);
            pstmt.setFloat(1, 11.99f);
            pstmt.setInt(2, key);
            pstmt.executeUpdate();
```

```
            keys.close();
            pstmt.close();
            con.close();

        } catch (SQLException e) {
            e.printStackTrace();
        }
    }
}
```

NOTE: At the time of this writing, not all drivers fully support the APIs used in this sample code. Consequently, the code has been compiled but not executed. It is included as an aid to understanding how the API can be used. In addition, SQL syntax and dialects may differ between DBMS implementations. It is therefore highly recommended that you consult your DBMS documentation to see the exact syntax you should use.

Chapter 5, "RowSet Tutorial," shows you how to use a rowset to provide updating and scrollability, among other things, and it also gives an example of using a rowset in an EJB component.

CHAPTER 4

MetaData Tutorial

THIS chapter shows you how to use the three metadata interfaces, DatabaseMeta-Data, ResultSetMetaData, and ParameterMetaData. A DatabaseMetaData object provides information about a database or a database management system (DBMS). The developers of the driver you are using implemented the DatabaseMetaData interface so that its methods return information that applies to your driver and the database with which it works. So, if you call the method supportsBatchUpdates, for example, the return value will tell you whether your database and driver support sending multiple update statements to the database as a batch. If the return value is false, an application that uses any of the methods associated with batch updates will not work.

A ResultSetMetaData object provides information about the columns in a particular ResultSet instance. One method in the ResultSetMetaData interface returns the number of columns in the ResultSet object as a whole, and the rest of the methods return information about a particular column in the ResultSet object. The column information includes the name of the column, what data type the column can hold, and everything from whether the column value is writable to whether the column value can be used as a search criterion in a WHERE clause. Note that because a RowSet object is derived from a ResultSet object, any of the ResultSetMetaData methods for getting information about a column in a Result-Set object can also be used to get information about a column in a RowSet object.

A ParameterMetaData object provides information about the parameters to a PreparedStatement object. Similar to a ResultSetMetaData object, a Parameter-MetaData object contains the number of parameters in the PreparedStatement object as a whole. However, the information in a ParameterMetaData object applies to the designated parameter in a PreparedStatement object rather than to the designated column in a ResultSet object. Parameter information includes the

3.0

data type of the parameter, whether the parameter can be NULL, whether the mode of the parameter is IN, INOUT, or OUT, and so on. Note that because a CallableStatement object is derived from a PreparedStatement object, everything said in this chapter about a ParameterMetaData object applies to CallableStatement parameters as well as to PreparedStatement parameters.

The chapters "DatabaseMetaData," starting on page 449, "ResultSetMetaData," starting on page 783, and "ParameterMetaData," starting on page 627, give basic information about these three interfaces, and we recommend that you familiarize yourself with them before going through this chapter. The emphasis here is on example code that puts together metadata methods in programs that illustrate their usefulness. We assume that readers of this chapter are familiar with the material in Chapter 2, "Basic Tutorial," and Chapter 3, "Advanced Tutorial."

This chapter includes the metadata features in the JDBC 1.0 API plus those that were added in the JDBC 2.0 core API and the JDBC 3.0 API. In general, the new metadata methods provide information about what new functionality is supported and which new data types can be used.

NOTE: Metadata is most often used by tools or developers who write programs that use advanced, nonstandard database features and by programs that dynamically discover database tables.

4.1   Using a `ResultSetMetaData` Object

When you send a SELECT statement in a JDBC application, you get back a ResultSet object containing the data that satisfies your criteria. You can get information about the columns in this ResultSet object by creating a ResultSetMetaData object and invoking ResultSetMetaData methods on it. The following code fragment, in which the variable *con* is a Connection object, creates the ResultSet object *rs* and then uses *rs* to create a ResultSetMetaData object that contains information about the columns in *rs*.

```
Statement stmt = con.createStatement();
ResultSet rs = stmt.executeQuery("select * from COFFEES");
ResultSetMetaData rsmd = rs.getMetaData();
```

You can now use *rsmd* to invoke `ResultSetMetaData` methods to access its information about the columns in *rs*. Except for the method `getColumnCount`, which gives the total number of columns in the result set, all of the `ResultSet-MetaData` methods return information about an individual column and therefore take one parameter indicating the number of the column for which information is desired.

4.1.1   Using the Method `getColumnCount`

Probably the most frequently used `ResultSetMetaData` method is `getColumnCount`. As just stated, this method tells you how many columns the result set has.

```
ResultSet rs = stmt.executeQuery("select * from COFFEES");
ResultSetMetaData rsmd = rs.getMetaData();
int numberOfColumns = rsmd.getColumnCount();
```

Since the query selected all of the columns in COFFEES, which has five columns, the variable *numberOfColumns* is assigned the value 5. This number is most often used in a `for` loop to iterate through the columns in a result set row, as in the following code fragment.

```
while (rs.next()) {
    for (int i = 1; i<= numberOfColumns; i++) {
        String s = rs.getString(i);
        System.out.println("Column " + i + ":  " + s);

        System.out.println("");
    }
}
```

Note that the `ResultSet` method used to retrieve all of the column values in this example is `getString`. This is an easy way to retrieve values when you do not know the type for each column but you know that no SQL99 data types are being used. See "Using the Method `getString`," on page 195, for an explanation of how to use the method `getString`. Note that if you want to be able to retrieve all data types, including SQL99 data types, you can use the method `getObject`. This is the only method guaranteed to retrieve all column values.

4.1.2   Sample Code 9

Sample Code 9 is the file SQLStatement.java. Because this code uses the methods getColumnCount and getString, as just described, it can be used as a template for simple queries. The query it currently contains is the example of a join used in "Basic Tutorial." It prints out the coffee names supplied by Acme, Inc. You can simply substitute another SELECT statement, and the results of that query will be printed out for you.

SQLStatement.java looks like this:

```
import java.sql.*;

public class SQLStatement  {

    public static void main(String args[]) {

        String url = "jdbc:mySubprotocol:myDataSource";
        Connection con;
        String query = "select SUPPLIERS.SUP_NAME, COFFEES.COF_NAME " +
                    "from COFFEES, SUPPLIERS " +
                    "where SUPPLIERS.SUP_NAME = 'Acme, Inc.' and " +
                    "SUPPLIERS.SUP_ID = COFFEES.SUP_ID";
        Statement stmt;

        try {
            Class.forName("myDriver.ClassName");

        } catch(java.lang.ClassNotFoundException e) {
            System.err.print("ClassNotFoundException: ");
            System.err.println(e.getMessage());
        }

        try {
            con = DriverManager.getConnection(url,
                            "myLogin", "myPassword");

            stmt = con.createStatement();

            ResultSet rs = stmt.executeQuery(query);
```

```
        ResultSetMetaData rsmd = rs.getMetaData();
        int numberOfColumns = rsmd.getColumnCount();
        int rowCount = 1;
        while (rs.next()) {
            System.out.println("Row " + rowCount + ":  ");
            for (int i = 1; i <= numberOfColumns; i++) {
                System.out.print("   Column " + i + ":  ");
                System.out.println(rs.getString(i));
            }
            System.out.println("");
            rowCount++;
        }
        stmt.close();
        con.close();

    } catch(SQLException ex) {
        System.err.print("SQLException: ");
        System.err.println(ex.getMessage());
    }
  }
}
```

Running this application with its current query produces this printout:

```
➡ Row 1:
➡     Column 1:  Acme, Inc.
➡     Column 2:  Colombian
➡
➡ Row 2:
➡     Column 1:  Acme, Inc.
➡     Column 2:  Colombian_Decaf
➡
```

4.1.3   Using Other **ResultSetMetaData** Methods

Let's suppose that the `select` statement that generated the `ResultSet` *rs* was in a stored procedure and that we do not know how many columns *rs* has or what the column names are. We can call the `ResultSetMetaData` methods `getColumnCount` and getColumnLabel on the object *rsmd* to find out how many columns *rs* has and what string is recommended as the label for each of the columns.

The following code fragment, which prints the column names on one line and then the contents of each row on succeeding lines, illustrates using the methods getColumnCount and getColumnLabel. You can see this code as used in a complete application in "Sample Code 10 and 11," starting on page 199.

```
Statement stmt = con.createStatement();
ResultSet rs = stmt.executeQuery(query);
ResultSetMetaData rsmd = rs.getMetaData();
int numberOfColumns = rsmd.getColumnCount();
for (int i = 1; i <= numberOfColumns; i++) {
    if (i > 1) { System.out.print(",   "); }
    String columnName = rsmd.getColumnLabel(i);
    System.out.print(columnName);
}
System.out.println("");
while (rs.next ()) {
    for (int i=1; i<=numberOfColumns; i++) {
        if (i > 1) { System.out.print(",   "); }
        String columnValue = rs.getString(i);
        System.out.print(columnValue);
    }
    System.out.println("");
}
stmt.close();
```

If this code fragment were run in a complete Java application, the output would look similar to this:

```
➥ COF_NAME,  SUP_ID,  PRICE,  SALES,  TOTAL
➥ Colombian,  101,  7.99,  175,  350
➥ French_Roast,  49,  8.99,  150,  300
➥ Espresso,  150,  9.99,  60,  120
➥ Colombian_Decaf,  101,  8.99,  155,  310
➥ French_Roast_Decaf,  49,  10.75,  90,  180
```

4.1.4   Getting Column Type Information

Two ResultSetMetaData methods provide information about the type of a result set column: getColumnType and getColumnTypeName. The method getColumnType tells you the JDBC type (the generic SQL type) for values stored in a specified column. It returns the JDBC type as an int; you can refer to the class java.sql.Types, on page 1035, to see which JDBC type that number represents. For example, the following code fragment gets the JDBC type for the second column in the ResultSet *rs*:

```
ResultSetMetaData rsmd = rs.getMetaData();
int jdbcType = rsmd.getColumnType(2);
```

If the second column stores values that have JDBC type INTEGER, *jdbcType* will be assigned the integer 4, which is java.sql.Types.INTEGER. Note that the recommended programming style is to use the JDBC type name rather than its integer value.

The method getColumnTypeName returns the name used by the DBMS for that JDBC type. "Getting Information about DBMS Data Types," starting on page 214, looks at the DatabaseMetaData method getTypeInfo, which gives information about the types used by a DBMS.

4.1.5   Sample Code 10 and 11

Sample Code 10 is the file PrintColumnTypes.java, and Sample Code 11 is the file PrintColumns.java. The following code defines the class PrintColumnTypes. This class consists of one method, printColTypes, that prints out a report containing the return values of the two methods getColumnType and getColumnTypeName. The method printColTypes, shown next, is called in the class PrintColumns, which is explained after the following code. Here is PrintColumnTypes.java:

```
import java.sql.*;

public class PrintColumnTypes {
    public static void printColTypes(ResultSetMetaData rsmd)
                                            throws SQLException {
        int columns = rsmd.getColumnCount();
        for (int i = 1; i <= columns; i++) {
```

```
        int jdbcType = rsmd.getColumnType(i);
        String name = rsmd.getColumnTypeName(i);
        System.out.print("Column " + i + " is JDBC type " + jdbcType);
        System.out.println(", which the DBMS calls " + name);
    }
  }
}
```

The class `PrintColumnTypes` does not contain a `main` method, so it cannot be executed by itself. It can be called by an application that does contain a `main` method, however, as is done in the application in the file `PrintColumns.java`, shown later.

As must be done in any JDBC application, `PrintColumns.java` loads the driver and establishes a connection with the DBMS. Next it creates the `ResultSet` object *rs* by executing a query and then creates the `ResultSetMetaData` object *rsmd* by calling the method `getMetaData` on *rs*. The `ResultSetMetaData` object *rsmd* is then used several times to get information about the `ResultSet` *rs*.

The method `printColTypes` (in the class `PrintColumnTypes`, shown above) uses *rsmd* three times. First it uses *rsmd* to call the method `getColumnCount`. The results of this method are used in a `for` loop that iterates through the columns in the `ResultSet` *rs*. Next, `printColTypes` invokes the methods `getColumnType` and `getColumnTypeName` on *rsmd*. As just mentioned, `printColTypes` uses the results of these two methods to print out a report for each column in *rs*, giving the JDBC type code number for that column and also the local DBMS name for that data type. The printout for `printColTypes` is the first part of the output for the application `PrintColumns`, shown later, and it is also shown here for convenience. The following printout represents what will be returned by most DBMSs.

```
➡ Column 1 is JDBC type 12, which the DBMS calls VARCHAR
➡ Column 2 is JDBC type 4, which the DBMS calls INTEGER
➡ Column 3 is JDBC type 8, which the DBMS calls DOUBLE PRECISION
➡ Column 4 is JDBC type 4, which the DBMS calls INTEGER
➡ Column 5 is JDBC type 4, which the DBMS calls INTEGER
➡
```

After passing *rsmd* to the method `printColTypes`, the application uses *rsmd* two more times. Like `printColTypes`, it invokes `getColumnCount` on *rsmd* in order

to use it to iterate through the columns in *rs*. Then it calls the method getColumn-
Name on *rsmd* to print out the column names in *rs*.

Finally, the application PrintColumns prints out the values in each row of *rs*.
The query that produced *rs* was select * from COFFEES, so all of the values in
the table COFFEES are printed. The printout follows the code in the file PrintCol-
umns.java, which is shown next.

```java
import java.sql.*;

class PrintColumns  {

    public static void main(String args[]) {

        String url = "jdbc:mySubprotocol:myDataSource";
        Connection con;
        String query = "select * from COFFEES";
        Statement stmt;

        try {
            Class.forName("myDriver.ClassName");

        } catch(java.lang.ClassNotFoundException e) {
            System.err.print("ClassNotFoundException: ");
            System.err.println(e.getMessage());
        }

        try {
            con = DriverManager.getConnection(url,
                                "myLogin", "myPassword");

            stmt = con.createStatement();

            ResultSet rs = stmt.executeQuery(query);
            ResultSetMetaData rsmd = rs.getMetaData();

            PrintColumnTypes.printColTypes(rsmd);
            System.out.println("");
                int numberOfColumns = rsmd.getColumnCount();
```

```java
            for (int i = 1; i <= numberOfColumns; i++) {
                if (i > 1) System.out.print(",  ");
                String columnName = rsmd.getColumnName(i);
                System.out.print(columnName);
            }
            System.out.println("");

            while (rs.next()) {
                for (int i = 1; i <= numberOfColumns; i++) {
                    if (i > 1) System.out.print(",  ");
                    String columnValue = rs.getString(i);
                    System.out.print(columnValue);
                }
                System.out.println("");
            }

            stmt.close();
            con.close();
        } catch(SQLException ex) {
            System.err.print("SQLException: ");
            System.err.println(ex.getMessage());
        }
    }
}
```

The output of this code will be similar to the following, with the values in the PRICE, SALES, and TOTAL columns varying according to what has been entered.

```
➥ Column 1 is JDBC type 12, which the DBMS calls VARCHAR
➥ Column 2 is JDBC type 4, which the DBMS calls INTEGER
➥ Column 3 is JDBC type 6, which the DBMS calls FLOAT
➥ Column 4 is JDBC type 4, which the DBMS calls INTEGER
➥ Column 5 is JDBC type 4, which the DBMS calls INTEGER
➥
➥ COF_NAME,  SUP_ID,  PRICE,  SALES,  TOTAL
➥ Colombian,  101,  7.99,  175,  350
➥ French_Roast,  49,  8.99,  150,  300
➥ Espresso,  150,  9.99,  60,  120
➥ Colombian_Decaf,  101,  8.99,  155,  310
➥ French_Roast_Decaf,  49,  9.99,  90,  180
```

4.1.6   Sample Code 12

Sample Code 12 is the file RSMetaDataMethods.java. In addition to using the method getColumnCount, this code sample illustrates using the following Result-SetMetaData methods:

```
getTableName
getColumnTypeName
isCaseSensitive
isWritable
```

These methods do what their names suggest. The method getTableName returns the name of the table from which this result set column was derived. The method getColumnTypeName returns the type name used by this particular DBMS for values stored in this result set column. The method isCaseSensitive returns true if a value stored in this column is case sensitive and false otherwise. The method isWritable returns true if it is possible for a write operation on a value stored in this column to succeed; otherwise it returns false.

The results of these methods are printed out for each column of the ResultSet rs. All of the results from the query select * from COFFEES are also printed out so that you can see the values to which the column information refers.

The following is the file RSMetaDataMethods.java.

```java
import java.sql.*;

public class RSMetaDataMethods {

    public static void main(String args[]) {

        String url = "jdbc:mySubprotocol:myDataSource";
        Connection con;
        Statement stmt;


        try {
            Class.forName("myDriver.ClassName");

        } catch(java.lang.ClassNotFoundException e) {
```

```java
            System.err.print("ClassNotFoundException: ");
            System.err.println(e.getMessage());
        }

        try {
            con = DriverManager.getConnection(url,
                                "myLogin", "myPassword");

            stmt = con.createStatement();
            ResultSet rs = stmt.executeQuery("select * from COFFEES");
            ResultSetMetaData rsmd = rs.getMetaData();

            int numberOfColumns = rsmd.getColumnCount();
            for (int i = 1; i <= numberOfColumns; i++) {
                String colName = rsmd.getColumnName(i);
                String tableName = rsmd.getTableName(i);
                String name = rsmd.getColumnTypeName(i);
                boolean caseSen = rsmd.isCaseSensitive(i);
                boolean w = rsmd.isWritable(i);
                System.out.println("Information for column " + colName);
                System.out.println("    Column is in table " + tableName);
                System.out.println("    DBMS name for type is " + name);
                System.out.println("    Is case sensitive:  " + caseSen);
                System.out.println("    Is possibly writable:  " + w);
                System.out.println("");
            }

            while (rs.next()) {
                for (int i = 1; i<=numberOfColumns; i++) {
                    String s = rs.getString(i);
                    System.out.print(s + "   ");
                }
                System.out.println("");
            }

            stmt.close();
            con.close();

        } catch(SQLException ex) {
```

```
        System.err.println("SQLException: " + ex.getMessage());
    }
  }
}
```

Here is the output of RSMetaDataMethods.java for one DBMS.

```
➥ Information for column COF_NAME
➥      Column is in table COFFEES
➥      DBMS name for type is VARCHAR
➥      Is case sensitive:  true
➥      Is possibly writable:  true
➥
➥ Information for column SUP_ID
➥      Column is in table COFFEES
➥      DBMS name for type is INTEGER
➥      Is case sensitive:  false
➥      Is possibly writable:  true
➥
➥ Information for column PRICE
➥      Column is in table COFFEES
➥      DBMS name for type is DOUBLE PRECISION
➥      Is case sensitive:  false
➥      Is possibly writable:  true
➥
➥ Information for column SALES
➥      Column is in table COFFEES
➥      DBMS name for type is INTEGER
➥      Is case sensitive:  false
➥      Is possibly writable:  true
➥
➥ Information for column TOTAL
➥      Column is in table COFFEES
➥      DBMS name for type is INTEGER
➥      Is case sensitive:  false
➥      Is possibly writable:  true
➥
➥ Colombian  101  7.99  175  350
➥ French_Roast  49  8.99  150  300
➥ Espresso  150  9.99  60  220
➥ Colombian_Decaf  101  8.99  155  310
➥ French_Roast_Decaf  49  10.75  90  180
```

4.1.7   Getting Other Information

Several `ResultSetMetaData` methods give you information relevant to columns that store numeric types:

```
isAutoIncrement
isCurrency
isSigned
getPrecision
getScale
```

These methods have names that are largely self-explanatory. (*Precision* is the total number of digits, and *scale* is the number of digits to the right of the decimal point.)

The method `isNullable` tells you whether you can use `null` as a value for a specified column, and `getColumnDisplaySize` gives you the limit for how many characters normally fit in a specified column.

2.0   ### 4.1.8   Using `ResultSetMetaData` Features

The JDBC 2.0 API added two new methods related to the `ResultSetMetaData` interface. The first is a method in the `PreparedStatement` interface that lets you get information about the `ResultSet` object that a `PreparedStatement` object will return without having to execute it first. This is possible because a `PreparedStatement` object is sent to the database and precompiled when it is created; therefore, a driver can ascertain what the result set will be and return a `ResultSetMetaData` object that describes its columns. A `Statement` object, on the other hand, is not sent to the database and compiled until it is executed. That is why the `getMetaData` method we have used up to this point is a `ResultSet` method. In the JDBC 1.0 API, you had to have a `ResultSet` object (the result of executing a query) on which to call the method `getMetaData`.

The `PreparedStatement` version of the method `getMetaData` will probably be used by a tool more often than a programmer. For example, a tool that generates code based on the results of a query might need information about the results before the query is executed. Or, a tool that provides a programmer with a default layout as a starting point for designing the display of a query's results might also use column information before the query is executed. Note that, depending on the driver and DBMS being used, calling this method may involve considerable overhead.

The second method added is the ResultSetMetaData method getColumn-ClassName. In the JDBC 2.0 API, it is possible not only to use an SQL user-defined type (UDT) as a column value but also to map it to a class in the Java programming language. When the method getObject is invoked to retrieve a UDT from a Result-Set object and a custom mapping has been set up for that UDT, the driver will use the custom mapping instead of the standard mapping. For a custom mapping, the driver returns an instance of the Java class that is the mapping of the UDT. (Chapter 37, "SQLData," starting on page 895, explains custom mapping.) The method getColumnClassName returns the fully qualified class name of the Java class to which the UDT is mapped. This class is always an implementation of the SQLData interface.

Suppose that you want to know the name of the class used for the custom mapping of a column value in a ResultSet object but you do not yet want to execute the PreparedStatement query that will produce it. The following code fragment demonstrates how to use the PreparedStatement method getMetaData and the ResultSetMetaData method getColumnClassName to obtain that information.

```
PreparedStatement pstmt = con.prepareStatement(
                           "SELECT LOCATION FROM STORES");
ResultSetMetaData rsmd = pstmt.getMetadata();
String className = rsmd.getColumnClassName(1);
```

The variable *rsmd* represents the ResultSetMetaData object that contains column information about the ResultSet object that will be produced when *pstmt* is executed. The variable *className* contains the fully qualified class name of the class to which the UDT values stored in the column STORES.LOCATION will be mapped.

4.1.9   Getting Other Information

The JDBC 2.0 core API added many new features to ResultSet objects, and it also added new methods for getting information about the new features. Some of these methods, such as getType and getConcurrency, are part of the ResultSet interface and return information about the particular ResultSet object that is invoking the method. For example, the following code fragment tests a result set to see that it is scrollable and updatable before attempting to move the cursor to the insert row and insert a new row. While on the insert row, the code provides a value for each column in the new row by using the appropriate updater method. Then it inserts the new row into the result set and database before moving the cursor back to the current row of the result set (the position of the cursor before it went to the insert row). The variable *address* is a Struct object; the variable *coffees* is an Array object; the variable *manager* is a Ref object.

```
ResultSet rs = stmt.executeQuery("SELECT * FROM STORES");
int type = rs.getType();
int concurrency = rs.getConcurrency();
if (type == ResultSet.TYPE_SCROLL_SENSITIVE ||
    type == ResultSet.TYPE_SCROLL_INSENSITIVE) {
    if (concurrency == ResultSet.CONCUR_UPDATABLE) {
        rs.moveToInsertRow();
        rs.updateInt("STORE_NO", 100004);
        rs.updateObject("LOCATION", address);
        rs.updateObject("COF_TYPES", coffees);
        rs.updateObject("MGR", manager);
        rs.insertRow();
        rs.moveToCurrentRow();
    }
}
```

Other new methods for getting information about ResultSet objects are part of the DatabaseMetaData interface. These methods are covered in the section "Features Added in the JDBC 2.0 Core API," on page 453.

Note that in the JDBC 3.0 API, the ResultSet interface got new updater methods for updating the SQL99 types represented by the interfaces Array, Blob, Clob, and Ref. Using the method updateObject is still correct, but if your DBMS supports the JDBC 3.0 API, the if loop in the preceding code fragment could have been written using the updater methods updateArray and updateRef, as shown in the following example.

```
if (concurrency == ResultSet.CONCUR_UPDATABLE) {
    rs.moveToInsertRow();
    rs.updateInt("STORE_NO", 100004);
    rs.updateObject("LOCATION", address);
    rs.updateArray("COF_TYPES", coffees);
    rs.updateRef("MGR", manager);
```

```
            rs.insertRow();
            rs.moveToCurrentRow();
    }
```

4.2   Using a **DatabaseMetaData** Object

The interface `DatabaseMetaData` has over 150 methods for getting information about a database or DBMS. See "DatabaseMetaData," starting on page 449, for an overview of this interface and an explanation of each method.

Once you have an open connection with a DBMS, you can create a `DatabaseMetaData` object that contains information about that database system. Using the `Connection` object *con,* the following line of code creates the `DatabaseMetaData` object *dbmd.*

```
    DatabaseMetaData dbmd = con.getMetaData();
```

You can now call `DatabaseMetaData` methods on *dbmd* to get information about the DBMS to which *con* is connected. The next part of this chapter describes these methods and the information they return.

4.2.1   Categories of **DatabaseMetaData** Methods

One way to organize `DatabaseMetaData` methods is by the types of their return values. There are four return types, or categories. The first three categories return a single value; the fourth category returns a result set with one to eighteen columns.

4.2.2   Methods That Return a **String**

The smallest category returns a `String` object. Some of these methods get information about the DBMS as a whole, such as the URL for the DBMS, the user name, the product name, the product version, the driver name, and the driver version. Others return information such as the character used to escape wildcard characters, the term the DBMS uses for *schema,* the term the DBMS uses for *catalog,* and the term the DBMS uses for *procedure.* Some methods return a `String` object, which is a comma-separated list. These methods give you lists of SQL keywords, numeric functions, string functions, system functions, and time/date functions.

As an example of this category, let us look at the method `getSearchStringEscape`. For some of the `DatabaseMetaData` methods, you can supply a search string pattern as a parameter. If, for instance, you wanted to use a table name such as Emp_Info as a search string parameter, you would need to indicate that the underscore character (_) was part of the name and not a wildcard character. To do this, you would need to precede the underscore with the driver's escape character. The method getSearchStringEscape tells you what that escape character is for your driver. This is demonstrated in the following code fragment.

```
Connection con = DriverManager.getConnection (url,
                          "myLogin", "myPassword");
DatabaseMetaData dbmd = con.getMetaData();
String escape = dbmd.getSearchStringEscape();
System.out.print("The search string escape for this ");
System.out.println("driver is " + escape);
con.close();
```

When this code fragment is put into a complete Java application and run, the output for one DBMS looks like this:

➥ The search string escape for this driver is \

Now we know that we need to use a backslash (\) as the escape character, as in "Emp_Info."

The method getSQLKeywords returns a String that is a comma-separated list of the keywords used by the DBMS that are not also SQL92 keywords. For one DBMS, the code fragment that follows will produce the output that follows it.

```
Connection con = DriverManager.getConnection (url,
                          "myLogin", "myPassword");
DatabaseMetaData dbmd = con.getMetaData();
String dbmsKeywords = dbmd.getSQLKeywords();
System.out.print("The keywords used by this DBMS that ");
System.out.println("are not also SQL92 keywords:  ");
System.out.println(dbmsKeywords);
con.close();
```

➥ The keywords used by this DBMS that are not also SQL92 keywords:
(Note that this output has been changed to break at commas.)
➥ arith_overflow,break,browse,bulk,char_convert,checkpoint,
➥ clustered,commit,compute,confirm,controlrow,data_pgs,
➥ database,dbcc,disk,dummy,dump,endtran,errlvl,

➡ errorexit,exit,fillfactor,
➡ holdlock,identity_insert,if,kill,lineno,load,mirror,mirrorexit,
➡ noholdlock,nonclustered,numeric_truncation,
➡ offsets,once,over,perm,permanent,plan,print,proc,processexit,
➡ raiserror,read,readtext,
➡ reconfigure,replace,reserved_pgs,return,role,rowcnt,
➡ rowcount,rule,save,setuser,shared,shutdown,some,
➡ statistics,stripe,syb_identity,syb_restree,
➡ syb_terminate,temp,textsize,tran,trigger,truncate,
➡ tsequal,used_pgs,user_option,waitfor,while,writetext

Several `DatabaseMetaData` methods let you find out which scalar functions a driver supports. The section "Support Scalar Functions," starting on page 1104, explains scalar functions and contains a list of them. Calling the method get-StringFunctions, for example, will return a `String` object containing a list of the string functions the driver supports, as shown in the following code fragment.

```
DatabaseMetaData dbmd = con.getMetaData();
String stringFunctions = dbmd.getStringFunctions();
System.out.println("String functions supported by this driver:");
System.out.println(stringFunctions);
```

The output for this particular DBMS and driver looks like this:

➡ The string functions supported by this driver:
(Note that this output has been changed to break at commas,)
➡ ASCII,CHAR,CONCAT,
➡ DIFFERENCE,LCASE,LEFT,LENGTH,LTRIM,REPEAT,RIGHT,RTRIM,
➡ SOUNDEX,SPACE,SUBSTRING,UCASE

The methods `getNumericFunctions`, `getSystemFunctions`, and `getTimeDate-Functions` also return a `String` object that is a comma-separated list of scalar functions.

4.2.3   Methods That Return an `int`

The next category of `DatabaseMetaData` methods returns an `int`, which is usually a limit of some sort that applies to the target DBMS with the current driver. These methods generally have the form `getMaxXXX` where XXX is what is being limited. You can find out the maximum number of characters allowed for a statement or for names (names include user name and names of tables, columns, cursors, schemas, catalogs, and procedures). You can also get the limit on the number of tables you can include in a SELECT statement, or the maximum number of columns you can have in a table, an index, a SELECT statement, a GROUP BY clause, or an ORDER BY clause. Other methods tell you how many connections you can have at one time, how many statements you can have active at the same time on a single connection, and how long an index can be.

The code fragment below finds out how long a column name may be:

```
DatabaseMetaData dbmd = con.getMetaData();
int len = dbmd.getMaxColumnNameLength();
String columnName = "AnExtraordinarilyLongColumnName";
if(columnName.length() > len) {
    System.out.print("The maximum number of characters allowed ");
    System.out.println("in a column name:   " + len);
    System.out.println(columnName + " has " + columnName.length());
}
```

The following is the output for one DBMS:

```
➥ The maximum number of characters allowed in a column name:   30
➥ AnExtraordinarilyLongColumnName has 31
```

4.2.4   Methods That Return a boolean

The category with the largest number of methods is the category that returns a boolean, that is, either true or false. The majority of these have the form supportsXXX, where XXX is a capability that the DBMS supports or does not support. For example, the following code fragment determines whether the DBMS and driver support the use of savepoints in transactions. If the return value is true, the code will set a savepoint; otherwise, the code will not use savepoints.

```
boolean supportsSavepoints = dbmd.supportsSavepoints();
if (supportsSavepoints()) {
    // code sets savepoints within the current transaction
    . . .
}
```

Looking at the interface definition for `DatabaseMetaData`, starting on page 458, will give you an overview of the methods in this category.

4.2.5   Methods That Return a `ResultSet` Object

The fourth category is the most complex. These methods return `ResultSet` objects that can be as simple as one column for each row returned or as complex as eighteen columns for each row returned. In the sample code following this, we will show you examples of using these methods and the results they return.

4.2.6   Sample Code 13

Sample Code 13 is the file `TableTypes.java`. This application depends on the method `getTableTypes`, which is a good example of a `DatabaseMetaData` method that returns a simple `ResultSet` object. Each row in the result set has only one column, which indicates one of the types of tables available in the DBMS. The method `getDatabaseProductName` is an example of a method that returns a `String` object. Here is the file `TableTypes.java`, which demonstrates the use of these two methods:

```java
import java.sql.*;

public class TableTypes  {

    public static void main(String args[]) {

        String url = "jdbc:mySubprotocol:myDataSource";
        Connection con;

        try {
            Class.forName("myDriver.ClassName");

        } catch(java.lang.ClassNotFoundException e) {
            System.err.print("ClassNotFoundException: ");
            System.err.println(e.getMessage());
        }

        try {
            con = DriverManager.getConnection(url,
```

```
                                    "myLogin", "myPassword");

            DatabaseMetaData dbmd = con.getMetaData();
            String dbmsName = dbmd.getDatabaseProductName();
            ResultSet rs = dbmd.getTableTypes();
            System.out.print("The following types of tables are ");
            System.out.println("available in " + dbmsName + ":  ");

            while (rs.next()) {
                String tableType = rs.getString("TABLE_TYPE");
                System.out.println("    " + tableType);
            }

            rs.close();
            con.close();

        } catch(SQLException ex) {
            System.err.print("SQLException: ");
            System.err.println(ex.getMessage());
        }
    }
}
```

The output from one driver and DBMS looks like this:

```
➥ The following types of tables are available in SQL Server:
➥     SYSTEM TABLE
➥     TABLE
➥     VIEW
```

4.2.7   Getting Information about DBMS Data Types

The method `getTypeInfo`, which returns one of the more complex `ResultSet` objects, tells you which SQL types a DBMS uses. If, for example, you want to create a table but are not sure about which types are available, you can get the information you need by calling the method `getTypeInfo`. This method tells you not only what data types the database uses but, as its name suggests, also gives information about them. The `ResultSet` object returned by the method `getTypeInfo` contains one row for each data type. The information in each row includes the type's name as used by the DBMS; its type code from the class `java.sql.Types`; what character, if any, is used before and after a literal to form a quoted literal; what parameters, if any, are used in a `CREATE` statement using this type; whether the type is nullable, case sensitive, or searchable; and so on. If a DBMS supports SQL99 data types, the result set includes one row for each SQL99 type that is supported.

4.2.8   Sample Code 14

Sample Code 14 is the file `TypeInfo.java`. This application prints out five of the result set columns produced by the `DatabaseMetaData` method `getTypeInfo`. In all, the result set has eighteen columns, two of which are not used. The columns used in this example code are `TYPE_NAME`, `DATA_TYPE`, `CREATE_PARAMS`, `NULLABLE`, and `CASE_SENSITIVE`.

```java
import java.sql.*;

public class TypeInfo {

    public static void main(String args[]) {

        String url = "jdbc:mySubprotocol:myDataSource";
        Connection con;
        DatabaseMetaData dbmd;

        try {
            Class.forName("myDriver.ClassName");

        } catch(java.lang.ClassNotFoundException e) {
            System.err.print("ClassNotFoundException: ");
            System.err.println(e.getMessage());
        }

        try {
            con = DriverManager.getConnection(url,
                            "myLogin", "myPassword");

            dbmd = con.getMetaData();
```

```
        ResultSet rs = dbmd.getTypeInfo();
        while (rs.next()) {
            String typeName = rs.getString("TYPE_NAME");
            short dataType = rs.getShort("DATA_TYPE");
            String createParams = rs.getString("CREATE_PARAMS");
            int nullable = rs.getInt("NULLABLE");
            boolean caseSensitive = rs.getBoolean("CASE_SENSITIVE");
            System.out.println("DBMS type " + typeName + ":");
            System.out.println("    java.sql.Types:  " + dataType);
            System.out.print("    parameters used to create: ");
            System.out.println(createParams);
            System.out.println("    nullable?:  " + nullable);
            System.out.print("    case sensitive?:  ");
            System.out.println(caseSensitive);
            System.out.println("");
        }

        con.close();

    } catch(SQLException ex) {
        System.err.println("SQLException: " + ex.getMessage());
    }
  }
}
```

If you run this code, you will get back results that show all the types available with your particular database system; the types available will vary from one DBMS to another. The value in the column DATA_TYPE, printed after "java.sql.Types:" in the output that follows, gives a number representing the JDBC type (the generic SQL type) to which the DBMS type corresponds. You can find this number and the name of the JDBC type it represents in the class java.sql.Types, on page 1035.

Note that each DBMS type is listed only once, but the java.sql.Types type code may be listed more than once. This will happen when more than one type used by the DBMS maps to the same JDBC type. In that case, the one listed first is the preferred type, and that is the one you should use.

The following is just part of the printout for the particular DBMS we are using to give you an idea of what it looks like.

```
➥ DBMS type bit:
➥       java.sql.Types:  -7
➥       parameters used to create: null
➥       nullable?:  0
➥       case sensitive?:  false
➥
➥ DBMS type tinyint:
➥       java.sql.Types:  -6
➥       parameters used to create: null
➥       nullable?:  1
➥       case sensitive?:  false
➥
➥ DBMS type image:
➥       java.sql.Types:  -4
➥       parameters used to create: null
➥       nullable?:  1
➥       case sensitive?:  false
➥
➥ DBMS type varchar:
➥       java.sql.Types:  12
➥       parameters used to create: max length
➥       nullable?:  1
➥       case sensitive?:  true
➥
```

Let's examine what this printout means by looking in detail at two of the types listed. First let's look at the type varchar line by line.

```
➥ DBMS type varchar:
```

This indicates that varchar is one of the DBMS types you can use for values in this database.

```
➥       java.sql.Types:  12
```

This column indicates that this type corresponds most closely to java.sql.Types.VARCHAR, which is indicated by the number 12. (The definition for the class Types, on page 1035, lists the JDBC type codes used to identify SQL types.)

```
➥       parameters used to create: max length
```

This column indicates that when this type is used in a CREATE TABLE statement, it must include a parameter indicating the maximum length, as shown in the following example, where the maximum length is set to 32 characters:

```
CREATE TABLE COFFEES
(COF_NAME VARCHAR(32),
 . . .
 . . . )
```

➥   nullable?: 1

The number 1 indicates that NULL values are allowed for this type. 0 means that nulls are not allowed for this type, and 2 means that it is not known whether NULL is allowed. (The explanation for the method getTypeInfo lists the possible values for the column NULLABLE, and the section on DatabaseMetaData fields, starting on page 551, gives the numbers that correspond to these possible values.)

➥   case sensitive?: true

This indicates that in this database system, the type varchar is case sensitive, which means that a value stored in a column of this type is case sensitive.

Now let's look at the entry for image:

```
➥ DBMS type image:
➥        java.sql.Types:   -4
➥        parameters used to create: null
➥        nullable?:  1
➥        case sensitive?:  false
```

This entry indicates that the DBMS has the type image and that it corresponds to java.sql.Types.LONGVARBINARY, which has the value -4. The other information in this entry means that for the type image, no parameters are used in the creation of the type, it may be a null, and it is not case sensitive.

4.2.9   Getting Information about Primary and Foreign Keys

The methods that return information about primary and foreign keys are further examples of DatabaseMetaData methods that return ResultSet objects. These methods are getPrimaryKeys, getImportedKeys, getExportedKeys, and getCross-

Reference. We will give examples using two of them to illustrate how they work in general.

If you specify a primary key in your statement creating a table, the DBMS will keep track of that primary key in a metadata table. The JDBC method getPrimaryKeys will return information stored in the DBMS about that primary key. The following create table statements demonstrate how to define a primary key:

```
create table COFFEES
(COF_NAME VARCHAR(32) NOT NULL,
SUP_ID INTEGER,
PRICE FLOAT,
SALES INTEGER,
TOTAL INTEGER,
primary key(COF_NAME))

create table SUPPLIERS
(SUP_ID INTEGER NOT NULL,
SUP_NAME VARCHAR(40),
STREET VARCHAR(40),
CITY VARCHAR(20),
STATE CHAR(2),
ZIP CHAR(5),
primary key(SUP_ID))
```

4.2.10 Sample Code 15

Sample Code 15 is the file PrimaryKeysSuppliers.java. If you have defined your tables specifying the primary keys, as illustrated, you can call the method getPrimaryKeys to get a description of the primary key columns in a table. For example, the following application defines a primary key in its CREATE TABLE statement and then prints out information about that primary key.

```
import java.sql.*;

public class PrimaryKeysSuppliers  {

    public static void main(String args[]) {
```

```java
String url = "jdbc:mySubprotocol:myDataSource";
Connection con;
String createString = "create table SUPPLIERSPK " +
                      "(SUP_ID INTEGER NOT NULL, " +
                      "SUP_NAME VARCHAR(40), " +
                      "STREET VARCHAR(40), " +
                      "CITY VARCHAR(20), " +
                      "STATE CHAR(2), " +
                      "ZIP CHAR(5), " +
                      "primary key(SUP_ID))";
Statement stmt;

try {
    Class.forName("myDriver.ClassName");

} catch(java.lang.ClassNotFoundException e) {
    System.err.print("ClassNotFoundException: ");
    System.err.println(e.getMessage());
}

try {
    con = DriverManager.getConnection(url,
                        "myLogin", "myPassword");

    stmt = con.createStatement();
    stmt.executeUpdate(createString);

    DatabaseMetaData dbmd = con.getMetaData();

    ResultSet rs = dbmd.getPrimaryKeys(
                                null, null, "SUPPLIERSPK");
    while (rs.next()) {
        String name = rs.getString("TABLE_NAME");
        String columnName = rs.getString("COLUMN_NAME");
        String keySeq = rs.getString("KEY_SEQ");
        String pkName = rs.getString("PK_NAME");
        System.out.println("table name :  " + name);
        System.out.println("column name:  " + columnName);
        System.out.println("sequence in key:  " + keySeq);
```

```
            System.out.println("primary key name:   " + pkName);
            System.out.println("");
        }

        rs.close();
        stmt.close();
        con.close();

    } catch(SQLException ex) {
        System.err.print("SQLException: ");
        System.err.println(ex.getMessage());
    }
  }
}
```

The output for this DBMS looks like this:

```
➥ table name :   SUPPLIERSPK
➥ column name:   SUP_ID
➥ sequence in key:   1
➥ primary key name:   null
➥
```

Note that primary keys, and therefore also foreign keys, can be more than one column. (Recall that a primary key uniquely identifies a row in a table, and it may take more than one column to do that. In fact, it is possible that all of the columns in a row could be included in the primary key.) If the primary key consists of multiple columns, the method getPrimaryKeys (as well as getExportedKeys, getImportedKeys, and getCrossReference) will describe each of them. The value in the column KEY_SEQ indicates which column is being described. For example, if there are two columns that constitute the primary key, a value of 2 in the KEY_SEQ column refers to the second column of the primary key. In the output above, the value in KEY_SEQ is 1, so this row of the result set is describing the first column in the primary key for the table SUPPLIERS. Of course, in this case, there is only one column serving as the primary key.

Defining a foreign key is similar to defining a primary key except that you also need to give the name of the table that it references. In other words, a foreign key is a column in one table that also occurs in another table, and in the other table that column is the primary key. In our tables COFFEES and SUPPLIERS, the column SUP_ID is the primary key in SUPPLIERS and the foreign key in COFFEES. Now we will once again create the COFFEES table, this time including a declaration of its foreign key and the table it references (the table in which that column is the primary key):

```
create table COFFEESFK
(COF_NAME VARCHAR(32) NOT NULL,
SUP_ID INTEGER,
PRICE FLOAT,
SALES INTEGER,
TOTAL INTEGER,
primary key(COF_NAME),
foreign key(SUP_ID) references SUPPLIERSPK)
```

4.2.11   Sample Code 16

Sample Code 16 is the file ForeignKeysCoffees.java. The method getImported-Keys tells you about the foreign keys imported into a table. In the table COFFEES, SUP_ID is an imported key, and it references the table SUPPLIERS, where SUP_ID is the primary key. Note that you must have created the table SUPPLIERSPK before you run ForeignKeysCoffees. This table is created in PrimaryKeysSuppliers, so if you run the code samples in order, you will have no problem. If you have not created SUPPLIERSPK, you will get an exception when you run ForeignKeysCoffees because the table it creates, COFFEESFK, refers to SUPPLIERSPK.

A call to the method getImportedKeys(null, null, COFFEESFK) gets a description of the column SUP_ID. A call to the method getExportedKeys(null, null, SUPPLIERSPK) will also get a description of the column SUP_ID. You can think of the column SUP_ID as being imported into COFFEESFK and exported from SUPPLIERSPK.

The following code sample illustrates using getImportedKeys.

```
import java.sql.*;

public class ForeignKeysCoffees  {

    public static void main(String args[]) {
```

```java
String url = "jdbc:mySubprotocol:myDataSource";
Connection con;
String createString = "create table COFFEESFK " +
                "(COF_NAME VARCHAR(32) NOT NULL, " +
                "SUP_ID INTEGER, " +
                "PRICE FLOAT, " +
                "SALES INTEGER, " +
                "TOTAL INTEGER, " +
                "primary key(COF_NAME), " +
                "foreign key(SUP_ID) references SUPPLIERSPK)";
Statement stmt;

try {
    Class.forName("myDriver.ClassName");

} catch(java.lang.ClassNotFoundException e) {
    System.err.print("ClassNotFoundException: ");
    System.err.println(e.getMessage());
}

try {
    con = DriverManager.getConnection(url,
                        "myLogin", "myPassword");

    stmt = con.createStatement();
    stmt.executeUpdate(createString);

    DatabaseMetaData dbmd = con.getMetaData();
    ResultSet rs = dbmd.getImportedKeys(null, null, "COFFEESFK");
    while (rs.next()) {
        String pkTable = rs.getString("PKTABLE_NAME");
        String pkColName = rs.getString("PKCOLUMN_NAME");
        String fkTable = rs.getString("FKTABLE_NAME");
        String fkColName = rs.getString("FKCOLUMN_NAME");
        short updateRule = rs.getShort("UPDATE_RULE");
        short deleteRule = rs.getShort("DELETE_RULE");
        System.out.print("primary key table name :  ");
        System.out.println(pkTable);
        System.out.print("primary key column name :  ");
```

```
                    System.out.println(pkColName);
                    System.out.print("foreign key table name :   ");
                    System.out.println(fkTable);
                    System.out.print("foreign key column name :   ");
                    System.out.println(fkColName);
                    System.out.println("update rule:   " + updateRule);
                    System.out.println("delete rule:   " + deleteRule);
                    System.out.println("");
                }

                rs.close();
                stmt.close();
                con.close();

        } catch(SQLException ex) {
            System.err.print("SQLException: ");
            System.err.println(ex.getMessage());
        }
    }
}
```

The output on the DBMS we are using looks like this:

➡ primary key table name :   SUPPLIERSPK
➡ primary key column name :   SUP_ID
➡ foreign key table name :   COFFEESFK
➡ foreign key column name :   SUP_ID
➡ update rule: 1
➡ delete rule: 1

The explanation in the reference section for the method `getImportedKeys` tells you that there are five possible values for the columns UPDATE_RULE and DELETE_RULE: `importedKeyNoAction`, `importedKeyCascade`, `importedKeySetNull`, `importedKeySetDefault`, and `importedKeyRestrict`. The value 1, returned for both the update rule and the delete rule, is `importedKeyRestrict`, which means that the column SUP_ID in table SUPPLIERSPK may not be updated or deleted because it has been imported to another table, in this case the table COFFEESFK. For example, if you try to delete the table SUPPLIERSPK, you will get an exception telling you that you cannot delete SUPPLIERSPK because another table references it.

You can find an explanation for the possible return values in the section "Data-baseMetaData Fields," starting on page 551.

4.3   Methods Added in the JDBC 2.0 Core API

The JDBC 2.0 core API added several methods to the DatabaseMetaData interface. Most of these methods tell you whether the driver supports a particular JDBC 2.0 feature.

4.3.1   Getting Information about ResultSet Objects

Many new features were added to the ResultSet interface, and corresponding methods telling whether the driver supports the feature were added to the DatabaseMeta-Data interface. For example, there are three types of ResultSet objects with respect to scrollability: those that are not scrollable, those that are scrollable and make visible the changes made to the data source while the ResultSet object is open, and those that are scrollable but do not make changes visible. The following code fragment finds out whether the driver supports the given ResultSet type.

```
DatabaseMetaData dbmd = con.getMetaData();
boolean scrollableInsensitive = dbmd.supportsResultSetType(
                            ResultSet.TYPE_SCROLL_INSENSITIVE);

boolean scrollableSensitive = dbmd.supportsResultSetType(
                            ResultSet.TYPE_SCROLL_SENSITIVE);
```

If *scrollableInsensitive* is true, the driver supports scrollable result sets that are not sensitive to changes made to the data source; if it is false, the driver does not support them. Similarly, if *scrollableSensitive* is true, this driver supports scrollable result sets that *are* sensitive to changes; otherwise, it does not.

The method supportsResultSetConcurrency indicates whether the driver supports a given concurrency mode in combination with a given result set type. For example, the following code fragment finds out whether the driver supports a result set that is scrollable and sensitive to changes in combination with being updatable.

```
DatabaseMetaData dbms = con.getMetaData();
boolean scrollableAndUpdatable = dbms.supportsResultSetConcurrency(
    ResultSet.TYPE_SCROLL_SENSITIVE, ResultSet.CONCUR_UPDATABLE);
```

Nine `DatabaseMetaData` methods return information about what changes to a result set are visible or can be detected. All of these methods take the type of result set as a parameter and return `true` if the functionality described by the method name is supported for the given type of result set. For example, three methods get information about updates: `ownUpdatesAreVisible`, `othersUpdates-AreVisible`, and `updatesAreDetected`. When `updatesAreDetected` returns `true`, it means that the `ResultSet` method `rowUpdated` will return `true` when updates to a row are visible. Three analogous methods get information about inserts, and three get information about deletes.

As an example, let's look at the method `ResultSet.rowInserted`. This method is called on a `ResultSet` object after a row has been inserted into it and while it is still open to see if the current row has been inserted into it. For instance, in the following code fragment, *b1* is `true` only if the fourth row of the `ResultSet` object *rs* has been inserted into *rs* and *rs* is also capable of detecting the insertion.

```
rs.absolute(4);
boolean b1 = rs.rowInserted();
```

The `DatabaseMetaData` method `insertsAreDetected` tells whether a `Result-Set` object of a given type can return `true` when the method `ResultSet.rowIn-serted` is called on it. Assuming that *b1* from the preceding code fragment is `true`, *b2* in the following line of code will be *true* if *rs* is a `ResultSet` object whose type is `TYPE_SCROLL_SENSITIVE`.

```
boolean b2 = dbms.insertsAreDetected(
                        ResultSet.TYPE_SCROLL_SENSITIVE);
```

4.3.2   Getting Other Information

Only three of the `DatabaseMetaData` methods added in the JDBC 2.0 core API return information about something other than result sets. The method `supports-BatchUpdates` indicates whether the DBMS supports sending multiple update statements to the database as a batch. The method `getConnection` retrieves the `Connection` object that produced this `DatabaseMetaData` object. Finally, the method getUDTs returns the UDTs (user-defined types) that have been defined in a particular schema.

4.4 Methods Added in the JDBC 3.0 API

Both methods and fields were added to the DatabaseMetaData interface in the JDBC 3.0 API. As with additions in the JDBC 2.0 API, the majority of methods check to see if new functionality added in the JDBC 3.0 API is supported. However, various other kinds of information are also now available.

4.4.1 Getting Information about ResultSet Objects

The JDBC 3.0 API introduced the capability of an application to choose whether a ResultSet object (cursor) remains open after the method commit has been called to end a transaction. This capability is commonly referred to as result set holdability. The ResultSet interface added the fields HOLD_CURSORS_OVER_COMMIT and CLOSE_CURSORS_AT_COMMIT, which can be used to specify the holdability of a ResultSet object. These constants can be supplied to the Connection methods that create Statement, PreparedStatement, and CallableStatement objects. They are also the possible values for the argument supplied to the DatabaseMetaData method supportsResultSetHoldability. In the following code fragment, the code first determines whether the driver supports ResultSet holdability. If so, it then creates a Statement object that will produce ResultSet objects with holdable cursors. The code also specifies the type and concurrency of the ResultSet objects that *stmt* will generate when it executes a query.

```
if (boolean b = dbms.supportsResultSetHoldability(
                        ResultSet.HOLD_CURSORS_OVER_COMMIT) {
    Statement.stmt = con.createStatement(
                        ResultSet.TYPE_SCROLL_INSENSITIVE,
                        ResultSet.CONCUR_UPDATABLE,
                        ResultSet.HOLD_CURSORS_OVER_COMMIT);
}
```

The method supportsMultipleOpenResults is another DatabaseMetaData method that gets information about keeping ResultSet objects open. In this case, however, the ResultSet objects are generated by a CallableStatement object calling the method execute. The method supportsMultipleOpenResults returns true if the driver supports having multiple `ResultSet` objects returned by a `Callable Statement` object remain open simultaneously.

```
if (dbmd.supportsMultipleOpenResults()) {
    cstmt.getMoreResults(Statement.KEEP_CURRENT_RESULT);
}
```

Other methods check whether the DBMS supports setting savepoints in a transaction, identifying parameters to a `CallableStatement` object by name, retrieving automatically generated keys, and the pooling of `PreparedStatement` objects.

For example, the following line of code finds out whether the DBMS supports statement pooling.

```
boolean stmtPooling = dbmd.supportsStatementPooling();
```

If the return value is `true`, an application can take advantage of the improved performance possibilities that pooling offers by making optimal use of `PreparedStatement` objects.

The following code fragment finds out whether named parameters are supported in `CallableStatement` objects. If so, it uses the name of a parameter rather than its index to indicate the parameter from which a value is being retrieved. The variable *dbmd* is the `DatabaseMetaData` object for the DBMS and driver being used, and *cstmt* is a `CallableStatement` object.

```
if (dbmd.supportsNamedParameters()) {
    String dept = cstmt.getString("DEPT");
    int id = cstmt.getInt("ID");

    String rank = cstmt.getString("RANK");
    . . .
}
```

Two new methods get information about the hierarchies for database objects. If the driver does not support type hierarchies, the return value for both methods is an empty `ResultSet` object. The first one is the method `getSuperTables`, which returns a `ResultSet` object describing the table hierarchies in a schema. Each row contains the name of the super table for a table that matches the name pattern, catalog, and schema pattern supplied as arguments to the method `getSuperTables`.

The second method is getSuperTypes, which returns a ResultSet object that describes the super types of the UDTs that match the catalog, schema pattern, and type name pattern supplied to it.

You will find a complete list of the API added to the DatabaseMetaData interface in "Methods and Fields Added in the JDBC 3.0 API," on page 455.

4.5 Using a ParameterMetaData Object

3.0

You use a ParameterMetaData object to get information about the parameters to a PreparedStatement object or a CallableStatement object. These parameters are indicated by the "?" parameter placeholders that are part of the SQL statement supplied to the Connection methods prepareStatement and prepareCall. For example, the following line of code creates a PreparedStatement object with two parameter placeholders.

```
PreparedStatement pstmt = con.prepareStatement(
        "SELECT ID FROM EMPLOYEES WHERE DEPT = ? and SALARY > ?");
```

The parameters are numbered by their ordinal position, so the first parameter is 1, the second parameter is 2, and so on. In the preceding example, parameter 1 is a value in the column DEPT; parameter 2 is a value in the column SALARY. The following code fragment finds out how many parameters the PreparedStatement *pstmt* has. First, it creates *pstmt* and uses it to create the ParameterMetaData object *pmd*, which contains information about the parameters in *pstmt*. Then it calls the method getColumnCount on *pmd* to find out how many parameters *pstmt* has.

```
PreparedStatement pstmt = con.prepareStatement(
            "UPDATE EMPLOYEES SET SALARY = ? WHERE LEVEL = ?");
ParameterMetaData pmd = pstmt.getParameterMetaData();
int count = pmd.getParameterCount();
```

The value of the variable *count* should be 2 because there are two parameter placeholders in the SQL statement defining *pstmt*. Generally, you already know how many parameters a statement has, so the main use for the method getParameterCount is to get the limit to be used in a for loop. You will see an example later in this section.

The method `getParameterCount` does not take a parameter because it returns information about all the parameters to a `PreparedStatement` object. All of the other methods in the `ParameterMetaData` interface take an ordinal number to indicate the parameter for which information is being requested. For example, the following lines of code get the data type for the first parameter in the preceding example, which is the data type for the column SALARY in the table EMPLOYEES. The code then gets the name the database uses for the data type in the column SALARY, which may be different because different DBMSs may use different names.

```
int type = pmd.getParameterType(1);
String typeName = pmd.getParameterTypeName(1);
```

If the column SALARY stores values of JDBC type INTEGER, the value of the variable *type* will be 4, the type code for INTEGER defined in `java.sql.Types`. The value of the variable *typeName* depends on what specific name the database uses.

If a parameter is a numeric value, you can call three `ParameterMetaData` methods to find out more about it. The following code fragment uses the method `getPrecision` to discover the number of decimal digits in the values stored in the column LEVEL, which is the precision for the second parameter. It also calls the method `getScale` to discover the number of digits to the right of the decimal point and the method `isSigned` to discover whether values can be signed numbers.

```
int totalDigits = pmd.getPrecision(2);
int digitsAfterDecimal = pmd.getScale(2);
boolean signedNumbersAllowed = pmd.isSigned(2);
```

Depending on how the table was originally defined, *totalDigits* could be, for example, 6; *digitsAfterDecimal* could be 2; and *signedNumbersAllowed* could be true. If our coffee entrepreneur had a large shipment of coffee returned and ended up with a negative sales amount for the week, he would need to know whether the *SALES* column in the *COFFEES* table can hold negative numbers.

If you wanted to find out the mode and nullability for all of the parameters in *pstmt*, you could use the following code fragment in an application.

```
int count = pmd.getParameterCount();
for (int i = 1; i <= count; i++) {
    int mode = pmd.getParameterMode(i);
    int nullable = pmd.isNullable(i);
    System.out.print("Parameter " + i + " has mode " + mode);
```

```
        System.out.println(" and nullability " + nullable);
    }
```

The return values for both `getParameterMode` and `isNullable` are constants defined in the interface `ParameterMetaData`. So, for example, in the preceding code fragment, the variable *mode* is `parameterModeIn` for an IN parameter, `parameterModeOut` for an OUT parameter, `parameterModeInOut` for an INOUT parameter, or `parameterModeUnknown` if the mode is unknown. Similarly, the variable *nullable* is `parameterNoNulls`, `parameterNullable`, or `parameterNullableUnknown`. The section "ParameterMetaData Fields," on page 635, gives more information about the exact meaning of these fields.

4.5.1 Sample Code

The following sample code uses many of the `ParameterMetaData` methods illustrated in the previous code fragments. For example, it uses the methods that apply to numeric parameters to see what restrictions apply to the parameter for the SALES column in the COFFEES table. Our coffee entrepreneur is especially interested in whether a negative number can be used in case a large return makes the net sales for a coffee negative for the week.

```java
import java.sql.*;

public class GetParamMetaData {
public static void main(String args[]) {

        String url = "jdbc:mySubProtocol:myDataSource";
        Connection con;
        PreparedStatement pstmt;
        ParameterMetaData pmd;

        String sql = "UPDATE COFFEES SET SALES = ? " +
                                    "WHERE COF_NAME = ?";

        try {
            Class.forName("myDriver.className");

        } catch(java.lang.ClassNotFoundException e) {
```

```
            System.err.print("ClassNotFoundException: ");
            System.err.println(e.getMessage());
        }

        try {
            con = DriverManager.getConnection(url,
                                "myLogin", "myPassword");

            pstmt = con.prepareStatement(sql);
            pmd = pstmt.getParameterMetaData();

            int totalDigits = pmd.getPrecision(1);
            int digitsAfterDecimal = pmd.getScale(1);
            boolean b = pmd.isSigned(1);
            System.out.println("The first parameter ");
            System.out.println("    has precision " + totalDigits);
            System.out.println("    has scale " + digitsAfterDecimal);
            System.out.println("    may be a signed number " + b);

            int count = pmd.getParameterCount();
            System.out.println("count is " + count);

            for (int i = 1; i <= count; i++) {
                int type = pmd.getParameterType(i);
                String typeName = pmd.getParameterTypeName(i);
                System.out.println("Parameter " + i + ":");
                System.out.println("    type is " + type);
                System.out.println("    type name is " + typeName);
            }

            pstmt.close():
            con.close();

        } catch (Exception e) {
        e.printStackTrace();
        }
    }
}
```

NOTE: At the time of this writing, not all drivers fully support the APIs used in this sample code. Consequently, the code has been compiled but not executed. It is included as an aid to understanding how the API can be used. In addition, SQL syntax and dialects may differ between DBMS implementations. It is therefore highly recommended that you consult your DBMS documentation to see the exact syntax you should use.

4.6   Generic Applications

DBMSs generally use standard SQL types. But if you want to write a generic application that works for all DBMSs, regardless of what data types they use, you can do so with the help of methods from `ResultSetMetaData` and `DatabaseMetaData`. The following sample code, `CreateNewTable.java`, is an example of this. It creates a table by prompting the user for the necessary input (table name, column name(s), and column type(s)) and then incrementally constructing a `CREATE TABLE` statement that works for the particular DBMS with which it is being run.

The key method in this application is the `DatabaseMetaData` method `getTypeInfo`, which is used to ascertain what types a DBMS uses and how these relate to the JDBC SQL types. The method `getTypeInfo` was explained in detail in the section "Getting Information about DBMS Data Types," starting on page 214.

We include this code because it is an example of a generic application, but even more importantly, because we want to make it possible for all readers to create the tables used in the tutorials no matter what data types their DBMSs may use.

"Sample Code 19, on page 244, contains code that is very similar, but instead of building a `CREATE TABLE` statement, it builds a `CREATE TYPE` statement. This is the code you can use to create user-defined types in Chapter 3, "Advanced Tutorial," starting on page 113.

4.6.1   Sample Code 17 and 18

Sample Code 17 is the file `DataType.java`; Sample Code 18 is the file `CreateNewTable.java`. The first step in writing this application is to build a vector based on the JDBC SQL types and UDTs that may be used as the data type for a column in the table to be created. (A Vector object, which can be thought of as a variable length array, defines methods for operating on its contents, such as add for adding an element, get for retrieving an element, and size for getting the number of elements it contains.) To make the application more manageable, we separated out the code for building the Vector object, which is called *dataTypes*, into the method get-DataTypes.

The base type for *dataTypes* is an instance of the class DataTypes. Each DataTypes object represents a data type and includes the four values needed for each type: the JDBC SQL type code number, the JDBC SQL type name, the local DBMS name, and the parameters for this type, if there are any, that must be included in the CREATE TABLE statement.

We opted to use a vector of classes because classes offer data encapsulation. The class DataTypes has five fields, one for each of the four values just mentioned plus a boolean to indicate whether any fields still need to be given values. It has one constructor that takes a JDBC SQL type code and a JDBC SQL type name, which are used to initialize instances of DataType. The local DBMS name and parameters are initially set to null. The fields are private, so they can be accessed only through the public methods defined in this class. There are get methods to retrieve the values for each of the fields, but there is only one set method. This method, called setLocalTypeAndParams, sets the values for localType and param, the two values that may vary from one DBMS to another. It also sets the variable *needsSetting* to false so that the status can be tested to prevent setting the values for localType and param again. (The method getTypeInfo may return more than one entry for the local type, and the first one is the one that should be used. Setting *needsSetting* to false guarantees that no subsequent entries can replace the first entry.) The field SQLType is the name of a constant defined in java.sql.Types; the field code is the value assigned to it. Values for these two fields can be set only at initialization.

Here is the definition for the class DataType, contained in the file DataType.java.

```java
public class DataType {

    private int code;
    private String SQLType;
    private String localType = null;
    private String params = null;
```

```
    private boolean needsSetting = true;
        public DataType(int code, String SQLType) {
        this.code = code;
        this.SQLType = SQLType;
        }

    public boolean needsToBeSet() {
        return needsSetting;
    }

    public int getCode() {
        return code;
    }

    public String getSQLType() {
        return SQLType;
    }

    public String getLocalType() {
        return localType;
    }

    public String getParams() {
        return params;
    }

    public void setLocalTypeAndParams(String local, String p) {
        if (needsSetting) {
            localType = local;
            params = p;
            needsSetting = false;
        }
    }
}
```

The Vector object *dataTypes* is initialized with instances of the class DataType. Each instance is created with an SQL type code (from the class java.sql.Types), the corresponding generic SQL type name, and two fields initialized with null. The values for these null fields will be set from the information returned by the method getTypeInfo.

After a call to the method getDataTypes returns the vector *dataTypes*, the rest of the application gets input from the user to build a CREATE TABLE statement. To get user input, we defined another method, getInput, which prints the prompt it is given and returns what the user types in response.

Whenever the user is asked to supply the type for a column name, a list of the SQL types from which to choose is printed on the screen. Type names are included in the list only if the DBMS has an equivalent type. This is tested by calling the method needsToBeSet on each instance of DataType. If the return value is false, indicating that a local DBMS type has been set for this particular SQL data type, then this data type is printed as part of the list presented to the user.

The application CreateNewTable.java looks like this:

```
import java.sql.*;
import java.util.*;

public class CreateNewTable {

    public static void main(String [] args) {
        String url = "jdbc:mySubprotocol:myDataSource";

        Connection con;
        Statement stmt;

        try {

            Class.forName("myDriver.ClassName");

        } catch(java.lang.ClassNotFoundException e) {
            System.err.print("ClassNotFoundException: ");
            System.err.println(e.getMessage());
        }

        try {

            con = DriverManager.getConnection(url,
                                "myLogin", "myPassword");
```

```
stmt = con.createStatement();

Vector dataTypes = getDataTypes(con);

String tableName;
String columnName;
String sqlType;
String prompt = "Enter the new table name and hit Return: ";
tableName = getInput(prompt);
String createTableString = "create table " + tableName + " (";

String commaAndSpace = ", ";
boolean firstTime = true;
while (true){
    System.out.println("");
    prompt = "Enter a column name " +
        "(or nothing when finished) \nand hit Return: ";
    columnName = getInput(prompt);
    if (firstTime) {
        if (columnName.length() == 0) {
            System.out.print("Need at least one column;");
            System.out.println(" please try again");
            continue;
        } else {
            createTableString += columnName + " ";
            firstTime = false;
        }
    } else if (columnName.length() == 0) {
            break;
    } else {
        createTableString += commaAndSpace
                        + columnName + " ";
    }

    String localTypeName = null;
    String paramString = "";

    while (true) {
        System.out.println("");
```

```java
System.out.println("LIST OF TYPES YOU MAY USE:   ");
boolean firstPrinted = true;
int length = 0;
for (int i = 0; i < dataTypes.size(); i++) {
    DataType dataType = (DataType)dataTypes.get(i);
    if (!dataType.needsToBeSet()) {
        if (!firstPrinted)
            System.out.print(commaAndSpace);
        else
            firstPrinted = false;
        System.out.print(dataType.getSQLType());
        length += dataType.getSQLType().length();
        if ( length > 50 ) {
            System.out.println("");
            length = 0;
            firstPrinted = true;
        }
    }
}
System.out.println("");

int index;
prompt = "Enter a column type " +
    "from the list and hit Return:   ";
sqlType = getInput(prompt);

for (index = 0; index < dataTypes.size(); index++) {
    DataType dataType =
                (DataType)dataTypes.get(index);
    if (dataType.getSQLType().equalsIgnoreCase(
            sqlType) && !dataType.needsToBeSet()) {
        break;
    }
}

localTypeName = null;
paramString = "";
if (index < dataTypes.size()) { // there was a match
    String params;
```

```
            DataType dataType =
                        (DataType)dataTypes.get(index);
            params = dataType.getParams();
            localTypeName = dataType.getLocalType();
            if (params != null) {
                prompt = "Enter " + params + ":  ";
                paramString = "(" + getInput(prompt) + ")";
            }
            break;
        }
        else {                  // use the name as given
            prompt = "Are you sure?  " +
                "Enter 'y' or 'n' and hit Return:  ";
            String check = getInput(prompt) + " ";
            check = check.toLowerCase().substring(0,1);
            if (check.equals("n"))
                continue;
            else {
                localTypeName = sqlType;
                break;
            }
        }
    }

    createTableString += localTypeName + paramString;

}
createTableString += ")";
System.out.println("");
System.out.print("Your CREATE TABLE statement as ");
System.out.println("sent to your DBMS:  ");
System.out.println(createTableString);
System.out.println("");

stmt.executeUpdate(createTableString);

stmt.close();
con.close();
```

```
        } catch(SQLException ex) {
            System.err.println("SQLException: " + ex.getMessage());
        }
    }


    private static Vector getDataTypes(Connection con)
                                                throws SQLException {
        String structName = null,
               distinctName = null,
               javaName = null;

        // create a vector of class DataType initialized with
        // the SQL code, the SQL type name, and two null entries
        // for the local type name and the creation parameter(s)

        Vector dataTypes = new Vector();
        dataTypes.add(new DataType(java.sql.Types.BIT, "BIT"));
        dataTypes.add(new DataType(java.sql.Types.TINYINT, "TINYINT"));
        dataTypes.add(new DataType(
                        java.sql.Types.SMALLINT, "SMALLINT"));
        dataTypes.add(new DataType(java.sql.Types.INTEGER, "INTEGER"));
        dataTypes.add(new DataType(java.sql.Types.BIGINT, "BIGINT"));
        dataTypes.add(new DataType(java.sql.Types.FLOAT, "FLOAT"));
        dataTypes.add(new DataType(java.sql.Types.REAL, "REAL"));
        dataTypes.add(new DataType(java.sql.Types.DOUBLE, "DOUBLE"));
        dataTypes.add(new DataType(java.sql.Types.NUMERIC, "NUMERIC"));
        dataTypes.add(new DataType(java.sql.Types.DECIMAL, "DECIMAL"));
        dataTypes.add(new DataType(java.sql.Types.CHAR, "CHAR"));
        dataTypes.add(new DataType(java.sql.Types.VARCHAR, "VARCHAR"));
        dataTypes.add(new DataType(
                        java.sql.Types.LONGVARCHAR, "LONGVARCHAR"));
        dataTypes.add(new DataType(java.sql.Types.DATE, "DATE"));
        dataTypes.add(new DataType(java.sql.Types.TIME,"TIME"));
        dataTypes.add(new DataType(
                        java.sql.Types.TIMESTAMP, "TIMESTAMP"));
        dataTypes.add(new DataType(java.sql.Types.BINARY, "BINARY"));
        dataTypes.add(new DataType(
                        java.sql.Types.VARBINARY, "VARBINARY"));
```

```
dataTypes.add(new DataType(java.sql.Types.LONGVARBINARY,
    "LONGVARBINARY"));
dataTypes.add(new DataType(java.sql.Types.NULL, "NULL"));
dataTypes.add(new DataType(java.sql.Types.OTHER, "OTHER"));
dataTypes.add(new DataType(java.sql.Types.BLOB, "BLOB"));
dataTypes.add(new DataType(java.sql.Types.CLOB, "CLOB"));

DatabaseMetaData dbmd = con.getMetaData();
ResultSet rs = dbmd.getTypeInfo();
while (rs.next()) {
    int codeNumber = rs.getInt("DATA_TYPE");
    String dbmsName = rs.getString("TYPE_NAME");
    String createParams = rs.getString("CREATE_PARAMS");

    if ( codeNumber == Types.STRUCT && structName == null )
        structName = dbmsName;
    else if (
            codeNumber == Types.DISTINCT && distinctName == null )
        distinctName = dbmsName;
    else if (
            codeNumber == Types.JAVA_OBJECT && javaName == null )
        javaName = dbmsName;
    else {
        for (int i = 0; i < dataTypes.size(); i++) {
            // find entry that matches the SQL code,
            // and if local type and params are not already set,
            // set them
            DataType type = (DataType)dataTypes.get(i);

            if (type.getCode() == codeNumber) {
                type.setLocalTypeAndParams(
                                    dbmsName, createParams);
            }
        }
    }
}

int[] types = {Types.STRUCT, Types.DISTINCT, Types.JAVA_OBJECT};
rs = dbmd.getUDTs(null, "%", "%", types);
```

```java
        while (rs.next()) {
            String typeName = null;
            DataType dataType = null;

            if ( dbmd.isCatalogAtStart() )
                typeName = rs.getString(1) + dbmd.getCatalogSeparator() +
                    rs.getString(2) + "." + rs.getString(3);
            else
                typeName = rs.getString(2) + "." + rs.getString(3) +
                    dbmd.getCatalogSeparator() + rs.getString(1);

            switch (rs.getInt(5)) {
            case Types.STRUCT:
                dataType = new DataType(Types.STRUCT, typeName);
                dataType.setLocalTypeAndParams(structName, null);
                break;
            case Types.DISTINCT:
                dataType = new DataType(Types.DISTINCT, typeName);
                dataType.setLocalTypeAndParams(distinctName, null);
                break;
            case Types.JAVA_OBJECT:
                dataType = new DataType(Types.JAVA_OBJECT, typeName);
                dataType.setLocalTypeAndParams(javaName, null);
                break;
            }
            dataTypes.add(dataType);
        }

        return dataTypes;
    }

    private static String getInput(String prompt) throws SQLException {

        System.out.print(prompt);
        System.out.flush();

        try {
            java.io.BufferedReader bin;
            bin = new java.io.BufferedReader(
                    new java.io.InputStreamReader(System.in));
```

```
        String result = bin.readLine();
        return result;

    } catch(java.io.IOException ex) {
        System.out.println("Caught java.io.IOException:");
        System.out.println(ex.getMessage());
        return "";
    }
  }
}
```

The following example is what you will see when you run `CreateNewTable`. This printout has our responses included in bold type.

```
➥ Enter the table name and hit Return: COFFEES
➥
➥ Enter a column name (or nothing when finished)
➥ and hit Return: COF_NAME
➥
➥ LIST OF TYPES YOU MAY USE:
➥ BIT
➥ TINYINT
➥ SMALLINT
➥ INTEGER
➥ FLOAT
➥ REAL
➥ NUMERIC
➥ DECIMAL
➥ CHAR
➥ VARCHAR
➥ LONGVARCHAR
➥ BINARY
➥ VARBINARY
➥ LONGVARBINARY
➥ NULL
➥
➥ Enter a column type from the list and hit Return:  VARCHAR
➥ Enter max length:  32
➥
➥ Enter a column name (or nothing when finished)
➥ and hit Return: SUP_ID
➥
```

➡ LIST OF TYPES YOU MAY USE:

(types omitted)

➡

➡ Enter a column type from the list and hit Return: **INTEGER**

➡

➡ Enter a column name (or nothing when finished)
➡ and hit Return: **PRICE**

➡

➡ LIST OF TYPES YOU MAY USE:

(types omitted)

➡

➡ Enter a column type from the list and hit Return: **FLOAT**

➡

➡ Enter a column name (or nothing when finished)
➡ and hit Return: **SALES**

➡

➡ LIST OF TYPES YOU MAY USE:

(types omitted)

➡

➡ Enter a column type from the list and hit Return: **INTEGER**

➡

➡ Enter a column name (or nothing when finished)
➡ and hit Return: **TOTAL**

➡

➡ LIST OF TYPES YOU MAY USE:

(types omitted)

➡

➡ Enter a column type from the list and hit Return: **INTEGER**

➡

➡ Enter a column name (or nothing when finished) and hit Return:

➡

➡ Your CREATE TABLE statement as sent to your DBMS:
➡ create table COFFEES (COF_NAME varchar(32), SUP_ID int, PRICE
   real, SALES int, TOTAL int)

4.6.2   Sample Code 19

Sample Code 19 is the file CreateNewType.java, which creates a user-defined type (UDT). You will need to run CreateNewType if your DBMS uses type names that are different from the generic JDBC type names used in CreateUDTs. Note that you can build only one CREATE TYPE statement at a time, so you will need to run CreateNew-Type three times to create the three UDTs created in CreateUDTs.

`CreateNewType.java` is similar to `CreateNewTable.java` except that it builds a `CREATE TYPE` statement instead of a `CREATE TABLE` statement and uses attribute names in the place of column names.

To run `CreateNewType`, follow these instructions:

UNIX or Microsoft Windows

```
javac CreateNewType.java
java CreateNewType
```

MacOS

Drag the `CreateNewType.java` file icon onto the Java Compiler icon.
Double-click the `CreateNewType.class` file icon.

When you run `CreateNewType`, it will first prompt you for whether you want to create a structured type or a distinct type. For a structured type, it will then prompt you for the name of the new structured type. Then it will prompt you for the following for as long as you keep entering attribute names:

- An attribute name

- The data type for the attribute

- If applicable, parameter(s) for the type

For a distinct type, it will prompt you for the name of the new distinct type. Then it will prompt you for the following:

- The data type

- If applicable, parameter(s) for the type

Some DBMSs may use a slightly different syntax for creating a new type, in which case you will get an error message indicating that there is a syntax error. If this happens, check the documentation for your driver to see the syntax it requires for creating a user-defined type. Then you simply need to change the line of code that initially assigns a `String` to the variable *createTypeString*. For example, if the syntax your DBMS uses is "CREATE TYPE. . . AS OBJECT" instead of "CREATE TYPE," change the code as shown.

Original:
```
String createTypeString = "create type " + typeName + " (";
```

Revised:
```
String createTypeString = "create type " + typeName + " as object (";
```

Similarly, if your DBMS uses the syntax "CREATE DISTINCT TYPE AS . . ." instead of "CREATE TYPE AS . . . " for creating a distinct type, you will need to modify the code as shown.

Original:
```
String createTypeString = "create type " + typeName;
```

Revised:
```
String createTypeString = "create distinct type " + typeName;
```

You do not need to worry about putting "AS" in the String createTypeString; it is put in later if you indicated that you are creating a distinct type.

Here is the generic code for creating a new user-defined type.

```java
import java.sql.*;
import java.util.*;

public class CreateNewType {

    public static void main(String [] args) {
        String url = "jdbc:mySubprotocol:myDataSource";

        Connection con;
        Statement stmt;
        try {
            Class.forName("myDriver.ClassName");

        } catch(java.lang.ClassNotFoundException e) {
            System.err.print("ClassNotFoundException: ");
            System.err.println(e.getMessage());
        }
```

```
try {
    con = DriverManager.getConnection(url,
                         "myLogin", "myPassword");

    stmt = con.createStatement();

    String typeToCreate = null;
    String prompt = "Enter 's' to create a structured type " +
                    "or 'd' to create a distinct type\n" +
                    "and hit Return: ";
    do {
        typeToCreate = getInput(prompt) + " ";
        typeToCreate =
                    typeToCreate.toLowerCase().substring(0, 1);
    } while ( !(typeToCreate.equals("s") ||
                typeToCreate.equals("d")) );

    Vector dataTypes = getDataTypes(con, typeToCreate);

    String typeName;
    String attributeName;
    String sqlType;
    prompt = "Enter the new type name and hit Return: ";
    typeName = getInput(prompt);
    String createTypeString = "create type " + typeName;
    if ( typeToCreate.equals("d") )
        createTypeString += " as ";
    else
        createTypeString += " (";

    String commaAndSpace = ", ";
    boolean firstTime = true;
    while (true){
        System.out.println("");
        prompt = "Enter an attribute name " +
            "(or nothing when finished) \nand hit Return: ";
        attributeName = getInput(prompt);
        if (firstTime) {
            if (attributeName.length() == 0) {
```

```java
            System.out.print("Need at least one attribute;");
            System.out.println(" please try again");
            continue;
        } else {
            createTypeString += attributeName + " ";
            firstTime = false;
        }
    } else if (attributeName.length() == 0) {
            break;
    } else {
        createTypeString += commaAndSpace
            + attributeName + " ";
    }

    String localTypeName = null;
    String paramString = "";
    while (true) {
        System.out.println("");
        System.out.println("LIST OF TYPES YOU MAY USE:   ");
        boolean firstPrinted = true;
        int length = 0;
        for (int i = 0; i < dataTypes.size(); i++) {
            DataType dataType = (DataType)dataTypes.get(i);
            if (!dataType.needsToBeSet()) {
                if (!firstPrinted)
                    System.out.print(commaAndSpace);
                else
                    firstPrinted = false;
                System.out.print(dataType.getSQLType());
                length += dataType.getSQLType().length();
                if ( length > 50 ) {
                    System.out.println("");
                    length = 0;
                    firstPrinted = true;
                }
            }
        }
        System.out.println("");
```

```
int index;
prompt = "Enter an attribute type " +
    "from the list and hit Return:  ";
sqlType = getInput(prompt);

for (index = 0; index < dataTypes.size(); index++) {
    DataType dataType =
                (DataType)dataTypes.get(index);
    if (dataType.getSQLType().equalsIgnoreCase(
                                sqlType) &&
        !dataType.needsToBeSet()) {
        break;
    }
}

localTypeName = null;
paramString = "";

if (index < dataTypes.size()) { // there was a match
    String params;
    DataType dataType =
                (DataType)dataTypes.get(index);
    params = dataType.getParams();
    localTypeName = dataType.getLocalType();
    if (params != null) {
        prompt = "Enter " + params + ":  ";

        paramString = "(" + getInput(prompt) + ")";
    }
    break;
}
    else {                    // use the name as given
        prompt = "Are you sure?  " +
            "Enter 'y' or 'n' and hit Return:  ";
        String check = getInput(prompt) + " ";
        check = check.toLowerCase().substring(0,1);
        if (check.equals("n"))
            continue;
```

```
                        else {
                        localTypeName = sqlType;
                        break;
                    }
                }
            }

        createTypeString += localTypeName + paramString;

        if ( typeToCreate.equals("d") ) break;
    }

    if ( typeToCreate.equals("s") ) createTypeString += ")";
    System.out.println("");
    System.out.print("Your CREATE TYPE statement as ");
    System.out.println("sent to your DBMS:   ");
    System.out.println(createTypeString);
    System.out.println("");

    stmt.executeUpdate(createTypeString);

    stmt.close();
    con.close();

} catch(SQLException ex) {
    System.err.println("SQLException: " + ex.getMessage());
}
}


private static Vector getDataTypes(
        Connection con, String typeToCreate) throws SQLException {

    String structName = null,
           distinctName = null,
           javaName = null;
    // create a vector of class DataType initialized with
    // the SQL code, the SQL type name, and two null entries
    // for the local type name and the creation parameter(s)
```

```
Vector dataTypes = new Vector();
dataTypes.add(new DataType(java.sql.Types.BIT, "BIT"));
dataTypes.add(new DataType(java.sql.Types.TINYINT, "TINYINT"));
dataTypes.add(new DataType(
                    java.sql.Types.SMALLINT, "SMALLINT"));
dataTypes.add(new DataType(java.sql.Types.INTEGER, "INTEGER"));
dataTypes.add(new DataType(java.sql.Types.BIGINT, "BIGINT"));
dataTypes.add(new DataType(java.sql.Types.FLOAT, "FLOAT"));
dataTypes.add(new DataType(java.sql.Types.REAL, "REAL"));
dataTypes.add(new DataType(java.sql.Types.DOUBLE, "DOUBLE"));
dataTypes.add(new DataType(java.sql.Types.NUMERIC, "NUMERIC"));
dataTypes.add(new DataType(java.sql.Types.DECIMAL, "DECIMAL"));
dataTypes.add(new DataType(java.sql.Types.CHAR, "CHAR"));
dataTypes.add(new DataType(java.sql.Types.VARCHAR, "VARCHAR"));
dataTypes.add(new DataType(
                java.sql.Types.LONGVARCHAR, "LONGVARCHAR"));
dataTypes.add(new DataType(java.sql.Types.DATE, "DATE"));
dataTypes.add(new DataType(java.sql.Types.TIME,"TIME"));
dataTypes.add(new DataType(
                    java.sql.Types.TIMESTAMP, "TIMESTAMP"));
dataTypes.add(new DataType(java.sql.Types.BINARY, "BINARY"));
dataTypes.add(new DataType(
                    java.sql.Types.VARBINARY, "VARBINARY"));
dataTypes.add(new DataType(
                java.sql.Types.LONGVARBINARY, "LONGVARBINARY"));
dataTypes.add(new DataType(java.sql.Types.NULL, "NULL"));
dataTypes.add(new DataType(java.sql.Types.OTHER, "OTHER"));
dataTypes.add(new DataType(java.sql.Types.BLOB, "BLOB"));
dataTypes.add(new DataType(java.sql.Types.CLOB, "CLOB"));
DatabaseMetaData dbmd = con.getMetaData();
ResultSet rs = dbmd.getTypeInfo();

while (rs.next()) {
    int codeNumber = rs.getInt("DATA_TYPE");
    String dbmsName = rs.getString("TYPE_NAME");
    String createParams = rs.getString("CREATE_PARAMS");

    if ( codeNumber == Types.STRUCT && structName == null )
      structName = dbmsName;
```

```
            else if ( codeNumber == Types.DISTINCT &&
                                        distinctName == null )
                distinctName = dbmsName;
            else if (
                    codeNumber == Types.JAVA_OBJECT && javaName == null )
                javaName = dbmsName;
            else {
                for (int i = 0; i < dataTypes.size(); i++) {
                    // find entry that matches the SQL code,
                    // and if local type and params are not already set,
                    // set them
                    DataType type = (DataType)dataTypes.get(i);
                    if (type.getCode() == codeNumber) {
                        type.setLocalTypeAndParams(
                                        dbmsName, createParams);
                    }
                }
            }
        }
    }


    if (typeToCreate.equals("s")) {
        int[] types = {Types.STRUCT, Types.DISTINCT,
                                        Types.JAVA_OBJECT};
        rs = dbmd.getUDTs(null, "%", "%", types);
        while (rs.next()) {
            String typeName = null;
            DataType dataType = null;

            if ( dbmd.isCatalogAtStart() )
                typeName = rs.getString(1) +
                        dbmd.getCatalogSeparator() +
                        rs.getString(2) + "." + rs.getString(3);
            else
                typeName = rs.getString(2) + "." + rs.getString(3) +
                    dbmd.getCatalogSeparator() + rs.getString(1);

            switch (rs.getInt(5)) {
            case Types.STRUCT:
                dataType = new DataType(Types.STRUCT, typeName);
```

```
                    dataType.setLocalTypeAndParams(structName, null);
                    break;
                case Types.DISTINCT:
                    dataType = new DataType(Types.DISTINCT, typeName);
                    dataType.setLocalTypeAndParams(distinctName, null);
                    break;
                case Types.JAVA_OBJECT:
                    dataType = new DataType(Types.JAVA_OBJECT, typeName);
                    dataType.setLocalTypeAndParams(javaName, null);
                    break;
                }
                dataTypes.add(dataType);
            }
        }

        return dataTypes;
    }

    private static String getInput(String prompt) throws SQLException {

        System.out.print(prompt);
        System.out.flush();

        try {
            java.io.BufferedReader bin;
            bin = new java.io.BufferedReader(
                        new java.io.InputStreamReader(System.in));

            String result = bin.readLine();
            return result;

        } catch(java.io.IOException ex) {
            System.out.println("Caught java.io.IOException:");
            System.out.println(ex.getMessage());
            return "";
        }
    }
}
```

CHAPTER 5

Rowset Tutorial

A RowSet object makes it easy to send tabular data over a network. It can also be used to provide scrollable result sets or updatable result sets when the underlying JDBC driver does not support them. This tutorial will walk you through examples of these uses. Because there can be so many variations in rowsets, the first part of this chapter gives a conceptual description of rowsets and their uses. The next part walks you through creating and using a rowset. The last part shows you how a rowset can be used in a distributed Enterprise JavaBeans™ (EJB™) application.

5.1 Types and Uses of Rowsets

The JDBC API includes the RowSet interface, which defines the core model on which all RowSet implementations are built. Any RowSet object contains a set of rows from a result set or some other source of tabular data, such as a file or spreadsheet. One of the main features of a RowSet object is that because it follows the Java-Beans model for properties and event notification, it is a JavaBeans component that can be combined with other components in an application. As is true with other Beans, application programmers will probably use a development tool to create a RowSet object and set its properties.

RowSet implementations, which may fill a variety of needs, fall into two broad categories: rowsets that are connected and those that are disconnected. A disconnected rowset gets a connection to a data source in order to fill itself with data or to propagate changes in data back to the data source, but most of the time it does not have a connection open. While it is disconnected, it does not need a JDBC driver or the full JDBC API, so its footprint is very small. Thus a disconnected rowset is an ideal format for sending data over a network to a thin client.

Because it is not continually connected to its data source, a disconnected rowset stores its data in memory. It needs to maintain metadata about the columns it contains and information about its internal state. It also needs a facility for making connections, for executing commands, and for reading and writing data to and from the data source. In addition, as part of writing data back to the target data source, a rowset needs to control the way in which its content is synchronized back to the data source. A connected rowset, by contrast, opens a connection and keeps it open for as long as the rowset is in use.

Although anyone can implement a rowset, driver vendors will probably provide the majority of implementations, including them as part of their products. To make it easier for anyone writing an implementation, Sun Microsystems and several experts from the database world are developing some standard RowSet implementations through the Java Community Process. The standard RowSet implementations specification, being developed as JSR 114, provides five core interfaces plus a standard reference implementation for each interface. Developers may extend these reference implementations or implement the interfaces in their own way. Standard implementations must all pass the compatability test kit (TCK) to ensure interoperability and portability. The following list describes the implementations and gives you an idea of some of the possibilities.

- JDBCRowSet—a connected rowset that serves mainly as a thin wrapper around a ResultSet object to make a JDBC driver look like a JavaBeans component.

- CachedRowSet—a disconnected rowset that caches its data in memory; not suitable for very large data sets, but an ideal way to provide thin Java clients with tabular data.

- WebRowSet—a disconnected rowset that caches its data in memory in the same manner as a CachedRowSet object. In addition, a WebRowSet object can read and write its data as an XML document. A WebRowSet object makes it easy to use a rowset in the context of Web services.

- FilteredRowSet—a disconnected rowset that can be set to filter its contents so that it exposes only a subset of its rows. The next method is implemented to skip any rows that are not in a specified range of rows.

- JoinRowSet—a disconnected rowset that can combine data from different rowsets into one rowset. This can be especially valuable when the data comes from different data sources.

These implementations are described in more detail in "Standard Implementations," on page 808.

5.2   Using a Rowset

As the conceptual description of rowsets pointed out, what you can do with a rowset depends on how it has been implemented. It can also depend on which properties have been set. The example rowsets used in this chapter are based on the Cached-RowSet interface implementation, but because they are used for different purposes, one rowset has several properties set whereas the other has only one. Among other things, this tutorial will show you which properties to use and when to use them.

Getting back to our owner of The Coffee Break chain, he has had one of his developers write an application that lets him project the effects of changing different coffee prices. To create this application, the developer hooked together various JavaBeans components, setting their properties to customize them for his application. The first JavaBeans component, called Projector, is one that the owner bought from an economic forecasting firm. This Bean takes all kinds of factors into account to project future revenues. Given the price and past sales performance of a coffee, it predicts the revenue the coffee is likely to generate and displays the results as a bar chart.

The second JavaBeans component is a CachedRowSet object. The owner wants to be able to look at different coffee pricing scenarios using his laptop, so the application is set up such that it creates a rowset that can be copied to the laptop's disc. The owner can later fire up the application on his laptop so that he can make updates to the rowset to test out various pricing strategies.

The third Bean is a form for displaying and updating ResultSet objects. The form can be used for displaying and updating our CachedRowSet object because a CachedRowSet object is simply a specialized implementation of the ResultSet interface.

The application has a graphical user interface that includes buttons for opening and closing the application. These buttons are themselves JavaBeans components that the programmer assembled to make the GUI for his application.

While he is at work, the owner can click on the form's New Data button to get a rowset filled with data. This is the work that requires the rowset to get a connection to the data source, execute its query, get a result set, and populate itself with the result set data. When this work is done, the rowset disconnects itself. The owner can now click on the Close button to save the disconnected rowset to his laptop's disc. At home or on an airplane, the owner can open the application on his laptop and click the button Open to copy the rowset from disc and start making updates using the form. The form displays the rowset, and he simply uses arrow keys or tabs to highlight the piece of data he wants to update. He uses the editing component of the form to type in new values, and the Projector Bean shows the effects of the new values in its bar chart. When he gets back to headquarters, the owner can copy his updated rowset to his office computer if he wants to propagate the updates back to the database.

As part of the implementation, the application programmer will do the following:

- Create the CachedRowSet Bean and set its properties
- Register the Projector Bean as a listener to the rowset
- Create the GUI for the application and implement the actions of the open and close buttons
- Specify the rowset as a property on the form Bean

The SunONE™ IDE and many other IDEs based on Java technology provide tools and wizards that allow you to build applications that leverage the component-based architecture provided by JavaBeans technology. These tools minimize the amount of code you have to write, thus making it much easier and faster to use a rowset in your applications. Note that much of the code shown in the examples in this chapter will probably be generated by a tool.

5.2.1   Creating a Rowset and Setting Properties

Because a programmer will generally use a Bean visual development tool to create a RowSet object and set its properties, the example code fragments shown here would most likely be executed by a Bean development tool. The main purpose of this section is to show you when and why you would want to set certain properties.

The code for creating a CachedRowSetImpl object simply uses the default constructor.

```
CachedRowSetImpl crset = new CachedRowSetImpl();
```

Now the programmer can set the CachedRowSetImpl object's properties to suit the owner's needs. The RowSet interface, which the CachedRowSet class implements, contains `get`/`set` methods for retrieving and setting properties. These properties and a `RowSet` object's event notification capabilities (explained in a later section) are what make a `RowSet` object a `JavaBeans` component. A rowset's properties include:

- Command
- Concurrency
- Type
- Data source name
- JDBC URL
- Data source user name
- Data source password
- Transaction isolation level
- Escape processing
- Maximum field size
- Maximum rows
- Query timeout
- Type map
- Provider

You are required to set only those properties that are needed for your particular use of a rowset. The following example uses several properties and explains why they are needed.

The owner wants the convenience of being able to make updates by scrolling to the rows he wants to update, so the property for the type of rowset is set to scrollable. The JDBC RowSet Implementations specification mandates that the `CachedRowSet` interface should be implemented so that it is by default `TYPE_SCROLL_INSENSITIVE`, which means that you do not need to set the rowset's type property. It does no harm to set it, however. Similarly, the default for the concurrency property is `ResultSet.CONCUR_UPDATABLE`.

The following lines of code ensure that the `CachedRowSet` object *crset* is scrollable and updatable.

```
crset.setType(ResultSet.TYPE_SCROLL_INSENSITIVE);
crset.setConcurrency(ResultSet.CONCUR_UPDATABLE);
```

The owner will want to make updates to the table COFFEES, so the programmer sets the rowset's command string with the query SELECT * FROM COFFEES. When the method execute is called, this command will be executed, and the rowset will be populated with the data in the table COFFEES. The owner can then use the rowset to make his updates. In order to execute its command, the rowset will need to make a connection with the database COFFEEBREAK, so the programmer also needs to set the properties required for that. If the DriverManager were being used to make a connection, he would set the properties for a JDBC URL, a user name, and a password. However, he wants to use the preferred means of getting a connection, which is to use a DataSource object, so he will set the properties for the data source name, the owner's user name, and the owner's password. For security, the programmer may opt to get the user name and password from the owner interactively at run time, in which case he would not need to set them as properties. (If you need a refresher on using a DataSource object to make a connection, see "Using a DataSource Object to Get a Connection," on page 168.) Here is the code a tool would generate to set the command string, the data source name, the user name, and the password properties for the CachedRowSet object *crset*.

```
crset.setCommand("SELECT * FROM COFFEES");
crset.setDataSourceName("jdbc/coffeesDB");
crset.setUsername("juanvaldez");
crset.setPassword("espresso");
```

Note that the String object set for the data source name is the logical name that the system administrator (or someone acting in that capacity) registered with a JNDI naming service as the logical name for the COFFEEBREAK database. A programmer just needs to get the logical name, in this case jdbc/coffeesDB, from the system administrator and use it to set the data source property. When the rowset makes a connection, it will use the information in its properties, so the programmer or tool will not need to do anything except execute the command string, which you will see later. Internally, the rowset gives the JNDI naming service the string the programmer set for the data source name property. Because jdbc/coffeesDB was previously bound to a DataSource object representing the database COFFEEBREAK, the naming service will return a DataSource object that the rowset can use to get a connection to COFFEEBREAK.

The programmer sets one more property, the transaction isolation level, which determines the transaction isolation level given to the connection that the rowset establishes. The owner does not want to read any data that has not been committed, so the programmer chooses the level TRANSACTION_READ_COMMITTED. The following line of code sets the rowset's property so that "dirty reads" will not be allowed.

```
crset.setTransactionIsolation(
          Connection.TRANSACTION_READ_COMMITTED);
```

The other properties are all optional for the owner, so the programmer does not set any others. For example, he does not need to set a type map because there are no custom mappings in the table COFFEES. If the owner has the programmer change the command string so that it gets data from a table that has user-defined types with custom mappings, then the type map property will need to be set.

One other property should be mentioned. The provider property specifies a SyncProvider object that determines how changes made to a disconnected rowset's data are propagated back to the underlying data source to synchronize the data in the rowset and the data source. One implementation uses an optimistic concurrency model; another implementation uses a pessimistic concurrency model. The default for a CachedRowSetImpl object is the optimistic concurrency implementation. The programmer in our scenario leaves the provider property as is because she does not expect there to be problems with users entering conflicting values into the COFFEEBREAK database. See "Updating a Rowset," on page 263 for explanations of optimistic concurrency and pessimistic concurrency.

5.2.2   Rowsets and Event Notification

Being a JavaBeans component, a RowSet object has the ability to participate in event notification. In the application we are considering, the Projector Bean needs to be notified when the rowset is updated, so it needs to be registered with the rowset as a listener. The developer who wrote the Projector Bean will already have implemented the three RowSetListener methods rowChanged, rowSetChanged, and cursorMoved. The implementations of these methods specify what the listener will do when an event occurs on the CachedRowSet object *crset*. The Projector Bean does not care about where the cursor is, so its implementation of cursorMoved is probably to do nothing. When one or more values in a row changes, the method rowChanged will be called on the listener. This method will probably check to see if the value in the PRICE or SALES columns has changed, and if either has changed, it will plug the appropriate value(s) into its projection model to get a value to display. The method rowSetChanged is invoked when the contents of the whole rowset change, which happens only when the rowset's command string has been changed and then executed. This method will probably have an implementation similar to that of the method rowChanged.

The following line of code registers *projector*, the bar chart component, as a listener for *crset*.

```
crset.addRowSetListener(projector);
```

Now that *projector* is registered as a listener with the rowset, it will be notified every time an event occurs on *crset*.

The programmer will use her development tool to bring one more component into the application, the editor that will be used to update the rowset. She does this by simply specifying *crset* as a property on the editor. This tells the editor to which component it should send the changes keyed into it.

5.2.3   Obtaining a Scrollable and Updatable Rowset

So far the programmer has created a CachedRowSetImpl object and set its properties. Now all she has to do in order to get a scrollable and updatable rowset is to call the method execute on the rowset. As a result of this call, the rowset does all of the following behind the scenes:

- Gets a connection to the COFFEEBREAK database, using the properties for the data source name, the user name, and the password
- Executes the query SELECT * FROM COFFEES, which has been set as its command string property
- Fills the rowset with the data from the result set produced by the query
- Closes the connection to the COFFEEBREAK database

The invocation that accomplishes all of this is the following single line of code.

```
crset.execute();
```

This produces a CachedRowSet object that contains the same data as the ResultSet object generated by the query SELECT * FROM COFFEES. In other words, they both contain the data in the table COFFEES. The difference is that because the application developer has set the properties on the rowset to make it scrollable and updatable, the owner can move the cursor to any position in the rowset and modify its data. This is true even if the ResultSet object from which the rowset got its data is not scrollable or updatable. In fact, it is especially when a JDBC driver does not support scrollable or updatable result sets that you might want to use a rowset as a means of getting those capabilities. The execute method's final act is to disconnect the CachedRowSet object from its data source.

5.2.4 Using a Rowset for Scrolling and Updating

Scrolling in a rowset is exactly the same as scrolling in a result set. The cursor is initially positioned before the first row in a newly populated rowset, and a call to the method next moves the cursor to the first row. Thus, to iterate through a rowset from first row to last row, you call the method next in a while loop, just as you would do for a ResultSet object. For example, the following code fragment iterates through the entire RowSet object *crset*, printing the name of every coffee in the table COF-FEES.

```
crset.execute();
while (crset.next()) {
    System.out.println(crset.getString("COF_NAME"));
}
```

With a non-scrollable rowset or result set, you are limited to iterating through the data once and in a forward direction. With scrolling, you can move the cursor in any direction and can go to a row as many times as you like. If you want a review of how to move the cursor, see the advanced tutorial section "Moving the Cursor in Scrollable Result Sets," on page 116.

The owner of The Coffee Break wanted a scrolling rowset so that he could easily make updates to a particular row. The following section illustrates moving the cursor to update a row.

5.2.5 Updating a Rowset

Updating a CachedRowSet object is similar to updating a ResultSet object. The updater methods and the methods insertRow and deleteRow are inherited from the ResultSet interface and are used in the same way.

For example, the owner has brought up the rowset, which contains the current data in the table COFFEES, on his laptop computer. He wants to change the price for French_Roast_Decaf, which is in the fifth row, so he moves the cursor there. The

GUI tool displaying the rowset will execute the following line of code to move the cursor to the fifth row.

```
crset.absolute(5);
```

The Projector Bean will be notified that the cursor has moved but will do nothing about it.

The owner now moves the cursor to the price, which is the third column, and changes the column's value to 10.49. In response, the GUI tool executes the following update statement.

```
crset.updateFloat(3, 10.49f);
```

Next the owner clicks on the ROW DONE button to indicate that he is finished making updates to the current row. This causes the GUI tool to execute the following line of code.

```
crset.updateRow();
```

The method rowChanged is called on the Projector Bean to notify it that a row in the rowset has changed. The Projector Bean determines whether the price and/or number of pounds sold has changed and, if so, plugs the most current price and number of pounds sold into its projection calculations. After it arrives at new projected values for revenue from sales of the affected coffee, it updates the bar chart to reflect the new values.

Now the owner moves to the previous row, which is the fourth row, changes the price to 9.49 and the sales amount to 500, and clicks the ROW DONE button. Note that the fourth column in the rowset contains the number of pounds sold in the last week. The GUI tool executes the following code.

```
crset.previous(-1); // or crset.absolute(4);
crset.updateFloat(3, 9.49f);
crset.updateInt(4, 500);
crset.updateRow();
```

So far the owner has updated the fourth and fifth rows in the rowset, but he has not updated the values in the database. If this had been a ResultSet object, both the result set and the database would have been updated with the call to the method updateRow. However, because this is a disconnected rowset, only the rowset itself has been updated, and the method `CachedRowSet.acceptChanges` has to be called for the updates to be made in the database. The owner will click the `UPDATE DATABASE` button if he wants to propagate his changes back to the database. The GUI tool will execute the following line of code.

```
crset.acceptChanges();
```

The application is implemented so that the `acceptChanges` method is not actually invoked until the owner returns to work and copies the updated rowset to his office computer. On the office machine, the rowset can create a connection for writing updated values back to the database. In addition to updating the database with the new values in rows four and five of the rowset, the `acceptChanges` method will set the values that the rowset keeps as its "original" values. Original values are the values the rowset had just before the current set of updates.

Before writing new values to the database, the rowset's writer component works behind the scenes to compare the rowset's original values with those in the database. If no one has changed values in the table, the rowset's original values and the values in the database should be the same. If there is no conflict, that is, the rowset's original values and the database's values match, the writer will generally write the updated values to the database. If there is a conflict, generally the writer does not change the data in the data source.

The writer's behavior depends on the `SyncProvider` implementation that has been set for the rowset's `provider` property. There are two standard implementations. One is implemented for pessimistic concurrency and will attempt to prevent conflicts by setting varying degrees of locks that prevent other users from accessing data in the data source. How the locks are set depends on the implementation. This pessimistic concurrency model assures a greater likelihood that the values in the data source will be synchronized with the updates in the rowset. However, it has the disadvantages of restricting access to the data source and of incurring the additional cost of setting locks.

The second SyncProvider implementation uses an optimistic concurrency model, which assumes that other users will never or seldom access the data in the data source that corresponds to the data in the rowset. It therefore allows more access and does not incur the expense of setting locks. The drawback to this approach is that it cannot guarantee that updates made to the rowset will be propagated back to the data source.

In addition to setting one of the standard `SyncProvider` implementations, a developer can set a third-party implementation as well. The pluggable synchronization mechanism allows other standard synchronization implementations, such as SyncML (`http://www.syncml.org/`), to be easily plugged in to a `RowSet` implementation.

When the data source is updated, the current values that the writer enters will be used as the original values when a new set of updates is made. For example, the price in the fifth row was 9.99 before it was updated to 10.49. The rowset's original price of 9.99 should match the price for `French_Roast_Decaf` coffee in the database. If it does, the writer can update the database price to 10.49 and change the rowset's original price to 10.49. The next time the price for `French_Roast_Decaf` is changed, the writer will compare the new original value (10.49) with the current value in the database.

In this example scenario you have seen how a rowset can be used to pass a set of rows to a thin client, in this case a laptop computer. You have also seen how a rowset can provide scrolling and updatability, which the JDBC driver used at the owner's office does not support. The next part of this chapter will show you how a rowset might be used in an EJB application.

5.3   An EJB Example

For this example, we assume that you are familiar with the concepts discussed in "Basic Tutorial" and "Advanced Tutorial," especially the sections on using the JDBC Optional Package API (`javax.sql` package). This EJB example gives only a high-level explanation of the EJB classes and interfaces used in it; if you want a more thorough explanation, you should see the EJB specification available at the following URL:

```
http://java.sun.com/products/ejb
```

Let's assume that the owner of The Coffee Break has set up an EJB application to make it easier for his managers to order coffee for their stores. The managers can bring up an order form that has two buttons: one button for viewing a table with the coffees and prices currently available and another button for placing an order.

The developer who designed the form used JavaBeans components to create the buttons, layout, and other components of the form. The application developer will use Enterprise JavaBeans components to make the buttons do their work. The EJB component (enterprise Bean) will be deployed in a container provided by an

EJB server. The container manages the life cycle of its enterprise Beans and also manages the boundaries of the transactions in which they participate. The EJB implementation also includes a `DataSource` class that works with an `XADataSource` class to provide distributed transactions.

5.3.1 A Distributed Application

An EJB application is always a distributed application, an application that distributes its work among different machines. An EJB application uses the three-tier model. The first tier is the client, which is typically a web browser. In our example, the client is a form running on The Coffee Break's intranet. The second tier, or middle tier, is made up of the EJB server and the JDBC driver. The third tier is one or more database servers.

The method `getCoffees` is one of the three methods that is implemented by our enterprise Bean, the class `CoffeesBean`. Let's look at the implementation of this method, which creates and populates a rowset, and then look at how its invocation and execution are spread out over the three tiers. This method will be explained in more detail later in this chapter.

```java
public RowSet getCoffees() throws SQLException {
    Connection con = null;
    try {
        con = ds.getConnection("managerID", "mgrPassword");
        Statement stmt = con.createStatement();
        ResultSet rs =  stmt.executeQuery(
                        "SELECT COF_NAME, PRICE FROM COFFEES");
        CachedRowSetImpl crset = new CachedRowSetImpl();
        crset.setConcurrency(ResultSet.CONCUR_READ_ONLY);
        crset.populate(rs);
        rs.close();
        stmt.close();
        return crset;
    }

    finally {
        if (con != null) con.close();
    }
```

```
    return null;
}
```

1. Client—invokes the method `getCoffees`

   The manager clicks the button `Display Coffee Prices` on The Coffee Break order form.

2. Middle tier—starts executing the method `getCoffees`

   The EJB server creates a connection to the DBMS server and sends the query to it.

3. DBMS server(s)—executes the query sent from the middle tier

   The DBMS server executes the query and returns a result set with coffee names and their prices to the middle-tier server.

4. Middle tier—finishes executing the method `getCoffees`

   The middle-tier server creates a rowset, populates it with the data from the result set returned by the DBMS, and returns the rowset to the client.

5. Client—the order form displays the rowset received from the middle tier

Note that a distributed application is not restricted to three tiers: It may have two tiers, a client and server. Also note that a distributed application is different from a distributed transaction. A distributed transaction, often referred to as a global transaction, is a transaction that involves two or more DBMS servers. A global transaction will always occur within the context of a distributed application because, by definition, it requires a client and at least two servers.

5.3.2   Differences in Rowsets

As you have just seen, the rowset used in our EJB example is a `CachedRowSetImpl` object that is created and populated on the middle-tier server. This disconnected rowset is then sent to a thin client. All of this is also true of the rowset in the laptop example, but there are some differences between the two rowsets. The main difference is that the rowset used in the order form for The Coffee Break is not updatable by the client; it is simply a list of coffees and their prices that the manager can look at. The default for the concurrency property is to be updatable, so the code needs to set it to read-only. Otherwise, the rowset used in the order form does not need to have any properties set. The method `getCoffees` gets a `DataSource` object and then uses it to get a connection, so the rowset does not need to perform these tasks. This means that the rowset does not use a data source name, user name, or password, and thus it does not need the properties for them set. The order form rowset also needs no command property because the `getCoffees` implementation executes the query to get coffee names and prices. Recall that, by contrast, the rowset in the laptop example created a connection, executed its command string, and populated itself with data by having its `execute` method invoked. The only `CachedRowSet` method used in the EJB example, other than `setConcurrency`, is `populate`, which just reads data from the `ResultSet` object passed to it and inserts the data into the rowset.

5.3.3 EJB and Distributed Transactions

In the EJB framework, one or more enterprise Beans can be deployed in a container, which manages the Beans. The container controls the life cycle of a Bean, and it also controls the boundaries of distributed transactions.

Every enterprise Bean has a transaction attribute to tell the container how it should be managed with regard to distributed transactions. The developer of the enterprise Bean in our example has given the Bean the transaction attribute `TX_REQUIRED`, which means that the Bean's methods must be executed in the scope of a global transaction. If the component that invokes one of the enterprise Bean's methods is already associated with a global transaction, the enterprise Bean method will be associated with that transaction. If not, the container must start a new distributed transaction and execute the enterprise Bean method in the scope of that transaction. When the method has completed, the container will commit the transaction.

The fact that the Bean's container manages the start and end of transactions has implications for the Bean's behavior. First, the Bean should not call the methods `commit` or `rollback`. Second, the Bean should not change the default setting for a connection's auto-commit mode. Because the `DataSource` object is implemented to work with distributed transactions, any connection it produces has its auto-commit mode disabled. This prevents the connection from automatically committing a transaction, which would get in the way of the container's management of the transaction. Summarizing, the Bean should leave the connection's auto-commit mode disabled and should not call the methods `commit` or `rollback`.

5.3.4   A Stateless SessionBean Object

The EJB component in this example is a stateless SessionBean object, which is the simplest kind of enterprise Bean. Being a session Bean means that it is an extension of the client that creates it, typically reading and updating data in a database on behalf of the client. A session Bean is created when a client begins its session and is closed when the client ends its session. Being stateless means that the Bean does not need to retain any information it might get from a client from one method invocation to the next. Therefore, any Bean instance can be used for any client.

For example, the enterprise Bean we will use has three methods. The first creates a CoffeesBean object, the second retrieves a table of coffees and prices, and the third places a manager's order. In general, because our enterprise Bean is a SessionBean object, it is created when a manager opens The Coffee Break order form and is closed when he/she quits it. It is stateless because it does not have to remember coffee prices or what the client ordered.

5.3.5   Overview of an EJB Application

An EJB application has four parts, which are described briefly in the following list. The enterprise Bean developer writes the first three, and anyone, including the enterprise Bean developer, may supply the fourth. The sections following this one show the code for each interface or class.

1. The remote interface—declares the methods that a client can call on the enterprise Bean

    In our example, the remote interface is the interface Coffees, which declares the methods getCoffees and placeOrder. The container generates an implementation of this interface that delegates to the class CoffeesBean. CoffeesBean, supplied by the developer, actually defines what the methods do. It is the third item in this list. Instances of the interface Coffees are EJBObjects.

2. The home interface—declares the method that creates a Coffees object

    In our example, the home interface is the interface CoffeesHome, which is registered with a JNDI naming service. It declares the method create and creates Coffees objects. The container implements this interface so that the method create delegates its work to the method ejbCreate, which is implemented by the CoffeesBean class.

3. The enterprise Bean class—the class that implements the methods used in the other parts of the application

> Instances of this class are enterprise Beans. In our example this class is `CoffeesBean`, which implements the methods `ejbCreate`, `getCoffees`, and `placeOrder`.

4. The client code—the class on the client that invokes the enterprise Bean object

> In our example, the client class is `CoffeesClient`. This class typically includes GUI components. For our example, if it were fully implemented, the `CoffeesClient` class would include buttons for invoking the methods `getCoffees` and `placeOrder`. It would also include a text editor for typing in the parameters for the method `placeOrder`. This class could have many different implementations, with or without GUI components, and it could be written by the enterprise Bean developer or anyone else.

Now let's look at some sample code for an EJB application. Note that we kept this example very simple in order to concentrate on the basic concepts.

5.3.6   The Remote Interface

The interface `Coffees` declares the methods that managers of The Coffee Break coffee houses can invoke. In other words, this interface contains the methods that a remote client can invoke.

This interface, which extends `EJBObject`, declares the methods `getCoffees` and `placeOrder`. It imports four packages because it uses elements from each one. Both methods can throw a `RemoteException` as well as an `SQLException` because they use methods from the package `java.rmi`, the package for remote method invocation on Java objects. The following code defines the interface `Coffees`.

```
import java.rmi.*;
import java.sql.*;
import javax.sql.*;
import javax.ejb.*;

public interface Coffees extends EJBObject {
   public RowSet getCoffees() throws RemoteException, SQLException;
   public void placeOrder(String cofName, int quantity, String MgrId)
```

```
        throws RemoteException, SQLException;
}
```

5.3.7   The Home Interface

The home interface CoffeesHome is a factory for Coffees objects. It declares only the single method create, which creates Coffees objects, thus making CoffeesHome the simplest possible form of the home interface. The method create may throw a RemoteException, from the java.rmi package, or a CreateException, from the javax.ejb package.

```
import java.rmi.*;
import javax.ejb.*;

public interface CoffeesHome extends javax.ejb.EJBHome {
   public Coffees create() throws RemoteException, CreateException;
}
```

5.3.8   The Client Class

So far you have seen two interfaces with one thing in common: These interfaces contain the methods that will be called by the client class. The two methods in Coffees are called in response to button clicks from a manager. The client calls the CoffesHome.create method to get a Coffees object it can use for invoking the methods defined on Coffees.

The first thing the CoffeesClient class does is to retrieve a CoffeesHome object that has been registered with a JNDI naming service. The CoffeesHome object has been bound to the logical name ejb/Coffees, so when ejb/Coffees is given to the method lookup, it returns a CoffeesHome object. Because the instance of CoffeesHome is returned in the form of an RMI (Remote Method Invocation) object, PortableRemoteObject, it has to be cast to a CoffeesHome object before being assigned to the variable *chome*. The method CoffeesHome.create can then be called on *chome* to create the Coffees object *coffees*. Once the client has a Coffees object, it can call the methods Coffees.getCoffees and Coffees.place-Order on it.

The methods invoked by a CoffeesClient object are implemented in the class CoffeesBean, which you will see next.

```java
import java.sql.*;
import javax.sql.*;
import javax.naming.*;
import javax.ejb.*;
import javax.rmi.*;

class CoffeesClient {

  public static void main(String[] args) {

    try {
      Context ctx = new InitialContext();
      Object obj = ctx.lookup("ejb/Coffees");
      CoffeesHome chome = (CoffeesHome)PortableRemoteObject.narrow(
                                        obj, CoffeesHome.class);

      Coffees coffees = chome.create();

      RowSet rset = coffees.getCoffees();

      // display the coffees for sale
      // get user input from GUI

      coffees.placeOrder("Colombian", 3, "12345");

      // repeat until user quits
    }

    catch (Exception e) {
      System.out.print(e.getClass().getName() + ":");
      System.out.println(e.getMessage());
    }
  }
}
```

5.3.9   The Enterprise Bean

The final part of our EJB component is the class `CoffeesBean`, which implements the methods that are declared in the interfaces `Coffees` and `CoffeesHome` and that are invoked in the class `CoffeesClient`. Note that it implements the `SessionBean` interface, but because it is a stateless `SessionBean` object, the implementations of the methods `ejbRemove`, `ejbPassivate`, and `ejbActivate` are empty. These methods apply to a `SessionBean` object with conversational state, but not to a stateless `SessionBean` object such as an instance of `CoffeesBean`. We will examine the code more closely after you have looked at it.

```java
import java.sql.*;
import javax.sql.*;
import javax.naming.*;
import javax.ejb.*;

public class CoffeesBean implements SessionBean {

    public CoffeesBean() {}

    public void ejbCreate() throws CreateException {
        try {
            ctx = new InitialContext();
            ds = (DataSource)ctx.lookup("jdbc/CoffeesDB");
        }
        catch (Exception e) {
            throw new CreateException();
        }
    }


    public RowSet getCoffees() throws SQLException {
        Connection con = null;

        try {
            con = ds.getConnection("managerID", "mgrPassword");
            Statement stmt = con.createStatement();
            ResultSet rs =  stmt.executeQuery("select * from coffees");
```

```
            CachedRowSetImpl rset = new CachedRowSetImpl();
            rset.populate(rs);

            rs.close();
            stmt.close();

            return rset;
        } finally {
            if (con != null) con.close();
        }
    }

    public void placeOrder(String cofName, int quantity, String MgrId)
                                            throws SQLException {
        Connection con = null;

        try {
            con = ds.getConnection("managerID", "mgrPassword");
            PreparedStatement pstmt = con.prepareStatement(
                        "insert into orders values (?, ?, ?)");
            pstmt.setString(1, cofName);
            pstmt.setInt(2, quantity);
            pstmt.setString(3, MgrId);
            pstmt.executeUpdate();

            pstmt.close();
        } finally {
            if (con != null) con.close();
        }
    }

    //
    // Methods inherited from SessionBean
    //
    public void setSessionContext(SessionContext sc) {
        this.sc = sc;
    }
```

```
    public void ejbRemove() {}

    public void ejbPassivate() {}

    public void ejbActivate() {}

    private SessionContext sc = null;
    private Context ctx = null;
    private DataSource ds = null;
}
```

CoffeesBean can be divided into the following steps:

1. Defining the default constructor

```
public CoffeesBean() {}
```

2. Defining the method ejbCreate

```
public void ejbCreate() throws CreateException {
    try {
        ctx = new InitialContext();
        ds = (DataSource)ctx.lookup("jdbc/CoffeesDB");
    } catch (Exception e) {
            throw new CreateException();
    }
}
```

The Context object *ctx* and the DataSource object *ds* are private fields originally set to null. This method retrieves an instance of the DataSource implementation that is associated with the logical name jdbc/CoffeesDB and assigns it to
ds. The DataSource object *ds* can be used to create connections to the database
COFFEEBREAK. This work is done once when the Bean is created to avoid doing it
over and over each time the methods getCoffees and placeOrder are called.

3. Defining the method getCoffees. We will break this method down into smaller
   units for examination.

```
public RowSet getCoffees() throws SQLException {
   Connection con != null;
   try {
      con = ds.getConnection("managerID", "mgrPassword");
      Statement stmt = con.createStatement();
      ResultSet rs =  stmt.executeQuery(
                            "SELECT COF_NAME, PRICE FROM COFFEES");
```

As the signature indicates, this method returns a RowSet object. It uses the DataSource object that the method ejbCreate obtained from the JNDI naming service to create a connection to the database that *ds* represents. Supplying a user name and password to the method DataSource.getConnection produces the Connection object *con*. This is a connection to the database COFFEEBREAK because when the system administrator deployed the DataSource object used to make the connection, she gave it the properties for the COFFEEBREAK database.

The code then creates a Statement object and uses it to execute a query. The query produces a ResultSet object that has the name and price for every coffee in the table COFFEES. This is the data that the client has requested.

```
CachedRowSetImpl crset = new CachedRowSetImpl();
crset.populate(rs);
```

The preceding code creates the CachedRowSetImpl object *crset* and populates it with the data that is in *rs*. This code assumes that the interface CachedRowSet has been defined and that it provides the method populate, which reads data from a ResultSet object and inserts it into a RowSet object. Now let's look at the rest of the implementation of the getCoffees method.

```
      rs.close();
      stmt.close();
      return rset;

   } finally { if (con != null) con.close();
   }
   return null;
```

The method getCoffees returns the newly populated CachedRowSetImpl object if the connection is made and the rowset is successfully filled with data. Otherwise, the getCoffees method returns null. There are two points to be made about these lines of code. First, the code contains a `finally` block that assures that even if there is an exception thrown, if the connection is not `null`, it will be closed and thereby recycled. Because the EJB server and JDBC driver being used implement connection pooling, a valid connection will automatically be put back into the pool of available connections when it is closed.

The second point is that the code does not enable the auto-commit mode, nor does it call the methods `commit` or `rollback`. The reason is that this enterprise Bean is operating within the scope of a distributed transaction, so the container will commit or roll back all transactions.

4. Defining the method `placeOrder`

```
public void placeOrder(String cofName, int quantity, String MgrId)
                                              throws SQLException {

    Connection con = null;

    try {
        con = ds.getConnection("managerID", "mgrPassword");
        PreparedStatement pstmt = con.prepareStatement(
                        "INSERT INTO ORDERS VALUES (?, ?, ?)");
        pstmt.setString(1, cofName);
        pstmt.setInt(2, quantity);
        pstmt.setString(3, MgrId);
        pstmt.executeUpdate();

        pstmt.close();
    }

    catch (SQLException e) {
        throw e;
    }
    finally {
        if (con != null) con.close();
    }
}
```

The method `placeOrder` gets values for the three input parameters and then sets them. After the manager clicks the PLACE ORDER button on the order form, he gets three blank spaces into which to type the coffee name, the number of pounds, and his ManagerID. For example, the manager might have typed "Colombian", 50, and "12345" in the blanks on his form. The server would get the following line of code:

```
coffees.placeOrder("Colombian", 50, "12345");
```

The `placeOrders` method would produce the following code:

```
pstmt.setString(1, "Colombian");
pstmt.setInt(2, 50);
pstmt.setString(3, "12345");
```

The following update statement would effectively be sent to the DBMS server to be executed.

```
INSERT INTO ORDERS VALUES ("Colombian", 50, "12345")
```

This would put a new row into the ORDERS table to record the manager's order.

As with the method `getCoffees`, the `placeOrders` method has a `finally` block to make sure that a valid connection is closed even if there is an exception thrown. This means that if the connection is valid, it will be returned to the connection pool to be reused.

The rest of the implementation deals with methods inherited from the `SessionBean` interface. The methods `ejbRemove`, `ejbPassivate`, and `ejbActivate` apply to `SessionBean` objects with state. Because `CoffeesBean` is a stateless `SessionBean` object, the implementations for these methods are empty.

Congratulations! You have finished the tutorials on the JDBC API. You can create tables, update tables, retrieve and process data from result sets, use prepared statements and stored procedures, and use transactions. You can also take advantage of more advanced functionality, such as using SQL99 data types, making batch updates, making programmatic updates, doing custom mapping, making a connection with a `DataSource` object, using connection pooling, using savepoints, using automatically generated keys, using distributed transactions, and using rowsets. In addition, you have seen how the JDBC API works with EJB technology and have been introduced to the four parts of an EJB application.

The reference chapters give more examples and more in-depth explanations of the features you have learned to use in these tutorials. Remember to take advantage of the glossary and the index as aids for getting information quickly.

Part Two

Part Two is the definitive reference for the complete JDBC 3.0 API. It contains a chapter for each class and interface, a chapter on mapping data types between SQL and the Java programming language, two appendices, a glossary, and an index. There is also a quick reference tear-out card inside the back cover. The reference chapters are arranged alphabetically for easy lookup.

Each reference chapter consists of three main parts. The first part is an overview of the class or interface. The second part is the definition of the class or interface, which lists constructors, methods, and/or fields in logical order. The third part contains in-depth explanations of each constructor, method, and/or field. These explanations are arranged alphabetically to make looking them up easier.

As was explained in Chapter 1, "Introduction," almost all of the methods in the JDBC API throw an SQLException if there is a problem accessing data. To save unnecessary repetition, method explanations do not include a THROWS section if the method throws an SQLException because of a problem with data access, which is the typical reason. An SQLException is explained if it is thrown for any reason other than a problem with data access. All other exceptions are explained in a THROWS section.

Referring to the sections "Suggested Order for Reading Chapters," on page 10, and "Where to Find Information by Topic," on page 11, may be helpful.

CHAPTER **6**

Array

6.1   Array Overview

THE Array interface represents the standard mapping of the SQL99 ARRAY type. An SQL99 ARRAY value, which is an array of elements that are all the same data type, is stored as a column value in a row of a database table.

In a standard implementation, a JDBC driver implements the Array interface using the SQL99 type LOCATOR(ARRAY) internally. Because a LOCATOR(ARRAY) value is a logical pointer designating an SQL ARRAY instance residing on a database server, an Array object contains a logical pointer to the array, not the elements of the array. Consequently, creating an Array object does not bring the ARRAY data over to the client machine from the server. SQL operations on an Array object, however, operate on the SQL ARRAY value stored on the server. This ability to operate on an SQL ARRAY value without bringing its data to the client can be a big boost for performance, especially when the ARRAY value has many elements. The driver uses LOCATOR(ARRAY) behind the scenes, so its use is completely transparent to the programmer writing JDBC applications.

Methods in the interfaces ResultSet, CallableStatement, and PreparedStatement allow a programmer to get and set the SQL99 type ARRAY in the same way that other data types are accessed. In other words, with the JDBC 2.0 API, an application uses the ResultSet.getArray and PreparedStatement.setArray methods to retrieve and store an ARRAY value the same way it uses getInt and setInt for an INTEGER value or getString and setString for a VARCHAR value.

Using JDBC methods, an application can operate on a java.sql.Array object to retrieve, update, and store the SQL ARRAY instance that it designates. It can also operate on the Array object using SQL commands. In these cases, all that resides on the client is a logical pointer to the ARRAY instance. However, if an application wants to operate on the elements of the ARRAY instance locally, it can bring the data of the ARRAY value to the client, referred to as *materializing* the data. Consequently, the main work of the Array interface, second only to mapping an SQL ARRAY instance to the Java programming language, is to materialize the elements of an ARRAY instance on the client. All of the methods in the interface Array, except for the two that retrieve information about the base type of the elements, materialize the elements of an array on the client. These methods are explained later in this chapter.

6.1.1   Creating an Array Object

The following code fragment illustrates creating an Array object, where *stmt* is a Statement object and the column SCORES stores values of SQL type ARRAY.

```
ResultSet rs = stmt.executeQuery(
                    "SELECT SCORES FROM STUDENTS WHERE ID = 1234");
rs.next();
Array scores = rs.getArray("SCORES");
```

The variable *scores* contains a logical pointer to the ARRAY value that is stored on the server. The value stored in the column SCORES in the current row of the result set *rs* is an SQL LOCATOR(ARRAY) value, which is mapped to *scores* by the ResultSet.getArray method. Even though *scores* does not contain the elements of the ARRAY value to which it points, methods called on *scores* will take effect on the ARRAY instance just as if they were being called on it directly. In a standard implementation, *scores* will remain valid until the transaction in which it was created is either committed or rolled back.

6.1.2   Getting Base Type Information

The base type of an array (the data type of all of the elements in the array) may be a built-in type or a user-defined type.

Two methods in the interface Array give information about the base type of an array: getBaseType and getBaseTypeName. Typically programmers are familiar with the database they access and would already know the base type of an array value, so these methods are generally used by tools or for unusual situations. These methods provide a way to get base type information when the method Array.getArray has been used to materialize an ARRAY object's element values on the client. If the method `Array.getResultSet` is used to materialize the elements, the same information retrieved by `getBaseType` and `getBaseTypeName` can be retrieved with the `ResultSetMetaData` methods `getColumnType` and `getColumn-TypeName`.

6.1.3   Materializing Array Data

Materializing an `Array` instance consists of physically copying the contents of an `ARRAY` value from the DBMS server to the client. Of the eight methods that materialize the values of an array, four materialize them as an array in the Java programming language, and four materialize them as a `ResultSet` object.

When values are materialized as a `ResultSet` object, they are logically stored in the result set as SQL values or, more precisely, as JDBC types (generic SQL types defined in the class `java.sql.Types`). When a value is retrieved from the result set using the getter methods in the `ResultSet` interface, the JDBC type is converted to a type in the Java programming language. The conversion done by the getter methods follows the standard mapping from a JDBC type to a type in the Java programming language, as shown in "JDBC Types Mapped to Java Types," on page 1087. For example, if the base type of an SQL `ARRAY` is `INTEGER`, that is the data type of the values in the result set. When the values are retrieved using the method `getInt`, each value returned will have been converted to an `int` in the Java programming language. If the base type of the array is unknown, the `ResultSetMetaData` methods mentioned previously can be called to determine the base type and thus the appropriate getter method to use.

A different mechanism is used when the elements are materialized by a call to the method `getArray`, which returns an array in the Java programming language. Since there are no methods like the getter methods in the `ResultSet` interface to perform conversions when the values are retrieved, the driver will have already converted the elements to a type in the Java programming language. Conceptually, the driver has called the method `getObject` on each element and put the resulting object into the array that will be returned. The data type for the elements is determined by the standard mapping from JDBC types to `Object` types, as shown in the table "JDBC Types Mapped to Java Object Types," on page 1089. For example, an array of JDBC `CHAR` values will be materialized as an array of `String` objects, and an array of JDBC `NUMERIC` values will be materialized as an array of `java.math.BigDecimal` objects.

There is one very important exception to this rule. If the base type of the array maps to a primitive type in the Java programming language, the base type of the returned array will be the primitive type rather than the Object type. For example, if the base type maps to a Java int, then the array returned will be an array of int values, not an array of Integer objects. This special treatment for primitive types makes it easier to manipulate the array values and also increases performance.

It should be noted that the return type for the getArray methods is Object, not Object [] (array of Object). The value returned by getArray may be an array of Object objects or an array of a primitive type, but it will always be an array. Therefore, to be general enough, the return value is considered simply as an array, which is an Object type.

If the base type of the array is a user-defined type (either a distinct type or a structured type), a programmer may choose to use a customized mapping rather than the standard mapping. This involves (1) creating a class that contains the custom mapping and (2) including an entry for the UDT in a type map. For more information on custom mapping, see "Creating a Custom Mapping," on page 896.

The type map entry may be handled in one of two ways. One way is to add the entry to the type map associated with a database connection and call the versions of Array.getArray and Array.getResultSet that do not take a type map parameter. When this is done, a UDT will be mapped according to the custom mapping indicated in the connection's type map rather than according to the standard mapping. The second way is to add an entry to a type map that is supplied as an argument to an Array.getArray or Array.getResultSet method. This type map supersedes a connection's type map if there is one. In fact, when a type map is supplied as a parameter, the connection's type map will never be used; either the given type map is used, or, if the UDT does not appear in the given type map, the standard mapping will be used. For a structured type, the standard mapping is to a Struct object, and for a distinct type, the standard mapping is to the built-in type on which the distinct type is based.

6.1.4   Four Versions of the Method getArray

All versions of the method Array.getArray materialize an SQL99 ARRAY value as an array in the Java programming language. This array contains the elements of the ARRAY mapped to Object objects in the Java programming language unless the base type maps to a primitive type, in which case the primitive type is used. Two methods return all of the array elements, and two return a slice of the array.

As mentioned previously, if the base type of an array is a structured type or a distinct type, the elements may be mapped using either the standard mapping or a custom mapping. Two versions of the method Array.getArray take a type map as a parameter. When a type map is supplied to one of these methods, the driver will use that one instead of the one associated with the connection to do the custom mapping.

6.1.5 Four Versions of the Method `getResultSet`

The `Array.getResultSet` methods materialize an array as a `ResultSet` object. This result set holds the elements of an SQL99 `ARRAY` value. Like the `Array.getArray` methods, two of the `Array.getResultSet` methods materialize all of the array elements, and two materialize a specified subarray.

All versions of the method `getResultSet` return a `ResultSet` object that contains one row for each element in the array or subarray. Each row has two columns, with the second column containing the array element value and the first column containing its array index. The rows in the result set are arranged in ascending order, with the ordering based on the index. Note that the index is the index into the SQL `ARRAY` in the database; it will not necessarily be the same as the row number in the result set.

As with the method `Array.getArray`, two versions of `Array.getResultSet` take a type map, which will be used for the custom mapping of each element if the base type is a UDT and if the UDT is named in the type map. The other two `getResultSet` methods do not take a type map, so they will always use the connection's type map for any custom mapping.

6.1.6 Using `Array` Methods

The following code fragment demonstrates the use of the methods `getBaseType` and `getBaseTypeName`. The code selects the column `SCORES` for the student with ID number 1234 and stores it in a result set with one row. For this example, the value in `SCORES` is an `ARRAY` value containing the semester test scores for student 1234. After placing the cursor on the first row of the result set with a call to the method `next`, the code creates an instance of `Array` (*scores*) that contains a logical pointer to the `ARRAY` value on the server that the value in the `SCORES` column of *rs* designates. The next line calls the method `getBaseTypeName` on *scores*, and the following line prints out the name for the base type of the array.

```
ResultSet rs = stmt.executeQuery(
                "SELECT SCORES FROM STUDENTS WHERE ID = 1234");
rs.next();
Array scores = rs.getArray("SCORES");
```

```
String elementType = scores.getBaseTypeName();
System.out.print("The array elements have SQL type ");
System.out.println(elementType);
```

If an application wants to work with the array elements locally, it can materialize the scores on the client. The following line of code materializes the elements of the array designated by *scores*:

```
int [] testScores = (int [])scores.getArray();
```

The variable *testScores* contains an array of the test scores for student 1234. Note that *testScores* is an array object in the Java programming language, not a java.sql.Array object. Note also that since the method Array.getArray returns an Object, the Object is cast to an array of int before being assigned to the variable *testScores*.

It is important not to confuse the method ResultSet.getArray with the method Array.getArray. The method ResultSet.getArray is called on a Result-Set object and returns an Array object. This Array object, a logical pointer designating an SQL99 ARRAY value, does not contain the elements of the ARRAY value. In contrast, the method Array.getArray is called on an Array object and returns an Object that is an array containing the elements of the SQL99 ARRAY value. In other words, the ResultSet method returns an Array object, and the Array method materializes the SQL99 ARRAY elements on the client.

With the scores materialized in an array in the Java programming language (in the variable *testScores*), we can calculate the average score. Assuming that *testScores* has at least one element, the following code fragment continues from the previous example to print out the elements in the array, calculate the mean, and print the result.

```
int length = testScores.length;
System.out.print("testScores contains:  ");
int sum = 0;
for (int i = 0; i < length; i++) {
    System.out.print(score[i] + "   ");
    sum = sum + score[i];
}
int av = sum / length;
System.out.println();
System.out.println("average score = " + av);
```

If this code were incorporated into a class with a `main` method and run, the output would look like this (assuming that these are the scores for student 1234):

```
➥ testScores contains:  89   97   95   83
➥ average score = 91
```

Note that in an array in the Java programming language, the index of the first element is 0. This is not true for the interface `Array` in the package `java.sql`. Instead, it follows the SQL99 convention of having the first element of an array be at index 1. This is also consistent with the numbering of columns in a result set, where the first column is column 1.

Two versions of the `getArray` method and two versions of the `getResultSet` method materialize only part of an array rather than all of it. These methods take two arguments, the first to indicate the index where the subarray starts and the second to indicate how many consecutive elements the subarray will contain. The following code fragment demonstrates using `getArray` to materialize a slice of an array.

```
ResultSet rs = stmt.executeQuery(
                    "SELECT SCORES FROM STUDENT WHERE ID = 1234");
rs.next();
Array scores = rs.getArray("SCORES");
int [] lastScores = (int [])scores.getArray(3, 2);
```

The variable *lastScores* contains the third and fourth scores (an array two elements long starting at index 3) earned by student 1234.

The following line of code, which uses the variable *scores* from the previous example, materializes the array elements as a result set instead of an array.

```
ResultSet data = scores.getResultSet();
```

The variable *data* is a `ResultSet` object that contains the elements of the ARRAY value designated by *scores*, and through it, a Java application can operate on the individual scores that *data* contains.

In the previous code, we used the `ResultSet` *rs*, returned by a SELECT statement, to create the `Array` instance *scores*. Then we used *scores* to materialize the array elements as the result set *data*. The following code fragment illustrates retrieving values from *data*. Even though *data* is a result set returned by one of the `Array.getResultSet` methods rather than a result set returned by a query, it is still a ResultSet object, and we use the normal getter methods in the ResultSet interface to retrieve values from it. The following code fragment uses the method ResultSet.getInt to retrieve the test score and array index from each row of *data.* Then it prints out each score with its corresponding array index.

```
while (data.next()) {
    int index = data.getInt(1);
    int score = data.getInt(2);
    System.out.println("Score at index " + index + " = " + score);
}
```

The output might look like this:

➥ Score at index 1 = 89
➥ Score at index 2 = 97
➥ Score at index 3 = 95
➥ Score at index 4 = 83

The previous example assumes that the user knows the base type for the array, which is the usual situation. In this case, the base type of the ARRAY value mapped to an int in the Java programming language, so the ResultSet method getInt was used to retrieve the elements of the array from the result set.

If the base type is not already known, there are several alternatives. One is to use a ResultSet method that will retrieve any data type. For example, if an application uses only JDBC 1.0 data types, the ResultSet method getString will retrieve any of those types as a String object. The problem with this is that if, for example, the value is a double, and it is to be operated on as a double, it will have to be converted from a String object to a double before it can be used. The ResultSet method getObject will retrieve any data type, including the new SQL99 types in the JDBC 2.0 API, as an object. This will not take advantage of the ability to use primitive types if the base type maps to a primitive type, but it will always work. It does, however, have a limitation similar to that of getString, in that the value retrieved generally needs to be converted before it is used. Yet another alternative is first to ascertain the base type and then to ascertain whether the base type is one of the primitive types by using a case statement or a series of if statements.

The following code fragment illustrates (1) using the method Array.getResultSet to materialize the elements on the client, (2) getting the data type of the elements, and then (3) using a case statement to determine if the data type is one of the primitive types in the Java programming language. Each case or if condition specifies which getter method to use, so if the condition is met, the corresponding getter method is called. This code fragment builds on the previous example, using *scores*, (an Array object) to create *data* (a ResultSet object), in which the elements of the SQL ARRAY value designated by *scores* are materialized.

```
ResultSet data = scores.getResultSet();
ResultSetMetaData rsmd = data.getMetaData();
int typeCode = rsmd.getColumnType(2);
// typeCode now contains the constant from java.sql.Types for the
// type of column 2
while (data.next()) {
    switch (typeCode) {
        case BIT:
            boolean element = data.getBoolean(2);
            . . . // do something
            break;
        case TINYINT:
            byte element = data.getByte(2);
            . . . // do something
            break;
        case SMALLINT:
            short element = data.getShort(2);
            . . . // do something
            break;
        case INTEGER:
            int element = data.getInt(2);
            . . . // do something
            break;
        case BIGINT:
            long element = data.getLong(2);
            . . . // do something
            break;
        case REAL:
            float element = data.getFloat(2);
            . . . // do something
            break;
```

```
        case DOUBLE:
            double element = data.getDouble(2);
            . . . // do something
            break;
        default:
            Object element = data.getObject(2);
            . . . // do something
    }
}
```

Because the data type is usually known, the general database programmer would probably not need to use a case statement such as the one in the previous example; it is much more likely that a tool would make use of it.

6.1.7   Storing Array Objects

An instance of the interface Array may be stored in a database by passing it as an input parameter to a prepared statement. The following code fragment creates the Array object *titles*, which maps the SQL99 ARRAY locator stored in the third column in the current row of the ResultSet object *rs*. Then it passes *titles* as a parameter to the PreparedStatement object *pstmt*.

```
Array titles = rs.getArray(3);
. . .
PreparedStatement pstmt = con.prepareStatement(
            "UPDATE AJAX_LTD SET TITLE = ? WHERE STATUS = 2");
pstmt.setArray(1, titles);
```

In the table AJAX_LTD in the row where the value for the column STATUS is 2, the column TITLE now stores the ARRAY value to which *titles* (indirectly) points.

The preceding code example shows how to store an instance of the interface java.sql.Array in a database. It is also possible to store an array object defined in the Java programming language. As with other data types, it is stored by passing it as a parameter to a prepared statement. The following code fragment creates the array *departments* and passes it to the database as a parameter to *pstmt*. Note that the PreparedStatement method setObject is used to pass array objects that are defined in the Java programming language. The method setArray is used only for passing instances of the interface java.sql.Array.

```
String [] departments = {"accounting", "personnel", "marketing"};
PreparedStatement pstmt = con.prepareStatement(
                "UPDATE AJAX_LTD SET DEPTS = ? WHERE ID = 0045");
pstmt.setObject(1, departments);
```

In the table AJAX_LTD, column DEPTS in the row where ID is 0045 now stores the array *departments*.

6.2   Array Interface Definition

2.0

```
package java.sql;
public interface Array {
    String getBaseTypeName() throws SQLException;
    int getBaseType() throws SQLException;
    java.lang.Object getArray() throws SQLException;
    java.lang.Object getArray(java.util.Map map) throws SQLException;
    java.lang.Object getArray(long index, int count)
                                              throws SQLException;
    java.lang.Object getArray(long index, int count, java.util.Map map)
                                              throws SQLException;
    ResultSet getResultSet() throws SQLException;
    ResultSet getResultSet(java.util.Map map) throws SQLException;
    ResultSet getResultSet(long index, int count) throws SQLException;
    ResultSet getResultSet(long index, int count, java.util.Map map)
                                              throws SQLException;
}
```

6.3   Array Methods

The following methods are defined in the java.sql.Array interface:

getArray

2.0

```
java.lang.Object getArray() throws SQLException
```

Materializes on the client the contents of the SQL ARRAY in the data source that this `Array` object designates. If the elements of the array are a user-defined type, they will be mapped using the type map associated with the connection. See "Materializing `Array` Data," on page 285, for information about how the contents are retrieved.

RETURNS:
an array in the Java programming language that contains the ordered elements of the SQL `ARRAY` value designated by this object

EXAMPLE:
```
Array names = rs.getArray("NAMES");
// names contains a locator designating the SQL ARRAY value on the
// server to which the value in the column "NAMES" in the current
// row of the ResultSet rs points
String [] namesArray = (String [])names.getArray();
// namesArray, an array of String, contains the elements in
// the SQL ARRAY value designated by names. The Object returned by
// getArray is cast to an array of String before being assigned
// to the variable namesArray.
```

2.0   getArray

```
java.lang.Object getArray(java.util.Map map) throws SQLException
```

Materializes the contents of the SQL `ARRAY` value designated by this `Array` object, using the `Map` object *map* for custom mapping the elements if they are a user-defined type named in *map*. If the base type of the array does not match a user-defined type in *map*, the standard mapping will be used instead. See "Materializing `Array` Data," on page 285, for information about how the contents are retrieved.

PARAMETERS:

map   the `Map` object that contains the mapping of SQL type
                           names to classes in the Java programming language

RETURNS:
an array in the Java programming language that contains the ordered elements of the SQL `ARRAY` value designated by this object

EXAMPLE:
```
Array names = rs.getArray("NAMES");
Object [] namesArray = (Object [])names.getArray(namesMap);
// namesArray is an array containing the elements in the SQL ARRAY
```

```
// designated by names. If the elements of the SQL ARRAY value were
// custom mapped, they were mapped according to namesMap.
```

getArray

```
java.lang.Object getArray(long index, int count) throws SQLException
```

Retrieves a slice of the SQL ARRAY value designated by this object, start-ing with the element at index *index* and containing up to *count* successive ele-ments. This method uses the type map associated with this connection for a custom mapping of the array elements. If the type map does not have an entry for the array's base type, the standard mapping is used.

PARAMETERS:

index	the index into the SQL array at which to start retrieving elements. The first index is 1, the second is 2, and so on.
count	the number of consecutive elements to retrieve

RETURNS:
an array in the Java programming language containing up to *count* consecutive elements of the SQL ARRAY value designated by this Array object, starting at index *index*

EXAMPLE:
```
String [] namesArray = (String [])names.getArray(1, 5);
// namesArray is an array containing the first five elements in the
// SQL ARRAY designated by names.
```

getArray

```
java.lang.Object getArray(long index, int count, java.util.Map map)
                                                      throws SQLException
```

Retrieves a slice of the SQL ARRAY value designated by this Array object, starting with the element at index *index* and containing up to *count* successive elements. This method uses the Map object *map* to map the elements of the ARRAY value unless its base type does not match a user-defined type in *map*, in which case it uses the standard mapping.

PARAMETERS:

index	the index into the SQL array at which to start retrieving elements. The first index is 1, the second is 2, and so on.
count	the number of consecutive elements to retrieve
map	the Map object that contains the mapping of SQL type names to classes in the Java programming language

RETURNS:
an array in the Java programming language containing up to *count* consecutive elements of the SQL ARRAY value designated by this Array object, starting at index *index*

EXAMPLE:
```
String [] namesArray = (String [])names.getArray(3, 2, namesMap);
// namesArray is an array containing the third and fourth elements
// of the SQL ARRAY value designated by names. If appropriate, the
// elements were mapped using namesMap.
```

getBaseType

`2.0`

```
int getBaseType() throws SQLException
```

Returns the JDBC type of the elements in the array designated by this Array object.

RETURNS:
a constant from the class java.sql.Types that is the type code for the elements in the SQL ARRAY value designated by this Array object

EXAMPLE:
```
int typeCode = scores.getBaseType();
// typeCode contains the type code for the elements in the ARRAY
// value designated by scores
```

getBaseTypeName

`2.0`

```
String getBaseTypeName() throws SQLException
```

Returns the type name used by this particular DBMS for the elements in the SQL ARRAY value designated by this Array object if the elements are a built-in type. If the elements are a user-defined type (UDT), this method returns the fully qualified SQL type name.

RETURNS:
a String that is the database-specific name for a built-in base type or the fully qualified SQL type name for a base type that is a UDT

EXAMPLE:
```
String typeName = scores.getBaseTypeName();
// If scores is an ARRAY of structured type instances, typeName
// contains the fully qualified SQL type name of the structured
// type; if scores represents an array of int, typeName contains
// the name used by this DBMS for an int.
```

getResultSet   2.0

```
ResultSet getResultSet() throws SQLException
```

Returns a result set that contains the elements of the ARRAY value designated by this Array object. If the base type is a UDT for which the connection's type map has an entry, the elements of the ARRAY value are mapped using the connection's type map; otherwise, the standard mapping is used.

The result set contains one row for each array element, with two columns in each row. The second column stores the element value; the first column stores the index into the array for that element. The rows are in ascending order corresponding to the order of the indices.

RETURNS:
a ResultSet object containing one row for each of the elements in the array designated by this Array object, with the rows in ascending order based on the indices

EXAMPLE:
```
ResultSet data = scores.getResultSet();
// data contains one row for each element in the array designated by
// scores
```

getResultSet   2.0

```
ResultSet getResultSet(java.util.Map map) throws SQLException
```

Returns a result set that contains the elements of the array designated by this `Array` object and uses the type map *map* for mapping the array elements. If the base type of the array does not match a user-defined type in *map*, the standard mapping will be used instead.

The result set contains one row for each array element, with two columns in each row. The second column stores the element value; the first column stores the index into the array for that element. The rows are in ascending order corresponding to the order of the indices.

PARAMETERS:

map   the `Map` object that contains the mapping of SQL type names to classes in the Java programming language

RETURNS:

a `ResultSet` object containing one row for each of the elements in the SQL ARRAY value designated by this `Array` object, with the rows in ascending order based on the indices

EXAMPLE:
```
ResultSet data = scores.getResultSet(typeMap);
// data contains one row for each element in the array designated by
// scores. typeMap was used to map the array elements.
```

2.0 getResultSet

```
ResultSet getResultSet(long index, int count) throws SQLException
```

Returns a result set holding the elements of the subarray that starts at index *index* and contains up to *count* successive elements. This method uses the connection's type map to map the elements of the array if the base type has an entry in the type map. Otherwise, this method uses the standard mapping for the base type.

The result set has one row for each element of the SQL ARRAY value designated by this `Array` object, with the first row containing the element at index *index*. The result set will have up to *count* rows in ascending order based on the indices. Each row has two columns: The second column stores the element value; the first column stores the index into the array for that element.

PARAMETERS:

index   the index into the SQL ARRAY value at which to start retrieving elements. The first index is 1, the second is 2, and so on.

count   the number of consecutive elements to include

RETURNS:
a ResultSet object containing up to *count* consecutive elements of the SQL array designated by this Array object, starting at index *index*

EXAMPLE:
```
ResultSet data = scores.getResultSet(1, 3);
// data is a result set with three rows, containing the elements at
// indices 1, 2, and 3
```

getResultSet

2.0

```
ResultSet getResultSet(long index, int count, java.util.Map map)
                                          throws SQLException
```

Returns a result set holding the elements of the subarray that starts at
index *index* and contains up to *count* successive elements. This method uses
the Map object *map* to map the elements of the array unless the base type of the
array does not match a user-defined type in *map*, in which case it uses the standard mapping.

The result set has one row for each element of the SQL ARRAY value designated by this Array object, with the first row containing the element at index
index. The result set will have up to *count* rows in ascending order based on
the indices. Each row has two columns: The second column stores the element
value; the first column stores the index into the array for that element.

PARAMETERS:

index   the index into the SQL ARRAY value at which to start re-
                             trieving elements. The first index is 1, the second is 2,
                             and so on.

count   the number of consecutive elements to include

map   the Map object that contains the mapping of SQL type
                             names to classes in the Java programming language

RETURNS:
a ResultSet object containing up to *count* consecutive elements of the SQL
ARRAY value designated by this Array object, starting at index *index*

EXAMPLE:
```
ResultSet data = scores.getResultSet(4, 2, typeMap);
// data is a result set with two rows, containing the elements at
// indices 4 and 5 (the fourth and fifth elements). typeMap was used
// to map the elements if the base type matches a type in typeMap.
```

CHAPTER 7

BatchUpdateException

7.1 BatchUpdateException Overview

THE class BatchUpdateException provides information about errors that occur during a batch update operation. It inherits all the methods from the class SQLException and adds the method getUpdateCounts. This exception is thrown by the Statement method executeBatch if one of the commands in the batch fails. If there are no errors, the executeBatch method returns an array of update counts, one for each command in the batch. If an error occurs, the BatchUpdateException object creates an array of update counts for all commands in the batch that were successfully executed before the error occurred. See "Sending Batch Updates," on page 961, for more detailed information.

7.1.1 What a BatchUpdateException Object Contains

Each BatchUpdateException object contains the following kinds of information:

- an array of update counts. This is an array of int, where each element is the update count for a command in a batch update that executed successfully before the error occurred.

- a description of the error. This is a String object that explains the error.

- an "SQLState" string. This is a String object identifying the warning, which follows the Open Group SQLState conventions. Values for the SQLState string are described in the Open Group SQL specification.

- an error code. This is an integer that is specific to each vendor. Normally this will be the actual error code returned by the underlying database.

- a chain to an SQLException object. This can be used if there is more than one error. Note that an exception chained to a BatchUpdateException is an SQLException rather than a BatchUpdateException.

The BatchUpdateException class defines five constructors for creating instances of BatchUpdateException, and it adds one method for determining which updates were successful before an error occurred during a batch update.

7.1.2   Retrieving BatchUpdateException Information

Information is retrieved from a BatchUpdateException object by getting each of its components. The method getMessage (inherited from SQLException, which inherited it from java.lang.Exception, which in turn inherited it from java.lang.Throwable) returns the description of the error. Methods defined in SQLException get two other components: getSQLState gets the SQLState value, and getErrorCode gets the warning code used by the database vendor. The method getUpdateCounts, defined in BatchUpdateException, retrieves the update counts for successful updates.

The following code fragment, which defines a method that displays errors in processing a batch update, could be invoked in a catch block. The while loop illustrates getting the components of the first BatchUpdateException object and then getting any subsequent ones that are chained to it:

```
private static void printUpdateErrors(BatchUpdateException b)
                                        throws SQLException {
    // When a BatchUpdateException object is caught, display the
    // error. It is possible for there to be multiple errors chained
    // together.
    if (b != null) {
        System.err.println("\n--- Batch Update Error---\n");
        int [] counts = b.getUpdateCounts();
        for (int i = 0; i < counts.length; i ++) {
            System.err.println(counts[i] + " ");
        }
        System.err.println("Message:  " + b.getMessage());
        System.err.println("SQLState: " + b.getSQLState());
        System.err.println("Vendor:   " + b.getErrorCode());
        System.err.println("");
    }
```

```
    SQLException s = b.getNextException();
    while (s != null) {
        System.err.println("Message:  " + s.getMessage());
        System.err.println("SQLState: " + s.getSQLState());
        System.err.println("Vendor:   " + s.getErrorCode());
        System.err.println("");
        s = s.getNextException();
    }
}
```

7.2   BatchUpdateException Class Definition

2.0

```
package java.sql;
public class BatchUpdateException extends java.sql.SQLException {
    public BatchUpdateException(String reason, String SQLState,
                                int vendorCode, int [] updateCounts);
    public BatchUpdateException(String reason, String SQLState,
                                              int [] updateCounts);
    public BatchUpdateException(String reason, int [] updateCounts);
    public BatchUpdateException(int [] updateCounts);
    public BatchUpdateException();
    public int[] getUpdateCounts();
}
```

7.3   BatchUpdateException Constructors

BatchUpdateException

2.0

```
public BatchUpdateException(String reason, String SQLState,
                            int vendorCode, int [] updateCounts)
```
Constructs a fully specified BatchUpdateException object.

PARAMETERS:

reason	a String object describing the exception
SQLState	a String object containing an Open Group code identifying the exception
vendorCode	an int indicating an exception code for a particular database vendor
updateCounts	an array of int, with each element indicating the update count for an SQL command that executed successfully before the exception was thrown

RETURNS:

a BatchUpdateException object initialized with *reason, SQLState, vendorCode*, and *updateCounts*

EXAMPLE:
```
int [] updates = {3, 1, 4};
BatchUpdateException b = new BatchUpdateException(
"Insert value list does not match column list", "21S01", 5,
                                            updates);
// b contains a BatchUpdateException object initialized with (1) the
// message "Insert value list does not match column list", (2) the
// SQL state "21S01", (3) the vendor code 5, and (4) the array
// updates, which contains the ints 3, 1, and 4
```

BatchUpdateException

2.0

```
public BatchUpdateException(String reason, String SQLState,
                                          int [] updateCounts)
```

Constructs a BatchUpdateException object initialized with *reason, SQL-State, updateCounts*, and 0 for the vendor code.

PARAMETERS:

reason	a String object describing the exception
SQLState	a String object containing an Open Group code identifying the exception
updateCounts	an array of int, with each element indicating the update count for an SQL command that executed successfully before this exception was thrown

RETURNS:
a BatchUpdateException object initialized with *reason*, *SQLState*, 0, and *updateCounts*

EXAMPLE:
```
int [] updates = {3, 1, 4};
BatchUpdateException b = new BatchUpdateException(
"Degree of derived table does not match column list", "21S02",
                                                    updates);
// b contains (1) a BatchUpdateException object initialized with the
// message "Degree of derived table does not match column list", (2)
// the SQL state "21S02", (3) the vendor code 0, and (4) an array
// containing the ints 3, 1, and 4
```

BatchUpdateException

2.0

```
public BatchUpdateException(String reason, int [] updateCounts)
```

Constructs a BatchUpdateException object initialized with *reason*, null for the SQLState, *updateCounts*, and 0 for the vendor code.

PARAMETERS:

reason	a String object describing the exception
updateCounts	an array of int, with each element indicating the update count for an SQL command that executed successfully before the exception was thrown

RETURNS:
a BatchUpdateException object initialized with *reason*, null, 0, and *updateCounts*

EXAMPLE:
```
int [] updates = {3, 1, 4};
BatchUpdateException b = new BatchUpdateException(
        "Insert value list does not match column list", updates);
// b contains a BatchUpdateException object initialized with (1) the
// message "Insert value list does not match column list", (2) the
// SQL state null, (3) the vendor code 0, and (4) an array containing
// the ints 3, 1, and 4
```

BatchUpdateException

`2.0`

```
public BatchUpdateException(int [] updateCounts)
```

Constructs a BatchUpdateException object initialized with null for the reason, null for the SQLState, *updateCounts*, and 0 for the vendor code.

PARAMETERS:

updateCounts   an array of int, with each element indicating the update count for an SQL command that executed successfully before the exception was thrown

RETURNS:

a BatchUpdateException object initialized with null, null, 0, and *updateCounts*

EXAMPLE:
```
int [] updates = {3, 1, 4};
BatchUpdateException b = new BatchUpdateException(updates);
// b contains a BatchUpdateException object initialized with (1)
// null, (2) null, (3) 0, and (4) an array containing the ints 3, 1,
and 4
```

BatchUpdateException

`2.0`

```
public BatchUpdateException()
```

Constructs a BatchUpdateException object initialized with null for the reason, null for the SQLState, null for the update count, and 0 for the vendor code.

RETURNS:

a BatchUpdateException object initialized with null, null, null, and 0

EXAMPLE:
```
BatchUpdateException b = new BatchUpdateException();
// b contains a BatchUpdateException object initialized with (1) the
// message null, the (2) SQL state null, (3) the vendor code 0, and
// (4) null for the array of update counts
```

7.4   `BatchUpdateException` Methods

7.4.1   Inherited Methods

The following methods are inherited from the class `java.lang.Exception`, which inherited them from the class `java.lang.Throwable`:

```
fillInStackTrace              getLocalizedMessage
getMessage                    printStackTrace
toString
```

The following methods are inherited from the class `java.sql.SQLException`:

```
getSQLState                   getErrorCode
getNextException              setNextException
```

7.4.2   Methods Defined in `BatchUpdateException`

The following method is defined in the class `java.sql.BatchUpdateException`:

getUpdateCounts   2.0

```
public int [] getUpdateCounts()
```

   Retrieves the update count for each statement in the batch update that executed successfully before this exception was thrown.
   After this exception is thrown, a driver that implements batch updates may or may not continue to process the commands remaining in a batch. If the driver continues processing commands, the array returned by this method will have as many elements as there are commands in the batch; otherwise, the array will have update counts only for commands that executed successfully before this `BatchUpdateException` object was thrown.

RETURNS:
an array of `int` containing the update counts for the commands that were executed successfully before an error occurred. Or, if the driver continues to execute commands after an error, one of the following for every command in the batch:

- an update count
- `Statement.SUCCESS_NO_INFO (-2)` if the command executed successfully but the number of rows affected is unknown
- `Statement.EXECUTE_FAILED (-3)` if the command failed to execute successfully

EXAMPLE:

```
// assuming the driver does not continue to process commands after
// an error, the print message is "Update Counts of Successful
// Commands: "; if the driver continues processing commands, the
// print message might be "Update Counts of All Commands: "
try {

    . . .

} catch(BatchUpdateException b) {
    System.err.println("Update Counts of Successful Commands: ");
    int [] updates = b.getUpdateCounts();
    for(int i = 0; i < updates.length; i++) {
        int c = updates[i];
        System.err.println("   Update Count " + (i+1) + " = " + c);
    }
}
```

CHAPTER 8

Blob 2.0

8.1 Blob Overview

A Blob object represents the Java programming language mapping of an SQL
BLOB (Binary Large Object). An SQL BLOB is a built-in type that stores a Binary
Large Object as a column value in a row of a database table. Methods in the interfaces ResultSet, CallableStatement, and PreparedStatement allow a programmer to access the SQL99 type BLOB in the same way that SQL92 built-in types are
accessed. In other words, an application uses methods such as getBlob and setBlob
for a BLOB value the same way it uses getInt and setInt for an INTEGER value or
getString and setString for a CHAR or VARCHAR value.

In a standard implementation, a JDBC driver implements the Blob interface
using the SQL type LOCATOR(BLOB) behind the scenes. A LOCATOR(BLOB) designates an SQL BLOB value residing on a database server, and operations on the locator achieve the same results as operations on the BLOB value itself. This means that
a client can operate on a Blob instance without ever having to materialize the BLOB
data on the client machine, which can improve performance significantly. Because
the driver uses LOCATOR(BLOB) behind the scenes, its use is completely transparent
to the programmer using a JDBC driver.

The standard behavior for a Blob instance is to remain valid until the transaction in which it was created is either committed or rolled back.

The Blob interface provides methods for getting the length of an SQL BLOB
value, for materializing a BLOB value on the client, for determining the position of
a pattern of bytes within a BLOB value, for updating all or part of a BLOB value, and
for truncating a BLOB value to a specified length.

8.1.1   Creating a Blob Object

The following code fragment illustrates creating a Blob object, where *stmt* is a Statement object:

```
Statement stmt = con.createStatement(
                        ResultSet.TYPE_SCROLL_INSENSITIVE,
                        ResultSet.CONCUR_READ_ONLY);
ResultSet rs = stmt.executeQuery("SELECT DATA FROM TABLE1");
if (rs.next() {
    rs.first();
        Blob blob = rs.getBlob("DATA");
}
```

The variable *blob* contains a logical pointer to the BLOB value that is stored in the column DATA in the first row of the result set *rs*. Even though *blob* does not actually contain the data in the BLOB value, an application can operate on *blob* as if it did. In other words, any changes an application makes to *blob* will also be made to the BLOB value in the database table. See "Locators and Updates," on page 313, for a more complete explanation.

8.1.2   Materializing Blob Data

Programmers can invoke methods in the JDBC API on a Blob object as if they were operating on the SQL BLOB it designates. However, if they want to operate on BLOB data, they must first materialize it on the client. The Blob interface provides two methods for materializing BLOB data: getBinaryStream, which materializes the BLOB value as an input stream, and getBytes, which materializes all or part of the BLOB value as an array of bytes. The following code fragment materializes all of the data in the BLOB value designated by *blob* as an input stream:

```
java.io.InputStream in = blob.getBinaryStream();
byte b;
while ((b = in.read()) > -1) {
    System.out.println(b);
}
// prints out all the bytes in the BLOB value that blob designates
```

The next code fragment also materializes all of the data in the BLOB value designated by *blob*, but it produces the data as an array of bytes instead of an input stream. The following example uses the method length, which returns the number of bytes in a Blob object.

```
long len = blob.length();
byte [] data = blob.getBytes(1, len);
for (int i = 0; i < len; i++) {
    byte b = data[i];
    System.out.println(b);
}
// prints out all the bytes in the BLOB value that blob designates
```

The variable *data* contains a copy of all of the bytes in the BLOB value that *blob* designates. This is true because the arguments passed to the method get-Bytes specify the entire BLOB value: The first argument tells it to return bytes starting with the first byte, and the second argument tells it to return the number of bytes in the length of the BLOB value.

The following lines of code illustrate materializing only part of the Blob object *blob*. The byte array *data* contains1024 bytes from *blob*, starting with the 256th byte in *blob*:

```
byte [] data = blob.getBytes(256, 1024);
byte b = data[0];
// data contains bytes 256 through 1280 of the BLOB value that blob
// designates; b contains the 256th byte
```

A point to keep in mind is that because of differences in SQL and the Java programming language, the first byte in a BLOB value is at position 1, whereas the first element of an array in the Java programming language is at index 0.

8.1.3   Storing a Blob Object

To store a Blob object in the database, an application passes it as a parameter to the PreparedStatement method setBlob. For example, the following code fragment stores the Blob object *stats* by passing it as the first input parameter to the Pre-paredStatement object *pstmt*:

```
Blob stats = rs.getBlob("STATS");
PreparedStatement pstmt = con.prepareStatement(
                    "UPDATE SIGHTINGS SET MEAS = ? WHERE AREA = 'NE'");
pstmt.setBlob(1, stats);
pstmt.executeUpdate();
```

The BLOB value designated by *stats* is now stored in the table SIGHTINGS in column MEAS in the row where column AREA contains NE.

8.1.4   Finding Patterns within a Blob Object

An application can see if a Blob object contains a given set of bytes using the two versions of the method position. One version searches for a given byte array, and the other version searches for a given Blob object within a Blob object. If either method finds a match, it returns the position at which the pattern of bytes begins.

3.0   8.1.5   Methods for Modifying a Blob Object

The methods setBytes and setBinaryStream, added in the JDBC 3.0 API, allow an application to make internal modifications to a Blob object.

The method setBytes has two versions for adding data to a Blob object. One adds all of a given byte array, and one adds a specified portion of a given byte array. Both methods take a parameter indicating the position in the Blob object at which to start inserting data. For example, the following code fragment writes the entire byte array *bytes* to the beginning of the Blob object blob1. In this case, *bytes* contains all of the bytes in the Blob object *blob2*, so the result is that *blob2* is written to the beginning of *blob1*. Note that if *blob2* is 1024 bytes long, the first 1024 bytes of *blob1* are overwritten by the 1024 bytes in *blob2*.

```
byte [] bytes = blob2.getBytes(1, blob2.length());
blob1.setBytes(1, bytes);
```

The following code fragment illustrates how to add only the specified portion of a byte array to a Blob object. In this case, the method setBytes takes two additional parameters to indicate the part of the byte array that is to be added. One indicates the offset into the byte array at which to start, and one indicates how many consecutive bytes from the byte array to include.

```
byte [] bytes = { . . . };
blob.setBytes(1, bytes, 0, 512);
```

So in the case just shown, the first 512 bytes of *blob* are overwriten with the first 512 bytes of *bytes*.

In addition to methods for adding bytes to a Blob object, the Blob interface supplies a method for deleting bytes. The method truncate shortens a Blob object by the number of bytes passed to it.

8.1.6 Locators and Updates

3.0

The standard implementation for a Blob object, which represents an SQL BLOB value, is to use an SQL LOCATOR type. A locator works as a pointer to the value stored in the database, and how a DBMS handles updates to an object implemented as a locator depends on the particular DBMS. Some DBMSs update the BLOB value in the database table, but some update only a copy of the BLOB value and do not change the value in the database. When the latter case is true, an application must update the BLOB value directly.

To find out how the DBMS being used handles updates to BLOB values, an application can call the DatabaseMetaData method locatorsUpdateCopy. If this method returns true, the application needs to update BLOB values in the database. The following code fragment shows how this can be done. It first retrieves a Blob object from the ResultSet object *rs* and changes its value to that of the byte array *val*. If the method locatorsUpdateCopy returns true, it then executes a Prepared-Statement object to update the value in the database. If the method locatorsUpdateCopy returns false, the code does nothing because the value has already been updated in the database.

```
byte[] val = {0, 1, 2, 3, 4};
. . .
Blob data = rs.getBlob("DATA");
int numWritten = data.setBytes(1, val);
if (dbmd.locatorsUpdateCopy() == true) {
    PreparedStatement pstmt = con.prepareStatement(
            "UPDATE statistics SET DATA = ? WHERE REGION = NE");
    pstmt.setBlob("DATA", data);
    pstmt.executeUpdate();
}
```

8.2   **Blob Interface Definition**

```
package java.sql;
public interface Blob {
```
2.0	`long length() throws SQLException;`
2.0	`java.io.InputStream getBinaryStream() throws SQLException;`
2.0	`byte[] getBytes(long pos, int length) throws SQLException;`
2.0	`long position(byte [] pattern, long start) throws SQLException;`
2.0	`long position(Blob pattern, long start) throws SQLException;`
3.0	`int setBytes(long pos, byte[] bytes) throws SQLException;`
3.0	`int setBytes(long pos, byte[] bytes, int offset, int len)`
	`                                    throws SQLException;`
3.0	`java.io.OutputStream setBinaryStream(long pos) throws SQLException;`
3.0	`void truncate(long len) throws SQLException;`

```
}
```

8.3   **Blob Methods**

2.0   **getBinaryStream**

```
InputStream getBinaryStream() throws SQLException
```

Materializes the `BLOB` value designated by this `Blob` object as a stream of uninterpreted bytes.

RETURNS:
an `InputStream` object with the data of the `BLOB` value designated by this `Blob` object

EXAMPLE:
```
InputStream in = blob.getBinaryStream();
// in has the data in the BLOB value that blob designates
```

2.0   **getBytes**

```
byte[] getBytes(long pos, int length) throws SQLException
```

Materializes part or all of the BLOB value that this Blob object designates as an array of bytes. The byte array contains up to *length* consecutive bytes starting at position *pos*.

PARAMETERS:

pos	the ordinal position in the BLOB value of the first byte to be extracted; the first byte is at position 1
length	the number of consecutive bytes to be copied

RETURNS:
a byte array with up to *length* consecutive bytes from the BLOB value pointed to by this Blob object, starting with the byte at position *pos*

EXAMPLE:
```
byte [] part = blob.getBytes(5, 100);
// part contains the fifth through 104th bytes, inclusive, as an
// array of bytes
```

length

2.0

```
long length() throws SQLException
```

Returns the number of bytes in the BLOB value designated by this Blob object.

RETURNS:
the length of the BLOB value designated by this Blob object, in bytes

EXAMPLE:
```
Blob blob = rs.getBlob(2);
long len = blob.length();
// len contains the number of bytes in the BLOB value designated by
// blob (the BLOB value in the second column of the current row of the
// ResultSet object rs)
```

position

2.0

```
long position(byte [] pattern, long start) throws SQLException
```

Determines the position at which the byte array *pattern* begins within the BLOB value that this Blob object represents. The search for *pattern* begins at position *start*.

PARAMETERS:

pattern	the byte array for which to search
start	the position in the BLOB value at which to begin searching; the first byte is at position 1

RETURNS:

a long indicating the position in the BLOB value at which the byte array *pattern* begins, which will be *start* or larger if the search, starting at position *start*, is successful; -1 otherwise

EXAMPLE:
```
byte [] part = blob1.getBytes(5, 100);
long beginning = blob2.position(part, 1024);
// if part, which is part of blob1, is contained in the BLOB value
// that blob2 designates, starting the search at position 1024 in
// blob2, beginning will contain the position at which part begins
```

position

2.0

```
long position(Blob pattern, long start) throws SQLException
```

Determines the byte position in the BLOB value designated by this Blob object at which *pattern* begins. The search begins at position *start*.

PARAMETERS:

pattern	the Blob object designating the BLOB value for which to search
start	the position in the BLOB value at which to begin searching; the first byte is at position 1, the second is at 2, and so on

RETURNS:

a long indicating the position at which the Blob object *pattern* begins, which will be *start* or larger if the search, starting at position *start*, is successful; -1 otherwise

EXAMPLE:
```
Blob blob2 = rs.getBlob(4);
long beginning = blob1.position(blob2, 512);
// if the BLOB value designated by blob2 is contained in the BLOB
// value designated by blob1, starting at position 512 or later,
```

```
// beginning will contain the position in blob1 at which blob2 begins
```

setBinaryStream

```
java.io.OutputStream setBinaryStream(long pos) throws SQLException
```

Retrieves a stream that can be used to write to the BLOB value designated by this Blob object. The stream is set to start writing at byte *pos*.

PARAMETERS:

pos   the position in the BLOB value at which to start writing; the first byte is 1, the second is 2, and so on

EXAMPLE:
```
byte [] b = { . . . };
java.io.OutputStream out = blob.setBinaryStream(1024);
out.write(b, 128, 256);
// out will write data from the byte array b, starting at
// offset 128 in b and writing 256 bytes. The 256 bytes from b will
// be written to the BLOB value that blob represents, starting at
// byte 1024 in blob.
```

setBytes

```
int setBytes(long pos, byte[] bytes) throws SQLException
```

Writes *bytes* to the BLOB value designated by this Blob object, starting to write at position *pos* in the BLOB value. This method returns the number of bytes that were successfully written.

PARAMETERS:

pos   the position in the BLOB value at which to start writing; the first byte is 1, the second is 2, and so on

bytes   the array of byte values to be written

RETURNS:
the number of bytes that were successfully written from *bytes* to the BLOB value represented by this Blob object

EXAMPLE:
```
byte [] bytes = { . . . };
```

```
int bytesWritten = blob.setBytes(512, bytes);
// Writes the byte array to the BLOB value that blob represents,
// starting at byte 512 in the BLOB value. If all the bytes were
// written successfully, the value of the variable bytesWritten will
// be the total number of bytes in the byte array.
```

3.0 setBytes

```
int setBytes(long pos, byte[] bytes, int offset, int len)
                                            throws SQLException
```

Writes all or part of *bytes* to the BLOB value designated by this Blob object, starting to write at position *pos* in the BLOB value. The bytes to be written start at element *offset* in the array *bytes*, and *len* bytes from *bytes* are written. This method returns the number of bytes that were successfully written.

PARAMETERS:

pos	the position in the BLOB value at which to start writing; the first byte is 1, the second is 2, and so on
bytes	the array of byte values to be written
offset	the offset into *bytes* at which to start reading the bytes to be written; the first element is 0, the second is 1, and so on
len	the number of bytes from the array *bytes* that is to be written to the BLOB value

RETURNS:
the number of bytes that were successfully written from *bytes* to the BLOB value represented by this Blob object

EXAMPLE:
```
Blob blob1 = rs1.getBlob(2);
long length = blob1.length();
byte [] bytes = blob1.getBytes(1, (int)length);
Blob blob2 = rs2.getBlob(4);
int bytesWritten = blob2.setBytes(512, bytes, 0, length);
// Retrieves all of the BLOB value represented by blob1 as an array
// of bytes and then writes it to the BLOB value that blob2
// represents. Writing begins at byte 512 of the BLOB value
// represented by blob2. If all the bytes were written successfully,
```

```
// the value of the variable bytesWritten will be the length of the
// BLOB value represented by blob1.
```

truncate

```
void truncate(long len) throws SQLException
```

Truncates the BLOB value designated by this Blob object so that it is *len* bytes in length. This method does nothing if the BLOB value is *len* bytes or less in length.

PARAMETERS:

len   the number of bytes to which the BLOB value is to be truncated

EXAMPLE:

```
blob3.truncate(1024);
// blob3 now contains the first 1024 bytes it had before this method
// was called (assuming it was at least 1024 bytes before the method
// truncate was called on it)
```

CHAPTER 9

CallableStatement

9.1 CallableStatement Overview

A CallableStatement object provides a way to call stored procedures in a standard way for all RDBMSs. A stored procedure is stored in a database; the *call* to the stored procedure is what a CallableStatement object contains. This call is written in an escape syntax that may take one of two forms: one form with a result parameter and the other without one. (See "SQL Escape Syntax in Statements," on page 958, for complete information on escape syntax.) A result parameter, a kind of OUT parameter, is the return value for the stored procedure. Both forms may have a variable number of parameters used for input (IN parameters), output (OUT parameters), or both (INOUT parameters). A question mark (?) serves as a placeholder for a parameter.

The syntax for invoking a stored procedure using the JDBC API is shown here.

- Calling a stored procedure with no parameters:

  ```
  {call procedure_name}
  ```

- Calling a stored procedure with one or more IN, OUT, or INOUT parameters:

  ```
  {call procedure_name(?, ?, ...)}
  ```

- Calling a procedure that returns a result parameter and may or may not take any IN, OUT, or INOUT parameters: (Note that the square brackets indicate that what is between them is optional; they are not themselves part of the syntax.)

```
{? = call procedure_name[(?, ?, ...)]}
```

Normally, anyone creating a `CallableStatement` object would already know that the DBMS being used supports stored procedures and what those procedures are. If one needed to check, however, various `DatabaseMetaData` methods will supply such information. For instance, the method `supportsStoredProcedures` will return `true` if the DBMS supports stored procedure calls, and the method `getProcedures` will return a description of the stored procedures available. See "DatabaseMetaData," on page 449, for more information.

The `CallableStatement` interface inherits `Statement` methods, which deal with SQL statements in general, and it also inherits `PreparedStatement` methods, which deal with setting `IN` parameters. The setter methods defined in the `PreparedStatement` interface take an `int` indicating the ordinal number of the column to be updated. In the JDBC 3.0 API, the `CallableStatement` interface adds a set of setter methods that take the parameter name to indicate which input parameter is being set.

All of the other methods defined in `CallableStatement` deal with `OUT` parameters or the output aspect of `INOUT` parameters: registering the JDBC types of the `OUT` parameters, retrieving values from them, or checking whether a returned value was JDBC `NULL`. As with `IN` parameters, the JDBC 3.0 API adds the ability to identify `OUT` parameters with a name instead of its ordinal number. Parameter names are discussed in more detail in "Named Parameters," on page 323.

9.1.1   Creating a `CallableStatement` Object

`CallableStatement` objects are created with the `Connection` method `prepareCall`. The following example, in which *con* is an active JDBC `Connection` object, creates an instance of `CallableStatement`.

```
CallableStatement cstmt = con.prepareCall(
                          "{call getTestData(?, ?)}");
```

The variable *cstmt* contains a call to the stored procedure `getTestData`, which is stored in the database. The stored procedure has two input parameters and no result parameter. Whether the ? placeholders are `IN`, `OUT`, or `INOUT` parameters depends on the signature of `getTestData`. This instance of a `CallableStatement` object was created using JDBC 1.0 API; consequently, any query in the stored procedure called by *cstmt* will produce a default `ResultSet` object (one that is non-scrollable and non-updatable).

By passing the appropriate `ResultSet` constants to the method `prepareCall`, it is possible to create `CallableStatement` objects that produce `ResultSet` objects that are scrollable and updatable, as the following code fragment demonstrates.

```
String sql = "{call getTestData(?, ?)}";
CallableStatement cstmt2 = con.prepareCall(sql,
    ResultSet.TYPE_SCROLL_INSENSITIVE, ResultSet.CONCUR_UPDATABLE);
```

The variable *cstmt2* contains the same call to the stored procedure `TestData` that *cstmt* does, but with *cstmt2*, any `resultSet` objects that `TestData` produces can be updated and are scrollable (although they will not be sensitive to updates made while they are open). Explanations for the constants used to indicate scrollability and updatability are given in "Types of Result Sets," on page 700, and "Concurrency Types," on page 701.

It is also possible to create `CallableStatement` objects that produce `ResultSet` objects that remain open after a transaction has been committed. The `CallableStatement` object `cstmt3`, created in the following code fragment, is the same as *cstmt2* from the previous example except that *cstmt3* will produce `ResultSet` objects that stay open after the `Connection` method `commit` is called.

```
String sql = "{call getTestData(?, ?)}";
CallableStatement cstmt2 = con.prepareCall(sql,
    ResultSet.TYPE_SCROLL_INSENSITIVE, ResultSet.CONCUR_UPDATABLE,
    ResultSet.HOLD_CURSORS_OVER_COMMIT);
```

The section "Result Set Holdability," on page 702, explains keeping `ResultSet` objects open and the constants that specify whether or not they are kept open.

9.1.2   Named Parameters

In the JDBC 3.0 API, the `CallableStatement` interface adds the convenience of being able to identify a parameter using its name instead of its ordinal position. This is especially useful for stored procedures that have a large number of parameters and some of those parameters have default values.

Parameter names correspond to the parameters named in a stored procedure's definition. You can get the parameter names for a specified stored procedure by calling the `DatabaseMetaData` method `getProcedureColumns`. This method returns a `ResultSet` object that includes the column `COLUMN_NAME`, which provides the parameter names for that particular stored procedure.

Note that a CallableStatement object must be consistent in the way it indicates parameters; that is, it must use only methods that take the parameter's name (a String object), or it must use only methods that take the parameter's ordinal position (an int). A CallableStatement object that mixes the two will throw an SQLException object.

An application can use named parameters only if the driver/database supports them. The DatabaseMetaData method supportsNamedParameters returns true if named parameters are supported.

9.1.3   IN Parameters

Passing in any IN parameter values to a CallableStatement object is done using setter methods. These methods include both the setter methods inherited from the PreparedStatement interface and those defined in the CallableStatement interface. The type of the value being passed in determines which setter method to use (setFloat to pass in a float value, setBoolean to pass in a boolean, and so on).

The following code fragment uses the setter methods that take the parameter number to indicate which parameter is to be set.

```
String sql = "{call updateStats(?, ?)}";
CallableStatement cstmt = con.prepareCall(sql);
cstmt.setInt(1, 398);
cstmt.setDoublel(2, 0.04395);
```

The result of the preceding lines of code is that the first ? placeholder parameter is set to 398, and the second one is set to 0.04395.

The next code fragment is identical to the preceding one except that it uses the setter methods that take a name to indicate the parameter to be set.

```
String sql = "{call updateStats(?, ?)}";
CallableStatement cstmt = con.prepareCall(sql);
cstmt.setInt("TRIALS", 398);
cstmt.setDouble("DILUTION", 0.04395);
```

In this case, the parameter named TRIALS is set to 398, and the parameter named DILUTION is set to 0.04395.

Of the stored procedures that use parameters, the vast majority use mainly IN parameters. Consequently, programmers will generally use setter methods to set parameter values far more often than they will use getter methods to retrieve parameter values.

9.1.4 Making Batch Updates

The ability to make batch updates is the same for CallableStatement objects as it is for PreparedStatement objects. In fact, a CallableStatement object is restricted to the same functionality that a PreparedStatement object has. More precisely, when using the batch update facility, a CallableStatement object can call only stored procedures that take input parameters or no parameters at all. Further, the stored procedure must return an update count. The CallableStatement.executeBatch method (inherited from PreparedStatement) will throw a BatchUpdateException if the stored procedure returns anything other than an update count or takes OUT or INOUT parameters.

The following code fragment illustrates using the batch update facility to associate two sets of parameters with a CallableStatement object.

```
CallableStatement cstmt = con.prepareCall(
                                "{call updatePrices(?, ?)}");
cstmt.setString("COF_NAME", "COLOMBIAN");
cstmt.setFloat("PRICE", 8.49f);
cstmt.addBatch();

cstmt.setString("COF_NAME", "COLOMBIAN_DECAF");
cstmt.setFloat("PRICE", 9.49f);
cstmt.addBatch();

int [] updateCounts = cstmt.executeBatch();
```

The variable *cstmt* contains a call to the stored procedure updatePrices with two sets of parameters associated with it. When *cstmt* is executed, two update statements will be executed together as a batch: one with the parameters Colombian and 8.49f, and a second one with the parameters Colombian_Decaf and 9.49f. (Note that an f after a number, as in 8.49f, tells the Java compiler that the value is a float; otherwise, the compiler assumes that a number with decimal digits is a double and will not allow it to be used as a float.)

9.1.5   OUT Parameters

If the stored procedure returns OUT parameters, the data type of each OUT parameter must be registered before the CallableStatement object can be executed. This is necessary because some DBMSs require the SQL type (which the JDBC type represents); the JDBC API itself does not require that the SQL type be registered. JDBC types, a set of generic SQL type identifiers that represent the most commonly used SQL types, are explained fully in the chapter "Mapping SQL and Java Types," on page 1065.

Registering the JDBC type is done with the method registerOutParameter. Then after the statement has been executed, the CallableStatement interface's getter methods can be used to retrieve OUT parameter values. The correct getter method to use is the type in the Java programming language that corresponds to the JDBC type registered for that parameter. (The standard mapping from JDBC types to Java types is shown in Table 50.1, on page 1087.) In other words, registerOutParameter uses a JDBC type (so that it matches the data type that the database will return), and the getter method casts this to a Java type.

To illustrate, the following code registers the OUT parameters, executes the stored procedure called by *cstmt*, and then retrieves the values returned in the OUT parameters. The method getByte retrieves a Java byte from the first OUT parameter, and getBigDecimal retrieves a java.math.BigDecimal object from the second OUT parameter. The method executeQuery is used to execute *cstmt* because the stored procedure that it calls returns a result set.

```
CallableStatement cstmt = con.prepareCall(
                                "{call getTestData(?, ?)}");
cstmt.registerOutParameter(1, java.sql.Types.TINYINT);
cstmt.registerOutParameter(2, java.sql.Types.DECIMAL);
ResultSet rs = cstmt.executeQuery();
. . . // Retrieve result set values with rs.getter methods
// Now retrieve OUT parameter values with cstmt.getter methods
byte x = cstmt.getByte(1);
java.math.BigDecimal n = cstmt.getBigDecimal(2);
```

Here is the same code fragment except that it uses the version of the methods registerOutParameter, getByte, and getBigDecimal that take a name instead of a number to indicate the parameter.

```
CallableStatement cstmt = con.prepareCall(
                                "{call getTestData(?, ?)}");
cstmt.registerOutParameter("AV_AGE", java.sql.Types.TINYINT);
```

```
cstmt.registerOutParameter("AV_SCORE", java.sql.Types.DECIMAL);
ResultSet rs = cstmt.executeQuery();
. . . // Retrieve result set values with rs.getter methods
// Now retrieve OUT parameter values
byte x = cstmt.getByte("AV_AGE");
java.math.BigDecimal n = cstmt.getBigDecimal("AV_SCORE");
```

If the stored procedure returns a result parameter, a form of OUT parameter, it is treated just like any other OUT parameter. Its data type must be registered with the method registerOutParameter, and its value is retrieved with the appropriate getter method. Note that because a result parameter comes first in a call to a stored procedure, its ordinal position is always 1.

The following code fragment retrieves the result parameter and the value of another OUT parameter. After creating the call to the stored procedure, it registers the type of the result (the first ? parameter) and of the other OUT parameter (the second ? parameter), and then it executes the stored procedure. Finally, it retrieves the value of the result parameter and of the other OUT parameter.

```
CallableStatement cstmt = con.prepareCall(
                          "{? = call getEmpData(?)}");
cstmt.registerOutParameter(1, java.sql.Types.VARCHAR);
cstmt.registerOutParameter(2, java.sql.Types.DECIMAL);
ResultSet rs = cstmt.executeQuery();
. . . // Retrieve result set values with rs.getter methods
// Now retrieve result and OUT parameter values with cstmt.getter
// methods
String empName = cstmt.getString(1);
java.math.BigDecimal salary = cstmt.getBigDecimal(2);
```

The following lines of code use the parameter name instead of ordinal position to retrieve the result and OUT parameter values.

```
String empName = cstmt.getString("EMP_NAME");
java.math.BigDecimal salary = cstmt.getBigDecimal("SALARY");
```

Both the ResultSet and CallableStatement interfaces have a set of getter methods for retrieving data of particular data types, but they have some significant differences. Whereas the getter methods defined in the ResultSet interface retrieve values from a result set column, the getter methods in the CallableStatement interface retrieve values from the OUT parameters and/or return value of a stored procedure. Another way the two interfaces differ is that unlike the ResultSet interface, the CallableStatement interface does not provide a special mechanism for retrieving large OUT values incrementally. More specifically, it does not have getter methods for streams of data, such as getAsciiStream or getBinaryStream. However, it does provide getter methods for retrieving the SQL99 data types BLOB and CLOB from result, OUT, or INOUT parameters. These methods are getBlob for retrieving BLOB (binary large object) values and getClob for retrieving CLOB (character large object) values.

9.1.6 Numbering of Parameters

When a method takes an int specifying which parameter to act upon (setter methods, getter methods, and the method registerOutParameter), that int refers to ? placeholder parameters only, with numbering starting at one. The parameter number does not refer to literal parameters that might be supplied to a stored procedure call. For example, the following code fragment illustrates a stored procedure call with one literal parameter and one ? parameter:

```
CallableStatement cstmt = con.prepareCall(
                            "{call getTestData(25, ?)}");
cstmt.registerOutParameter(1, java.sql.Types.TINYINT);
```

In this code, the first argument to registerOutParameter, the int 1, refers to the first ? parameter (and in this case, the only ? parameter). It does not refer to the literal 25, which is the first parameter to the stored procedure.

As noted previously, when a stored procedure has a result parameter, which always comes first, its ordinal position is 1. In the following code fragment, there are two ? placeholder parameters, the first being the result parameter and the second being an OUT parameter.

```
CallableStatement cstmt = con.prepareCall(
                            "{? = call getTestData(25, ?)}");
cstmt.registerOutParameter(1, java.sql.Types.VARCHAR);
cstmt.registerOutParameter(2, java.sql.Types.TINYINT);
```

9.1.7 INOUT Parameters

A parameter that supplies input as well as accepts output (an INOUT parameter) requires a call to the appropriate setter method in addition to a call to the method registerOutParameter. The setter method sets a parameter's value as an input parameter, and the method registerOutParameter registers its JDBC type as an output parameter. The setter method provides a Java value that the driver converts to a JDBC value before sending it to the database. The JDBC type of this IN value and the JDBC type supplied to the method registerOutParameter should be the same. If they are not the same, they should at least be types that are compatible, that is, types that can be mapped to each other. Then, to retrieve the output value, a corresponding getter method is used. For example, a parameter whose Java type is byte should use the method setByte to assign the input value, should supply a TINYINT as the JDBC type to registerOutParameter, and should use getByte to retrieve the output value. ("Mapping SQL and Java Types," on page 1065, contains tables of type mappings.)

The following example assumes that there is a stored procedure reviseTotal whose only parameter is an INOUT parameter. The method setByte sets the parameter to 25, which the driver will send to the database as a JDBC TINYINT. Next registerOutParameter registers the parameter as a JDBC TINYINT. After the stored procedure is executed, a new JDBC TINYINT value is returned, and the method getByte will retrieve this new value as a Java byte. Since the stored procedure called in this example returns an update count, the method executeUpdate is used.

```
CallableStatement cstmt = con.prepareCall(
                               "{call reviseTotal(?)}");
cstmt.setByte(1, (byte)25);
cstmt.registerOutParameter(1, java.sql.Types.TINYINT);
cstmt.executeUpdate();
byte x = cstmt.getByte(1);
```

9.1.8 Retrieving OUT Parameters after Results

Because of limitations imposed by some DBMSs, it is recommended that for maximum portability, all of the results in a ResultSet object generated by the execution of a CallableStatement object should be retrieved before OUT parameters are retrieved. When all values have been retrieved from a result set, the method `Result-Set.next` will return `false`.

If a `CallableStatement` object returns multiple `ResultSet` objects (which is possible only if it is executed with a call to the method `execute`), all of the results should be retrieved before `OUT` parameters are retrieved. In this case, to be sure that all results have been accessed, the `Statement` methods `getResultSet`, `getUpdateCount`, and `getMoreResults` need to be called until there are no more results. When all results have been exhausted, the method `getMoreResults` returns `false`, and the method `getUpdateCount` returns `-1`. See "Executing Special Kinds of Statements," on page 965, for more information.

After all values have been retrieved from `ResultSet` objects (using `Result-Set.getter` methods), and after it has been determined that there are no more update counts, values from `OUT` parameters can be retrieved (using `Call-ableStatement.getter` methods).

9.1.9   Retrieving NULL Values as OUT Parameters

The value returned to an `OUT` parameter may be JDBC `NULL`. When this happens, the JDBC `NULL` value will be converted so that the value returned by a `getter` method will be `null`, `0`, or `false`, depending on the `getter` method type. As with `ResultSet` objects, the only way to know whether a value of `0` or `false` was originally JDBC `NULL` is to test it with the method `wasNull`, which returns `true` if the last value read by a `getter` method was JDBC `NULL`, and `false` otherwise. For example, the following code fragment tests to see whether the last value retrieved was SQL `NULL` in the database and acts accordingly.

```
int num = cstmt.getInt(3);
boolean b = cstmt.wasNull();
if (b = true) {
    . . . // handle null value
} else {
    . . . // do something else
}
```

The `ResultSet` section "NULL Result Values," on page 722, contains more information.

9.1.10   Getting Information about Parameters

3.0

The `CallableStatement` interface inherits the `PreparedStatement` method `getPa-rameterMetaData`, which can be called on a `CallableStatement` object to get a `ParameterMetaData` object with information about its parameters. (See "Parameter-MetaData," on page 627.) For example, the following code fragment uses the `Call-ableStatement` object *cstmt* to create a `ParameterMetaData` object *paramInfo*, which it then uses to retrieve the mode (IN, OUT, or INOUT) of each of the parameters in *cstmt*.

```
CallableStatement cstmt = con.prepareCall(
                          "{call updateScores(?, ?, ?)}");
ParameterMetaData paramInfo = cstmt.getParameterMetaData();
int count = paramInfo.getParameterCount();
for (int i = 1; i <= count; i++) {
    int mode = paramInfo.getParameterMode(i);
    System.Out.println("Parameter " + i + " has mode " + mode);
}
```

9.2   CallableStatement Definition

```
package java.sql;
public interface CallableStatement extends PreparedStatement {
    void registerOutParameter(int parameterIndex, int jdbcType)
                                              throws SQLException;
    void registerOutParameter(String parameterName, int jdbcType)
                                              throws SQLException;
    void registerOutParameter(int parameterIndex, int jdbcType,
                                   int scale) throws SQLException;
    void registerOutParameter(String parameterName, int jdbcType,
                                   int scale) throws SQLException;
    void registerOutParameter(int parameterIndex, int jdbcType,
                              String typeName) throws SQLException;
    void registerOutParameter(String parameterName, int jdbcType,
                              String typeName) throws SQLException;
    boolean wasNull() throws SQLException;
    //=============================================================
    // Methods for accessing results and out parameters:
    //=============================================================
```

```
        String getString(int parameterIndex) throws SQLException;
  3.0   String getString(String parameterName) throws SQLException;
        boolean getBoolean(int parameterIndex) throws SQLException;
  3.0   boolean getBoolean(String parameterName) throws SQLException;
        byte getByte(int parameterIndex) throws SQLException;
  3.0   byte getByte(String parameterName) throws SQLException;
        short getShort(int parameterIndex) throws SQLException;
  3.0   short getShort(String parameterName) throws SQLException;
        int getInt(int parameterIndex) throws SQLException;
  3.0   int getInt(String parameterName) throws SQLException;
        long getLong(int parameterIndex) throws SQLException;
  3.0   long getLong(String parameterName) throws SQLException;
        float getFloat(int parameterIndex) throws SQLException;
  3.0   float getFloat(String parameterName) throws SQLException;
        double getDouble(int parameterIndex) throws SQLException;
  3.0   double getDouble(String parameterName) throws SQLException;
  2.0   java.math.BigDecimal getBigDecimal(int parameterIndex)
                                                  throws SQLException;
  3.0   java.math.BigDecimal getBigDecimal(String parameterName)
                                                  throws SQLException;
        java.math.BigDecimal getBigDecimal(int parameterIndex, int scale)
                                throws SQLException; (Deprecated)
        byte[] getBytes(int parameterIndex) throws SQLException;
  3.0   byte[] getBytes(String parameterName) throws SQLException;
        java.sql.Date getDate(int parameterIndex) throws SQLException;
  3.0   java.sql.Date getDate(String parameterName) throws SQLException;
  2.0   java.sql.Date getDate(int parameterIndex, java.util.Calendar cal)
                                                  throws SQLException;
  3.0   java.sql.Date getDate(String parameterName,
                        java.util.Calendar cal) throws SQLException;
        java.sql.Time getTime(int parameterIndex) throws SQLException;
  3.0   java.sql.Time getTime(String parameterName) throws SQLException;
  2.0   java.sql.Time getTime(int parameterIndex, java.util.Calendar cal)
                                                  throws SQLException;
  3.0   java.sql.Time getTime(String parameterName,
                        java.util.Calendar cal) throws SQLException;
        java.sql.Timestamp getTimestamp(int parameterIndex)
                                                  throws SQLException;
  3.0   java.sql.Timestamp getTimestamp(String parameterName)
                                                  throws SQLException;
  2.0   java.sql.Timestamp getTimestamp(int parameterIndex,
```

```
                         java.util.Calendar cal) throws SQLException;
3.0   java.sql.Timestamp getTimestamp(String parameterName,
                         java.util.Calendar cal) throws SQLException;
3.0   java.net.URL getURL(int parameterIndex) throws SQLException;
3.0   java.net.URL getURL(String parameterName) throws SQLException;
      Object getObject(int parameterIndex) throws SQLException;
3.0   Object getObject(String parameterName) throws SQLException;
2.0   Object getObject(int parameterIndex, java.util.Map map)
                                                throws SQLException;
3.0   Object getObject(String parameterName, java.util.Map map)
                                                throws SQLException;

      //===========================================================
      // Methods for accessing SQL99 types as results and out parameters:
      //===========================================================
2.0   Array getArray(int parameterIndex) throws SQLException;
3.0   Array getArray(String parameterName) throws SQLException;
2.0   Blob getBlob(int parameterIndex) throws SQLException;
3.0   Blob getBlob(String parameterName) throws SQLException;
2.0   Clob getClob(int parameterIndex) throws SQLException;
3.0   Clob getClob(String parameterName) throws SQLException;
2.0   Ref getRef(int parameterIndex) throws SQLException;
3.0   Ref getRef(String parameterName) throws SQLException;

      //===========================================================
      // Methods for setting named parameters:
      //===========================================================
3.0   void setBoolean(String parameterName, boolean x)
                                                throws SQLException;
3.0   void setByte(String parameterName, byte x) throws SQLException;
3.0   void setShort(String parameterName, short x) throws SQLException;
3.0   void setInt(String parameterName, int x) throws SQLException;
3.0   void setLong(String parameterName, long x) throws SQLException;
3.0   void setFloat(String parameterName, float x) throws SQLException;
3.0   void setDouble(String parameterName, double x) throws SQLException;
3.0   void setBigDecimal(String parameterName, java.math.BigDecimal x)
                                                throws SQLException;
3.0   void setString(String parameterName, String x) throws SQLException;
3.0   void setBytes(String parameterName, byte x[]) throws SQLException;
3.0   void setDate(String parameterName, java.sql.Date x) throws
                                                SQLException;
```

```
3.0   void setTime(String parameterName, java.sql.Time x)
                                              throws SQLException;
3.0   void setTimestamp(String parameterName, java.sql.Timestamp x)
                                              throws SQLException;
3.0   void setAsciiStream(String parameterName, java.io.InputStream x,
                                 int length) throws SQLException;
3.0   void setBinaryStream(String parameterName, java.io.InputStream x,
                                 int length) throws SQLException;
3.0   void setCharacterStream(String parameterName, java.io.Reader
                          reader, int length) throws SQLException;
3.0   void setDate(String parameterName, java.sql.Date x,
                       java.util.Calendar cal) throws SQLException;
3.0   void setTime(String parameterName, java.sql.Time x,
                       java.util.Calendar cal) throws SQLException;
3.0   void setTimestamp(String parameterName, java.sql.Timestamp x,
                       java.util.Calendar cal) throws SQLException;
3.0   void setURL(String parameterName, java.net.URL val)
                                              throws SQLException;
3.0   void setObject(String parameterName, Object x, int targetJdbcType,
                                 int scale) throws SQLException;
3.0   void setObject(String parameterName, Object x, int targetJdbcType)
                                              throws SQLException;

3.0   void setObject(String parameterName, Object x) throws SQLException;
3.0   void setNull(String parameterName, int jdbcType)
                                              throws SQLException;
3.0   void setNull(String parameterName, int jdbcType, String typeName)
                                              throws SQLException;
}
```

9.3   CallableStatement Methods

9.3.1   Inherited Methods and Fields

The following methods are inherited from `java.sql.Statement`:

JDBC 1.0 methods:

cancel	getMoreResults	setCursorName
clearWarnings	getQueryTimeout	setEscapeProcessing
close	getResultSet	setMaxFieldSize
getMaxFieldSize	getUpdateCount	setMaxRows
getMaxRows	getWarnings	setQueryTimeout

JDBC 2.0 methods:

clearBatch	getFetchDirection	getResultSetType
executeBatch	getFetchSize	setFetchDirection
getConnection	getResultSetConcurrency	setFetchSize

JDBC 3.0 methods:

execute	getGeneratedKeys	getResultSetHoldability
executeUpdate	getMoreResults	

The following fields are inherited from java.sql.Statement:

JDBC 3.0 fields:

CLOSE_ALL_RESULTS	KEEP_CURRENT_RESULT	SUCCESS_NO_INFO
CLOSE_CURRENT_RESULT	NO_GENERATED_KEYS	
EXECUTE_FAILED	RETURN_GENERATED_KEYS	

The following methods are inherited from java.sql.PreparedStatement:

JDBC 1.0 methods:

clearParameters	setByte	setObject
execute	setBytes	setShort
executeQuery	setDate	setString
executeUpdate	setDouble	setTime
setAsciiStream	setFloat	setTimestamp
setBigDecimal	setInt	setUnicodeStream
setBinaryStream	setLong	
setBoolean	setNull	

JDBC 2.0 methods:

addBatch	setCharacterStream	setRef
setArray	setClob	setTime
setBlob	setDate	setTimestamp

JDBC 3.0 methods:

getParameterMetaData	setURL

9.3.2   Methods Defined in CallableStatement

The following methods are defined in the interface java.sql.CallableStatement:

getArray

2.0   Array **getArray**(int *parameterIndex*) throws SQLException

3.0   Array **getArray**(String *parameterName*) throws SQLException

Retrieves a JDBC ARRAY value from parameter *parameterIndex* (or *parameterName*) as an Array object in the Java programming language.

PARAMETERS:

parameterIndex or	1 indicates the first parameter, 2 the second, and so on
parameterName	String object indicating the parameter name in the stored procedure definition

RETURNS:
the parameter value as an Array object in the Java programming language. If the value was SQL NULL, the value null will be returned.

EXAMPLE:
```
Array ids = cstmt.getArray(2);
// gets the second OUT parameter as an Array object
```
or
```
Array ids = cstmt.getArray("IDS");
// gets the parameter IDS as an Array object
```

getBigDecimal   DEPRECATED

java.math.BigDecimal **getBigDecimal**(int *parameterIndex*, int *scale*)
                                                    throws SQLException

Retrieves a JDBC NUMERIC value from parameter *parameterIndex* as a java.math.BigDecimal object with *scale* digits to the right of the decimal point.

NOTE: This method has been deprecated. If you are using a JDBC 2.0 or 3.0 driver, use the version of the method getBigDecimal that does not take an argument for the scale and returns a java.math.BigDecimal value with full precision.

PARAMETERS:

parameterIndex	1 indicates the first parameter, 2 the second, and so on
scale	the number of digits to the right of the decimal point

RETURNS:
the parameter value as a java.math.BigDecimal object. If the value is SQL
NULL, the value returned is null.

EXAMPLE:
```
java.math.BigDecimal n = cstmt.getBigDecimal(2, 6);
// gets the second OUT parameter as a java.math.BigDecimal object
// with 6 digits to the right of the decimal point
```

getBigDecimal

```
java.math.BigDecimal getBigDecimal(int parameterIndex)
                                          throws SQLException
```
2.0

```
java.math.BigDecimal getBigDecimal(String parameterName)
                                          throws SQLException
```
3.0

Gets a JDBC NUMERIC value from parameter *parameterIndex* (or *parameterName*) as a java.math.BigDecimal object with as many digits to the right of
the decimal point as the value contains.

PARAMETERS:

parameterIndex	1 indicates the first parameter, 2 the second, and so on
or	
parameterName	String object indicating the parameter name in the stored procedure definition

RETURNS:
the parameter value as a java.math.BigDecimal object with full precision. If
the value is SQL NULL, the value returned is null.

EXAMPLE:
```
java.math.BigDecimal n = cstmt.getBigDecimal(1);
// gets the first OUT parameter as a java.math.BigDecimal object
// with as many digits to the right of the decimal point as are in
// the parameter value
```
or
```
java.math.BigDecimal n = cstmt.getBigDecimal("AV_AGE");
// gets the AV_AGE parameter as a java.math.BigDecimal object
// with as many digits to the right of the decimal point as are in
// the parameter value
```

getBlob

2.0   Blob **getBlob**(int *parameterIndex*) throws SQLException

3.0   Blob **getBlob**(String *parameterName*) throws SQLException

Retrieves a JDBC BLOB value from parameter *parameterIndex* (or *param-eterName*) as a Blob object in the Java programming language.

PARAMETERS:

parameterIndex or	1 indicates the first parameter, 2 the second, and so on
parameterName	String object indicating the parameter name in the stored procedure definition

RETURNS:
the parameter value as a Blob object in the Java programming language. If the value was SQL NULL, the value null will be returned.

EXAMPLE:
```
Blob stats = cstmt.getBlob(2);
// gets the second OUT parameter as a Blob object
or
Blob stats = cstmt.getBlob("STATS");
// gets the second OUT parameter as a Blob object
```

getBoolean

---

boolean **getBoolean**(int *parameterIndex*) throws SQLException

3.0   boolean **getBoolean**(String *parameterName*) throws SQLException

Retrieves a JDBC BIT or BOOLEAN value from parameter *parameterIndex* (or *parameterName*) as a boolean in the Java programming language.

PARAMETERS:

parameterIndex or	1 indicates the first parameter, 2 the second, and so on
parameterName	String object indicating the parameter name in the stored procedure definition

RETURNS:
the parameter value as a `boolean` in the Java programming language. If the value was SQL `NULL`, the value `false` will be returned.

EXAMPLE:
```
boolean b = cstmt.getBoolean(1);
// gets the first OUT parameter as a Java boolean
```
or
```
boolean b = cstmt.getBoolean("NEEDS_UPDATE");
// gets the value in the NEEDS_UPDATE parameter as a Java boolean
```

getByte

```
byte getByte(int parameterIndex) throws SQLException
```

```
byte getByte(String parameterName) throws SQLException
```

`3.0`

Retrieves a JDBC `TINYINT` value from parameter *parameterIndex* (or *parameterName*) as a byte in the Java programming language.

PARAMETERS:

parameterIndex	1 indicates the first parameter, 2 the second, and so on
or	
parameterName	`String` object indicating the parameter name in the stored procedure definition

RETURNS:
the parameter value as a Java byte. If the value was SQL `NULL`, the value returned is 0.

EXAMPLE:
```
byte q = cstmt.getByte(2); // gets the second OUT parameter as a byte
```
or
```
byte q = cstmt.getByte("DATA");
// gets the value of the DATA parameter as a byte
```

getBytes

```
byte[] getBytes(int parameterIndex) throws SQLException
```

```
byte[] getBytes(String parameterName) throws SQLException
```

`3.0`

Retrieves a JDBC BINARY, VARBINARY, or LONGVARBINARY value from parameter *parameterIndex* (or *parameterName*) as an array of byte values in the Java programming language.

PARAMETERS:

parameterIndex or	1 indicates the first parameter, 2 the second, and so on
parameterName	String object indicating the parameter name in the stored procedure definition

RETURNS:

the parameter value as a Java byte[]. If the value was SQL NULL, the value returned is null.

EXAMPLE:
```
byte [] q = cstmt.getBytes(1);
// gets the first OUT parameter as an array of bytes
or
byte [] q = cstmt.getBytes("READINGS");
// gets the value of the READINGS parameter as an array of bytes
```

getClob

2.0   Clob **getClob**(int *parameterIndex*) throws SQLException

3.0   Clob **getClob**(String *parameterName*) throws SQLException

Retrieves a JDBC CLOB value from parameter *parameterIndex* (or *parameterName*) as a Clob object in the Java programming language.

PARAMETERS:

parameterIndex or	1 indicates the first parameter, 2 the second, and so on
parameterName	String object indicating the parameter name in the stored procedure definition

RETURNS:

the parameter value as a Clob object in the Java programming language. If the value was SQL NULL, the value null will be returned.

EXAMPLE:
```
Clob summary = cstmt.getClob(2);
// gets the second OUT parameter as a Clob object
```

or
```
Clob summary = cstmt.getClob("SUMMARY");
// gets the value of the SUMMARY parameter as a Clob object
```

getDate

```
java.sql.Date getDate(int parameterIndex) throws SQLException
```

```
java.sql.Date getDate(String parameterName) throws SQLException
```
3.0

Retrieves a JDBC DATE value from parameter *parameterIndex* (or *parameterName*) as a java.sql.Date object.

PARAMETERS:

parameterIndex 1 indicates the first parameter, 2 the second, and so on
or
parameterName   String object indicating the parameter name in the stored procedure definition

RETURNS:

the parameter value as a java.sql.Date object. If the value was SQL NULL, the value returned is null.

EXAMPLE:
```
Date d = cstmt.getDate(3);
// gets the third OUT parameter as a java.sql.Date object
```
or
```
Date d = cstmt.getDate("HIRE_DATE");
// gets the value of the HIRE_DATE parameter as a
// java.sql.Date object
```

getDate

```
java.sql.Date getDate(int parameterIndex, java.util.Calendar cal)
                                        throws SQLException
```
2.0

```
java.sql.Date getDate(String parameterName, java.util.Calendar cal)
                                        throws SQLException
```
3.0

Retrieves a JDBC DATE value from parameter *parameterIndex* (or *parameterName*) as a java.sql.Date object, using *cal* to construct an appropriate millisecond value for the Date object when the underlying database does not store time zone information. If no Calendar object is specified, the default time zone is used.

PARAMETERS:

parameterIndex or	1 indicates the first parameter, 2 the second, and so on
parameterName	String object indicating the parameter name in the stored procedure definition
cal	the Calendar object to use to construct the Date object

RETURNS:

the parameter value as a java.sql.Date object. If the value was SQL NULL, the value returned is null.

EXAMPLE:
```
Date d = cstmt.getDate(3, myCal);
// gets the third OUT parameter as a java.sql.Date object, using
// myCal to construct the date if the underlying database does not
// store time zone information
```
or
```
Date d = cstmt.getDate("DUE_DATE", myCal);
// gets the value of the DUE_DATE parameter as a java.sql.Date
// object, using myCal to construct the date if the underlying
// database does not store time zone information
```

getDouble

```
double getDouble(int parameterIndex) throws SQLException
```

3.0

```
double getDouble(String parameterName) throws SQLException
```

Retrieves a JDBC DOUBLE or JDBC FLOAT value from parameter *parameterIndex* (or *parameterName*) as a double in the Java programming language.

PARAMETERS:

parameterIndex or	1 indicates the first parameter, 2 the second, and so on
parameterName	String object indicating the parameter name in the stored procedure definition

RETURNS:
the parameter value as a double in the Java programming language. If the value was SQL NULL, the value returned is 0.

EXAMPLE:
```
double measurement = cstmt.getDouble(2);
// gets the second OUT parameter as a double
or
double measurement = cstmt.getDouble("CENTIMETERS");
// gets the value of the CENTIMETERS parameter as a double
```

getFloat

```
float getFloat(int parameterIndex) throws SQLException
```

```
float getFloat(String parameterName) throws SQLException
```

3.0

Retrieves a JDBC FLOAT value from parameter *parameterIndex* (or *parameterName*) as a float in the Java programming language.

PARAMETERS:

parameterIndex	1 indicates the first parameter, 2 the second, and so on
or	
parameterName	String object indicating the parameter name in the stored procedure definition

RETURNS:
the parameter value as a float in the Java programming language. If the value was SQL NULL, the value returned is 0.

EXAMPLE:
```
float cost = cstmt.getFloat(1);
// gets the first OUT parameter as a float
or
float costf = cstmt.getFloat("COST");
// gets the value of the COST parameter as a float
```

getInt

```
int getInt(int parameterIndex) throws SQLException
```

```
int getInt(String parameterName) throws SQLException
```

3.0

Retrieves a JDBC INTEGER value from parameter *parameterIndex* (or *parameterName*) as an int in the Java programming language.

PARAMETERS:

parameterIndex   1 indicates the first parameter, 2 the second, and so on
or
parameterName   String object indicating the parameter name in the stored procedure definition

RETURNS:
the parameter value as an int in the Java programming language. If the value was SQL NULL, the value returned is 0.

EXAMPLE:
```
int age = cstmt.getInt(2); // gets the second OUT parameter as an int
or
int age = cstmt.getInt("AGE");
// gets the value of the AGE parameter as an int
```

getLong

```
long getLong(int parameterIndex) throws SQLException
```

```
long getLong(String parameterName) throws SQLException
```

3.0

Retrieves a JDBC BIGINT value from parameter *parameterIndex* (or *parameterName*) as a long in the Java programming language.

PARAMETERS:

parameterIndex   1 indicates the first parameter, 2 the second, and so on
or
parameterName   String object indicating the parameter name in the stored procedure definition

RETURNS:
the parameter value as a long in the Java programming language. If the value was SQL NULL, the value returned is 0.

EXAMPLE:
```
long distance = cstmt.getLong(2);
// gets the second OUT parameter as a long
or
long distance = cstmt.getLong("DISTANCE");
// gets the value of the DISTANCE parameter as a long
```

getObject

```
Object getObject(int parameterIndex) throws SQLException

Object getObject(String parameterName) throws SQLException
```

3.0

Retrieves the value of parameter *parameterIndex* (or *parameterName*) as an instance of Object in the Java programming language. If the parameter is a UDT with a custom mapping, the driver will use the connection's type map for custom mapping.

This method returns a Java object whose type corresponds to the JDBC type that was registered for this parameter using the method registerOutParameter. By registering the target JDBC type as java.sql.Types.OTHER, this method may be used to read database-specific abstract data types. This is discussed in detail in "Dynamic Data Access," on page 1084.

PARAMETERS:

parameterIndex	1 indicates the first parameter, 2 the second, and so on
or	
parameterName	String object indicating the parameter name in the stored procedure definition

RETURNS:
a java.lang.Object object holding the OUT parameter value. If the parameter was SQL NULL, the value null will be returned.

EXAMPLE:
```
Object obj = cstmt.getObject(2);
// gets the second OUT parameter as the type that was registered for
// this parameter
```

or

```
Object obj = cstmt.getObject("INFO");
// gets the value of the INFO parameter as the type that was
// registered for this parameter
```

The following example demonstrates using an object after it has been retrieved:

```
if (obj instanceOf Wombat) {
    Wombat w = (Wombat)obj;
    w.burrow();
}
```

SEE:
java.sql.Types
"JDBC Types Mapped to Java Object Types," on page 1089

getObject

2.0

```
Object getObject(int parameterIndex, java.util.Map map)
                                        throws SQLException
```

3.0

```
Object getObject(String parameterName, java.util.Map map)
                                        throws SQLException
```

Retrieves the value of parameter *parameterIndex* (or *parameterName*) as an instance of Object in the Java programming language and uses *map* for the custom mapping of the parameter value. If the parameter is a UDT with no entry in *map*, the driver will use the standard mapping.

This method returns a Java object whose type corresponds to the JDBC type that was registered for this parameter using the method registerOutParameter. By registering the target JDBC type as java.sql.Types.OTHER, this method may be used to read database-specific abstract data types. This is discussed in detail in "Dynamic Data Access," on page 1084.

PARAMETERS:

parameterIndex	1 indicates the first parameter, 2 the second, and so on
or	
parameterName	String object indicating the parameter name in the stored procedure definition

map   a java.util.Map object that contains the mapping from
                               SQL type names for user-defined types to classes in the
                               Java programming language

RETURNS:
a java.lang.Object object holding the OUT parameter value. If the parameter
was SQL NULL, the value null will be returned.

EXAMPLE:
```
Object obj = cstmt.getObject(2, map);
// gets the second OUT parameter as the type that was registered for
// this parameter. If the OUT parameter is a UDT with a custom mapping
// that is entered in map, the OUT parameter will be custom mapped
// using the mapping specified in map.
```
or
```
Object obj = cstmt.getObject("ADDRESS", map);
// gets the value of the ADDRESS parameter as the type that was
// registered for this parameter. If the OUT parameter is a UDT with
// a custom mapping that is entered in map, the OUT parameter will
// be custom mapped using the mapping specified in map.
```

The following example demonstrates using an object after it has been
retrieved:

```
if (obj instanceOf Wombat) {
    Wombat w = (Wombat)obj;
    w.sleep();
}
```

SEE:
java.sql.Types
"JDBC Types Mapped to Java Object Types," on page 1089.

getRef

```
Ref getRef(int parameterIndex) throws SQLException
```
2.0

```
Ref getRef(String parameterName) throws SQLException
```
3.0

Retrieves a JDBC REF(<structured-type>) value from parameter *parameterIndex* (or *parameterName*) as a Ref object in the Java programming lan-

guage.

PARAMETERS:

parameterIndex	1 indicates the first parameter, 2 the second, and so on
or	
parameterName	String object indicating the parameter name in the stored procedure definition

RETURNS:
the parameter value as a Ref object in the Java programming language. If the value was SQL NULL, the value null will be returned.

EXAMPLE:
```
Ref ref = cstmt.getRef(2);
// gets the second OUT parameter as a Ref object, which points to a
// user-defined structured type
```
or
```
Ref ref = cstmt.getRef("REF_ADDRESS");
// gets the REF_ADDRESS parameter as a Ref object, which points to a
// user-defined structured type
```

getShort

```
short getShort(int parameterIndex) throws SQLException
```

`3.0`

```
short getShort(String parameterName) throws SQLException
```

Retrieves a JDBC SMALLINT value from parameter *parameterIndex* (or *parameterName*) as a short in the Java programming language.

PARAMETERS:

parameterIndex	1 indicates the first parameter, 2 the second, and so on
or	
parameterName	String object indicating the parameter name in the stored procedure definition

RETURNS:
the parameter value as a short in the Java programming language. If the value was SQL NULL, the value returned is 0.

EXAMPLE:
```
short count = cstmt.getShort(1);
// gets the first OUT parameter as a short
```

or

```
short count = cstmt.getShort("COUNT");
// gets the value of the COUNT parameter as a short
```

getString

String **getString**(int *parameterIndex*) throws SQLException

String **getString**(String *parameterName*) throws SQLException

Retrieves a JDBC CHAR, VARCHAR, or LONGVARCHAR value from parameter *parameterIndex* (or *parameterName*) as a String in the Java programming language.

For the fixed-length type JDBC CHAR, the String object returned will have exactly the same value the JDBC CHAR value had in the database, including any padding added by the database.

PARAMETERS:

parameterIndex or	1 indicates the first parameter, 2 the second, and so on
parameterName	String object indicating the parameter name in the stored procedure definition

RETURNS:
the parameter value as a String object in the Java programming language. If the value was SQL NULL, the value returned is null.

EXAMPLE:
```
String name = cstmt.getString(2);
// gets the second OUT parameter as a String object
or
String name = cstmt.getString("NAME");
// gets the value of the NAME parameter as a String object
```

getTime

java.sql.Time **getTime**(int *parameterIndex*) throws SQLException

java.sql.Time **getTime**(String *parameterName*) throws SQLException

Retrieves a JDBC TIME value from parameter *parameterIndex* (or *parameterName*) as a java.sql.Time object.

PARAMETERS:

parameterIndex	1 indicates the first parameter, 2 the second, and so on
or	
parameterName	String object indicating the parameter name in the stored procedure definition

RETURNS:
the parameter value as a java.sql.Time object. If the value was SQL NULL, the value returned is null.

EXAMPLE:
```
Time arrival = cstmt.getTime(4);
// gets the fourth OUT parameter as a java.sql.Time object
```
or
```
Time arrival = cstmt.getTime("ARR_TIME");
// gets the value of the ARR_TIME parameter as a java.sql.Time object
```

getTime

2.0
```
java.sql.Time getTime(int parameterIndex, java.util.Calendar cal)
                                                  throws SQLException
```

3.0
```
java.sql.Time getTime(String parameterName, java.util.Calendar cal)
                                                  throws SQLException
```

Retrieves a JDBC TIME value from parameter *parameterIndex* (or *parameterName*) as a java.sql.Time object, using *cal* to construct an appropriate millisecond value for the Time object when the underlying database does not store time zone information. If no Calendar object is specified, the default time zone is used.

PARAMETERS:

parameterIndex	1 indicates the first parameter, 2 the second, and so on
or	
parameterName	String object indicating the parameter name in the stored procedure definition
cal	the Calendar object to use to construct the Time object

RETURNS:
the parameter value as a `java.sql.Time` object. If the value was SQL `NULL`, the value returned is `null`.

EXAMPLE:
```
java.sql.Time depart = cstmt.getTime(2, myCal);
// gets the second OUT parameter as a java.sql.Time object, using
// myCal to construct the time
```
or
```
java.sql.Time depart = cstmt.getTime("DEPART_TIME", myCal);
// gets the value of the DEPART_TIME parameter as a java.sql.Time
//object, using myCal to construct the time
```

getTimestamp

```
java.sql.Timestamp getTimestamp(int parameterIndex)
                                        throws SQLException;
```

```
java.sql.Timestamp getTimestamp(String parameterName)
                                        throws SQLException;
```
`3.0`

Retrieves a JDBC `TIMESTAMP` value from parameter *parameterIndex* (or *parameterName*) as a `java.sql.Timestamp` object.

PARAMETERS:

parameterIndex	1 indicates the first parameter, 2 the second, and so on
or	
parameterName	String object indicating the parameter name in the stored procedure definition

RETURNS:
the parameter value as a `java.sql.Timestamp` object. If the value was SQL `NULL`, the value returned is `null`.

EXAMPLE:
```
Timestamp ts = cstmt.getTimestamp(2);
// gets the second OUT parameter as a java.sql.Timestamp object
```

getTimestamp

```
java.sql.Timestamp getTimestamp(int parameterIndex,
```
`2.0`

```
                              java.util.Calendar cal) throws SQLException
```

3.0   java.sql.Timestamp **getTimestamp**(String *parameterName*,
```
                              java.util.Calendar cal) throws SQLException
```

Retrieves a JDBC TIMESTAMP value from parameter *parameterIndex* (or *parameterName*) as a java.sql.Timestamp object, using *cal* to construct an appropriate millisecond value for the Timestamp object when the underlying database does not store time zone information. If no Calendar object is specified, the default time zone is used.

PARAMETERS:

parameterIndex or	1 indicates the first parameter, 2 the second, and so on
parameterName	String object indicating the parameter name in the stored procedure definition
cal	the Calendar object to use to construct the Timestamp object

RETURNS:
the parameter value as a java.sql.Timestamp object. If the value was SQL NULL, the value returned is null.

EXAMPLE:
```
java.sql.Timestamp sunrise = cstmt.getTimestamp(3, myCal);
// gets the third OUT parameter as a java.sql.Timestamp object, using
// myCal to construct the timestamp
```
or
```
java.sql.Timestamp sunrise = cstmt.getTimestamp("SUNRISE", myCal);
// gets the value of the SUNRISE parameter as a java.sql.Timestamp
// object, using myCal to construct the timestamp
```

getURL

3.0   java.net.URL **getURL**(int *parameterIndex*) throws SQLException;

3.0   java.net.URL **getURL**(String *parameterName*) throws SQLException;

Retrieves the JDBC DATALINK value from parameter *parameterIndex* (or *parameterName*) as a java.net.URL object.

PARAMETERS:

parameterIndex   1 indicates the first parameter, 2 the second, and so on

or

parameterName   String object indicating the parameter name in the stored procedure definition

RETURNS:

the parameter value as a java.net.URL object. If the value was SQL NULL, the value returned is null.

THROWS:

SQLException if the java.net.URL object is malformed

EXAMPLE:

```
java.net.URL url = cstmt.getURL(2);
// gets the second OUT parameter as a java.net.URL object
```

or

```
java.net.URL url = cstmt.getURL("RECEIVER");
// gets the value of the "RECEIVER" parameter as a java.net.URL
// object
```

registerOutParameter

```
void registerOutParameter(int parameterIndex, int jdbcType)
                                              throws SQLException
```

```
void registerOutParameter(String parameterName, int jdbcType)
                                              throws SQLException
```

3.0

Registers the OUT parameter in ordinal position *parameterIndex* (or the parameter *parameterName)* to the JDBC type *jdbcType*. All OUT parameters must be registered before a stored procedure is executed.

The JDBC type specified by *jdbcType* for an OUT parameter determines the Java type that must be used in the getter method used to retrieve the value of that parameter. See "JDBC Types Mapped to Java Types," on page 1087.

If the JDBC type expected to be returned to this output parameter is specific to this particular database, *jdbcType* should be java.sql.Types.OTHER. The method CallableStatement.getObject will retrieve the value.

PARAMETERS:

parameterIndex   1 indicates the first parameter, 2 the second, and so on

or

parameterName	String object indicating the parameter name in the stored procedure definition
jdbcType	the JDBC type code defined by java.sql.Types. If the parameter is of type NUMERIC or DECIMAL, the version of registerOutParameter that accepts a scale value should be used.

EXAMPLE:
```
cstmt.registerOutParameter(3, Types.TIMESTAMP);
// registers the third parameter to be of type JDBC TIMESTAMP
```
or
```
cstmt.registerOutParameter("ARRIVAL", Types.TIMESTAMP);
// registers the ARRIVAL parameter to be of type JDBC TIMESTAMP
```

SEE:
java.sql.Types

registerOutParameter

```
void registerOutParameter(int parameterIndex, int jdbcType,
                                    int scale) throws SQLException
```

```
void registerOutParameter(String parameterName, int jdbcType,
                                    int scale) throws SQLException
```
3.0

Registers the OUT parameter in ordinal position *parameterIndex* (or the parameter *parameterName*) to be of JDBC type *jdbcType*. This method must be called before executing a stored procedure.

The JDBC type specified by *jdbcType* for an OUT parameter determines the Java type that must be used in the getter method used to retrieve the value of that parameter. See "JDBC Types Mapped to Java Types," on page 1087.

This version of registerOutParameter should be used when the parameter is of JDBC type NUMERIC or DECIMAL.

PARAMETERS:

parameterIndex or	1 indicates the first parameter, 2 the second, and so on
parameterName	String object indicating the parameter name in the stored procedure definition
jdbcType	the JDBC type code defined by java.sql.Types

scale   the desired number of digits to the right of the decimal
                            point. It must be greater than or equal to zero.

EXAMPLE:
```
cstmt.registerOutParameter(3, Types.NUMERIC, 4);
// registers the third parameter to be of type NUMERIC with
// 4 digits after the decimal point
```

SEE:
```
java.sql.Types
```

registerOutParameter

```
void registerOutParameter(int parameterIndex, int jdbcType,
                          String typeName) throws SQLException
```
2.0

```
void registerOutParameter(String parameterName, int jdbcType,
                          String typeName) throws SQLException
```
3.0

Registers the parameter in ordinal position *parameterIndex* (or the
parameter *parameterName*) to be of JDBC type *jdbcType*. This version of the
method registerOutParameter should be used for registering OUT parameters that are user-named or SQL REF types. The user-named types include the
JDBC types STRUCT, DISTINCT, JAVA_OBJECT, and named array types. This
method must be called before executing a stored procedure with such an OUT
parameter.

The JDBC type specified by *jdbcType* for an OUT parameter determines
the Java type that must be used in the getter method used to read the value of
that parameter. See "JDBC Types Mapped to Java Types," on page 1087.

This version of registerOutParameter is intended for use with user-
named and REF OUT parameters; however, it may be used to register a parameter of any JDBC type. The driver will ignore *typeName* if *jdbcType* is not
STRUCT, DISTINCT, JAVA_OBJECT, or REF.

PARAMETERS:

parameterIndex or	1 indicates the first parameter, 2 the second, and so on
parameterName	String object indicating the parameter name in the stored procedure definition
jdbcType	one of the following type codes in java.sql.Types: STRUCT, DISTINCT, JAVA_OBJECT, or REF

| typeName | the fully qualified SQL name of the user-named type being used as an OUT parameter; for a REF type, the fully qualified name of the structured type to which it refers |

EXAMPLE:
```
cstmt.registerOutParameter(3, Types.STRUCT, "SchemaName.AUTHOR");
// registers the third parameter, which has the SQL name of
// SchemaName.AUTHOR, to be of type STRUCT
```

SEE:
```
java.sql.Types
```

setAsciiStream

3.0

```
void setAsciiStream(String parameterName, java.io.InputStream fin,
                                  int length) throws SQLException
```

Sets the parameter *parameterName* to the input stream object *fin*, from which *length* bytes will be read and sent to the database.

This is useful when a very large ASCII value is input to a LONGVARCHAR parameter. JDBC will read the data from the stream as needed until it reaches end-of-file. The JDBC driver will do any necessary conversion from ASCII to the database CHAR format.

NOTE: This stream object can be either a standard stream object in the Java programming language or the programmer's own subclass that implements the standard interface.

PARAMETERS:

parameterName	String object indicating the parameter name in the stored procedure definition
fin	the java.io.InputStream object that contains the input data in ASCII format
length	the number of bytes to be read from the stream and sent to the database. Note that if the stream contains more or fewer bytes than are specified in *length*, an exception is thrown.

THROWS:
SQLException if the number of bytes read and sent to the database is not equal to the number of bytes specified

EXAMPLE:
```
pstmt.setAsciiStream("BIO", fin, 4096);
// sets the parameter BIO to the input stream fin;
// 4096 bytes will be read
pstmt.setAsciiStream("BIO", (new StringBufferInputStream(text)),
                    text.length()); // to get accurate length
```

setBigDecimal

3.0

```
void setBigDecimal(String parameterName, java.math.BigDecimal n)
                                        throws SQLException
```

Sets parameter *parameterName* to *n*. The driver converts this to a JDBC NUMERIC value when it sends it to the database.

PARAMETERS:

parameterName	String object indicating the parameter name in the stored procedure definition
n	an instance of the class java.math.BigDecimal to which the parameter will be set

EXAMPLE:
```
java.math.BigDecimal n = new java.math.BigDecimal(1234.56789);
pstmt.setBigDecimal("DISTANCE", n);
// sets parameter DISTANCE to 1234.56789
```

setBinaryStream

3.0

```
void setBinaryStream(String parameterName, java.io.InputStream fin,
                            int length) throws SQLException
```

Sets the parameter *parameterName* to the input stream object *fin*, from which *length* bytes will be read and sent to the database.

This is useful when a very large binary value is input to a LONGVARBINARY parameter. JDBC will read the data from the stream as needed until it reaches end-of-file.

NOTE: This stream object can be either a standard stream object in the Java programming language or the programmer's own subclass that implements the standard interface.

PARAMETERS:

parameterName	String object indicating the parameter name in the stored procedure definition
fin	the java.io.InputStream object that contains the input data in binary form
length	the number of bytes to be read from the stream and sent to the database. Note that if the stream contains more or less bytes than are specified in *length*, an exception is thrown.

THROWS:

SQLException if the number of bytes read and sent to the database is not equal to the number of bytes specified

EXAMPLE:

```
pstmt.setBinaryStream("DATA", fin, 10000);
// sets the parameter DATA to the input stream fin;
// 10000 bytes will be read and sent to the database
```

setBoolean
`3.0`

void **setBoolean**(String *parameterName*, boolean *b*) throws SQLException

Sets parameter *parameterName* to *b*, a Java boolean value. The driver converts this to a JDBC BIT or BOOLEAN value when it sends it to the database.

PARAMETERS:

parameterName	String object indicating the parameter name in the stored procedure definition
b	the parameter value—either true or false

EXAMPLE:

```
pstmt.setBoolean("NEEDS_SUP", false);
// sets the parameter NEEDS_SUP to false
```

setByte
`3.0`

void **setByte**(String *parameterName*, byte *x*) throws SQLException

Sets parameter *parameterName* to *x*, a Java byte value. The driver converts this to a JDBC TINYINT value when it sends it to the database.

PARAMETERS:

parameterName	String object indicating the parameter name in the stored procedure definition
x	the parameter value to be set

EXAMPLE:
```
pstmt.setByte("STATUS", (byte)0); // sets the STATUS parameter to 0
```

setBytes

`3.0`

```
void setBytes(String parameterName, byte x[]) throws SQLException
```

Sets parameter *parameterName* to *x[]*, a Java array of bytes. The driver converts this to a JDBC VARBINARY or LONGVARBINARY value (depending on the argument's size relative to the driver's limits on VARBINARY values) when it sends it to the database.

PARAMETERS:

parameterName	String object indicating the parameter name in the stored procedure definition
x	a Java array of bytes

EXAMPLE:
```
byte x[] = {1, 2, 3, 4, 5};
pstmt.setBytes("DATA", x); // sets the DATA parameter to the array x
```

setCharacterStream

`3.0`

```
void setCharacterStream(String parameterName, java.io.Reader reader,
                         int length) throws SQLException
```

Sets the parameter *parameterName* to the Reader stream object *reader*, from which *length* characters will be read and sent to the database.

This is useful when a very large Unicode value is input to a LONGVARCHAR parameter. JDBC will read the data from the stream as needed until it reaches end-of-file. The JDBC driver will do any necessary conversion from Unicode to the database char format.

This stream object can be either a standard stream object in the Java programming language or the programmer's own subclass that implements the standard interface.

PARAMETERS:

parameterName	String object indicating the parameter name in the stored procedure definition
reader	the java.io.Reader object that contains the input data in Unicode form
length	the number of characters to be read from the stream and sent to the database. Note that if the stream contains more or less characters than are specified in *length*, an exception is thrown.

THROWS:

java.sql.SQLException if *length* is greater or less than the number of characters in *reader*

EXAMPLE:
```
pstmt.setCharacterStream("COMMENT", reader, 10000);
// sets the COMMENT parameter to the Reader stream reader;
// 10000 characters will be read
```

setDate

```
void setDate(String parameterName, java.sql.Date x) throws SQLException
```

Sets parameter *parameterName* to *x*. The driver converts this to a JDBC DATE value when it sends it to the database.

PARAMETERS:

parameterName	String object indicating the parameter name in the stored procedure definition
x	a java.sql.Date object

EXAMPLE:
```
Date x = new Date(980366400000L);
pstmt.setDate("START_DATE, x);
// sets the START_DATE parameter to 2001-01-24, using the time zone
// of the virtual machine running the application to calculate the
// date
```

setDate

```
void setDate(String parameterName, java.sql.Date x,
```

java.util.Calendar *cal*) throws SQLException

Sets parameter *parameterName* to *x*. When the DBMS does not store time zone information, the driver will use *cal* to construct a JDBC DATE value, which it will then send to the database. With a Calendar object, the driver can calculate the date taking into account a custom time zone. If no Calendar object is specified, the driver uses the time zone of the Virtual Machine that is running the application.

PARAMETERS:

parameterName	String object indicating the parameter name in the stored procedure definition
x	a java.sql.Date object
cal	the Calendar object the driver will use to construct the date

EXAMPLE:
```
Date x = new Date(980366400000L);
pstmt.setDate("DATE_REC", x, cal);
// sets the first parameter to 2001-01-24, taking into account the
// time zone specified in cal
```

setDouble

3.0

void **setDouble**(String *parameterName*, double *x*) throws SQLException

Sets parameter *parameterName* to *x*. The driver converts this to a JDBC DOUBLE value when it sends it to the database.

PARAMETERS:

parameterName	String object indicating the parameter name in the stored procedure definition
x	the double value to which the parameter will be set

EXAMPLE:
```
pstmt.setDouble("AVG", 3958325.89);
// sets AVG parameter to 3958325.89
```

setFloat

3.0

void **setFloat**(String *parameterName*, float *x*) throws SQLException

Sets parameter *parameterName* to *x*. The driver converts this to a JDBC REAL value when it sends it to the database.

PARAMETERS:

parameterName	String object indicating the parameter name in the stored procedure definition
x	the float value to which the parameter will be set

EXAMPLE:
```
pstmt.setFloat("LENGTH", 18.0f); // sets LENGTH parameter to 18.0f
```

3.0   setInt

```
void setInt(String parameterName, int x) throws SQLException
```

Sets parameter *parameterName* to *x*. The driver converts this to a JDBC INTEGER value when it sends it to the database.

PARAMETERS:

parameterName	String object indicating the parameter name in the stored procedure definition
x	the int value to which the parameter will be set

EXAMPLE:
```
pstmt.setInt("AGE", 18); // sets AGE parameter to 18
```

3.0   setLong

```
void setLong(String parameterName, long x) throws SQLException
```

Sets parameter *parameterName* to *x*. The driver converts this to a JDBC BIGINT value when it sends it to the database.

PARAMETERS:

parameterName	String object indicating the parameter name in the stored procedure definition
x	the long value to which the parameter will be set

EXAMPLE:
```
pstmt.setLong(2, 18000000L); // sets second parameter to 18000000
```

setNull

`3.0`

void **setNull**(String *parameterName*, int *jdbcType*) throws SQLException

Sets parameter *parameterName* to JDBC NULL (the generic SQL NULL defined in java.sql.Types). Note that the JDBC type of the parameter to be set to JDBC NULL must be specified.

PARAMETERS:

parameterName	String object indicating the parameter name in the stored procedure definition
jdbcType	a JDBC type code defined by java.sql.Types

EXAMPLE:
```
pstmt.setNull("COUNT", java.sql.Types.INTEGER);
// sets the COUNT parameter, whose type is JDBC INTEGER, to JDBC
// NULL
```

Note that it is also possible to set the value of an input parameter to JDBC NULL using setter methods if the data type being set is an object type in the Java programming language.

The following example sets the second parameter, a String value, to JDBC NULL:
```
pstmt.setString(2, null);
```

SEE:
java.sql.Types

setNull

`3.0`

void **setNull**(String *parameterName*, int *jdbcType*, String *typeName*)
                                         throws SQLException

Sets parameter *parameterName* to JDBC NULL (the generic SQL NULL defined in java.sql.Types). This version of setNull should be used to set parameters that are REF or user-named types. User-named types include STRUCT, DISTINCT, JAVA_OBJECT, and named array types.

Note that the JDBC type of the parameter to be set to SQL NULL must be specified. To be portable, an application must give the JDBC type code and the fully qualified SQL type name when setting a REF or user-defined parameter to SQL NULL. Although this method is intended for setting parameters whose type is REF or a user-defined type, it can be used to set a parameter of any JDBC type to NULL. If the parameter to be set does not have a user-named or REF type, the driver ignores the *typeName* parameter. If a driver does not need the type code and type name information, it may ignore both *jdbcType* and *typeName*.

PARAMETERS:

parameterName	String object indicating the parameter name in the stored procedure definition
jdbcType	a JDBC type code defined by java.sql.Types; if not REF, STRUCT, DISTINCT, or JAVA_OBJECT, the driver will ignore the parameter *typeName*
typeName	the fully qualified name of the parameter being set. If *jdbcType* is REF, *typeName* should be the fully qualified name of the structured type that the REF parameter identifies. If *jdbcType* is not REF, STRUCT, DISTINCT, or JAVA_OBJECT, the driver will ignore this parameter.

EXAMPLE:
```
pstmt.setNull("BREED", java.sql.Types.REF, "schemaName.PUG");
// sets the BREED parameter, a JDBC REF value that references the
// SQL structured type schemaName.PUG, to SQL NULL
```

SEE:
java.sql.Types

setObject

`3.0`

```
void setObject(String parameterName, Object x, int targetJdbcType,
                                     int scale) throws SQLException
```

Sets parameter *parameterName* to *x*. The driver converts *x* to *targetJdbcType* before sending it to the database. If *targetJdbcType* is NUMERIC or DECIMAL, *scale* indicates the number of digits to the right of the decimal point; for all other data types, *scale* is ignored.

This form of the method setObject should be used when the target JDBC type is DECIMAL or NUMERIC.

Note that the setter methods for specific types convert their arguments to the JDBC type that is the default mapping for that particular type. Methods other than setObject do not, however, perform any general data type conversions. A setObject method can take any type (in the form of a generic Object

object) and convert it to the specified JDBC type before sending it to the database. In order to be objects, values for built-in types need to be expressed in their `java.lang` equivalents. For example, an `int` needs to be an instance of class `Integer`.

This method may be used to pass database-specific abstract data types by using a driver-specified Java type for *x* and using `java.sql.Types.OTHER` for *targetJdbcType*.

PARAMETERS:

parameterName	`String` object indicating the parameter name in the stored procedure definition
x	an instance of a Java `Object` containing the input parameter value
targetJdbcType	an integer constant representing the JDBC type (as defined in `java.sql.Types`) to be sent to the database. The *scale* argument may further qualify this type.
scale	the number of digits to the right of the decimal point. This applies only to `java.sql.Types.DECIMAL` and `java.sql.Types.NUMERIC` types. For all other types, this value will be ignored.

EXAMPLE:
```
Object x = new Integer(1234);
pstmt.setObject("MICRONS", x, java.sql.Types.DECIMAL, 5);
// sets MICRONS parameter to 1234.00000 after converting it to a JDBC
// DECIMAL
```

SEE:
```
java.sql.Types
```
"Using setObject" on page 651

setObject

3.0

```
void setObject(String parameterName, Object x, int targetJdbcType)
                                              throws SQLException
```

Sets parameter *parameterName* to *x* and assumes a scale of zero. The driver converts *x* to *targetJdbcType* before sending it to the database.

Note that the `setter` methods for specific types convert their arguments to the JDBC type that is the default mapping for that particular type. Methods other than `setObject` do not, however, perform any general data type conversions. A `setObject` method can take any type (in the form of a generic `Object` object) and convert it to the specified JDBC type before sending it to the database. In order to be objects, values for built-in types need to be expressed in their `java.lang` class equivalents. For example, an `int` needs to be an instance of class `Integer`.

This method may be used to pass database-specific abstract data types by using a driver-specified Java type for *x* and using `java.sql.Types.OTHER` for *targetJdbcType*.

PARAMETERS:

parameterName	`String` object indicating the parameter name in the stored procedure definition
x	an instance of a Java `Object` containing the input parameter value
targetJdbcType	an integer constant representing the JDBC type (as defined in `java.sql.Types`) to be sent to the database

EXAMPLE:
```
Object x = new Integer(1234);
pstmt.setObject("SCORE", x, java.sql.Types.VARCHAR);
// sets SCORE parameter to 1234 and converts it to JDBC type VARCHAR
```

SEE:
`java.sql.Types`
"Using setObject" on page 651

setObject
`3.0`

```
void setObject(String parameterName, Object x) throws SQLException
```

Sets parameter *parameterName* to *x* and converts it using the standard mapping of Java `Object` types to JDBC types before sending it to the database. This standard mapping is shown in the table "Java Object Types Mapped to JDBC Types," on page 1090.

PARAMETERS:

parameterName	`String` object indicating the parameter name in the stored procedure definition
x	an instance of a Java `Object` containing the input parameter value

EXAMPLE:
```
Object x = new Long(1234567890345000);
```

```
pstmt.setObject("ORDER_NO", x);
// sets the first parameter to 1234567890345000
```

SEE:
"Using setObject" on page 651

setShort

`3.0`

void **setShort**(String *parameterName*, short *x*) throws SQLException

Sets parameter *parameterName* to *x*. The driver converts this to a JDBC SMALLINT value when it sends it to the database.

PARAMETERS:

parameterName	String object indicating the parameter name in the stored procedure definition
x	the short value to which the parameter will be set

EXAMPLE:
```
pstmt.setShort("TYPE", (short)8); // sets TYPE parameter to 8
```

setString

`3.0`

void **setString**(String *parameterName*, String *x*) throws SQLException

Sets parameter *parameterName* to *x*. The driver converts this to a JDBC VARCHAR or LONGVARCHAR value (depending on the argument's size relative to the driver's limits on VARCHARs) when it sends it to the database.

PARAMETERS:

parameterName	String object indicating the parameter name in the stored procedure definition
x	the String object in the Java programming language to which the parameter will be set

EXAMPLE:
```
String x = "Happy Days"
pstmt.setString("TITLE", x);
// sets TITLE parameter to "Happy Days"
```

3.0 setTime

```
void setTime(String parameterName, java.sql.Time x) throws SQLException
```

Sets parameter *parameterName* to *x*. The driver converts this to a JDBC TIME value when it sends it to the database.

PARAMETERS:

parameterName	String object indicating the parameter name in the stored procedure definition
x	the java.sql.Time object to which the parameter will be set

EXAMPLE:
```
Time t = new Time(3456934567L);
pstmt.setTime("START", t);
```

SEE:
java.sql.Time

3.0 setTime

```
void setTime(String parameterName, java.sql.Time x,
                      java.util.Calendar cal) throws SQLException
```

Sets parameter *parameterName* to *x*. When the DBMS does not store time zone information, the driver will use *cal* to construct a JDBC TIME value, which it will then send to the database. With a Calendar object, the driver can calculate the time taking into account a custom time zone. If no Calendar object is specified, the driver uses the time zone of the Virtual Machine that is running the application.

PARAMETERS:

parameterName	String object indicating the parameter name in the stored procedure definition
x	the java.sql.Time object to which the parameter will be set
cal	the Calendar object the driver will use to calculate the time

EXAMPLE:
```
Time t = new Time(23502938562L);
pstmt.setTime("TOTALS", t, cal); //sets TOTALS parameter to t, using
```

```
// cal to calculate the time
```

SEE:
java.sql.Time

setTimestamp

3.0

```
void setTimestamp(String parameterName, java.sql.Timestamp x)
                                          throws SQLException
```

Sets parameter *parameterName* to *x*. The driver converts this to a JDBC TIMESTAMP value when it sends it to the database.

PARAMETERS:

parameterName	String object indicating the parameter name in the stored procedure definition
x	a java.sql.Timestamp object

EXAMPLE:
```
Timestamp ts = new Timestamp(25035912512350392L);
pstmt.setTimestamp("RECD", ts); // sets RECD parameter to ts
```

SEE:
java.sql.Timestamp

setTimestamp

3.0

```
void setTimestamp(String parameterName, java.sql.Timestamp x,
                    java.util.Calendar cal) throws SQLException
```

Sets parameter *parameterName* to *x*. When the DBMS does not store time zone information, the driver will use *cal* to construct a Timestamp object, which it converts to an SQL TIMESTAMP value and then sends to the database. With a Calendar object, the driver can calculate the Timestamp object taking into account a custom time zone. If no Calendar object is specified, the driver uses the time zone of the Virtual Machine that is running the application.

PARAMETERS:

parameterName	String object indicating the parameter name in the stored procedure definition

x	the java.sql.Timestamp object to which the parameter will be set
cal	the Calendar object the driver will use to construct the Timestamp object

EXAMPLE:
```
Timestamp ts = new Timestamp(2934581625910L);
pstmt.setTimestamp("SHIPPED", ts, cal); // sets SHIPPED parameter
// to ts, using cal to construct the timestamp
```

SEE:
```
java.sql.Timestamp
```

3.0   setURL

```
void setURL(String parameterName, java.net.URL val)
                                        throws SQLException;
```

Sets the parameter *parameterName* to the given java.net.URL object. The driver converts *val* to an SQL DATALINK value when it sends it to the database.

PARAMETERS:

parameterIndex or	1 indicates the first parameter, 2 the second, and so on
parameterName	String object indicating the parameter name in the stored procedure definition
val	the java.net.URL object to which the parameter will be set

THROWS:
SQLException if the java.net.URL object is malformed

EXAMPLE:
```
java.net.URL val = new java.net.URL("http://gizmos.com/orders");
pstmt.setURL("RECEIVER", val);
```

wasNull

```
boolean wasNull() throws SQLException
```

Indicates whether or not the last OUT parameter read had the value SQL

NULL. Note that this method should be called only after calling one of the getter methods; otherwise, there is no value to use in determining whether it is
null or not.

RETURNS:
true if the last parameter read was SQL NULL; false otherwise

EXAMPLE:
```
String s = cstmt.getString(2);
boolean b = cstmt.wasNull(); // b is true if s was SQL NULL
```

CHAPTER 10

Clob 2.0

10.1 Clob Overview

A Clob object represents the Java programming language mapping of an SQL
CLOB (Character Large Object). An SQL CLOB is a built-in type that stores a Character
Large Object as a column value in a row of a database table. Methods in the
interfaces ResultSet, CallableStatement, and PreparedStatement allow a programmer
to access the SQL99 type CLOB in the same way that more basic SQL types
are accessed. In other words, an application uses methods such as getClob and set-
Clob for a CLOB value the same way it uses getInt and setInt for an INTEGER value
or getString and setString for a CHAR or VARCHAR value.

The standard implementation is for a JDBC driver to implement the Clob
interface using the SQL type LOCATOR(CLOB) behind the scenes. A LOCATOR(CLOB)
designates an SQL CLOB residing on a database server, and operations on the locator
achieve the same results as operations on the CLOB itself. This means that a client
can operate on a Clob instance without ever having to bring the CLOB data over
to the client machine. The driver uses LOCATOR(CLOB) behind the scenes, making
its use completely transparent to the JDBC programmer. Being able to operate on
a CLOB value without having to bring its contents over to the client can be a real
boost in efficiency, especially if the CLOB value is very large.

The standard behavior for a Clob instance is to remain valid until the transaction
in which it was created is either committed or rolled back.

The interface Clob provides methods for getting the length of an SQL CLOB
value, for materializing the data in a CLOB value on the client, and for searching for
a substring or CLOB object within a CLOB value. The JDBC 3.0 API added methods
for updating a CLOB value programmatically and also a method for truncating a 3.0
CLOB value.

10.1.1   Creating a Clob Object

The following code fragment illustrates creating a Clob object, where *rs* is a
ResultSet object:

```
Clob clob = rs.getClob(1);
```

The variable *clob* can now be used to operate on the CLOB value that is stored
in the first column of the result set *rs*.

10.1.2   Materializing Clob Data

Programmers can invoke Clob methods on a Clob object as if they were operating
on the SQL CLOB value it represents. However, if they want to operate on CLOB data,
they must first materialize the data of the CLOB value on the client. In other words,
they must retrieve the CLOB value's data and put it in memory on the client in the
form of a Java object. The Clob interface provides three ways to do this:

1. getAsciiStream materializes the CLOB value as a byte stream containing Ascii
   bytes

   ```
   Clob notes = rs.getClob("NOTES");
   java.io.InputStream in = notes.getAsciiStream();
   byte b = in.read();
   // in contains the characters in the CLOB value designated by
   // notes as Ascii bytes; b contains the first character as an Ascii
   // byte
   ```

2. getCharacterStream materializes the CLOB value as a stream of Unicode characters

   ```
   Clob notes = rs.getClob("NOTES");
   java.io.Reader reader = notes.getCharacterStream();
   int c = reader.read();
   // c contains the first character in the CLOB value that notes
   // represents
   ```

3. getSubString materializes all or part of the CLOB value as a String object

```
Clob notes = rs.getClob(4);
String substring = notes.getSubString(10, 5);
// substring contains five characters, starting with the tenth
// character of the CLOB value that notes represents

long len = notes.length();
String substring = notes.getSubString(1, (int)len);
// substring contains all of the characters in the CLOB value that
// notes represents
```

10.1.3 Storing a Clob Object

To store a Clob object in the database, it is passed as a parameter to the Prepared-Statement method setClob. For example, the following code fragment stores the Clob object *notes* by passing it as the first input parameter to the PreparedStatement object *pstmt*:

```
Clob notes = rs.getClob("NOTES");
PreparedStatement pstmt = con.prepareStatement(
        "UPDATE SALES_STATS SET COMMENTS = ? WHERE SALES > 500000");
pstmt.setClob(1, notes);
pstmt.executeUpdate();
```

The CLOB value designated by *notes* is now stored in the table SALES_STATS in column COMMENTS in every row where the value in the column SALES is greater than 500000.

10.1.4 Updating a Clob Object

The JDBC 3.0 API adds five methods to the Clob interface, all of which modify a CLOB value in some way. One method truncates a CLOB value to a given length, and the other four add data to it. Two methods add data directly by writing all or part of a given String object at a specified position in the CLOB value. The other two return a stream that will write to the CLOB value starting at a specified position. The stream can read data in and then call its write method to write its contents to the CLOB value. The key concept is that when the write method for these streams is invoked, the streams will automatically write to the Clob object that created them, and they will begin writing at the position specified when they were created.

The method `setString` has two versions, one for adding an entire `String` object and one for adding part of a `String` object. The following code fragment illustrates inserting all of a `String` object. It writes the `String` object *str* to the `Clob` object *clob*, starting at the 128th character in *clob*. The variable *charsWritten* will be `str.length()`.

```
Clob clob = rs.getClob(2);
String str = "Time waits for no man--or woman.";
int charsWritten = clob.setString(128, str);
```

Note that the characters in *clob* will be overwritten by those in *str*. In other words, the first character in *str* will replace the character at position 128 in *clob*, the second character in *str* will replace character 129 in *clob*, and so on.

The second version of the method `setString` takes the same two parameters as the first version plus two additional parameters to specify the part of a `String` object that is to be added to a `CLOB` value. The third parameter is an `int` giving the offset into *str*, which indicates the first character in *str* to be inserted into *clob*. The fourth parameter is an `int` indicating the number of consecutive characters, starting from the offset, that will be written to *clob*. In this case, *charsWritten* should equal 49, the number of characters from *str* to be written.

```
Clob clob = rs.getClob("SUMMARY");
String str = "This study shows that even when you are slow, " +
                "you are not always right.";
int charsWritten = clob.setString(clob.length() + 1, str, 22, 49);
```

At this point, *clob* should have "even when you are slow, you are not always right." appended to it. Note that the first character in a `String` object is at position 0, so the twenty-third character in *str* is at offset 22.

The methods `setAsciiStream` and `setCharacterStream` both create a stream that will write to the `Clob` object that invoked them. The difference is that `setAsciiStream` writes characters as Ascii bytes, and `setCharacterStream` writes Unicode characters. For example, the following code fragment creates a `java.io.Writer` object that is set to write Unicode characters, beginning after the last character in *clob*. In this case,

```
Clob clob = rs.getClob(4);
java.io.Writer writer = clob.setCharacterStream(clob.length() + 1);
```

10.1.5   Locators and Updates

3.0

The standard implementation for a `Clob` object, which represents an SQL `CLOB` value, is to use an SQL `LOCATOR` type. A locator works as a pointer to the value stored in the database, and how a DBMS handles updates to an object implemented as a locator depends on the particular DBMS. When a `Clob` method like `setString` changes the value of a `Clob` object, some DBMSs update the `CLOB` value in the database table, but some update only a copy of the `CLOB` value and do not change the value in the database. When the latter case is true, an application must update the `CLOB` value directly.

To find out how the DBMS handles updates to `CLOB` values, an application can call the `DatabaseMetaData` method `locatorsUpdateCopy`. If this method returns `true`, the application needs to update `CLOB` values in the database. The following code fragment is an example of how this can be done. It first retrieves a `Clob` object from the `ResultSet` object *rs* and changes its value to that of the `String` *descrip*. If the method `locatorsUpdateCopy` returns `true`, it then executes a `PreparedStatement` object to update the `CLOB` value in the database. If the method `locatorsUpdateCopy` returns `false`, the code in the `if` block does nothing because the value has already been updated in the database.

```
Clob clob = rs.getClob(2);
String descrip = "History of civilization from 1200 to 1800.";
int charsWritten = clob.setString(128, descrip);
if (dbmd.locatorsUpdateCopy() == true) {
    PreparedStatement pstmt = con.prepareStatement(
        "UPDATE COURSES SET DESCRIP = ? WHERE NAME = ?");
    pstmt.setClob("DESCRIP", descrip);
    pstmt.setString("NAME", "History_1B");
    pstmt.executeUpdate();
}
```

10.2   Clob Interface Definition

```
package java.sql;
public interface java.sql.Clob {
    long length() throws SQLException;
    InputStream getAsciiStream() throws SQLException;
    Reader getCharacterStream() throws SQLException;
```

`2.0` String **getSubString**(long *pos*, int *length*) throws SQLException;

`2.0` long **position**(String *searchstr*, long *start*) throws SQLException;
`2.0` long **position**(Clob *searchstr*, long *start*) throws SQLException;

`3.0` int **setString**(long *pos*, String *str*) throws SQLException;
`3.0` int **setString**(long *pos*, String *str*, int *offset*, int *len*)
                                             throws SQLException;
`3.0` java.io.OutputStream **setAsciiStream**(long *pos*) throws SQLException;
`3.0` java.io.Writer **setCharacterStream**(long *pos*) throws SQLException;
`3.0` void **truncate**(long *len*) throws SQLException;
    }

10.3   Clob Methods

`2.0` ### getAsciiStream

InputStream **getAsciiStream**() throws SQLException

Materializes the CLOB value designated by this Clob object as a stream of Ascii bytes.

RETURNS:
an InputStream object with all the data in the CLOB value designated by this Clob object as Ascii bytes

EXAMPLE:
java.io.InputStream in = clob.getAsciiStream();
byte b = in.read();
// in has all of the characters in the CLOB value designated by
// clob as Ascii bytes; b designates the first character as an Ascii
// byte

`2.0` ### getCharacterStream

Reader **getCharacterStream**() throws SQLException

Materializes the CLOB value designated by this Clob object as a stream of Unicode characters.

RETURNS:
a Reader object with all the data in the CLOB value designated by this Clob object as Unicode characters

EXAMPLE:
```
Reader read = clob.getCharacterStream();
// read has all the data in the CLOB value designated by clob
// as Unicode characters
```

getSubString

2.0

```
String getSubString(long pos, int length) throws SQLException
```

Returns a copy of the portion of the CLOB value represented by this Clob object that starts at position *pos* and has up to *length* consecutive characters.

PARAMETERS:

pos	the position of the first char to extract from the CLOB value designated by this Clob object; the initial position is 1
length	the number of consecutive characters to be copied

RETURNS:
a String object containing a copy of up to *length* consecutive characters from the CLOB value represented by this Clob object, starting with the char at position *pos*

EXAMPLE:
```
String substr = clob.getSubString(1, 100);
// substr contains the first 100 characters (those in positions 1
// through 100, inclusive) in the CLOB value designated by clob
```

length

2.0

```
long length() throws SQLException
```

Returns the number of characters in the CLOB value designated by this Clob object.

RETURNS:
the length in characters of the CLOB value that this Clob object represents

EXAMPLE:
```
Clob clob = rs.getClob(3);
long len = clob.length();
// len contains the number of characters in the CLOB value
// designated by clob
```

2.0 position

```
long position(Clob searchstr, long start) throws SQLException
```

Determines the character position at which the Clob object *searchstr* begins within the CLOB value that this Clob object represents. The search begins at position *start*.

PARAMETERS:

searchstr	the Clob object for which to search
start	the position at which to begin searching; the first character is at position 1, the second character is at position 2, and so on

RETURNS:
the position at which the Clob object *searchstr* begins, which will be *start* or larger if the search is successful; -1 otherwise

EXAMPLE:
```
Clob clob1 = rs1.getClob(1);
Clob clob2 = rs2.getClob(4);
long beginning = clob1.position(clob2, 1024);
// if clob2 is contained in clob1 starting at position 1024 or later,
// beginning will contain the position at which clob2 begins
```

2.0 position

```
long position(String searchstr, long start) throws SQLException
```

Determines the position at which the String *searchstr* begins within the

CLOB value that this Clob object represents. The search begins at position *start*.

PARAMETERS:

searchstr   the String object for which to search

start   the position at which to begin searching; the first character is at position 1, the second character is at position 2, and so on

RETURNS:

the position at which the String object *searchstr* begins, which will be *start* or larger if the search, starting at position *start*, is successful; -1 otherwise

EXAMPLE:
```
String searchstr= clob.getSubString(5, 100);
long beginning = clob.position(searchstr, 1024);
// if searchstr is contained in clob from position 1024 on, beginning
// will contain the position at which searchstr begins
```

setAsciiStream

3.0

```
java.io.OutputStream setAsciiStream(long pos) throws SQLException
```

Returns a java.io.OuputStream object that can write Ascii bytes to the CLOB value that this Clob object represents. The output stream will start writing at position *pos* in the CLOB value.

PARAMETERS:

pos   the position in the CLOB value at which the new Output-Stream object will begin writing; the first character is at position 1

RETURNS:

an OutputStream object that can write Ascii encoded characters to the CLOB value, starting at the designated position in the CLOB value

EXAMPLE:
```
java.io.OutputStream out = clob.setAsciiStream(256);
FileInputStream in = new FileInputStream("asciifile.txt");
byte [] buf = byte[256];
in.read(buf, 0, 256);
out.write(buf, 0, 256);
// out writes 256 Ascii bytes from buf, starting with byte 0 in
```

```
// buf. The OutputStream object out begins writing at byte 256 in
// the CLOB value.
```

setCharacterStream
`3.0`

```
java.io.Writer setCharacterStream(long pos) throws SQLException
```

Returns a java.io.Writer object that can be used to write Unicode characters to the CLOB value that this Clob object represents. The Writer object will start writing at position *pos* in the CLOB value.

PARAMETERS:

pos   the position in the CLOB value at which the new Writer object will begin writing; the first character is at position 1

RETURNS:
a Writer object to which Unicode characters can be written

EXAMPLE:
```
java.io.Writer writer = clob.setCharacterStream(1);
// Unicode characters can be written to writer, and then writer can
// be used to write the Unicode characters to clob, starting at the
// beginning of clob
```

setString
`3.0`

```
int setString(long pos, String str) throws SQLException
```

Inserts *str* into the CLOB value that this Clob object represents, starting at position *pos*.

PARAMETERS:

pos   the position in the CLOB value at which to start writing *str*; the first character is at position 1

str   the String object that will be inserted into the CLOB value

RETURNS:
an int indicating how many characters were written

EXAMPLE:
```
String str = "Introduction: ";
int charsWritten = clob.setString(0, str);
// str is prepended to clob, and charsWritten is 15
```

setString

3.0

```
int setString(long pos, String str, int offset, int len)
                                        throws SQLException
```

Inserts the designated portion of *str* into the CLOB value that this Clob object represents, starting at position *pos*. The portion of *str* to be inserted starts at *offset* and continues for *len* consecutive characters.

PARAMETERS:

pos	the position in the CLOB value at which to start writing the designated portion of *str*; the first character is at position 1
str	the String object that contains the characters to be inserted into the CLOB value
offset	an int indicating the offset into *str* at which to start reading. This determines the beginning of the characters to be inserted into the CLOB value. The first character is at offset of 0.
len	an int indicating the number of consecutive characters from *str*, with the first character being at position *offset*, to be inserted into the CLOB value

RETURNS:
an int indicating how many characters were written

EXAMPLE:
```
String str = "The end is near.";
int charsWritten = clob.setString(clob.length() + 1, str, 0, 7);
// "The end" is appended to clob, and charsWritten is 7
```

truncate

3.0

```
void truncate(long len) throws SQLException
```

Truncates the CLOB value that this Clob object represents so that it is *len* bytes long. If the length of the CLOB value is *len* bytes or less, this method does nothing.

PARAMETERS:

len   a long indicating the number of bytes to which the BLOB
                          value is to be truncated

EXAMPLE:
```
clob.truncate(1024);
// The CLOB value that clob represents now has only the first 1024
// bytes. Byte 1025 and all bytes following it have been deleted.
```

CHAPTER 11

Connection

11.1 `Connection` Overview

A `Connection` object represents a connection with a database. A connection session includes the SQL statements that are executed and the results that are returned over that connection. A single application can have one or more connections with a single database, or it can have connections with many different databases.

A user can get information about a `Connection` object's database by invoking the `Connection.getMetaData` method. This method returns a `DatabaseMetaData` object that contains information about the database's tables, the SQL grammar it supports, its stored procedures, the capabilities of this connection, and so on. Readers who want more information can check "DatabaseMetaData," on page 449.

11.1.1 Opening a Connection

The traditional way to establish a connection with a database is to call the method `DriverManager.getConnection`, which takes a string containing a URL. The `DriverManager` class, referred to as the JDBC management layer, attempts to locate a driver that can connect to the database represented by the given URL. The `DriverManager` class maintains a list of registered `Driver` classes, and when the method `getConnection` is called, it checks with each driver in the list until it finds one that can connect to the database specified in the URL. The `Driver` method `connect` uses this URL to actually establish the connection.

A user can bypass the JDBC management layer and call `Driver` methods directly. This could be useful in the rare case that two drivers can connect to a database and the user wants to explicitly select a particular driver. Normally, however, it is much easier to just let the `DriverManager` class handle opening a connection. The chapters "Driver," on page 603 and "DriverManager," on page 611 give more detailed information.

The following code exemplifies opening a connection to a database located at the URL `jdbc:odbc:wombat` with a user ID of oboy and 12Java as the password:

```
String url = "jdbc:odbc:wombat";
Connection con = DriverManager.getConnection(url, "oboy", "12Java");
```

2.0

The `DataSource` interface is the preferred alternative to the `DriverManager` for establishing a connection. When a `DataSource` class has been implemented appropriately, a `DataSource` object can be used to produce `Connection` objects that participate in connection pooling, distributed transactions, or both. See Chapter 16, "DataSource," starting on page 565, for more information and to see example code for creating a connection using a `DataSource` object. Refer to the section "Advantages of Using JNDI," on page 575, to see why using a `DataSource` object is the preferred alternative for creating a connection.

An application uses a `Connection` object produced by a `DataSource` object in essentially the same way it uses a `Connection` object produced by the `DriverManager`. There are some differences, however. If the `Connection` object is a pooled connection, an application should include a `finally` block to assure that the connection is closed even if an exception is thrown. That way a valid connection will always be put back into the pool of available connections. See Chapter 24, "PooledConnection," starting on page 637, for more information on `Connection` objects that participate in connection pooling. The section "Application Code for Connection Pooling," on page 637, gives an example of a `finally` block that closes a connection.

If a `Connection` object is part of a distributed transaction, an application should not call the methods `Connection.commit` or `Connection.rollback`, nor should it turn on the connection's auto-commit mode. These would interfere with the transaction manager's handling of the distributed transaction. See Chapter 48, "XAConnection," starting on page 1039, for more information.

11.1.2 URLs in General Use

When an application uses the `DriverManager` to create a `Connection` object, it must supply a URL to the `DriverManager.getConnection` method. Since URLs often cause some confusion, we will first give a brief explanation of URLs in general and then go on to a discussion of JDBC URLs.

A URL (Uniform Resource Locator) gives information for locating a resource on the Internet. It can be thought of as an address.

The first part of a URL specifies the protocol used to access information, and it is always followed by a colon. Some common protocols are `ftp`, which specifies "file transfer protocol," and `http`, which specifies "hypertext transfer protocol." If the protocol is `file`, it indicates that the resource is in a local file system rather than on the Internet. The following example URLs illustrate these three protocols.

```
ftp://java.sun.com/docs/apidocs.zip
http://java.sun.com/products/JDK/CurrentRelease
file:/home/haroldw/docs/tutorial.html
```

The rest of a URL, everything after the first colon, gives information about where the data source is located. If the protocol is `file`, the rest of the URL is the path for the file. For the protocols `ftp` and `http`, the rest of the URL identifies the host and may optionally give a path to a more specific site. For example, here is the URL for the home page for the Java platforms. This URL identifies only the host:

```
http://www.java.sun.com
```

By navigating from this home page, you can go to many other pages, one of which is the JDBC home page. The URL for the JDBC home page is more specific and looks like this:

```
http://www.java.sun.com/products/jdbc
```

11.1.3 JDBC URLs

A JDBC URL provides a way of identifying a data source so that the appropriate driver will recognize it and establish a connection with it. Driver writers are the ones who actually determine what the JDBC URL that identifies a particular driver will be. Users do not need to worry about how to form a JDBC URL; they simply use the URL supplied with the drivers they are using. JDBC's role is to recommend some conventions for driver writers to follow in structuring their JDBC URLs.

Since JDBC URLs are used with various kinds of drivers, the conventions are, of necessity, very flexible. First, they allow different drivers to use different schemes for naming databases. The odbc subprotocol, for example, lets the URL contain attribute values (but does not require them).

Second, JDBC URLs allow driver writers to encode all necessary connection information within them. This makes it possible, for example, for an applet that wants to talk to a given database to open the database connection without requiring the user to do any system administration chores.

Third, JDBC URLs allow a level of indirection. This means that the JDBC URL may refer to a logical host or database name that is dynamically translated to the actual name by a network naming system. This allows system administrators to avoid specifying particular hosts as part of the JDBC name. There are a number of different network name services (such as DNS, NIS, and DCE), and there is no restriction about which ones can be used.

The standard syntax for JDBC URLs is shown here. It has three parts, which are separated by colons.

```
jdbc:<subprotocol>:<subname>
```

The three parts of a JDBC URL are broken down as follows:

1. jdbc—the protocol. The protocol in a JDBC URL is always jdbc.

2. <subprotocol>—the name of the driver or the name of a database connectivity mechanism, which may be supported by one or more drivers. A prominent example of a subprotocol name is odbc, which has been reserved for URLs that specify ODBC–style data source names. For example, to access a database through a JDBC–ODBC bridge, one might use a URL such as the following:

   ```
   jdbc:odbc:fred
   ```

   In this example, the subprotocol is odbc, and the subname fred is a local ODBC data source.

   If one wants to use a network name service (so that the database name in the JDBC URL does not have to be its actual name), the naming service can be the subprotocol. So, for example, one might have a URL like:

   ```
   jdbc:dcenaming:accounts-payable
   ```

In this example, the URL specifies that the local DCE naming service should resolve the database name `accounts-payable` into a more specific name that can be used to connect to the real database.

3. `<subname>`—a way to identify the data source. The subname can vary, depending on the subprotocol, and it can have any internal syntax the driver writer chooses, including a subsubname. The point of a subname is to give enough information to locate the data source. In the previous example, `fred` is enough because ODBC provides the remainder of the information. A data source on a remote server requires more information, however. If the data source is to be accessed over the Internet, for example, the network address should be included in the JDBC URL as part of the subname and should adhere to the following standard URL naming convention:

```
//hostname:port/subsubname
```

Supposing that `dbnet` is a protocol for connecting to a host on the Internet, a JDBC URL might look like this:

```
jdbc:dbnet://wombat:356/fred
```

11.1.4   The odbc Subprotocol

The subprotocol `odbc` is a special case. It has been reserved for URLs that specify ODBC-style data source names and has the special feature of allowing any number of attribute values to be specified after the subname (the data source name). The full syntax for the odbc subprotocol is:

```
jdbc:odbc:<data-source-name>[;<attribute-name>=<attribute-value>]*
```

Thus all of the following are valid jdbc:odbc names:

```
jdbc:odbc:qeor7
jdbc:odbc:wombat
jdbc:odbc:wombat;CacheSize=20;ExtensionCase=LOWER
jdbc:odbc:qeora;UID=kgh;PWD=fooey
```

11.1.5 Registering Subprotocols

A driver developer can reserve a name to be used as the subprotocol in a JDBC URL. When the `DriverManager` class presents this name to its list of registered drivers, the driver for which this name is reserved should recognize it and establish a connection to the database it identifies. For example, "odbc" is reserved for the JDBC–ODBC Bridge. If there were a Miracle Corporation, it might want to register "miracle" as the subprotocol for the JDBC driver that connects to its Miracle DBMS so that no one else would use that name.

Sun Microsystems is acting as an informal registry for JDBC subprotocol names. To register a subprotocol name, send e-mail to:

```
jdbc@sun.com
```

11.1.6 Sending SQL Statements

Once a connection is established, it is used to pass SQL statements to its underlying database. The JDBC API does not put any restrictions on the kinds of SQL statements that can be sent; this provides a great deal of flexibility, allowing the use of database-specific statements or even non-SQL statements. It requires, however, that the user be responsible for making sure that the underlying database can process the SQL statements being sent and suffer the consequences if it cannot. For example, an application that tries to send a stored procedure call to a DBMS that does not support stored procedures will be unsuccessful and will generate an exception.

The JDBC API provides three interfaces for sending SQL statements to the database, and corresponding methods in the `Connection` interface create instances of them. The interfaces for sending SQL statements and the `Connection` methods that create them are as follows:

1. `Statement`—created by the `Connection.createStatement` methods. A `Statement` object is used for sending SQL statements with no parameters.

2. `PreparedStatement`—created by the `Connection.prepareStatement` methods. A `PreparedStatement` object is used for precompiled SQL statements. These can take one or more parameters as input arguments (IN parameters). `PreparedStatement` has a group of methods that set the value of IN parameters, which are sent to the database when the statement is executed. `PreparedStatement` extends `Statement` and therefore includes `Statement` methods. A `PreparedStatement` object has the potential to be more efficient than a `Statement` object because it has been precompiled and temporarily stored for future use. Therefore, in order to improve performance, a `PreparedStatement` object is

sometimes used for an SQL statement that is executed many times.

3. `CallableStatement`—created by the `Connection.prepareCall` methods. `CallableStatement` objects are used to execute SQL stored procedures—a group of SQL statements that is called by name, much like invoking a function. A `CallableStatement` object inherits methods for handling IN parameters from `PreparedStatement`; it adds methods for handling OUT and INOUT parameters.

The following list gives a quick way to determine which `Connection` method is appropriate for creating different types of SQL statements:

- `createStatement` methods—for a simple SQL statement with no parameters

- `prepareStatement` methods—for an SQL statement that is executed repeatedly

- `prepareCall` methods—for a call to a stored procedure

The basic versions of these methods (the ones that take no `ResultSet` constants as arguments) create statements that will produce default `ResultSet` objects; that is, they produce `ResultSet` objects that are not scrollable and that cannot be updated. By using versions of the methods `createStatement`, `prepareStatement`, and `prepareCall` that take additional parameters for specifying the type of result set and the concurrency level, it is possible to create statements that will produce result sets that are scrollable, updatable, or both. The section "Types of Result Sets," on page 700, explains the different types of `ResultSet` objects and the constants that specify them. The section "Concurrency Types," on page 701, does the same for concurrency levels.

Another feature that determines the behavior of a result set is its *holdability*, that is, its ability to remain open after the `Connection` method `commit` has been called. Some DBMSs automatically close a `ResultSet` object when the transaction in which it was created is committed. New versions of the `Connection` methods for creating statements together with new constants in the `ResultSet` interface, added in the JDBC 3.0 API, make it possible to specify the holdability of result sets that the newly created statements will produce.

"Creating Different Types of Result Sets," on page 705, gives examples of how to create `ResultSet` objects using the new versions of the `Connection` methods for creating statements.

An application can set the holdability of ResultSet objects produced by statements that a connection creates by calling the Connection method setHoldability. For example, in the following code fragment, the Connection object *con* first creates the Statement object *stmt1*, which will produce ResultSet objects that are scrollable, are sensitive to changes made by others, are updatable, and have cursors that remain open across commits. Then *con* sets its holdability so that statements it creates will produce ResultSet objects whose cursors are closed when the method commit is called. Consequently, ResultSet objects produced by *stmt2* will not remain open across commits. Finally, the code checks the holdability that ResultSet objects will have when they are produced by statements that *con* creates.

```
Statement stmt = con.createStatement(
                    ResultSet.TYPE_SCROLL_SENSITIVE,
                    ResultSet.CONCUR_UPDATABLE,
                    ResultSet.HOLD_CURSORS_OVER_COMMIT);
... //
con.setHoldability(ResultSet.CLOSE_CURSORS_AT_COMMIT);
Statement stmt2 = con.createStatement();
int holdability = con.getHoldability();
```

11.1.7 Transactions

A transaction consists of one or more statements that have been executed, completed, and then either committed or rolled back. When the method commit or rollback is called, the current transaction ends and another one begins.

Generally a new Connection object is in auto-commit mode by default, meaning that when a statement is completed, the method commit will be called on that statement automatically. In this case, since each statement is committed individually, a transaction consists of only one statement. If auto-commit mode has been disabled, a transaction will not terminate until the method commit or rollback is called explicitly, so it will include all the statements that have been executed since the last invocation of either commit or rollback. In this second case, all the statements in the transaction are committed or rolled back as a group.

The beginning of a transaction requires no explicit call; it is implicitly initiated after disabling auto-commit mode or after calling the methods commit or rollback. The method commit makes permanent any changes an SQL statement makes to a database, and it also releases any locks held by the transaction. The method rollback will discard those changes.

Sometimes a user doesn't want one change to take effect unless another one does also. This can be accomplished by disabling auto-commit and grouping both updates into one transaction. If both updates are successful, then the `commit` method is called, making the effects of both updates permanent; if one fails or both fail, then the `rollback` method is called, restoring the values that existed before the updates were executed.

Most JDBC drivers will support transactions. In order to be designated JDBC Compliant, a JDBC driver must support transactions.

The JDBC 2.0 Optional Package API made it possible for `Connection` objects to be part of a distributed transaction, a transaction that involves connections to more than one DBMS server. When a `Connection` object is part of a distributed transaction, a transaction manager determines when the methods `commit` or `rollback` are called on it. Thus, when a `Connection` object is participating in a distributed transaction, an application should not do anything that affects when a connection begins or ends.

In order to be able to participate in distributed transactions, a `Connection` object must be produced by a `DataSource` object that has been implemented to work with the middle-tier server's distributed transaction infrastructure. Unlike `Connection` objects produced by the `DriverManager`, a `Connection` object produced by such a `DataSource` object will automatically have its auto-commit mode disabled. A standard implementation of a `DataSource` object, on the other hand, will produce `Connection` objects that are exactly the same as those produced by the `DriverManager` class. The section "DataSource Implementations," on page 571, discusses the different ways the `DataSource` interface can be implemented.

11.1.8 Transaction Isolation Levels

If a DBMS supports transaction processing, it will have some way of managing potential conflicts that can arise when two transactions are operating on a database at the same time. A user can specify a transaction isolation level to indicate what level of care the DBMS should exercise in resolving potential conflicts. For example, what happens when one transaction changes a value and a second transaction reads that value before the change has been committed or rolled back? Should that be allowed, given that the changed value read by the second transaction will be invalid if the first transaction is rolled back? A JDBC user can instruct the DBMS to allow a value to be read before it has been committed (a "dirty read") with the following code, where *con* is the current connection:

```
con.setTransactionIsolation(TRANSACTION_READ_UNCOMMITTED);
```

The higher the transaction isolation level, the more care is taken to avoid conflicts. The Connection interface defines five levels, with the lowest specifying that transactions are not supported at all and the highest specifying that while one transaction is operating on a database, no other transactions may make any changes to the data read by that transaction. TRANSACTION_READ_UNCOMMITTED, used in the previous example, is one level up from the lowest level. Typically, the higher the level of isolation, the slower the application executes (due to increased locking overhead and decreased concurrency between users). The developer must balance the need for performance/concurrent access with the need for data consistency when making a decision about what isolation level to use. Of course, the level that can actually be supported depends on the capabilities of the underlying DBMS.

When a new Connection object is created, its transaction isolation level depends on the driver, but normally it is the default for the underlying data source. A user may call the method setTransactionIsolation to change the transaction isolation level, and the new level will be in effect for the rest of the connection session. To change the transaction isolation level for just one transaction, one needs to set it before executing any statements in the transaction and then reset it after the transaction terminates. Changing the transaction isolation level during a transaction is not recommended because it will trigger an immediate call to the method commit, causing any changes up to that point to be made permanent.

11.1.9   Using Savepoints

An application can gain finer-grained control over a transaction by using savepoints, represented in the JDBC API by the Savepoint interface. A savepoint is a point within a transaction that marks an intermediate point to which a transaction may be rolled back. In a transaction with no savepoints set, calling the rollback method rolls back the entire transaction. If a savepoint has been set, however, the application can control whether the entire transaction is rolled back or if only part of the transaction is rolled back to the named point. Multiple savepoints may be set for a transaction, and the Savepoint object supplied to the method rollback indicates the point to which the rollback takes effect. In other words, everything in the current transaction before the savepoint will be saved; everything after it will be rolled back.

The JDBC 3.0 API added the Savepoint interface and also several Connection methods for setting, releasing, and using Savepoint objects. Two versions of the Connection method setSavepoint create Savepoint objects and set them at the point in the current transaction where they were created. Another Connection method, `releaseSavepoint`, removes a `Savepoint` object. An application uses a `Savepoint` object by passing it to the `Connection` method `rollback`, thereby indicating the point to which the transaction should be rolled back. "Savepoint," starting on page 889, gives a more complete explanation, including code examples showing how to create, use, and release `Savepoint` objects.

11.1.10 Freeing DBMS Resources

It is recommended that programmers explicitly close connections and statements they have created when they are no longer needed.

A programmer writing code in the Java programming language and not using any outside resources does not need to worry about memory management. The garbage collector automatically removes objects when they are no longer being used and frees the memory they were using. Periodically, it will recycle discarded objects, making the memory they currently occupy available for quick reuse.

However, if an application uses external resources, as it does when it accesses a DBMS with the JDBC API, the garbage collector has no way of knowing the status of those resources. It will still recycle discarded objects, but if there is plenty of free memory in the Java heap, it may garbage collect infrequently even though the (small) amount of Java garbage is holding open large amounts of expensive database resources. Therefore, it is recommended that programmers explicitly close all statements (with the method `Statement.close`) and all connections (with the method `Connection.close`) as soon as they are no longer needed, thereby freeing DBMS resources as early as possible. Even though closing a `Connection` object closes all of the statements it created, it is better to close statements explicitly as soon as possible rather than waiting to close the connection. This applies especially to applications that are intended to work with different DBMSs because of variations from one DBMS to another.

Note that the method `Connection.isClosed` is guaranteed to return `true` only when it is called after the method `Connection.close` has been called. As a result, a programmer cannot depend on this method to indicate whether a connection is valid or not. Instead, a typical JDBC client can determine that a connection is invalid by catching the exception that is thrown when a JDBC operation is attempted.

11.1.11 Using Type Maps

2.0

The two new SQL99 data types that are user-defined types (UDTs), SQL structured types and `DISTINCT` types, can be custom mapped to a class in the Java programming language. Like all the SQL99 data types, they have standard mappings, but a programmer may create a custom mapping as well. The fact that there is a custom mapping for a particular UDT is declared in a `java.util.Map` object. This `Map` object may be the one that is associated with a connection, or it may be one that is passed to a method.

A programmer declares a custom mapping by adding an entry to a `Map` object. This entry must contain two things: (1) the name of the UDT to be mapped and (2) the `Class` object for the class in the Java programming language to which the UDT is to be mapped. The class itself, which must implement the `SQLData` interface, will contain the specific mappings.

Each `Connection` object created using a driver that supports custom mapping will have an empty type map to which custom mappings may be added. This type map is an instance of the interface `java.util.Map`, which is new in the Java 2 platform and replaces `java.util.Dictionary`. Until custom map entries are added to this type map, all operations for `STRUCT` and `DISTINCT` values will use the standard mappings shown in the table "JDBC Types Mapped to Java Types," on page 1087.

The following code fragment, in which *con* is a `Connection` object and `ADDRESSES` is an SQL structured type, demonstrates retrieving the type map associated with *con* and adding a new entry to it. After the type map is modified, it is set as the new type map for *con*.

```
java.util.Map map = con.getTypeMap();
map.put("SchemaName.ADDRESSES", Addresses.class);
con.setTypeMap();
```

The `Map` object *map*, the type map associated with *con*, now contains at least one custom mapping (or more if any mappings have already been added). The programmer will have previously created the class `Addresses`, probably using a tool to generate it. Note that it is an error to supply a class that does not implement the interface `SQLData`. The class `Addresses`, which does implement `SQLData`, will have a field for each attribute in `ADDRESSES`, and whenever a value of type `ADDRESSES` is operated on by a method in the Java programming language, the default will be to map it to an instance of the class `Addresses`. The type map associated with a connection is the default type map in the sense that a method will use it if no other type map is explicitly passed to it.

Note that the name of the UDT should be the fully qualified name. For some DBMSs, this will be of the form `catalogName.schemaName.UDTName`. Many DBMSs, however, do not use this form and, for example, use a schema name but no catalog name. Programmers need to be sure that they are using the form appropriate for their particular DBMS. The `DatabaseMetaData` methods `getCatalogs`, `getCatalogTerm`, `getCatalogSeparator`, `getSchemas`, and `getSchemaTerm` give information about a DBMS's catalogs, schemas, preferred terms, and the separator it uses.

Instead of modifying the existing type map, an application can replace it with a completely different type map. This is done with the `Connection` method `setTypeMap`, as shown in the following code fragment. It creates a new type map, gives it two entries (each with an SQL UDT name and the class to which values of that type should be mapped), and then installs the new type map as the one associated with the `Connection` *con*.

```
java.util.Map newConnectionMap = new java.util.HashMap();
newConnectionMap.put(
            "SchemaName.UDTName1", ClassName1.class);
newConnectionMap.put(
            "SchemaName.UDTName2", ClassName2.class);
con.setTypeMap(newConnectionMap);
```

The `Map` object *newConnectionMap* now replaces the type map originally associated with the `Connection` *con*, and it will be used for custom type mappings unless it is itself replaced. Note that the example uses the default constructor for the class `HashMap` to create the new type map. This class is one of many implementations of `java.util.Map` provided in the Java 2 platform API, and one of the others could have been used as well. Also note that the example uses `ClassName.class` to indicate the `Class` object rather than the method `Class.forName("ClassName")`. Either is correct, but using `ClassName.class` has the advantage of being checked at compile time., whereas `Class.forName("ClassName")` will not be checked until run time.

In the previous examples, the type map associated with a connection was modified to contain additional mappings or set to be a different type map altogether. In either case, though, the connection's type map is the default for custom mapping JDBC types to types in the Java programming language. The next example will show how to supersede the connection's type map by supplying a method with a different type map.

Methods whose implementations may involve a custom mapping for UDTs have two versions, one that takes a type map and one that does not. If a type map is passed to one of these methods, the given type map will be used instead of the one associated with the connection. For example, the `Array` methods `getArray` and `getResultSet` have versions that take a type map and versions that do not. If a type map is passed to a method, it will map the array elements using the given type map. If no type map is specified, the method will use the type map associated with the connection.

The capability for supplying a type map to a method makes it possible for values of the same user-defined type to have different mappings. For example, if two applications are using the same connection and operating on the same column value, one could use the type map associated with the connection, and the other could use a different type map by supplying it as an argument to the appropriate method.

The following code fragment creates a new type map and provides it as a parameter to the `Array` method `getArray`.

```
java.util.Map arrayMap = new java.util.HashMap();
arrayMap.put("SchemaName.DIMENSIONS", Dimensions.class);
Dimensions [] d = (Dimensions [])array.getArray(arrayMap);
```

In the second line, the new type map *arrayMap* is given an entry with the fully qualified name of an SQL structured type (`SchemaName.DIMENSIONS`) and the Java class object (`Dimensions.class`). This establishes the mapping between the Java type `Dimensions` and the SQL type `DIMENSIONS`. In the third line, *arrayMap* is specified as the type map to use for mapping the contents of this `Array` object, whose base type is `SchemaName.DIMENSIONS`.

The method `getArray` will materialize the elements of the SQL99 `ARRAY` value designated by *array*, with each element being mapped according to the mapping specified in *arrayMap*. In other words, each element, which is a value of type `Schema.DIMENSIONS`, will be translated to an instance of the class `Dimensions` by mapping the attributes of each `DIMENSIONS` value to the fields of a `Dimensions` object. If the base type of the array does not match the UDT named in *arrayMap*, the driver will convert the array's elements according to the standard mapping. If no type map is specified to the method `getArray`, the driver uses the mapping indicated in the connection's type map. If that type map has no entry for `Schema.DIMENSIONS`, the driver will use the standard mapping instead.

For a complete discussion of custom mapping, see Chapter 37, "SQLData," starting on page 895.

11.2   Connection Interface Definition

```java
package java.sql;
public interface Connection {


//====================================================================
//                 Methods for creating statements:
//====================================================================


    Statement createStatement() throws SQLException;
    PreparedStatement prepareStatement(String sql)
                                                throws SQLException;
    CallableStatement prepareCall(String sql) throws SQLException;
    Statement createStatement(int resultSetType,
                    int resultSetConcurrency) throws SQLException;
    PreparedStatement prepareStatement(String sql, int resultSetType,
                    int resultSetConcurrency) throws SQLException;
    CallableStatement prepareCall(String sql, int resultSetType,
                    int resultSetConcurrency) throws SQLException;


//====================================================================
//                 Methods relating to transactions:
//====================================================================


    void setAutoCommit(boolean enableAutoCommit) throws
                                    SQLException;
    boolean getAutoCommit() throws SQLException;
    void commit() throws SQLException;
    void rollback() throws SQL exception;
    void close() throws SQLException;
    boolean isClosed() throws SQLException;


//====================================================================
//                 Advanced features:
//====================================================================


    DatabaseMetaData getMetaData() throws SQLException;
    void setReadOnly(boolean readOnly) throws SQLException;
```

```
        boolean isReadOnly() throws SQLException;
        void setCatalog(String catalog) throws SQLException;
        String getCatalog() throws SQLException;
        SQLWarning getWarnings() throws SQLException;
        void clearWarnings() throws SQLException;
  2.0   void setTypeMap(java.util.Map map) throws SQLException;
  2.0   java.util.Map getTypeMap() throws SQLException;
        void setTransactionIsolation(int level) throws SQLException;
        int getTransactionIsolation() throws SQLException;
        String nativeSQL(String query) throws SQLException;


  //===================================================================
  //                    JDBC 3.0 API features:
  //===================================================================


  3.0   void setHoldability(int holdability) throws SQLException;
  3.0   int getHoldability() throws SQLException;
  3.0   Savepoint setSavepoint() throws SQLException;
  3.0   Savepoint setSavepoint(String name) throws SQLException;
  3.0   void rollback(Savepoint savepoint) throws SQLException;
  3.0   void releaseSavepoint(Savepoint savepoint) throws SQLException;
  3.0   Statement createStatement(int resultSetType,
                        int resultSetConcurrency,
                        int resultSetHoldability)
                                            throws SQLException;
  3.0   PreparedStatement prepareStatement(String sql, int resultSetType,
                        int resultSetConcurrency,
                        int resultSetHoldability)
                                            throws SQLException;
  3.0   CallableStatement prepareCall(String sql, int resultSetType,
                        int resultSetConcurrency,
                        int resultSetHoldability)
                                            throws SQLException;
  3.0   PreparedStatement prepareStatement(String sql,
                        int autoGeneratedKeys) throws SQLException;
  3.0   PreparedStatement prepareStatement(String sql,
                        int [] columnIndexes) throws SQLException;
  3.0   PreparedStatement prepareStatement(String sql,
                        String [] columnNames) throws SQLException;
```

```
//=======================================================================
//          Fields defining transaction isolation levels:
//=======================================================================

    int TRANSACTION_NONE              = 0;
    int TRANSACTION_READ_UNCOMMITTED  = 1;
    int TRANSACTION_READ_COMMITTED    = 2;
    int TRANSACTION_REPEATABLE_READ   = 4;
    int TRANSACTION_SERIALIZABLE      = 8;
}
```

11.3 Connection Methods

clearWarnings

```
void clearWarnings() throws SQLException
```

Clears all warnings that have been reported by calls on this connection. After a call to the method clearWarnings, calls to the method getWarnings will return null until a new warning is reported for this connection.

EXAMPLE:
```
con.clearWarnings();
```

close

```
void close() throws SQLException
```

Releases a Connection object's DBMS and JDBC resources immediately instead of waiting for them to be released automatically.

A connection is automatically closed when it is garbage collected; however, depending on this feature is not recommended. Certain fatal errors also result in a closed connection.

The recommended programming style is to close any Connection objects explicitly when they are no longer needed; this releases DBMS resources as soon as possible.

EXAMPLE:
```
con.close();
```

commit

```
void commit() throws SQLException
```

Makes permanent all changes made to the database since the previous call to the method `commit` or `rollback` and releases any database locks currently held by this `Connection` object.

A `Connection` object produced by the `DriverManager` or by a basic implementation of the `DataSource` interface will be in auto-commit mode by default, and all its SQL statements will automatically be executed and committed as individual transactions. To execute and commit multiple statements as one transaction, auto-commit must be disabled (by calling `setAutoCommit(false)`) and the method `commit` must then be called explicitly.

A `Connection` object that can participate in distributed transactions (one produced by a `DataSource` object with the appropriate implementation) has its auto-commit mode disabled by default. An application should not call the method `commit` on such a `Connection` object while it is participating in a distributed transaction.

THROWS:
`SQLException` if called on a `Connection` object that is associated with a distributed transaction

EXAMPLE:
```
con.commit();
```

createStatement

```
Statement createStatement() throws SQLException
```

Creates a `Statement` object, which is the type of statement normally used to execute SQL statements without parameters. This method creates a `Statement` object that will produce a default `ResultSet` object (one that is not scrollable and is read-only). See the `Connection` method `prepareStatement` for information about when it is more efficient to use a `PreparedStatement` object for a simple SQL statement.

RETURNS:
a newly created `Statement` object that will produce a non-scrollable and non-updatable result set

EXAMPLE:
```
Connection con = DriverManager.getConnection(url, "xyz", "");
```

```
Statement stmt = con.createStatement();
ResultSet rs = stmt.executeQuery("SELECT a, b, c FROM Table1");
```

createStatement

2.0

```
Statement createStatement(int resultSetType, int resultSetConcurrency)
                                                  throws SQLException
```

Creates a Statement object that will produce ResultSet objects of type *resultSetType* and concurrency level *resultSetConcurrency*. This version of the createStatement method is the one to use if scrollable and/or updatable result sets are desired.

See the Connection method prepareStatement for information about when it is more efficient to use a PreparedStatement object for a simple SQL statement.

PARAMETERS:

resultSetType   one of the ResultSet constants indicating the type of result set: TYPE_FORWARD_ONLY, TYPE_SCROLL_INSEN-SITIVE, or TYPE_SCROLL_SENSITIVE

resultSetConcurrency one of the ResultSet constants indicating a result set's concurrency level; either CONCUR_READ_ONLY or CONCUR_UPDATABLE

RETURNS:

a newly created Statement object that will produce result sets with the given type and concurrency level

THROWS:

SQLException if the arguments supplied are not ResultSet constants specifying the type and concurrency

EXAMPLE:

```
Connection con = DriverManager.getConnection(url, "xyz", "");
Statement stmt = con.createStatement(
    ResultSet.TYPE_SCROLL_SENSITIVE, ResultSet.CONCUR_UPDATABLE);
ResultSet rs = stmt.executeQuery("SELECT a, b, c FROM Table1");
// stmt creates a result set that is scrollable, updatable, and
// generally sensitive to changes made while the result set is open
```

SEE:

"Types of Result Sets," on page 700
"Concurrency Types," on page 701

createStatement

3.0

Statement **createStatement**(int *resultSetType*, int *resultSetConcurrency*,
        int *resultSetHoldability*) throws SQLException

Creates a Statement object that will produce ResultSet objects of type *resultSetType*, concurrency level *resultSetConcurrency*, and holdability *resultSetHoldability*. Applications use this version of the createStatement method to set the holdability of the ResultSet objects that will be produced by the new Statement object. This method allows the default result set type, concurrency, and holdability to be overridden.

See the Connection method prepareStatement for information about when it is more efficient to use a PreparedStatement object for a simple SQL statement.

PARAMETERS:

resultSetType   one of the ResultSet constants indicating the type of
                      result set:

> ResultSet.TYPE_FORWARD_ONLY,
>
> ResultSet.TYPE_SCROLL_INSENSITIVE,
>
> ResultSet.TYPE_SCROLL_SENSITIVE

resultSetConcurrency one of the ResultSet constants indicating a result set's
                      concurrency level;

> ResultSet.CONCUR_READ_ONLY
>
> ResultSet.CONCUR_UPDATABLE

resultSetHoldability one of the ResultSet constants indicating a result set's
                      holdability;

> ResultSet.HOLD_CURSORS_OVER_COMMIT
>
> ResultSet.CLOSE_CURSORS_AT_COMMIT

RETURNS:

a newly created Statement object that will produce result sets with the given type, concurrency level, and holdability

THROWS:

SQLException if the arguments supplied to specify the type, concurrency, and holdability are not the ResultSet constants allowed

EXAMPLE:

```
Statement stmt = con.createStatement(
    ResultSet.TYPE_SCROLL_SENSITIVE, ResultSet.CONCUR_UPDATABLE,
    ResultSet.HOLD_CURSORS_OVER_COMMIT);
ResultSet rs = stmt.executeQuery("SELECT a, b, c FROM Table1");
```

```
// rs is scrollable, is updatable, is generally sensitive to changes
// made while the result set is open, and will remain open across
// commits
```

SEE:
"Types of Result Sets," on page 700
"Concurrency Types," on page 701
"Result Set Holdability," on page 702

getAutoCommit

```
boolean getAutoCommit() throws SQLException
```

When a `Connection` object is in auto-commit mode, its SQL statements are committed automatically right after they are executed. This means that each statement is treated as a separate transaction and that any changes it produces are either made permanent or discarded immediately. It also means that no locks are retained in the underlying database. If the connection is not in auto-commit mode (the method `getAutoCommit` returns `false`), a transaction will include all the SQL statements that have been executed since the last call to the method `commit` or `rollback` and will not terminate until either the `commit` or `rollback` method is called again.

A new connection produced by the `DriverManager` class or a basic implementation of the `DataSource` interface will be in auto-commit mode by default. This is not true for a connection produced by a `DataSource` object that is implemented to work with a middle-tier distributed transaction infrastructure. The default for such a connection is to have its auto-commit mode disabled so as not to interfere with the transaction manager's control of transaction boundaries.

RETURNS:
`true` if the connection is in auto-commit mode or `false` if it is not

EXAMPLE:
```
boolean b = myConnection.getAutoCommit();
```

getCatalog

```
String getCatalog() throws SQLException
```

Retrieves this `Connection` object's catalog name. The definition of a catalog name depends on the particular DBMS, but in general, it is the outermost level of qualification for the name of a database object. For example, a table can be referred to as "tableName," "databaseName.tableName," or "database-Name.userName.tableName." In this example, "databaseName.user-Name.tableName" is the fully qualified name, and "databaseName" is the catalog name. The fully qualified name can be expressed as "catalog.schema.tableName," where *catalog* is generally the database, and *schema* is generally the name of the user. For most databases, a new connection session begins in the database's default catalog, and in most cases, a user would not want to change it.

RETURNS:
a `String` object representing the `Connection` object's catalog name; `null` if there is none

EXAMPLE:
`String s = myConnection.getCatalog();`

3.0   getHoldability

`int getHoldability() throws SQLException`

Retrieves the holdability that is the default for `ResultSet` objects that are produced by statements created using this `Connection` object.

If the `Connection` method `setHoldability` has not been called to set the default holdability, the value returned will be the default holdability for the DBMS. Note that this is the same value returned by the `DatabaseMetaData` method `getResultSetHoldability`.

RETURNS:
an `int` indicating the default holdability of `ResultSet` objects that statements created by this `Connection` object will produce; one of
`ResultSet.HOLD_CURSORS_OVER_COMMIT` or
`ResultSet.CLOSE_CURSORS_AT_COMMIT`

EXAMPLE:
`int holdability = con.getHoldability();`

getMetaData

DatabaseMetaData **getMetaData**() throws SQLException

    Retrieves a DatabaseMetaData object containing information about the connection's database, including a description of the database's tables, its stored procedures, the SQL grammar that the DBMS supports, and the capabilities of the connection. This object is used to access information about the database by calling DatabaseMetaData methods on it.

RETURNS:
a DatabaseMetaData object for this connection

EXAMPLE:
DatabaseMetaData dbmd = myConnection.getMetaData();

SEE:
"DatabaseMetaData Overview," starting on page 449

getTransactionIsolation

int **getTransactionIsolation**() throws SQLException

    Retrieves the transaction isolation level for this Connection object. The transaction isolation level of a newly created Connection object depends on the connection's driver. If the driver supports transaction isolation levels, it will be the default for the underlying database unless it has been changed. See "Transaction Isolation Levels," on page 393, for a discussion of transaction isolation levels.

RETURNS:
an int representing the connection's current transaction isolation mode. Valid values, in ascending order, are TRANSACTION_NONE, TRANSACTION_READ_UNCOMMITTED, TRANSACTION_READ_COMMITTED, TRANSACTION_REPEATABLE_READ, and TRANSACTION_SERIALIZABLE.

EXAMPLE:
int x = myConnection.getTransactionIsolation();

2.0

getTypeMap

```
java.util.Map getTypeMap() throws SQLException
```

Retrieves the type map associated with this `Connection` object. Only drivers that implement the custom mapping facility of the JDBC 2.0 core API will return a `Map` object. The type map of a newly created `Connection` object will be empty; entries may be added to it at any time.

When a method such as `getObject` is invoked to retrieve a UDT and no type map is passed to it, the driver will check in the connection's type map to see if there is an entry for the UDT. If there is, the driver will map the UDT to the class specified in the connection's type map. If there is no matching entry, the driver will use the standard mapping.

RETURNS:
the `java.util.Map` object associated with this `Connection` object, which will be empty until entries are added

EXAMPLE:
```
Connection con = DriverManager.getConnection(URL);
java.util.Map map = con.getTypeMap();
map.put("SchemaName.UDTTypeName", UddtName.class);
// retrieves this Connection object's type map and makes an entry
// in it
```

SEE:
"Creating a Custom Mapping," on page 896

getWarnings

```
SQLWarning getWarnings() throws SQLException
```

Gets the first warning reported by calls on this `Connection` object. Subsequent warnings will be chained to the first `SQLWarning`. This method does not clear warnings.

RETURNS:
the first `SQLWarning`; `null` if there have been no warnings reported or if the method `clearWarnings` has been called and there have been no subsequent warnings reported

EXAMPLE:
```
SQLWarning w = con.getWarnings(); // get first warning
```

```
while(w != null) {
    System.out.println("Warning = " + w);
    w = w.getNextWarning();
    // gets any warnings chained to the first one and prints out the
    // class name and message for all warnings
}
```

SEE:
`java.sql.SQLWarning`, starting on page 945

isClosed

`boolean isClosed() throws SQLException`

Indicates whether this `Connection` object has been closed. A connection is closed if the method `close` has been called on it or if certain fatal errors have occurred. This method is guaranteed to return `true` only when it is called after the method `Connection.close` has been called.

This method generally cannot be called to determine whether a connection with a data source is valid or invalid. A typical JDBC client can determine that a connection is invalid by catching the exception that is thrown when a JDBC operation is attempted.

RETURNS:
`true` if the connection is closed or `false` if it is still open

EXAMPLE:
```
if (!con.isClosed() {
    con.close();
}
boolean b = con.isClosed(); // b is guaranteed to be true
```

isReadOnly

`boolean isReadOnly() throws SQLException`

Being in read-only mode is a suggestion to the database that it can optimize performance by not worrying about write operations; it does not mean that the connection is prevented from writing to the database. It is expected that the default value for read-only is `false`; however, if a driver allows no

updates to a database (the database is read-only), then a call to the method
isReadOnly should return true.

RETURNS:
true if the connection is in read-only mode; false otherwise

EXAMPLE:
```
boolean b = con.isReadOnly();
```

nativeSQL

```
String nativeSQL(String query) throws SQLException
```

Translates *query* into the native query language of the underlying DBMS
and returns it as a String object.

PARAMETERS:
query   String containing an SQL statement

RETURNS:
the native form of *query* as a String object in the Java programming language

EXAMPLE:
```
String query = "INSERT INTO Table1 (a, b, c)
                VALUES (10013, 'Washington', {d '1999-01-01'})";
String nativeForm = con.nativeSQL(query);
// The variable nativeForm contains a String object with query
// translated into the query language of the underlying database.
// For example, if the DBMS is Oracle, the variable nativeForm would
// contain a String object similar to the following:
//     "insert into Table1 (a, b, c)
//      values (10013, 'Washington', '01-JAN-99')"
// The escape syntax {d '1999-01-01'} signals the driver to
// translate the date into native syntax.
```

SEE:
"SQL Escape Syntax in Statements," on page 958

prepareCall

```
CallableStatement prepareCall(String sql) throws SQLException
```

Creates a `CallableStatement` object that contains *sql* and that will produce `ResultSet` objects that are non-scrollable and non-updatable. An SQL stored procedure call statement is handled by creating a `CallableStatement` object for it. The `CallableStatement` object has methods for setting up its IN and OUT parameters, and it also provides methods for executing the stored procedure.

NOTE: This method is optimized for handling stored procedure call statements. Some drivers may send the call statement to the database when the method `prepareCall` creates a `CallableStatement`; others may wait until the `CallableStatement` object is executed. This has no direct effect on users; however, it does affect which methods throw certain `SQLException` objects.

PARAMETERS:

sql   an SQL statement that may contain one or more ? parameter placeholders. Optimally, this should be a call to a stored procedure, but any SQL statement will be accepted.

RETURNS:

a new default `CallableStatement` object containing the given precompiled SQL statement

EXAMPLE:
```
CallableStatement cstmt = con.prepareCall(
                    "{call revisePrices(?, ?)}");
```

prepareCall   2.0

```
CallableStatement prepareCall(String sql, int resultSetType,
                    int resultSetConcurrency) throws SQLException
```

Creates a `CallableStatement` object that contains *sql* and that will produce `ResultSet` objects of type *resultSetType* and with a concurrency level of *resultSetConcurrency*. An SQL stored procedure call statement is handled by creating a `CallableStatement` object for it. The `CallableStatement` object has methods for setting up its IN and OUT parameters, and it also provides methods for executing the stored procedure.

NOTE: This method is optimized for handling stored procedure call statements. Some drivers may send the call statement to the database when the method prepareCall creates a CallableStatement; others may wait until the CallableStatement object is executed. This has no direct effect on users; however, it does affect which methods throw certain SQLException objects.

PARAMETERS:

sql	an SQL statement that may contain one or more ? parameter placeholders. Optimally, this should be a call to a stored procedure, but any SQL statement will be accepted.
resultSetType	one of the constants in the ResultSet interface indicating the type of a result set: TYPE_FORWARD_ONLY, TYPE_SCROLL_INSENSITIVE, or TYPE_SCROLL_SENSITIVE
resultSetConcurrency	one of the constants in the ResultSet interface indicating the concurrency level of a result set; either CONCUR_READ_ONLY or CONCUR_UPDATABLE

RETURNS:

a newly created CallableStatement object that will call stored procedures and, if the stored procedure contains a query, that will produce result sets with the given type and concurrency level

THROWS:

SQLException if the arguments supplied to specify the type and concurrency are not the ResultSet constants allowed

EXAMPLE:

```
Connection con = DriverManager.getConnection(url, "xyz", "");
String sql = "{call getPrices(?, ?)}";
CallableStatement cstmt = con.prepareCall(sql,
    Result.Set.TYPE_SCROLL_SENSITIVE, ResultSet.CONCUR_UPDATABLE);
cstmt.setString(1, "Colombian");
cstmt.setInt(2, 5430);
cstmt.registerOutParameter(2, java.sql.Types.INTEGER);

ResultSet rs = cstmt.executeQuery();
// cstmt creates a result set that is scrollable, updatable, and
// generally sensitive to changes made while the result set is open
```

SEE:

"Types of Result Sets," on page 700
"Concurrency Types," on page 701

prepareCall

3.0

```
CallableStatement prepareCall(String sql, int resultSetType,
                int resultSetConcurrency, int resultSetHoldability)
                                        throws SQLException
```

Creates a `CallableStatement` object that will produce `ResultSet` objects of type *resultSetType*, concurrency level *resultSetConcurrency*, and holdability *resultSetHoldability*. Applications use this version of the prepare-Call method to set the holdability of `ResultSet` objects that will be produced by the new `CallableStatement` object.

PARAMETERS:

sql
a `String` object that is the call to a database stored procedure; may contain one or more ? placeholder parameters

resultSetType
one of the `ResultSet` constants indicating the type of result set:

> ResultSet.TYPE_FORWARD_ONLY
> ResultSet.TYPE_SCROLL_INSENSITIVE
> ResultSet.TYPE_SCROLL_SENSITIVE

resultSetConcurrency one of the `ResultSet` constants indicating a result set's concurrency level:

> ResultSet.CONCUR_READ_ONLY
> ResultSet.CONCUR_UPDATABLE

resultSetHoldability one of the `ResultSet` constants indicating a result set's holdability:

> ResultSet.HOLD_CURSORS_OVER_COMMIT
> ResultSet.CLOSE_CURSORS_AT_COMMIT

RETURNS:
a newly created `CallableStatement` object that will produce result sets with the given type, concurrency level, and holdability

THROWS:
`SQLException` if the arguments supplied to specify the type, concurrency, and holdability are not the `ResultSet` constants allowed

EXAMPLE:
```
String sql = "{call getInfo(?, ?, ?)}";
CallableStatement cstmt = con.prepareCall(sql,
    ResultSet.TYPE_SCROLL_SENSITIVE, ResultSet.CONCUR_UPDATABLE,
    ResultSet.HOLD_CURSORS_OVER_COMMIT);
```

```
cstmt.setInt("CUST_ID", 003456);
cstmt.setInt("ORDER_NO", 09835710);
cstmt.setString("SUPPLIER", "Acme, Inc.");
ResultSet rs = cstmt.executeUpdate();
// rs is scrollable, is updatable, is generally sensitive to changes
// made while the result set is open, and will remain open across
// commits
```

SEE:
"Types of Result Sets," on page 700
"Concurrency Types," on page 701
"Result Set Holdability," on page 702

prepareStatement

PreparedStatement **prepareStatement**(String *sql*) throws SQLException

Creates a PreparedStatement object containing *sql*. A SQL statement can be precompiled and stored in a PreparedStatement object whether it has IN parameters or not. Expert programmers can use this object to efficiently execute a statement multiple times. PreparedStatement objects cannot contain SQL statements with OUT parameters; those require CallableStatement objects. See the method prepareCall.

NOTE: This method is optimized for handling parametric SQL statements that benefit from precompilation. If the driver supports precompilation, the method prepareStatement will send the statement to the database for precompilation. If the driver does not support precompilation, the statement may not be sent to the database until the PreparedStatement object is executed. This has no direct effect on users; however, it does affect which methods throw certain SQLException objects.

PARAMETERS:

sql   An SQL statement that may contain one or more ? IN parameter placeholders. It may not contain OUT or IN-OUT parameter placeholders.

RETURNS:
a new precompiled PreparedStatement object containing the given SQL statement

EXAMPLE:
```
PreparedStatement pstmt = con.prepareStatement(
```

```
                "UPDATE DEPARTMENTS SET NAME = ? WHERE ID = ?");
```

prepareStatement

3.0

```
PreparedStatement prepareStatement(String sql, int autoGeneratedKeys)
                                            throws SQLException
```

Creates a default PreparedStatement object that has the capability to retrieve keys that the DBMS generates automatically when a new row is inserted into a table. The constant *autoGeneratedKeys* tells the driver whether it should make automatically generated keys available for retrieval. This argument is ignored if *sql* in not an INSERT statement.

NOTE: This method is optimized for handling parametric SQL statements that benefit from precompilation. If the driver supports precompilation, this method will send *sql* to the database to be precompiled. If the driver does not support precompilation, *sql* may not be sent to the database until this PreparedStatement object is executed. This has no direct effect on users, but it does affect which methods throw certain SQLException objects.

The default for ResultSet objects created using the returned PreparedStatement object is to be non-scrollable (TYPE_FORWARD_ONLY) and non-updatable (CONCUR_READ_ONLY).

PARAMETERS:

sql	a String object that is the SQL statement to be sent to the database; may contain one or more ? IN placeholder parameters
autoGeneratedKeys	one of the Statement constants indicating whether the driver should make automatically generated keys available for retrieval: Statement.NO_GENERATED_KEYS or Statement.RETURN_GENERATED_KEYS

RETURNS:
a new PreparedStatement object containing the precompiled SQL statement and having the ability to retrieve keys that the DBMS generates automatically

THROWS:
SQLException if the second argument is not a Statement constant indicating whether automatically generated keys should be available for retrieval

EXAMPLE:
```
String sql = "INSERT INTO AUTHORS VALUES (?, ?, ?)";
```

```
PreparedStatement pstmt = con.prepareStatement(sql,
                                Statement.RETURN_GENERATED_KEYS);
// The driver is alerted to make any keys generated by the DBMS
// available for retrieval
```

SEE:
"Retrieving Automatically Generated Keys," on page 954

3.0 **prepareStatement**

```
PreparedStatement prepareStatement(String sql, int [] columnIndexes)
                                            throws SQLException
```

Creates a default `PreparedStatement` object that has the capability to retrieve automatically generated keys from the columns designated by *col-umnIndexes*. This array contains the indexes of the columns in the target table that contain the automatically generated keys that should be made available. This array is ignored if *sql* is not an `INSERT` statement.

An SQL statement with or without `IN` parameters can be precompiled and stored in a `PreparedStatement` object. This object can then be used for efficiently executing the statement multiple times.

NOTE: This method is optimized for handling parametric SQL statements that benefit from precompilation. If the driver supports precompilation, this method will send *sql* to the database to be precompiled. If the driver does not support precompilation, *sql* may not be sent to the database until this `PreparedStatement` object is executed. This has no direct effect on users, but it does affect which methods throw certain `SQLException` objects.

The default for `ResultSet` objects created using the returned `PreparedStatement` object is to be non-scrollable (`TYPE_FORWARD_ONLY`) and non-updatable (`CONCUR_READ_ONLY`).

PARAMETERS:

sql   a `String` object that is the SQL statement to be sent to the database; may contain one or more ? `IN` placeholder parameters

columnIndexes   an `int` array containing the indexes of columns in the inserted row or rows that should be available for retrieval

RETURNS:

a new `PreparedStatement` object than contains the precompiled SQL statement and that has the ability to retrieve automatically generated keys from the designated columns

THROWS:

`SQLException` if *columnIndexes* is not an `int` array of column indexes

EXAMPLE:
```
String sql = "INSERT INTO AUTHORS VALUES (?, ?, ?)";
int [] keyIndexes = {1};
PreparedStatement pstmt = con.prepareStatement(sql, keyIndexes);
// The driver is alerted to make available for retrieval the key
// generated by the DBMS that is stored in the first column
```

SEE:
"Retrieving Automatically Generated Keys," on page 954

prepareStatement

2.0

```
PreparedStatement prepareStatement(String sql, int resultSetType,
                        int resultSetConcurrency) throws SQLException
```

Creates a `PreparedStatement` object that contains *sql* and that will produce `ResultSet` objects with type *resultSetType* and concurrency level *resultSetConcurrency*. An SQL statement with or without IN parameters can be precompiled and stored in a `PreparedStatement` object. Expert programmers can use this object to efficiently execute a statement multiple times.

`PreparedStatement` objects cannot contain SQL statements with OUT parameters; those require `CallableStatement` objects. See the method `prepareCall`.

NOTE: This method is optimized for handling parametric SQL statements that benefit from precompilation. If the driver supports precompilation, the method `prepareStatement` will send the statement to the database for precompilation. If the driver does not support precompilation, the statement may not be sent to the database until the `PreparedStatement` object is executed. This has no direct effect on users; however, it does affect which methods throw certain `SQLException` objects.

PARAMETERS:

sql	an SQL statement that may contain one or more ? IN parameter placeholders. It may not contain OUT or INOUT parameter placeholders.
resultSetType	one of the `ResultSet` constants indicating the type of result set: `TYPE_FORWARD_ONLY`, `TYPE_SCROLL_INSEN-SITIVE`, or `TYPE_SCROLL_SENSITIVE`
resultSetConcurrency	one of the `ResultSet` constants indicating the concurrency level of a result set: `CONCUR_READ_ONLY` or `CONCUR_UPDATABLE`

RETURNS:

a newly created `PreparedStatement` object that contains the given SQL statement and, if the SQL statement is a query, that produces result sets with the given type and concurrency level

EXAMPLE:

```
Connection con = DriverManager.getConnection(url, "xyz", "");
String sql = "SELECT NAME FROM DEPARTMENTS WHERE ID = ?";
PreparedStatement pstmt = con.prepareStatement(sql,
    ResultSet.TYPE_SCROLL_SENSITIVE, ResultSet.CONCUR_UPDATABLE);
pstmt.setInt(1, 1553);

ResultSet rs = pstmt.executeQuery();
// pstmt creates a result set that is scrollable, updatable, and
// generally sensitive to changes made while the result set is open
```

SEE:

"Types of Result Sets," on page 700
"Concurrency Types," on page 701

prepareStatement

3.0

```
PreparedStatement prepareStatement(String sql, int resultSetType,
            int resultSetConcurrency, int resultSetHoldability)
                                        throws SQLException
```

Creates a `PreparedStatement` object that will produce `ResultSet` objects of type *resultSetType*, concurrency level *resultSetConcurrency*, and holdability *resultSetHoldability*. An application uses this version of the prepareStatement method if it wants to set the holdability of result sets that the new `PreparedStatement` object will produce. This method allows the default result set type, concurrency, and holdability to be overwritten.

PARAMETERS:

sql	a `String` object that is the SQL statement to be sent to the database; may contain one or more ? `IN` placeholder parameters
resultSetType	one of the `ResultSet` constants indicating the type of result set:

> `ResultSet.TYPE_FORWARD_ONLY,`
> `ResultSet.TYPE_SCROLL_INSENSITIVE`
> `ResultSet.TYPE_SCROLL_SENSITIVE`

resultSetConcurrency	one of the `ResultSet` constants indicating a result set's concurrency level:

> `ResultSet.CONCUR_READ_ONLY` or
> `ResultSet.CONCUR_UPDATABLE`

resultSetHoldability	one of the `ResultSet` constants indicating a result set's holdability:

> `ResultSet.HOLD_CURSORS_OVER_COMMIT`
> `ResultSet.CLOSE_CURSORS_AT_COMMIT`

RETURNS:

a newly created `PreparedStatement` object that will produce result sets with the given type, concurrency level, and holdability

EXAMPLE:

```
String sql = "SELECT NAME FROM DEPARTMENTS WHERE ID = ?";
PreparedStatement pstmt = con.prepareStatement(sql,
    ResultSet.TYPE_SCROLL_SENSITIVE, ResultSet.CONCUR_UPDATABLE,
    ResultSet.HOLD_CURSORS_OVER_COMMIT);
pstmt.setInt(1, 1553);

ResultSet rs = pstmt.executeQuery();
// rs is scrollable, is updatable, is generally sensitive to changes
// made while the result set is open, and will remain open across
// commits
```

SEE:

"Types of Result Sets," on page 700
"Concurrency Types," on page 701
"Result Set Holdability," on page 702

prepareStatement

3.0

PreparedStatement **prepareStatement**(String *sql*, String [] *columnNames)*
                                                    throws SQLException

Creates a default PreparedStatement object that has the capability to retrieve automatically generated keys from the columns designated by *columnNames*. This array contains the names of the columns in the target table that contain the automatically generated keys that should be made available. This array is ignored if *sql* is not an INSERT statement.

An SQL statement with or without IN parameters can be precompiled and stored in a PreparedStatement object. This object can then be used for efficiently executing the statement multiple times.

NOTE: This method is optimized for handling parametric SQL statements that benefit from precompilation. If the driver supports precompilation, this method will send *sql* to the database to be precompiled. If the driver does not support precompilation, *sql* may not be sent to the database until this PreparedStatement object is executed. This has no direct effect on users, but it does affect which methods throw certain SQLException objects.

The default for ResultSet objects created using the returned PreparedStatement object is to be non-scrollable (TYPE_FORWARD_ONLY) and non-updatable (CONCUR_READ_ONLY).

PARAMETERS:

sql	a String object that is the SQL statement to be sent to the database; may contain one or more ? IN placeholder parameters
columnNames	a String array containing the names of columns in the inserted row or rows that should be available for retrieval

RETURNS:
a new PreparedStatement object that contains the precompiled SQL statement and that has the ability to retrieve automatically generated keys from the designated columns

THROWS:
SQLException if *columnNames* is not a String array of column names

EXAMPLE:
```
String sql = "INSERT INTO AUTHORS VALUES (?, ?, ?)";
String [] keyColNames = {"ID"};
PreparedStatement pstmt = con.prepareStatement(sql, keyColNames);
```

```
// The driver is alerted to make keys generated by the DBMS in the
// column ID available for retrieval
```

SEE:
"Retrieving Automatically Generated Keys," on page 954

releaseSavepoint

3.0

```
void releaseSavepoint(Savepoint savepoint) throws SQLException
```

Removes *savepoint* from the current transaction. Any reference to *savepoint* after it has been removed will cause an SQLException to be thrown.

PARAMETERS:

savepoint   the Savepoint object to be removed from the current transaction

THROWS:
SQLException if a reference to the given Savepoint object is made after the Savepoint object has been removed

EXAMPLE:
```
Savepoint savepoint2 = con.setSavepoint(savepoint2);
// ...
con.releaseSavepoint(savepoint2);
// removes savepoint2 from the current transaction
```

rollback

```
void rollback() throws SQLException
```

Undoes all changes made in the current transaction and releases any database locks currently held by this Connection object. This method should be used only when auto-commit mode has been disabled.

THROWS:
SQLException if called when auto-commit mode is enabled

EXAMPLE:
```
con.rollback; // any changes to the database in the current
              // transaction are undone
```

3.0

rollback

---

void **rollback**(Savepoint *savepoint*) throws SQLException

Undoes the changes in the current transaction that come after *savepoint* was created. Any changes made before *savepoint* will remain.

PARAMETERS:

savepoint   a Savepoint object marking an intermediate point in the current transaction

THROWS:
SQLException if called when auto-commit mode is enabled

EXAMPLE:
```
// ... update 1
// ... update 2
Savepoint savepoint1 = con.setSavepoint(savepoint1);
// ... update 3
Savepoint savepoint2 = con.setSavepoint(savepoint2);
// ... update 4
con.rollback(savepoint2);
// undoes update 4
```

setAutoCommit

---

void **setAutoCommit**(boolean *enableAutoCommit*) throws SQLException

Sets the connection's auto-commit mode to *enableAutoCommit*.

When Connection objects are in auto-commit mode, individual SQL statements are committed automatically when the statement is completed. To be able to group SQL statements into transactions and commit them or roll them back as a unit, auto-commit must be disabled by calling the method set-AutoCommit with false as its argument. When auto-commit is disabled, the user must call either the commit or rollback method explicitly to end a transaction.

The commit occurs when the statement completes or the next execute occurs, whichever comes first. In the case of statements returning a ResultSet object, the statement completes when the last row of a non-scrollable result set has been retrieved or the ResultSet object has been closed. In advanced cases, a single statement may return multiple results as well as output parameter values. In this case, the commit may occur when all results and output parameter values have been retrieved, or the commit may occur after each result is retrieved.

This method should not be called on a `Connection` object while it is part of a distributed transaction because that will conflict with the transaction manager's control of transaction boundaries.

PARAMETERS:

enableAutoCommit   either `true` to enable auto-commit mode or `false` to disable auto-commit mode

THROWS:

`SQLException` if called to enable auto-commit mode on a `Connection` object while it is associated with a distributed transaction

EXAMPLE:
```
myConnection.setAutoCommit(false); // disables auto-commit mode
```

setCatalog

```
void setCatalog(String catalog) throws SQLException
```

Sets the catalog name for this `Connection` object to *catalog*. The definition of a catalog name depends on the particular DBMS, but in general, it is the outermost level of qualification for the name of a database object. For example, a table can be referred to as "tableName," "databaseName.tableName," or "databaseName.userName.tableName." In this example, "databaseName.userName.tableName" is the fully qualified name, and "databaseName" is the catalog name. The fully qualified name can be expressed as "catalog.schema.tableName," where *catalog* is generally the database, and *schema* is generally the name of the user.

A catalog name identifies a particular section of a database, so setting the catalog name selects a subspace of the `Connection` object's database to work in. Normally a user will work in the default catalog and will not use this method.

If the driver does not support catalogs, it will silently ignore this request.

PARAMETERS:

catalog   a `String` object representing a catalog name

EXAMPLE:
```
myConnection.setCatalog("myCatalogName");
```

setHoldability

```
void setHoldability(int holdability) throws SQLException
```

Sets the holdability that is the default for `ResultSet` objects that are produced by statements created using this `Connection` object.

PARAMETERS:

holdability   `int` indicating the default holdability of `ResultSet` objects that statements created by this `Connection` object will produce; one of `ResultSet.HOLD_CURSORS_OVER_COMMIT` or `ResultSet.CLOSE_CURSORS_AT_COMMIT`

THROWS:

`SQLException` if the given argument is not a `ResultSet` constant indicating holdability or the given holdability is not supported

EXAMPLE:

```
DatabaseMetaData dbMetada = con.getMetaData();
if (dbMetadata.supportsResultSetHoldability(
                        ResultSet.HOLD_CURSORS_OVER_COMMIT) {
    con.setHoldability(ResultSet.HOLD_CURSORS_OVER_COMMIT);
}
Statement stmt = con.createStatement();
ResultSet rs = stmt.executeQuery("SELECT a, b FROM TABLE1");
// rs will remain open after the method commit has been called
```

SEE:

"Result Set Holdability," on page 702

setReadOnly

```
void setReadOnly(boolean readOnly) throws SQLException
```

Sets this `Connection` object to read-only mode when *readOnly* is `true` and disables read-only mode when *readOnly* is `false`.

It is recommended that this method be called prior to execution of statements on a connection.

Note that read-only mode is only a hint to the driver to enable database optimizations; calling `setReadOnly(true)` does not necessarily cause writes to be prohibited.

PARAMETERS:

readOnly   either `true` to enable read-only mode or `false` to dis-
                                able read-only mode

EXAMPLE:
```
myConnection.setReadOnly(true);
// enables read-only mode but does not prohibit writes
```

setSavepoint

`3.0`

```
Savepoint setSavepoint() throws SQLException
```

Creates an unnamed `Savepoint` object in the current transaction. The DBMS will automatically create a numeric identifier for the new `Savepoint` object. Trying to set a savepoint in a transaction when auto-commit mode is enabled will cause an `SQLException` object to be thrown.

RETURNS:
an unnamed `Savepoint` object

THROWS:
`SQLException` if this `Connection` object is in auto-commit mode when the method `setSavepoint` is called

EXAMPLE:
```
con.setAutoCommit(false); // disable auto-commit mode
//... update 1
//... update 2
Savepoint s1 = con.setSavepoint();
//... update 3
// creates and sets s1 after update 2
```

SEE:
"Retrieving a Savepoint Object Identifier," on page 891

setSavepoint

`3.0`

```
Savepoint setSavepoint(String name) throws SQLException
```

Creates a `Savepoint` object with the name *name* in the current transaction. Trying to set a savepoint in a transaction when auto-commit mode is enabled will cause an SQLException object to be thrown.

PARAMETERS:

name   a String containing the name with which the new
         Savepoint object will be initialized

RETURNS:

a Savepoint object initialized with the name *name*

THROWS:

SQLException if this Connection object is in auto-commit mode when the
method setSavepoint is called

EXAMPLE:
```
con.setAutoCommit(false); // disable auto-commit mode
//... update 1
Savepoint s1 = con.setSavepoint("savepoint1");
//...update 2
// creates and sets s1, which is named "Savepoint1", after the first
// update and before the second update. If con.rollback(s1) is
// called, the first update will remain, and the second update will
// be removed.
```

SEE:
"Retrieving a Savepoint Object Identifier," on page 891

setTransactionIsolation

```
void setTransactionIsolation(int level) throws SQLException
```

Sets the transaction isolation level of this Connection object to *level* (if
the underlying database supports setting transaction isolation values). The
parameter *level* must be one of the TRANSACTION_* constants defined in the
Connection interface.

This method generates an SQLException if the DBMS cannot support the
isolation level requested and cannot substitute a higher level of isolation.

If this method is called while in the middle of a transaction, any changes
up to that point will be committed.

PARAMETERS:

level   one of the following Connection constants:
TRANSACTION_READ_UNCOMMITTED,
TRANSACTION_READ_COMMITTED,
TRANSACTION_REPEATABLE_READ, or
TRANSACTION_SERIALIZABLE. (TRANSACTION_NONE cannot
be used because it specifies that transactions are not sup-
ported.)

THROWS:

SQLException if this Connection object requests a transaction isolation level
that the DBMS does not support and the DBMS cannot substitute a higher
transaction isolation level

EXAMPLE:

```
myConnection.setTransactionIsolation(
                    Connection.TRANSACTION_READ_COMMITTED);
// prohibits "dirty reads"
```

SEE:

"Connection Fields," on page 428

setTypeMap   2.0

```
void setTypeMap(java.util.Map, map) throws SQLException
```

Installs *map* as this Connection object's type map, replacing the type map
with which this Connection object was created. Only drivers that implement
the custom mapping facility will allow the setting of a Map object.

PARAMETERS:

map   a java.util.Map object that contains the mapping from
SQL type names for user-defined types to classes in the
Java programming language

EXAMPLE:

```
java.util.Map map2 = new HashMap();
map2.put("SQLSchema.SQLName", ClassImplementingSQLData.class);
myConnection.setTypeMap(map2);
// creates a new type map, makes an entry in it, and installs it as
// the new type map for this connection
```

SEE:
"Creating a Custom Mapping," on page 896

11.4 Connection Fields

The constant values defined in the `Connection` interface are used as parameters to the `Connection` method `setTransactionIsolation`. They are also the possible return values for the `DatabaseMetaData` method `getDefaultTransactionIsolation`, which returns the default transaction isolation level of the underlying database.

TRANSACTION_NONE

```
public static final int TRANSACTION_NONE = 0
```

Transactions are not supported.

TRANSACTION_READ_UNCOMMITTED

```
public static final int TRANSACTION_READ_UNCOMMITTED = 1
```

Specifies that "dirty reads," nonrepeatable reads, and phantom reads can occur. This level allows a row changed by one transaction to be read by another transaction before any changes in that row have been committed. If any of the changes are rolled back, the second transaction will have retrieved an invalid row.

TRANSACTION_READ_COMMITTED

```
public static final int TRANSACTION_READ_COMMITTED = 2
```

Specifies that "dirty reads" are prevented; however, nonrepeatable reads and phantom reads can occur. In other words, this level only prohibits a transaction from reading a row with uncommitted changes in it.

TRANSACTION_REPEATABLE_READ

```
public static final int TRANSACTION_REPEATABLE_READ = 4
```

Specifies that "dirty reads" and nonrepeatable reads are prevented; phantom reads can occur. This level prohibits a transaction from reading a row with uncommitted changes in it, and it also prohibits the situation where one transaction reads a row, a second transaction alters the row, and the first transaction rereads the row, getting different values the second time.

TRANSACTION_SERIALIZABLE

```
public static final int TRANSACTION_SERIALIZABLE = 8
```

Specifies that "dirty reads," nonrepeatable reads, and phantom reads are all prevented. This level includes the prohibitions in TRANSACTION_REPEATABLE_READ and further prohibits the situation where one transaction reads all rows that satisfy a WHERE condition, a second transaction inserts a row that satisfies that WHERE condition, and the first transaction rereads for the same condition, retrieving the additional "phantom" row in the second read.

CHAPTER 12

ConnectionEvent javax.sql

12.1 ConnectionEvent Overview

A ConnectionEvent object, part of the event model for pooled connections, informs a component managing the pooling of connections that an event has occurred on a PooledConnection object. The ConnectionEvent object always contains the PooledConnection object that generated the event, and if an error occurred, it also contains the SQLException that explains the event.

Application programmers never use the ConnectionEvent interface directly. Like other parts of the connection pooling mechanism, it is handled entirely behind the scenes. Generally, the driver creates a ConnectionEvent object, and the application server works with other parts of the infrastructure to manage the pooling of connections.

In order for the component managing the pool of connections to be notified of events that occur on PooledConnection objects, it must become a *listener*. This is done by implementing the ConnectionEventListener interface and by being registered with all of the relevant PooledConnection objects via the method Pooled-Connection.addConnectionEventListener. It is the JDBC driver that notifies the listener when an event occurs on a PooledConnection object.

When a listener is notified about an event on a PooledConnection object, it knows that an application is no longer using the pooled connection that the PooledConnection object represents. If the connection was closed, the listener will return it to the pool of available connections; if an error occurred, it is unfit for future use (because, for example, the server crashed), so the listener will not return it to the connection pool.

The ConnectionEvent interface provides two constructors and one method. When a pooled connection is closed, the event created is initialized with the

431

PooledConnection object that is being closed. When an error occurs on a pooled connection, the instance of ConnectionEvent that is created contains the connection on which the error occurred and also the SQLException object that is about to be thrown. The method getSQLException retrieves the exception about to be thrown if there is one.

Note that it is possible for a method to throw an SQLException object that is not fatal to the connection and therefore does not cause a ConnectionEvent object to be created. For example, if an SQLException object is thrown because of a constraint violation, the driver will not generate a ConnectionEvent object.

12.2 ConnectionEvent Interface Definition

```
package javax.sql;
public class ConnectionEvent extends java.util.EventObject {
    ConnectionEvent(PooledConnection con);
    ConnectionEvent(PooledConnection con, java.sql.SQLException ex);
    java.sql.SQLException getSQLException();
}
```

12.3 ConnectionEvent Constructors

ConnectionEvent

public **ConnectionEvent**(PooledConnection *con*)

Constructs a new ConnectionEvent object initialized with *con*. The SQLException field defaults to null. When *con* is closed by an application, the JDBC driver will use this constructor to create a ConnectionEvent object internally as part of the connection pool management mechanism. The driver will supply this ConnectionEvent object to the listener's connectionClosed method.

PARAMETERS:

con   the PooledConnection object that was closed by the application using it

EXAMPLE:
```
con.close();
```

```
// application closes the Connection object con, which represents a
// pooled connection
ConnectionEvent event = new ConnectionEvent(con);
// the JDBC driver creates event internally
listener.connectionClosed(event);
// the JDBC driver passes event to the listener method corresponding
// to the event
```

ConnectionEvent

public **ConnectionEvent**(PooledConnection *con*, java.sql.SQLException *ex*)

Constructs a new ConnectionEvent object initialized with *con* and *ex*. When a fatal error occurs on *con*, the JDBC driver will use this constructor to create a ConnectionEvent object internally as part of the connection pool management mechanism. The driver will supply this ConnectionEvent object to the listener's connectionErrorOccurred method.

PARAMETERS:

con	the PooledConnection object that was terminated by a fatal error
ex	the SQLException object that will be thrown as a result of a fatal connection error

EXAMPLE:
```
ConnectionEvent event = new ConnectionEvent(con, ex);
// the JDBC driver creates event internally when a fatal error occurs
// on the Connection con
listener.connectionErrorOccurred(event);
// the JDBC driver passes event to the listener method corresponding
// to the event
```

12.4   ConnectionEvent Methods

12.4.1   Methods Inherited from `java.util.EventObject`

The `ConnectionEvent` class inherits the following methods from `java.util.Event-Object`:

```
getSource              toString
```

12.4.2   Methods Defined in `javax.sql.ConnectionEvent`

The `javax.sql.ConnectionEvent` class defines the following method:

getSQLException

```
public java.sql.SQLException getSQLException()
```

> Retrieves the `SQLException` object with which this `ConnectionEvent` object was initialized. This method is called by a listener registered with the source of this `ConnectionEvent` object after the method `ConnectionEventListener.connectionErrorOccurred` has been called on it.

RETURNS:
the `SQLException` object that will be thrown as a result of a fatal connection error; `null` if this `ConnectionEvent` object was not initialized with an exception

EXAMPLE:
```
java.sql.SQLException ex = event.getSQLException();
// event is a ConnectionEvent object
```

CHAPTER **13**

ConnectionEventListener

13.1 ConnectionEventListener Overview

A ConnectionEventListener object, referred to as a *listener*, is a component that wants to be notified about events that occur on a PooledConnection object. Generally it is a connection pooling module that needs to know when a PooledConnection object can be reused or when it should be discarded. It implements the Connection-EventListener interface and is registered as a listener with all of the PooledConnection objects that it manages. A connection pooling module, software in the middle tier between a client and a database server, will usually be provided by a JDBC driver vendor or server vendor. Connection pooling is all done internally, as is true of event notification, so the user is aware of neither. Those who want more information about connection pooling and the connection pooling event model, should see Chapter 24, "PooledConnection," starting on page 637, and Chapter 12, "ConnectionEventListener," starting on page 435. However, application programmers do not use the ConnectionEventListener interface directly and may choose not to read this chapter or the other chapters on interfaces related to connection pooling.

13.1.1 Methods for Event Notification

The ConnectionEventListener interface provides two methods, one for each type of event that can occur on a pooled connection. The driver invokes these methods on the registered listener(s). It calls the method connectionClosed when an application closes its representation of a pooled connection. When a fatal connection error has occurred, the driver calls the method connectionErrorOccurred just before it throws the SQLException to the application that is using the PooledConnection object.

In both cases, the driver supplies a ConnectionEvent object as the parameter to the method. The method called tells the listener what kind of event occurred, and the ConnectionEvent object tells it which connection was affected. If the method invoked on the listener is connectionErrorOccurred, the event will also contain the SQLException object that the driver will throw.

13.1.2 Registering a ConnectionEventListener Object

The component managing a pool of connections needs to be registered with each PooledConnection object in the pool. This is accomplished by having the connection pooling module add itself as a listener to each newly created PooledConnection object.

The following code fragment, where *ds* is a ConnectionPoolDataSource object and *listener* is a component managing the pool containing *pcon1, pcon2*, and *pcon3*, registers *listener* with three PooledConnection objects. Note that an application programmer would never write this code; it is all part of the internal implementation of connection pooling. This code would be part of the DataSource implementation on a middle-tier server.

```
PooledConnection pcon1 = ds.getPooledConnection(
                                    "userName", "password");
pcon1.addConnectionEventListener(listener);

PooledConnection pcon2 = ds.getPooledConnection(
                                    "userName", "password");
pcon2.addConnectionEventListener(listener);

PooledConnection pcon3 = ds.getPooledConnection(
                                    "userName", "password");
pcon3.addConnectionEventListener(listener);
```

13.2 ConnectionEventListener Interface Definition

```
package javax.sql;
public class ConnectionEventListener extends java.util.EventListener {
    void connectionClosed(ConnectionEvent event);
    void connectionErrorOccurred(ConnectionEvent event);
}
```

13.3 ConnectionEventListener Methods

connectionClosed

void **connectionClosed**(ConnectionEvent *event*)

Notifies this ConnectionEventListener object that an application using the PooledConnection object specified in *event* has closed the connection, making it available for reuse. The driver calls this method after the application calls the method close on the PooledConnection object.

PARAMETERS:

event   the ConnectionEvent object indicating the PooledConnection object that was closed by the application using it

EXAMPLE:
```
con.close();
// application closes the Connection object con, which represents a
// pooled connection
ConnectionEvent event = new ConnectionEvent(con);
// the JDBC driver creates event internally
listener.connectionClosed(event);
// the JDBC driver notifies the listener that con has been closed
```

connectionErrorOccurred

void **connectionErrorOccurred**(ConnectionEvent *event*)

Notifies this ConnectionEventListener object that a fatal connection error occurred on the PooledConnection object specified in *event*, thus making it unusable. The driver calls this method on the listener just after the error occurs and before it throws the SQLException to the application using the PooledConnection object. A fatal error is an error that makes the PooledConnection object unusable.

PARAMETERS:

event   the ConnectionEvent object containing the PooledConnection object that had a fatal error and the SQLException object that will be thrown

EXAMPLE:
```
// server crashes while the PooledConnection object con is open
ConnectionEvent event = new ConnectionEvent(con);
// the JDBC driver creates event internally
listener.connectionErrorOccurred(event);
// the JDBC driver notifies the listener that con is no longer
// usable because of a fatal connection error
```

CHAPTER 14

ConnectionPoolDataSource

14.1 ConnectionPoolDataSource Overview

A ConnectionPoolDataSource object is a factory for PooledConnection objects. A PooledConnection object represents a physical connection that is cached in memory; thus it can be reused, which saves the overhead of having to create a new physical connection whenever an application calls for a new connection. The operations on ConnectionPoolDataSource objects are completely internal, so the ConnectionPoolDataSource interface is not part of the API used by application programmers. Driver vendors use it in their implementation of connection pooling.

The ConnectionPoolDataSource interface is almost identical to the DataSource interface, having a similar set of methods. The properties described in the section "Properties," on page 566, apply to the ConnectionPoolDataSource interface as well as to the DataSource interface. Another similarity is that, like a DataSource object, a ConnectionPoolDataSource object is registered with a JNDI naming service.

14.1.1 Connection and PooledConnection Objects

When an application calls the DataSource.getConnection method, the return value is always a Connection object. That Connection object can vary, however, depending on the implementation of the DataSource class. When the DataSource class is a basic implementation, the getConnection method called on an instance of it will return a Connection object that is a physical connection to a data source. But when the DataSource class implements connection pooling, the Connection object that the method getConnection returns to the application is actually a handle to a PooledConnection object. This handle delegates most of the work of the connection to the underlying `PooledConnection` object, which is a physical connection, so the application is never aware that its `Connection` object is not a regular physical connection.

When a `DataSource` class implements connection pooling, a different sequence of events occurs when the method `getConnection` is invoked. Rather than immediately creating a new `Connection` object, the connection pooling module checks to see if there is a `PooledConnection` object available for reuse in the pool of connections. If there is, that `PooledConnection` object is used to create a new `Connection` object to return to the application. If there is no reusable `Pooled-Connection` object, a `ConnectionPoolDataSource` object will be used to create one. In either case, a reusable `PooledConnection` object will have the method `PooledConnection.getConnection` called on it to create the `Connection` object to return to the application.

See Chapter 24, "PooledConnection," starting on page 637, for a detailed explanation of connection pooling.

14.1.2   Reusing Statements

The JDBC 3.0 API makes it possible for an application to reuse `PreparedStatement` objects, thereby offering another means of increasing efficiency. With the new specification, a `PooledConnection` object can have a pool of `PreparedStatement` objects associated with it. This allows the reuse of a `PreparedStatement` object similar to the way a pool of `PooledConnection` objects allows the reuse of a connection. Connection pooling and statement pooling are available to an application only if these features are implemented by the infrastructure on which the application is running. The JDBC API places no restrictions on who can implement statement pooling, so it may be implemented by the application server, the driver, or the underlying data source.

The important point is that pooling mechanisms, either connection pooling or statement pooling, operate purely in the background and do not in any way affect application code. In fact, the specification requires that the reuse of `Prepared-Statement` objects by `PooledConnection` objects be completely transparent to an application. This means that an application using a `PreparedStatement` object must create it and close it for each use. If statement pooling is implemented, closing a `PreparedStatement` object returns it to the pool of statements rather than actually closing it. The next time the application creates the `PreparedStatement` object, the pooled one can be reused.

The JDBC 3.0 specification provides for statement pooling by defining a set of standard properties that apply to `PooledConnection` objects. These properties specify how many physical connections (`PooledConnection` objects) should be in the initial pool, how many should always be available, how long they can be idle before being closed, and so on. The property that applies to statement pooling, `maxStatements`, specifies the total number of `PreparedStatement` objects that a `PooledConnection` object should keep open in its pool of statements. Figure 14.1 gives a logical view of statement pooling.

Figure 14.1: Logical View of `PreparedStatement` Objects Reused by `PooledConnection` Objects

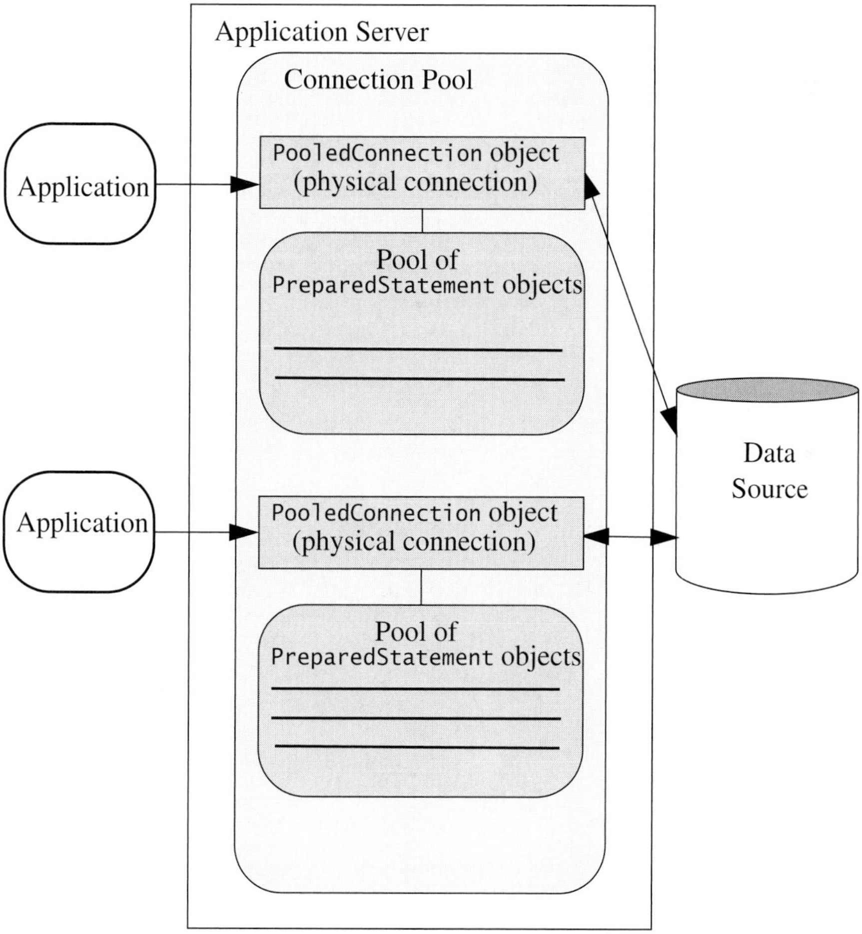

14.1.3   Properties for Connection and Statement Pooling

The properties set in a `ConnectionPoolDataSource` implementation apply to the `PooledConnection` objects that an instance of `ConnectionPoolDataSource` creates. The values set for these properties determine the configuration of connection pooling and statement pooling.

`PooledConnection` properties are part of a `ConnectionPoolDataSource` implementation; an application never uses them directly. An implementation may define additional properties, but if it does, it must make sure that all property names are unique. An implementation must also provide getter and setter methods for all of the properties it uses, regardless of whether they are implementation-specific properties or standard ones.

Table 14.1 shows the standard properties that a `ConnectionPoolDataSource` implementation may set for a `PooledConnection` object.

Table 14.1: Standard Connection Pool Properties

PROPERTY NAME	TYPE	DESCRIPTION
maxStatements	int	The total number of statements the pool should keep open. 0 (zero) indicates that caching of statements is disabled.
initialPoolSize	int	The number of physical connections the pool should contain when it is created.
minPoolSize	int	The minimum number of physical connections in the pool.
maxPoolSize	int	The maximum number of physical connections the pool should contain. 0 (zero) indicates no maximum size.
maxIdleTime	int	The number of seconds that a physical connection should remain unused in the pool before it is closed. 0 (zero) indicates no time limit.
propertyCycle	int	The interval, in seconds, that the pool should wait before enforcing the policy defined by the values currently assigned to these connection pool properties.

If a vendor, Gizmo, Inc., were writing a class implementing the `Connection-PoolDataSource` interface, the code for creating the `ConnectionPoolDataSource` object and setting its properties might look like the following.

```
GizmoConnectionPoolDS gcpds = new GizmoConnectionPoolDS();
gcpds.setMaxStatements(30);
gcpds.setInitialPoolSize(12);
gcpds.setMinPoolSize(1);
gcpds.setMaxPoolSize(0); // no upper limit on pool size
gcpds.setMaxIdleTime(0); // no limit
gcpds.setPropertyCycle(300);
```

An application server that is managing a pool of `PooledConnection` objects uses these properties to determine how to manage the pool. Because the getter and setter methods for properties are defined in `ConnectionPoolDataSource` implementations and are not part of the JDBC API, they are not available to clients. If there is a need to access the properties, such as, for example, when a tool is generating a list of them, they can be obtained through introspection.

14.1.4 Closing a Pooled Statement

As stated previously, an application using pooled statements must create `Prepared-Statement` objects and close them just as if it were using non-pooled statements. If an application creates several `PreparedStatement` objects but neglects to close them, they will not be recycled even if statement pooling is implemented. In other words, an application must close a pooled statement in order for the statement to be available for reuse. An application can close a `Statement` object (and therefore a `PreparedStatement` object) in two ways: by calling the `close` method on the statement or calling the `close` method on the connection. When an application calls the method `PreparedStatement.close` on a pooled statement, the logical statement it is using is closed, but the physical statement is made available for reuse in the statement pool.

Closing a connection closes not only the connection but also all of the statements created by that connection. Thus, when an application calls the method `Connection.close` on a pooled connection, it closes the `Connection` object it is using and also the logical `PreparedStatement` object it is using. However, the underlying physical connection, a `PooledConnection` object, is returned to the connection pool. Similarly, the physical `PreparedStatement` object is returned to the statement pool.

14.2   ConnectionPoolDataSource Interface Definition

```
package javax.sql;
public abstract interface ConnectionPoolDataSource {
    public javax.sql.PooledConnection getPooledConnection()
                                    throws java.sql.SQLException;
    public javax.sql.PooledConnection getPooledConnection(
                    java.lang.String user, java.lang.String password)
                                    throws java.sql.SQLException;
    public void setLoginTimeout(int seconds);
                                    throws java.sql.SQLException;
    public int getLoginTimeout() throws java.sql.SQLException;
    public void setLogWriter(java.io.PrintWriter out)
                                    throws java.sql.SQLException;
    public java.io.PrintWriter getLogWriter()
                                    throws java.sql.SQLException;
}
```

14.3   ConnectionPoolDataSource Methods

NOTE: A vendor's implementation of a `ConnectionPoolDataSource` object must include methods for getting and setting all of a `ConnectionPoolDataSource` object's properties in addition to the methods listed in this section.

getLoginTimeout

```
public int getLoginTimeout() throws java.sql.SQLException
```

Retrieves the maximum number of seconds that this `ConnectionPool-DataSource` object can wait while attempting to connect to a database. A value of zero means that the timeout is the default system timeout if there is one; otherwise, zero means that there is no timeout.

The default is for a newly created `ConnectionPoolDataSource` object to have a login timeout of zero.

RETURNS:
an `int` representing the maximum number of seconds that this `Connection-PoolDataSource` object can wait to connect to a data source

EXAMPLE:
```
int limit = ds.getLoginTimeout();
```

getLogWriter

```
public java.io.PrintWriter getLogWriter();
                              throws java.sql.SQLException
```

Retrieves the character output stream to which all logging and tracing messages for this `ConnectionPoolDataSource` object will be printed. This includes messages printed by the methods of this `ConnectionPoolDataSource` object and also messages printed by methods of other objects manufactured by this `ConnectionPoolDataSource` object.

RETURNS:
the log writer for this `ConnectionPoolDataSource` object; `null` if the log writer has been disabled

EXAMPLE:
```
java.io.PrintWriter logWriter = ds.getLogWriter();
```

getPooledConnection

```
public javax.sql.PooledConnection getPooledConnection()
                              throws java.sql.SQLException
```

Attempts to establish a connection to the data source that this `ConnectionPoolDataSource` object represents.

RETURNS:
a `PooledConnection` object that is a physical connection to the data source that this `ConnectionPoolDataSource` object represents

EXAMPLE:
```
// jdbc/pool/EmployeeDB has been registered with a JNDI naming
// service
ConnectionPoolDataSource ds =
    (ConnectionPoolDataSource)ctx.lookup("jdbc/pool/EmployeeDB");
PooledConnection con = ds.getPooledConnection();
// con is a physical connection to the data source that ds represents
// (the data source for which the logical name is
// jdbc/pool/EmployeeDB)
```

getPooledConnection

```
public javax.sql.PooledConnection getPooledConnection(java.lang.String
    user, java.lang.String password) throws java.sql.SQLException
```

Attempts to establish a connection to the data source that this ConnectionPoolDataSource object represents.

PARAMETERS:

user   the database user on whose behalf the connection is being made

password   the user's password

RETURNS:

a PooledConnection object that is a physical connection to the data source that this ConnectionPoolDataSource object represents

EXAMPLE:
```
// jdbc/pool/EmployeeDB has been registered with a JNDI naming
// service
ConnectionPoolDataSource ds =
    (ConnectionPoolDataSource)ctx.lookup("jdbc/pool/EmployeeDB");
Connection con = ds.getConnection("archibald", "lullaby");
```

setLoginTimeout

```
public void setLoginTimeout(int seconds);
                                    throws java.sql.SQLException
```

Sets to *seconds* the maximum number of seconds that this Connection-

PoolDataSource object can wait for a connection to be established. A value of zero specifies that the timeout is the default system timeout if there is one; otherwise, zero specifies that there is no timeout.

The default login timeout for a newly created DataSource object is zero.

PARAMETERS:

seconds   the maximum number of seconds that this Connection-PoolDataSource object can wait for a connection to be established; 0 to set the timeout to the default system timeout, if there is one, or else 0 to specify no timeout limit

EXAMPLE:
```
ds.setLoginTimeout(30);
// sets the timeout limit for ds to 30 seconds
ds.setLoginTimeout(0);
// sets the timeout limit for ds to the default system timeout; if
// there is no system default, sets the timeout to have no limit
```

setLogWriter

```
public void setLogWriter(java.io.PrintWriter out)
                                        throws java.sql.SQLException
```

Sets to *out* the character output stream to which all logging and tracing messages for this ConnectionPoolDataSource object will be printed. The messages that will be printed to *out* include those printed by the methods of this ConnectionPoolDataSource object and also messages printed by methods of other objects manufactured by this ConnectionPoolDataSource object.

PARAMETERS:

out   the java.io.PrintWriter object to which logging and tracing messages will be sent; null to disable logging and tracing

EXAMPLE:
```
ds.setLogWriter(out);
// logging and tracing messages for ds and any objects manufactured
// by ds will be printed to out

ds.setLogWriter(null);
// no logging or tracing messages will be printed
```

CHAPTER 15

DatabaseMetaData

15.1 DatabaseMetaData Overview

THE interface `java.sql.DatabaseMetaData` provides information about a database as a whole. More precisely, it provides information about a DBMS and its driver working together. For example, many `DatabaseMetaData` methods indicate whether a certain functionality is supported. In some cases, a driver might implement a feature that the DBMS itself does not support. So, if either the DBMS or the driver supports the functionality, the `DatabaseMetaData` method should return `true`.

An application or tool creates an instance of `DatabaseMetaData` and then uses that instance to call `DatabaseMetaData` methods to retrieve information about a database. Other metadata interfaces are `ResultSetMetaData`, which provides information about the columns in a result set, and `ParameterMetaData`, which provides information about the parameters in a `PreparedStatement` object.

In addition to defining a great many methods, the `DatabaseMetaData` interface defines a number of fields. Some of the `DatabaseMetaData` methods return a `ResultSet` object, and the fields, which are by definition constants, serve as possible values for columns in some of those `ResultSet` objects. For example, one of the columns in the `ResultSet` object returned by the method `getProcedures` is `PROCEDURE_TYPE`. The three possible values for this column are the fields `procedureResultUnknown`, `procedureNoResult`, and `procedureReturnsResult`. These constants say whether a given procedure returns a result.

The `DatabaseMetaData` interface is used mostly by driver and tool developers. A driver implements the `DatabaseMetaData` methods so that each method gives the appropriate response for the DBMS and the driver working together. Tool developers use the `DatabaseMetaData` methods to discover how their applications should deal with the underlying database. Users who simply send SQL statements to a database with which they are familiar generally do not need to call methods from this interface. When users do call `DatabaseMetaData` methods, they are typically checking whether a particular feature is supported.

For more information and complete code examples of how to use the `DatabaseMetaData` interface, see "Using a `DatabaseMetaData` Object," on page 209.

15.1.1   Creating a `DatabaseMetaData` Object

A `DatabaseMetaData` object is created with the `Connection` method `getMetaData`, as in the following code, where *con* is a `Connection` object.

```
DatabaseMetaData dbmd = con.getMetaData();
```

The variable *dbmd* contains a `DatabaseMetaData` object that can be used to get information about the database to which *con* is connected. This is done by calling a `DatabaseMetaData` method on *dbmd*, as is done in the following code fragment.

```
int n = dbmd.getMaxTableNameLength();
```

If the `Connection` object *con* is connected to a database called `HumanRelations`, the variable *n* indicates the maximum number of characters that can be used to name a table in `HumanRelations`.

The method `getConnection` allows an application to discover which connection created a `DatabaseMetaData` object. For example, in the following code fragment, *dbmd* is created by the `Connection` object *con*. Thus, the values for *con* and *x* will be the same.

```
DatabaseMetaData dbmd = con.getMetaData();
Connection x = dbmd.getConnection();
```

15.1.2   `ResultSet` Objects as Return Values

Many of the `DatabaseMetaData` methods return lists of information in the form of a `ResultSet` object. A `ResultSet` object returned by a `DatabaseMetaData` method is the same standard `ResultSet` object returned by a query. Data is retrieved from these `ResultSet` objects using the normal `ResultSet.getter` methods, such as `getString` and `getInt`. For example, the following code illustrates retrieving the values returned by the method `getSchemas`. This method returns a `ResultSet` object that has only one column, and that column stores a `String` object. Each row of the result set is the name of a schema that is available in this database.

```
ResultSet rs = dbmd.getSchemas();
while (rs.next()) {
    String s = rs.getString(1);
    System.out.println("Schema name = " + s);
}
```

As is always true of getter methods in the `ResultSet` interface, if one is called on a data type that requires a conversion that the driver does not support, the getter method will throw an `SQLException`. Table 27.1, "Use of ResultSet getter Methods to Retrieve JDBC Types," on page 699, shows the conversions that are supported by `ResultSet` getter methods.

Methods that are supposed to return a `ResultSet` object but fail to do so should throw an `SQLException`. Any `ResultSet` object is a legal return value, including one that is empty. A DBMS may define additional columns for a `ResultSet` object that is returned by a `DatabaseMetaData` method.

15.1.3 String Patterns as Arguments

Some `DatabaseMetaData` methods take as an argument a `String` object that serves as a search pattern. These arguments all have "Pattern" as the last part of the variable name, such as in *schemaPattern*, *tableNamePattern*, *columnNamePattern*, and *procedureNamePattern*. Within one of these search patterns, an underscore (_) calls for a match of any single character, and a percent sign (%) calls for a match of zero or more characters. Supplying `null` signifies that this criterion should not be used in the search. For example, if `null` is specified to a method for the catalog and schema parameters, the method will search all catalogs and all schemas. Note that if a database does not support a particular search criterion, such as catalog or schema, `null` must be supplied for that criterion.

If the method `getProcedures` were invoked with the following arguments, it would return information about procedures that are in any schema and whose names start with "REPLACE":

```
ResultSet rs = dbmd.getProcedures(null, null, "REPLACE%");
```

Thus, if there were procedures named REPLACE_PRICE, REPLACEMENT_UPDATE, and REPLACE, they would all be described in the ResultSet object *rs*; REPLACING_NO_SALES and AUTOREPLACE, however, would not be included.

Note that identifier name patterns are case-sensitive. What needs to be matched is the identifier name as it is stored in the database. Some databases, for example, store identifiers in their catalogs as all uppercase or all lowercase. This is true even if the identifier name was mixed case in the statement that created it. For example, consider the following statement:

```
CREATE TABLE newCars
(Model CHAR(10))
```

The table identifier newCars may be stored as NEWCARS in some databases; therefore, to access information about it using metadata methods, it may be necessary to use all uppercase characters in the search pattern.

The only sure way to make patterns database-independent is to discover the way identifiers are stored (with DatabaseMetaData methods), and then use the appropriate case in identifier name patterns.

DatabaseMetaData has several methods for determining whether identifier names are stored in the database as lowercase, mixed case, or uppercase:

- storesLowerCaseIdentifiers
- storesLowerCaseQuotedIdentifiers
- storesMixedCaseIdentifiers
- storesMixedCaseQuotedIdentifiers
- storesUpperCaseIdentifiers
- storesUpperCaseQuotedIdentifiers
- supportsMixedCaseIdentifiers
- supportsMixedCaseQuotedIdentifiers

If the methods with "QuotedIdentifiers" in their names return true, they allow nonalphanumeric characters if those characters are enclosed in quotation marks.

15.1.4 Pseudo Columns

Some of the variables in DatabaseMetaData (bestRowNotPseudo, bestRowPseudo, bestRowUnknown, versionColumnNotPseudo, versionColumnPseudo, and version-

ColumnUnknown) indicate whether a column is a pseudo column. A pseudo column is a column that is generated by the database. A typical example is the ROWID column used by several database systems. This column contains identification numbers for rows in a result set. These identification numbers are not entered by the user; they are calculated by the database and stored in the pseudo column ROWID, which is not included as part of the result set returned to the user. Another example is a DBMS that, for designated tables, automatically increments identification numbers and assigns them as primary keys. The DBMS maintains a special pseudo column to keep track of the last number assigned. When a row is added to the table, the DBMS increments the last number in its pseudo column and assigns the new number to the appropriate column. In this case, the generated identification number is entered in a regular table column, whereas the number to increment is maintained in a pseudo column.

15.1.5   Features Added in the JDBC 2.0 Core API

The following features were added to the DatabaseMetaData interface as part of the JDBC 2.0 core API:

- Methods getting information about the update capabilities of the DBMS and driver, and about the visibility of changes:

  - supportsBatchUpdates

    This method returns true if the driver supports batch updates.

  - deletesAreDetected, insertsAreDetected, updatesAreDetected

    These methods indicate whether a change that is visible in a ResultSet object can be detected by calling the ResultSet methods rowDeleted, rowInserted, or rowUpdated. For example, if an update can be seen in a result set that is open and the method DatabaseMetaData.updatesAreDetected returns true, then the method ResultSet.rowUpdated will return true when called on that row.

  - ownDeletesAreVisible, ownInsertsAreVisible, ownUpdatesAreVisible

    These methods indicate whether the changes made via a ResultSet object are visible via the ResultSet object. For example, if a result set inserts a row into itself and the new row appears without having to close and reopen the result set, then the method ownInsertsAreVisible will return true.

- othersDeletesAreVisible, othersInsertsAreVisible, othersUpdatesAre-Visible

    These methods indicate whether a change made to a ResultSet object via others (another transaction or another result set in the same transaction as the one being modified) will be visible to the modified result set while it is open. For example, if another transaction inserts a row into a result set and the new row appears without having to close and reopen the result set, then the method othersInsertsAreVisible will return true.

- Methods relating to the new kinds of ResultSet objects:

  - supportsResultSetType

    This method returns true if the driver supports the given ResultSet type.

  - supportsResultSetConcurrency

    This method returns true if the driver supports the given concurrency type in combination with the given ResultSet type.

- Methods that retrieve other information:

  - getUDTs

    This method returns a ResultSet object containing a description of the user-defined types (UDTs) that have been defined for a particular schema. In order to use a UDT as a column value in a table, it must first be defined as part of a schema.

  - getConnection

    This method returns the Connection object that produced this DatabaseMetaData object.

4. New JDBC types (defined in the class java.sql.Types) as possible values in the ResultSet objects returned by the following DatabaseMetaData methods:

  - getTypeInfo (JDBC 1.0)

    additional possible values for the column DATA_TYPE:
    ARRAY, BLOB, CLOB, DISTINCT, JAVA_OBJECT, REF, STRUCT

  - getColumns (JDBC 1.0)

    additional possible values for the column DATA_TYPE:
    ARRAY, BLOB, CLOB, DISTINCT, JAVA_OBJECT, REF, STRUCT

- getProcedureColumns (JDBC 1.0)

  additional possible values for the column DATA_TYPE:
  ARRAY, BLOB, CLOB, DISTINCT, JAVA_OBJECT, REF, STRUCT

- getBestRowIdentifier (JDBC 1.0)

  additional possible values for the column DATA_TYPE:
  ARRAY, BLOB, CLOB, DISTINCT, JAVA_OBJECT, REF, STRUCT

- getUDTs (JDBC 2.0)

  possible values for the column DATA_TYPE:
  DISTINCT, STRUCT, JAVA_OBJECT

15.1.6 Getting Advanced Type Information

2.0

The JDBC 2.0 core API added new data types and also new methods to get information about them.

You can get a list of the user-defined types (UDTs) that have been created for your database by calling the DatabaseMetaData method getUDTs. For example, the following code fragment gets a list of all the STRUCT objects defined in a particular schema.

```
DatabaseMetaData dbmd = con.getMetaData();
int [] types = {Types.STRUCT};
ResultSet udtrs = dbmd.getUDTs(
                    "catalog-name", "schema-name", "%", types);
while(udtrs.next()) {
    String name = udtrs.getString("TYPE_NAME");
}
```

15.1.7 Methods and Fields Added in the JDBC 3.0 API

3.0

The JDBC 3.0 API added new functionality and enhancements to existing functionality. The new methods and fields in the DatabaseMetaData interface either give access to additional information or indicate whether the DBMS supports a new functionality. The following list itemizes the new DatabaseMetaData API and briefly summarizes what it does.

- Methods indicating whether new functionality is supported. These methods all return true or false.

  - supportsGetGeneratedKeys

This method returns `true` if the driver can return the keys that the DBMS creates automatically when new rows are added to a table

- supportsMultipleOpenResults

  This method returns `true` if a `CallableStatement` object can return more than one `ResultSet` object and keep them open simultaneously.

- supportsNamedParameters

  This method returns `true` if the DBMS supports using a name (as opposed to using the ordinal number) to specify the parameter when calling the `CallableStatement.getter` methods.

- supportsResultSetHoldability

  This method returns `true` if the DBMS supports the given holdability (either `ResultSet.HOLD_CURSORS_OVER_COMMIT` or `ResultSet.CLOSE_CURSORS_AT_COMMIT`).

- supportsSavepoints

  This method returns `true` if the DBMS supports setting savepoints to mark intermediate points in a transaction.

- supportsStatementPooling

  This method returns `true` if the DBMS supports the pooling of `PreparedStatement` objects.

- API related to UDTs

  - getSuperTypes

    This method returns a description of the super type for each UDT defined in a given schema in the database.

  - getAttributes

    This method returns a description of the given attribute for a UDT.

- API for getting other information

  - locatorsUpdateCopy

    This method returns `true` if the updates made to `BLOB` or `CLOB` data are made only to a copy and not to the `BLOB` or `CLOB` value in the database. This method returns `false` if updates change the `BLOB` or `CLOB` value in the database.

- `getSuperTables`

  This method returns a description of the super tables for a given table defined in the database.

- `getDatabaseMajorVersion`

  This method returns the major version number for the underlying database.

- `getDatabaseMinorVersion`

  This method returns the minor version number for the underlying database.

- `getJDBCMajorVersion`

  This method returns the major JDBC version number for this driver.

- `getJDBCMinorVersion`

  This method returns the minor JDBC version number for this driver.

- `getSQLStateType`

  This method returns the type of `SQLSTATE` that is returned by the method `SQLException.getSQLState`.

- Fields Used in Return Values

  - Possible return values for the method `getSQLStateType`

    - `sqlStateXOpen`
    - `sqlStateSQL99`

    The method `SQLException.getSQLState` returns an SQL state, and the method `getSQLStateType` finds out which of these two constants describes the type of SQL state being returned.

  - Possible values for the column `NULLABLE` in the `ResultSet` object returned by the method `getAttributes`

    - `attributeNoNulls`
      Attributes of the specified UDTs might not be able to be `NULL`.
    - `attributeNullable`
      Attributes of the specified UDTs can definitely be `NULL`.
    - `attributeNullableUnknown`
      It is not known whether attributes of the specified UDTs can be `NULL`.

15.1.8   Methods Modified in the JDBC 3.0 API

Some existing methods were modified to add support for type hierarchies. These methods all return a `ResultSet` object that describes the database object that matches the given catalog, schema, and other criteria. One or more columns has been added to each `ResultSet` object to hold the additional hierarchy information. The return values of the following `DatabaseMetaData` methods have been modified:

- getTables

- getColumns

- getUDTs

- getSchemas

15.2   DatabaseMetaData Interface Definition

```
package java.sql;
public interface DatabaseMetaData {


//===================================================================
// Methods that get minor information about the target database:
//===================================================================

    boolean allProceduresAreCallable() throws SQLException;
    boolean allTablesAreSelectable() throws SQLException;
    String getURL() throws SQLException;
    String getUserName() throws SQLException;
    boolean isReadOnly() throws SQLException;
    boolean nullsAreSortedHigh() throws SQLException;
    boolean nullsAreSortedLow() throws SQLException;
    boolean nullsAreSortedAtStart() throws SQLException;
    boolean nullsAreSortedAtEnd() throws SQLException;
    String getDatabaseProductName() throws SQLException;
    String getDatabaseProductVersion() throws SQLException;
    String getDriverName() throws SQLException;
    String getDriverVersion() throws SQLException;
    int getDriverMajorVersion();
    int getDriverMinorVersion();
```

```
           boolean usesLocalFiles() throws SQLException;
           boolean usesLocalFilePerTable() throws SQLException;
           boolean supportsMixedCaseIdentifiers() throws SQLException;
           boolean storesLowerCaseIdentifiers() throws SQLException;
           boolean storesUpperCaseIdentifiers() throws SQLException;
           boolean storesMixedCaseIdentifiers() throws SQLException;
           boolean supportsMixedCaseQuotedIdentifiers() throws SQLException;
           boolean storesUpperCaseQuotedIdentifiers() throws SQLException;
           boolean storesLowerCaseQuotedIdentifiers() throws SQLException;
           boolean storesMixedCaseQuotedIdentifiers() throws SQLException;
           String getIdentifierQuoteString() throws SQLException;
           String getSQLKeywords() throws SQLException;
           String getNumericFunctions() throws SQLException;
           String getStringFunctions() throws SQLException;
           String getSystemFunctions() throws SQLException;
           String getTimeDateFunctions() throws SQLException;
           String getSearchStringEscape() throws SQLException;
           String getExtraNameCharacters() throws SQLException;
           String getSchemaTerm() throws SQLException;
           String getProcedureTerm() throws SQLException;
           String getCatalogTerm() throws SQLException;
           boolean isCatalogAtStart() throws SQLException;
           String getCatalogSeparator() throws SQLException;
           int getDefaultTransactionIsolation() throws SQLException;

   [2.0]   Connection getConnection() throws SQLException;

   [3.0]   int getResultSetHoldability() throws SQLException;
   [3.0]   int getDatabaseMajorVersion() throws SQLException;
   [3.0]   int getDatabaseMinorVersion() throws SQLException;
   [3.0]   int getJDBCMajorVersion() throws SQLException;
   [3.0]   int getJDBCMinorVersion() throws SQLException;

   [3.0]   int getSQLStateType() throws SQLException;


   //================================================================
   Methods describing which features are supported:
   //================================================================
```

```
boolean supportsAlterTableWithAddColumn() throws SQLException;
boolean supportsAlterTableWithDropColumn() throws SQLException;
boolean supportsColumnAliasing() throws SQLException;
boolean nullPlusNonNullIsNull() throws SQLException;
boolean supportsConvert() throws SQLException;
boolean supportsConvert(int fromType, int toType)
                                                    throws SQLException;
boolean supportsTableCorrelationNames() throws SQLException;
boolean supportsDifferentTableCorrelationNames()
                                                    throws SQLException;
boolean supportsExpressionsInOrderBy() throws SQLException;
boolean supportsOrderByUnrelated() throws SQLException;
boolean supportsGroupBy() throws SQLException;
boolean supportsGroupByUnrelated() throws SQLException;
boolean supportsGroupByBeyondSelect() throws SQLException;
boolean supportsLikeEscapeClause() throws SQLException;
boolean supportsMultipleResultSets() throws SQLException;
boolean supportsMultipleTransactions() throws SQLException;
boolean supportsNonNullableColumns() throws SQLException;
boolean supportsMinimumSQLGrammar() throws SQLException;
boolean supportsCoreSQLGrammar() throws SQLException;
boolean supportsExtendedSQLGrammar() throws SQLException;
boolean supportsANSI92EntryLevelSQL() throws SQLException;
boolean supportsANSI92IntermediateSQL() throws SQLException;
boolean supportsANSI92FullSQL() throws SQLException;
boolean supportsIntegrityEnhancementFacility() throws SQLException;
boolean supportsOuterJoins() throws SQLException;
boolean supportsFullOuterJoins() throws SQLException;
boolean supportsLimitedOuterJoins() throws SQLException;
boolean supportsSchemasInDataManipulation() throws SQLException;
boolean supportsSchemasInProcedureCalls() throws SQLException;
boolean supportsSchemasInTableDefinitions() throws SQLException;
boolean supportsSchemasInIndexDefinitions() throws SQLException;
boolean supportsSchemasInPrivilegeDefinitions()
                                                    throws SQLException;
boolean supportsCatalogsInDataManipulation() throws SQLException;
boolean supportsCatalogsInProcedureCalls() throws SQLException;
boolean supportsCatalogsInTableDefinitions() throws SQLException;
boolean supportsCatalogsInIndexDefinitions() throws SQLException;
```

```
        boolean supportsCatalogsInPrivilegeDefinitions()
                                              throws SQLException;
        boolean supportsPositionedDelete() throws SQLException;
        boolean supportsPositionedUpdate() throws SQLException;
        boolean supportsSelectForUpdate() throws SQLException;
        boolean supportsStoredProcedures() throws SQLException;
        boolean supportsSubqueriesInComparisons() throws SQLException;
        boolean supportsSubqueriesInExists() throws SQLException;
        boolean supportsSubqueriesInIns() throws SQLException;
        boolean supportsSubqueriesInQuantifieds() throws SQLException;
        boolean supportsCorrelatedSubqueries() throws SQLException;
        boolean supportsUnion() throws SQLException;
        boolean supportsUnionAll() throws SQLException;
        boolean supportsOpenCursorsAcrossCommit() throws SQLException;
        boolean supportsOpenCursorsAcrossRollback() throws SQLException;
        boolean supportsOpenStatementsAcrossCommit() throws SQLException;
        boolean supportsOpenStatementsAcrossRollback() throws SQLException;
        boolean supportsTransactions() throws SQLException;
        boolean supportsTransactionIsolationLevel(int level)
                                              throws SQLException;
```

```
 2.0    boolean supportsBatchUpdates() throws SQLException;
 2.0    boolean supportsResultSetType(int type) throws SQLException;
 2.0    boolean supportsResultSetConcurrency(int type, int concurrency)
                                              throws SQLException;
```

```
 3.0    boolean supportsSavepoints() throws SQLException;
 3.0    boolean supportsNamedParameters() throws SQLException;
 3.0    boolean supportsMultipleOpenResults() throws SQLException;
 3.0    boolean supportsGetGeneratedKeys() throws SQLException;
 3.0    boolean supportsResultSetHoldability() throws SQLException;
 3.0    boolean supportsStatementPooling() throws SQLException;
 3.0    boolean locatorsUpdateCopy() throws SQLException;
```

```
    //===================================================================
    //   Methods that expose various limitations based on the target
    //   database with the current driver.
```

```
//    Unless otherwise specified, a result of zero means there is
//    no limit or the limit is not known.
//======================================================================

    int getMaxBinaryLiteralLength() throws SQLException;
    int getMaxCharLiteralLength() throws SQLException;
    int getMaxColumnNameLength() throws SQLException;
    int getMaxColumnsInGroupBy() throws SQLException;
    int getMaxColumnsInIndex() throws SQLException;
    int getMaxColumnsInOrderBy() throws SQLException;
    int getMaxColumnsInSelect() throws SQLException;
    int getMaxColumnsInTable() throws SQLException;
    int getMaxConnections() throws SQLException;
    int getMaxCursorNameLength() throws SQLException;
    int getMaxIndexLength() throws SQLException;
    int getMaxSchemaNameLength() throws SQLException;
    int getMaxProcedureNameLength() throws SQLException;
    int getMaxCatalogNameLength() throws SQLException;
    int getMaxRowSize() throws SQLException;
    boolean doesMaxRowSizeIncludeBlobs() throws SQLException;
    int getMaxStatementLength() throws SQLException;
    int getMaxStatements() throws SQLException;
    int getMaxTableNameLength() throws SQLException;
    int getMaxTablesInSelect() throws SQLException;
    int getMaxUserNameLength() throws SQLException;


//======================================================================
// Methods specifying whether data definition statements can be
// part of a transaction and what happens if they are:
//======================================================================

    boolean supportsDataDefinitionAndDataManipulationTransactions()
                                                 throws SQLException;
    boolean supportsDataManipulationTransactionsOnly()
                                                 throws SQLException;
    boolean dataDefinitionCausesTransactionCommit()throws SQLException;
    boolean dataDefinitionIgnoredInTransactions() throws SQLException;
```

```
//===================================================================
//     Methods that return ResultSet objects to describe
//     database objects:
//===================================================================

    ResultSet getProcedures(String catalog, String schemaPattern,
                    String procedureNamePattern) throws SQLException;
    ResultSet getProcedureColumns(String catalog, String schemaPattern,
                String procedureNamePattern, String columnNamePattern)
                                               throws SQLException;
    ResultSet getTables(String catalog, String schemaPattern,
        String tableNamePattern, String types[]) throws SQLException;
    ResultSet getSchemas() throws SQLException;
    ResultSet getCatalogs() throws SQLException;
    ResultSet getTableTypes() throws SQLException;
    ResultSet getColumns(String catalog, String schemaPattern,
                    String tableNamePattern, String columnNamePattern)
                                               throws SQLException;
    ResultSet getColumnPrivileges(String catalog, String schema,
        String table, String columnNamePattern) throws SQLException;
    ResultSet getTablePrivileges(String catalog, String schemaPattern,
                String tableNamePattern) throws SQLException;
    ResultSet getBestRowIdentifier(String catalog, String schema,
        String table, int scope, boolean nullable) throws SQLException;
    ResultSet getVersionColumns(String catalog, String schema,
                String table) throws SQLException;
    ResultSet getPrimaryKeys(String catalog, String schema,
                String table) throws SQLException;
    ResultSet getImportedKeys(String catalog, String schema,
                String table) throws SQLException;
    ResultSet getExportedKeys(String catalog, String schema,
                String table) throws SQLException;
    ResultSet getCrossReference(String primaryCatalog,
                    String primarySchema, String primaryTable,
                    String foreignCatalog, String foreignSchema,
                    String foreignTable) throws SQLException;
    ResultSet getTypeInfo() throws SQLException;
    ResultSet getIndexInfo(String catalog, String schema, String table,
            boolean unique, boolean approximate) throws SQLException;
```

`2.0` ResultSet **getUDTs**(String catalog, String schemaPattern,
             String typeNamePattern, int [] types) throws SQLException;

`3.0` ResultSet **getSuperTypes**(String catalog, String schemaPattern,
                  String typeNamePattern) throws SQLException;
`3.0` ResultSet **getSuperTables**(String catalog, String schemaPattern,
                  String tableNamePattern) throws SQLException;
`3.0` ResultSet **getAttributes**(String catalog, String schemaPattern,
             String typeNamePattern, String attributeNamePattern)
                                        throws SQLException;

```
//===================================================================
//     Methods relating to modifications to ResultSet objects:
//===================================================================
```

`2.0` boolean **deletesAreDetected**(int type) throws SQLException;
`2.0` boolean **insertsAreDetected**(int type) throws SQLException;
`2.0` boolean **updatesAreDetected**(int type) throws SQLException;
`2.0` boolean **othersDeletesAreVisible**(int type) throws SQLException;
`2.0` boolean **othersInsertsAreVisible**(int type) throws SQLException;
`2.0` boolean **othersUpdatesAreVisible**(int type) throws SQLException;

`2.0` boolean **ownDeletesAreVisible**(int type) throws SQLException;
`2.0` boolean **ownInsertsAreVisible**(int type) throws SQLException;
`2.0` boolean **ownUpdatesAreVisible**(int type) throws SQLException;

```
//===================================================================
//     Fields used as possible values returned by
//     DatabaseMetaData methods:
//===================================================================
```

```
    // Possible values for getProcedureColumns
    public final static int procedureColumnUnknown = 0;
    public final static int procedureColumnIn = 1;
    public final static int procedureColumnInOut = 2;
    public final static int procedureColumnResult = 3;
    public final static int procedureColumnOut = 4;
    public final static int procedureColumnReturn = 5;
    public final static int procedureNoNulls = 0;
```

```
public final static int procedureNullable = 1;
public final static int procedureNullableUnknown = 2;

// Possible values for getProcedures
public final static int procedureResultUnknown = 0;
public final static int procedureNoResult = 1;
public final static int procedureReturnsResult = 2;

// Possible values for getColumns
public final static int columnNoNulls = 0;
public final static int columnNullable = 1;
public final static int columnNullableUnknown = 2;

// Possible values for getBestRowIdentifier
public final static int bestRowTemporary = 0;
public final static int bestRowTransaction = 1;
public final static int bestRowSession = 2;
public final static int bestRowUnknown = 0;
public final static int bestRowNotPseudo = 1;
public final static int bestRowPseudo = 2;
// Possible values for getVersionColumns
public final static int versionColumnUnknown = 0;
public final static int versionColumnNotPseudo = 1;
public final static int versionColumnPseudo = 2;

// Possible values for getImportedKeys, getExportedKeys, and
// getCrossReference
public final static int importedKeyCascade = 0;
public final static int importedKeyRestrict = 1;
public final static int importedKeySetNull = 2;
public final static int importedKeyNoAction = 3;
public final static int importedKeySetDefault = 4;
public final static int importedKeyInitiallyDeferred = 5;
public final static int importedKeyInitiallyImmediate = 6;
public final static int importedKeyNotDeferrable = 7;

// Possible values for getTypeInfo
public final static int typeNoNulls = 0;
public final static int typeNullable = 1;
public final static int typeNullableUnknown = 2;
```

```
public final static int typePredNone = 0;
public final static int typePredChar = 1;
public final static int typePredBasic = 2;
public final static int typeSearchable = 3;


// Possible values for getIndexInfo
public final static short tableIndexStatistic = 0;
public final static short tableIndexClustered = 1;
public final static short tableIndexHashed = 2;
public final static short tableIndexOther = 3;


// Possible values for getSQLStateType
public final static int sqlStateXOpen = 1;
public final static int sqlStateSQL99 = 2;


// Possible values for getAttributes
public final static short attributeNoNulls = 0;
public final static short attributeNullable = 1;
public final static short attributeNullableUnknown = 2;
}
```

15.3 DatabaseMetaData Methods

allProceduresAreCallable

```
boolean allProceduresAreCallable() throws SQLException
```

Checks whether the current user has the required security rights to call all the procedures returned by the method getProcedures.

RETURNS:
true if so; false otherwise

EXAMPLE:
```
DatabaseMetaData dbmd = myConnection.getMetaData();
boolean b = dbmd.allProceduresAreCallable();
```

allTablesAreSelectable

```
boolean allTablesAreSelectable() throws SQLException
```

Checks whether the current user can use a SELECT statement with all of the tables returned by the method getTables.

RETURNS:
true if so; false otherwise

EXAMPLE:
```
boolean b = dbmd.allTablesAreSelectable();
```

dataDefinitionCausesTransactionCommit

```
boolean dataDefinitionCausesTransactionCommit()throws SQLException
```

Checks whether a data definition statement within a transaction forces the transaction to commit.

RETURNS:
true if so; false otherwise

EXAMPLE:
```
boolean b = dbmd.dataDefinitionCausesTransactionCommit();
```

dataDefinitionIgnoredInTransactions

```
boolean dataDefinitionIgnoredInTransactions() throws SQLException
```

Checks whether a data definition statement within a transaction is ignored.

RETURNS:
true if so; false otherwise

EXAMPLE:
```
boolean b = dbmd.dataDefinitionIgnoredInTransactions();
```

deletesAreDetected

`2.0`

```
boolean deletesAreDetected(int type) throws SQLException
```

     Checks whether a deletion that is visible in a `ResultSet` object of type *type* can be detected by calling the method `ResultSet.rowDeleted`. A deletion is visible under two conditions: (1) the row is removed or (2) an empty row (a "hole") replaces the deleted row. When `deletesAreDetected` returns `true`, a "hole" replaces the deleted row. When `deletesAreDetected` returns `false`, it means that deleted rows are removed from the `ResultSet` object.

PARAMETERS:

type   an `int` indicating the type of the `ResultSet` object:
                                `ResultSet.TYPE_FORWARD_ONLY`,
                                `ResultSet.TYPE_SCROLL_INSENSITIVE`, or
                                `ResultSet.TYPE_SCROLL_SENSITIVE`

RETURNS:
`true` if a "hole" replaces a visible deleted row; `false` if a visible deleted row is simply removed

EXAMPLE:
```
boolean b = dbmd.deletesAreDetected(
                        ResultSet.TYPE_SCROLL_SENSITIVE);
```

SEE:
"Detecting Changes," on page 719

doesMaxRowSizeIncludeBlobs

```
boolean doesMaxRowSizeIncludeBlobs() throws SQLException
```

     Checks whether the value returned by the method `getMaxRowSize` includes `LONGVARCHAR` and `LONGVARBINARY` blobs, that is, whether blobs are counted as part of the row size. Whether it includes `BLOB` and `CLOB` objects is implementation-defined.

RETURNS:
`true` if so; `false` otherwise

EXAMPLE:
```
boolean b = dbmd.doesMaxRowSizeIncludeBlobs();
```

getAttributes

3.0

```
ResultSet getAttributes(String catalog, String schemaPattern,
        String typeNamePattern, String attributeNamePattern)
                                          throws SQLException
```

Returns a `ResultSet` object that describes the specified attribute of the given type (a user-definted type (UDT) or `REF` value) that is available in the given schema and catalog.

Descriptions are returned only for attributes that match the given attribute name pattern and where the catalog, schema, and type also match those given. They are ordered by `TYPE_SCHEM`, `TYPE_NAME`, and `ORDINAL_POSITION`. This description does not contain inherited attributes.

PARAMETERS:

catalog	a `String` object representing a catalog name, which must match the catalog name as it is stored in the database; "" retrieves those without a catalog; `null` indicates that the catalog name should not be used to narrow the search
schemaPattern	a `String` object representing a schema name pattern, which must match the schema name as it is stored in the database; "" retrieves those without a schema; `null` indicates that the schema name should not be used to narrow the search
typeNamePattern	a `String` object representing a type name pattern, which must match the type name as it is stored in the database
attributeNamePattern	a `String` representing the name pattern of an attribute, which must match the attribute name as it is declared in the database

RETURNS:
a `ResultSet` object, with each row being a description of an attribute

Each row in the `ResultSet` object has the following columns:

1. TYPE_CAT   String indicating the type catalog; may be `null`
2. TYPE_SCHEM   String object giving the schema of the type
3. TYPE_NAME   String object giving the type name used by the data source
4. DATA_TYPE   short indicating the generic SQL data type from `java.sql.Types`

5. `ATTR_NAME`	`String` giving the attribute name
6. `ATTR_TYPE_NAME`	`String` giving the data source-dependent type name. For a UDT, the type name is fully qualified. For a `REF` value, the type name is fully qualified and represents the target type of the reference type.
7. `ATTR_SIZE`	`int` indicating the column size. For char or date types, this is the maximum number of characters; for numeric or decimal types, this is precision.
8. `DECIMAL_DIGITS`	`int` indicating the number of fractional digits
9. `NUM_PREC_RADIX`	`int` indicating the radix (typically 10 or 2)
10. `NULLABLE`	`int` indicating whether a column can be `NULL` The possible values are:
•`attributeNoNulls`	—might not allow `NULL` values
•`attributeNullable`	—definitely allows `NULL` values
•`attributeNullableUnknown`	—whether `NULL` values are allowed is unknown
11. `REMARKS`	`String` describing the column; may be `null`
12. `ATTR_DEF`	`String` indicating the default value; may be `null`
13. `SQL_DATA_TYPE`	`int`; unused
14. `SQL_DATETIME_SUB`	`int`; unused
15. `CHAR_OCTET_LENGTH`	`int` that for char types indicates the maximum number of bytes in the column
16. `ORDINAL_POSITION`	`int` indicating the index of the column in the table, with numbering starting at 1
17. `IS_NULLABLE`	`String` indicating whether the column can contain a `NULL` value; "NO" means that the column definitely does not allow `NULL` values; "YES" means that the column might allow `NULL` values. An empty string means that the nullability is unknown.
18. `SCOPE_CATALOG`	`String` indicating the catalog of the table that is the scope of a reference attribute; `null` when `DATA_TYPE` is not `REF`
19. `SCOPE_SCHEMA`	`String` indicating the schema of the table that is the scope of a reference attribute; `null` when `DATA_TYPE` is not `REF`
20. `SCOPE_TABLE`	`String` indicating the name of the table that is the scope of a reference attribute; `null` when `DATA_TYPE` is not `REF`

21. SOURCE_DATA_TYPE   short indicating the source type of a DISTINCT type or a user-generated REF type. The short is a type code defined in java.sql.Types. The column value will be null if DATA_TYPE is not DISTINCT or a user-generated REF

EXAMPLE:
```
ResultSet rs = dbmd.getAttributes("MYCATALOG", "MYSCHEMA%",
            "MYUDTNAME%", "MYATTRIBUTENAME%");
```

getBestRowIdentifier

```
ResultSet getBestRowIdentifier(String catalog, String schema,
     String table, int scope, boolean nullable) throws SQLException
```

Gets a description of a table's optimal set of columns that uniquely identifies a row. The descriptions are ordered by the column SCOPE.

PARAMETERS:

catalog   a String object representing a catalog name; "" retrieves those without a catalog; null indicates that the catalog name should not be used to narrow the search

schema   a String object representing a schema name; "" retrieves those without a schema; null indicates that the schema name should not be used to narrow the search

table   a String object representing a table name

scope   an int representing the scope of interest; one of bestRowTemporary, bestRowTransaction, or bestRowSession

nullable   true to indicate that columns that are nullable may be included; false to exclude columns that can be null

RETURNS:
a ResultSet object, with each row being a description of a column that belongs to the optimal set of columns that uniquely identifies a row. This set may consist of one or more columns, and it may include pseudo columns.

Each column description has the following columns:

1. SCOPE   short indicating the actual scope of the result The possible values are:

•bestRowTemporary	—very temporary; this column is the best identifier for this row only while the row is being used
•bestRowTransaction	—this column is the best identifier for this row for the remainder of the current transaction
•bestRowSession	—this column is the best identifier for this row for the remainder of the current session
2. COLUMN_NAME	String object giving the column name
3. DATA_TYPE	short indicating the generic SQL data type from java.sql.Types
4. TYPE_NAME	String object giving the type name used by the data source
5. COLUMN_SIZE	int giving the precision
6. BUFFER_LENGTH	int; not used
7. DECIMAL_DIGITS	short indicating the scale
8. PSEUDO_COLUMN	short indicating whether this is a pseudo column, such as an Oracle ROWID The possible values are:
•bestRowUnknown	—may or may not be a pseudo column
•bestRowNotPseudo	—is NOT a pseudo column
•bestRowPseudo	—is a pseudo column

EXAMPLE:
```
ResultSet rs = dbmd.getBestRowIdentifier("MYCATALOG", "MYSCHEMA",
            "TABLE1", DatabaseMetaData.bestRowSession, false);
```

getCatalogs

```
ResultSet getCatalogs() throws SQLException
```

Gets the catalog names available in this database. The results are ordered by catalog name.

RETURNS:
a ResultSet object, with each row representing a catalog name available in this database

The `ResultSet` object has the following column:

1. `TABLE_CAT`   `String` object containing a catalog name

EXAMPLE:
```
ResultSet rs = dbmd.getCatalogs();
```

getCatalogSeparator

```
String getCatalogSeparator() throws SQLException
```

Gets the `String` object used to separate a catalog name and a schema name or a schema name and table name.

RETURNS:
a `String` object containing the separator string

EXAMPLE:
```
String s = dbmd.getCatalogSeparator();
```

getCatalogTerm

```
String getCatalogTerm() throws SQLException
```

Gets the database vendor's preferred term for `catalog`.

RETURNS:
a `String` object containing the vendor term for `catalog`

EXAMPLE:
```
String s = dbmd.getCatalogTerm();
```

getColumnPrivileges

```
ResultSet getColumnPrivileges(String catalog, String schema,
        String table, String columnNamePattern) throws SQLException
```

Gets a description of the access rights for a table's columns. Descriptions of privileges are returned only if all of the following are true: the catalog name of the column's table matches *catalog*, the schema name of the column's table matches *schema,* the column's table name matches *table,* and the column name matches *columnNamePattern.* The descriptions are ordered by the columns COLUMN_NAME and PRIVILEGE.

Note that getColumnPrivileges will return privileges that were set for the column and also those that were set for the table.

PARAMETERS:

catalog	a String object representing a catalog name; "" retrieves column privileges in tables without a catalog; null indicates that the catalog name should not be used to narrow the search
schema	a String object representing a schema name; "" retrieves column privileges in tables without a schema; null indicates that the schema name should not be used to narrow the search
table	a String object representing a table name
columnNamePattern	a String object representing a column name pattern

RETURNS:

a ResultSet object, with each row being a description of a column's privileges

Each privilege description has the following columns:

1. TABLE_CAT   String object giving the table catalog, which may be null
2. TABLE_SCHEM   String object giving the table schema, which may be null
3. TABLE_NAME   String object giving the table name
4. COLUMN_NAME   String object giving the column name
5. GRANTOR   String object giving the grantor of access, which may be null
6. GRANTEE   String object giving the grantee of access
7. PRIVILEGE   String object naming the type of access (SELECT, INSERT, UPDATE, REFERENCES, and so on)
8. IS_GRANTABLE   String object; YES indicates that the grantee is permitted to grant access to others, NO indicates that the grantee cannot grant access to others, and null indicates that it is unknown

SEE:

"String Patterns as Arguments," on page 451

getColumns

```
ResultSet getColumns(String catalog, String schemaPattern,
                String tableNamePattern, String columnNamePattern)
                                            throws SQLException
```

Gets a description of the table columns available in catalog *catalog*.

Descriptions of columns are returned only if the table schema name matches *schemaPattern*, the table name matches *tableNamePattern*, and the column name matches *columnNamePattern*. The descriptions are ordered by the columns TABLE_SCHEM, TABLE_NAME, and ORDINAL_POSITION.

If the driver supports the new data types available in the JDBC 2.0 API, they will be included as rows in the ResultSet object this method returns.

PARAMETERS:

catalog	a String object representing a catalog name; "" retrieves columns for tables without a catalog; null indicates that the catalog name should not be used to narrow the search
schemaPattern	a String object representing a schema name pattern; "" retrieves columns for tables without a schema; null indicates that the schema name should not be used to narrow the search
tableNamePattern	a String object representing a table name pattern
columnNamePattern	a String object representing a column name pattern

RETURNS:

a ResultSet object, with each row being a description of a table column

Each row in the ResultSet object has the following fields:

1.	TABLE_CAT	String object giving the table catalog, which may be null
2.	TABLE_SCHEM	String object giving the table schema, which may be null
3.	TABLE_NAME	String object giving the table name
4.	COLUMN_NAME	String object giving the column name
5.	DATA_TYPE	short indicating the JDBC (SQL) data type from java.sql.Types
6.	TYPE_NAME	String object giving the local type name used by the data source

7. COLUMN_SIZE	int indicating the column size. For char or date types, this is the maximum number of characters; for numeric or decimal types, this is the precision.
8. BUFFER_LENGTH	is not used
9. DECIMAL_DIGITS	int indicating the number of fractional digits
10. NUM_PREC_RADIX	int indicating the radix, which is typically either 10 or 2
11. NULLABLE	int indicating whether a column can be NULL The possible values are:
•columnNoNulls	—NULL values might not be allowed
•columnNullable	—NULL values are definitely allowed
•columnNullableUnknown	—whether NULL values are allowed is unknown
12. REMARKS	String object containing an explanatory comment on the column; may be null
13. COLUMN_DEF	String object containing the default value for the column; may be null
14. SQL_DATA_TYPE	int; currently unused
15. SQL_DATETIME_SUB	int; currently unused
16. CHAR_OCTET_LENGTH	int indicating the maximum number of bytes in the column (for char types only)
17. ORDINAL_POSITION	int indicating the index of the column in a table; the first column is 1, the second column is 2, and so on
18. IS_NULLABLE	String object; either NO indicating that the column definitely does not allow NULL values, YES indicating that the column might allow NULL values, or an empty string ("") indicating that nullability is unknown
19. SCOPE_CATALOG	String object giving the catalog of the table that is the scope of a reference attribute; null if DATA_TYPE is not REF
20. SCOPE_SCHEMA	String object giving the schema of the table that is the scope of a reference attribute; null if DATA_TYPE is not REF

3.0

3.0

21. SCOPE_TABLE	String object giving the table name that is the scope of a reference attribute; null if DATA_TYPE is not REF	3.0
22. SOURCE_DATA_TYPE	short giving the SQL type from java.sql.Types that is the source type of a distinct type or user-generated Ref type; null if DATA_TYPE is not DISTINCT or a user-generated REF	3.0

EXAMPLE:
```
ResultSet rs = dbmd.getColumns(null, null, "EMPLOYEES", "%NAME");
```

SEE:
"String Patterns as Arguments," on page 451

getConnection

2.0

```
Connection getConnection() throws SQLException
```

Retrieves the Connection object that produced this DatabaseMetaData object.

RETURNS:
the Connection object that created this DatabaseMetaData object

EXAMPLE:
```
DatabaseMetaData dbmd = con.getMetaData();
Connection c = dbmd.getConnection();
// c represents the same Connection object that con represents
```

getCrossReference

```
ResultSet getCrossReference(String primaryCatalog,
        String primarySchema, String primaryTable,
        String foreignCatalog, String foreignSchema,
        String foreignTable) throws SQLException
```

Describes how one table imports the keys of another table.

Gets a description of the foreign key columns in the table *foreignTable*. These foreign key columns reference the primary key columns of the table *primaryTable*. In other words, the foreign keys in *foreignTable* are the primary keys in *primaryTable*. The descriptions are ordered by the columns FKTABLE_CAT, FKTABLE_SCHEM, FKTABLE_NAME, and KEY_SEQ.

This method does not return information about candidate keys.

PARAMETERS:

primaryCatalog	a String object representing the catalog name of the table that contains the primary key; "" retrieves those without a catalog; null indicates that the catalog name should not be used to narrow the search
primarySchema	a String object representing the schema name of the table that contains the primary key; "" retrieves those without a schema; null indicates that the schema name should not be used to narrow the search
primaryTable	a String object representing the name of the table that contains the primary key (the key exported to table *foreignTable*, where it becomes the foreign key)
foreignCatalog	a String object representing the catalog name of the table that contains the foreign key; "" retrieves those without a catalog; null indicates that the catalog name should not be used to narrow the search
foreignSchema	a String object representing the schema name of the table that contains the foreign key; "" retrieves those without a schema; null indicates that the schema name should not be used to narrow the search
foreignTable	a String object representing the name of the table that contains the foreign key (the primary key imported from table *primaryTable*)

RETURNS:

a ResultSet object, with each row being a description of a foreign key column

Each description has the following columns:

1. PKTABLE_CAT   String object giving the catalog of the primary key's table, which may be null
2. PKTABLE_SCHEM   String object giving the schema of the primary key's table, which may be null
3. PKTABLE_NAME   String object giving the table name of the primary key, which is *primaryTable*
4. PKCOLUMN_NAME   String object giving the column name of the primary key

5. FKTABLE_CAT | String object giving the catalog name (which may be null) of *foreignTable* (which may be null)

6. FKTABLE_SCHEM | String object giving the schema name (which may be null) of *foreignTable* (which may be null)

7. FKTABLE_NAME | String object giving the table name of the foreign key

8. FKCOLUMN_NAME | String object giving the column name of the foreign key

9. KEY_SEQ | short indicating the sequence number within the foreign key (useful if the foreign key consists of more than one column)

10. UPDATE_RULE | short indicating what happens to the foreign key when the primary key is updated
The possible values are:

- importedKeyNoAction —if a primary key has been imported by another table, it cannot be updated

- importedKeyCascade —if a primary key has been updated, change the foreign key to agree with it

- importedKeySetNull —if a primary key has been updated, change the foreign key to null

- importedKeySetDefault —if a primary key has been updated, change the foreign key to its default value

- importedKeyRestrict —same as importedKeyNoAction (for ODBC 2.x compatibility)

11. DELETE_RULE | short indicating what happens to the foreign key when the primary key is deleted
The possible values are:

- importedKeyNoAction —if a primary key has been imported by another table, it cannot be deleted

- importedKeyCascade —if a primary key has been deleted, delete rows that contain the foreign key

- importedKeySetNull —if a primary key has been deleted, change the foreign key to null

- importedKeySetDefault —if a primary key has been deleted, change the foreign key to its default value

- importedKeyRestrict —same as importedKeyNoAction (for ODBC 2.x compatibility)

12. FK_NAME | String object containing the name of the foreign key, which may be null

13. PK_NAME	String object containing the name of the primary key, which may be null
14. DEFERRABILITY	short indicating whether the evaluation of foreign key constraints can be deferred until commit

Possible values are:

•importedKeyInitiallyDeferred	See SQL92 for definition
•importedKeyInitiallyImmediate	See SQL92 for definition
•importedKeyNotDeferrable	See SQL92 for definition

EXAMPLE:
```
ResultSet rs = dbmd.getCrossReference("MYPRIMARYCATALOG",
    "MYPRIMARYSCHEMA", "MYPRIMARYTABLE","MYFOREIGNCATALOG",
    "MYFOREIGNSCHEMA", "MYFOREIGNTABLE");
```

`3.0`

getDatabaseMajorVersion

```
int getDatahaseMajorVersion() throws SQLException
```

Retrieves the major version number of the underlying database.

RETURNS:
an int indicating the underlying database's major version number

EXAMPLE:
```
int majorVersion = dbmd.getDatabaseMajorVersion();
```

`3.0`

getDatabaseMinorVersion

```
int getDatahaseMinorVersion() throws SQLException
```

Retrieves the minor version number of the underlying database.

RETURNS:
an int indicating the underlying database's minor version number

EXAMPLE:
```
int minorVersion = dbmd.getDatabaseMinorVersion();
```

getDatabaseProductName

```
String getDatabaseProductName() throws SQLException
```

Gets the product name for this database.

RETURNS:
a `String` object representing the database product name

EXAMPLE:
```
String s = dbmd.getDatabaseProductName();
```

getDatabaseProductVersion

```
String getDatabaseProductVersion() throws SQLException
```

Gets the version for this database product.

RETURNS:
a `String` object representing the database version

EXAMPLE:
```
String s = dbmd.getDatabaseProductVersion();
```

getDefaultTransactionIsolation

```
int getDefaultTransactionIsolation() throws SQLException
```

Gets the database's default transaction isolation level. The values are the constants defined in `java.sql.Connection`.

RETURNS:
an `int` representing the default transaction isolation level. Possible values are
> TRANSACTION_NONE,
> TRANSACTION_READ_UNCOMMITTED,
> TRANSACTION_READ_COMMITTED,
> TRANSACTION_REPEATABLE_READ, and
> TRANSACTION_SERIALIZABLE.

EXAMPLE:
```
int level = dbmd.getDefaultTransactionIsolation();
```

SEE:
"Connection Fields," on page 428

getDriverMajorVersion

`int getDriverMajorVersion()`

Gets this JDBC driver's major version number.

RETURNS:
an `int` representing this JDBC driver's major version number

EXAMPLE:
`int n = dbmd.getDriverMajorVersion();`

getDriverMinorVersion

`int getDriverMinorVersion()`

Gets this JDBC driver's minor version number.

RETURNS:
an `int` representing this JDBC driver's minor version number

EXAMPLE:
`int n = dbmd.getDriverMinorVersion();`

getDriverName

`String getDriverName() throws SQLException`

Gets the name of this JDBC driver.

RETURNS:
a `String` object representing this JDBC driver's name

EXAMPLE:
`String s = dbmd.getDriverName();`

getDriverVersion

```
String getDriverVersion() throws SQLException
```

Gets the version of this JDBC driver. This method combines the major and minor version numbers into a version string.

RETURNS:
a String object representing this JDBC driver's version, which includes its major and minor version numbers

EXAMPLE:
```
String s = dbmd.getDriverVersion();
```

getExportedKeys

```
ResultSet getExportedKeys(String catalog, String schema,
          String table) throws SQLException
```

Gets a description of the foreign key columns that reference the primary key columns in table *table* (the keys exported by *table*). The descriptions are ordered by the columns FKTABLE_CAT, FKTABLE_SCHEM, FKTABLE_NAME, and KEY_SEQ.

This method does not return information about candidate keys.

PARAMETERS:

catalog	a String object representing a catalog name; "" retrieves those without a catalog; null indicates that the catalog name should not be used to narrow the search
schema	a String object representing a schema name; "" retrieves those without a schema; null indicates that the schema name should not be used to narrow the search
table	a String object representing the name of the table from which primary keys have been exported. These keys become foreign keys in the tables which import them.

RETURNS:
a ResultSet object, with each row being a description of a foreign key column

Each description has the following columns:
1. PKTABLE_CAT   String object giving the catalog name of table *table*, which may be null

2. PKTABLE_SCHEM	`String` object giving the schema name of table `table`, which may be `null`
3. PKTABLE_NAME	`String` object giving the table name of table `table`
4. PKCOLUMN_NAME	`String` object giving the column name of the primary key
5. FKTABLE_CAT	`String` object giving the table catalog name (which may be `null`) of the foreign key that was exported from table `table` (which may be `null`)
6. FKTABLE_SCHEM	`String` object giving the table schema name (which may be `null`) of the foreign key that was exported from table `table` (which may be `null`)
7. FKTABLE_NAME	`String` object giving the table name of the foreign key (the table to which the key was exported from table `table`)
8. FKCOLUMN_NAME	`String` object giving the column name of the foreign key (the key that was exported from table `table`)
9. KEY_SEQ	`short` indicating the sequence number within the foreign key (useful if the foreign key consists of more than one column)
10. UPDATE_RULE	`short` indicating what happens to the foreign key when the primary key is updated The possible values are:
•`importedKeyNoAction`	—if a primary key has been imported by another table, it cannot be updated
•`importedKeyCascade`	—if a primary key has been updated, change the foreign key to agree with it
•`importedKeySetNull`	—if a primary key has been updated, change the foreign key to `null`
•`importedKeySetDefault`	—if a primary key has been updated, change the foreign key to its default value
•`importedKeyRestrict`	—the same as `importedKeyNoAction` (for ODBC 2.x compatibility)
11. DELETE_RULE	`short` indicating what happens to the foreign key when the primary key is deleted The possible values are:
•`importedKeyNoAction`	—if a primary key has been imported by another table, it cannot be deleted
•`importedKeyCascade`	—if a primary key has been deleted, delete rows that contain the foreign key

• importedKeySetNull	—if a primary key has been deleted, change the foreign key to null
• importedKeySetDefault	—if a primary key has been deleted, change the foreign key to its default value
• importedKeyRestrict	—the same as importedKeyNoAction (for ODBC 2.x compatibility).
12. FK_NAME	String object containing the name of the foreign key, which may be null
13. PK_NAME	String object containing the name of the primary key, which may be null
14. DEFERRABILITY	short indicating whether the evaluation of foreign key constraints can be deferred until commit
	Possible values are:
• importedKeyInitiallyDeferred	See SQL92 for a definition
• importedKeyInitiallyImmediate	See SQL92 for a definition
• importedKeyNotDeferrable	See SQL92 for a definition

EXAMPLE:
```
ResultSet rs = dbmd.getExportedKeys(
                        "MYCATALOG", "MYSCHEMA", "TABLE1");
```

SEE:
```
getImportedKeys
```

getExtraNameCharacters

```
String getExtraNameCharacters() throws SQLException
```

Gets the "extra" characters that can be used in unquoted identifier names (those beyond a - z,0 - 9, and _). These characters are the ASCII special characters, such as @, %, and so on, that can be used in names. Note that this method does not necessarily return the unicode characters of all the NLS characters accepted as identifier names.

RETURNS:
a String object containing the extra ASCII characters

EXAMPLE:
```
String s = dbmd.getExtraNameCharacters();
```

getIdentifierQuoteString

```
String getIdentifierQuoteString() throws SQLException
```

Gets the string used to quote SQL identifiers. This returns a space (" ") if identifier quoting isn't supported. A JDBC Compliant driver always uses a double quote character (").

RETURNS:
a String object representing the quoting string or a space if the database does not support quoting identifiers

EXAMPLE:
```
String s = dbmd.getIdentifierQuoteString();
```

getImportedKeys

```
ResultSet getImportedKeys(String catalog, String schema,
          String table) throws SQLException
```

Gets a description of the primary key columns that are referenced by the foreign key columns in table *table* (the primary keys imported by table *table*). The descriptions are ordered by the columns PKTABLE_CAT, PKTABLE_SCHEM, PKTABLE_NAME, and KEY_SEQ.

This method does not return information about candidate keys.

PARAMETERS:

catalog	a String object representing a catalog name; "" retrieves those without a catalog; null indicates that the catalog name should not be used to narrow the search
schema	a String object representing a schema name; "" retrieves those without a schema; null indicates that the schema name should not be used to narrow the search
table	a String object representing the name of a table that has foreign keys. (It imports primary keys from another table.)

RETURNS:
a ResultSet object, with each row being a description of a primary key column

Each description has the following columns:

1. PKTABLE_CAT — String object giving the name of the catalog (which may be null) for the table containing the primary key being imported to table *table*

2. PKTABLE_SCHEM — String object giving the name of the schema (which may be null) for the table containing the primary key being imported to table *table*

3. PKTABLE_NAME — String object giving the table name of the primary key being imported to table *table*

4. PKCOLUMN_NAME — String object giving the column name of the primary key being imported

5. FKTABLE_CAT — String object giving the name of the catalog (which may be null) for table *table*, the table containing the foreign key

6. FKTABLE_SCHEM — String object giving the name of the schema (which may be null) for table *table*, the table containing the foreign key

7. FKTABLE_NAME — String object giving the name of table *table*, the table containing the foreign key

8. FKCOLUMN_NAME — String object giving the column name of the foreign key

9. KEY_SEQ — short indicating the sequence number within the foreign key (useful if the foreign key consists of more than one column)

10. UPDATE_RULE — short indicating what happens to the foreign key when the primary key is updated

The possible values are:

- importedKeyNoAction — if a primary key has been imported by another table, it cannot be updated

- importedKeyCascade — if a primary key has been updated, change the foreign key to agree with it

- importedKeySetNull — if a primary key has been updated, change the foreign key to null

- importedKeySetDefault — if a primary key has been updated, change the foreign key to its default value

- importedKeyRestrict — the same as importedKeyNoAction (for ODBC 2.x compatibility)

| 11. DELETE_RULE | short indicating what happens to the foreign key when the primary key is deleted |
| | The possible values are: |

•importedKeyNoAction	—if a primary key has been imported by another table, it cannot be deleted
•importedKeyCascade	—if a primary key has been deleted, delete rows that contain the foreign key
•importedKeySetNull	—if a primary key has been deleted, change the foreign key to null
•importedKeySetDefault	—if a primary key has been deleted, change the foreign key to its default value
•importedKeyRestrict	—the same as importedKeyNoAction (for ODBC 2.x compatibility)

12. FK_NAME	String object containing the name of the foreign key, which may be null
13. PK_NAME	String object containing the name of the primary key, which may be null
14. DEFERRABILITY	short indicating whether the evaluation of foreign key constraints can be deferred until commit
	Possible values are:

•importedKeyInitiallyDeferred	See SQL92 for a definition
•importedKeyInitiallyImmediate	See SQL92 for a definition
•importedKeyNotDeferrable	See SQL92 for a definition

EXAMPLE:
```
ResultSet rs = dbmd.getImportedKeys(
                    "MYCATALOG", "MYSCHEMA", "TABLE1");
```

SEE:
getExportedKeys

"Sample Code 16," on page 222, for a complete example

getIndexInfo

```
ResultSet getIndexInfo(String catalog, String schema, String table,
        boolean unique, boolean approximate) throws SQLException
```

Gets a description of a table's indices and statistics. The descriptions are ordered by the following columns: NON_UNIQUE, TYPE, INDEX_NAME, and

ORDINAL_POSITION.

PARAMETERS:

catalog	String object representing a catalog name; "" retrieves those without a catalog; null indicates that the catalog name should not be used to narrow the search
schema	String object representing a schema name; "" retrieves those without a schema; null indicates that the schema name should not be used to narrow the search
table	String object representing the name of the table for which index and statistics information is being requested
unique	true means that only indices for unique values will be returned; false means that all indices will be returned regardless of whether they are unique or not
approximate	true means that results are allowed to reflect approximate or out-of-date values; false requests that results be accurate

RETURNS:

a ResultSet object, with each row being a description of an index column

Each row of the ResultSet object has the following columns:

1.	TABLE_CAT	String object giving the table catalog name; may be null
2.	TABLE_SCHEM	String object giving the table schema name; may be null
3.	TABLE_NAME	String object giving the table name
4.	NON_UNIQUE	true means that index values can be non-unique; false means that index values must be unique or that TYPE is tableIndexStatistic
5.	INDEX_QUALIFIER	String object giving the index catalog, which may be null; null when TYPE is tableIndex-Statistic
6.	INDEX_NAME	String object giving the index name; null when TYPE is tableIndexStatistic
7.	TYPE	short indicating the index type The possible values are:

•tableIndexStatistic	—identifies table statistics that are returned in conjunction with a table's index descriptions

•`tableIndexClustered`	—identifies this index as a clustered index
•`tableIndexHashed`	—identifies this index as a hashed index
•`tableIndexOther`	—identifies this index as some other style of index
8. ORDINAL_POSITION	short indicating the column sequence number within the index; 0 is returned when TYPE is `tableIndexStatistic`
9. COLUMN_NAME	String object giving the column name; `null` when TYPE is `tableIndexStatistic`
10. ASC_OR_DESC	String object indicating the column sort sequence. A indicates ascending; D indicates descending; `null` indicates that a sort sequence is not supported or that TYPE is `tableIndexStatistic`.
11. CARDINALITY	int indicating the number of unique values in the index. When TYPE is `tableIndexStatistic`, however, it indicates the number of rows in the table.
12. PAGES	int indicating the number of pages used for the current index. When TYPE is `tableIndexStatistic`, however, it indicates the number of pages used for the table.
13. FILTER_CONDITION	String object giving the filter condition, if any; may be `null`

EXAMPLE:
```
ResultSet rs = dbmd.getIndexInfo(
               "MYCATALOG", "MYSCHEMA", "TABLE1", false, false);
```

getJDBCMajorVersion

`3.0`

```
int getJDBCMajorVersion() throws SQLException
```

Retrieves the JDBC major version number for this driver.

RETURNS:
an `int` indicating the JDBC major version number

EXAMPLE:
```
int majorVersion = dbmd.getJDBCMajorVersion();
```

getJDBCMinorVersion

3.0

```
int getJDBCMinorVersion() throws SQLException
```

Retrieves the JDBC minor version number for this driver.

RETURNS:
an int indicating the JDBC minor version number for this driver

EXAMPLE:
```
int minorersion = dbmd.getJDBCMinorVersion();
```

getMaxBinaryLiteralLength

```
int getMaxBinaryLiteralLength() throws SQLException
```

Gets the maximum number of hexadecimal characters allowed in an inline binary literal.

RETURNS:
an int representing the maximum number of hex characters; 0 if there is no limit or the limit is unknown

EXAMPLE:
```
int max = dbmd.getMaxBinaryLiteralLength();
```

getMaxCatalogNameLength

```
int getMaxCatalogNameLength() throws SQLException
```

Gets the maximum number of characters allowed in a catalog name.

RETURNS:
an int representing the maximum number of characters; 0 if there is no limit or the limit is unknown

EXAMPLE:
```
int max = dbmd.getMaxCatalogNameLength();
```

getMaxCharLiteralLength

```
int getMaxCharLiteralLength() throws SQLException
```

Gets the maximum number of characters allowed in a character literal.

RETURNS:
an int representing the maximum number of characters; 0 if there is no limit or the limit is unknown

EXAMPLE:
```
int max = dbmd.getMaxCharLiteralLength();
```

getMaxColumnNameLength

```
int getMaxColumnNameLength() throws SQLException
```

Gets the maximum number of characters allowed in a column name.

RETURNS:
an int representing the maximum number of characters; 0 if there is no limit or the limit is unknown

EXAMPLE:
```
int max = dbmd.getMaxColumnNameLength();
```

getMaxColumnsInGroupBy

```
int getMaxColumnsInGroupBy() throws SQLException
```

Gets the maximum number of columns allowed in a GROUP BY clause.

RETURNS:
an int representing the maximum number of columns; 0 if there is no limit or the limit is unknown

EXAMPLE:
```
int max = dbmd.getMaxColumnsInGroupBy();
```

getMaxColumnsInIndex

```
int getMaxColumnsInIndex() throws SQLException
```

Gets the maximum number of columns allowed in an index.

RETURNS:
an int representing the maximum number of columns; 0 if there is no limit or the limit is unknown

EXAMPLE:
```
int max = dbmd.getMaxColumnsInIndex();
```

getMaxColumnsInOrderBy

```
int getMaxColumnsInOrderBy() throws SQLException
```

Gets the maximum number of columns allowed in an ORDER BY clause.

RETURNS:
an int representing the maximum number of columns; 0 if there is no limit or the limit is unknown

EXAMPLE:
```
int max = dbmd.getMaxColumnsInOrderBy();
```

getMaxColumnsInSelect

```
int getMaxColumnsInSelect() throws SQLException
```

Gets the maximum number of columns allowed in a SELECT clause.

RETURNS:
an int representing the maximum number of columns; 0 if there is no limit or the limit is unknown

EXAMPLE:
```
int max = dbmd.getMaxColumnsInSelect();
```

getMaxColumnsInTable

int **getMaxColumnsInTable**() throws SQLException

    Gets the maximum number of columns allowed in a table.

RETURNS:
an int representing the maximum number of columns; 0 if there is no limit or the limit is unknown

EXAMPLE:
int max = dbmd.getMaxColumnsInTable();

getMaxConnections

int **getMaxConnections**() throws SQLException

    Gets the maximum number of active connections to this database that can be made through this driver instance.

RETURNS:
an int representing the maximum number of connections; 0 if there is no limit or the limit is unknown

EXAMPLE:
int max = dbmd.getMaxConnections();

getMaxCursorNameLength

int **getMaxCursorNameLength**() throws SQLException

    Gets the maximum number of characters allowed in a cursor name.

RETURNS:
an int representing the maximum number of characters; 0 if there is no limit or the limit is unknown

EXAMPLE:
int max = dbmd.getMaxCursorNameLength();

getMaxIndexLength

```
int getMaxIndexLength() throws SQLException
```

Gets the maximum number of bytes allowed in an index.

RETURNS:
an int representing the maximum number of bytes; 0 if there is no limit or the limit is unknown

EXAMPLE:
```
int max = dbmd.getMaxIndexLength();
```

getMaxProcedureNameLength

```
int getMaxProcedureNameLength() throws SQLException
```

Gets the maximum number of characters allowed in a procedure name.

RETURNS:
an int representing the maximum number of characters; 0 if there is no limit or the limit is unknown

EXAMPLE:
```
int max = dbmd.getMaxProcedureNameLength();
```

getMaxRowSize

```
int getMaxRowSize() throws SQLException
```

Gets the maximum number of bytes allowed in a single row.

RETURNS:
an int representing the maximum number of bytes; 0 if there is no limit or the limit is unknown

EXAMPLE:
```
int max = dbmd.getMaxRowSize();
```

getMaxSchemaNameLength

```
int getMaxSchemaNameLength() throws SQLException
```

Gets the maximum number of characters allowed in a schema name.

RETURNS:
an int representing the maximum number of characters; 0 if there is no limit or the limit is unknown

EXAMPLE:
```
int max = dbmd.getMaxSchemaNameLength();
```

getMaxStatementLength

```
int getMaxStatementLength() throws SQLException
```

Gets the maximum number of characters allowed in an SQL statement.

RETURNS:
an int representing the maximum number of characters; 0 if there is no limit or the limit is unknown

EXAMPLE:
```
int max = dbmd.getMaxStatementLength();
```

getMaxStatements

```
int getMaxStatements() throws SQLException
```

Gets the maximum number of active statements to this database that may be open on one connection at the same time.

RETURNS:
an int representing the maximum number of statements allowed on one Connection object; 0 if there is no limit or the limit is unknown

EXAMPLE:
```
int max = dbmd.getMaxStatements();
```

getMaxTableNameLength

```
int getMaxTableNameLength() throws SQLException
```

Gets the maximum number of characters allowed in a table name.

RETURNS:
an int representing the maximum number of characters; 0 if there is no limit or the limit is unknown

EXAMPLE:
```
int max = dbmd.getMaxTableNameLength();
```

getMaxTablesInSelect

```
int getMaxTablesInSelect() throws SQLException
```

Gets the maximum number of tables allowed in a SELECT clause.

RETURNS:
an int representing the maximum number of tables; 0 if there is no limit or the limit is unknown

EXAMPLE:
```
int max = dbmd.getMaxTablesInSelect();
```

getMaxUserNameLength

```
int getMaxUserNameLength() throws SQLException
```

Gets the maximum number of characters allowed in a user name.

RETURNS:
an int representing the maximum number of characters; 0 if there is no limit or the limit is unknown

EXAMPLE:
```
int max = dbmd.getMaxUserNameLength();
```

getNumericFunctions

String **getNumericFunctions**() throws SQLException

Gets the Open Group CLI names for this database's math functions.

RETURNS:
a String object that is a comma-separated list of math functions; 0 if there is no limit or the limit is unknown

EXAMPLE:
String s = dbmd.getNumericFunctions();

getPrimaryKeys

ResultSet **getPrimaryKeys**(String *catalog*, String *schema*,
            String *table*) throws SQLException

Gets a description of the primary key columns in *table*. Descriptions are returned only if all of the following are true: the table's catalog name matches *catalog*, the table's schema name matches *schema*, and the column's table name matches *table*. The descriptions are ordered by the column COLUMN_NAME.
This method does not return any information about candidate keys.

PARAMETERS:

catalog	a String object representing a catalog name; "" retrieves primary key columns in tables without a catalog; null indicates that the catalog name should not be used to narrow the search
schema	a String object representing a schema name; "" retrieves primary key columns in tables without a schema; null indicates that the schema name should not be used to narrow the search
table	a String object representing the name of the table whose primary key columns will be described

RETURNS:
a ResultSet object, with each row being a description of the given table's primary key column(s)

Each primary key column description has the following columns:

1. TABLE_CAT   String object giving the table catalog, which may be null

2. TABLE_SCHEM   String object giving the table schema, which may be null

3. TABLE_NAME   String object giving the name of the table whose primary key columns are described in this ResultSet object

4. COLUMN_NAME   String object giving the name of the column being described

5. KEY_SEQ   short giving the sequence number within a primary key (useful if the primary key consists of more than one column)

6. PK_NAME   String object giving the primary key name, which may be null

EXAMPLE:
```
ResultSet rs = dbmd.getPrimaryKeys("MYCATALOG", "MYSCHEMA",
                                   "TABLE1");
```

SEE:
"Sample Code 15," on page 219, for a complete example

getProcedureColumns

```
ResultSet getProcedureColumns(String catalog, String schemaPattern,
            String procedureNamePattern, String columnNamePattern)
                                        throws SQLException
```

Gets a description of the input, output, and results associated with certain stored procedures available in catalog *catalog*. The input, output, and results include the IN, OUT, and INOUT parameters; the return value, if there is one; and the columns in a ResultSet object generated by the execution of a stored procedure.

Descriptions are returned for input, output, and results associated with all stored procedures that satisfy the following criteria: the procedure schema name matches *schemaPattern*, the procedure name matches *procedureName-Pattern*, and the column name matches *columnNamePattern*. The descriptions are ordered by the columns PROCEDURE_SCHEM and PROCEDURE_NAME. Within this, the stored procedure's return value, if any, is first. Next are the parameter descriptions in call order. Last are the descriptions of result set columns, given in column number order.

PARAMETERS:

catalog	a String object representing a catalog name; "" retrieves procedures without a catalog; null indicates that the catalog name should not be used to narrow the search
schemaPattern	a String object representing a schema name pattern; "" retrieves procedures without a schema; null indicates that the schema name should not be used to narrow the search
procedureNamePattern	a String object representing a procedure name pattern
columnNamePattern	a String object representing the name pattern of a column in a ResultSet object that was generated by the stored procedure

RETURNS:

a ResultSet object, with each row describing one of the following: a parameter for this stored procedure, the return value for this stored procedure, or a column in a ResultSet object derived from this stored procedure

Each row in the ResultSet object has the following columns:

1. PROCEDURE_CAT — String object giving the procedure catalog name, which may be null

2. PROCEDURE_SCHEM — String object giving the procedure schema name, which may be null

3. PROCEDURE_NAME — String object giving the procedure name

4. COLUMN_NAME — String object giving the result set column name or the parameter name

5. COLUMN_TYPE — short indicating what this row describes. The possible values are:

   •procedureColumnUnknown — kind of column unknown

   •procedureColumnIn — column contains an IN parameter

   •procedureColumnInOut — column contains an INOUT parameter

   •procedureColumnOut — column contains an OUT parameter

   •procedureColumnReturn — column contains the return value for the procedure

   •procedureColumnResult — column is a result column in a ResultSet object

6. DATA_TYPE — short indicating the JDBC (SQL) data type from java.sql.Types

7. TYPE_NAME	String object giving the local type name used by the data source
8. PRECISION	int indicating the total number of digits
9. LENGTH	int indicating the length of data in bytes
10. SCALE	short indicating the number of digits to the right of the decimal point
11. RADIX	int indicating the radix
12. NULLABLE	short indicating whether this column can contain a null value. The possible values are:

•procedureNoNulls	—null values are not allowed
•procedureNullable	—null values are allowed
•procedureNullableUnknown	—not known whether null values are allowed

| 13. REMARKS | String object containing an explanatory comment on the parameter or column. This column may be null. |

Note that some databases may not return the parameter or ResultSet column descriptions for a procedure.

EXAMPLE:
```
ResultSet rs = getProcedureColumns("MYCATALOG", "MYSCHEMA%",
                          "MYPROCEDURE%", "MYCOLUMN%");
```

SEE:
java.sql.Types
"String Patterns as Arguments," on page 451

getProcedures

```
ResultSet getProcedures(String catalog, String schemaPattern,
        String procedureNamePattern) throws SQLException
```

Gets a description of the stored procedures available in catalog *catalog*. Only descriptions of those procedures whose schema name matches *schemaPattern* and whose procedure name matches *procedureNamePattern* are returned. The descriptions are ordered by the columns PROCEDURE_SCHEM and PROCEDURE_NAME.

PARAMETERS:

catalog	a String object representing a catalog name; "" retrieves procedures without a catalog; null indicates that the catalog name should not be used to narrow the search
schemaPattern	a String object representing a schema name pattern; "" retrieves procedures without a schema; null indicates that the schema name should not be used to narrow the search
procedureNamePattern	a String object representing a procedure name pattern

RETURNS:

a ResultSet object, with each row being a description of a stored procedure

Each procedure description has the following columns:

1. PROCEDURE_CAT   String object giving the procedure catalog, which may be null
2. PROCEDURE_SCHEM   String object giving the procedure schema, which may be null
3. PROCEDURE_NAME   String object giving the procedure name
4. Reserved for future use
5. Reserved for future use
6. Reserved for future use
7. REMARKS   String object containing an explanatory comment on the procedure. This column may be null.
8. PROCEDURE_TYPE   short indicating the kind of procedure. The possible values are:

•procedureResultUnknown   —procedure may return a result
•procedureNoResult   —procedure does not return a result
•procedureReturnsResult   —procedure returns a result

EXAMPLE:
```
ResultSet rs = getProcedures("MYCATALOG", "MYSCHEMA%",
                                        "MYPROCEDURE%");
```

SEE:
"String Patterns as Arguments," on page 451

getProcedureTerm

```
String getProcedureTerm() throws SQLException
```

Gets the database vendor's preferred term for "procedure."

RETURNS:
a String object containing the vendor term for "procedure"

EXAMPLE:
```
String s = dbmd.getProcedureTerm();
```

getResultSetHoldability

`3.0`

```
int getResutlSetHoldatility() throws SQLException
```

Retrieves the default holdability of ResultSet objects for this database.

RETURNS:
an int indicating the default holdability of ResultSet objects, which is either
ResultSet.HOLD_CURSORS_OVER_COMMIT or
ResultSet.CLOSE_CURSORS_AT_COMMIT

EXAMPLE:
```
int holdability = dbmd.getResultSetHoldability();
```

getSchemas

```
ResultSet getSchemas() throws SQLException
```

Gets the schema names available in this database. The results are ordered by schema name.

RETURNS:
a ResultSet object, with each row representing a schema name available in this database and the catalog name for the schema

The ResultSet object has the following columns:
1. TABLE_SCHEM   String object containing a schema name
2. TABLE_CATALOG   String object containing the catalog name for   `3.0`
                        the schema in TABLE_SCHEM; may be null

EXAMPLE:
```
ResultSet rs = dbmd.getSchemas();
```

getSchemaTerm

```
String getSchemaTerm() throws SQLException
```
Gets the database vendor's preferred term for "schema."

RETURNS:
a String object containing the vendor term for "schema"

EXAMPLE:
```
String s = dbmd.getSchemaTerm();
```

getSearchStringEscape

```
String getSearchStringEscape() throws SQLException
```

Gets the string that can be used to escape "_"or "%" wildcards in the string search pattern used for search parameters.

The character "_" represents any single character. The character "%" represents any sequence of zero or more characters.

RETURNS:
a String object that is used to escape wildcard characters

EXAMPLE:
```
String s = dbmd.getSearchStringEscape();
```

SEE:
"Methods That Return a String," on page 209, for a more complete example

getSQLKeywords

```
String getSQLKeywords() throws SQLException
```

Gets a list of all a database's keywords that are NOT also SQL–92 keywords.

RETURNS:
a String object that is a comma-separated list of keywords used by the database that are not also SQL–92 keywords

EXAMPLE:
```
String s = dbmd.getSQLKeywords();
```

getSQLStateType

3.0

```
int getSQLStateType() throws SQLException
```

Retrieves the SQLSTATE returned by the method `SQLException.getSQL-State`, which must be either X/Open (now known as Open Group) SQL CLI or SQL99.

RETURNS:
an `int` indicating the type of `SQLSTATE`, which is either
```
DatabaseMetaData.SQL_STATE_XOPEN or
DatabaseMetaData.SQL_STATE_SQL99
```

EXAMPLE:
```
int sqlStateType = dbmd.getSQLStateType();
```

getStringFunctions

```
String getStringFunctions() throws SQLException
```

Gets the Open Group CLI names for this database's string functions.

RETURNS:
a `String` object that is a comma-separated list of string functions

EXAMPLE:
```
String s = dbmd.getStringFunctions();
```

getSuperTables

3.0

```
ResultSet getSuperTables(String catalog, String schemaPattern,
                         String tableNamePattern) throws SQLException
```

Returns a `ResultSet` object that describes the table hierarchies defined in the given schema and catalog.

Descriptions are returned only for tables that match the given table name pattern and where the given catalog and schema also match. The table name parameter may be a fully qualified name, in which case, the `catalog` and `schemaPattern` parameters are ignored. If a table does not have a super table, it is not listed here. Super tables have to be defined in the same catalog and schema as the sub tables. Therefore, the type description does not need to include this information for the super table.

PARAMETERS:

catalog	a String object representing a catalog name, which must match the catalog name as it is stored in the database; "" retrieves those without a catalog; null indicates that the catalog name should not be used to narrow the search
schemaPattern	a String object representing a schema name pattern, which must match the schema name as it is stored in the database; "" retrieves those without a schema; null indicates that the schema name should not be used to narrow the search
tableNamePattern	a String object representing a table name pattern; may be a fully qualified name, in which case the the *catalog* and *schemaPattern* parameters are ignored

RETURNS:

a ResultSet object, with each row being a description of a super table for a table that matches the given criteria; an empty ResultSet object if the driver does not support table hierarchies

Each row in the ResultSet object has the following columns:

1. TABLE_CAT   String indicating the table catalog; may be null
2. TABLE_SCHEM   String object giving the schema of the table
3. TABLE_NAME   String object giving the table name used by the data source
4. SUPERTABLE_NAME String indicating the name of the direct super table

EXAMPLE:
```
ResultSet rs = dbmd.getSuperTables("MYCATALOG", "MYSCHEMA%",
                "MYTABLENAME%");
```

getSuperTypes

```
ResultSet getSuperTypes(String catalog, String schemaPattern,
                    String typeNamePattern) throws SQLException
```

Returns a `ResultSet` object that describes the hierarchies for the given user-defined type (UDT) defined in the given schema and catalog. Only the immediate super type/sub type relationship is modeled.

Descriptions are returned only for UDTs that match the given type name pattern and where the given catalog and schema also match. The type name parameter may be a fully qualified name, in which case, the *catalog* and *schemaPattern* parameters are ignored. If a UDT does not have a super type, it is not listed in the `ResultSet` object that is returned.

PARAMETERS:

catalog	a `String` object representing a catalog name, which must match the catalog name as it is stored in the database; "" retrieves those without a catalog; `null` indicates that the catalog name should not be used to narrow the search
schemaPattern	a `String` object representing a schema name pattern, which must match the schema name as it is stored in the database; "" retrieves those without a schema; `null` indicates that the schema name should not be used to narrow the search
typeNamePattern	a `String` object representing a UDT name pattern; may be a fully qualified name, in which case the the *catalog* and *schemaPattern* parameters are ignored

RETURNS:

a `ResultSet` object, with each row being a description of the direct super type for a UDT that matches the given criteria; an empty `ResultSet` object if the driver does not support type hierarchies

Each row in the `ResultSet` object describes a UDT and its direct super type. Each row has the following columns:

1.	TYPE_CAT	`String` indicating the UDT's catalog; may be `null`
2.	TYPE_SCHEM	`String` object giving the schema of the UDT
3.	TYPE_NAME	`String` object giving the type name of the UDT used by the data source
4.	SUPERTYPE_CAT	`String` indicating the catalog of the direct super type; may be `null`
5.	SUPERTYPE_SCHEM	`String` indicating the schema of the direct super type; may be `null`

6. SUPERTYPE_NAME   String indicating the name of the direct super
                          type

EXAMPLE:
```
ResultSet rs = dbmd.getSuperTypes("MYCATALOG", "MYSCHEMA%",
            "MYTYPENAME%");
```

getSystemFunctions

```
String getSystemFunctions() throws SQLException
```

Gets the Open Group CLI names for this database's system functions.

RETURNS:
a String object that is a comma-separated list of system functions

EXAMPLE:
```
String s = dbmd.getSystemFunctions();
```

getTablePrivileges

```
ResultSet getTablePrivileges(String catalog, String schemaPattern,
            String tableNamePattern) throws SQLException
```

Gets a description of the access rights for each table available in catalog
catalog. Descriptions of privileges are returned only if all of the following are
true: the table's catalog name matches *catalog,* the table's schema name
matches *schemaPattern,* and the column's table name matches *tableName-*
Pattern. The descriptions are ordered by the columns TABLE_SCHEM,
TABLE_NAME, and PRIVILEGE.

Note that the method getTablePrivileges returns privileges that were set
at the table level and also those that were set at the column level. A table privilege applies to one or more columns in a table; it cannot be assumed that a
table privilege applies to all columns. In some RDBMSs a table privilege
applies to all columns, but this is not necessarily true for all RDBMSs.

PARAMETERS:

catalog   a String object representing a catalog name; "" re-
                          trieves columns in tables without a catalog; null indi-
                          cates that the catalog name should not be used to
                          narrow the search

schemaPattern	a String object representing a schema name pattern; "" retrieves privileges in tables without a schema; null indicates that the schema name should not be used to narrow the search
tableNamePattern	a String object representing a table name pattern

RETURNS:

a ResultSet object, with each row being a description of the access rights for a table

Each privilege description has the following columns:

1.	TABLE_CAT	String object giving the table catalog, which may be null
2.	TABLE_SCHEM	String object giving the table schema, which may be null
3.	TABLE_NAME	String object giving the table name
4.	GRANTOR	String object giving the grantor of access, which may be null
5.	GRANTEE	String object giving the grantee of access
6.	PRIVILEGE	String object naming the type of access (SELECT, INSERT, UPDATE, REFERENCES, and so on)
7.	IS_GRANTABLE	String object; YES indicates that the grantee is permitted to grant access to others, NO indicates that the grantee cannot grant access to others, and null indicates that it is unknown

EXAMPLE:
```
ResultSet rs = dbmd.getTablePrivileges(
                      "MYCATALOG", "MYSCHEMA%", "EMPLOY%");
```

SEE:
"String Patterns as Arguments," on page 451

getTables

```
ResultSet getTables(String catalog, String schemaPattern,
     String tableNamePattern, String types[]) throws SQLException
```

Gets a description of the tables available in catalog *catalog*. Only descriptions of those tables whose catalog name matches *catalog*, whose schema name matches *schemaPattern*, and whose table name matches *tableNamePattern* are returned. The descriptions are ordered by the columns TABLE_TYPE, TABLE_SCHEM, and TABLE_NAME.

PARAMETERS:

catalog	a String object representing a catalog name; "" retrieves tables without a catalog; null indicates that the catalog name should not be used to narrow the search
schemaPattern	a String object representing a schema name pattern; "" retrieves tables without a schema; null indicates that the schema name should not be used to narrow the search
tableNamePattern	a String object representing a table name pattern
types[]	a list of String objects representing the types of tables to include; null indicates that all table types should be returned. Typical types of tables are "TABLE", "SYSTEM TABLE", "VIEW", "GLOBAL TEMPORARY", "LOCAL TEMPORARY", "ALIAS", and "SYNONYM".

RETURNS:

a ResultSet object, with each row being a description of a table

Each table description has the following columns:

1.	TABLE_CAT	String object giving the table catalog, which may be null
2.	TABLE_SCHEM	String object giving the table schema, which may be null
3.	TABLE_NAME	String object giving the table name
4.	TABLE_TYPE	String object giving the table type. Typical types are "TABLE", "VIEW", "SYSTEM TABLE", "GLOBAL TEMPORARY", "LOCAL TEMPORARY", "ALIAS", "SYNONYM".
5.	REMARKS	String object containing an explanatory comment on the table, which may be null
6.	TYPE_CAT	String object giving the types catalog; may be null
7.	TYPE_SCHEMA	String object giving the types schema; may be null
8.	TYPE_NAME	String object giving the type name; may be null

9. SELF_REFERENCING_ COL_NAME	String object giving the name of the designated "identifier" column of a typed table; may be null
10. REF_GENERATION	String object specifying how values in SELF_REFERENCING_COL_NAME are created. Values are "SYSTEM", "USER", or "DERIVED"; may be null

Note that some databases may not return information for all tables.

EXAMPLE:
```
String [] tableTypes = { "TABLE", "VIEW" };
ResultSet rs = dbmd.getTables(
             "MYCATALOG", "MYSCHEMA%", "MYTABLE%", tableTypes);
```

SEE:
"String Patterns as Arguments," on page 451

getTableTypes

```
ResultSet getTableTypes() throws SQLException
```

Gets the table types available in this database system. The results are ordered by table type.

RETURNS:
a ResultSet object, with each row representing a table type available in this DBMS

Each row of the ResultSet object has a single String column that is a table type. The ResultSet object has the following column:

1. TABLE_TYPE	String object containing a table type, such as "TABLE", "VIEW", "SYSTEM TABLE", "GLOBAL TEMPORARY", "LOCAL TEMPORARY", "ALIAS", "SYNONYM"

EXAMPLE:
```
ResultSet rs = dbmd.getTableTypes();
```

SEE:
"Sample Code 13," on page 213, for a complete example

getTimeDateFunctions

```
String getTimeDateFunctions() throws SQLException
```

Gets the Open Group CLI names for this database's time and date functions.

RETURNS:
a `String` object that is a comma-separated list of time and date functions

EXAMPLE:
```
String s = dbmd.getTimeDateFunctions();
```

getTypeInfo

```
ResultSet getTypeInfo() throws SQLException
```

Gets a description of all the data types supported by this database. If both the driver and DBMS support the new data types available with the JDBC 2.0 API and 3.0 API, these new data types will be included. Each row describes a DBMS data type with the name of `TYPE_NAME`. The type in the column `DATA_TYPE` is the JDBC SQL type that is the best mapping for this local DBMS type. For example, if a DBMS supports types that can be a class in the Java programming language, a row will describe that type. The `DATA_TYPE` column for that row will contain the constant `java.sql.Types.JAVA_OBJECT`, and the `TYPE_NAME` column will contain whatever term is used by the database for that type, such as `JavaObject` or `Serialized`.

Multiple DBMS types can map to a single JDBC type when, for example, the DBMS defines different types that are similar. Conversely, a single DBMS type can map to multiple JDBC types if the vendor's specific type is general enough to provide the functionality of multiple JDBC data types.

A description of the user-defined data types that have been defined for this DBMS can be retrieved by calling the method `DatabaseMetaData.getUDTs`.

The results are ordered first by `DATA_TYPE` and then by how closely the local type matches the definition of `DATA_TYPE`. Therefore, if two or more rows have the same value for the column `DATA_TYPE`, the first row gives the best local type to use for the JDBC type in `DATA_TYPE`.

RETURNS:
a `ResultSet` object, with each row being a description of a local DBMS type

Each row in the `ResultSet` object has the following columns:

1. TYPE_NAME — `String` object giving the local DBMS name for a type supported by this DBMS

2. DATA_TYPE — `short` indicating the JDBC (SQL) data type from `java.sql.Types` that corresponds to the local data type in column TYPE_NAME. If there is more than one row for a data type, the first entry is the preferred one.

3. PRECISION — `int` indicating the maximum precision

4. LITERAL_PREFIX — `String` object giving the prefix used to quote a literal; may be `null`

5. LITERAL_SUFFIX — `String` object giving the suffix used to quote a literal; may be `null`

6. CREATE_PARAMS — `String` object giving the parameters used in creating the type; may be `null`

7. NULLABLE — `int` indicating whether a column can be NULL
   The possible values are:
   - `typeNoNulls` — does not allow NULL values
   - `typeNullable` — allows NULL values
   - `typeNullableUnknown` — nullability unknown

8. CASE_SENSITIVE — `true` to indicate that the type is case sensitive; `false` indicates that it is not case sensitive

9. SEARCHABLE — `short` indicating whether it is possible to use a WHERE clause based on this type
   The possible values are:
   - `typePredNone` — no WHERE clauses can be based on this type
   - `typePredChar` — only a WHERE . . . LIKE clause can be based on this type
   - `typePredBasic` — all WHERE clauses except WHERE . . . LIKE can be based on this type
   - `typeSearchable` — all WHERE clauses can be based on this type

10. UNSIGNED_ATTRIBUTE — `true` indicates that the type is unsigned; `false` indicates that it is signed

11. FIXED_PREC_SCALE — `true` indicates that the type can be a money value; `false` indicates that it cannot

12. AUTO_INCREMENT — `true` indicates that the type can be used for an auto-increment value; `false` indicates that it cannot

13.	LOCAL_TYPE_NAME	String object containing the localized version of the type name; may be null
14.	MINIMUM_SCALE	short indicating the minimum scale supported
15.	MAXIMUM_SCALE	short indicating the maximum scale supported
16.	SQL_DATA_TYPE	int; unused
17.	SQL_DATETIME_SUB	int; unused
18.	NUM_PREC_RADIX	int indicating the radix, which is usually 2 or 10

EXAMPLE:
ResultSet rs = dbmd.getTypeInfo();

SEE:
"Sample Code 14," on page 215, for a complete example

getUDTs

`2.0`

```
ResultSet getUDTs(String catalog, String schemaPattern,
        String typeNamePattern, int [] types) throws SQLException
```

Gets a description of the user-defined types (UDTs) defined in a particular schema. A UDT (an SQL structured type, DISTINCT type, or JAVA_OBJECT type) must be defined as part of a particular database schema before it can be used in a schema table definition. Only descriptions of the UDTs specified in *types* that match *catalog, schemaPattern,* and *typeNamePattern* will be returned by this method. If the parameter *typeNamePattern* is a fully qualified name, *catalog* and *schemaPattern* will be ignored.

The rows in the ResultSet object returned by this method are ordered first by the contents of the column DATA_TYPE and then by the content of the columns TYPE_SCHEM and TYPE_NAME. If the driver does not support UDTs or no matching UDTs are found, an empty ResultSet object will be returned.

If the value returned for the column DATA_TYPE is java.sql.Types.STRUCT or java.sql.Types.DISTINCT, the value for the column CLASS_NAME will be the fully qualified class name of a class in the Java programming language. When a value is retrieved from a table column of this STRUCT or DISTINCT type with a call to the method getObject, a JDBC Compliant driver will manufacture instances of this class. Thus, for structured types, the value for the column CLASS_NAME defaults to the JDBC type java.sql.Struct, and for distinct types, it defaults to the built-in type on which the distinct type is based. A driver may return a subtype of the class named by CLASS_NAME. The value in the CLASS_NAME column reflects a custom type mapping when one is used.

PARAMETERS:

catalog	a String object representing a catalog name; "" retrieves tables without a catalog; null indicates that the catalog name should not be used to narrow the search
schemaPattern	a String object representing a schema name pattern; "" retrieves UDTs without a schema; null indicates that the schema name should not be used to narrow the search
typeNamePattern	a String object representing a type name pattern; may be a fully qualified name (in which case the parameters *catalog* and *schemaPattern* are ignored)
types[]	an array of type int representing the data types to include, which must be one or more of the JDBC types Types.JAVA_OBJECT, Types.STRUCT, or Types.DISTINCT; null indicates that all types should be returned

RETURNS:

a ResultSet object, with each row being a description of a UDT

Each row in the ResultSet object has the following columns:

1. TYPE_CAT — String object giving the catalog for this UDT; may be null
2. TYPE_SCHEM — String object giving the schema for this UDT; may be null
3. TYPE_NAME — String object giving the SQL type name of this UDT, which is the name used in a CREATE TABLE statement to specify a column of this type
4. CLASS_NAME — String object giving the class name in the Java programming language for this UDT
5. DATA_TYPE — short indicating the JDBC (generic SQL) data type defined in java.sql.Types
6. REMARKS — String object containing an explanatory comment about the UDT
7. BASE_TYPE — short from java.sql.Types giving the source type of a DISTINCT type or the type that implements the user-generated reference type of the SELF_REFERENCING_COLUMN of a structured type; null if DATA_TYPE is not DISTINCT or STRUCT with REFERENCE_GENERATION = USER_DEFINED

3.0

EXAMPLE:
```
int [] types = {java.sql.Types.DISTINCT};
ResultSet rs = dbmd.getUDTs("MYCATALOG", "MYSCHEMA%", %, types);
// rs will contain one row for every SQL DISTINCT type defined in
// the schema whose name begins with MYCATALOG.MYSCHEMA
```

SEE:
"String Patterns as Arguments," on page 451

getURL

```
String getURL() throws SQLException
```

Gets the URL for this database.

RETURNS:
a String object representing the URL for this database or null if the URL cannot be generated

EXAMPLE:
```
String s = dbmd.getURL();
```

getUserName

```
String getUserName() throws SQLException
```

Gets the user name as known to the database.

RETURNS:
a String object representing one's database user name

EXAMPLE:
```
String s = dbmd.getUserName();
```

getVersionColumns

```
ResultSet getVersionColumns(String catalog, String schema,
                            String table) throws SQLException
```

Gets a description of the columns in a table that are automatically updated when any value in a row is updated. The column descriptions are not ordered.

PARAMETERS:

catalog	a `String` object representing a catalog name; "" retrieves those without a catalog; `null` indicates that the catalog name should not be used to narrow the search
schema	a `String` object representing a schema name; "" retrieves those without a schema; `null` indicates that the schema name should not be used to narrow the search
table	a `String` object representing a table name

RETURNS:

a `ResultSet` object, with each row being a description of a table column that is automatically updated whenever a value in a row is updated

Each column description has the following columns:

1. SCOPE — short; not used
2. COLUMN_NAME — String object giving the column name
3. DATA_TYPE — short indicating a JDBC (SQL) data type from `java.sql.Types`.
4. TYPE_NAME — String object giving the local type name used by the data source
5. COLUMN_SIZE — int giving the precision
6. BUFFER_LENGTH — int indicating the length of the column value in bytes
7. DECIMAL_DIGITS — short indicating the scale
8. PSEUDO_COLUMN — short indicating whether this is a pseudo column, such as an Oracle `ROWID`
   The possible values are:

•versionColumnUnknown	—may or may not be a pseudo column
•versionColumnNotPseudo	—is NOT a pseudo column
•versionColumnPseudo	—is a pseudo column

EXAMPLE:
```
ResultSet rs = dbmd.getVersionColumns("MYCATALOG", "MYSCHEMA",
                                      "MYTABLE");
```

insertsAreDetected
2.0

```
boolean insertsAreDetected(int type) throws SQLException
```

Checks whether an inserted row is detected by a ResultSet object of type *type*. If inserted rows are detected, the following are true: (1) a row that is inserted into the ResultSet object appears in that ResultSet object without having to close and reopen it, and (2) the method ResultSet.rowInserted will return true when it is called on the result set, and the current row was inserted after the result set was opened.

PARAMETERS:

type   an int indicating the type of the ResultSet object: TYPE_FORWARD_ONLY, TYPE_SCROLL_INSENSITIVE, or TYPE_SCROLL_SENSITIVE

RETURNS:
true if the method ResultSet.rowInserted returns true when called on a ResultSet object of the given type that contains a visible row insertion; false if the method ResultSet.rowInserted returns false under the same conditions

EXAMPLE:
```
boolean b = dbmd.insertsAreDetected(
                          ResultSet.TYPE_SCROLL_SENSITIVE);
```

SEE:
"Detecting Changes," on page 719

isCatalogAtStart

```
boolean isCatalogAtStart() throws SQLException
```

Checks whether a catalog name appears at the start of a fully qualified table name. If it is not at the beginning, it appears at the end.

RETURNS:
true if the catalog name appears at the start of a fully qualified table name; false if it appears at the end

EXAMPLE:
```
boolean b = dbmd.isCatalogAtStart();
```

isReadOnly

```
boolean isReadOnly() throws SQLException
```

Checks whether the database is in read-only mode.

RETURNS:
true if so; false otherwise

EXAMPLE:
```
boolean b = dbmd.isReadOnly();
```

locatorsUpdateCopy

3.0

```
boolean locatorsUpdateCopy() throws SQLException
```

Indicates whether updates made to a BLOB or CLOB value are made on a copy or directly to the BLOB or CLOB value.

RETURNS:
true if updates are made to a copy of a BLOB or CLOB value; false if updates are made directly to the BLOB or CLOB value in the database

nullPlusNonNullIsNull

```
boolean nullPlusNonNullIsNull() throws SQLException
```

Checks whether the concatenation of a NULL value and a non-NULL value results in a NULL value. A JDBC Compliant driver always returns true.

RETURNS:
true if so; false otherwise

EXAMPLE:
```
boolean b = dbmd.nullPlusNonNullIsNull();
```

nullsAreSortedAtEnd

```
boolean nullsAreSortedAtEnd() throws SQLException
```

Checks whether NULL values are sorted at the end regardless of sort order.

RETURNS:
true if so; false otherwise

EXAMPLE:
```
boolean b = dbmd.nullsAreSortedAtEnd();
```

nullsAreSortedAtStart

```
boolean nullsAreSortedAtStart() throws SQLException
```

Checks whether NULL values are sorted at the start regardless of sort order.

RETURNS:
true if so; false otherwise

EXAMPLE:
```
boolean b = dbmd.nullsAreSortedAtStart();
```

nullsAreSortedHigh

```
boolean nullsAreSortedHigh() throws SQLException
```

Retrieves whether NULL values are sorted high. Sorted high means that NULL values sort higher than any other value in a domain. In an ascending order, if this method returns true, NULL values will appear at the end. By contrast, the method nullsAreSortedAtEnd indicates whether NULL values are sorted at the end regardless of sort order.

RETURNS:
true if so; false otherwise

EXAMPLE:
```
boolean b = dbmd.nullsAreSortedHigh();
```

nullsAreSortedLow

```
boolean nullsAreSortedLow() throws SQLException
```

Retrieves whether NULL values are sorted low. Sorted low means that NULL values sort lower than any other value in a domain. In an ascending order, if this method returns true, NULL values will appear at the beginning. By contrast, the method nullsAreSortedAtStart indicates whether NULL values are sorted at the beginning regardless of sort order.

RETURNS:
true if so; false otherwise

EXAMPLE:
```
boolean b = dbmd.nullsAreSortedLow();
```

othersDeletesAreVisible

2.0

```
boolean othersDeletesAreVisible(int type) throws SQLException
```

Checks whether the rows deleted from the specified type of result set via another transaction or another ResultSet object in the same transaction are visible without first closing and then reopening the result set.

For a TYPE_FORWARD_ONLY ResultSet object, this method determines whether deletes are visible when the result set is materialized incrementally by the DBMS. Note that if the rows in a ResultSet object are sorted, then incremental materialization may not be possible and changes will not be visible, even if this method returns true.

PARAMETERS:

type   an int indicating the type of the ResultSet object: TYPE_FORWARD_ONLY, TYPE_SCROLL_INSENSITIVE, or TYPE_SCROLL_SENSITIVE

RETURNS:
true if rows deleted by others are visible; false otherwise

EXAMPLE:
```
boolean b = dbmd.othersDeletesAreVisible(
                         ResultSet.TYPE_SCROLL_INSENSITIVE);
```

SEE:
"Visibility of Changes Made by Others," on page 716

2.0

othersInsertsAreVisible

```
boolean othersInsertsAreVisible(int type) throws SQLException
```

Checks whether the rows inserted into the specified type of result set via others (another transaction or another ResultSet object in the same transaction) are visible without first closing and then reopening the result set.

For a TYPE_FORWARD_ONLY ResultSet object, this method determines whether deletes are visible when the result set is materialized incrementally by the DBMS. Note that if the rows in a ResultSet object are sorted, then incremental materialization may not be possible and changes will not be visible, even if this method returns true.

PARAMETERS:

type   an int indicating the type of the ResultSet object:
                        TYPE_FORWARD_ONLY, TYPE_SCROLL_INSENSITIVE, or
                        TYPE_SCROLL_SENSITIVE

RETURNS:
true if rows inserted by others are visible; false otherwise

EXAMPLE:
```
boolean b = dbmd.othersInsertsAreVisible(
                                ResultSet.TYPE_FORWARD_ONLY);
```

SEE:
"Visibility of Changes Made by Others," on page 716

2.0

othersUpdatesAreVisible

```
boolean othersUpdatesAreVisible(int type) throws SQLException
```

Checks whether the rows updated in the specified type of result set via others (another transaction or another ResultSet object in the same transaction) are visible without first closing and then reopening the result set.

For a TYPE_FORWARD_ONLY ResultSet object, this method determines whether updates are visible when the result set is materialized incrementally by the DBMS. Note that if the rows in a ResultSet object are sorted, then incremental materialization may not be possible and changes will not be visible, even if this method returns true.

PARAMETERS:

type   an `int` indicating the type of the `ResultSet` object:
                                                `TYPE_FORWARD_ONLY`, `TYPE_SCROLL_INSENSITIVE`, or
                                                `TYPE_SCROLL_SENSITIVE`

RETURNS:
`true` if rows updated by others are visible; `false` otherwise

EXAMPLE:
```
boolean b = dbmd.othersUpdatesAreVisible(
                            ResultSet.TYPE_SCROLL_SENSITIVE);
```

SEE:
"Visibility of Changes Made by Others," on page 716

ownDeletesAreVisible   2.0

```
boolean ownDeletesAreVisible(int type) throws SQLException
```

Checks whether the rows deleted via the specified type of result set are
visible via that result set while it is still open. A deletion is visible if the row is
removed from the result set or if an empty row (a "hole") replaces the deleted
row.

PARAMETERS:

type   an `int` indicating the type of the `ResultSet` object; one
                                                of `TYPE_FORWARD_ONLY`, `TYPE_SCROLL_INSENSITIVE`, or
                                                `TYPE_SCROLL_SENSITIVE`

RETURNS:
`true` if a `ResultSet` object's own deletions are visible without having to close
and reopen the result set; `false` otherwise

EXAMPLE:
```
boolean b = dbmd.ownDeletesAreVisible(
                            ResultSet.TYPE_SCROLL_INSENSITIVE);
```

SEE:
"Visibility of a Result Set's Own Changes," on page 718

ownInsertsAreVisible

boolean **ownInsertsAreVisible**(int *type*) throws SQLException

Checks whether rows inserted via the specified type of result set are visible via that result set while it is still open. An insertion is visible if it appears in the result set immediately after the method insertRow is invoked.

PARAMETERS:

type   an int indicating the type of the ResultSet object; one of TYPE_FORWARD_ONLY, TYPE_SCROLL_INSENSITIVE, or TYPE_SCROLL_SENSITIVE

RETURNS:
true if a ResultSet object's own insertions are visible without having to close and reopen the result set; false otherwise

EXAMPLE:
boolean b = dbmd.ownInsertionsAreVisible(
                                        ResultSet.TYPE_SCROLL_SENSITIVE);

SEE:
"Visibility of a Result Set's Own Changes," on page 718

ownUpdatesAreVisible

boolean **ownUpdatesAreVisible**(int *type*) throws SQLException

Checks whether column values updated via the specified type of result set are visible via that result set while it is still open. An update is visible if a getter method that is called on the updated column returns the new value. Updates are not visible if a getter method returns the original value of an updated column.

PARAMETERS:

type   an int indicating the type of the ResultSet object; one of TYPE_FORWARD_ONLY, TYPE_SCROLL_INSENSITIVE, or TYPE_SCROLL_SENSITIVE

RETURNS:
true if a ResultSet object's own updates are visible without having to close and reopen the result set; false otherwise

EXAMPLE:
```
boolean b = dbmd.ownUpdatesAreVisible(
                                ResultSet.TYPE_FORWARD_ONLY);
```

SEE:
"Visibility of a Result Set's Own Changes," on page 718

storesLowerCaseIdentifiers

```
boolean storesLowerCaseIdentifiers() throws SQLException
```

Checks whether the DBMS (1) treats mixed-case unquoted SQL identifiers used in SQL statements as case-insensitive and (2) stores them as all lowercase in its metadata tables.

RETURNS:
true if so; false otherwise

EXAMPLE:
```
boolean b = dbmd.storesLowerCaseIdentifiers();
```

storesLowerCaseQuotedIdentifiers

```
boolean storesLowerCaseQuotedIdentifiers() throws SQLException
```

Checks whether the DBMS (1) treats mixed-case quoted SQL identifiers used in SQL statements as case-insensitive and (2) stores them as all lowercase in its metadata tables.

RETURNS:
true if so; false otherwise

EXAMPLE:
```
boolean b = dbmd.storesLowerCaseQuotedIdentifiers();
```

storesMixedCaseIdentifiers

```
boolean storesMixedCaseIdentifiers() throws SQLException
```

Checks whether the DBMS (1) treats mixed-case unquoted SQL identifiers used in SQL statements as case-insensitive and (2) stores them in mixed case in its metadata tables.

RETURNS:
true if so; `false` otherwise

EXAMPLE:
```
boolean b = dbmd.storesMixedCaseIdentifiers();
```

storesMixedCaseQuotedIdentifiers

```
boolean storesMixedCaseQuotedIdentifiers() throws SQLException
```

Checks whether the DBMS (1) treats mixed-case quoted SQL identifiers used in SQL statements as case-insensitive and (2) stores them in mixed case in its metadata tables.

RETURNS:
true if so; `false` otherwise

EXAMPLE:
```
boolean b = dbmd.storesMixedCaseQuotedIdentifiers();
```

storesUpperCaseIdentifiers

```
boolean storesUpperCaseIdentifiers() throws SQLException
```

Checks whether the DBMS (1) treats mixed-case unquoted SQL identifiers used in SQL statements as case-insensitive and (2) stores them in all uppercase in its metadata tables.

RETURNS:
true if so; `false` otherwise

EXAMPLE:
```
boolean b = dbmd.storesUpperCaseIdentifiers();
```

storesUpperCaseQuotedIdentifiers

```
boolean storesUpperCaseQuotedIdentifiers() throws SQLException
```

Checks whether the DBMS (1) treats mixed-case quoted SQL identifiers used in SQL statements as case-insensitive and (2) stores them as all uppercase in its metadata tables.

RETURNS:
true if so; false otherwise

EXAMPLE:
```
boolean b = dbmd.storesUpperCaseQuotedIdentifiers();
```

supportsAlterTableWithAddColumn

```
boolean supportsAlterTableWithAddColumn() throws SQLException
```

Checks whether the database supports ALTER TABLE with add column.

RETURNS:
true if so; false otherwise

EXAMPLE:
```
boolean b = dbmd.supportsAlterTableWithAddColumn();
```

supportsAlterTableWithDropColumn

```
boolean supportsAlterTableWithDropColumn() throws SQLException
```

Checks whether the database supports ALTER TABLE with drop column.

RETURNS:
true if so; false otherwise

EXAMPLE:
```
boolean b = dbmd.supportsAlterTableWithDropColumn();
```

supportsANSI92EntryLevelSQL

```
boolean supportsANSI92EntryLevelSQL() throws SQLException
```

Checks whether the database supports ANSI–92 entry level SQL grammar. All JDBC Compliant drivers must return true.

RETURNS:
true if so; false otherwise

EXAMPLE:
`boolean b = dbmd.supportsANSI92EntryLevelSQL();`

supportsANSI92FullSQL

`boolean supportsANSI92FullSQL() throws SQLException`

Checks whether the database supports ANSI–92 full SQL grammar.

RETURNS:
true if so; false otherwise

EXAMPLE:
`boolean b = dbmd.supportsANSI92FullSQL();`

supportsANSI92IntermediateSQL

`boolean supportsANSI92IntermediateSQL() throws SQLException`

Checks whether the database supports ANSI–92 intermediate SQL grammar.

RETURNS:
true if so; false otherwise

EXAMPLE:
`boolean b = dbmd.supportsANSI92IntermediateSQL();`

2.0 supportsBatchUpdates

`boolean supportsBatchUpdates() throws SQLException`

Checks whether this database supports sending multiple updates to the database as a unit (a batch).

RETURNS:
true if so; false otherwise

EXAMPLE:
```
boolean b = dbmd.supportsBatchUpdates();
```

supportsCatalogsInDataManipulation

```
boolean supportsCatalogsInDataManipulation() throws SQLException
```

Checks whether this database supports using a catalog name in a data manipulation statement.

RETURNS:
true if so; false otherwise

EXAMPLE:
```
boolean b = dbmd.supportsCatalogsInDataManipulation();
```

supportsCatalogsInIndexDefinitions

```
boolean supportsCatalogsInIndexDefinitions() throws SQLException
```

Checks whether this database supports using a catalog name in an index definition statement.

RETURNS:
true if so; false otherwise

EXAMPLE:
```
boolean b = dbmd.supportsCatalogsInIndexDefinitions();
```

supportsCatalogsInPrivilegeDefinitions

```
boolean supportsCatalogsInPrivilegeDefinitions()
                                              throws SQLException
```

Checks whether this database supports using a catalog name in a privilege definition statement.

RETURNS:
true if so; `false` otherwise

EXAMPLE:
`boolean b = dbmd.supportsCatalogsInPrivilegeDefinitions();`

supportsCatalogsInProcedureCalls

`boolean supportsCatalogsInProcedureCalls() throws SQLException`

Checks whether this database supports using a catalog name in a procedure call statement.

RETURNS:
true if so; `false` otherwise

EXAMPLE:
`boolean b = dbmd.supportsCatalogsInProcedureCalls();`

supportsCatalogsInTableDefinitions

`boolean supportsCatalogsInTableDefinitions() throws SQLException`

Checks whether this database supports using a catalog name in a table definition statement.

RETURNS:
true if so; `false` otherwise

EXAMPLE:
`boolean b = dbmd.supportsCatalogsInTableDefinitions();`

supportsColumnAliasing

`boolean supportsColumnAliasing() throws SQLException`

Checks whether the database supports column aliasing. If true, the SQL AS clause can be used to provide names for computed columns or to provide alias names for columns as required. A JDBC Compliant driver always returns true.

RETURNS:
true if so; false otherwise

EXAMPLE:
```
boolean b = dbmd.supportsColumnAliasing();
```

supportsConvert

```
boolean supportsConvert() throws SQLException
```

Checks whether the database supports the scalar function CONVERT for the conversion of one JDBC type to another. The JDBC types are the generic SQL data types defined in java.sql.Types, on page 1033.

RETURNS:
true if so; false otherwise

EXAMPLE:
```
boolean b = dbmd.supportsConvert();
```

SEE:
"Support Scalar Functions," on page 1104

supportsConvert

```
boolean supportsConvert(int fromType, int toType)
                                                throws SQLException
```

Checks whether the database supports the scalar function CONVERT for conversions between the JDBC types *fromType* and *toType*. The JDBC types are the generic SQL data types defined in java.sql.Types, on page 1033.

PARAMETERS:

fromType	the JDBC type to convert from
toType	the JDBC type to convert to

RETURNS:
true if so; false otherwise

EXAMPLE:
```
boolean b = dbmd.supportsConvert(TIMESTAMP, CHAR);
```

SEE:
java.sql.Types
"Support Scalar Functions," on page 1104

supportsCoreSQLGrammar

boolean **supportsCoreSQLGrammar**() throws SQLException

Checks whether the database supports the ODBC Core SQL grammar.

RETURNS:
true if so; false otherwise

EXAMPLE:
boolean b = dbmd.supportsCoreSQLGrammar();

supportsCorrelatedSubqueries

boolean **supportsCorrelatedSubqueries**() throws SQLException

Checks whether this database supports correlated subqueries. A JDBC Compliant driver always returns true.

RETURNS:
true if so; false otherwise

EXAMPLE:
boolean b = dbmd.supportsCorrelatedSubqueries();

supportsDataDefinitionAndDataManipulationTransactions

boolean **supportsDataDefinitionAndDataManipulationTransactions**()
                                                    throws SQLException

Checks whether this database supports both data definition and data manipulation statements within a transaction.

RETURNS:
true if so; false otherwise

EXAMPLE:
```
boolean b =
    dbmd.supportsDataDefinitionAndDataManipulationTransactions();
```

supportsDataManipulationTransactionsOnly

```
boolean supportsDataManipulationTransactionsOnly() throws SQLException
```

Checks whether this database supports only data manipulation statements within a transaction.

RETURNS:
true if so; false otherwise

EXAMPLE:
```
boolean b = dbmd.supportsDataManipulationTransactionsOnly();
```

supportsDifferentTableCorrelationNames

```
boolean supportsDifferentTableCorrelationNames() throws SQLException
```

Checks whether it is true that if table correlation names are supported, they are restricted to be different from the names of the tables.

RETURNS:
true if so; false otherwise

EXAMPLE:
```
boolean b = dbmd.supportsDifferentTableCorrelationNames();
```

supportsExpressionsInOrderBy

```
boolean supportsExpressionsInOrderBy() throws SQLException
```

Checks whether the database supports expressions in ORDER BY lists.

RETURNS:
true if so; false otherwise

EXAMPLE:
```
boolean b = dbmd.supportsExpressionsInOrderBy();
```

supportsExtendedSQLGrammar

boolean **supportsExtendedSQLGrammar**() throws SQLException

Checks whether the database supports the ODBC Extended SQL grammar.

RETURNS:
true if so; false otherwise

EXAMPLE:
boolean b = dbmd.supportsExtendedSQLGrammar();

supportsFullOuterJoins

boolean **supportsFullOuterJoins**() throws SQLException

Checks whether the database supports full nested outer joins.

RETURNS:
true if so; false otherwise

EXAMPLE:
boolean b = dbmd.supportsFullOuterJoins();

3.0

supportsGetGeneratedKeys

boolean **supportsGetGeneratedKeys**() throws SQLException

Indicates whether keys that are automatically generated when a new row is inserted into a table can be retrieved.

RETURNS:
true if automatically generated keys can be retrieved; false otherwise

supportsGroupBy

boolean **supportsGroupBy**() throws SQLException

Checks whether the database supports some form of the GROUP BY clause.

RETURNS:
true if so; false otherwise

EXAMPLE:
```
boolean b = dbmd.supportsGroupBy();
```

supportsGroupByBeyondSelect

```
boolean supportsGroupByBeyondSelect() throws SQLException
```

Checks whether a GROUP BY clause can use columns that are not in the SELECT clause, provided that it specifies all the columns in the SELECT clause.

RETURNS:
true if so; false otherwise

EXAMPLE:
```
boolean b = dbmd.supportsGroupByBeyondSelect();
```

supportsGroupByUnrelated

```
boolean supportsGroupByUnrelated() throws SQLException
```

Checks whether a GROUP BY clause can use columns that are not in the SELECT clause.

RETURNS:
true if so; false otherwise

EXAMPLE:
```
boolean b = dbmd.supportsGroupByUnrelated();
```

supportsIntegrityEnhancementFacility

```
boolean supportsIntegrityEnhancementFacility() throws SQLException
```

Checks whether the database supports the SQL Integrity Enhancement Facility.

RETURNS:
true if so; false otherwise

EXAMPLE:
```
boolean b = dbmd.supportsIntegrityEnhancementFacility();
```

supportsLikeEscapeClause

```
boolean supportsLikeEscapeClause() throws SQLException
```

Checks whether the database supports specifying a LIKE escape clause. A JDBC Compliant driver always returns true.

RETURNS:
true if so; false otherwise

EXAMPLE:
```
boolean b = dbmd.supportsLikeEscapeClause();
```

SEE:
"SQL Escape Syntax in Statements," on page 958

supportsLimitedOuterJoins

```
boolean supportsLimitedOuterJoins() throws SQLException
```

Checks whether the database provides limited support for outer joins. Note that this method returns true if the method supportsFullOuterJoins returns true.

RETURNS:
true if so; false otherwise

EXAMPLE:
```
boolean b = dbmd.supportsLimitedOuterJoins();
```

supportsMinimumSQLGrammar

```
boolean supportsMinimumSQLGrammar() throws SQLException
```

Checks whether the database supports the ODBC Minimum SQL grammar. All JDBC Compliant drivers must return true.

RETURNS:
true if so; false otherwise

EXAMPLE:
```
boolean b = dbmd.supportsMinimumSQLGrammar();
```

supportsMixedCaseIdentifiers

```
boolean supportsMixedCaseIdentifiers() throws SQLException
```

Checks whether the DBMS treats mixed-case unquoted SQL identifiers used in SQL statements as case sensitive and, as a result, stores them in mixed case in its metadata tables. A JDBC Compliant driver will always return false.

RETURNS:
true if so; false otherwise

EXAMPLE:
```
boolean b = dbmd.supportsMixedCaseIdentifiers();
```

supportsMixedCaseQuotedIdentifiers

```
boolean supportsMixedCaseQuotedIdentifiers() throws SQLException
```

Checks whether the database treats mixed-case quoted SQL identifiers used in SQL statements as case sensitive and, as a result, stores them in mixed case in its metadata tables. A JDBC Compliant driver will always return true.

RETURNS:
true if so; false otherwise

EXAMPLE:
```
boolean b = dbmd.supportsMixedCaseQuotedIdentifiers();
```

supportsMultipleOpenResults

3.0

```
boolean supportsMultipleOpenResults() throws SQLException
```

Indicates whether it is possible to have more than one ResultSet object returned from a `CallableStatement` object open at the same time.

RETURNS:
true if a `CallableStatement` object may return multiple `ResultSet` objects that are open simultaneously; `false` otherwise

EXAMPLE:
```
boolean b = dbmd.supportsMultipleOpenResults();
```

supportsMultipleResultSets

```
boolean supportsMultipleResultSets() throws SQLException
```

Checks whether the database supports multiple result sets from a single execute statement.

RETURNS:
true if retrieving multiple `ResultSet` objects from the execution of a single `CallableStatement` object is supported; `false` otherwise

EXAMPLE:
```
boolean b = dbmd.supportsMultipleResultSets();
```

supportsMultipleTransactions

```
boolean supportsMultipleTransactions() throws SQLException
```

Checks whether there can be multiple transactions open at once (on different connections).

RETURNS:
true if so; `false` otherwise

EXAMPLE:
```
boolean b = dbmd.supportsMultipleTransactions();
```

3.0   supportsNamedParameters

```
boolean supportsNamedParameters() throws SQLException
```

Indicates whether this database supports using the parameter name to specify a parameter to a `CallableStatement` object.

RETURNS:
`true` if a parameter to a `CallableStatement` object may be designated by its name; `false` otherwise

EXAMPLE:
`boolean b = dbmd.supportsNamedParameters();`

supportsNonNullableColumns

`boolean supportsNonNullableColumns() throws SQLException`

Checks whether the database supports defining columns as nonnullable. A JDBC Compliant driver will always return `true`.

RETURNS:
`true` if so; `false` otherwise

EXAMPLE:
`boolean b = dbmd.supportsNonNullableColumns();`

supportsOpenCursorsAcrossCommit

`boolean supportsOpenCursorsAcrossCommit() throws SQLException`

Checks whether this database supports having cursors remain open across commits. Note that a return value of `false` does not mean that cursors are always closed on commit; rather, `false` means that cursors are not always left open across commits.

RETURNS:
`true` if cursors always remain open after commits; `false` if cursors are sometimes or always closed on commit

EXAMPLE:
`boolean b = dbmd.supportsOpenCursorsAcrossCommit();`

supportsOpenCursorsAcrossRollback

`boolean supportsOpenCursorsAcrossRollback() throws SQLException`

Checks whether this database supports having cursors remain open across rollbacks. Note that a return value of `false` does not mean that cursors are always closed on rollback; rather, `false` means that cursors are not always left open across rollbacks.

RETURNS:
`true` if cursors always remain open after rollbacks; `false` if cursors are sometimes or always closed on rollback

EXAMPLE:
`boolean b = dbmd.supportsOpenCursorsAcrossRollback();`

supportsOpenStatementsAcrossCommit

`boolean supportsOpenStatementsAcrossCommit() throws SQLException`

Checks whether this database supports having statements remain open across commits. Note that a return value of `false` does not mean that statements are always closed on commit; rather, `false` means that statements are not always left open across commits.

RETURNS:
`true` if statements always remain open across commits; `false` if statements are sometimes or always closed on commit

EXAMPLE:
`boolean b = dbmd.supportsOpenStatementsAcrossCommit();`

supportsOpenStatementsAcrossRollback

`boolean supportsOpenStatementsAcrossRollback() throws SQLException`

Checks whether this database supports having statements remain open across rollbacks. Note that a return value of `false` does not mean that statements are always closed on rollback; rather, `false` means that statements are not always left open across rollbacks.

RETURNS:
`true` if statements always remain open across rollbacks; `false` if statements are sometimes or always closed on rollback

EXAMPLE:
```
boolean b = dbmd.supportsOpenStatementsAcrossRollback();
```

supportsOrderByUnrelated

```
boolean supportsOrderByUnrelated() throws SQLException
```

Checks whether an ORDER BY clause can use columns that are not in the SELECT clause.

RETURNS:
true if so; false otherwise

EXAMPLE:
```
boolean b = dbmd.supportsOrderByUnrelated();
```

supportsOuterJoins

```
boolean supportsOuterJoins() throws SQLException
```

Checks whether the database supports some form of outer join.

RETURNS:
true if so; false otherwise

EXAMPLE:
```
boolean b = dbmd.supportsOuterJoins();
```

supportsPositionedDelete

```
boolean supportsPositionedDelete() throws SQLException
```

Checks whether this database supports positioned DELETE statements.

RETURNS:
true if so; false otherwise

EXAMPLE:
```
boolean b = dbmd.supportsPositionedDelete();
```

supportsPositionedUpdate

boolean **supportsPositionedUpdate**() throws SQLException

Checks whether this database supports positioned UPDATE statements.

RETURNS:
true if so; false otherwise

EXAMPLE:
boolean b = dbmd.supportsPositionedUpdate();

supportsResultSetConcurrency

`2.0`

boolean **supportsResultSetConcurrency**(int *type*, int *concurrency*)
                                                    throws SQLException

Checks whether this database supports the concurrency level *concurrency* in combination with ResultSet type *type*.

PARAMETERS:

type	an int indicating the type of the ResultSet object; one of the constants defined in the ResultSet interface: TYPE_FORWARD_ONLY, TYPE_SCROLL_INSENSITIVE, or TYPE_SCROLL_SENSITIVE
concurrency	an int indicating the concurrency level of the Result-Set object; one of the constants defined in ResultSet: CONCUR_READ_ONLY or CONCUR_UPDATABLE

RETURNS:
true if so; false otherwise

EXAMPLE:
boolean b = dbmd.supportsResultSetConcurrency(
                        ResultSet.TYPE_SCROLLABLE_INSENSITIVE,
                        ResultSet.CONCUR_UPDATABLE);

SEE:
"Concurrency Types," on page 701

supportsResultSetHoldability

3.0

```
boolean supportsResultSetHoldability(int holdability)
                                        throws SQLException
```

Indicates whether this database supports the given result set holdability.

PARAMETERS:

holdability   an int indicating the holdability of a ResultSet object; must be one of the following constants defined in the ResultSet interface:
ResultSet.HOLD_CURSORS_OVER_COMMIT or
ResultSet.CLOSE_CURSORS_AT_COMMIT

RETURNS:
true if the database supports holdability for result sets; false otherwise

EXAMPLE:
```
boolean b = dbmd.supportsResultSetHoldability(
                        ResultSet.HOLD_CURSORS_OVER_COMMIT);
```

SEE:
"Result Set Holdability," on page 702

supportsResultSetType

2.0

```
boolean supportsResultSetType(int type) throws SQLException
```

Checks whether this database supports the ResultSet type type.

PARAMETERS:

type   an int indicating the type of the ResultSet object; one of the constants defined in the ResultSet interface:
TYPE_FORWARD_ONLY, TYPE_SCROLL_INSENSITIVE, or
TYPE_SCROLL_SENSITIVE

RETURNS:
true if so; false otherwise

EXAMPLE:
```
boolean b = dbmd.supportsResultSetType(
                        ResultSet.TYPE_SCROLLABLE_SENSITIVE);
```

SEE:
"Types of Result Sets," on page 700
"Concurrency Types," on page 701

supportsSavepoints

`boolean` **`supportsSavepoints`**`() throws SQLException`

Indicates whether this database supports setting savepoints within a transaction.

RETURNS:
`true` if the database supports savepoints; `false` otherwise

EXAMPLE:
`boolean b = dbmd.supportsSavepoints();`

SEE:
"Using Savepoints," on page 394

supportsSchemasInDataManipulation

`boolean` **`supportsSchemasInDataManipulation`**`() throws SQLException`

Checks whether this database supports using a schema name in a data manipulation statement.

RETURNS:
`true` if so; `false` otherwise

EXAMPLE:
`boolean b = dbmd.supportsSchemasInDataManipulation();`

supportsSchemasInIndexDefinitions

`boolean` **`supportsSchemasInIndexDefinitions`**`() throws SQLException`

Checks whether this database supports using a schema name in an index definition statement.

RETURNS:
true if so; `false` otherwise

EXAMPLE:
`boolean b = dbmd.supportsSchemasInIndexDefinitions();`

supportsSchemasInPrivilegeDefinitions

`boolean supportsSchemasInPrivilegeDefinitions() throws SQLException`

Checks whether this database supports using a schema name in a privilege definition statement.

RETURNS:
true if so; `false` otherwise

EXAMPLE:
`boolean b = dbmd.supportsSchemasInPrivilegeDefinitions();`

supportsSchemasInProcedureCalls

`boolean supportsSchemasInProcedureCalls() throws SQLException`

Checks whether this database supports using a schema name in a procedure call statement.

RETURNS:
true if so; `false` otherwise

EXAMPLE:
`boolean b = dbmd.supportsSchemasInProcedureCalls();`

supportsSchemasInTableDefinitions

`boolean supportsSchemasInTableDefinitions() throws SQLException`

Checks whether this database supports using a schema name in a table definition statement.

RETURNS:
true if so; `false` otherwise

EXAMPLE:
```
boolean b = dbmd.supportsSchemasInTableDefinition();
```

supportsSelectForUpdate

```
boolean supportsSelectForUpdate() throws SQLException
```

Checks whether this database supports SELECT FOR UPDATE statements.

RETURNS:
true if so; false otherwise

EXAMPLE:
```
boolean b = dbmd.supportsSelectForUpdate();
```

supportsStatementPooling

```
boolean supportsStatementPooling() throws SQLException
```

Indicates whether this database supports the pooling of PreparedStatement objects.

RETURNS:
true if the database supports statement pooling; false otherwise

EXAMPLE:
```
boolean b = dbmd.supportsStatementPooling();
```

SEE:
"Reusing Statements," on page 440

supportsStoredProcedures

```
boolean supportsStoredProcedures() throws SQLException
```

Checks whether this database supports stored procedure calls using the stored procedure escape syntax.

RETURNS:
true if so; false otherwise

EXAMPLE:
```
boolean b = dbmd.supportsStoredProcedures();
```

SEE:
"SQL Escape Syntax in Statements," on page 958
"CallableStatement Overview," starting on page 321

supportsSubqueriesInComparisons

```
boolean supportsSubqueriesInComparisons() throws SQLException
```

Checks whether this database supports subqueries in comparison expressions. A JDBC Compliant driver always returns `true`.

RETURNS:
true if so; false otherwise

EXAMPLE:
```
boolean b = dbmd.supportsSubqueriesInComparisons();
```

supportsSubqueriesInExists

```
boolean supportsSubqueriesInExists() throws SQLException
```

Checks whether this database supports subqueries in EXISTS expressions.

RETURNS:
true if so; false otherwise

EXAMPLE:
```
boolean b = dbmd.supportsSubqueriesInExists();
```

supportsSubqueriesInIns

```
boolean supportsSubqueriesInIns() throws SQLException
```

Checks whether this database supports subqueries in IN statements. A JDBC Compliant driver always returns `true`.

RETURNS:
true if so; false otherwise

EXAMPLE:
```
boolean b = dbmd.supportsSubqueriesInIns();
```

supportsSubqueriesInQuantifieds

```
boolean supportsSubqueriesInQuantifieds() throws SQLException
```

    Checks whether this database supports subqueries in quantified expressions. A JDBC Compliant driver always returns true.

RETURNS:
true if so; false otherwise

EXAMPLE:
```
boolean b = dbmd.supportsSubqueriesInQuantifieds();
```

supportsTableCorrelationNames

```
boolean supportsTableCorrelationNames() throws SQLException
```

    Checks whether this database supports table correlation names. A JDBC Compliant driver always returns true.

RETURNS:
true if so; false otherwise

EXAMPLE:
```
boolean b = dbmd.supportsTableCorrelationNames();
```

supportsTransactionIsolationLevel

```
boolean supportsTransactionIsolationLevel(int level)
                                        throws SQLException
```

    Checks whether this database supports *level*.

PARAMETERS:

level   int representing one of the constants defined in ja-
                                va.sql.Connection; possible values are
                                TRANSACTION_NONE, TRANSACTION_READ_UNCOMMITTED,
                                TRANSACTION_READ_COMMITTED, TRANSACTION_REPEAT-
                                ABLE_READ, or TRANSACTION_SERIALIZABLE

RETURNS:
true if this database supports the given transaction isolation level; false otherwise

EXAMPLE:
```
boolean b = dbmd.supportsTransactionIsolationLevel(
                                TRANSACTION_SERIALIZABLE);
```

SEE:
"Connection Fields," on page 450

supportsTransactions

```
boolean supportsTransactions() throws SQLException
```

Checks whether this database supports transactions. If this method returns
false, the method commit does nothing, and the transaction isolation level is
TRANSACTION_NONE. Drivers that are JDBC Compliant are required to support
transactions.

RETURNS:
true if this database supports transactions; false otherwise

EXAMPLE:
```
boolean b = dbmd.supportsTransactions();
```

supportsUnion

```
boolean supportsUnion() throws SQLException
```

Checks whether this database supports SQL UNION.

RETURNS:
true if so; false otherwise

EXAMPLE:
```
boolean b = dbmd.supportsUnion();
```

supportsUnionAll

```
boolean supportsUnionAll() throws SQLException
```

Checks whether this database supports SQL UNION ALL.

RETURNS:
true if so; false otherwise

EXAMPLE:
```
boolean b = dbmd.supportsUnionAll();
```

2.0

updatesAreDetected

```
boolean updatesAreDetected(int type) throws SQLException
```

Checks whether the specified type of result set detects an updated row. If updated rows are detected, the following will be true: (1) updates made via a ResultSet object are visible via that ResultSet object without having to close and reopen it, and (2) the method ResultSet.rowUpdated will return true when it is called on the result set after the current row has been updated.

PARAMETERS:

type   an int indicating the type of the ResultSet object:
                                TYPE_FORWARD_ONLY, TYPE_SCROLL_INSENSITIVE, or
                                TYPE_SCROLL_SENSITIVE

RETURNS:
true if the method ResultSet.rowUpdated returns true when called on a ResultSet object of the given type that contains visible row updates; false if the method ResultSet.rowUpdated returns false under the same conditions

EXAMPLE:
```
boolean b = dbmd.updatesAreDetected(
                        ResultSet.TYPE_SCROLL_SENSITIVE);
```

SEE:
"Detecting Changes," on page 719

usesLocalFilePerTable

```
boolean usesLocalFilePerTable() throws SQLException
```

Checks whether this database uses a separate local file to store each table.

RETURNS:
true if the database uses a local file for each table; false otherwise

EXAMPLE:
```
boolean b = dbmd.usesLocalFilePerTable();
```

usesLocalFiles

```
boolean usesLocalFiles() throws SQLException
```

Checks whether the database stores tables in a local file.

RETURNS:
true if so; false otherwise

EXAMPLE:
```
boolean b = dbmd.usesLocalFiles();
```

15.4 DatabaseMetaData Fields

The DatabaseMetaData interface defines the following fields, which are used as column values in the ResultSet objects returned by certain DatabaseMetaData methods. The interface definition section for DatabaseMetaData lists these fields grouped by the methods for which they are possible return values. This section lists the fields alphabetically.

attributeNoNulls

3.0

```
public final static short attributeNoNulls = 0
```

A possible value for column NULLABLE in the ResultSet object returned by the method getAttributes.
Indicates that NULL values might not be allowed for attributes of a UDT.

attributeNullable

```
public final static short attributeNullable = 1
```

A possible value for column `NULLABLE` in the `ResultSet` object returned by the method `getAttributes`.

Indicates that `NULL` values are definitely allowed for attributes of a UDT.

attributeNullableUnknown

```
public final static short attributeNullableUnknown = 2
```

A possible value for column `NULLABLE` in the `ResultSet` object returned by the method `getAttributes`.

Indicates that it is not know whether `NULL` values are allowed for attributes of a UDT.

bestRowNotPseudo

```
public final static int bestRowNotPseudo = 1
```

A possible value for column `PSEUDO_COLUMN` in the `ResultSet` object returned by the method `getBestRowIdentifier`.

Indicates that the best row identifier is not a pseudo column.

bestRowPseudo

```
public final static int bestRowPseudo = 2
```

A possible value for column `PSEUDO_COLUMN` in the `ResultSet` object returned by the method `getBestRowIdentifier`.

Indicates that the best row identifier is a pseudo column.

bestRowSession

```
public final static int bestRowSession = 2
```

A possible value for column SCOPE in the ResultSet object returned by the method getBestRowIdentifier.

Indicates that the best row identifier is valid for the remainder of the current session.

bestRowTemporary

```
public final static int bestRowTemporary = 0
```

A possible value for column SCOPE in the ResultSet object returned by the method getBestRowIdentifier.

Indicates that the best row identifier is very temporary, being valid only while using this row.

bestRowTransaction

```
public final static int bestRowTransaction = 1
```

A possible value for column SCOPE in the ResultSet object returned by the method getBestRowIdentifier.

Indicates that the best row identifier is valid for the remainder of the current transaction.

bestRowUnknown

```
public final static int bestRowUnknown = 0
```

A possible value for column PSEUDO_COLUMN in the ResultSet object returned by the method getBestRowIdentifier.

Indicates that the best row identifier may or may not be a pseudo column.

columnNoNulls

```
public final static int columnNoNulls = 0
```

A possible value for column NULLABLE in the ResultSet object returned by the method getColumns.
Indicates that a column might not allow NULL values.

columnNullable

```
public final static int columnNullable = 1
```

A possible value for column NULLABLE in the ResultSet object returned by the method getColumns.
Indicates that a column definitely allows NULL values.

columnNullableUnknown

```
public final static int columnNullableUnknown = 2
```

A possible value for column NULLABLE in the ResultSet object returned by the method getColumns.
Indicates that it is not known whether a column allows NULL values.

importedKeyCascade

```
public final static int importedKeyCascade = 0
```

A possible value for the columns UPDATE_RULE and DELETE_RULE in the ResultSet objects returned by the methods getImportedKeys, getExported-Keys, and getCrossReference.
For the column UPDATE_RULE, it indicates that when the primary key is updated, the foreign key (imported key) is changed to agree with it.
For the column DELETE_RULE, it indicates that when the primary key is deleted, rows that imported that key are deleted.

importedKeyInitiallyDeferred

```
public final static int importedKeyInitiallyDeferred = 5
```

A possible value for the column DEFERRABILITY in the ResultSet objects returned by the methods getImportedKeys, getExportedKeys, and getCross-Reference.

Indicates deferrability. See SQL–92 for a definition.

importedKeyInitiallyImmediate

```
public final static int importedKeyInitiallyImmediate = 6
```

A possible value for the column DEFERRABILITY in the ResultSet objects returned by the methods getImportedKeys, getExportedKeys, and getCross-Reference.

Indicates deferrability. See SQL–92 for a definition.

importedKeyNoAction

```
public final static int importedKeyNoAction = 3
```

A possible value for the columns UPDATE_RULE and DELETE_RULE in the ResultSet objects returned by the methods getImportedKeys, getExported-Keys, and getCrossReference.

For the columns UPDATE_RULE and DELETE_RULE, it indicates that if the primary key has been imported by another table, then it cannot be updated or deleted.

importedKeyNotDeferrable

```
public final static int importedKeyNotDeferrable = 7
```

A possible value for the column DEFERRABILITY in the ResultSet objects returned by the methods getImportedKeys, getExportedKeys, and getCross-Reference.

Indicates deferrability. See SQL–92 for a definition.

importedKeyRestrict

```
public final static int importedKeyRestrict = 1
```

A possible value for the columns UPDATE_RULE and DELETE_RULE in the ResultSet objects returned by the methods getImportedKeys, getExported-Keys, and getCrossReference.

For the column UPDATE_RULE, it indicates that a primary key may not be updated if it has been imported by another table as a foreign key.

For the column DELETE_RULE, it indicates that a primary key may not be deleted if it has been imported by another table as a foreign key.

importedKeySetDefault

```
public final static int importedKeySetDefault = 4
```

A possible value for the columns UPDATE_RULE and DELETE_RULE in the ResultSet objects returned by the methods getImportedKeys, getExported-Keys, and getCrossReference.

For the columns UPDATE_RULE and DELETE_RULE, it indicates that if the primary key has been updated or deleted, then the foreign key (imported key) should be set to the default value.

importedKeySetNull

```
public final static int importedKeySetNull = 2
```

A possible value for the columns UPDATE_RULE and DELETE_RULE in the ResultSet objects returned by the methods getImportedKeys, getExported-Keys, and getCrossReference.

For the columns UPDATE_RULE and DELETE_RULE, it indicates that if the primary key has been updated or deleted, then the foreign key (imported key) is changed to NULL.

procedureColumnIn

```
public final static int procedureColumnIn = 1
```

A possible value for column COLUMN_TYPE in the ResultSet object returned by the method getProcedureColumns.

Indicates that this row of the ResultSet object describes an IN parameter.

procedureColumnInOut

public final static int **procedureColumnInOut** = 2

A possible value for column COLUMN_TYPE in the ResultSet object returned by the method getProcedureColumns.

Indicates that this row of the ResultSet object describes an INOUT parameter.

procedureColumnOut

public final static int **procedureColumnOut** = 4

A possible value for column COLUMN_TYPE in the ResultSet object returned by the method getProcedureColumns.

Indicates that this row of the ResultSet object describes an OUT parameter.

procedureColumnResult

public final static int **procedureColumnResult** = 3

A possible value for column COLUMN_TYPE in the ResultSet object returned by the method getProcedureColumns.

Indicates that this row describes a result column in a ResultSet object produced by a stored procedure.

procedureColumnReturn

public final static int **procedureColumnReturn** = 5

A possible value for column COLUMN_TYPE in the ResultSet object

returned by the method `getProcedureColumns`.
Indicates that this row describes a procedure's return value.

procedureColumnUnknown

```
public final static int procedureColumnUnknown = 0
```

A possible value for column `COLUMN_TYPE` in the `ResultSet` object
returned by the method `getProcedureColumns`.
Indicates that the type of the column described in this row is unknown.

procedureNoNulls

```
public final static int procedureNoNulls = 0
```

A possible value for column `NULLABLE` in the `ResultSet` object returned
by the method `getProcedureColumns`.
Indicates that the procedure does not allow `NULL` values.

procedureNoResult

```
public final static int procedureNoResult = 1
```

A possible value for column `PROCEDURE_TYPE` in the `ResultSet` object
returned by the method `getProcedures`.
Indicates that the procedure does not return a result.

procedureNullable

```
public final static int procedureNullable = 1
```

A possible value for column `NULLABLE` in the `ResultSet` object returned
by the method `getProcedureColumns`.
Indicates that the procedure allows `NULL` values.

procedureNullableUnknown

```
public final static int procedureNullableUnknown = 2
```

A possible value for column NULLABLE in the ResultSet object returned by the method getProcedureColumns.
Indicates that it is not known whether the procedure allows NULL values.

procedureResultUnknown

```
public final static int procedureResultUnknown = 0
```

A possible value for column PROCEDURE_TYPE in the ResultSet object returned by the method getProcedures.
Indicates that it is not known whether the procedure returns a result.

procedureReturnsResult

```
public final static int procedureReturnsResult = 2
```

A possible value for column PROCEDURE_TYPE in the ResultSet object returned by the method getProcedures.
Indicates that the procedure returns a result.

sqlStateSQL99

`3.0`

```
public final static int sqlStateSQL99 = 2
```

A possible return value for the method getSQLStateType.
Indicates that the type of SQLState returned by the method SQLException.getSQLState is SQL99.

sqlStateXOpen

`3.0`

```
public final static int sqlStateXOpen = 1
```

A possible return value for the method `getSQLStateType`.

Indicates that the type of SQLState returned by the method `SQLException.getSQLState` is X/Open (now known as Open Group) SQL CLI .

tableIndexClustered

```
public final static short tableIndexClustered = 1
```

A possible value for column TYPE in the ResultSet object returned by the method `getIndexInfo`.

Indicates that this table index is a clustered index.

tableIndexHashed

```
public final static short tableIndexHashed = 2
```

A possible value for column TYPE in the ResultSet object returned by the method `getIndexInfo`.

Indicates that this table index is a hashed index.

tableIndexOther

```
public final static short tableIndexOther = 3
```

A possible value for column TYPE in the ResultSet object returned by the method `getIndexInfo`.

Indicates that what is returned in conjunction with a table's index descriptions is not a clustered index, a hashed index, or table statistics; it is something other than these.

tableIndexStatistic

```
public final static short tableIndexStatistic = 0
```

A possible value for column TYPE in the ResultSet object returned by the method `getIndexInfo`.

Indicates that this column contains table statistics that are returned in conjunction with a table's index descriptions.

typeNoNulls

`public final static int typeNoNulls = 0`

A possible value for column `NULLABLE` in the `ResultSet` object returned by the method `getTypeInfo`.

Indicates that `NULL` values are not allowed for this data type.

typeNullable

`public final static int typeNullable = 1`

A possible value for column `NULLABLE` in the `ResultSet` object returned by the method `getTypeInfo`.

Indicates that a `NULL` value is allowed for this data type.

typeNullableUnknown

`public final static int typeNullableUnknown = 2`

A possible value for column `NULLABLE` in the `ResultSet` object returned by the method `getTypeInfo`.

Indicates that it is not known whether `NULL` values are allowed for this data type.

typePredBasic

`public final static int typePredBasic = 2`

A possible value for column `SEARCHABLE` in the `ResultSet` object returned by the method `getTypeInfo`.

Indicates that one can base all WHERE search clauses except WHERE . . . LIKE on this type.

typePredChar

```
public final static int typePredChar = 1
```

A possible value for column SEARCHABLE in the ResultSet object returned by the method getTypeInfo.
Indicates that the only WHERE search clause that can be based on this type is WHERE . . . LIKE.

typePredNone

```
public final static int typePredNone = 0
```

A possible value for column SEARCHABLE in the ResultSet object returned by the method getTypeInfo.
Indicates that WHERE search clauses are not supported for this type.

typeSearchable

```
public final static int typeSearchable = 3
```

A possible value for column SEARCHABLE in the ResultSet object returned by the method getTypeInfo.
Indicates that all WHERE search clauses can be based on this type.

versionColumnNotPseudo

```
public final static int versionColumnNotPseudo = 1
```

A possible value for column PSEUDO_COLUMN in the ResultSet object returned by the method getVersionColumns.
Indicates that this column, which is automatically updated when any

value in a row is updated, is *not* a pseudo column.

versionColumnPseudo

```
public final static int versionColumnPseudo = 2
```

A possible value for column PSEUDO_COLUMN in the ResultSet object returned by the method getVersionColumns.

Indicates that this column, which is automatically updated when any value in a row is updated, is a pseudo column.

versionColumnUnknown

```
public final static int versionColumnUnknown = 0
```

A possible value for column PSEUDO_COLUMN in the ResultSet object returned by the method getVersionColumns.

Indicates that this column, which is automatically updated when any value in a row is updated, may or may not be a pseudo column.

CHAPTER **16**

DataSource ⛁ 2.0

16.1 DataSource Overview

A DataSource object is the representation of a data source in the Java programming language. In basic terms, a data source is a facility for storing data. It can be as sophisticated as a complex database for a large corporation or as simple as a file with rows and columns. A data source can reside on a remote server, or it can be on a local desktop machine. Applications access a data source using a connection, and a DataSource object can be thought of as a factory for connections to the particular data source that the DataSource instance represents. The DataSource interface provides two methods for establishing a connection with a data source.

Using a DataSource object is the preferred alternative to using the DriverManager for establishing a connection to a data source. They are similar to the extent that the DriverManager class and DataSource interface both have methods for creating a connection, methods for getting and setting a timeout limit for making a connection, and methods for getting and setting a stream for logging.

Their differences are more significant than their similarities, however. Unlike the DriverManager, a DataSource object has properties that identify and describe the data source it represents. Also, a DataSource object works with a Java™ Naming and Directory Interface™ (JNDI) naming service and is created, deployed, and managed separately from the applications that use it. A driver vendor will provide a class that is a basic implementation of the DataSource interface as part of its JDBC driver product. What a system administrator does to register a DataSource object with a JNDI naming service is described in "Creating and Registering a DataSource Object," on page 568; what an application does to get a connection to a data source using a DataSource object registered with a JNDI naming service is described in "Connecting to a Data Source," on page 570.

Being registered with a JNDI naming service gives a `DataSource` object two major advantages over the `DriverManager`. First, an application does not need to hard code driver information, as it does with the `DriverManager`. A programmer can choose a logical name for the data source and register the logical name with a JNDI naming service. The application uses the logical name, and the JNDI naming service will supply the `DataSource` object associated with the logical name. The `DataSource` object can then be used to create a connection to the data source it represents. More is said about how to use JNDI and what its advantages are later in this chapter.

The second major advantage is that the `DataSource` facility allows developers to implement a `DataSource` class to take advantage of features such as connection pooling and distributed transactions. Connection pooling can increase performance dramatically by reusing connections rather than creating a new physical connection each time a connection is requested. Chapter 24, "PooledConnection," starting on page 637, explains connection pooling in detail. The ability to use distributed transactions enables an application to do the heavy duty database work of large enterprises. Chapter 48, "XAConnection," starting on page 1039, and Chapter 49, "XADataSource," starting on page 1055, explain distributed transactions. In this chapter, the section "DataSource Implementations," on page 571, gives a general, conceptual description of how the `DataSource` interface is implemented to work with connection pooling and distributed transactions.

Although an application may use either the `DriverManager` or a `DataSource` object to get a connection, using a `DataSource` object offers significant advantages and is the recommended way to establish a connection.

16.1.1 Properties

A `DataSource` object has a set of properties that identify and describe the real world data source that it represents. These properties include information such as the location of the database server, the name of the database, the network protocol to use to communicate with the server, and so on. `DataSource` properties follow the JavaBeans design pattern and are usually set when a `DataSource` object is deployed.

To encourage uniformity among `DataSource` implementations from different vendors, the JDBC 2.0 API specified a standard set of properties and a standard name for each property. Table 16.1: gives the standard name, the data type, and a description for each of the standard properties. Note that a `DataSource` implementation does not have to support all of these properties; the table just shows the standard name that an implementation should use when it supports a property.

Table 16.1:   Standard Data Source Properties

Property Name	Type	Description
databaseName	String	the name of a particular database on a server
dataSourceName	String	the logical name for the underlying XADataSource or Connection-PoolDataSource object; used only when pooling of connections or distributed transactions are implemented
description	String	a description of this data source
networkProtocol	String	the network protocol used to communicate with the server
password	String	the user's database password
portNumber	int	the port number where a server is listening for requests
roleName	String	the initial SQL rolename
serverName	String	the database server name
user	String	the user's account name

A DataSource object will, of course, have to support all of the properties that the data source it represents needs for making a connection, but the only property that all DataSource implementations are required to support is the description property. This standardizing of properties makes it possible, for instance, for a utility to be written that lists available data sources, giving a description of each along with the other property information that is available.

A `DataSource` object is not restricted to using only those properties specified in Table 16.1. A vendor may add its own properties, in which case it should give each new property a vendor-specific name.

If a `DataSource` object supports a property, it must supply getter and setter methods for it. The following code fragment illustrates the methods that a vendor implementation of the `DataSource` interface, *vds* in this example, would need to include if it supports, for example, the property `serverName`.

```
vds.setServerName("my_database_server");
String serverName = vds.getServerName();
```

Properties will most likely be set by a developer or system administrator using a GUI tool as part of the installation of the data source. Users connecting to the data source do not get or set properties. This is enforced by the fact that the `Data-Source` interface does not include the getter and setter methods for properties; they are supplied only in a particular implementation. The effect of including getter and setter methods in the implementation but not the public interface creates some separation between the management API for `DataSource` objects and the API used by applications. Management tools can get at properties by using introspection.

16.1.2   Using JNDI

JNDI provides a uniform way for an application to find and access remote services over the network. The remote service may be any enterprise service, including a messaging service or an application-specific service, but, of course, a JDBC application is interested mainly in a database service. Once a `DataSource` object is created and registered with a JNDI naming service, an application can use the JNDI API to access that `DataSource` object, which can then be used to connect to the data source it represents.

16.1.3   Creating and Registering a `DataSource` Object

A `DataSource` object is usually created, deployed, and managed separately from the Java applications that use it. For example, the following code fragment creates a `DataSource` object, sets its properties, and registers it with a JNDI naming service. Note that a `DataSource` object for a particular data source is created and deployed by a developer or system administrator, not the user. The class `VendorDataSource` would most likely be supplied by a driver vendor. (The code example in "Connecting to a Data Source," on page 570, shows the code that a user would write to get a connection.) Note also that a GUI tool will probably be used to deploy a DataSource object, so the following code, shown here mainly for illustration, is what such a tool would execute.

```
VendorDataSource vds = new VendorDataSource();

vds.setServerName("my_database_server");
vds.setDatabaseName("my_database");
vds.setDescription("the data source for inventory and personnel");

Context ctx = new InitialContext();
ctx.bind("jdbc/AcmeDB", vds);
```

The first four lines represent API from a vendor's class VendorDataSource, an implementation of the javax.sql.DataSource interface. They create a DataSource object, *vds*, and set its serverName, databaseName, and description properties. The fifth and sixth lines use JNDI API to register *vds* with a JNDI naming service. The fifth line calls the default InitialContext constructor to create a Java object that references the initial JNDI naming context. System properties, which are not shown here, tell JNDI which naming service provider to use. The last line associates *vds* with a logical name for the data source that *vds* represents.

The JNDI namespace consists of an initial naming context and any number of subcontexts under it. It is hierarchical, similar to the directory/file structure in many file systems, with the initial context being analogous to the root of a file system and subcontexts being analogous to subdirectories. The root of the JNDI hierarchy is the initial context, here represented by the variable *ctx*. Under the initial context there may be many subcontexts, one of which is jdbc, the JNDI subcontext reserved for JDBC data sources. (The logical data source name may be in the subcontext jdbc or in a subcontext under jdbc.) The last element in the hierarchy is the object being registered, analogous to a file, which in this case is a logical name for a data source. The result of the preceding six lines of code is that the VendorDataSource object *vds* is associated with jdbc/AcmeDB. The following section shows how an application uses this to connect to a data source.

16.1.4 Connecting to a Data Source

In the previous section, a `DataSource` object, *vds*, was given properties and bound to the logical name `AcmeDB`. The following code fragment shows application code that uses this logical name to connect to the database that *vds* represented. The code then uses the connection to print lists with the name and title of each member of the sales and customer service departments.

```
Context ctx = new InitialContext();
DataSource ds = (DataSource)ctx.lookup("jdbc/AcmeDB");
Connection con = ds.getConnection("genius", "abracadabra");
con.setAutoCommit(false);
PreparedStatement pstmt = con.prepareStatement(
            "SELECT NAME, TITLE FROM PERSONNEL WHERE DEPT = ?");
pstmt.setString(1, "SALES");
ResultSet rs = pstmt.executeQuery();

System.out.println("Sales Department:");
while (rs.next()) {
    String name = rs.getString("NAME");
    String title = rs.getString("TITLE");
    System.out.println(name + "    " + title);
}
pstmt.setString(1, "CUST_SERVICE");
ResultSet rs = pstmt.executeQuery();

System.out.println("Customer Service Department:");
while (rs.next()) {
    String name = rs.getString("NAME");
    String title = rs.getString("TITLE");
    System.out.println(name + "    " + title);
}
con.commit();
pstmt.close();
con.close();
```

The first two lines use JNDI API; the third line uses `DataSource` API. After the first line creates an instance of `javax.naming.Context` for the initial naming context, the second line calls the method `lookup` on it to get the `DataSource` object associated with jdbc/AcmeDB. Recall that in the previous code fragment, the last line of code associated jdbc/AcmeDB with *vds*, so the object returned by the lookup method refers to the same DataSource object that *vds* represented. However, the return value for the method lookup is a reference to a Java Object, the most generic of objects, so it must be cast to the more narrow DataSource before it can be assigned to the DataSource variable *ds*.

At this point *ds* refers to the same data source that *vds* referred to previously, the database *my_database* on the server *my_database_server*. Therefore, in the third line of code, calling the method DataSource.getConnection on *ds* and supplying it with a user name and password is enough to create a connection to *my_database*.

The rest of the code fragment uses a single transaction to execute two queries and print the results of each query. The DataSource implementation in this case is a basic implementation included with the JDBC driver. If the DataSource class had been implemented to work with an XADataSource implementation, and the preceding code example was executed in the context of a distributed transaction, the code could not have called the method Connection.commit, as is explained in the section "Application Code in Distributed Transactions," on page 1039. It also would not have set the auto-commit mode to false because that would have been unnecessary. The default for newly created connections that can participate in distributed transactions is to have auto-commit mode turned off. The next section will discuss the three broad categories of DataSource implementations.

In addition to the version of getConnection that takes a user name and password, the DataSource interface provides a version of the method Data-Source.getConnection that takes no parameters. It is available for situations where a data source does not require a user name and password because it uses a different security mechanism or where a data source does not restrict access.

16.1.5 DataSource Implementations

The DataSource interface may be implemented to provide three different kinds of connections. As a result of DataSource objects working with a JNDI service provider, all connections produced by a DataSource object offer the advantages of portability and easy maintenance, which are explained later in this chapter. Implementations of DataSource that work with implementations of the more specialized ConnectionPoolDataSource and XADataSource interfaces produce connections that are pooled or that can be used in distributed transactions. The following list summarizes the three general categories of classes that implement the `Data-Source` interface:

1. Basic `DataSource` class

   - provided by: driver vendor

   - advantages: portability, easy maintenance

2. `DataSource` class implemented to provide connection pooling

   - provided by: application server vendor or driver vendor

   - works with: a `ConnectionPoolDataSource` class, which is always provided by a driver vendor

   - advantages: portability, easy maintenance, increased performance

3. `DataSource` class implemented to provide distributed transactions

   - provided by: application server vendor, such as an EJB server vendor

   - works with: an `XADataSource` class, which is always provided by a driver vendor

   - advantages: portability, easy maintenance, ability to participate in distributed transactions

   Note that a `DataSource` implementation that supports distributed transactions is almost always implemented to support connection pooling as well.

An instance of a class that implements the `DataSource` interface represents one particular data source. Every connection produced by that instance will reference the same data source. In a basic `DataSource` implementation, a call to the method `DataSource.getConnection` returns a `Connection` object that, like the `Connection` object returned by the `DriverManager` facility, is a physical connection to the data source. Appendix A of the specification for the JDBC 2.0 Optional Package API (available at `http://java.sun.com/products/jdbc`) gives a sample implementation of a basic `DataSource` class.

`DataSource` objects that implement connection pooling likewise produce a connection to the particular data source that the `DataSource` class represents. The `Connection` object that the method `DataSource.getConnection` returns, however, is a handle to a `PooledConnection` object rather than being a physical connection. An application uses the `Connection` object just as it usually does and is generally unaware that it is in any way different. Connection pooling has no effect whatever on application code except that a pooled connection should always be explicitly closed. When an application closes a connection, the connection joins a pool of reusable connections. The next time `DataSource.getConnection` is called, a handle to one of these pooled connections will be returned if one is available. Because it avoids creating a new physical connection every time one is requested, connection pooling can help to make applications run significantly faster. Connection pooling is generally used, for example, by a Web server that supports servlets and JavaServer™ Pages.

A `DataSource` class can likewise be implemented to work with a distributed transaction environment. An EJB server, for example, supports distributed transactions and requires a `DataSource` class that is implemented to interact with it. In this case, the `DataSource.getConnection` method returns a `Connection` object that can be used in a distributed transaction. As a rule, EJB servers provide a `DataSource` class that supports connection pooling as well as distributed transactions. Like connection pooling, transaction management is handled internally, so using distributed transactions is easy. The only requirement is that when a transaction is distributed (involves two or more data sources), the application cannot call the methods `commit` or `rollback`. It also cannot put the connection in auto-commit mode. The reason for these restrictions is that a transaction manager begins and ends a distributed transaction under the covers, so an application cannot do anything that would affect when a transaction begins or ends.

Suppose that an EJB component (an enterprise Bean) invokes a method that sends a query to a remote DBMS server to check the positions of the securities in a portfolio. If there is a change in the quantity or price of a security, another enterprise Bean is used to update the database on a different DBMS server. The programmer who deploys the enterprise Beans specifies that both enterprise Beans need to be in the context of a distributed transaction because two different data sources are involved. The transaction manager will internally start a distributed transaction, so when the following code fragment is run, it is already in the context of a distributed transaction. Because the `Connection` object *con* was produced by a `DataSource` class that implements distributed transactions, it will by default have its auto-commit mode turned off.

The code gets a connection, updates a table, and then closes the connection without calling the method `commit` on it. This is the case because the transaction manager will check with the DBMS servers, and if they both vote to commit, the transaction manager will commit the entire distributed transaction. If one DBMS server votes not to commit, the transaction manager will roll back the entire transaction.

Assuming that the first part, or branch, of the distributed transaction has already executed, the following code fragment shows the second branch of the distributed transaction. The `DataSource` object used in the code, *ds*, produces connections to the `Portfolio` database that can be used in distributed transactions and that participate in connection pooling.

```
try {
    Connection con = ds.getConnection("BHD", "fortune");

    PreparedStatement pstmt = con.prepareStatement(
            "UPDATE SECURITIES SET PRICE = ? WHERE SYMBOL = ?");
    pstmt.setBigDecimal(1, new BigDecimal(54.125));
    pstmt.setString(2, "GYQ");
    pstmt.executeUpdate();

    pstmt.close();
} catch (SQLException ex) {
    // . . . handle exception
} finally {
    if (con != null) con.close();
}
```

Note that this code assumes that *con* is a pooled connection and therefore uses a `finally` block to close it. This ensures that if the connection is valid, it will be put back into the connection pool even if an exception is thrown. This is explained more fully in "Application Code for Connection Pooling," on page 637.

16.1.6 Logging and Tracing

The `DataSource` interface provides methods that allow a user to get and set the character stream to which tracing and error logging will be written. A user can trace a specific data source on a given stream, or multiple data sources can write log messages to the same stream provided that the stream is set for each data source. Log messages that are written to a log stream specific to a `DataSource` object are not written to the log stream maintained by the `DriverManager`.

A new `DataSource` object will have logging disabled by default, so it must set a log writer if logging is to be done. The following lines of code set the log writer for the `DataSource` object *ds*.

```
java.io.PrintWriter out = new java,io.Printwriter();
ds.setLogWriter(out);
```

The log writer can be disabled with the following line of code.

```
ds.setLogWriter(null);
```

The following line of code retrieves the character output stream to which logging and tracing messages are written.

```
java.io.PrintWriter writer = ds.getLogWriter();
```

The variable *writer* will be `null` if no log writer has been set for *ds* or if the log writer has been disabled (set to `null`).

16.1.7 Advantages of Using JNDI

There are major advantages to connecting to a data source using a `DataSource` object registered with a JNDI naming service rather than using the `DriverManager` facility. The first is that it makes code more portable. With the `DriverManager`, the name of a JDBC driver class, which usually identifies a particular driver vendor, is included in application code. This makes the application specific to that vendor's driver product and thus non-portable.

Another advantage is that it makes code much easier to maintain. If any of the necessary information about the data source changes, only the relevant `Data-Source` properties need to be modified, not every application that connects to that data source. For example, if a database is moved to a different server and uses a different port number, only the `DataSource` object's `serverName` and `portNumber` properties need to be updated. A system administrator could keep all existing code usable with the following code fragment. In practice, a system administrator would probably use a GUI tool to set the properties, so this code fragment illustrates the code a tool might execute internally.

```
Context ctx = new InitialContext()
VendorDataSource vds = (VendorDataSource)ctx.lookup("jdbc/AcmeDB");
vds.setServerName("my_new_database_server");
vds.setPortNumber("940");
```

The application programmer would not need to do anything to keep all of the applications using the data source running smoothly.

Yet another advantage is that applications using a DataSource object to get a connection will automatically benefit from connection pooling if the DataSource class has been implemented to support connection pooling. Likewise, an application will automatically be able to use distributed transactions if the DataSource class has been implemented to support them.

16.2   DataSource Interface Definition

```
package javax.sql;
public abstract interface DataSource {
    public java.sql.Connection getConnection()
                                    throws java.sql.SQLException;
    public java.sql.Connection getConnection(java.lang.String user,
            java.lang.String password) throws java.sql.SQLException;
    public void setLoginTimeout(int seconds)
                                    throws java.sql.SQLException;
    public int getLoginTimeout() throws java.sql.SQLException;
    public void setLogWriter(java.io.PrintWriter out)
                                    throws java.sql.SQLException;
    public java.io.PrintWriter getLogWriter()
                                    throws java.sql.SQLException;
}
```

16.3   DataSource Methods

NOTE: A vendor's implementation of a DataSource object must include methods for getting and setting all of a DataSource object's properties in addition to the methods listed in this section.

The following methods are defined in the interface javax.sql.DataSource:

getConnection

```
public java.sql.Connection getConnection()
                                    throws java.sql.SQLException
```

Attempts to establish a connection to the data source that this `DataSource` object represents.

RETURNS:
a `Connection` object that is a connection to the data source that this `DataSource` object represents. When this `DataSource` object is implemented to work with a connection pooling module, the `Connection` object it produces will participate in connection pooling; when it is implemented to work with a distributed transaction infrastructure, the `Connection` object will be able to participate in distributed transactions. Generally a `DataSource` class that is implemented to work with distributed transactions will be implemented to work with connection pooling as well.

EXAMPLE:
```
// jdbc/CoffeesDB has been registered with a JNDI naming service
DataSource ds = (DataSource)ctx.lookup("jdbc/CoffeesDB");
Connection con = ds.getConnection();
```

getConnection

```
public java.sql.Connection getConnection(java.lang.String user,
        java.lang.String password) throws java.sql.SQLException
```

Attempts to establish a connection to the data source that this `DataSource` object represents.

PARAMETERS:

user	the data source user on whose behalf the connection is being made
password	the user's password

RETURNS:
a `Connection` object that is a connection to the data source that this `DataSource` object represents. When this `DataSource` object is implemented to work with a connection pooling module, the `Connection` object it produces will participate in connection pooling; when it is implemented to work with a distributed transaction infrastructure, the `Connection` object will be able to participate in dis-

tributed transactions. Generally a DataSource class that is implemented to work with distributed transactions will be implemented to work with connection pooling as well.

EXAMPLE:
```
// jdbc/CoffeesDB has been registered with a JNDI naming service
DataSource ds = (DataSource)ctx.lookup("jdbc/CoffeesDB");
Connection con = ds.getConnection("archibald", "jdbc4all");
```

getLoginTimeout

```
public int getLoginTimeout() throws java.sql.SQLException
```

Retrieves the maximum number of seconds that this DataSource object can wait while attempting to connect to the data source it represents. A value of zero means that the timeout is the default system timeout if there is one; otherwise, zero means that there is no timeout.

The default is for a newly created DataSource object to have a login timeout of zero.

RETURNS:
an int representing the maximum number of seconds that this DataSource object can wait to connect to a database

EXAMPLE:
```
int limit = ds.getLoginTimeout();
// limit will be 0 unless a different timeout limit has been set for
// logging in
```

getLogWriter

```
public java.io.PrintWriter getLogWriter();
                                    throws java.sql.SQLException
```

Retrieves the character output stream to which all logging and tracing messages for the data source that this DataSource object represents will be printed. This includes messages printed by the methods of this DataSource object and also messages printed by methods of other objects manufactured by this DataSource object.

RETURNS:
the log writer for this `DataSource` object; `null` if the log writer has been disabled

EXAMPLE:
```
java.io.PrintWriter logWriter = ds.getLogWriter();
```

setLoginTimeout

```
public void setLoginTimeout(int seconds);
                                    throws java.sql.SQLException
```

Sets the maximum number of seconds that this `DataSource` object can wait for a connection to be established to *seconds*. A value of zero specifies that the timeout is the default system timeout if there is one; otherwise, zero specifies that there is no timeout.

The default login timeout for a newly created `DataSource` object is zero.

PARAMETERS:

seconds   the maximum number of seconds that this `DataSource` object can wait for a connection to be established; 0 to set the timeout to the default system timeout, if there is one, or else 0 to specify no timeout limit

EXAMPLE:
```
ds.setLoginTimeout(30);
// sets the timeout limit for ds to 30 seconds
ds.setLoginTimeout(0);
// sets the timeout limit for ds to the default system timeout; if
// there is no system default, sets the timeout to have no limit
```

setLogWriter

```
public void setLogWriter(java.io.PrintWriter out)
                                    throws java.sql.SQLException
```

Sets the character output stream to which all logging and tracing messages for this `DataSource` object will be printed to *out*. The messages that will be printed to *out* include those printed by the methods of this `DataSource` object and also messages printed by methods of other objects manufactured by this DataSource object.

PARAMETERS:

out   the java.io.PrintWriter object to which logging and
                         tracing messages will be sent; null to disable logging
                         and tracing

EXAMPLE:

```
ds.setLogWriter(out);
// logging and tracing messages for ds and any objects manufactured
// by ds will be printed to out

ds.setLogWriter(null);
// no logging or tracing messages will be printed
```

CHAPTER **17**

DataTruncation

17.1 DataTruncation Overview

THE class DataTruncation, a subclass of SQLWarning, provides information
when a data value is unexpectedly truncated. Under some circumstances, only part
of a data field will be read from or written to a database. How this is handled will
depend on the circumstances. In general, when data is unexpectedly truncated
while being read from a database, an SQLWarning is reported, whereas unexpected
data truncation during a write operation to a database will generally cause an
SQLException to be thrown.

17.1.1 Data Truncation with No Warning or Exception

If an application imposes a limit on the size of a field (using the Statement method
setMaxFieldSize) and attempts to read or write a field larger than the limit, the data
will be silently truncated to that size limit. In this case, even though the data is truncated, no SQLException will be thrown, and no SQLWarning will be reported.

For maximum portability, an application should set the maximum field size to
at least 256 bytes.

17.1.2 Data Truncation on Reads

The application programmer does not need to be concerned about data truncation
exceptions when reading data from a database. The JDBC API does not require the
programmer to pass in fixed-size buffers; instead, Java allocates appropriate data
space as needed. This means that the JDBC API puts no limits on the size of data
that can be read and accommodates varying field sizes.

17.1.3   Data Truncation on Writes

It is possible that an application may attempt to send more data to a database than the driver or the database is prepared to accept. In this case, the failing method should throw a DataTruncation object as an SQLException. It should be noted that even when a data truncation exception has been thrown, the data has still been sent to the database, and depending on the driver, the truncated data may have been written.

17.1.4   What a DataTruncation Object Contains

Each DataTruncation object contains the following kinds of information:

- the string "Data truncation" to describe the warning or exception
- an "SQLState" string set to "01004"
- a boolean to indicate whether a column or parameter was truncated
- an int giving the index of the column or parameter that was truncated
- a boolean to indicate whether the truncation occurred on a read or a write operation
- an int indicating the number of bytes that should have been transferred
- an int indicating the number of bytes that were actually transferred
- a chain to the next SQLWarning or SQLException object, which can be used if there is more than one warning or exception

17.1.5   Retrieving DataTruncation Information

The method getWarnings will retrieve the first SQLWarning. The interfaces Connection, Statement (including PreparedStatement and CallableStatement), and ResultSet all have their own versions of the method getWarnings to retrieve the first SQLWarning or DataTruncation object reported. Any subsequent warnings are retrieved by calling the SQLWarning method getNextWarning.

The first DataTruncation object thrown as an SQLException object can be caught in a catch block. Second and subsequent exceptions are retrieved by calling the SQLException method getNextException.

Once a DataTruncation object has been accessed, the information stored in it is retrieved by calling the following methods: getMessage, getSQLState, getIndex, getParameter, getRead, getDataSize, and getTransferSize.

The `DataTruncation` class defines one constructor for creating instances of `DataTruncation`. The inherited methods `getMessage` and `getSQLState` return the default values with which every `DataTruncation` object is initialized: `getMessage` returns "Data truncation", and `getSQLState` returns "01004". The five methods for getting components specific to this class return the values supplied to the constructor.

17.2 DataTruncation Class Definition

```
package java.sql;
public class DataTruncation extends SQLWarning {
    public DataTruncation(int index, boolean parameter,
                    boolean read, int dataSize, int transferSize);
    public int getIndex();
    public boolean getParameter();
    public boolean getRead();
    public int getDataSize();
    public int getTransferSize();
}
```

17.3 DataTruncation Constructor

The following constructor is defined in `java.sql.DataTruncation`:

DataTruncation

```
public DataTruncation(int index, boolean parameter,
                boolean read, int dataSize, int transferSize)
```

Constructs a fully specified `DataTruncation` object.

PARAMETERS:

index   an `int` indicating the index of the parameter or column in which data was truncated

parameter	true to indicate that the value truncated is a parameter value; false to indicate that the value truncated is a column value
read	true to indicate that data was truncated while being read from the database; false to indicate that data was truncated while being written to the database
dataSize	an int indicating the number of bytes that should have been read or written
transferSize	an int indicating the number of bytes that were actually read or written

RETURNS:

a DataTruncation object initialized with "Data truncation", "01004", *index*, *parameter*, *read*, *dataSize*, and *transferSize*

EXAMPLE:

```
DataTruncation dt = new DataTruncation(3, false, false, 1000, 255);
// dt contains a DataTruncation object with the message "Data trunca-
// tion", the SQLState of "01004", and the information that only 255
// bytes out of 1000 were written to column 3
```

17.4 DataTruncation Methods

17.4.1 Inherited Methods

The following methods are inherited from the class java.lang.Exception, which inherited them from the class java.lang.Throwable:

```
fillInStackTrace
getMessage
printStackTrace
toString
```

The following methods are inherited from the class java.sql.SQLException:

```
getSQLState
getErrorCode
getNextException
setNextException
```

The following methods are inherited from the class `java.sql.SQLWarning`:

```
getNextWarning
setNextWarning
```

17.4.2 Methods Defined in `DataTruncation`

The following methods are defined in the class `java.sql.DataTruncation`:

getDataSize

```
public int getDataSize()
```

Gets the number of bytes of data that should have been transferred. This number may be approximate if data conversions were performed. The value will be -1 if the size is unknown.

RETURNS:
an `int` indicating the number of bytes of data that should have been transferred or -1 if the size is unknown

EXAMPLE:
```
int numberOfBytes = myDataTruncation.getDataSize();
```

getIndex

```
public int getIndex()
```

Gets the index of the column or parameter that was truncated. This may be -1 if the column or parameter index is unknown, in which case the `parameter` and `read` fields should be ignored.

RETURNS:
an `int` representing the `DataTruncation` object's `index` value or -1 if the index of the column or parameter is unknown

EXAMPLE:
```
int ix = myDataTruncation.getIndex();
```

getParameter

public boolean **getParameter**()

Indicates whether data truncation occurred in a parameter or a result set column. The parameter field should be ignored if the method getIndex returns -1.

RETURNS:
true if data truncation occurred in a parameter or false if it occurred in a result set column

EXAMPLE:
boolean b = myDataTruncation.getParameter();

SEE:
DataTruncation.getIndex

getRead

public boolean **getRead**()

Indicates whether the data truncation occurred during a read or a write operation. If the method getIndex returns -1, the read field should be ignored.

RETURNS:
true if data truncation occurred during a read from the database or false if it occurred during a write to the database

EXAMPLE:
boolean b = myDataTruncation.getRead();

SEE:
DataTruncation.getIndex

getTransferSize

public int **getTransferSize**()

Gets the number of bytes of data actually transferred. This number may be -1 if the size is unknown.

RETURNS:

an int indicating the number of bytes that were actually transferred or -1 if the size is unknown

EXAMPLE:

```
int numberOfBytes = myDataTruncation.getTransferSize();
```

CHAPTER 18

Date

18.1 Date Overview

THE class java.sql.Date represents an SQL DATE value. The JDBC API does not use the class java.util.Date because it contains both date and time information, and the type SQL DATE contains only date information (year, month, and day). The class java.sql.Date is implemented as a thin wrapper around java.util.Date that uses only the date part. The class java.sql.Time works in a similar fashion, using only the time part of java.util.Date. The class java.sql.Timestamp is likewise a wrapper around java.util.Date, but because an SQL TIMESTAMP has not only date and time information but also a nanoseconds component, java.sql.Timestamp uses all parts of java.util.Date and adds a nanoseconds field.

A java.sql.Date object is a long representing the number of milliseconds before or after January 1, 1970, 00:00:00 GMT. (A long value of 0 is January 1, 1970, 00:00:00 GMT, the zero epoch in the Java programming language.) When an SQL DATE is retrieved from a result set or stored procedure, the driver converts the database's representation of the date to a long representing a milliseconds value. The driver also normalizes the time components of the date (sets them to zero) before returning a java.sql.Date object to an application. An application that creates a java.sql.Date object should likewise explicitly normalize it, thus making it possible to make meaningful comparisons of Date objects in Java applications. An application can normalize a Date object by constructing a Calendar object to represent the date and setting the hour, minutes, seconds, and milliseconds to zero. Another even more compelling reason to construct a Calendar object is that it will provide the desired milliseconds value to supply to the Date constructor. The next section gives an example of the complete process.

The java.sql.Date class adds the method toString for formatting and the method ValueOf for parsing so that the JDBC escape syntax for date values can be used. See "SQL Escape Syntax in Statement Objects," starting on page 958, for information about the escape syntax for dates.

18.1.1   Creating a Date Object

Date objects can be created in two ways: using the constructor or using the method valueOf.

1. The constructor creates a Date object from a long value. The following code demonstrates how to use a java.util.Calendar object to arrive at the correct number of milliseconds for creating a particular date. The Calendar object should always have its HOUR, MINUTE, SECOND, and MILLISECOND fields set to 0, as shown in the following code.

```
import java.util.*;

public class Cal {
    public static void main(String [] args) {

        Calendar cal = Calendar.getInstance();
        cal.set(Calendar.YEAR, 2004);
        cal.set(Calendar.MONTH, Calendar.JANUARY);
        cal.set(Calendar.DATE, 24);
        cal.set(Calendar.HOUR, 0);
        cal.set(Calendar.MINUTE, 0);
        cal.set(Calendar.SECOND, 0);
        cal.set(Calendar.MILLISECOND, 0);

        long millis = cal.getTime().getTime();
        java.sql.Date d = new java.sql.Date(millis);

        System.out.println("millis = " + millis);
        System.out.println("Date d = " + d);
    }
}
```

Running this code produces the following output.

```
➥ millis = 980366400000
➥ Date d = 2004-01-24
```

The preceding example illustrates the following features:

- You can use constants for setting the month, which was done in the preceding code example and is the recommended practice, or you can use `int` values (January is 0, February is 1, and so on).
- The call `cal.getTime().getTime()` returns a milliseconds value. The first invocation of `getTime` converts the `Calendar` object to a `java.util.Date` object, and the next call to the `getTime` method converts the `Date` object to its milliseconds value.
- The method `Calendar.getInstance` returns a `Calendar` object with its fields set to the current time and date. All of the time components should be set to 0. If you do not set one of the time components to 0, the millisecond value used to construct a new `Date` object will include the milliseconds value for that time component and will affect the comparison of `Date` objects.

Note that if a number literal is supplied to the `Date` constructor, it should include `L` at the end of the number to indicate a `long`. Otherwise, the compiler will interpret it as an `int` and reject a number that is larger than 2147483647 or smaller than – 2147483648.

2. The method `valueOf` creates a `Date` object by converting a string to a `Date` object. Note that the `String` object used as the argument must have the form `"yyyy-mm-dd"`.

```
Date d = Date.valueOf("1999-05-31");
```

The variable *d* contains a `Date` object representing May 31, 1999.

The method `java.sql.Date.setTime`, which takes a `long` as its parameter and overrides the method `java.util.Date.setTime`, can be used to change the date of a `Date` object after it has been created.

18.1.2 Deprecated Methods

A `java.sql.Date` object includes the time components inherited from `java.util.`
`Date`, but the hours, minutes, and seconds in a `java.sql.Date` object should not be
accessed. Toward this end, in Java 2 SDK, Standard Edition, and Java 2 SDK, Enterprise Edition, the following methods have been deprecated:

```
getHours
getMinutes
getSeconds
setHours
setMinutes
setSeconds
```

Trying to use the methods inherited from `java.util.Date` to set or get a time component in a `java.sql.Date` object will generate an exception.

The constructor that uses a year, month, and day to construct a `Date` object has
also been deprecated; the constructor that takes a milliseconds value should be
used instead.

18.1.3 Retrieving a `Date` Object

A `Date` object is retrieved using either the method `ResultSet.getDate` or `CallableStatement.getDate`. As an example, the following code fragment, in which
stmt is a `Statement` object, uses `ResultSet.getDate` to retrieve the date of sale
number 0038542.

```
ResultSet rs = stmt.executeQuery(
        "SELECT DATE FROM SALES WHERE SALE_NO = 0038542");
rs.next();
java.sql.Date date = rs.getDate("DATE");
```

The variable *date* contains a `long` equal to the number of milliseconds before
or after January 1, 1970, 00:00:00 GMT that the SQL DATE object represents. Its
time components were all set to 0 by the driver.

18.1.4 Advanced Features

The number of milliseconds in a `java.sql.Date` object always takes into account a
time zone, which can, of course, affect the date. In the examples up to this point, the

driver has used the default time zone, the time zone of the Java virtual machine running an application. The JDBC 2.0 core API added new versions of the getDate methods in the ResultSet and CallableStatement interfaces that take a java.util.Calendar object, in which time zone information can be stored with an appropriate instance of the TimeZone class. The PreparedStatement method setDate also has a new version that uses a Calendar object for time zone information, as does the RowSet.setDate method in the JDBC Optional Package API.

When the ResultSet.getDate and CallableStatement.getDate methods are called, the driver converts a JDBC DATE instance, which is generally a string, to a java.sql.Date object, which is a milliseconds value. In order to calculate the milliseconds, the driver takes into account the time zone of the date, information a DBMS may or may not store. Because a Date object itself has no way to keep track of time zone information, the driver relies on a java.util.Calendar object to get this information when the DBMS does not supply it. If no Calendar object is supplied, the driver will use the default Calendar, whose time zone is that of the Java virtual machine that is running the application. If the DBMS does provide time zone information, the driver will simply use that and ignore a Calendar object that may have been passed to it. Therefore, to be portable, an application should supply a Calendar object to a getDate method, thereby not relying on the DBMS to supply a time zone but still being able to use the time zone supplied by a DBMS when one is available. The situation is analogous for the PreparedStatement.setDate method.

The following code fragment illustrates using a Calendar object to retrieve a date for Japan Standard Time.

```
ResultSet rs = stmt.executeQuery(
    "SELECT DATE FROM BROADCAST_SCHED WHERE ID = 3959817");
java.util.Calendar cal = java.util.Calendar.getInstance();
java.util.TimeZone tz = java.util.TimeZone.getTimeZone("JST");
cal.setTimeZone(tz);
rs.next();
Date broadcastDate = rs.getDate("DATE", cal);
```

After creating an instance of Calendar, the example code gets the time zone for Japan Standard Time and assigns it to a TimeZone object. Then it sets the Calendar instance with that TimeZone object and passes the Calendar to the method getDate. The driver will use the time zone information in Calendar to calculate the date, with the result that the variable *broadcastDate* contains a Date object that is accurate for Japan Standard Time.

18.2   Date Class Definition

```
package java.sql;
public class Date extends java.util.Date {
    public Date(int year, int month, int day);
    public Date(long date);
    public void setTime(long date);
    public static Date valueOf(String s);
    public String toString();
}
```

18.3   Date Constructors

Date   **DEPRECATED**
_____

```
public Date(int year, int month, int day)
```

Constructs a java.sql.Date object initialized with *year*, *month*, and *day* to represent a date value that can be used as an SQL DATE value.

This constructor has been deprecated; in its place, use the constructor that takes a long.

PARAMETERS:

year	a Java int representing the year minus 1900
month	a Java int from 0 to 11 (0 is January; 11 is December)
day	a Java int from 1 to 31

RETURNS:
a java.sql.Date object representing a date

EXAMPLE:
```
Date d = new Date(100, 0, 1); // d represents January 1, 2000
```

Date

public **Date**(long *millis*)

Constructs a java.sql.Date object from *millis*, a milliseconds time value, to represent a date value that can be used as an SQL DATE value.

Because java.sql.Date is a subclass of java.util.Date, it inherits a time component, which should be set to 00:00:00. See "Creating a Date Object," on page 590, for an example of the recommended way to create a Date object.

If any of the following methods is called on a java.sql.Date object, it will throw a java.lang.IllegalArgumentException: getHours, getMinutes, getSeconds, setHours, setMinutes, or setSeconds. In the JDBC 2.0 API, these methods are deprecated.

PARAMETERS:

millis   a long in the Java programming language representing the number of milliseconds since January 1, 1970, 00:00:00 GMT. A negative value represents the number of milliseconds before January 1, 1970, 00:00:00 GMT.

RETURNS:
a java.sql.Date object representing a date

EXAMPLE:
Date d = new Date(4875329593045L); // d represents 2124-06-29
Date d2 = new Date(-4875329593045L); // d2 represents 1815-07-05

18.4 Date Methods

The following methods are inherited from the class java.util.Date:

after	before	clone
compareTo	equals	getDate
getDay	getMonth	getTime
getTimezoneOffset	getYear	hashCode
parse	setDate	setMonth
setYear	toGMTString	toLocaleString
UTC		

The following methods are inherited from the class java.lang.Object:

finalize	getClass	notify
notifyAll	wait	

The following methods are defined in the class `java.sql.Date`:

setTime

```
public void setTime(long millis)
```

Sets this `Date` object to *millis*.

PARAMETERS:

millis   a long representing the number of milliseconds after
                        January 1, 1970, 00:00:00 GMT; a negative number
                        represents the number of milliseconds *before* January
                        1, 1970, 00:00:00 GMT

EXAMPLE:
```
Date d = new Date(920494875325L); // d represents 1999-03-03
d.setTime(9538156237483L); // d now represents 2272-04-01
```

toString

```
public String toString()
```

Formats this `Date` object as a `String` object in the JDBC date escape format yyyy-mm-dd. This method ignores any time components (hours, minutes,
seconds) contained in a `Date` object. It uses the default time zone in determining the `String` representation of the milliseconds value; therefore, this method
should not be used with dates in other time zones.

RETURNS:
A `String` object with the format "yyyy-mm-dd"

EXAMPLE:
```
Date d = new Date(2136543210L);
String s = d.toString(); // s contains "1970-01-25"
```

valueOf

```
public static Date valueOf(String s)
```

Converts *s*, a string in JDBC date escape format, to a `java.sql.Date` value (a milliseconds value). The time components included in `java.util.Date` are set to 0. The driver will use the time zone of the Java virtual machine running the application to calculate the number of milliseconds; therefore, this method should not be used with dates in other time zones.

PARAMETERS:

s   a `String` object in the format "yyyy-mm-dd", which is referred to as the *date escape format*

RETURNS:

a `Date` object representing the year, month, and day specified in the given `String` object

EXAMPLE:
```
String s = new String("2000-01-01");
java.sql.Date d = java.sql.Date.valueOf(s);
// d contains a Date object representing January 1, 2000 in the time
// zone of the Java virtual machine running the application.
```

CHAPTER 19

Distinct Types 2.0

19.1 Distinct Types Overview

A distinct type is a user-defined SQL type that is based on a built-in type. The `java.sql.Types.DISTINCT` typecode is used to denote values whose type is distinct. The standard mapping for a `DISTINCT` value is the Java data type to which its underlying SQL type is mapped. It is retrieved using the getter method that would be used to retrieve its underlying type and stored using the setter method appropriate to the underlying type. In other words, in the Java programming language, a distinct type is treated as if its data type were that of its underlying type.

19.1.1 Creating a Distinct Type Object

Since a distinct type is a UDT, it must first be defined in SQL using the SQL statement `CREATE TYPE` or `CREATE DISTINCT TYPE`. The following SQL statement creates the UDT `MONEY` from the SQL type `NUMERIC`.

```
CREATE TYPE MONEY AS NUMERIC(10, 2)
```

Once the new type has been defined, it can be used as the data type for a column in a database table or as the data type for an attribute of an SQL structured type. Assuming that the column `PRICE` holds values of type `MONEY`, the following code fragment will select the values in the column `PRICE` and retrieve the value in the first row of the result set *rs*.

```
ResultSet rs = stmt.executeQuery("SELECT PRICE FROM PRICE_LIST");
rs.first();
java.math.BigDecimal price = rs.getBigDecimal("PRICE");
```

The variable *price* is of type BigDecimal because an SQL NUMERIC type maps to a java.math.BigDecimal in the Java programming language. Consequently, the ResultSet method getBigDecimal is used to retrieve values of type MONEY.

19.1.2 Storing Distinct Objects

An instance of a distinct type may be stored in a database by passing it as an input parameter to a prepared statement. Continuing the previous example, the following code fragment illustrates retrieving a value from the table PRICE_LIST, raising it by 25 percent, and then returning it to the table.

```
ResultSet rs = stmt.executeQuery(
        "SELECT PRICE FROM PRICE_LIST WHERE SKU = 1034093982");
rs.next();
java.math.BigDecimal price = rs.getBigDecimal("PRICE");
price = price.multiply(new java.math.BigDecimal(1.25));
PreparedStatement pstmt = con.prepareStatement(
        "UPDATE PRICE_LIST SET PRICE = ? WHERE SKU = 1034093982");
pstmt.setBigDecimal(1, price);
pstmt.executeUpdate();
```

In PRICE_LIST in the row where the column SKU is 1034093982, the column PRICE now stores the MONEY value that represents the new price.

19.1.3 Using Distinct Data Types

The following SQL statement creates the distinct type SSN to be used for social security numbers. It is defined to be a CHAR with length 9 because this nine-digit number is used only for identification and should never be manipulated as a number.

```
CREATE TYPE SSN AS CHAR(9);
```

The following code fragment uses the new data type SSN as the data type for the column ID in the table CLIENTS. It also uses the type MONEY, defined in the previous section, as the type for the column ACCT_VALUE.

```
CREATE TABLE CLIENTS
(
LAST_NAME VARCHAR(40),
```

```
FIRST_NAME VARCHAR(40),
ID SSN,
ACCT_VALUE MONEY
)
```

Assuming that the table CLIENTS has been created and populated with data, the following code fragment demonstrates correcting the social security number and updating the account value for client Owen Ng. A JDBC CHAR maps to a String in the Java programming language, so the method updateString is used to make the correction. The method updateBigDecimal updates the account value because the underlying type of MONEY (the data type for the column ACCT_VALUE) is NUMERIC, which maps to BigDecimal.

```
ResultSet rs = stmt.executeQuery(
              "SELECT SSN, ACCT_VALUE WHERE " +
              "LAST_NAME = 'NG' AND FIRST_NAME = 'OWEN'");
rs.next();
rs.updateString("SSN", "249803645");
rs.updateBigDecimal("ACCT_VALUE",
                  new java.math.BigDecimal(345678.90));
rs.updateRow();
```

19.1.4 Custom Mapping of Distinct Types

A distinct data type may optionally be mapped to a class in the Java programming language. Insofar as a distinct type may be thought of as a structured type with only one attribute, the custom mapping of a distinct type is just like the mapping of a structured type. The one attribute is mapped to a field of the Java class mapping the distinct type. Chapter 44, "Struct," starting on page 997, and Chapter 37, "SQL-Data," starting on page 895, give more information about custom mapping.

When a distinct type has a custom mapping, it should be retrieved with the method ResultSet.getObject or CallableStatement.getObject and stored with the method PreparedStatement.setObject. Assuming that a custom mapping has been set up in which the SQL type MONEY is mapped to the Java class Money, the following code fragment uses the method getObject to retrieve the MONEY value stored in the column PRICE as an instance of the class Money. Because getObject returns an Object, it is cast to the class Money before being assigned to the variable *price*. The method setObject will map the Money object *price* back to its SQL MONEY data type before sending it to the database.

```
ResultSet rs = stmt.executeQuery(
        "SELECT PRICE FROM PRICE_LIST WHERE SKU = 1034093982");
rs.next();
Money price = (Money)rs.getObject("PRICE");
price = price.increase(.25);
PreparedStatement pstmt = con.prepareStatement(
        "UPDATE PRICE_LIST SET PRICE = ? WHERE SKU = 1034093982");
pstmt.setObject(1, price);
pstmt.executeUpdate();
```

The preceding code example assumes that the method increase has been defined on the class Money, and it is used to increase the price by 25 percent.

CHAPTER 20

Driver

20.1 Driver Overview

IN most cases, only developers writing drivers will need to understand the `java.sql.Driver` interface. It provides six methods. One method sets up a connection between a driver and a database, and the others give information about the driver or get information necessary for making a connection to a database. A JDBC driver provides a class, called the `Driver` class, that implements the `Driver` interface.

Methods on the `Driver` class most often work behind the scenes, being called by the generic `java.sql.DriverManager` class. For example, an application using the `DriverManager` class to establish a connection with a database calls the `DriverManager.getConnection` method. The driver manager then calls the `Driver` method `connect` on each registered driver in turn, and the first driver that can make the connection is the one to do it. See "DriverManager," on page 611, for a more detailed explanation. It is possible, however, for users to bypass the `DriverManager` and call the `connect` method directly if they want to specify that a particular driver be used. Similarly, although it is possible for anyone to call `getPropertyInfo`, most users will probably never call it. Its intended purpose is to allow a GUI tool to find out what information it should prompt the human user for in order to be able to make a connection. Note that JDBC 2.0 drivers also provide a separate `DataSource` class that developers may call directly to make a connection to a database. This mechanism is recommended over the use of the `Driver` class directly.

20.1.1 Loading and Registering a Driver

A `Driver` class should be implemented with a static section, known as a static initializer, that automatically does two things when it is loaded: (1) creates an instance of itself and (2) registers that instance by calling the method `DriverManager.registerDriver`. See the section "Implement a Static Initializer," on page 1102, for an example. When a `Driver` class includes this static section, the user can simply invoke the method `Class.forName`, supplying the class name of the driver as a string, to load and register a driver. For example, the following code loads and registers the `Driver` class `foo.bah.Driver`:

```
Class.forName("foo.bah.Driver");
```

20.1.2 JDBC Implementation Alternatives

The `DriverManager` framework allows for multiple database drivers, and there are various choices for JDBC driver implementations. One alternative is an implementation of JDBC on top of ODBC, called a JDBC–ODBC bridge. Java Software provides such a bridge as part of the Java 2 SDK, Standard Edition, and the Java 2 SDK, Enterprise Edition. Since the JDBC API is patterned after the ODBC API, this implementation is small and efficient.

   Another useful driver, called a net driver, is one that goes directly to a DBMS-independent network protocol supported by a database middleware server. A JDBC net driver is a very small and fast all Java client-side implementation, and it speaks to many databases via the middleware server. Several vendors have implemented JDBC net drivers.

   A third alternative is a driver that is even smaller and more efficient because it works directly with a particular DBMS. This implementation, known as a two-tier driver, has nothing intervening between the driver and the underlying data source. In contrast, the JDBC–ODBC bridge and JDBC net drivers require various intermediate components.

   There are two variations of two-tier drivers: those that are all-Java drivers and those that are not. A two-tier driver that is all-Java is the ideal JDBC driver, since it is platform-independent and can be automatically installed.

   Figure 20.1 illustrates driver implementation alternatives, showing the `java.sql.Driver` interface working between the `DriverManager` class and the various JDBC driver implementations.

Figure 20.1JDBC Driver Implementations

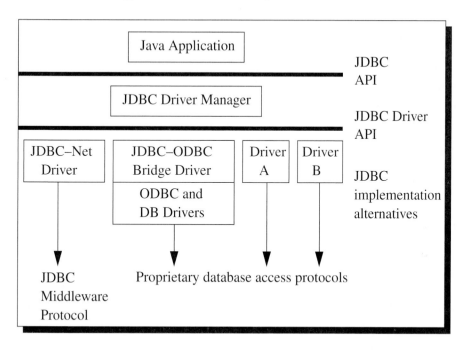

Although it is still possible to use the `DriverManager` class to connect to a driver, the `DataSource` interface, introduced in the JDBC 2.0 Optional Package API, offers a preferred way to connect to a driver. See Chapter 16, "DataSource," starting on page 565, for an explanation.

20.2 Driver Interface Definition

```
package java.sql;
public interface Driver {
    Connection connect(String url, java.util.Properties info)
                                              throws SQLException;
    boolean acceptsURL(String url) throws SQLException;
    DriverPropertyInfo[] getPropertyInfo(String url,
                  java.util.Properties info) throws SQLException;
    int getMajorVersion();
```

```
    int getMinorVersion();
    boolean jdbcCompliant();
}
```

20.3 Driver Methods

acceptsURL

```
boolean acceptsURL(String url) throws SQLException
```

> Tests to see if this driver understands the subprotocol specified in *url*.
> Typically, drivers will return `true` if they understand the URL and `false` if they do not.

PARAMETERS:

url   The URL of the database to which to connect

RETURNS:
true if this driver can connect to *url* and `false` if it cannot

EXAMPLE:
```
boolean b = myDriver.acceptsURL(url);
```

connect

```
Connection connect(String url, java.util.Properties info)
                                        throws SQLException
```

> Tries to make a database connection to *url*. The `Driver` class implemented by a driver vendor will return `null` if it is the wrong kind of driver to connect to *url*. This might not be uncommon because when the JDBC Driver Manager is asked to connect to a given URL, it passes the URL to each loaded `Driver` class in turn. The first `Driver` class may be the correct one to make the connection, but often it will not be. In that case, the `Driver` class returns `null` and the DriverManager passes the URL to the next `Driver` class, and so on.

PARAMETERS:

url	The URL of the database to which to connect
info	A list of arbitrary string tag/value pairs as connection arguments; normally at least a "user" and "password" property should be included in Properties

RETURNS:

a Connection object that represents a connection to the database located at *url* or null if the driver realizes it is the wrong kind of driver to connect to *url*. The driver will raise an SQLException if it is the right driver to connect to the given URL but has trouble connecting to the database.

EXAMPLE:
```
Connection con = myDriver.connect(url, info);
```

getMajorVersion

```
int getMajorVersion()
```

Returns the driver's major version number, which should initially be 1.

RETURNS:
the driver's major version number

EXAMPLE:
```
int x = d.getMajorVersion(); // x = 1 to begin with
```

SEE:
getMinorVersion

getMinorVersion

```
int getMinorVersion()
```

Returns the driver's minor version number, which should initially be 0.

RETURNS:
the driver's minor version number

EXAMPLE:
```
int x = d.getMajorVersion();
int y = d.getMinorVersion();
System.out.println("This driver version is " + x + "." + y);
```

Printout:
➥ This driver version is 1.0   // initial version

getPropertyInfo

DriverPropertyInfo[] **getPropertyInfo**(String *url*,
                       java.util.Properties *info*) throws SQLException

    The getPropertyInfo method is intended to allow a generic GUI tool to discover the properties for which it should prompt a human user in order to get enough information to connect to a database.

    The second argument should be null the first (and generally only) time this method is called. The second argument is included so that it is possible for an application to process input and present the human user with a list of properties from which to choose. Depending on the values the human has supplied so far, it is conceivable that additional values may be needed. In such cases, and assuming that the application has been written to handle the results of multiple calls to getPropertyInfo, it may be necessary to iterate through several calls to getPropertyInfo. If the application uses the information it gets to fill in values for a java.util.Properties object, then that object can be supplied to getPropertyInfo in subsequent calls to the method.

    The properties returned by this method will often correspond to the properties that are set on a javax.sql.DataSource object for this driver.

PARAMETERS:

url	The URL of the database to which to connect
info	null; on second and later invocations, a java.sql.DriverPropertyInfo object that contains a proposed list of tag/value pairs that will be sent when the method Driver.connect is called

RETURNS:
an array of java.sql.DriverPropertyInfo objects describing possible properties. This may be an empty array if no properties are required.

EXAMPLE:
String url = "jdbc:miracle:winners";
DriverPropertyInfo [] propArray = myDriver.getPropertyInfo(
                                                    url, null);

SEE:
DriverPropertyInfo

jdbcCompliant

```
boolean jdbcCompliant()
```

    Tests whether this driver can be designated JDBC Compliant. A driver may report `true` only if it passes the JDBC compliance tests; otherwise, it is required to return `false`. JDBC compliance requires full support for the JDBC 1.0 API and full support for SQL92 Entry Level.

    This method is not intended to encourage the development of JDBC drivers that are not compliant; rather, it recognizes that some vendors are interested in using the JDBC API and framework for lightweight databases that do not support full database functionality or for special databases, such as those for document information retrieval, where an SQL implementation may not be feasible.

RETURNS:
`true` if this driver passes minimum requirements for being designated JDBC Compliant

EXAMPLE:
```
boolean b = myDriver.jdbcCompliant();
```

SEE:
Appendix A "For Driver Writers"

CHAPTER 21

DriverManager

21.1 DriverManager Overview

THE DriverManager class is the traditional management layer of JDBC, working between the user and the drivers. It keeps track of the drivers that are available and handles establishing a connection between a database and the appropriate driver. In addition, the DriverManager class attends to things like driver login time limits and the printing of log and tracing messages.

For simple applications, the only method in this class that a general programmer needs to use directly is DriverManager.getConnection. As its name implies, this method establishes a connection to a database. An application may call the DriverManager methods getDriver, getDrivers, and registerDriver as well as the Driver method connect, but in most cases it is better to let the DriverManager class manage the details of establishing a connection.

21.1.1 Keeping Track of Available Drivers

The DriverManager class maintains a list of Driver classes that have registered themselves by calling the method DriverManager.registerDriver. All Driver classes should be written with a static section (a static initializer) that creates an instance of the class and then registers it with the DriverManager class when it is loaded. Thus, a user would not normally call DriverManager.registerDriver directly; it should be called automatically by a Driver class when it is loaded. A Driver class is loaded, and therefore automatically registered with the DriverManager, in one of two ways:

1. By calling the method `Class.forName`. This explicitly loads the driver class. Since it does not depend on any external setup, this way of loading a driver is the recommended one for using the `DriverManager` framework. The following code loads the class `acme.db.Driver`:

```
Class.forName("acme.db.Driver");
```

If `acme.db.Driver` has been written so that loading it causes an instance to be created and also calls `DriverManager.registerDriver` with that instance as the parameter (as it should do), then it is in the `DriverManager`'s list of drivers and available for creating a connection.

2. By adding the `Driver` class to the `java.lang.System` property `jdbc.drivers`. This is a list of driver classnames, separated by colons, that the `DriverManager` class loads. When the `DriverManager` class is initialized, it looks for the system property "`jdbc.drivers`," and if the user has entered one or more drivers, the `DriverManager` class attempts to load them. The following code illustrates how a programmer might enter three driver classes in ~/.hotjava/properties (HotJava loads these into the system properties list on startup):

```
jdbc.drivers=foo.bah.Driver:wombat.sql.Driver:bad.test.ourDriver
```

The first call to a `DriverManager` method will automatically cause these driver classes to be loaded.

Note that this second way of loading drivers requires a preset environment that is persistent. If there is any doubt about that being the case, it is safer to call the method `Class.forName` to explicitly load each driver. This is also the right method to use to bring in a particular driver since once the `DriverManager` class has been initialized, it will never recheck the `jdbc.drivers` property list.

In both of these cases, it is the responsibility of the newly loaded `Driver` class to register itself by calling `DriverManager.registerDriver`. As mentioned, this should be done automatically when the class is loaded.

For security reasons, the JDBC management layer will keep track of which class loader provided which driver. Then, when the `DriverManager` class is opening a connection, it will use only drivers that come from the local file system or from the same class loader as the code issuing the request for a connection.

21.1.2 Establishing a Connection

Once the `Driver` classes have been loaded and registered with the `DriverManager` class, they are available for establishing a connection with a database. When a request for a connection is made with a call to the `DriverManager.getConnection` method, the `DriverManager` tests each driver in turn to see if it can establish a connection.

It may sometimes be the case that more than one JDBC driver is capable of connecting to a given URL. For example, when connecting to a given remote database, it might be possible to use a JDBC–ODBC bridge driver, a JDBC-to-generic-network-protocol driver, or a driver supplied by the database vendor. In such cases, the order in which the drivers are tested is significant because the `DriverManager` will use the first driver it finds that can successfully connect to the given URL.

First, the `DriverManager` tries to use each driver in the order it was registered. (The drivers listed in `jdbc.drivers` are always registered first.) It will skip any drivers that are untrusted code unless they have been loaded from the same source as the code that is trying to open the connection.

It tests the drivers by calling the method `Driver.connect` on each one in turn, passing them the URL that the user originally passed to the method `DriverManager.getConnection`. The first driver that recognizes the URL makes the connection.

At first glance this may seem inefficient, but it requires only a few procedure calls and string comparisons per connection since it is unlikely that dozens of drivers will be loaded concurrently.

The following code is an example of all that is normally needed to set up a connection with a driver such as a JDBC–ODBC bridge driver.

```
Class.forName("jdbc.odbc.JdbcOdbcDriver"); //loads the driver
String url = "jdbc:odbc:fred";
Connection con = DriverManager.getConnection(
                                url, "userID", "passwd");
```

The variable *con* represents a connection to the data source "fred" that can be used to create and execute SQL statements.

With the addition of the JDBC 2.0 Optional Package API, a `DataSource` object can be used to establish a connection with a data source. The `DriverManager` can still be used, but a `DataSource` object offers several advantages over the `DriverManager` and is the preferred alternative. Developers who are writing Enterprise JavaBeans components, however, should always use a DataSource object instead of the DriverManager. Using a properly implemented DataSource object is the only way to get connections that are pooled and that can participate in distributed transactions. See Chapter 16, "DataSource," starting on page 565, for more information.

21.1.3 DriverManager Methods Are Static

All DriverManager methods are declared static, which means that they operate on the class as a whole and not on particular instances. In fact, the constructor for DriverManager is declared private to prevent users from instantiating it. Logically, there is one instance of the DriverManager class. This means that methods are called by qualifying them with DriverManager, as in the following line of code.

```
DriverManager.setLogWriter(out);
```

21.2 DriverManager Class Definition

```
package java.sql;
public class DriverManager {
    private static DriverManager();
    public static Connection getConnection(String url,
                java.util.Properties info) throws SQLException;
    public static Connection getConnection(String url,
                String user, String password) throws SQLException;
    public static Connection getConnection(String url)
                                            throws SQLException;
    public static Driver getDriver(String url) throws SQLException;
    public static void registerDriver(java.sql.Driver
                                driver) throws SQLException;
    public static void deregisterDriver(Driver driver) throws
                                                SQLException;
    public static java.util.Enumeration getDrivers();
    public static void setLoginTimeout(int seconds);
    public static int getLoginTimeout();
    public static void setLogStream(java.io.PrintStream out);
                                            (Deprecated)
```

```
      public static java.io.PrintStream getLogStream(); (Deprecated)
 2.0  public static void setLogWriter(java.io.PrintWriter out);
 2.0  public static java.io.PrintWriter getLogWriter();
      public static void println(String message);
}
```

21.3 DriverManager Methods

deregisterDriver

```
public static void deregisterDriver(Driver driver) throws SQLException
```

Removes the first entry for *driver* (if one exists) from the DriverManager's list of registered drivers. If there are duplicate entries, only the first one is removed. If there is no entry for *driver*, deregisterDriver does nothing. (Its definition specifies that it throws an SQLException, but this is only included for future use if needed.) For security reasons, applets can deregister drivers only from their own classloaders.

Normally users do not call either registerDriver or deregisterDriver; the easiest way to keep track of which drivers have been registered is by simply leaving registration up to the drivers and never deregistering them.

PARAMETERS:

driver   the JDBC driver to drop

EXAMPLE:

```
DriverManager.deregisterDriver(d);
```

getConnection

There are three forms of the method getConnection. All three take a URL as a parameter; one takes a java.util.Properties object in addition, and one takes a password and user in addition. A URL may contain a user, password, and attributes, in which case all the information is contained in the URL, making the other parameters unnecessary. In order to allow applets to access databases in a generic way, we recommend that as much connection information as possible be encoded as part of the JDBC URL and that driver writers keep their use of `java.util.Properties` to a minimum. As a general rule, the more information contained in the URL the better, especially for Internet connections.

Since the only difference in the three forms is the parameter list, they are grouped together to avoid unnecessary repetition.

```
public static Connection getConnection(String url)
                                                  throws SQLException;
public static Connection getConnection(String url,
              java.util.Properties info) throws SQLException;
public static Connection getConnection(String url,
              String user, String password) throws SQLException;
```

Attempts to establish a connection to the database identified in *url*. The `DriverManager` attempts to select an appropriate driver from the set of registered JDBC drivers by calling the `Driver` method `connect` on each driver in turn, passing it *url* as the parameter to the method `connect`. The connection is made with the first driver to recognize *url*.

PARAMETERS:

url	a JDBC URL of the form `jdbc:subprotocol:subname`
info	an instance of the class `java.util.Properties` that contains a list of strings that are key/value pairs. If this parameter is used, it will normally include at least a user and password.
user	the database user on whose behalf the connection is being made
password	the user's password

RETURNS:
a `Connection` object that represents a connection to the database specified in *url*

EXAMPLE 1:
```
String url = "jdbc:myDriverProtocol:http://xyzcorp.com." +
             "myLogin.myPassword:123/personnel/employees";
DriverManager.getConnection(url);
```

EXAMPLE 2:
```
// normally only an application that prompts the user for input
// in order to get enough information to make a connection would use
// this version of getConnection, and it would set up the properties
// in info
```

```
String url = "jdbc:odbc:myDataSourceName";
DriverManager.getConnection(url, info);
```

SEE:
DriverPropertyInfo and Driver.getPropertyInfo

EXAMPLE 3:
```
String url = "jdbc:myDriverProtocol://acme.com/personnel/" +
             "employees";
DriverManager.getConnection(url, "myLogin", "myPassword");
```

getDriver

```
public static Driver getDriver(String url) throws SQLException
```

Attempts to locate a driver that understands *url*. A user might want to call getDriver directly in the rare case where the Driver object rather than a connection is desired.

PARAMETERS:

url   a JDBC URL of the form jdbc:subprotocol:subname.
                        If the method DriverManager.getConnection was
                        called, this should be the same URL that was passed to
                        it.

RETURNS:
a driver that understands *url* and can connect to the subprotocol it specifies

EXAMPLE:
```
String url = "jdbc:odbc:superdb";
Driver d = DriverManager.getDriver(url);
```

getDrivers

```
public static java.util.Enumeration getDrivers()
```

Retrieves a list of registered drivers. Although a user can invoke this method, most users would never call it.

RETURNS:
an Enumeration object containing a list of the JDBC drivers that have been loaded by the caller's class loader. These are the drivers that are available to the caller for making a connection to a database.

EXAMPLE:
```
Enumeration e = DriverManager.getDrivers();
```

getLoginTimeout

```
public static int getLoginTimeout()
```

Indicates how many seconds a driver will wait to log in to a database before it times out.

RETURNS:
the maximum time in seconds that a driver can wait when attempting to log in to a database

EXAMPLE:
```
int x = DriverManager.getLoginTimeout();
```

getLogStream   DEPRECATED

```
public static java.io.PrintStream getLogStream()
```

Indicates where log and tracing messages will be printed.
This method has been deprecated; the method getLogWriter should be used instead.

RETURNS:
the PrintStream object that will be used by the DriverManager and all drivers for printing their logging and tracing messages

EXAMPLE:
```
java.io.PrintStream outStream = DriverManager.getLogStream();
```

getLogWriter

```
public static java.io.PrintWriter getLogWriter()
```

Retrieves the `PrintWriter` object that will be used by the `DriverManager` and all drivers for printing their logging and tracing messages.

This method should be used in place of the method `getLogStream`, which has been deprecated.

RETURNS:
the `PrintWriter` object where log and tracing messages will be printed

EXAMPLE:
```
java.io.PrintWriter writer = DriverManager.getLogWriter();
```

println

```
public static void println(String message)
```

Prints *message* to the current JDBC log stream.

PARAMETERS:
message   a log or tracing message

EXAMPLE:
```
DriverManager.println("Loading driver d");
```

registerDriver

```
public static void registerDriver(java.sql.Driver driver)
                                        throws SQLException
```

Adds *driver* to the list of drivers that the `DriverManager` maintains. The `DriverManager` will test each driver in the list to find the first one that recognizes the JDBC URL passed to the method `DriverManager.getConnection`.

Normally, a user will not call this method directly; it will be called by a driver when it is being loaded. The definition of a JDBC `Driver` class should include a static section such that when the `Driver` class is loaded, it creates an instance of itself and then calls the method `registerDriver` with that instance as the parameter *driver*.

Registering a driver adds an entry to the end of the list maintained by the DriverManager class, and this list is scanned from beginning to end. Note that duplicate registrations result in duplicate entries. A programmer who explicitly creates a new driver instance and registers it will create an unnecessary duplicate that will appear in the DriverManager's list of drivers twice.

PARAMETERS:

driver   a JDBC Driver class that has been loaded

EXAMPLE:
```
Class.forName("MyDriver");
// the user calls Class.forName() to load the Driver class MyDriver
Driver d = new Driver("MyDriver");
DriverManager.registerDriver(d);
// d is a new instance of MyDriver that is registered with the
// DriverManager
```

setLoginTimeout

```
public static void setLoginTimeout(int seconds)
```

Sets to *seconds* the maximum time that a driver can wait to log in to a database before timing out.

PARAMETERS:

seconds   the maximum time in seconds that a driver can wait when it is attempting to log in to a database

EXAMPLE:
```
DriverManager.setLoginTimeout(10);
// a driver will timeout after waiting 10 seconds to log in
```

setLogStream   DEPRECATED

```
public static void setLogStream(java.io.PrintStream out)
```

Sets the print stream for logging and tracing messages to *out*. This method has been deprecated; the method setLogWriter should be used instead.

PARAMETERS:

out   the print stream to which logging and tracing messages
                                    will be printed

EXAMPLE:
```
DriverManager.setLogStream(System.out);
// sets the logging and tracing print stream to the standard output
// stream
DriverManager.setLogStream(null); // shuts off the log stream
```

setLogWriter

2.0

```
public static void setLogWriter(java.io.PrintWriter out)
```

Sets the logging/tracing `Writer` used by the `DriverManager` and all drivers
to *out*. This method should be used in place of the deprecated method `set-
LogStream`.

To turn logging and tracing off, supply `null` as the argument to the
method `setLogWriter`.

Note that if an application sets the writer with the method `setLogWriter`
and also uses a JDBC 1.0 driver that uses the method `getLogStream`, it is
likely that the application will not see debugging information written by that
driver. This minor versioning problem occurs because the method `setLog-
Writer` cannot create a `PrintStream` object that will be returned by the
method `getLogStream`.

Starting with the Java 2 SDK, Standard Edition, version 1.3 release, this
method checks to see whether there is an `SQLPermission` object granting permission to set the logging stream. If a `SecurityManager` exists and its `check-
Permission` method denies setting a logging stream, this method throws a
`java.lang.SecurityException`.

PARAMETERS:

out   the print writer to which logging and tracing messages
                                    will be printed; may be `null` to disable logging and
                                    tracing

THROWS:
`java.lang.SecurityException` if a security manager exists and the method
`SecurityManager.checkPermission` denies setting the log writer

EXAMPLE:

```
DriverManager.setLogWriter(out); // sets writer to out
DriverManager.setLogWriter(null); // disables logging and tracing
```

SEE:
"SQLPermission," on page 941

CHAPTER 22

DriverPropertyInfo

22.1 DriverPropertyInfo Overview

T HE class DriverPropertyInfo is used only by advanced programmers who need to interact with a driver to discover and supply properties for connections. Its function is to be the return value for the method Driver.getPropertyInfo, which returns an array of DriverPropertyInfo objects. This method allows a generic GUI tool to discover what properties it should prompt a human user for in order to get enough information to connect to a database.

The class consists of a constructor and five fields; there are no methods. It can therefore be thought of as being similar to a struct.

22.1.1 Creating a DriverPropertyInfo Object

An instance of DriverPropertyInfo is created using the constructor, which takes two arguments:

```
DriverPropertyInfo info = new DriverPropertyInfo("fred", "foo");
```

The variable *info* contains a DriverPropertyInfo object initialized with "fred" as its name field and "foo" as its value field. The other three fields are initialized with their default values, which are the following:

```
description    null
required       false
choices        null
```

22.1.2   Getting and Setting Fields

Since there are no set methods, a new value for a field is simply assigned to it, as in the following example:

```
info.required = true;
```

Similarly, since there are no getter methods, the value of a field is accessed by simply using the field in an expression, as in the following example:

```
if(info.required) { // if required == true, do something
    . . . .
}
```

22.2   DriverPropertyInfo Class Definition

```
package java.sql;
public class DriverPropertyInfo {
    public DriverPropertyInfo(String name, String value);
    public String name;
    public String description = null;
    public boolean required = false;
    public String value;
    public String[] choices = null;
}
```

22.3   DriverPropertyInfo Constructor

DriverPropertyInfo

```
public DriverPropertyInfo(String name, String value);
```

Constructs a DriverPropertyInfo object with the field name initialized to *name* and the field value initialized to *value*. Other fields are initialized with their default values: description and choices are null; required is false.

PARAMETERS:

name	a String object indicating the name of the property
value	a String object indicating the current value; null if the current value is not known

EXAMPLE:
```
DriverPropertyInfo info2 = new DriverPropertyInfo("xyz", "abc");
```

22.4 DriverPropertyInfo Fields

choices

```
public String[] choices = null;
```

An array of String objects, with each String object representing a possible value for the field DriverPropertyInfo.value. This field is used only if the value for the field value may be selected from a particular set of values. If there are no choices, this field should be null.

description

```
public String description = null;
```

A String object giving a brief description of the property. It may be null, which is the default.

name

```
public String name;
```

A String object that is the name of the property.

required

```
public boolean required = false;
```

Indicates whether a value must be supplied for this property. It is required if it must be used by the method `Driver.connect` in order to make a connection. The property is required if `required` is `true`; `false` indicates that it is optional.

value

```
public String value = null;
```

A `String` object specifying the current value of the property. This is based on a combination of three things: (1) the information supplied to `getPropertyInfo`, (2) the Java environment, and (3) any driver-supplied default values. It may be `null` if no value is known.

CHAPTER 23

ParameterMetaData 〔3.0〕

23.1 ParameterMetaData Overview

THE ParameterMetaData interface, one of the interfaces added in the JDBC 3.0 API, lets a developer get information about the parameter in a prepared statement. For example, it provides methods for finding out the number of parameters, the data type of a parameter, whether a parameter can be null, whether a parameter is an IN, OUT, or INOUT parameter, and so on.

23.1.1 Creating a ParameterMetaData Object

A PreparedStatement object creates a ParameterMetaData object. This is true because a ParameterMetaData object contains information about a specific PreparedStatement object, and it thus makes sense that a PreparedStatement object creates the ParameterMetaData object that describes it. The PreparedStatement method getParameterMetaData both creates and returns a ParameterMetaData object, as shown in the following code fragment.

```
PreparedStatement pstmt = con.prepareStatement(
            "UPDATE EMPLOYEES SET SALARY = ? WHERE LEVEL = ?");
ParameterMetaData paramInfo = pstmt.getParameterMetaData();
```

The ParameterMetaData object *paramInfo* now contains information about the two parameters for *pstmt*. The next section shows how to access that information.

23.1.2 Getting Information from a `ParameterMetaData` Object

The `ParameterMetaData` interface provides methods for getting information from a `ParameterMetaData` object. For example, the following line of code uses *paramInfo*, created in the previous code fragment, to get the number of parameters in the `PreparedStatement` object *pstmt*.

```
int count = paramInfo.getParameterCount();
```

The method `getParameterCount` is the only method in the `ParameterMetaData` interface that takes no parameters. All of the other methods take an `int` that indicates the ordinal number of the parameter to which the information applies. Numbering starts at one, so the first parameter is 1, the second parameter is 2, and so on. In the following line of code, for example, the method `getParameterType` returns the data type of the second parameter.

```
int typeCode = paramInfo.getParameterType(2);
```

The variable *typeCode* represents the JDBC type code, defined in `java.sql.Types`, that indicates the data type of the second parameter in *pstmt*. The method `getParameterTypeName` returns the database-specific name for the data type, which could be different. For example, the JDBC type code might be `DOUBLE`, whereas the database-specific type name might be `DOUBLE PRECISION`. (See "JDBC Types Mapped to Database-specific SQL Types," on page 1093, to see what database-specific data types correspond to JDBC types.)

Another method dealing with data types is `getParameterClassName`. This method returns the class name for instances of `Object` that can be passed to the method `PreparedStatement.setObject` to set a value for the designated parameter.

Three methods give information about numeric parameters. The method `getPrecision` returns the number of decimal digits in the designated parameter. The method `getScale` returns the number of digits to the right of the decimal point. The method `isSigned` returns `true` if the designated parameter can be a signed number and `false` if it cannot.

`ParameterMetaData` defines several constants, which serve as the return values for either the method `isNullable` or the method `getParameterMode`. For the method `isNullable`, the constants indicate that the parameter can be null, cannot be null, or that the nullability is unknown. The constants for `getParameterMode` indicate that the parameter is an IN, OUT, or INOUT parameter or that its mode is unknown.

The following code fragmemt demonstrates using the ParameterMetaData object *paramInfo* to get the mode and type for all of the parameters.

```
int count = paramInfo.getParameterCount();
for (int i = 1; i <= count; i++) {
    int mode = paramInfo.getParameterMode(i);
    int type = paramInfo.getParameterType(i);
    System.out.print("Parameter " + i + " has mode " + mode);
    System.out.println("and JDBC type " + type);
}
```

The return value for the method getParameterMode is an int that corresponds to the fields defined in the interface ParameterMetaData. The return value for the method getParameterType is a type code, which is an int. The interface java.sql.Types provides the JDBC type name that corresponds to each type code.

See the section "Parameter Metadata," on page 650, for another example of how to use ParameterMetaData methods.

23.1.3 Using Parameter Metadata Wisely

Retreiving metadata of any kind can be expensive, so it should be used with caution. Many of the methods in the DatabaseMetaData, ResultSetMetaData, and ParameterMetaData interfaces involve highly complicated and intensive searches that can degrade the performance of both an application and the data source it is using. Therefore, an application should retrieve metadata prudently.

The purpose of a prepared statement is to allow the data source to "prepare" an SQL statement, that is, to compile an SQL statement before it is executed. This lets the data source check for problems with the statement and prepare a plan for executing it efficiently. However, not all data sources prepare a statement the same way, and some do not prepare them at all. If a data source does not precompile SQL statements, the ParameterMetaData methods will not be able to return results until after a PreparedStatement object has been executed.

23.2   ParameterMetaData Interface Definition

```java
package java.sql;
public interface ParameterMetaData {

//===============================================================
// Constants that are the possible return values for isNullable
//===============================================================

    public static final int parameterNoNulls = 0;
    public static final int parameterNullable = 1;
    public static final int parameterNullableUnknown = 2;


//===============================================================
// Constants that are the possible return values for getParameterMode
//===============================================================

    public static final int parameterModeUnknown = 0;
    public static final int parameterModeIn = 1;
    public static final int parameterModeInOut = 2;
    public static final int parameterModeOut = 4;


//===============================================================
        //Methods for retrieving parameter information
//===============================================================

    int getParameterCount() throws SQLException;
    int isNullable(int param) throws SQLException;
    boolean isSigned(int param) throws SQLException;
    int getPrecision(int param) throws SQLException;
    int getScale(int param) throws SQLException;
    int getParameterType(int param) throws SQLException;
    String getParameterTypeName(int param) throws SQLException;
    String getParameterClassName(int param) throws SQLException;
    int getParameterMode(int param) throws SQLException;
}
```

23.3 **ParameterMetaData Methods**

getParameterClassName

3.0

`String `**`getParameterClassName`**`(int `*`param`*`) throws SQLException`

Retrieves the fully qualified name of the Java class whose instances may be passed to the method `PreparedStatement.setObject` to set the value for the designated parameter in the `PreparedStatement` object for which this `ParameterMetaData` object contains information.

PARAMETERS:

param   an `int` indicating the parameter for which information is being retrieved. 1 is the first parameter, 2 is the second parameter, and so on.

RETURNS:

a `String` indicating the fully qualified class name for instances that may be passed to `PreparedStatement.setObject` to set the value for the designated parameter

EXAMPLE:
```
String name = p.getParameterClassName(2);
// Retrieves the class name for objects that can be passed to
// PreparedStatement.getObject to set a value for the second
// parameter
```

getParameterCount

3.0

`int `**`getParameterCount`**`() throws SQLException`

Retrieves the number of parameters in the `PreparedStatement` object for which this `ParameterMetaData` object contains information.

RETURNS:

an `int` indicating the number of parameters

EXAMPLE:
```
int count = p.getParameterCount();
// Retrieves the number of parameters in the PreparedStatement object
// for which p contains information
```

getParameterMode

```
int getParameterMode(int param) throws SQLException
```

Retrieves the mode of the designated parameter in the `PreparedStatement` object for which this `ParameterMetaData` object contains information.

PARAMETERS:

param   an `int` indicating the parameter for which information is being retrieved. 1 is the first parameter, 2 is the second parameter, and so on.

RETURNS:

a constant indicating whether the mode of the designated parameter is `IN`, `OUT`, or `INOUT`; must be one of the following:

```
ParameterMetaData.parameterModeIn
ParameterMetaData.parameterModeInOut
ParameterMetaData.parameterModeOut
```

EXAMPLE:

```
int mode = p.getParameterMode(3);
// Retrieves the mode of the third parameter
```

getParameterType

```
int getParameterType(int param) throws SQLException
```

Retrieves the JDBC type of the designated parameter in the `PreparedStatement` object for which this `ParameterMetaData` object contains information.

PARAMETERS:

param   an `int` indicating the parameter for which information is being retrieved. 1 is the first parameter, 2 is the second parameter, and so on.

RETURNS:

an `int` indicating the JDBC type code of the designated parameter; must be one of the constants defined in `java.sql.Types`

EXAMPLE:

```
int jdbcType = p.getParameterType(3);
// Retrieves the JDBC type of the third parameter
```

getParameterTypeName

```
String getParameterTypeName(int param) throws SQLException
```

Retrieves the database-specific type name of the designated parameter in the `PreparedStatement` object for which this `ParameterMetaData` object contains information.

PARAMETERS:

param   an `int` indicating the parameter for which information is being retrieved. 1 is the first parameter, 2 is the second parameter, and so on.

RETURNS:

a `String` giving the name used by the database for the data type of the designated parameter

EXAMPLE:

```
int databaseName = p.getParameterTypeName(1);
// Retrieves the type name used by the database for values that may
// be assigned to the first parameter
```

getPrecision

```
int getPrecision(int param) throws SQLException
```

Retrieves the number of decimal digits for values in the designated parameter in the `PreparedStatement` object for which this `ParameterMetaData` object contains information.

PARAMETERS:

param   an `int` indicating the parameter for which information is being retrieved. 1 is the first parameter, 2 is the second parameter, and so on.

RETURNS:

an `int` indicating the number of decimal digits in values assigned to the designated parameter

EXAMPLE:

```
int precision = p.getPrecision(4);
// Retrieves the precision of the fourth parameter
```

getScale

`int getScale(int param) throws SQLException`

Retrieves the number of digits to the right of the decimal point for values in the designated parameter in the PreparedStatement object for which this ParameterMetaData object contains information.

PARAMETERS:

param   an int indicating the parameter for which information is being retrieved. 1 is the first parameter, 2 is the second parameter, and so on.

RETURNS:

an int indicating the number of digits to the right of the decimal point in values assigned to the designated parameter

EXAMPLE:
```
int scale = p.getPrecision(2);
// Retrieves the scale of the second parameter
```

isNullable

`int isNullable(int param) throws SQLException`

Retrieves whether null values are allowed in the designated parameter in the PreparedStatement object for which this ParameterMetaData object contains information.

PARAMETERS:

param   an int indicating the parameter for which information is being retrieved. 1 is the first parameter, 2 is the second parameter, and so on.

RETURNS:

a constant indicating the nullability of the designated parameter; must be one of the following:
```
ParameterMetaData.parameterNoNulls
ParameterMetaData.parameterNullable
ParameterMetaData.parameterNullabilityUnknown
```

EXAMPLE:
```
int nullability = p.isNullable(2);
// Retrieves the nullability of the second parameter
```

isSigned

3.0

```
boolean isSigned(int param) throws SQLException
```

Retrieves whether signed numbers can be values for the designated parameter in the `PreparedStatement` object for which this `ParameterMetaData` object contains information.

PARAMETERS:

param   an `int` indicating the parameter for which information is being retrieved. 1 is the first parameter, 2 is the second parameter, and so on.

RETURNS:

`true` if the parameter may contain signed numbers; `false` if it cannot

EXAMPLE:

```
int signed = p.isSigned(1);
// Retrieves whether the first parameter may be a signed number
```

23.4 ParameterMetaData Fields

parameterModeIn

3.0

```
static int parameterModeIn
```

The constant indicating an `IN` parameter. This is one of the possible return values for the method `getParameterMode`.

parameterModeInOut

3.0

```
static int parameterModeInOut
```

The constant indicating an `INOUT` parameter. This is one of the possible return values for the method `getParameterMode`.

parameterModeOut

`3.0`

```
static int parameterModeOut
```

The constant indicating an OUT parameter. This is one of the possible return values for the method getParameterMode.

parameterModeUnknown

`3.0`

```
static int parameterModeUnknown
```

The constant indicating that the mode of the parameter is unknown. This is one of the possible return values for the method getParameterMode.

parameterNoNulls

`3.0`

```
static int parameterNoNulls
```

The constant indicating that the parameter does not allow NULL values. This is one of the possible return values for the method isNullable.

parameterNullable

`3.0`

```
static int parameterNullable
```

The constant indicating that the parameter allows NULL values. This is one of the possible return values for the method isNullable.

parameterNullableUnknown

`3.0`

```
static int parameterNullableUnknown
```

The constant indicating that it is not known whether the parameter allows NULL values. This is one of the possible return values for the method isNullable.

CHAPTER 24

PooledConnection

24.1 `PooledConnection` Overview

A `PooledConnection` object is a key component in the mechanism for providing a pool of connections to a data source. A `DataSource` object, which represents a particular real world data source, can be implemented so that the connections it produces are reusable. For example, if the `DataSource` object *ds* represents XYZ database, each connection that *ds* returns when `ds.getConnection` is called will be a connection to XYZ. If the `DataSource` class of which *ds* is an instance implements connection pooling, then each connection that the method `ds.getConnection` returns will be a connection to XYZ that can be used and reused. In other words, when an application closes its connection to XYZ, the connection goes to a connection pool instead of being physically closed. The next time the application calls `ds.getConnection`, it will get a connection to XYZ from the pool of connections, which might very well be the same physical connection it used previously. In fact, if an application has only one connection produced by *ds* open at a time, it could conceivably use the same connection to XYZ over and over again.

24.1.1 Application Code for Connection Pooling

Because connection pooling is done completely behind the scenes, it impacts application code in only two ways.

First, in order to get a pooled connection, an application must use a `Data-Source` object rather than the `DriverManager` class to get a connection. Any `Data-Source` object, including one that supports connection pooling, is registered with a JNDI service provider by someone performing the role of system administrator. Once a `DataSource` object that implements connection pooling is registered, the application retrieves it from the JNDI naming service in the same standard way an application retrieves a basic DataSource object. The DataSource object retrieved in the following code fragment represents the data source XYZ because the system administrator did two things: (1) set the DataSource object's properties so that it gets connections to XYZ and (2) registered it with the logical name of xyz with a JNDI naming service. The DataSource object is implemented to do connection pooling, so it will create connections to XYZ that can be recycled. For an explanation of the JNDI code, see "Connecting to a Data Source," on page 570.

```
javax.naming.Context ctx = new InitialContext();
javax.sql.DataSource ds =
                (DataSource)ctx.lookup("jdbc/xyz");
```

The variable *ds* now represents a DataSource object on which an application can call the method getConnection to obtain a connection to the data source XYZ.

The second impact connection pooling has on application code is that an application should close the connection explicitly. It is always good programming practice to close a connection, but with connection pooling, it is even more important. Unless the method close is called on a pooled connection, it will not be put back into the connection pool. Therefore, to guarantee that an open connection is recycled, programmers should include a finally block that closes it. That way, even if an exception is thrown, the connection will be closed. The following code fragment uses the DataSource object *ds* to get a connection to the data source XYZ, does some work, and then closes the connection. The finally statement checks to see if the connection is valid, and if so, it closes the connection.

```
Connection con = null;
try {
    con = ds.getConnection("rosap", "perfect");

    // ... code to do the application's work

} catch (SQLException ex) {
    // ... code to handle an SQLException
} finally {
    if (con != null) con.close();
}
```

Calling the method `close` on the `Connection` object *con* does not close the connection to XYZ; it puts *con* in the pool of connections so that it can be used again. Calling the method `close` in a `finally` statement ensures that a valid connection will be closed and recycled even if an exception is thrown.

An application obtains and uses a pooled connection in exactly the same way it obtains and uses a non-pooled connection. If the `DataSource` object is implemented to provide connection pooling, calling the method `getConnection` on it will automatically return a connection that participates in connection pooling. Thus, other than using a `DataSource` object to get a connection and a `finally` statement to close a connection, connection pooling has no effect at all on application code. Because this is all of the knowledge that is required to use connection pooling, the general database programmer may decide not to read the rest of this chapter. The same is true for the related chapters dealing with pooled connections ("ConnectionPoolDataSource," "ConnectionEvent," and "ConnectionEventListener"). The other chapters and the remainder of this one present more detailed information that is aimed primarily at a developer implementing a pooled connection facility.

24.1.2 How Connection Pooling Works

The previous section gave a very high level explanation of what connection pooling does. This section concentrates more on the operations that take place internally to make it work. Because the `DataSource` class may be implemented to support connection pooling in many different ways, this section describes the work that needs to be done in general terms rather than giving precise details of how it should be done.

All of the operations to accomplish connection pooling are implemented by a server or driver vendor and are typically used in the middle tier. Either an application server vendor or a driver vendor can provide a `DataSource` class that implements connection pooling. A driver vendor will provide implementations of the `PooledConnection` and `ConnectionPoolDataSource` interfaces as part of its JDBC 2.0 driver product. The `ConnectionEvent` class is already implemented in the JDBC 2.0 API. The `ConnectionEventListener` interface will be implemented by the same vendor that supplied the `DataSource` implementation.

Connection pooling takes place in a three-tier architecture. The first tier is the client, typically a Web browser. The second tier (the middle tier) will contain the JDBC driver and application code as well as the server code that manages connection pooling. The third tier will be the data source(s) where data is stored and from which data is to be retrieved.

As a general summary, connection pooling is a mechanism whereby physical connections to a data source are cached in memory. When an application requests a new connection to the data source, it will get one of the connections from this pool if one is available. Only if no existing connection is available will a new physical connection be created, and the new connection will be one that can be pooled. A pooled connection is not destroyed when an application closes its representation of the connection; instead, it is returned to the pool of connections where it is available for reuse.

For simplicity, connection pooling can be broken down into the following steps. The first list (steps 1 - 3) shows the sequence of events when a `PooledConnection` object is available for recycling. The second list (steps 4 - 5) shows what happens when a new `PooledConnection` object has to be created.

1. An application calls the `DataSource.getConnection` method.

2. The middle-tier server calls a `lookup` method internally to see if there is a `PooledConnection` instance available in the cache of connections that the pooled connection facility maintains in memory.

3. If a `PooledConnection` object is available, the method `PooledConnection.get-Connection` is called on it.

    This produces the `java.sql.Connection` object that the `DataSource.get-Connection` method will return to the application. This `Connection` object is not a new physical connection, however; it is a handle to the existing `Pooled-Connection` object that created it. When the application invokes a method on the handle, most of the work will be delegated to the underlying physical connection that the `PooledConnection` object represents.

4. The pooled connection facility's internal data structure will be updated to reflect that the existing `PooledConnection` object is being used and is not currently available.

5. The pooled connection facility (also referred to as the connection pooling module or connection pooling manager) will register itself with the `PooledConnection` object as a listener.

    This means that the driver will notify the connection pooling module when the `Connection` object is closed by the application or is unusable because of a fatal error.

What has been described so far is what happens when a `PooledConnection` object is available to satisfy an application's request for a connection. If there is no `PooledConnection` object currently available, the step of creating a new `PooledConnection` object is added. The following list gives the sequence when no `PooledConnection` object is available in the pool.

1. An application calls the `DataSource.getConnection` method.

2. The middle-tier server calls a `lookup` method internally to see if there is a `PooledConnection` instance available in the cache of connections that the pooled connection facility maintains in memory.

3. If no `PooledConnection` object is available, the connection pooling module on the middle-tier server calls the `ConnectionPoolDataSource.getPooledConnection` method.

   This creates a new physical connection to the data source.

4. The method `PooledConnection.getConnection` is called on the newly created `PooledConnection` object.

   This produces the `java.sql.Connection` object that the `DataSource.getConnection` method will return to the application. This `Connection` object is not a new physical connection, however; it is a handle to the existing `PooledConnection` object that created it.

5. The pooled connection facility's internal data structure will be updated to reflect that the existing `PooledConnection` object is being used and is not currently available.

6. The pooled connection facility will register itself with the `PooledConnection` object as a listener.

7. The `DataSource.getConnection` method that the application called will return the new `Connection` object to the application.

8. When the application closes the `Connection` object that it has been using, the handle becomes unusable and the `PooledConnection` object to which it refers will become available for reuse.

24.1.3 The Life Cycle of a `PooledConnection` Object

First, it is important to understand the difference between a `Connection` object created by the `DataSource.getConnection` method and one created by the `PooledCon-`

nection.getConnection method. When an application invokes the DataSource.getConnection method, it will get back a Connection object. This Connection object can be three different things, depending on the implementation of the DataSource class. With a basic implementation, the Connection object returned to an application represents a physical database connection. But when the DataSource class implements connection pooling, the Connection object that is returned by the DataSource.getConnection method is actually produced by the PooledConnection.getConnection method and is a temporary handle for the PooledConnection object that created it. The application can use the handle to access the underlying physical connection that the PooledConnection object represents, and the application is never aware that it has not been using a regular connection. (For information about the third kind of Connection object that can be returned by the method DataSource.getConnection, see Chapter 49, "XAData-Source," starting on page 1055.)

As stated previously, a PooledConnection object is created by the middle-tier server when an application requests a connection and there is no PooledConnection object available. During its lifetime, a PooledConnection object will usually produce a series of Connection objects. As long as the application maintains the connection, the PooledConnection object that produced it is unavailable; that is, it cannot produce another connection. But when the application closes its Connection object, the PooledConnection object becomes available for reuse.

Note that when an application closes a Connection object that is a handle to a PooledConnection object, the Connection object is effectively closed, but the PooledConnection object is not. When connection pooling has been implemented, the Connection.close method will trigger the connection pooling event mechanism. The JDBC driver will create a ConnectionEvent object and pass it to the ConnectionEventListener.connectionClosed method. This method is called on the connection pooling manager, which is registered as a listener for the PooledConnection object. The connection pooling manager can call the EventObject.getSource method on the ConnectionEvent object to find out which PooledConnection object had its handle closed. The connection pooling manager can then update its internal data structure to reflect that the PooledConnection object is being cached and is available to create another Connection object.

A PooledConnection object itself is closed when the connection pooling manager calls the method PooledConnection.close on it. This tells the driver that the connection pooling manager is finished using the physical connection, which the driver then closes. The PooledConnection object itself becomes unusable and will be routinely garbage collected.

A PooledConnection object is typically closed during an orderly shutdown of the middle-tier server or when the connection cache is being reinitialized. It will also be closed when the event notification mechanism is triggered by a fatal error, such as when the server crashes. In this case, the driver creates a ConnectionEvent object and calls the method ConnectionEventListener.connectionErrorOccurred on the connection pooling manager, passing it the newly created event. The connection pooling manager will call the EventObject.getSource method on the event to learn the source of the exception, and it will call the ConnectionEvent.getSQLException method on the event to learn which exception the driver will throw. Because the connection is no longer usable, the connection pooling manager will call the PooledConnection.close method on it.

A PooledConnection object may also be closed if it has not been used for a specified period of time. The property maxIdleTime, which was added to the ConnectionPoolDataSource interface in the JDBC 3.0 API, allows a developer implementing a connection pooling mechanism to supply a time limit for how long a connection may remain idle. If the maxIdleTime property has been set and the connection pool manager has been implemented to support it, the connection pool manager will close a PooledConnection object that sits idle for longer than the specified time limit.

A particular PooledConnection object can have only one Connection object open at a time, and that is the one most recently created. An existing Connection object will automatically be closed if the server calls the method PooledConnection.getConnection again. The purpose of allowing the server to invoke the method getConnection a second time is to give the application server a way to take a connection away from an application and give it to someone else. This will probably rarely happen, but the capability is there.

24.2 **PooledConnection** Interface Definition

```
package javax.sql;
public abstract interface PooledConnection {
    java.sql.Connection getConnection() throws java.sql.SQLException;
    void close() throws java.sql.SQLException;

    //================================================================
    //          methods for JavaBeans event model
    //================================================================
```

```
void addConnectionEventListener(ConnectionEvent Listener listener);
void removeConnectionEventListener(
                                    ConnectionEventListener listener);
}
```

24.3 `PooledConnection` Methods

addConnectionEventListener

```
void addConnectionEventListener(ConnectionEventListener listener)
```

Registers *listener* as an object that will be notified of events affecting this `PooledConnection` object.

PARAMETERS:

listener   software in the middle tier that manages connection pooling and wants to be notified when a significant event occurs in the life of this `PooledConnection` object; *listener* will have implemented the `Connection-EventListener` interface

EXAMPLE:
```
pcon.addConnectionEventListener(listener);
// listener will be notified whenever an event occurs on the
// PooledConnection object pcon
```

close

```
void close() throws SQLException
```

Closes this `PooledConnection` object, which closes the underlying physical connection it represents.

EXAMPLE:
```
pcon.close();
```

getConnection

```
java.sql.Connection getConnection() throws SQLException
```

Creates an object handle for the physical data source connection that this `PooledConnection` object represents.

RETURNS:
a `Connection` object that is a handle for this `PooledConnection` object

EXAMPLE:
```
Connection con = pcon.getConnection();
// con is a handle for the physical data source connection that the
// PooledConnection object pcon represents
```

removeConnectionEventListener

```
void removeConnectionEventListener(ConnectionEventListener listener)
```

Removes *listener* as an object that will be notified of events affecting this `PooledConnection` object.

PARAMETERS:

listener   software on the middle tier that manages connection pooling and wants to be notified when a significant event occurs in the life of this `PooledConnection` object; *listener* will have implemented the `Connection-EventListener` interface and been registered as a listener with this `PooledConnection` object

EXAMPLE:
```
pcon.removeConnectionEventListener(listener);
// listener will no longer be notified whenever an event occurs on
// the PooledConnection object pcon
```

CHAPTER 25

PreparedStatement

25.1 PreparedStatement Overview

THE PreparedStatement interface inherits from Statement and differs from it in two ways:

1. Instances of PreparedStatement contain an SQL statement that has already been compiled. This is what makes a statement "prepared."

2. The SQL statement contained in a PreparedStatement object may have one or more IN parameters. An IN parameter is a parameter whose value is not specified when the SQL statement is created. Instead, the statement has a question mark (?) as a placeholder for each IN parameter. The ? is also known as a parameter marker or parameter placeholder. An application must set a value for each parameter marker in a prepared statement before executing the prepared statement.

Because PreparedStatement objects are precompiled, their execution can be faster than that of Statement objects. Consequently, an SQL statement that is executed many times is often created as a PreparedStatement object to increase efficiency.

Being a subclass of Statement, PreparedStatement inherits all the functionality of Statement. In addition, it adds a set of methods that are needed for setting the values to be sent to the database in place of the placeholders for IN parameters. Also, the three methods execute, executeQuery, and executeUpdate are modified so that they take no argument. The Statement forms of these methods (the forms that take an SQL statement parameter) cannot be used with a PreparedStatement object.

25.1.1 Creating `PreparedStatement` Objects

The following code fragment, where *con* is a `Connection` object, creates a `PreparedStatement` object containing an SQL update statement with two placeholders for IN parameters:

```
PreparedStatement pstmt = con.prepareStatement(
                  "UPDATE table4 SET m = ? WHERE x = ?");
```

The object *pstmt* now contains the statement "UPDATE table4 SET m = ? WHERE x = ?", which has already been sent to the DBMS and been prepared for execution.

As with `Statement` objects, it is possible to create a `PreparedStatement` object that contains a query rather than an update statement; in fact, this is often done to improve efficiency for SQL statements that are executed many times. Using the version of the method `prepareStatement` introduced in the JDBC 2.0 API, the `PreparedStatement` object can produce `ResultSet` objects that are scrollable and updatable. For example, the following code fragment creates a `PreparedStatement` object such that each time it is executed, it will produce a `ResultSet` object that is scrollable and updatable.

```
PreparedStatement pstmt2 = con.prepareStatement(
      "SELECT a, b, c FROM Table1", ResultSet.TYPE_SCROLL_SENSITIVE,
      ResultSet.CONCUR_UPDATABLE);
ResultSet rs = pstmt2.executeQuery();
```

The object that *rs* represents is a result set with all the values stored in columns a, b, and c of Table1, and *rs* is scrollable and can be updated. Each time *pstmt2* is executed, it will produce a result set that is scrollable and updatable.

"Using a Prepared Statement to Create Result Sets," on page 707, gives more details and examples.

25.1.2 Passing IN Parameters

Before a `PreparedStatement` object is executed, the value of each parameter marker must be set. This is done by calling the appropriate setter method for the type of the value being set, such as `setString` or `setInt`. For example, if the parameter is of type `long` in the Java programming language, the method to use is `setLong`. The first argument to the setter methods is the *ordinal position* of the parameter to be set, with numbering starting at 1. The second argument is the *value* to which the parameter is to be set. For example, the following code sets the first parameter to 123456789 and the second parameter to 100000000:

```
pstmt.setLong(1, 123456789L);
pstmt.setLong(2, 100000000L);
```

Once a parameter value has been set for a given statement, it can be used for multiple executions of that statement until it is cleared by a call to the method clear-Parameters or until a new value is set.

When a connection has its auto-commit mode enabled, each statement is committed automatically when it is completed. Some database systems do not retain prepared statements across commits, so for them, the driver will have to recompile the prepared statement after each commit. This means that for these DBMSs, it may actually be less efficient to use a PreparedStatement object in place of a Statement object that is executed many times.

Using *pstmt*, the PreparedStatement object created above, the following code illustrates setting values for the two parameter placeholders and executing *pstmt* 10 times. In this example, the first parameter is set to "Hi" and remains constant. The second parameter is set to a different value each time around the for loop, starting with 0 and ending with 9.

```
pstmt.setString(1, "Hi");
for (int i = 0; i < 10; i++) {
    pstmt.setInt(2, i);
    int rowCount = pstmt.executeUpdate();
}
```

Features added in the JDBC 2.0 API make it possible to set a parameter placeholder with an SQL99 data type, as shown in the following example, where *statistics* is a Blob object representing an SQL BLOB value, and *departments* is an Array object representing an SQL ARRAY value.

```
PreparedStatement pstmt = con.prepareStatement(
                    "UPDATE Table3 SET Stats = ? WHERE Depts = ?");
pstmt.setBlob(1, statistics);
pstmt.setArray(2, departments);
```

25.1.3   Parameter Metadata

The `ParameterMetaData` interface (see the chapter "ParameterMetaData," on page 627), added in the JDBC 3.0 API, makes it possible to get information about a `PreparedStatement` object's parameters. For example, it has methods that retrieve information about whether a parameter can be `null`, whether a parameter can be a signed number, what data type a parameter is, and so on. The following code fragment returns a `ParameterMetaData` object that contains information about the parameters in the `PreparedStatement` object *pstmt*. After getting the number of parameters, the code gets the database-specific type name for each of the parameters and prints them out.

```
PreparedStatement pstmt = con.prepareStatement(
        "INSERT INTO QUOTAS (ID, LAST, FIRST, DEPT, QUOTA) " +
            "VALUES (?, ?, ?, ?, ?)";

ParameterMetaData paramInfo = pstmt.getParameterMetaData();
int numberOfParams = paramInfo.getParameterCount();
for (int i = 1; i <= numberOfParams; i++) {
    String dbType = paramInfo.getParameterTypeName(i);
    System.out.println("Param " + i " is DBMS type " + dbType);
}
```

Because retrieving metadata can degrade performance, it should be done judiciously. See "Using Parameter Metadata Wisely," on page 629, for more information.

25.1.4   Data Type Conformance on IN Parameters

The setter methods each name a specific data type in the Java programming language (`setLong`, `setString`, and so on). They also implicitly specify a JDBC type because the driver will map the Java type to its corresponding JDBC type (following the mapping specified in "Java Types Mapped to JDBC Types," on page 1088) and send that JDBC type to the database. For example, the following code fragment sets the second parameter of the `PreparedStatement` object *pstmt* to 44, with a Java type of `short`:

```
pstmt.setShort(2, 44);
```

The driver will send 44 to the database as a JDBC SMALLINT, which is the standard mapping from a Java short.

It is the programmer's responsibility to make sure that the type in the Java programming language for each IN parameter maps to a JDBC type that is compatible with the JDBC data type expected by the database. Consider the case where the database expects a JDBC SMALLINT. If the method setByte is used, the driver will send a JDBC TINYINT to the database. This will probably work because many database systems convert from one related type to another, and generally a TINYINT can be used anywhere a SMALLINT is used. However, for an application to work with the most database systems possible, it is best to use types in the Java programming language that correspond to the exact JDBC types expected by the database. If the expected JDBC type is SMALLINT, using setShort instead of set-Byte will make an application more portable. The table "Java Types Mapped to JDBC Types," on page 1088, can be used to determine which setter method to use.

25.1.5 Using setObject

A programmer can explicitly convert an input parameter to a particular JDBC type by using the method setObject. This method can take a third argument, which specifies the target JDBC type. The driver will convert the Object in the Java programming language to the specified JDBC type before sending it to the database.

If no JDBC type is given, the driver will simply map the Java Object to its default JDBC type (using the table "Java Object Types Mapped to JDBC Types," on page 1090) and then send it to the database. This is similar to what happens with the regular setter methods; in both cases, the driver maps the Java type of the value to the appropriate JDBC type before sending it to the database. The difference is that the setter methods use the standard mapping shown in the table "Java Types Mapped to JDBC Types," on page 1088, whereas the setObject method uses the mapping shown in the table "Java Object Types Mapped to JDBC Types," on page 1090.

The capability of the method setObject to accept any Java object allows an application to be generic and accept input for a parameter at run time. In this situation the type of the input is not known when the application is compiled. By using setObject, the application can accept any Java object type as input and convert it to the JDBC type expected by the database. The table "Conversions by set-Object," on page 1091, shows all the possible conversions that the method setObject can perform.

2.0

The JDBC 2.0 core API added a new setObject method that applies to a user-defined type (UDT) that has been custom mapped to a class in the Java programming language. The custom mapping of an SQL UDT is specified in a class that implements the SQLData interface. When a UDT instance is retrieved from the database via the method getObject, it will be mapped to an instance of the Java class that implemented SQLData for it. When that custom-mapped instance is passed to the method setObject, setObject will call the SQLOutput.writeObject method that is defined in the appropriate SQLData implementation, thereby converting the instance of a Java class back to an SQL UDT.

The details of custom mapping are hidden from the user. When an application invokes the method setObject, the value being stored will automatically be custom mapped if there is a custom mapping for it. As a result, code in which the method setObject performs a custom mapping looks identical to code in which setObject uses the standard mapping. UDTs can only be stored using the setObject method, which is a way of ensuring that UDTs with a custom mapping are mapped appropriately. Chapter 37, "SQLData," starting on page 895, gives a complete explanation of custom mapping.

In all of the cases discussed so far, the value passed to the method setObject was originally an SQL data type that was retrieved from a table column. Before returning it to the database, the driver needed to convert it back to its SQL data type. If a database is one of the new generation of Java-aware DBMSs, called a Java relational DBMS, it can store an instance of a class defined in the Java programming language as well as values defined in SQL. A class instance may be stored as a serialized Java object or in some other format defined by the DBMS.

The following example shows the use of the method setObject to store *emp*, an instance of the class Employee. After the salary field of *emp* is increased by 50 percent, *emp* is sent back to the database. The column EMPLOYEE in the table PERSONNEL stores instances of Employee.

```
emp.salary = emp.salary * 1.5;
PreparedStatement pstmt = con.prepareStatement(
    "UPDATE PERSONNEL SET EMPLOYEE = ? WHERE EMPLOYEE_NO = 300485");
pstmt.setObject(1, emp);
pstmt.executeUpdate();
```

Note that the syntax in this example is the same as that in the JDBC 1.0 API and is also the same as that used to store instances of UDTs that have been custom mapped.

25.1.6 Sending JDBC `NULL` as an IN Parameter

The `setNull` method allows a programmer to send a JDBC `NULL` (a generic SQL `NULL`) value to the database as an IN parameter. Note, however, that one must still specify the JDBC type of the parameter.

A JDBC `NULL` will also be sent to the database when a Java `null` value is passed to a setter method (if it takes Java objects as arguments). The method `setObject`, however, can take a `null` value only if the JDBC type is specified.

25.1.7 Sending Very Large IN Parameters

The methods `setBytes` and `setString` are capable of sending unlimited amounts of data. Sometimes, however, it is preferable to pass large amounts of data in smaller chunks. This can be accomplished by setting an IN parameter to a Java input stream. When the statement is executed, the JDBC driver will make repeated calls to this input stream, reading its contents and transmitting those contents as the actual parameter data.

The JDBC 1.0 API provides two methods for setting IN parameters to input streams: `setBinaryStream` for streams containing uninterpreted bytes and `setAsciiStream` for streams containing ASCII characters. A third method, `setUnicodeStream` for streams containing Unicode characters, has been deprecated; the JDBC 2.0 core API method `setCharacterStream` should be used in its place. These stream methods take one more argument than the other setter methods because the total length of the stream must be specified. This is necessary because some database systems need to know the total transfer size before any data is sent.

The following code illustrates using a stream to send the contents of a file as an IN parameter.

```
java.io.File file = new java.io.File("/tmp/data");
int fileLength = file.length();
java.io.InputStream fin = new java.io.FileInputStream(file);
java.sql.PreparedStatement pstmt = con.prepareStatement(
                "UPDATE Table5 SET stuff = ? WHERE index = 4");
pstmt.setBinaryStream (1, fin, fileLength);
pstmt.executeUpdate();
```

When the statement executes, the input stream `fin` will get called repeatedly to deliver up its data.

Another way to send large IN parameters to the database is to use SQL99 types like BLOB and CLOB. This is different from using streams in that BLOB and CLOB values are originally retrieved from the database, where they were created as SQL types. Using streams makes it possible to send the contents of a file written in the Java programming language to the database.

2.0

25.1.8 Using PreparedStatement Objects in Batch Updates

The JDBC 2.0 core API provides the ability to send multiple updates to the database for execution as a batch. The Statement method addBatch is given an SQL update statement as a parameter, and the SQL statement is added to the Statement object's list of commands to be executed in the next batch. (See "Sending Batch Updates," on page 961, for a fuller explanation.) The interface PreparedStatement has its own version of the method addBatch, which adds a set of parameters to the batch, as shown in the following code fragment.

```
PreparedStatement pstmt = con.prepareStatement(
            "UPDATE Table4 SET History = ? WHERE ID = ?");
pstmt.setClob(1, clob1);
pstmt.setLong(2, 350985839);
pstmt.addBatch();

pstmt.setClob(1, clob2);
pstmt.setLong(2, 350985840);
pstmt.addBatch();

int [] updateCounts = pstmt.executeBatch();
```

When the PreparedStatement object in *pstmt* is executed, it will be executed twice, once with the parameters clob1 and 350985839, and a second time with the parameters clob2 and 350985840. If either update command returns anything other than a single update count, the method executeBatch will throw an exception.

3.0

25.1.9 Pooling Prepared Statements

One of the reasons for creating a PreparedStatement object is to enhance performance for statements that will be executed multiple times. Performance can be further enhanced by pooling PreparedStatement objects, which the JDBC 3.0 specification makes possible. When a PreparedStatement object is pooled, it is not destroyed when it is executed. Instead it is returned to a pool so that it can be used again and again, thus saving the overhead of creating a new statement each time it is used.

From the developer's viewpoint, using a `PreparedStatement` object that is pooled is exactly the same as using one that is not pooled. An application creates a `PreparedStatement` object, sets its parameters (if any), executes it, and closes it in exactly the same way. This means that after a `PreparedStatement` object is closed, even if it is being pooled, it must be created again for the next use. The only difference is that there should be an improvement in efficiency when a pooled statement is used multiple times.

An application can check to see if the driver supports statement pooling by calling the `DatabaseMetaData` method `supportsStatementPooling`. If the return value is `true`, the application can use `PreparedStatement` objects armed with that knowledge.

Pooling of `PreparedStatement` objects is done completely behind the scenes and is available only if connection pooling is available. See "Reusing Statements," on page 440, for an explanation of how statement pooling works.

25.2 PreparedStatement Interface Definition

```
package java.sql;
public interface PreparedStatement extends Statement {
    ResultSet executeQuery() throws SQLException;
    int executeUpdate() throws SQLException;


    //==============================================================
    //          JDBC 1.0 methods for setting parameters
    //==============================================================


    void setNull(int parameterIndex, int jdbcType) throws SQLException;
    void setNull(int parameterIndex, int jdbcType, String typeName)
                                            throws SQLException;
    void setBoolean(int parameterIndex, boolean x) throws SQLException;
    void setByte(int parameterIndex, byte x) throws SQLException;
    void setShort(int parameterIndex, short x) throws SQLException;
    void setInt(int parameterIndex, int x) throws SQLException;
    void setLong(int parameterIndex, long x) throws SQLException;
```

```
    void setFloat(int parameterIndex, float x) throws SQLException;
    void setDouble(int parameterIndex, double x) throws SQLException;
    void setBigDecimal(int parameterIndex, java.math.BigDecimal x)
                                                    throws SQLException;
    void setString(int parameterIndex, String x) throws SQLException;
    void setBytes(int parameterIndex, byte x[]) throws SQLException;
    void setDate(int parameterIndex, java.sql.Date x) throws
                                                        SQLException;
    void setTime(int parameterIndex, java.sql.Time x)
                                                throws SQLException;
    void setTimestamp(int parameterIndex, java.sql.Timestamp x)
                                                throws SQLException;
    void setAsciiStream(int parameterIndex, java.io.InputStream x, int
                                    length) throws SQLException;
    void setUnicodeStream(int parameterIndex, java.io.InputStream x, int
                                    length) throws SQLException;
    void setBinaryStream(int parameterIndex, java.io.InputStream x, int
                                    length) throws SQLException;
    void clearParameters() throws SQLException;


    //================================================================
    //          JDBC 2.0 and 3.0 methods for setting parameters
    //================================================================
```

2.0	```void setArray(int parameterIndex, Array x) throws SQLException;```
2.0	```void setBlob(int parameterIndex, Blob x) throws SQLException;```
2.0	```void setCharacterStream(int parameterIndex, java.io.Reader reader,``` ``` int length) throws SQLException;```
2.0	```void setClob(int parameterIndex, Clob x) throws SQLException;```
2.0	```void setDate(int parameterIndex, java.sql.Date x,``` ``` java.util.Calendar cal) throws SQLException;```
2.0	```void setRef(int parameterIndex, Ref x) throws SQLException;```
2.0	```void setTime(int parameterIndex, java.sql.Time x,``` ``` java.util.Calendar cal) throws SQLException;```
2.0	```void setTimestamp(int parameterIndex, java.sql.Timestamp x,``` ``` java.util.Calendar cal) throws SQLException;```
3.0	```void setURL(int parameterIndex, URL x) throws SQLException;```

```
    //================================================================
    //                  JDBC 1.0 advanced features
    //================================================================
```

```
    void setObject(int parameterIndex, Object x, int targetJdbcType,
                                        int scale) throws SQLException;
    void setObject(int parameterIndex, Object x, int targetJdbcType)
                                                  throws SQLException;
    void setObject(int parameterIndex, Object x) throws SQLException;
    boolean execute() throws SQLException;


    //=============================================================
    //                  JDBC 2.0 advanced features
    //=============================================================


    void addBatch() throws SQLException;
    ResultSetMetaData getMetaData() throws SQLException;
    void setNull(int parameterIndex, int SQLtype, String typeName)
                                                  throws SQLException;


    //=============================================================
    //                  JDBC 3.0 advanced features
    //=============================================================


    ParameterMetaData getParameterMetaData() throws SQLException;
}
```

25.3 PreparedStatement Methods

The following methods are inherited from the interface java.sql.Statement:

JDBC 1.0 methods:

cancel	getMoreResults	setCursorName
clearWarnings	getQueryTimeout	setEscapeProcessing
close	getResultSet	setMaxFieldSize
getMaxFieldSize	getUpdateCount	setMaxRows
getMaxRows	getWarnings	setQueryTimeout

JDBC 2.0 methods:

addBatch	getFetchDirection	getResultSetType
clearBatch	getFetchSize	setFetchDirection
executeBatch	getResultSetConcurrency	setFetchSize
getConnection		

JDBC 3.0 methods:

execute	getGeneratedKeys	getResultSetHoldability
executeUpdate	getMoreResults	

The following fields are inherited from `java.sql.Statement`:

JDBC 3.0 fields:

CLOSE_ALL_RESULTS	KEEP_CURRENT_RESULT	SUCCESS_NO_INFO
CLOSE_CURRENT_RESULT	NO_GENERATED_KEYS	
EXECUTE_FAILED	RETURN_GENERATED_KEYS	

The following methods are defined in the interface `java.sql.PreparedStatement`:

addBatch

---

void **addBatch**() throws SQLException

Adds a set of parameters to this `PreparedStatement` object's list of commands to be sent to the database for execution as a batch.

EXAMPLE:
```
pstmt.addBatch();
```

SEE:
"Using `PreparedStatement` Objects in Batch Updates," on page 654, for an example

clearParameters

---

void **clearParameters**() throws SQLException

Clears the values set for the `PreparedStatement` object's IN parameters and releases the resources used by those values.

In general, parameter values remain in force for repeated use of a statement. Setting a new parameter value will automatically clear its previous value. In some cases, however, it is useful to immediately release the resources used by the current parameter values by calling the method `clearParameters`.

EXAMPLE:
```
pstmt.clearParameters();
```

execute

```
boolean execute() throws SQLException
```

Executes the SQL statement contained in the PreparedStatement object and indicates whether the first result is a result set, an update count, or there are no results.

This method will execute any PreparedStatement object, but it is designed to handle a complex SQL statement that returns multiple result sets or a statement whose contents are unknown because it is being executed dynamically.

Note that when the execute method is used, one must call the method getResultSet or getUpdateCount to retrieve the first result and then getMore-Results to move to any subsequent result(s).

This version of the execute method does not override the execute method in the Statement interface; the Java compiler treats it as a different method because it takes no parameters and thus has a different signature. Programmers should act as if it does override the Statement version, however. Using the method PreparedStatement.execute with a query parameter is not appropriate and will throw an SQLException.

RETURNS:
true if the first result is a result set; false if it is an update count or there is no result

THROWS:
SQLException if an argument is supplied to this method

EXAMPLE:
```
boolean b = pstmt.execute();
```

SEE:
"Executing Special Kinds of Statements," on page 965, for a fuller description

executeQuery

```
ResultSet executeQuery() throws SQLException
```

Executes a prepared SQL query and returns the result set in a `ResultSet` object. This method should be used only for SQL statements that return a result set; any other result will cause an exception.

This version of the `executeQuery` method does not override the `executeQuery` method in the `Statement` interface; the Java compiler treats it as a different method because it takes no parameters and thus has a different signature. Programmers should act as if it does override the `Statement` version, however. Using the method `PreparedStatement.executeQuery` with a query parameter is not appropriate and will throw an `SQLException`.

RETURNS:
the result set generated by the SQL statement contained in the calling `PreparedStatement` object

THROWS:
`SQLException` if the SQL statement contained in this `PreparedStatement` object returns anything other than a result set or if an argument is supplied to this method

EXAMPLE:
```
ResultSet rs = pstmt.executeQuery();
```

executeUpdate

```
int executeUpdate() throws SQLException
```

Executes an SQL `INSERT`, `UPDATE`, or `DELETE` statement and returns the number of rows that were affected. This method can also be used to execute SQL statements that have no return value, such as DDL statements that create or drop tables.

This method should be used for updates and data definition language statements only; an `SQLException` will be thrown if a result set is returned.

This version of the `executeUpdate` method does not override the `executeUpdate` method in the `Statement` interface; the Java compiler treats it as a different method because it takes no parameters and thus has a different signature. However, programmers should act as if this method does override the `Statement` version. Using the method `PreparedStatement.executeUpdate` with a query parameter is not appropriate and will throw an `SQLException`.

RETURNS:
an `int` indicating the number of rows that were affected; 0 indicates that zero rows were affected or that a DDL statement was executed.

THROWS:
SQLException if an argument is supplied to this method

EXAMPLE:
```
int rowCount = pstmt.executeUpdate();
```

getMetaData

2.0

```
ResultSetMetaData getMetaData() throws SQLException
```

Retrieves a ResultSetMetaData object with information about the number, types, and properties of the columns in the ResultSet object that will be returned when this PreparedStatement object is executed. ResultSetMetaData methods can be used to get information about the number, types, and properties of the result set's columns.

A Statement object must be executed and a ResultSet object returned before metadata information about that result set can be obtained. Because a PreparedStatement object is precompiled, however, it is possible to know about the ResultSet object that it will return without having to execute it. Consequently, it is possible to invoke the method getMetaData on a PreparedStatement object before it has been executed. This is in contrast to executing a statement and then invoking the ResultSet.getMetaData method on the ResultSet object that is returned.

NOTE: Using this method may be expensive for some drivers due to lack of underlying DBMS support for this feature.

RETURNS:
a ResultSetMetaData object for this PreparedStatement object, which contains information about the columns in the result set that will be returned when this PreparedStatement object is executed; may be null if the driver cannot return a ResultSetMetaData object

EXAMPLE:
```
PreparedStatement pstmt = con.prepareStatement(
                                      "SELECT * FROM COFFEES");
ResultSetMetaData rsmd = pstmt.getMetaData();
int count = rsmd.getColumnCount;
// If the result set that will be returned when pstmt is executed
// has five columns, count will be 5.
```

getParameterMetaData

ParameterMetaData **getParameterMetaData**() throws SQLException

Retrieves a ParameterMetaData object with information about the number, types, and properties of the parameters for this PreparedStatement object. ParameterMetaData methods can be used to access information in the ParameterMetaData object.

RETURNS:
a ParameterMetaData object with information about this PreparedStatement object's parameters

EXAMPLE:
ParameterMetaData pstmtInfo = pstmt.getParameterMetaData();
// pstmtInfo contains information about the parameters in pstmt

setArray

void **setArray**(int *parameterIndex*, Array *x*) throws SQLException

Sets parameter number *parameterIndex* to *x*, an Array object in the Java programming language. The driver converts this to a JDBC ARRAY value when it sends it to the database.

PARAMETERS:
parameterIndex	1 indicates the first parameter, 2 the second, and so on
x	the Array value to be set as a parameter

EXAMPLE:
pstmt.setArray(3, addresses);
// sets the third parameter to the Array object addresses

setAsciiStream

void **setAsciiStream**(int *parameterIndex*, java.io.InputStream *fin*,
                                    int *length*) throws SQLException

Sets the parameter in position *parameterIndex* to the input stream object *fin*, from which *length* bytes will be read and sent to the database.

This is useful when a very large ASCII value is input to a LONGVARCHAR parameter. JDBC will read the data from the stream as needed until it reaches end-of-file. The JDBC driver will do any necessary conversion from ASCII to the database CHAR format.

NOTE: This stream object can be either a standard stream object in the Java programming language or the programmer's own subclass that implements the standard interface.

PARAMETERS:

parameterIndex	1 indicates the first parameter, 2 the second, and so on
fin	the java.io.InputStream object that contains the input data in ASCII format
length	the number of bytes to be read from the stream and sent to the database. Note that if the stream contains more or fewer bytes than are specified in *length*, an exception is thrown.

THROWS:

SQLException if the number of bytes read and sent to the database is not equal to the number of bytes specified

EXAMPLE:
```
pstmt.setAsciiStream(3, fin, 4096);
// sets the third parameter to the input stream fin;
// 4096 bytes will be read
```

setBigDecimal

```
void setBigDecimal(int parameterIndex, java.math.BigDecimal n)
                                              throws SQLException
```

Sets parameter number *parameterIndex* to *n*. The driver converts this to a JDBC NUMERIC value when it sends it to the database.

PARAMETERS:

parameterIndex	1 is the first parameter, 2 is the second, and so on
n	an instance of the class java.math.BigDecimal to which the parameter will be set

EXAMPLE:
```
java.math.BigDecimal n = new java.math.BigDecimal(1234.56789);
pstmt.setBigDecimal(2, n); // sets second parameter to 1234.56789
```

setBinaryStream

```
void setBinaryStream(int parameterIndex, java.io.InputStream fin,
                            int length) throws SQLException
```

Sets the parameter in position *parameterIndex* to the input stream object *fin*, from which *length* bytes will be read and sent to the database.

This is useful when a very large binary value is input to a LONGVARBINARY parameter. JDBC will read the data from the stream as needed until it reaches end-of-file.

NOTE: This stream object can be either a standard stream object in the Java programming language or the programmer's own subclass that implements the standard interface.

PARAMETERS:

parameterIndex	1 indicates the first parameter, 2 the second, and so on
fin	the java.io.InputStream object that contains the input data in binary form
length	the number of bytes to be read from the stream and sent to the database. Note that if the stream contains more or less bytes than are specified in *length*, an exception is thrown.

THROWS:

SQLException if the number of bytes read and sent to the database is not equal to the number of bytes specified

EXAMPLE:

```
pstmt.setBinaryStream(2, fin, 10000);
// sets the second parameter to the input stream fin;
// 10000 bytes will be read and sent to the database
```

setBlob

```
void setBlob(int parameterIndex, Blob x) throws SQLException
```

Sets parameter number *parameterIndex* to *x*, a Blob object in the Java programming language. The driver converts this to a JDBC BLOB value when it sends it to the database.

PARAMETERS:

parameterIndex	1 indicates the first parameter, 2 the second, and so on

x   the Blob value to be set as a parameter

EXAMPLE:
```
pstmt.setBlob(1, sightings);
// sets the third parameter to the Blob object sightings
```

setBoolean

```
void setBoolean(int parameterIndex, boolean b) throws SQLException
```

Sets parameter number *parameterIndex* to *b*, a Java boolean value. The driver converts this to a JDBC BIT or BOOLEAN value when it sends it to the database.

PARAMETERS:
parameterIndex	1 indicates the first parameter, 2 the second, and so on
b	the parameter value—either true or false

EXAMPLE:
```
pstmt.setBoolean(3, false); // sets the third parameter to false
```

setByte

```
void setByte(int parameterIndex, byte x) throws SQLException
```

Sets parameter number *parameterIndex* to *x*, a Java byte value. The driver converts this to a JDBC TINYINT value when it sends it to the database.

PARAMETERS:
parameterIndex	1 indicates the first parameter, 2 the second, and so on
x	the parameter value to be set

EXAMPLE:
```
pstmt.setByte(2, (byte)31); // sets the second parameter to 31
```

setBytes

```
void setBytes(int parameterIndex, byte x[]) throws SQLException
```

Sets parameter number *parameterIndex* to *x[]*, a Java array of bytes. The driver converts this to a JDBC VARBINARY or LONGVARBINARY value (depending on the argument's size relative to the driver's limits on VARBINARY values) when it sends it to the database.

PARAMETERS:

parameterIndex	1 is the first parameter, 2 is the second, and so on
x	a Java array of bytes

EXAMPLE:
```
byte x[] = {1, 2, 3, 4, 5};
pstmt.setBytes(1, x); // sets the first parameter to the array x
```

setCharacterStream

`2.0`

```
void setCharacterStream(int parameterIndex, java.io.Reader reader,
                                 int length) throws SQLException
```

Sets the parameter in position *parameterIndex* to the Reader stream object *reader*, from which *length* characters will be read and sent to the database.

This is useful when a very large Unicode value is input to a LONGVARCHAR parameter. JDBC will read the data from the stream as needed until it reaches end-of-file. The JDBC driver will do any necessary conversion from Unicode to the database char format.

This stream object can be either a standard stream object in the Java programming language or the programmer's own subclass that implements the standard interface.

PARAMETERS:

parameterIndex	1 indicates the first parameter, 2 the second, and so on
reader	the java.io.Reader object that contains the input data in Unicode form
length	the number of characters to be read from the stream and sent to the database. Note that if the stream contains more or less characters than are specified in *length*, an exception is thrown.

THROWS:
java.sql.SQLException if *length* is greater or less than the number of characters in *reader*

EXAMPLE:
```
pstmt.setCharacterStream(2, reader, 10000);
```

```
// sets the second parameter to the Reader stream reader;
// 10000 characters will be read
```

setClob

2.0

```
void setClob(int parameterIndex, Clob x) throws SQLException
```

Sets parameter number *parameterIndex* to *x*, a Clob object in the Java programming language. The driver converts this to a JDBC CLOB value when it sends it to the database.

PARAMETERS:

parameterIndex	1 indicates the first parameter, 2 the second, and so on
x	the Clob object to be set as a parameter

EXAMPLE:
```
pstmt.setClob(2, comments);
// sets the second parameter to the Clob object comments
```

setDate

```
void setDate(int parameterIndex, java.sql.Date x) throws SQLException
```

Sets parameter number *parameterIndex* to *x*. The driver converts this to a JDBC DATE value when it sends it to the database.

PARAMETERS:

parameterIndex	1 is the first parameter, 2 is the second, and so on
x	a java.sql.Date object

EXAMPLE:
```
Date x = new Date(980366400000L);
pstmt.setDate(1, x);
// sets the first parameter to 2001-01-24, using the time zone of
// the virtual machine running the application to calculate the date
```

setDate

2.0

```
void setDate(int parameterIndex, java.sql.Date x,
                java.util.Calendar cal) throws SQLException
```

Sets parameter number *parameterIndex* to *x*. When the DBMS does not store time zone information, the driver will use *cal* to construct a JDBC DATE value, which it will then send to the database. With a Calendar object, the driver can calculate the date taking into account a custom time zone. If no Calendar object is specified, the driver uses the time zone of the Virtual Machine that is running the application.

PARAMETERS:

parameterIndex	1 is the first parameter, 2 is the second, and so on
x	a java.sql.Date object
cal	the Calendar object the driver will use to construct the date

EXAMPLE:
```
Date x = new Date(980366400000L);
pstmt.setDate(1, x, cal);
// sets the first parameter to 2001-01-24, taking into account the
// time zone specified in cal
```

setDouble

```
void setDouble(int parameterIndex, double x) throws SQLException
```

Sets parameter number *parameterIndex* to *x*. The driver converts this to a JDBC DOUBLE value when it sends it to the database.

PARAMETERS:

parameterIndex	1 is the first parameter, 2 is the second, and so on
x	the double value to which the parameter will be set

EXAMPLE:
```
pstmt.setDouble(1, 3958325.89);
// sets first parameter to 3958325.89
```

setFloat

```
void setFloat(int parameterIndex, float x) throws SQLException
```

Sets parameter number *parameterIndex* to *x*. The driver converts this to a JDBC REAL value when it sends it to the database.

PARAMETERS:

parameterIndex	1 is the first parameter, 2 is the second, and so on
x	the float value to which the parameter will be set

EXAMPLE:
```
pstmt.setFloat(2, 18.0f); // sets second parameter to 18.0f
```

setInt

```
void setInt(int parameterIndex, int x) throws SQLException
```

Sets parameter number *parameterIndex* to *x*. The driver converts this to a JDBC INTEGER value when it sends it to the database.

PARAMETERS:

parameterIndex	1 is the first parameter, 2 is the second, and so on
x	the int value to which the parameter will be set

EXAMPLE:
```
pstmt.setInt(2, 18); // sets second parameter to 18
```

setLong

```
void setLong(int parameterIndex, long x) throws SQLException
```

Sets parameter number *parameterIndex* to *x*. The driver converts this to a JDBC BIGINT value when it sends it to the database.

PARAMETERS:

parameterIndex	1 is the first parameter, 2 is the second, and so on
x	the long value to which the parameter will be set

EXAMPLE:
```
pstmt.setLong(2, 18000000L); // sets second parameter to 18000000
```

setNull

```
void setNull(int parameterIndex, int jdbcType) throws SQLException
```

Sets parameter number *parameterIndex* to JDBC NULL (the generic SQL

NULL defined in `java.sql.Types`). Note that the JDBC type of the parameter to be set to JDBC NULL must be specified.

PARAMETERS:

parameterIndex	1 is the first parameter, 2 is the second, and so on
jdbcType	a JDBC type code defined by `java.sql.Types`

EXAMPLE:
```
pstmt.setNull(2, java.sql.Types.INTEGER);
// sets the second parameter, whose type is JDBC INTEGER, to JDBC
// NULL
```

Note that it is also possible to set the value of an input parameter to JDBC NULL using setter methods if the type being set is an object type in the Java programming language.

The following example sets the second parameter, a `String` value, to JDBC NULL:
```
pstmt.setString(2, null);
```

SEE:
`java.sql.Types`

2.0   **setNull**

```
void setNull(int parameterIndex, int jdbcType, String typeName)
                                              throws SQLException
```

Sets parameter number *parameterIndex* to JDBC NULL (the generic SQL NULL defined in `java.sql.Types`). This version of `setNull` should be used to set parameters that are REF or user-named types. User-named types include STRUCT, DISTINCT, JAVA_OBJECT, and named array types.

Note that the JDBC type of the parameter to be set to SQL NULL must be specified. To be portable, an application must give the JDBC type code and the fully qualified SQL type name when setting a REF or user-defined parameter to SQL NULL. Although this method is intended for setting parameters whose type is REF or a user-defined type, it can be used to set a parameter of any JDBC type to NULL. If the parameter to be set does not have a user-named or REF type, the driver ignores the *typeName* parameter. If a driver does not need the type code and type name information, it may ignore both *jdbcType* and *typeName*.

PARAMETERS:

parameterIndex	1 is the first parameter, 2 is the second, and so on
jdbcType	a JDBC type code defined by `java.sql.Types`; if not REF, STRUCT, DISTINCT, or JAVA_OBJECT, the driver will ignore the parameter *typeName*
typeName	the fully qualified name of the parameter being set. If *jdbcType* is REF, *typeName* should be the fully qualified name of the structured type that the REF parameter identifies. If *jdbcType* is not REF, STRUCT, DISTINCT, or JAVA_OBJECT, the driver will ignore this parameter.

EXAMPLE:
```
pstmt.setNull(2, java.sql.Types.REF, "schemaName.DOG");
// sets the second parameter, a JDBC REF value that references the
// SQL structured type schemaName.DOG, to SQL NULL
```

SEE:
```
java.sql.Types
```

setObject

```
void setObject(int parameterIndex, Object x, int targetJdbcType,
                                    int scale) throws SQLException
```

Sets parameter number *parameterIndex* to *x*. The driver converts *x* to *targetJdbcType* before sending it to the database. If *targetJdbcType* is NUMERIC or DECIMAL, *scale* indicates the number of digits to the right of the decimal point; for all other data types, *scale* is ignored.

This form of the method setObject should be used when the target JDBC type is DECIMAL or NUMERIC.

Note that the setter methods for specific types convert their arguments to the JDBC type that is the default mapping for that particular type. Methods other than setObject do not, however, perform any general data type conversions. A setObject method can take any type (in the form of a generic Object object) and convert it to the specified JDBC type before sending it to the database. In order to be objects, values for built-in types need to be expressed in their java.lang equivalents. For example, an int needs to be an instance of class Integer.

This method may be used to pass database-specific abstract data types by using a driver-specified Java type for *x* and using java.sql.Types.OTHER for *targetJdbcType*.

PARAMETERS:

parameterIndex	1 is the first parameter, 2 is the second, and so on
x	an instance of a Java Object containing the input parameter value
targetJdbcType	an integer constant representing the JDBC type (as defined in java.sql.Types) to be sent to the database. The *scale* argument may further qualify this type.
scale	the number of digits to the right of the decimal point. This applies only to java.sql.Types.DECIMAL and java.sql.Types.NUMERIC types. For all other types, this value will be ignored.

EXAMPLE:
```
Object x = new Integer(1234);
pstmt.setObject(1, x, java.sql.Types.DECIMAL, 5);
// sets first parameter to 1234.00000 after converting it to a JDBC
// DECIMAL
```

SEE:
java.sql.Types
"Using setObject," on page 651

setObject

```
void setObject(int parameterIndex, Object x, int targetJdbcType)
                                            throws SQLException
```

Sets parameter number *parameterIndex* to *x* and assumes a scale of zero. The driver converts *x* to *targetJdbcType* before sending it to the database.

Note that the setter methods for specific types convert their arguments to the JDBC type that is the default mapping for that particular type. Methods other than setObject do not, however, perform any general data type conversions. A setObject method can take any type (in the form of a generic Object object) and convert it to the specified JDBC type before sending it to the database. In order to be objects, values for built-in types need to be expressed in their java.lang class equivalents. For example, an int needs to be an instance of class Integer.

This method may be used to pass database-specific abstract data types by using a driver-specified Java type for *x* and using java.sql.Types.OTHER for *targetJdbcType*.

PARAMETERS:

parameterIndex	1 is the first parameter, 2 is the second, and so on
x	an instance of a Java `Object` containing the input parameter value
targetJdbcType	an integer constant representing the JDBC type (as defined in `java.sql.Types`) to be sent to the database

EXAMPLE:
```
Object x = new Integer(1234);
pstmt.setObject(1, x, java.sql.Types.VARCHAR);
// sets first parameter to 1234 and converts it to JDBC type VARCHAR
```

SEE:
java.sql.Types

"Using setObject," on page 651

setObject

```
void setObject(int parameterIndex, Object x) throws SQLException
```

Sets parameter number *parameterIndex* to *x* and converts it using the standard mapping of Java `Object` types to JDBC types before sending it to the database. This standard mapping is shown in the table "Java Object Types Mapped to JDBC Types," on page 1090.

PARAMETERS:

parameterIndex	1 is the first parameter, 2 is the second, and so on
x	an instance of a Java `Object` containing the input parameter value

EXAMPLE:
```
Object x = new Integer(1234);
pstmt.setObject(1, x);
// sets the first parameter to 1234 and converts it to a JDBC INTEGER
```

SEE:
"Using setObject," on page 651

setRef

2.0

```
void setRef(int parameterIndex, Ref x) throws SQLException
```

Sets parameter number *parameterIndex* to *x*, a Ref object in the Java programming language. The driver converts this to a JDBC REF value when it sends it to the database.

PARAMETERS:

parameterIndex	1 indicates the first parameter, 2 the second, and so on
x	the Ref value to be set as a parameter

EXAMPLE:
```
pstmt.setRef(3, ref);
// sets the third parameter to the Ref object ref
```

setShort

```
void setShort(int parameterIndex, short x) throws SQLException
```

Sets parameter number *parameterIndex* to *x*. The driver converts this to a JDBC SMALLINT value when it sends it to the database.

PARAMETERS:

parameterIndex	1 is the first parameter, 2 is the second, and so on
x	the short value to which the parameter will be set

EXAMPLE:
```
pstmt.setShort(2, (short)8); // sets second parameter to 8
```

setString

```
void setString(int parameterIndex, String x) throws SQLException
```

Sets parameter number *parameterIndex* to *x*. The driver converts this to a JDBC VARCHAR or LONGVARCHAR value (depending on the argument's size relative to the driver's limits on VARCHARs) when it sends it to the database.

PARAMETERS:

parameterIndex	1 is the first parameter, 2 is the second, and so on
x	the String object in the Java programming language to which the parameter will be set

EXAMPLE:
```
String x = "Happy days are here again"
pstmt.setString(2, x); // sets second parameter to "Happy days ..."
```

setTime

```
void setTime(int parameterIndex, java.sql.Time x) throws SQLException
```

Sets parameter number *parameterIndex* to *x*. The driver converts this to a JDBC TIME value when it sends it to the database.

PARAMETERS:

parameterIndex	1 is the first parameter, 2 is the second, and so on
x	the java.sql.Time object to which the parameter will be set

EXAMPLE:
```
Time t = new Time(3456934567L);
pstmt.setTime(2, t);
```

SEE:
```
java.sql.Time
```

setTime

2.0

```
void setTime(int parameterIndex, java.sql.Time x,
                        java.util.Calendar cal) throws SQLException
```

Sets parameter number *parameterIndex* to *x*. When the DBMS does not store time zone information, the driver will use *cal* to construct a JDBC TIME value, which it will then send to the database. With a Calendar object, the driver can calculate the time taking into account a custom time zone. If no Calendar object is specified, the driver uses the time zone of the Virtual Machine that is running the application.

PARAMETERS:

parameterIndex	1 is the first parameter, 2 is the second, and so on
x	the java.sql.Time object to which the parameter will be set
cal	the Calendar object the driver will use to calculate the time

EXAMPLE:
```
Time t = new Time(23502938562L);
pstmt.setTime(2, t, cal);
```

SEE:
java.sql.Time

setTimestamp

```
void setTimestamp(int parameterIndex, java.sql.Timestamp x)
                                            throws SQLException
```

Sets parameter number *parameterIndex* to *x*. The driver converts this to a JDBC TIMESTAMP value when it sends it to the database.

PARAMETERS:

parameterIndex	1 is the first parameter, 2 is the second, and so on
x	a java.sql.Timestamp object

EXAMPLE:
```
Timestamp ts = new Timestamp(25035912512350392L);
pstmt.setTimestamp(1, ts);
```

SEE:
java.sql.Timestamp

2.0 setTimestamp

```
void setTimestamp(int parameterIndex, java.sql.Timestamp x,
                  java.util.Calendar cal) throws SQLException
```

Sets parameter number *parameterIndex* to *x*. When the DBMS does not store time zone information, the driver will use *cal* to construct a JDBC Timestamp value, which it then sends to the database. With a Calendar object, the driver can calculate the Timestamp object taking into account a custom time zone. If no Calendar object is specified, the driver uses the time zone of the Virtual Machine that is running the application.

PARAMETERS:

parameterIndex	1 is the first parameter, 2 is the second, and so on
x	the java.sql.Timestamp object to which the parameter will be set
cal	the Calendar object the driver will use to construct the TIMESTAMP object

EXAMPLE:
```
Timestamp ts = new Timestamp(2934581625910L);
pstmt.setTimestamp(2, ts, cal);
```

SEE:
```
java.sql.Timestamp
```

setUnicodeStream   DEPRECATED

```
void setUnicodeStream(int parameterIndex, java.io.InputStream fin,
                                    int length) throws SQLException
```

Sets the parameter in position *parameterIndex* to the input stream object *fin*, from which *length* bytes will be read and sent to the database.

This is useful when a very large Unicode value is input to a LONGVARCHAR parameter. JDBC will read the data from the stream as needed until it reaches end-of-file. The JDBC driver will do any necessary conversion from Unicode to the database CHAR format. A Unicode character is two bytes, with the first byte being the high byte and the second byte the low byte.

NOTE: This stream object can be either a standard Java stream object or the programmer's own subclass that implements the standard interface.

NOTE: This method has been deprecated. Use the method setCharacter-Stream for streams of Unicode characters.

PARAMETERS:

parameterIndex	1 indicates the first parameter, 2 the second, and so on
fin	the java.io.InputStream object that contains the input data in Unicode format
length	the number of bytes to be read from the stream and sent to the database. Note that if the stream contains more or fewer bytes than are specified in *length*, an exception is thrown.

THROWS:
SQLException if the number of bytes read and sent to the database is not equal to the number of bytes specified

EXAMPLE:
```
pstmt.setUnicodeStream(1, fin, 256);
// sets the first parameter to the input stream fin;
// 256 bytes will be read
```

setURL

```
void setURL(int parameterIndex, URL x) throws SQLException
```

Sets parameter number *parameterIndex* to *x*. The driver converts this to a JDBC DATALINK value when it sends it to the database.

PARAMETERS:

parameterIndex   1 is the first parameter, 2 is the second, and so on

x   a java.sql.URL object

EXAMPLE:

```
URL url = new URL("http://whizzies.com/whiz/");
pstmt.setURL(1, url);
// Sets the first parameter of pstmt to url
```

CHAPTER 26

Ref 2.0

26.1 Ref Overview

THE Ref interface is the mapping of an SQL REF(<structured type>) to the Java programming language. An SQL REF value is a logical pointer to an instance of a structured type. For example, if PERSON is an SQL structured type, a REF(PERSON) value is a reference to an instance of PERSON. SQL REF(PERSON) values can reference only instances of PERSON, and each one uniquely identifies a particular instance of PERSON.

The interfaces Blob, Clob, and Array all use locators internally in a standard implementation, which means that they represent a database value on the client without having to materialize the value's data on the client. The Ref interface likewise designates a database value without materializing its data on the client.

Even though a Ref object and an SQL LOCATOR are both logical pointers, they differ significantly. Whereas an SQL LOCATOR is transient and exists only on a client, an SQL REF object is persistent and can exist on both a client and a server. It exists on the client as a Ref object, and it exists on the server as a value assigned to a column in a database table.

An SQL REF value and a primary key likewise have a surface similarity but are really very different. They both uniquely identify a row in a table, but that is where the similarity ends. First, a REF value is always a single value, and it always identifies an instance of an SQL structured type. A primary key, on the other hand, may consist of one or more columns from the row it identifies, and it is not restricted to identifying only one kind of row.

Second, there are differences in how they are typically created. Both may be created either automatically by the DBMS or by a person, but a REF value is generally created by a DBMS. Some DBMSs, but not all, also automatically create a key for a row when it is added to a table, and this key often serves as the row's primary key. However, for DBMSs that do not automatically generate keys, a person such as a database administrator must create primary keys by coming up with some algorithm for deciding which column or columns constitute a unique identifier for a row.

A third difference is that an SQL REF value is both permanent and unique, whereas a primary key may not be. If, for instance, the primary key for a table is an ID number, and an employee is deleted from the table, it is possible to reuse that employee's ID number for a different employee added to the table later. A REF value, on the other hand, can never be reused; it is a persistent value stored in a special table that can never identify any value other than the instance of the particular structured type for which it was created.

Unlike instances of Blob, Clob, and Array, which are valid during a single transaction only, the lifetime of a Ref instance is the session in which it was created. Note that the life cycle of a Ref instance is not the same as that of the SQL REF value that it represents: A Ref instance lasts only for the duration of a connection, whereas the SQL REF value lasts indefinitely, existing for as long as the table in which it is stored exists.

The Ref interface has four methods. One returns the fully qualified SQL type name of the SQL structured type instance that the Ref value identifies, two retrieve the structured type that the Ref object references, and one sets the structured type that a Ref object references to a given value.

26.1.1 Creating an SQL Reference

An SQL REF(<structured type>) exists only under certain conditions. First, the SQL structured type that it references, being a user-defined type, must be properly set up in the database. Next, references to instances of the structured type must be properly set up. This involves creating a special table for the structured type and then populating it with instances of the structured type. The following list explains in more detail the three steps that must be accomplished before an SQL REF(<structured type>) can be used:

1. Create an SQL structured type using the command CREATE TYPE.
   (Note that DBMSs may vary in the syntax they use. For example, some DBMSs use CREATE TYPE AS OBJECT.)

   The following SQL statement creates the structured type WRITER.

```
CREATE TYPE WRITER
(
    LAST_NAME VARCHAR(40),
    FIRST_NAME VARCHAR(40),
    PUBLISHER VARCHAR(50),
    TYPE VARCHAR(50)
);
```

2. Create a table for the instances of the SQL structured type and for the REF values (unique identifiers) that will identify them.

The following table definition creates the table WRITERS, which will contain instances of the type WRITER and also a REF value for each instance of WRITER.

```
CREATE TABLE WRITERS OF WRITER
    (REF IS OID SYSTEM GENERATED);
```

"Storing Instances of a Structured Type," on page 1000, gives a more complete description of this table.

3. Add instances of the structured type to the table. The DBMS will automatically generate a REF object for each instance and store it in the table's OID column. The following INSERT INTO statement adds one instance of WRITER to the table WRITERS. The REF(WRITER) value that the DBMS generates and stores in the column OID will permanently identify this instance of the type WRITER.

```
INSERT INTO WRITERS (LAST_NAME, FIRST_NAME, PUBLISHER, TYPE) VALUES
(
    "JOYCE",
    "JAMES",
    "AWL",
    "FICTION"
);
```

The table WRITERS now contains a row in which the value for the column OID is a REF(WRITER) value that can be used to reference the instance of WRITER in which the column values (attributes) are "JOYCE", "JAMES", "AWL", and "FICTION".

Once the table WRITERS has been set up, a REF(WRITER) value can be used as a value for columns or attributes that are type REF(WRITER). For example, in the following SQL table definition, the column AUTHOR is declared to be of type REF(WRITER). This means that one of the values stored in the OID column of the table WRITERS can be used as a value in the column AUTHOR.

```
CREATE TABLE BOOKS
(
    BOOK_ID NUMERIC(6),
    TITLE VARCHAR(50),
    AUTHOR REF(WRITER)
);
```

In the following SQL definition of the structured type NOVEL, the attribute AUTHOR is declared to be of type REF(WRITER). As was true with the table definition, this means that values used for the attribute AUTHOR must be values from the OID column of the table WRITERS.

```
CREATE TYPE NOVEL
(
    TITLE VARCHAR(100),
    AUTHOR REF(WRITER)
);
```

See Chapter 44, "Struct," starting on page 997, for more information about creating and using SQL structured types.

26.1.2   Creating a Ref Object

A DBMS automatically creates an SQL REF(<structured type>) value each time a new instance of a structured type is added to the table for that structured type. This section illustrates creating a Ref object, which represents a REF(<structured type>) value in the Java programming language.

The following code fragment creates the Ref object *joyce*, where *stmt* is a Statement object and the table WRITERS is the table of WRITER instances and their corresponding REF(WRITER) values, defined in the previous section. Note that, like the command for creating an SQL structured type, the command for creating a table of structured type instances may vary from one DBMS to another.

```
ResultSet rs = stmt.executeQuery("SELECT OID FROM WRITERS WHERE
                                    LAST_NAME = 'JOYCE'");
rs.next();
Ref joyce = rs.getRef("OID");
```

The variable *joyce* now designates the REF(WRITER) value that is stored in column OID in the current row of *rs*. It is logically a pointer to the instance of the structured type WRITER in which the value for the column LAST_NAME is JOYCE. In a standard implementation, *joyce* will remain valid while the session, or connection, on which it was created remains open.

26.1.3 Storing a Ref Object

A Ref object may be stored in a database by simply passing it as an input parameter to a PreparedStatement object. The following code fragment creates the Ref variable *joyce*, as was done in the previous example, and then passes it as a parameter to the PreparedStatement object *pstmt*.

```
Ref joyce = rs.getRef("OID");
PreparedStatement pstmt = con.prepareStatement(
        "UPDATE BOOKS SET AUTHOR = ? WHERE BOOK_ID = ?");
pstmt.setRef(1, joyce);
pstmt.setLong(2, 002764);
```

The column AUTHOR in the row of the table BOOKS where BOOK_ID is 002764 now stores the REF(WRITER) value that *joyce* represents. Note that the driver converts *joyce* from a Ref object to an SQL REF(WRITER) value before using it to update the AUTHOR column in the table BOOKS.

26.1.4 Dereferencing a Ref Object

An application that has obtained a Ref object may want to dereference it, that is, to retrieve the attributes of the structured type that the Ref object references. Sample code 29 shows one way to dereference a Ref object. In this example, the Ref object references a REF(WRITER) value, which identifies a row in the table WRITERS. The code prints out the column values for each row in WRITERS. Each row of WRITERS is an instance of the structured type WRITER, and each column value is an attribute of that instance.

The code first gets the ResultSet object *rs* for the table BOOKS. One of the columns in *rs*, AUTHOR, is a Ref object representing a REF(WRITER). After retrieving the Ref object *author* from a row in *rs*, the code next retrieves the ResultSet object *rs2* for the table WRITERS. The variable *author*, stored in the column OID, uniquely identifies one of the rows in WRITERS. Thus, *rs2* is produced by selecting the columns from WRITERS where the value in the column OID is *author*. To dereference *author*, the code retrieves the column values from *rs2*.

In short, each time the code retrieves a REF(WRITER) value, it stores it in the variable *author* and then uses it to select a row in the table WRITERS. The attributes for the instance of WRITER that *author* represents are then retrieved and printed out.

26.1.5   Sample Code 30

This code shows one way to dereference a Ref object.

```
import java.sql.*;

public class Dereference {

    public static void main(String [] args) {
        String url = "jdbc:mySubprotocol:myDataSource";

        Connection con = null;
        try {
            Class.forName("myDriver.ClassName");

        } catch(java.lang.ClassNotFoundException e) {
            System.err.print("ClassNotFoundException: ");
            System.err.println(e.getMessage());
        }
        try {
            con = DriverManager.getConnection(url,
                            "myLogin", "myPassword");

            Statement stmt = con.createStatement();
            ResultSet rs = stmt.executeQuery("SELECT * FROM BOOKS");
            while (rs.next()) {
```

```
        int id = rs.getInt("BOOK_ID");
        String title = rs.getString("TITLE");
        Ref author = rs.getRef("AUTHOR");

        PreparedStatement pstmt = con.prepareStatement(
            "SELECT LAST_NAME, FIRST_NAME, PUBLISHER, TYPE " +
            "FROM WRITERS WHERE OID = ?");
        pstmt.setRef(1, author);
        ResultSet rs2 = pstmt.executeQuery();
        rs2.next();
        String last = rs2.getString("LAST_NAME");
        String first = rs2.getString("FIRST_NAME");
        String publisher = rs2.getString("PUBLISHER");
        String type = rs2.getString("TYPE");

        System.out.println(id + "   " + title + "   " + first +
            " " + last + "   " + publisher + "   " + type);
        rs2.close();
        pstmt.close();
    }

    stmt.close();
} catch(SQLException ex) {
    System.err.println("SQLException: " + ex.getMessage());
} finally {
            if (con != null) con.close();
        }
    }
}
```

NOTE: At the time of this writing, not all drivers fully support the APIs used in this sample code. Consequently, the code has been compiled but not executed. It is included as an aid to understanding how the API can be used. In addition, SQL syntax and dialects may differ between DBMS implementations. It is therefore highly recommended that you consult your DBMS documentation to see the exact syntax you should use.

3.0

The JDBC 3.0 API greatly simplifies dereferencing a Ref object by adding the method getObject. There are two versions of the getObject method, both of which retrieve the structured type that a Ref object references. Both versions map the structured type to a Java Object. If there is no type map specifying a custom mapping, the structured type is mapped to a Struct object. If there is a type map, either one that is associated with the connection or one that is passed to the method getObject, the structured type is custom mapped using the type map. In a typical custom mapping, each attribute in an SQL structured type is mapped to a field in a Java class.

The following code fragment uses the getObject method that takes no type map as an argument. In this example, the assumption is that there is no custom mapping for the structured type that *author* references. As a result, the structured type is mapped to a Struct object, which is the default mapping.

Note that an application can check whether the connection's type map has an entry for the structured type referenced by a Ref object. The application needs to call the Ref method getBaseTypeName to get the fully qualified name of the SQL structured type being referenced. It also needs to call the Connection method get-TypeMap. If the return value for getBaseTypeName is contained in an entry in the Map object returned by getTypeMap, there is a custom mapping for the structured type.

Here is an example of dereferencing a Ref object using the method getObject.

```
Ref author = rs.getRef("AUTHOR");
Struct struct = (Struct)author.getObject();
Object [] objs = struct.getAttributes();
for (int i = 0; i < objs.length; i++) {
        Object obj = objs[i];
        System.out.println("Attribute " + (i+1) + " is " + obj);
}
```

Each attribute will be printed on a separate line with its ordinal number.

The following code fragment uses the getObject method that takes a type map as an argument. In this type map, the structured type WRITER is mapped to the class `Author`. The attributes in `WRITER` are mapped to the fields in `Author`, which are `lastName`, `firstName`, `publisher`, and `type`, in that order.

```
Ref author = rs.getRef("AUTHOR");
Author auth = (Author)author.getObject(myTypeMap);
String lastName = auth.lastName;
String firstName = auth.firstName;
String publisher = auth.publisher;
String type = auth.type;
}
```

The `Author` object *auth* contains fields that map the attributes of the structured type referenced by the `Ref` object *author*. As a result, accessing the field values in *auth* retrieves the attribute values.

26.1.6 Modifying a Ref Object

The `setObject` method, added in the JDBC 3.0 API, makes it possible to make changes in the structured type that a `Ref` object references. For example, continuing with the preceding example, the following lines of code get the attributes of `WRITER` as fields in the `Author` object *auth* and change the `type` field to `"biography"`. The last line sets the `Ref` object *author* to *auth*. The driver will convert *auth*, with its new value for `type`, back to the SQL structured type `WRITER`. Each field in *auth* will be mapped to an attribute in `WRITER`, with the order always being the order in which the attributes were defined when `WRITER` was created. Thus, the value of the field `type` will become the value of the fourth attribute in `WRITER`.

```
Ref author = rs.getRef("AUTHOR");
Author auth = (Author)author.getObject(myTypeMap);
auth.type = "biography";
author.setObject(auth);
```

26.2 Ref Interface Definition

```
package java.sql;
public interface Ref {
```

`2.0` String **getBaseTypeName**() throws SQLException;

`3.0` Object **getObject**() throws SQLException;
`3.0` Object **getObject**(java.util.Map map) throws SQLException;
`3.0` void **setObject**(Object object) throws SQLException;
}

26.3 Ref Methods

`2.0`   ### getBaseTypeName

String **getBaseTypeName**() throws SQLException

Retrieves the fully qualified type name for the SQL structured type that is referenced by this Ref object.

RETURNS:
the fully qualified type name for the base type (an SQL structured type) to which this Ref object refers

EXAMPLE:
```
Ref ref = rs.getRef(3);
String baseTypeName = ref.getBaseTypeName();
// ref represents the SQL reference stored in column 3 of the
// ResultSet object rs. baseTypeName contains the fully qualified
// SQL name of the structured type to which ref refers.
```

`3.0`   ### getObject

Object **getObject**() throws SQLException

Retrieves the SQL structured type that is referenced by this Ref object. If the connection's type map has an entry for the structured type, the instance is custom mapped to the Java class indicated in the type map. Otherwise, the structured type instance is mapped to a Struct object, which is the default mapping.

RETURNS:
the SQL structured type to which this Ref object refers

EXAMPLE:
```
Struct struct = (Struct)ref.getObject();
// ref is a Ref object. It retrieves the structured type it
// references as an Object and casts it to a Struct object before
// assigning it to the variable struct. The structured type is
// mapped to a Struct object because there is no custom mapping in
// the connection's type map.
```

getObject

`3.0`

```
Object getObject(java.util.Map map) throws SQLException
```

Retrieves the SQL structured type that is referenced by this `Ref` object and custom maps it to the Java class indicated in *map*.

PARAMETERS:

map   a `java.util.Map` object that contains the mapping to use, which consists of the fully qualified name of the SQL structured type being referenced and the class object for the `SQLData` implementation to which the SQL structured type will be mapped

RETURNS:
a Java `Object` that is the custom mapping for the SQL structured type to which this `Ref` object refers

EXAMPLE:
```
Author auth = (Author)ref.getObject(map);
// ref is a Ref object. Author is the Java class to which the
// structured type that ref references is mapped. Because getObject
// returns an Object, its return value is cast to an Author object
// before being assigned to the variable auth.
```

setObject

`3.0`

```
void setObject(Object value) throws SQLException
```

Sets the structured type instance that this `Ref` object references to *value*. The driver converts *value* to an SQL structured type before sending it to the database.

PARAMETERS:

value   a Java `Object` that represents the SQL structured type
                                 instance that this `Ref` object will reference

EXAMPLE:
```
ref.setObject(value);
// ref is a Ref object that references an instance of an SQL
// structured type. value is either a Struct object containing the
// SQL structured type's attributes or a Java class object to which
// the structured type has been custom mapped.
```

CHAPTER 27

ResultSet

27.1 ResultSet Overview

A ResultSet object represents a database result set. A result set is a table of rows and columns that contains the results of executing an SQL query. In other words, it contains the rows that satisfy the conditions of the query. The data stored in a ResultSet object is retrieved through a set of getter methods that allows access to the various columns of the current row. The ResultSet.next method is used to move to the next row of the ResultSet object, making it the new current row.

The general form of a result set is a table with column headings and the corresponding values returned by a query. For example, if the query is SELECT a, b, c FROM Table1, the result set will have the following form:

```
a               b                c
----------      ------------     -----------
12345           Cupertino        2459723.495
83472           Redmond          1.0
83492           Boston           35069473.43
```

The following code fragment is an example of executing an SQL statement that will return a collection of rows, with column a as an int, column b as a String, and column c as a float:

```
java.sql.Statement stmt = con.createStatement();
ResultSet rs = stmt.executeQuery("SELECT a, b, c FROM Table1");
while (rs.next()) {
    // retrieve and print the values for the current row
    int i = rs.getInt("a");
```

```
        String s = rs.getString("b");
        float f = rs.getFloat("c");
        System.out.println("ROW = " + i + " " + s + " " + f);
    }
```

27.1.1 Rows and Columns

A relational database is made up of tables, with each table consisting of rows and columns. A row in a relational database table can be thought of as representing an instance of the entity that the table represents. For example, if there is a table of employees, each row will contain information about a particular employee. Each piece of data about the employee is stored in a column, so, for instance, the table of employees could have columns for an identification number, a name, a salary, and a date of hire. The columns in a row would contain the ID number, name, salary, and date of hire for a particular employee.

A result set is also a table with rows and columns, but it contains only the column values from a database table that satisfy the conditions of a query. In other words, a result set row will contain a subset of the columns in the underlying database table (unless the query selects everything in the table, in which case the result set table will include all of the column values for every row in the database table). In the past, a column value in a relational database table (and consequently in a result set table) had to be atomic; that is, it could be only one indivisible value. For instance, an array could not be a column value because an array may be made up of multiple elements. With the advent of SQL99 data types, however, the permissible content of table columns has expanded dramatically. It is now possible for an array or even a user-defined structured type to be a column value. Because this new capability allows a relational database to store instances of complex types as column values, it makes a relational database more like an object database, blurring the distinction between relational and object databases. Programmers can take advantage of these new data types if they use a driver that supports SQL99 types.

27.1.2 Cursors

A ResultSet object maintains a cursor, which points to its current row of data. The cursor moves down one row each time the method next is called. When a ResultSet object is first created, the cursor is positioned before the first row, so the first call to the next method puts the cursor on the first row, making it the current row.

ResultSet rows can be retrieved in sequence from top to bottom as the cursor moves down one row with each successive call to the method next. This ability to move its cursor only forward is the default behavior for a ResultSet and is the only cursor movement possible with drivers that implement only the JDBC 1.0 API. This kind of result set has the type ResultSet.TYPE_FORWARD_ONLY and is referred to as a forward-only result set.

If a driver implements the cursor movement methods in the JDBC API, its result sets can be scrollable. A scrollable result set's cursor can move both forward and backward as well as to a particular row. The following methods move the cursor backward, to the first row, to the last row, to a particular row number, to a specified number of rows from the current row, and so on: previous, first, last, absolute, relative, afterLast, and beforeFirst. An explanation and example of how to make a result set scrollable will be presented in the section "Creating Different Types of Result Sets," on page 705.

When a cursor is positioned on a row in a ResultSet object (not before the first row or after the last row), that row becomes the current row. This means that any methods called while the cursor is positioned on the current row will (1) operate on values in that row (methods such as getter and updater methods), (2) operate on the row as a whole (such as the methods updateRow, insertRow, deleteRow, and refreshRow), or (3) use that row as a starting point for moving to other rows (such as the method relative).

How long a cursor remains valid depends on its holdability. Cursors that are not holdable are closed when a transaction is committed or rolled back. A holdable cursor is valid until the ResultSet object or its parent Statement object is closed.

27.1.3 Cursor Movement Examples

As stated in the previous section, the standard cursor movement for forward-only result sets is to use the method next to iterate through each row of a result set once from top to bottom. With scrollable result sets, it is possible to revisit a row or to iterate through the result set multiple times. This is possible because the cursor can be moved before the first row at any time (with the method beforeFirst). The cursor can begin another iteration through the result set with the method next. The following example positions the cursor before the first row and then iterates forward through the contents of the result set. The methods getString and getFloat retrieve the column values for each row until there are no more rows, at which time the method next returns the value false.

```
rs.beforeFirst();
while (rs.next()) {
    System.out.println(rs.getString("EMP_NO") +
                        " " + rs.getFloat("SALARY");
}
```

It is also possible to iterate through a result set backwards, as is shown in the next example. The cursor is first moved to the very end of the result set (with the method afterLast), and then the method previous is invoked within a while loop to iterate through the contents of the result set by moving to the previous row with each iteration. The method previous returns false when there are no more rows, so the loop ends after all the rows have been visited.

```
rs.afterLast();
while (rs.previous()) {
    System.out.println(rs.getString("EMP_NO") +
                        " " + rs.getFloat("SALARY");
}
```

The interface ResultSet offers still other ways to iterate through the rows of a scrollable result set. Care should be taken, however, to avoid incorrect alternatives such as the one illustrated in the following example:

```
// incorrect!
while (!rs.isAfterLast()) {
    rs.relative(1);
    System.out.println(
            rs.getString("EMP_NO") + " " + rs.getFloat("SALARY"));
}
```

This example attempts to iterate forward through a scrollable result set and is incorrect for several reasons. One error is that if ResultSet.isAfterLast is called when the result set is empty, it will return a value of false since there is no last row. The loop body will be executed, which is not what is wanted. An additional problem occurs when the cursor is positioned before the first row of a result set that contains data. In this case, calling rs.relative(1) is erroneous because there is no current row. The method relative moves the cursor the specified number of rows from the current row, and it must be invoked only while the cursor is on the current row.

The following code fragment fixes the problems in the previous example. Here a call to the method `ResultSet.first` is used to distinguish the case of an empty result set from one that contains data. Because `ResultSet.isAfterLast` is called only when the result set is non-empty, the loop control works correctly. Since `ResultSet.first` initially positions the cursor on the first row, the method `ResultSet.relative(1)` steps through the rows of the result set as expected.

```
if (rs.first()) {
    while (!rs.isAfterLast()) {
        System.out.println(
            rs.getString("EMP_NO") + " " + rs.getFloat("SALARY"));
        rs.relative(1);
    }
}
```

27.1.4 Determining the Number of Rows in a Result Set

2.0

With the cursor movement methods, it is easy to see how many rows a scrollable `ResultSet` object contains. All that is necessary is to go to the last row of the result set and get the number of that row. In the following example, *rs* will have one row for each employee.

```
ResultSet rs = stmt.executeQuery(
                "SELECT LAST_NAME, FIRST_NAME FROM EMPLOYEES");
rs.last();
int numberOfRows = rs.getRow();
System.out.println("XYZ, Inc. has " + numberOfRows + " employees");
rs.beforeFirst();
while (rs.next()) {
    . . . // retrieve first and last names of each employee
}
```

Although not as convenient, it is also possible to find out how many rows a non-scrollable result set has. The following example shows one way to determine the number of rows.

```
ResultSet rs = stmt.executeQuery("SELECT COUNT(*) FROM EMPLOYEES");
rs.next();
int count = rs.getInt(1);
```

```
System.out.println("XYZ, Inc. has " + count + " employees");

ResultSet rs2 = stmt.executeQuery(
                "SELECT LAST_NAME, FIRST_NAME FROM EMPLOYEES");
while (rs2.next()) {
    . . . // retrieve first and last names of each employee
}
```

With the scrollable result set, the cursor was just repositioned to start iterating through the same result set to retrieve its data. In the preceding example, however, one query is needed to get the count, and another query is needed to get a result set with the data that is desired. Both queries must, of course, produce result sets of the same size for the count to be accurate.

A second way to determine the number of rows in a forward-only result set is to iterate through the result set, incrementing a variable with each iteration, which is shown in the following example. Because an application can iterate through a forward-only result set just once, the same query needs to be executed twice. In the iteration through the first *rs*, the number of rows is counted; in the iteration through the second *rs*, the data is retrieved.

```
ResultSet rs = stmt.executeQuery(
                "SELECT LAST_NAME, FIRST_NAME FROM EMPLOYEES");
int count = 0;
while (rs.next()) {
    count++;
}
System.out.println("Company XYZ has " + count " employees.");
rs = stmt.executeQuery(
                "SELECT LAST_NAME, FIRST_NAME FROM EMPLOYEES");
while (rs.next()) {
    . . . // retrieve first and last names of each employee
}
```

27.1.5 Retrieving Column Values

The `ResultSet.getter` methods provide the means for retrieving column values from the current row. For maximum portability with forward-only result sets, values should be retrieved from left to right, and column values should be read only once. With scrollable result sets, however, there are no such restrictions.

Either the column name or the column number can be used to designate the column from which to retrieve data. For example, if the second column of a ResultSet object *rs* is named TITLE, and it stores values as strings, either of the following will retrieve the value stored in that column:

```
String s = rs.getString(2);
String s = rs.getString("TITLE");
```

Note that columns are numbered from left to right starting with column 1. Also, column names used as input to getter methods are case insensitive.

The option of using the column name was provided so that a user who specifies column names in a query can use those same names as the arguments to getter methods. If, on the other hand, the SELECT statement does not specify column names (as in "SELECT * FROM TABLE1" or in cases where a column is derived) and the column names are not known, column numbers need to be used.

In some cases, it is possible for an SQL query to return a result set that has more than one column with the same name. If a column name is used as the parameter to a getter method, that method will return the value of the first matching column name. Thus, if there are multiple columns with the same name, one needs to use a column index to be sure that the correct column value is retrieved. It may also be slightly more efficient to use column numbers. If the name of a column is known but not its index, the method findColumn can be used to find the column number.

On the other hand, using the column name has its advantages. Using the column number in application code introduces a dependency on the order in which columns happen to have been defined in the table. Using the column name avoids such a dependency. Also, using column names is often more convenient because column names are more meaningful than column numbers.

Information about the columns in a ResultSet object, including their names, is available by calling the method ResultSet.getMetaData. The ResultSetMetaData object returned gives the number, types, and properties of its ResultSet object's columns. Refer to "ResultSetMetaData," on page 783, for more information.

27.1.6 Which Method to Use for Retrieving Values

JDBC drivers support type coercion. When a getter method is invoked, the driver attempts to convert the underlying JDBC (SQL) data type to the corresponding type in the Java programming language and then returns a suitable value. For example, if the getter method is getString, and the data type of the data in the underlying database is VARCHAR, the JDBC driver will convert the VARCHAR value to a String object in the Java programming language. That String object will be the value returned by getString.

2.0

The JDBC 2.0 API added getter methods for retrieving the data types defined in the SQL99 specification. These methods work the same way that the getter methods in the JDBC 1.0 API work; that is, they map the SQL99 JDBC type to a type in the Java programming language and return that type. For example, the method getClob retrieves a JDBC CLOB value from the database and returns a Clob object, which is an instance of the java.sql.Clob interface.

3.0

A new data type was added to the JDBC 3.0 API, so the corresponding getter methods were added to the ResultSet interface. The new data type is a JDBC DATALINK, which is defined in the Types interface; the new methods are the two version of getURL, one taking a column index, and one taking a column name. For more information on the DATALINK type, see "DATALINK," on page 1078.

Table 27.1 shows which JDBC types a getter method is *allowed* to retrieve and which JDBC types are *recommended* for it to retrieve. A small x indicates a legal getter method for a particular data type; a large, bold **x** indicates the recommended getter method for a data type. For example, any of the JDBC 1.0 getter methods except getBytes or getBinaryStream can be used to retrieve the value of a LONGVARCHAR, but getAsciiStream and getCharacterStream are recommended. (Note that the method getUnicodeStream was deprecated in the JDBC 2.0 API; the method getCharacterStream should be used in its place.)

27.1.7 Using the Method getObject

As shown in Table 27.1, the method getObject will retrieve any data type. This is possible because Object, being the type from which every other object type in the Java programming language is derived, is the most generic type. This is especially useful when the underlying data type is a database-specific type or when a generic application needs to be able to accept any data type. The method getObject, as would be expected from its name, returns a Java Object that must be narrowed if it is to be used as a more specific type. In other words, it must be cast from its generic Object type to its more derived type before it can be used as

Table 27.1: Use of `ResultSet` getter Methods to Retrieve JDBC Types

	TINYINT	SMALLINT	INTEGER	BIGINT	REAL	FLOAT	DOUBLE	DECIMAL	NUMERIC	BIT	BOOLEAN	CHAR	VARCHAR	LONGVARCHAR	BINARY	VARBINARY	LONGVARBINARY	DATE	TIME	TIMESTAMP	CLOB	BLOB	ARRAY	REF	DATALINK	STRUCT	JAVA_OBJECT
getByte	**X**	x	x	x	x	x	x	x	x	x		x	x	x													
getShort	x	**X**	x	x	x	x	x	x	x	x		x	x	x													
getInt	x	x	**X**	x	x	x	x	x	x	x		x	x	x													
getLong	x	x	x	**X**	x	x	x	x	x	x		x	x	x													
getFloat	x	x	x	x	**X**	x	x	x	x	x		x	x	x													
getDouble	x	x	x	x	x	**X**	**X**	x	x	x		x	x	x													
getBigDecimal	x	x	x	x	x	x	x	**X**	**X**	x		x	x	x													
getBoolean	x	x	x	x	x	x	x	x	x	**X**	**X**	x	x	x													
getString	x	x	x	x	x	x	x	x	x	x		**X**	**X**	x	x	x	x	x	x	x					x		
getBytes															**X**	**X**	x										
getDate												x	x	x				**X**		x							
getTime												x	x	x					**X**	x							
getTimestamp												x	x	x				x	x	**X**							
getAsciiStream												x	x	**X**	x	x	x										
getUnicodeStream												x	x	**X**	x	x	x										
getBinaryStream															x	x	**X**										
getCharacterStream												x	x	**X**	x	x	x										
getClob																					**X**						
getBlob																						**X**					
getArray																							**X**				
getRef																								**X**			
getURL																									**X**		
getObject	x	x	x	x	x	x	x	x	x	x	x	x	x	x	x	x	x	x	x	x	x	x	x	x	x	**X**	**X**

2.0

that derived type. The following code fragment illustrates using the getObject method to retrieve a Struct value from the column ADDRESS in the current row of the ResultSet object *rs*. The Object that getObject returns is cast to a Struct object before it is assigned to the variable *address*.

```
Struct address = (Struct)rs.getObject("ADDRESS");
```

The method getObject is not only the one method capable of retrieving values of any data type but also the only getter method that does custom mapping. Therefore, to be custom mapped, a data type has to be retrieved with the method getObject. The two SQL data types that can be custom mapped are the user-defined types, SQL structured types and DISTINCT types. A JDBC DISTINCT value is normally retrieved with the getter method appropriate for its underlying type, but if it has a custom mapping, it must be retrieved by the method getObject in order to be custom mapped. A JDBC STRUCT can only be retrieved with the method getObject, guaranteeing that if there is a custom mapping for a JDBC STRUCT value, it will be used.

2.0

27.1.8   Types of Result Sets

Results sets may have different levels of functionality. For example, they may be scrollable or non-scrollable. A scrollable result set has a cursor that moves both forward and backward and can be moved to a particular row. Also, result sets may be sensitive or insensitive to changes made while they are open; that is, they may or may not reflect changes to column values that are modified in the database. A developer should always keep in mind the fact that adding capabilities to a ResultSet object incurs additional overhead, so it should be done only as necessary.

Based on the capabilities of scrollability and sensitivity to changes, there are three types of result sets available with the JDBC 2.0 core API. The following constants, defined in the ResultSet interface, are used to specify these three types of result sets:

1. TYPE_FORWARD_ONLY

   • The result set is non-scrollable; its cursor moves forward only, from top to bottom.

   • The view of the data in the result set depends on whether the DBMS materializes results incrementally.

2. TYPE_SCROLL_INSENSITIVE

- The result set is scrollable: Its cursor can move forward or backward and can be moved to a particular row or to a row whose position is relative to its current position.

- The result set generally does not show changes to the underlying database that are made while it is open. The membership, order, and column values of rows are typically fixed when the result set is created.

3. TYPE_SCROLL_SENSITIVE

- The result set is scrollable; its cursor can move forward or backward and can be moved to a particular row or to a row whose position is relative to its current position.

- The result set is sensitive to changes made while it is open. If the underlying column values are modified, the new values are visible, thus providing a dynamic view of the underlying data. The membership and ordering of rows in the result set may be fixed or not, depending on the implementation.

The section "Creating Different Types of Result Sets," on page 705, presents examples of how to create these three types of result sets.

27.1.9 Concurrency Types

2.0

A result set may have different update capabilities. As with scrollability, making a ResultSet object updatable increases overhead and should be done only when necessary. That said, it is often more convenient to make updates programmatically, and that can be done only if a result set is made updatable. The JDBC 2.0 core API offers two update capabilities, specified by the following constants in the ResultSet interface:

1. CONCUR_READ_ONLY

- Indicates a result set that *cannot* be updated programmatically

- The one concurrency type available to drivers that implement only the JDBC 1.0 API

- Offers the highest level of concurrency (allows the largest number of simultaneous users). When a ResultSet object with read-only concurrency needs to set a lock, it uses a read-only lock. This allow users to read data but not to change it. Because there is no limit to the number of read-only locks that may be held on data at one time, there is no limit to the number of concurrent users unless the DBMS or driver imposes one.

2. `CONCUR_UPDATABLE`

- Indicates a result set that *can* be updated programmatically

- Available to drivers that implement the JDBC 2.0 core API

- Reduces the level of concurrency. Updatable results sets may use write-only locks so that only one user at a time has access to a data item. This eliminates the possibility that two or more users might change the same data, thus ensuring database consistency. However, the price for this consistency is a reduced level of concurrency.

To allow a higher level of concurrency, an updatable result set may be implemented so that it uses an optimistic concurrency control scheme. This implementation assumes that conflicts will be rare and avoids using write-only locks, thereby permitting more users concurrent access to data. Before committing any updates, it determines whether a conflict has occurred by comparing rows either by value or by a version number. If there has been an update conflict between two transactions, one of the transactions will be aborted in order to maintain consistency. Optimistic concurrency control implementations can increase concurrency; however, if there are too many conflicts, they may actually reduce performance.

`3.0`

27.1.10 Result Set Holdability

The `ResultSet` property *holdability* determines whether a `ResultSet` object (cursor) is closed when a transaction is committed. When the `Connection` method `commit` is called, either explicitly or automatically (because auto-commit mode is enabled), it can close all the `ResultSet` objects that were created in the current transaction. If this is not the desired behavior, an application can specify that cursors remain open across commits by using one of the `ResultSet` constants added in the JDBC 3.0 API.

The following `ResultSet` constants specify a `ResultSet` object's holdability:

- `ResultSet.HOLD_CURSORS_OVER_COMMIT`
  Any `ResultSet` objects (cursors) in the current transaction will remain open when the transaction is committed.

- `ResultSet.CLOSE_CURSORS_AT_COMMIT`
  Any `ResultSet` objects (cursors) in the current transaction will be closed when the transaction is committed.

An application uses these constants with `Connection` methods, which can be done in two ways: when it creates a new statement or when it sets a connection's holdability property. For example, the following code fragment, in which *ds* is a `DataSource` object, creates a `Statement` object that will produce `ResultSet` objects that are scrollable, not sensitive to changes made by others, not updatable, and whose cursors will be closed when the current transaction is committed.

```
Connection con = ds.getConnection();
Statement.stmt = con.createStatement(
                        ResultSet.TYPE_SCROLL_INSENSITIVE,
                        ResultSet.CONCUR_READ_ONLY,
                        ResultSet.CLOSE_CURSORS_AT_COMMIT);
```

Another way to set result set holdability is to set a `Connection` object's holdability property. This property affects all of the `Statement`, `PreparedStatement`, and `CallableStatement` objects that are created using the `Connection` object, which in turn affects the holdability of the `ResultSet` objects they produce. For example, in the following code fragment, in which *con* is an active `Connection` object, the `ResultSet` object *rs* will keep its cursor open across commits.

```
con.setHoldability(ResultSet.HOLD_CURSORS_OVER_COMMIT);
Statement stmt = con.createStatement();
ResultSet rs = stmt.executeQuery(SELECT * FROM AUTHORS);
```

The default holdability of a `ResultSet` object depends on the implementation of the driver and the underlying DBMS. An application can call the `DatabaseMetaData` method `getResultSetHoldability` to get the default holdability for any result sets returned by the DBMS. If the `Connection` method `getHoldability` is called and `Connection.setHoldability` has not yet been called, the return value will be the default value returned by the `DatabaseMetaData` method `getResultSetHoldability`. If `Connection.getHoldability` is called after `Connection.setHoldability` has been called, the return value will be the one supplied to the method `setHoldability`. In effect, this value becomes the new default holdability for any `ResultSet` objects that can trace their parentage back to the `Connection` object.

27.1.11 Providing Performance Hints

2.0

Many DBMSs and drivers are optimized to give the best performance under various circumstances, which means that generally a database programmer is best advised to use their default settings. However, for programmers who may want to fine-tune database performance for a particular application, the JDBC 2.0 API provides methods that give hints to the driver for making access to result set data more efficient. These performance hints are exactly that, just hints; a JDBC Compliant driver may choose to ignore them.

The following two hints give the driver suggestions for improving performance:

1. The number of rows that should be fetched from the database each time new rows are needed

    The number of rows to be fetched is called the *fetch size*, and it can be set by two different methods: `Statement.setFetchSize` and `ResultSet.setFetchSize`. The statement that creates a `ResultSet` object sets the default fetch size for that `ResultSet` object, using the `Statement` method `setFetchSize`. The following code fragment sets the fetch size for the `ResultSet` object *rs* to 25. Until the fetch size is changed, any result set created by the `Statement` object *stmt* will automatically have a fetch size of 25.

    ```
    Statement stmt = con.createStatement();
    stmt.setFetchSize(25);
    ResultSet rs = stmt.executeQuery(SELECT * FROM EMPLOYEES);
    ```

    A result set can, at any time, change its default fetch size by setting a new fetch size with the `ResultSet` version of the method `setFetchSize`. Continuing from the previous code fragment, the following line of code changes the fetch size of *rs* to 50:

    ```
    rs.setFetchSize(50);
    ```

    Normally the most efficient fetch size is already the default for the driver. The method `setFetchSize` simply allows a programmer to experiment to see if a certain fetch size is more efficient than the default for a particular application.

2. The direction in which rows will be processed

The interface `ResultSet` defines the following three constants for specifying the direction in which to process rows: FETCH_FORWARD, FETCH_REVERSE, and FETCH_UNKNOWN. As with the fetch size, there are two methods for setting the fetch direction, one in the interface `Statement` and the other in the interface `ResultSet`. The statement that creates the result set determines the default fetch direction by using the `Statement` method `setFetchDirection`. The following code fragment sets the fetch direction for the `ResultSet` object *rs* so that it will process rows from the bottom up. Until the fetch direction is changed, any result set created by the `Statement` object *stmt* will automatically have a fetch direction of backward.

```
Statement stmt = con.createStatement();
stmt.setFetchDirection(FETCH_REVERSE);
ResultSet rs = stmt.executeQuery(SELECT * FROM EMPLOYEES);
```

A result set can, at any time, change its default fetch direction by setting a new fetch direction with the `ResultSet` method `setFetchDirection`. Continuing from the previous code fragment, the following line of code changes the fetch direction of *rs* to forward.

```
rs.setFetchDirection(FETCH_FORWARD);
```

The `ResultSet` object *rs* will hint that the driver process rows in a forward direction. This hint will be in effect until the method `ResultSet.setFetchDirection` is again called on *rs* to change the suggested fetch direction.

As with the fetch size, drivers are commonly optimized to use the most efficient fetch direction, and changing the default may actually work against this optimization. The method `setFetchDirection` simply allows a programmer to try to fine-tune an application for even better performance.

27.1.12 Creating Different Types of Result Sets

A result set is created by executing a query, and the type of result set depends on the arguments that are supplied to the `Connection` method `createStatement` (or `prepareStatement` or `prepareCall`). The following code fragment, which uses only JDBC 1.0 API, supplies no arguments to the method `createStatement` and thus creates a default `ResultSet` object, one that is forward-only and uses read-only concurrency.

```
Connection con = DriverManager.getConnection(
                   "jdbc:my_subprotocol:my_subname");
Statement stmt = con.createStatement();
ResultSet rs = stmt.executeQuery(
               "SELECT EMP_NO, SALARY FROM EMPLOYEES");
```

The variable *rs* represents a `ResultSet` object that contains the values for the columns `EMP_NO` and `SALARY` from every row in the table `EMPLOYEES`. This result set is not scrollable, so only the method `next` can be used to move the cursor from the top down through the rows of the result set. The `ResultSet` object *rs* cannot be updated, and since no performance hints were given, the driver is free to do whatever it thinks will produce the best performance. The transaction isolation level was likewise not set, so *rs* will use the default transaction isolation level of the underlying database. (See "Transaction Isolation Levels," on page 393, for an explanation of transaction isolation levels.)

The next example uses API introduced in JDBC 2.0 to create a scrollable result set that is sensitive to updates (by specifying `Result-Set.TYPE_SCROLL_SENSITIVE`) and that is updatable (by specifying `Result-Set.CONCUR_UPDATABLE`).

```
Connection con = DriverManager.getConnection(
                        "jdbc:my_subprotocol:my_subname");

Statement stmt = con.createStatement(
                        ResultSet.TYPE_SCROLL_SENSITIVE,
                        ResultSet.CONCUR_UPDATABLE);
stmt.setFetchSize(25);

ResultSet rs2 = stmt.executeQuery(
                        "SELECT EMP_NO, SALARY FROM EMPLOYEES");
```

The variable *rs2* contains the same values as *rs*, from the previous example, but unlike *rs*, it is scrollable, updatable, and sensitive to changes in the underlying table's data. It also hints that the driver should fetch 25 rows from the database each time new rows are needed. Each time the `Statement` object *stmt* is executed, it will create a result set that is scrollable, is updatable, is sensitive to changes in its data, and has a fetch size of 25. The result set may change its fetch size, but it cannot change its type or concurrency.

As stated previously, there is a cost to making a result set scrollable or updatable, so it is good practice to create result sets with these features only when they are needed.

27.1.13 Using a Prepared Statement to Create Result Sets

Because PreparedStatement and CallableStatement objects inherit the methods defined in the Statement interface, they, too, can create different types of ResultSet objects.

The following code fragment creates a result set using a PreparedStatement object instead of a Statement object. The result set has the same attributes as in the previous example, except that a transaction isolation level is set for the connection.

```
Connection con = DriverManager.getConnection(
                        "jdbc:my_subprotocol:my_subname");
con.setTransactionIsolation(
                Connection.TRANSACTION_READ_COMMITTED);

PreparedStatement pstmt = con.prepareStatement(
        "SELECT EMP_NO, SALARY FROM EMPLOYEES WHERE EMP_NO = ?",
        ResultSet.TYPE_SCROLL_SENSITIVE,
        ResultSet.CONCUR_UPDATABLE);
pstmt.setFetchSize(25);
pstmt.setString(1, "1000010");

ResultSet rs3 = pstmt.executeQuery();
```

The variable *rs3* contains the values from the columns EMP_NO and SALARY for the row where the value for EMP_NO is 1000010. The ResultSet object *rs3* is like *rs2* in that it is scrollable, is updatable, is sensitive to changes in its data, and hints that the driver should fetch 25 rows at a time from the database. It is different in that its connection specifies that dirty reads (reading values before they are committed) will be prevented. Because no transaction isolation level was set for *rs2*, it will by default have the isolation level of the underlying database.

27.1.14 Requesting Features That Are Not Supported

With the addition of new functionality in the JDBC 2.0 API, it is possible for an application to request features that a DBMS or driver do not support. If the driver does not support scrollable result sets, for example, it may return a forward-only result set. Also, some queries will return a result set that cannot be updated, so requesting an updatable result set would have no effect for those queries. A general rule is that a query should include the primary key as one of the columns it selects, and it should reference only one table.

New methods in the JDBC 2.0 API let an application discover which result set features a driver supports. If there is any doubt about whether a feature is supported, it is advisable to call these methods before requesting the feature. The following `DatabaseMetaData` methods indicate whether a driver supports a given result set type or a given result set concurrency:

- `DatabaseMetaData.supportsResultSetType`—returns a boolean indicating whether the driver supports the given result set type
- `DatabaseMetaData.supportsResultSetConcurrency`—returns a boolean indicating whether the driver supports the given concurrency type in combination with the given result set type

The following `ResultSet` methods return the result set type and result set concurrency for the particular result set on which the method is called:

- `ResultSet.getType`—returns the type of this result set
- `ResultSet.getConcurrency`—returns the concurrency mode of this result set

If an application specifies a scrollable result set and the driver does not support scrolling, the driver will issue a warning on the `Connection` object that produced the statement and return a result set that is forward-only. Even if the driver supports scrollable result sets, it is possible for an application to request a scrollable type that the driver does not support. In such a case, the driver will issue an `SQLWarning` on the `Connection` object that produced the statement and return a scrollable result set of a type that it does support, even if it differs from the exact type requested. For example, if an application requests a TYPE_SCROLL_SENSITIVE result set and the driver does not support that type, it could return a TYPE_SCROLL_INSENSITIVE result set if it supports that type. The driver would also alert the application that it did not return the exact type requested by issuing an

SQLWarning on the Connection object that produced the statement requesting the unsupported result set type.

Similarly, if an application specifies an updatable result set, a driver that does not support updatable result sets will issue an SQLWarning on the Connection object that produced the statement and return a read-only result set. If the application requests both an unsupported result set type and an unsupported concurrency type, the driver should choose the result set type first.

In some situations, a driver may need to choose an alternate result set type or concurrency type at statement execution time. For example, a SELECT statement that contains a join over multiple tables might produce a result set that is not updatable. In such a situation, the driver will issue an SQLWarning on the Statement, PreparedStatement, or CallableStatement object that tried to create the result set instead of issuing it on the Connection object. The driver will then choose an appropriate result set type and/or concurrency type according to the guidelines in the preceding two paragraphs.

27.1.15 Updating Column Values

2.0

A ResultSet object may be updated (have its rows modified, inserted, or deleted) programmatically if its concurrency type is CONCUR_UPDATABLE. The JDBC 2.0 API adds updater methods and various other methods to the ResultSet interface so that rows can be programmatically updated in both the ResultSet object and the database.

The updater methods make it possible to update values in a result set without using SQL commands. There is an updater method for each data type, and as with the getter and setter methods, there is an updater method for each data type in the Java programming language. As with the setter methods, the driver converts this data type to an SQL data type before sending it to the database. So, for example, the method updateBoolean sends a JDBC BIT value to the database, and the method updateCharacterStream sends a JDBC LONGVARCHAR value to the database.

The updater methods take two parameters, the first to indicate which column is to be updated and the second to give the value to assign to the specified column. As is true with the getter methods, the column can be specified by giving either its name or its column index. If an application retrieved a value from a result set by using the column name, it will generally use the column name when it wants to update that value. Similarly, if the getter method was given a column index to retrieve a value, the corresponding updater method will generally use the column index to update that value.

Note that the column index used with ResultSet methods refers to the column number in the result set, not the column number in the database table, which might well be different. (The column numbers will be the same only in the case where all of a table's columns are selected.) In both result set tables and database tables, the index for the first column is 1, the index for the second column is 2, and so on.

In the following code fragment, the value in the third column of the ResultSet object *rs* is retrieved using the method getInt, and the method updateInt is used to update that column value with an int value of 88:

```
int n = rs.getInt(3); // n contains the value in column 3 of rs
. . .
rs.updateInt(3, 88); // the value in column 3 of rs is set to 88
int n = rs.getInt(3); // n = 88
```

If the third column is named SCORES, the following lines of code will also update the third column of the ResultSet object *rs* by assigning it the int value 88:

```
int n = rs.getInt("SCORES");
. . .
rs.updateInt("SCORES", 88);
```

The updater methods update a value in the current row of the result set, but they do not update the value in the underlying database table. It is the method updateRow that updates the database. It is very important that the updateRow method be called while the cursor is still on the current row (the row to be updated). In fact, if an application moves the cursor before it calls updateRow, the driver must discard the update, and neither the result set nor the database will be updated.

An application may explicitly cancel the updates to a row by calling the method cancelRowUpdates. To take effect, it must be called after an updater method is called and before the method updateRow is called. If cancelRowUpdates is called at any other time, it has no effect.

The following example demonstrates updating the second and third columns in the fourth row of the ResultSet object *rs*. Since updates affect the current row, the cursor is first moved to the row to be updated, which in this case is the fourth row. Next the method updateString is called to change the value in the second column of *rs* to 321 Kasten. The method updateFloat changes the value in the third column of *rs* to 10101.0. Finally, the method updateRow is called to update the row in the database that contains the two modified column values.

```
rs.absolute(4);
rs.updateString(2, "321 Kasten");
rs.updateFloat(3, 10101.0f);
rs.updateRow();
```

If the second column is named ADDRESS and the third column is named AMOUNT, the following code will have exactly the same effect as the previous example.

```
rs.absolute(4);
rs.updateString("ADDRESS", "321 Kasten");
rs.updateFloat("AMOUNT", 10101.0f);
rs.updateRow();
```

In addition to making updates programmatically, the JDBC 2.0 core API provides the ability to send batch updates. The batch update facility operates through a Statement object, which is explained in the section "Sending Batch Updates," on page 961.

27.1.16 Deleting a Row

2.0

The JDBC 2.0 API provides the method deleteRow so that a row in a ResultSet object can be deleted using only methods in the Java programming language. This method deletes the current row, so before calling deleteRow, an application must position the cursor on the row it wants to delete. Unlike the updater methods, which affect only a row in the result set, this method affects both the current row in the result set and the underlying row in the database. The following two lines of code remove the first row of the ResultSet object *rs* and also delete the underlying row from the database (which may or may not be the first row of the database table).

```
rs.first();
rs.deleteRow();
```

27.1.17 Inserting Rows

2.0

New rows may be inserted into a result set table and into the underlying database table using methods added in the JDBC 2.0 core API. To make this possible, the API defines the concept of an *insert row*. This is a special row, associated with the result set but not part of it, that serves as a staging area for building the row that is to be inserted. To access the insert row, an application calls the ResultSet method moveToInsertRow, which positions the cursor on the insert row. Then it calls the appropriate updater methods to add column values to the insert row. When all of the columns of the row to be inserted have been set, the application calls the method insertRow. This method adds the insert row to both the result set and the underlying database simultaneously. Finally, the application needs to position the cursor on a row back in the result set.

The following code fragment demonstrates these steps for inserting a new row.

```
rs.moveToInsertRow();
rs.updateObject(1, myArray);
rs.updateInt(2, 3857);
rs.updateString(3, "Mysteries");
rs.insertRow();
rs.first();
```

Several details deserve attention. First, it is possible to retrieve values from the insert row using getter methods in the ResultSet interface. Until a value has been assigned to the insert row with an updater method, however, its contents are undefined. Therefore, if a getter method is called after the moveToInsertRow method has been called but before an updater method has been called, the value it returns will be undefined.

Second, calling an updater method on the insert row is different from calling it on a row in the ResultSet object. When the cursor is on a row in a result set, a call to an updater method changes a value in the result set. When the cursor is on the insert row, a call to an updater method updates a value in the insert row but does nothing to the result set. In both cases, though, the updater method has no effect on the underlying database.

Third, calling the method insertRow, which adds the insert row to both the result set and database, may throw an SQLException if the number of columns in the insert row does not match the number of columns in the database table. For example, if a column is not given a value by calling an updater method, an SQLException will be thrown unless that column allows null values. Also, if the result set is missing a column, that, too, will cause an SQLException to be thrown unless the column allows null values.

Fourth, a result set keeps track of where its cursor was positioned when the cursor moved to the insert row. As a result, a call to the method Result-Set.moveToCurrentRow will return the cursor to the row that was the current row immediately before the method moveToInsertRow was called. The other cursor movement methods also work from the insert row, including those that use positioning relative to the current row.

27.1.18 Positioned Updates

Before the JDBC 2.0 API made programmatic updates available in the Java programming language, the only way to change a row that had been fetched with a result set was to use what is called a *positioned update*. A positioned update is done with SQL commands and requires a named cursor to indicate the result set row in which updates are to be made.

The Statement interface provides the method setCursorName, which allows an application to specify a cursor name for the cursor associated with the next result set produced by a statement. This name can then be used in SQL positioned update or delete statements to identify the current row in the ResultSet object generated by the statement. In order to enable a positioned update or delete on a result set, the query that produces it must have the following form:

```
SELECT . . . FROM . . . WHERE . . . FOR UPDATE . . .
```

Including the words "FOR UPDATE" ensures that the cursor has the proper isolation level to support an update.

After the method executeQuery has been called on the statement, the cursor name for the resulting ResultSet object can be obtained by calling the ResultSet method getCursorName. If a DBMS allows positioned updates or positioned deletes, the name of the cursor can be supplied as a parameter to the SQL command for updates or deletes. A Statement object other than the one that created the ResultSet object must be used for the positioned update. The following code fragment, in which *stmt* and *stmt2* are two different Statement objects, demonstrates the form for naming a cursor and then using it in an SQL update statement:

```
stmt.setCursorName("x");
ResultSet rs = stmt.executeQuery(
```

```
            "SELECT . . . FROM . . . WHERE . . . FOR UPDATE . . .")
String cursorName = rs.getCursorName;
int updateCount = stmt2.executeUpdate(
               "UPDATE . . . WHERE CURRENT OF " + cursorName);
```

Note that just because the method getCursorName has been invoked on a ResultSet object does not necessarily mean that it can be updated using a ResultSet updater method. In order to update a ResultSet object using the updater methods, the executeQuery statement that produces the result set must include the specification CONCUR_UPDATABLE. Positioned updates, however, are possible for a result set created without this specification if all the proper steps are taken: (1) a cursor is named, (2) the SQL query that produces the result set is of the form SELECT . . . FROM . . . WHERE . . . FOR UPDATE . . ., and (3) the SQL update statement is of the form UPDATE . . . WHERE CURRENT OF <cursorName>.

Not all DBMSs support positioned updates. To verify that a DBMS supports positioned updates, an application can call the DatabaseMetaData methods supportsPositionedDelete and supportsPositionedUpdate to discover whether a particular connection supports these operations. When they are supported, the DBMS/driver must ensure that rows selected are properly locked so that positioned updates do not result in update anomalies or other concurrency problems.

27.1.19 Queries That Produce Updatable Result Sets

Some queries will produce result sets that cannot be updated no matter what the result set type. For example, a query that does not select the primary key column might generate a result set that cannot be updated. Because of differences in database implementations, the JDBC 2.0 core API does not specify an exact set of SQL queries that must yield updatable result sets. Instead it defines a set of criteria that should generally produce updatable result sets for JDBC Compliant drivers that support updatability. If queries adhere to the following guidelines, a developer can generally expect that they will produce updatable result sets:

1. The query references only a single table in the database.

2. The query does not contain a join operation or a GROUP BY clause.

3. The query selects the primary key of the table it references.

If inserts are to be performed on the result set, an SQL query should satisfy conditions 1 through 3 plus the following three additional conditions:

4. The user has read/write database privileges on the table.

5. The query selects all of the nonnullable columns in the underlying table.

6. The query selects all columns that do not have a default value.

The fourth and fifth conditions are necessary because a row to be inserted into a table must have a value for each column in the table unless the column accepts null values or default values. If the result set on which insertion operations are to be performed does not contain every column that requires a value, the insertion will fail.

Result sets created by means other than the execution of a query, such as those returned by several methods in the DatabaseMetaData interface, are not scrollable or updatable, nor are they required to be.

27.1.20 What Is Visible to Transactions

A result set can "see" only what is visible to its surrounding transaction, so it is important to lay some groundwork by establishing what is visible to a transaction. First, as might seem obvious, a transaction can always see the changes (updates, inserts, deletes) it makes itself. Second, a transaction may or may not be able to see the changes made by other transactions, depending on the restrictions imposed by the transaction isolation levels of each. (Refer to the section "Connection Fields," starting on page 428, to see what the different transaction isolation levels are.)

For example, suppose that two transactions, A and B, are accessing the same table in a database. If both A and B have a transaction isolation level of TRANSACTION_READ_UNCOMMITTED, all of the changes that B makes will be visible to A, and all of the changes that A makes will be visible to B. Being the lowest level of transaction isolation, TRANSACTION_READ_UNCOMMITED provides a high level of concurrency but also allows changes to be read before they have been committed. Thus, it is possible for A to update a value and for B to read that value before A has committed it. If A's transaction is then rolled back, B will have made a "dirty read," meaning that the value B read is no longer valid. In this situation, a result set that is TYPE_SCROLL_SENSITIVE and that is open in transaction A will show the changes that B makes and vice versa.

Now suppose that A and B both have a transaction isolation level of TRANSACTION_READ_COMMITTED. This level prohibits reading a value that has changed until after it has been committed, so neither A nor B will be able to make a "dirty read." In this situation, a sensitive result set open in transaction A will not show uncommitted changes that B makes, but it will reflect a value updated by B after B commits the change. A sensitive result set open in B will likewise show changes that A makes after A commits them.

Finally, suppose that A and B have the most restrictive of all transaction isolation levels, TRANSACTION_SERIALIZABLE. This means that A and B will not see any of the changes made by the other transaction. As a result, a result set open in A will not see any of the changes made by B, even if A's result set is TYPE_SCROLL_SENSITIVE. Similarly, changes made by A will not be visible to a result set open in B, even if it is nominally sensitive to changes. The point here is that even when a ResultSet object is TYPE_SCROLL_SENSITIVE, it can reflect changes made while it is open only when those changes are visible to its transaction.

27.1.21 Visibility of Changes Made by Others

Changes that are visible to a transaction are always visible to any type of result set that is opened *after* changes are made. How a result set deals with changes that are made *while it is open*, however, is quite a different matter and depends on the type of the change, the type of the result set, and the transaction isolation level of the surrounding transaction. This section will discuss a result set's ability to see changes made by other result sets or Statement objects in the same transaction or by other transactions. The next section will cover the visibility of a result set's own changes.

For purposes of this discussion, "others" means "other transactions or other objects (such as Statement or ResultSet objects) in the same transaction." Changes include updates, deletions, and insertions. An update sets a single column value, whereas insertions and deletions apply to an entire row of a result set, not just a column value.

The following list describes what changes made by others (after a result set has been opened) are visible to each type of ResultSet object:

- **Non-scrollable Result Sets**

    A non-scrollable result set cannot see the changes made by others unless it can be materialized incrementally. A result set that is not scrollable must have its rows read from top to bottom and cannot be read again. When a result set is materialized incrementally, data values are not actually retrieved from the DBMS until they are needed. Thus, if a change occurs before the affected value in a result set is retrieved with a getter method, the value retrieved from the DBMS will reflect the update; otherwise, it will not.

Most DBMSs have the ability to materialize query results incrementally, but there are some queries for which incremental materialization is impossible. For example, if the results are to be sorted, the entire result set may need to be produced and sorted before the first row in the result set can be returned to an application. In this circumstance, a ResultSet object that is TYPE_FORWARD_ONLY will not be able to reflect changes made by others.

Three methods in the interface DatabaseMetaData tell whether inserts, updates, and deletes made by others are visible when the DBMS materializes the result set incrementally: othersUpdatesAreVisible, othersDeletesAre-Visible, and othersInsertsAreVisible. (The word "others" in these methods refers to other objects in the same transaction and to other transactions.) Note that these methods return true if the DBMS is capable of incremental materialization; it is possible that they will return true even when incremental materialization is impossible because the results need to be sorted before being returned.

• **Scroll-insensitive Result Sets**

A scroll-insensitive ResultSet object never sees changes that are made by others while it is open. Once opened, it is static with regard to changes made by others; that is, its membership, ordering, and row values are fixed, and nothing can be changed. For example, suppose that B is a static result set that is open and that A is a separate transaction. If A deletes a row that is visible in B, the deleted row will continue to be visible in B.

• **Scroll-sensitive Result Sets**

A scroll-sensitive ResultSet object always reflects the updates to column values made by others provided those updates are visible to its enclosing transaction. (See "What Is Visible to Transactions," on page 715, for an explanation of what is visible to a result set's enclosing transaction.) Usually an update of a column value simply sets a new value and does not affect rows, and such updates are always visible. Sometimes, however, setting a new value does affect rows, and those updates may or may not be visible.

There are various ways an update can affect rows. It is difficult to give definitive examples because, in some cases, the same action may have different effects, varying with how a particular DBMS is implemented. For example, if another transaction changes the value of a primary key, that could have the effect of deleting the row in one result set but not in another. In a DBMS where the primary key is necessary to identify a row, an attempt to reread a row using the old primary key will fail, giving the appearance that the row has been deleted. If a DBMS uses a ROWID number to identify rows, however, it is still possible to reread a row even after another transaction has changed the row's primary key. In the second case, the row does not appear to be deleted.

When another transaction or another result set explicitly deletes a row that appears in a scroll-sensitive result set, this creates a special situation. The result set may just delete the row, or it may delete the row but keep a blank row as a placeholder. The blank row placeholder, sometimes referred to as a "hole," allows an application to continue using absolute positioning to move the cursor because it preserves the row numbering.

In summary, the visibility of changes made by others while a result set is open depends first on what type of result set it is. Scroll-sensitive result sets reflect changes the most, with updates to column values always being visible. Scroll-insensitive result sets are at the other end of the spectrum, generally with no changes being visible. For forward-only result sets, it is possible for changes by others to be visible, but this is true only if the DBMS can materialize result sets incrementally. The next factor is the type of change and how it affects rows in the result set. Last, the visibility of changes made by others while a result set is open depends on what is visible to the result set's enclosing transaction, which is determined by the transaction isolation level of the other transactions operating concurrently.

27.1.22 Visibility of a Result Set's Own Changes

When an application executes a query and creates a ResultSet object, updates it makes to that result set while it is open may or may not be reflected in the result set itself. If updates are visible, calling the appropriate getter method after an updater method has been called will return the new updated value. If the getter method returns the original value, the result set's own updates are not visible to it.

In similar fashion, inserts are visible if a new row appears in the result set immediately after a call to the method insertRow without having to close and reopen the result set. Deletions are visible if deleted rows are either removed from the result set or replaced by an empty row (a hole in the result set).

The capability for a result set to see its own changes can vary among DBMSs and JDBC drivers. Therefore, to verify that a result set's own changes are visible, an application can call the following DatabaseMetaData methods: ownUpdates-AreVisible, ownInsertsAreVisible, and ownDeletesAreVisible.

The following code fragment, in which *con* is a Connection object, demonstrates how an application can determine whether a ResultSet object that is TYPE_SCROLL_SENSITIVE can see its own updates.

```
DatabaseMetaData dbmd = con.getMetaData();
    . . .


if (dbmd.ownUpdatesAreVisible(ResultSet.TYPE_SCROLL_SENSITIVE)) {
        // if true (changes are visible), do something
}
```

27.1.23 Detecting Changes

2.0

The ability of a result set to detect changes is orthogonal to its ability to make changes visible. This means that just because a change is visible in a result set does not guarantee that the result set can detect the change. The ResultSet interface provides the following methods to determine whether a visible update, delete, or insert has affected a row since the result set was opened: rowUpdated, rowDeleted, and rowInserted.

Not all types of result sets can use these methods successfully, so the interface DatabaseMetaData provides methods to check whether a driver can detect changes for a particular type of result set. For example, in the following code fragment, in which *dbmd* is a DatabaseMetaData object, the method rowDeleted will be called on *rs* (a ResultSet object of type TYPE_SCROLL_SENSITIVE) only if a ResultSet object that is TYPE_SCROLL_SENSITIVE can successfully call the method ResultSet.rowDeleted to detect visible row deletions:

```
if (dbmd.deletesAreDetected(ResultSet.TYPE_SCROLL_SENSITIVE)) {
        boolean b = rs.rowDeleted();
}
```

If *b* is true, two things are true: (1) a TYPE_SCROLL_SENSITIVE ResultSet object can successfully call the ResultSet method rowDeleted to detect "holes" in itself and (2) the current row of *rs* is an empty row serving as a placeholder for a row that was deleted.

The interface DatabaseMetaData also has corresponding methods for the ResultSet methods rowUpdated and rowInserted. Given a result set type, the method DatabaseMetaData.updatesAreDetected will tell whether the ResultSet method rowUpdated can be used successfully; the method DatabaseMeta-

Data.insertsAreDetected will tell whether the ResultSet method rowInserted can be used successfully by the given type of result set.

2.0

27.1.24 Refetching a Row

The ResultSet method refreshRow allows an application to refetch a row from the database and thereby see the very latest values stored in that row. This method is very useful if an application needs to see up-to-the-second changes and the driver is prefetching and caching multiple rows at a time. A row that is cached may not reflect the very latest changes made to a row, even when the result set is sensitive and updates are visible.

The method refreshRow is useful, but it can be expensive. Although it is called on the current row of the result set, it may actually refresh the number of rows specified in the fetch size, which could be quite large. Even if the fetch size is set to one, invoking the method refreshRow costs something. For these reasons, calling refreshRow frequently will likely slow performance, so applications should use it only when necessary.

27.1.25 Using Streams for Very Large Row Values

The JDBC 2.0 interfaces Blob and Clob are the mapping of the SQL99 data types BLOB (Binary Large Object) and CLOB (Character Large Object) in the Java programming language. With the availability of these data types, databases will undoubtedly start using them to store very large binary or character objects. If this is the case, the ResultSet methods getBlob and getClob should be used to retrieve them.

Using only the JDBC 1.0 API, a ResultSet object still makes it possible to retrieve arbitrarily large LONGVARBINARY or LONGVARCHAR data. The methods get-Bytes and getString return data as one large chunk (up to the limits imposed by the return value of Statement.getMaxFieldSize). It is possible to retrieve this large chunk of data in smaller, fixed-size chunks. This is done by having the ResultSet class return java.io.Input streams from which data can be read in chunks. Note that these streams must be accessed immediately because they will be closed automatically when the next getter method is called on the ResultSet object. (This behavior is not a limitation of the JDBC API but rather a constraint on large blob access imposed by the underlying implementations in some database systems.)

The JDBC 1.0 API has three separate methods for getting streams, each with a different return value:

- **getBinaryStream** — returns a stream that simply provides the raw bytes from the database without any conversion

- **getAsciiStream** — returns a stream that provides one-byte ASCII characters. This method can be more efficient for a DBMS that stores characters in ASCII format.

- **getUnicodeStream** — returns a stream that provides two-byte Unicode characters. This method, though still available, has been deprecated in favor of the new method getCharacterStream. (See below.)

The following method for retrieving streams of both ASCII and Unicode characters was added in the JDBC 2.0 core API:

- **getCharacterStream** — returns a java.io.Reader object that provides Unicode characters. No matter how a DBMS stores characters, the driver will return them as a stream of Unicode characters.

Note that the stream returned by getAsciiStream returns a stream of bytes in which each byte is an ASCII character. This differs from getCharacterStream, which returns a stream of two-byte Unicode characters. The method getCharacterStream can be used for both ASCII and Unicode characters because the driver will convert ASCII characters to Unicode before it returns a Reader object. If you must use getUnicodeStream because your DBMS and driver do not support the JDBC 2.0 API, note also that JDBC Unicode streams return big-endian data; that is, they expect data with the high byte first and the low byte second. This conforms to the standard endian defined by the Java programming language, which is important if a program is to be portable. Refer to *The Java™ Virtual Machine Specification*, by Tim Lindholm and Frank Yellin, for more detailed information about big-endian order.

The following code fragment demonstrates how to use the getAsciiStream method.

```
java.sql.Statement stmt = con.createStatement();
ResultSet rs = stmt.executeQuery("SELECT x FROM Table2");
// Now retrieve the column 1 results in 4 K chunks:
byte [] buff = new byte[4096];
while (rs.next()) {
    java.io.InputStream fin = rs.getAsciiStream(1);
```

```
        for (;;) {
            int size = fin.read(buff);
            if (size == -1) { // at end of stream
                    break;
            }


            // Send the newly-filled buffer to some ASCII output stream
            output.write(buff, 0, size);
        }
    }
}
```

27.1.26 NULL Result Values

To determine whether a given result value is JDBC NULL, one must first read the column and then use the method ResultSet.wasNull. This is true because a JDBC NULL retrieved by one of the ResultSet.getter methods may be converted to either null, 0, or false, depending on the type of the value.

The following list shows which values are returned by the various getter methods when they have retrieved a JDBC NULL.

- null—for those getter methods that return objects in the Java programming language (getString, getBigDecimal, getBytes, getDate, getTime, getTime-stamp, getAsciiStream, getCharacterStream, getUnicode-Stream, getBinaryStream, getObject, getArray, getBlob, getClob, and getRef)

- 0 (zero)—for getByte, getShort, getInt, getLong, getFloat, and getDouble

- false—for getBoolean

For example, if the method getInt returns 0 from a column that allows null values, an application cannot know for sure whether the value in the database was 0 or NULL until it calls the method wasNull, as shown in the following code fragment, where *rs* is a ResultSet object.

```
int n = rs.getInt(3);
boolean b = rs.wasNull();
```

If *b* is true, the value stored in the third column of the current row of *rs* is JDBC NULL. The method wasNull checks only the last value retrieved, so to determine whether *n* was NULL, wasNull had to be called before another getter method was invoked.

27.1.27 Optional or Multiple Result Sets

Normally SQL statements are executed using either executeQuery (which returns a single ResultSet) or executeUpdate (which can be used for database modification statements, which return a count of the rows updated, or for data definition language statements). However, under some circumstances an application may not know whether a given statement will return a result set until the statement has executed. In addition, some stored procedures may return several different result sets and/or update counts.

To accommodate these situations, the JDBC API provides a mechanism so that an application can execute a statement and then process an arbitrary collection of result sets and update counts. This mechanism is based on first calling a fully general execute method, and then calling three other methods, getResultSet, getUpdateCount, and getMoreResults. These methods allow an application to explore the statement results one at a time and to determine whether a given result was a ResultSet object or an update count. Most programmers will never need to use these methods. For those who do, a full explanation with a code example can be found in "Executing Special Kinds of Statements," on page 965.

27.1.28 Closing a ResultSet Object

Normally, nothing needs to be done to close a ResultSet object; it is automatically closed by the Statement object that generated it when that Statement object is closed, is re-executed, or is used to retrieve the next result from a sequence of multiple results. The method close is provided so that a ResultSet object can be closed explicitly, thereby immediately releasing the resources held by the ResultSet object. This could be necessary when several statements are being used and the automatic close does not occur soon enough to prevent database resource conflicts.

27.1.29 JDBC Compliance

2.0

Drivers that are JDBC Compliant should normally support scrollable result sets, but they are not required to do so. The intent is for JDBC drivers to implement scrollable result sets using the support provided by the underlying database systems. If the

DBMS does not provide support for scrollability, then the driver may omit this feature.

Making scrollability optional is not meant to encourage omitting it. It is simply meant to minimize the complexity of implementing JDBC drivers for data sources that do not support scrollability. Indeed, the recommended alternative is for a driver to implement scrollability as a layer on top of the DBMS. One way to do this is to implement a result set as a rowset. JDBC RowSet objects, part of the JDBC Optional Package API, are discussed in detail in Chapter 29, "RowSet," starting on page 797.

27.2 ResultSet Interface Definition

```
package java.sql;
public interface ResultSet {
    void close() throws SQLException;
    boolean wasNull() throws SQLException;


    //============================================================
    // Methods for accessing results by column number:
    //============================================================


    String getString(int columnIndex) throws SQLException;
    boolean getBoolean(int columnIndex) throws SQLException;
    byte getByte(int columnIndex) throws SQLException;
    short getShort(int columnIndex) throws SQLException;
    int getInt(int columnIndex) throws SQLException;
    long getLong(int columnIndex) throws SQLException;
    float getFloat(int columnIndex) throws SQLException;
    double getDouble(int columnIndex) throws SQLException;
    java.math.BigDecimal getBigDecimal(int columnIndex)
                                          throws SQLException;
    java.math.BigDecimal getBigDecimal(int columnIndex, int scale)
                             throws SQLException; (Deprecated)
    byte[] getBytes(int columnIndex) throws SQLException;
    java.sql.Date getDate(int columnIndex) throws SQLException;
    java.sql.Date getDate(int columnIndex, java.util.Calendar cal)
                                          throws SQLException;
    java.sql.Time getTime(int columnIndex) throws SQLException;
```

```
2.0   java.sql.Time getTime(int columnIndex, java.util.Calendar cal)
                                            throws SQLException;
      java.sql.Timestamp getTimestamp(int columnIndex)
                                            throws SQLException;
2.0   java.sql.Timestamp getTimestamp(int columnIndex,
                          java.util.Calendar cal) throws SQLException;
      java.io.InputStream getAsciiStream(int columnIndex)
                                            throws SQLException;
      java.io.InputStream getUnicodeStream(int columnIndex)
                                   throws SQLException; (Deprecated)
      java.io.InputStream getBinaryStream(int columnIndex)
                                            throws SQLException;
2.0   java.io.Reader getCharacterStream(int columnIndex)
                                            throws SQLException;
      Object getObject(int columnIndex) throws SQLException;
2.0   Object getObject(int columnIndex, java.util.Map map)
                                            throws SQLException;
2.0   Array getArray(int columnIndex) throws SQLException;
2.0   Blob getBlob(int columnIndex) throws SQLException;
2.0   Clob getClob(int columnIndex) throws SQLException;
2.0   Ref getRef(int columnIndex) throws SQLException;
3.0   java.net.URL getURL(int columnIndex) throws SQLException;


      //===========================================================
      // Methods for accessing results by column name:
      //===========================================================


      String getString(String columnName) throws SQLException;
      boolean getBoolean(String columnName) throws SQLException;
      byte getByte(String columnName) throws SQLException;
      short getShort(String columnName) throws SQLException;
      int getInt(String columnName) throws SQLException;
      long getLong(String columnName) throws SQLException;
      float getFloat(String columnName) throws SQLException;
      double getDouble(String columnName) throws SQLException;
2.0   java.math.BigDecimal getBigDecimal(String columnName)
                                            throws SQLException;
      java.math.BigDecimal getBigDecimal(String columnName, int scale)
                                   throws SQLException; (Deprecated)
```

```
          byte[] getBytes(String columnName) throws SQLException;
          java.sql.Date getDate(String columnName) throws SQLException;
 2.0      java.sql.Date getDate(String columnName, java.util.Calendar cal)
                                               throws SQLException;
          java.sql.Time getTime(String columnName) throws SQLException;
 2.0      java.sql.Time getTime(String columnName, java.util.Calendar cal)
                                               throws SQLException;
          java.sql.Timestamp getTimestamp(String columnName)
                                               throws SQLException;
 2.0      java.sql.Timestamp getTimestamp(String columnName,
                          java.util.Calendar cal) throws SQLException;
          java.io.InputStream getAsciiStream(String columnName)
                                               throws SQLException;
          java.io.InputStream getUnicodeStream(String columnName)
                                       throws SQLException; (Deprecated)
          java.io.InputStream getBinaryStream(String columnName)
                                               throws SQLException;
 2.0      java.io.Reader getCharacterStream(String columnName)
                                               throws SQLException;
          Object getObject(String columnName) throws SQLException;
 2.0      Object getObject(String columnName, java.util.Map map)
                                               throws SQLException;
 2.0      Array getArray(String columnName) throws SQLException;
 2.0      Blob getBlob(String columnName) throws SQLException;
 2.0      Clob getClob(String columnName) throws SQLException;
 2.0      Ref getRef(String columnName) throws SQLException;
 3.0      java.net.URL getURL(String columnName) throws SQLException;


          //=========================================================
          // Methods for moving the cursor or determining cursor position:
          //=========================================================


          boolean next() throws SQLException;
 2.0      boolean previous() throws SQLException;
 2.0      boolean first() throws SQLException;
 2.0      boolean last() throws SQLException;
 2.0      boolean absolute(int row) throws SQLException;
```

`2.0` boolean **relative**(int rows) throws SQLException;

`2.0` void **afterLast**() throws SQLException;
`2.0` void **beforeFirst**() throws SQLException;
`2.0` void **moveToCurrentRow**() throws SQLException;
`2.0` void **moveToInsertRow**() throws SQLException;
`2.0` boolean **isFirst**() throws SQLException;
`2.0` boolean **isBeforeFirst**() throws SQLException;
`2.0` boolean **isLast**() throws SQLException;
`2.0` boolean **isAfterLast**() throws SQLException;
`2.0` int **getRow**() throws SQLException;


```
//============================================================
// Methods for updating column values by column number:
//============================================================
```

`2.0` void **updateString**(int columnIndex, String x) throws SQLException;
`2.0` void **updateBoolean**(int columnIndex, boolean x) throws SQLException;
`2.0` void **updateByte**(int columnIndex, byte x) throws SQLException;
`2.0` void **updateShort**(int columnIndex, short x) throws SQLException;
`2.0` void **updateInt**(int columnIndex, int x) throws SQLException;
`2.0` void **updateLong**(int columnIndex, long x) throws SQLException;
`2.0` void **updateFloat**(int columnIndex, float x) throws SQLException;
`2.0` void **updateDouble**(int columnIndex double x) throws SQLException;
`2.0` void **updateBigDecimal**(int columnIndex, java.math.BigDecimal x)
                                          throws SQLException;
`2.0` void **updateBytes**(int columnIndex, byte [] x) throws SQLException;
`2.0` void **updateDate**(int columnIndex, java.sql.Date x)
                                          throws SQLException;
`2.0` void **updateTime**(int columnIndex, java.sql.Time x)
                                          throws SQLException;
`2.0` void **updateTimestamp**(int columnIndex, java.sql.Timestamp x)
                                          throws SQLException;
`2.0` void **updateAsciiStream**(int columnIndex, java.io.InputStream x,
                              int length) throws SQLException;
`2.0` void **updateCharacterStream**(int columnIndex, java.io.Reader x,
                              int length) throws SQLException;

```
2.0    void updateBinaryStream(int columnIndex, java.io.InputStream x,
                                        int length) throws SQLException;
2.0    void updateNull(int columnIndex) throws SQLException;
2.0    void updateObject(int columnIndex, java.lang.Object x, int scale)
                                        throws SQLException;
2.0    void updateObject(int columnIndex, java.lang.Object x)
                                        throws SQLException;
3.0    void updateRef(String columnIndex, java.sql.Ref x)
                                        throws SQLException;
3.0    void updateBlob(String columnIndex, java.sql.Blob x)
                                        throws SQLException;
3.0    void updateClob(String columnIndex, java.sql.Clob x)
                                        throws SQLException;
3.0    void updateArray(String columnIndex, java.sql.Array x)
                                        throws SQLException;


       //===========================================================
       // Methods for updating column values by column name:
       //===========================================================

2.0    void updateString(String columnName, String x) throws SQLException;
2.0    void updateBoolean(String columnName, boolean x)
                                        throws SQLException;
2.0    void updateByte(String columnName, byte x) throws SQLException;
2.0    void updateShort(String columnName, short x) throws SQLException;
2.0    void updateInt(String columnName, int x) throws SQLException;
2.0    void updateLong(String columnName, long x) throws SQLException;
2.0    void updateFloat(String columnName, float x) throws SQLException;
2.0    void updateDouble(String columnName double x) throws SQLException;
2.0    void updateBigDecimal(String columnName, java.math.BigDecimal x)
                                        throws SQLException;
2.0    void updateBytes(String columnName, byte [] x) throws SQLException;
2.0    void updateDate(String columnName, java.sql.Date x)
                                        throws SQLException;
2.0    void updateTime(String columnName, java.sql.Time x)
                                        throws SQLException;
2.0    void updateTimestamp(String columnName, java.sql.Timestamp x)
                                        throws SQLException;
2.0    void updateAsciiStream(String columnName, java.io.InputStream x,
                                        int length) throws SQLException;
```

```
2.0   void updateCharacterStream(String columnName, java.io.Reader x,
                                      int length) throws SQLException;
2.0   void updateBinaryStream(String columnName,java.io.InputStream x,
                                      int length) throws SQLException;
2.0   void updateNull(String columnName) throws SQLException;
2.0   void updateObject(String columnName, java.lang.Object x, int scale)
                                                throws SQLException;
2.0   void updateObject(String columnName, java.lang.Object x)
                                                throws SQLException;
3.0   void updateRef(String columnName, java.sql.Ref x)
                                                throws SQLException;
3.0   void updateBlob(String columnName, java.sql.Blob x)
                                                throws SQLException;
3.0   void updateClob(String columnName, java.sql.Clob x)
                                                throws SQLException;
3.0   void updateArray(String columnName, java.sql.Array x)
                                                throws SQLException;


      //===========================================================
      // Methods involving rows:
      //===========================================================


2.0   void updateRow() throws SQLException;
2.0   void insertRow() throws SQLException;
2.0   void deleteRow() throws SQLException;
2.0   void cancelRowUpdates() throws SQLException;
2.0   void refreshRow() throws SQLException;

2.0   boolean rowUpdated() throws SQLException;
2.0   boolean rowInserted() throws SQLException;
2.0   boolean rowDeleted() throws SQLException;


      //===========================================================
      // Methods pertaining to the result set:
      //===========================================================


2.0   int getType() throws SQLException;
2.0   int getConcurrency() throws SQLException;
2.0   Statement getStatement() throws SQLException;
```

```
        String getCursorName() throws SQLException;
2.0     int getFetchDirection() throws SQLException;
2.0     void setFetchDirection(int direction) throws SQLException;
2.0     int getFetchSize() throws SQLException;
2.0     void setFetchSize(int rows) throws SQLException;
        ResultSetMetaData getMetaData() throws SQLException;
        SQLWarning getWarnings() throws SQLException;
        void clearWarnings() throws SQLException;
        int findColumn(String columnName) throws SQLException;


        //==============================================================
        // ResultSet fields:
        //==============================================================


2.0     public static final int FETCH_FORWARD          = 1000;
2.0     public static final int FETCH_REVERSE          = 1001;
2.0     public static final int FETCH_UNKNOWN          = 1002;


2.0     public static final int TYPE_FORWARD_ONLY      = 1003;
2.0     public static final int TYPE_SCROLL_INSENSITIVE = 1004;
2.0     public static final int TYPE_SCROLL_SENSITIVE  = 1005;
2.0     public static final int CONCUR_READ_ONLY       = 1007;
2.0     public static final int CONCUR_UPDATABLE       = 1008;


3.0     public static final int HOLD_CURSORS_OVER_COMMIT = 1;
3.0     public static final int CLOSE_CURSORS_AT_COMMIT  = 2;
}
```

27.3 ResultSet Methods

NOTE: All updater methods and all getter methods that retrieve a column value
have two versions, one that takes a column name and one that takes a column number. Since this is the only difference between them, the two versions have been combined into one entry to avoid unnecessary repetition. Also, since in every case the
first parameter is the column number or column name, those are explained here and
are not repeated in the individual method explanations. All of the updater methods
and some of the getter methods take additional parameters; if there are additional
parameters, they are explained in the individual method explanations.

The first parameter for every updater method and for each getter method that retrieves a column value is one of the following:

columnIndex the number of the column in the current row that is to be updated or from which data is to be retrieved. The first column is 1, the second column is 2, and so on

or

columnName the name of the column in the current row that is to be updated or from which data is to be retrieved

absolute

2.0

```
boolean absolute(int row) throws SQLException
```

Moves the cursor to row *row* in this ResultSet object. The variable *row* may be positive, negative, or zero.

If *row* is positive, the cursor is moved *row* rows from the beginning of the result set. The first row is 1, the second row is 2, and so on; thus, calling absolute(1) is the same as calling the method first. If *row* is greater than the number of rows in the ResultSet object, the cursor is positioned after the last row.

If *row* is negative, the cursor is moved *row* rows from the end of the result set. The last row is −1, the next-to-last row is −2, and so on; thus, calling absolute(-1) is the same as calling the method last. If *row* is greater than the number of rows in the ResultSet object, the cursor is positioned before the first row.

If *row* is 0, the cursor is positioned before the first row.

This method should be called only on ResultSet objects that are scrollable (type TYPE_SCROLL_SENSITIVE or TYPE_SCROLL_INSENSITIVE). If this method is called on a TYPE_FORWARD_ONLY ResultSet object, it will throw an SQLException.

PARAMETERS:
row an int indicating the row to which the cursor should be moved; may be positive, negative, or 0

RETURNS:
true if the cursor is moved to a position in this ResultSet object; false if the cursor is before the first row or after the last row

THROWS:
SQLException if the type of this ResultSet object is TYPE_FORWARD_ONLY

EXAMPLE:
```
boolean b = rs.absolute(-3);
// If rs has 300 rows, the cursor will be on row 298 and b will be
// true. If rs has 2 rows, the cursor will be before the first row
// and b will be false.
```

afterLast

```
void afterLast() throws SQLException
```

Moves the cursor to the end of this ResultSet object, just after the last row. This method has no effect if the result set contains no rows.

This method should be called only on ResultSet objects that are scrollable (type TYPE_SCROLL_SENSITIVE or TYPE_SCROLL_INSENSITIVE).

THROWS:
SQLException if the type of this ResultSet object is TYPE_FORWARD_ONLY

EXAMPLE:
```
rs.afterLast();
// the cursor is after the last row of rs
```

beforeFirst

```
void beforeFirst() throws SQLException
```

Moves the cursor to the front of this ResultSet object, just before the first row. This method has no effect if the result set contains no rows.

This method should be called only on ResultSet objects that are scrollable (type TYPE_SCROLL_SENSITIVE or TYPE_SCROLL_INSENSITIVE).

THROWS:
SQLException if the type of this ResultSet object is TYPE_FORWARD_ONLY

EXAMPLE:
```
rs.beforeFirst();
// the cursor is before the first row of rs
```

cancelRowUpdates

void **cancelRowUpdates**() throws SQLException

> Rolls back the updates made to a row if it is invoked after calling one of the updater methods and before calling the method updateRow. If no updates have been made or updateRow has already been called, then this method has no effect.

THROWS:
SQLException if this method is called when the cursor is on the insert row or if this ResultSet object has a concurrency of CONCUR_READ_ONLY

EXAMPLE:
rs.cancelRowUpdates();

clearWarnings

void **clearWarnings**() throws SQLException

> Clears any warnings reported on this ResultSet object. After calling the method clearWarnings, a call to getWarnings will return null until a new warning is reported for this ResultSet object.

EXAMPLE:
rs.clearWarnings();

close

void **close**() throws SQLException

> Immediately releases a ResultSet object's database and JDBC resources.
> A ResultSet object is automatically closed by the Statement object that generated it when that Statement object is closed, re-executed, or used to retrieve the next result from a sequence of multiple results. A ResultSet object is also automatically closed when it is garbage collected. The method close is used to close a ResultSet object immediately instead of waiting for it to be closed automatically.

EXAMPLE:
rs.close();

deleteRow

`2.0`

```
void deleteRow() throws SQLException
```

Deletes the current row from this `ResultSet` object and also deletes the row from the underlying database.

THROWS:
`SQLException` if this method is called on a `ResultSet` object that is not updatable or when the cursor is before the first row, after the last row, or on the insert row

EXAMPLE:
```
rs.deleteRow();
// the current row of rs has been deleted from rs and from the
// underlying database table
```

findColumn

```
int findColumn(String columnName) throws SQLException
```

Retrieves the column index for the column *columnName* in this `ResultSet` object. The driver will do a case-insensitive search for *columnName* in its attempt to map it to the column's index.

PARAMETERS:
columnName   the name of a column in this ResultSet object

RETURNS:
the column index for *columnName*

EXAMPLE:
```
int columnIndex = rs.findColumn("ID");
String s = rs.getString(columnIndex);
// columnIndex contains the column number for the rs column named ID
or
String s = rs.getString(rs.findColumn("ID"));
```

first

`2.0`

```
boolean first() throws SQLException
```

Moves the cursor to the first row in this ResultSet object.

This method should be called only on ResultSet objects that are scrollable (type TYPE_SCROLL_SENSITIVE or TYPE_SCROLL_INSENSITIVE).

RETURNS:
true if the cursor is on a valid row; false if there are no rows in this ResultSet object

THROWS:
SQLException if the type of this ResultSet object is TYPE_FORWARD_ONLY

EXAMPLE:
```
boolean b = rs.first();
// If rs has at least one row, the cursor is on the first row and
// b is true. If rs has no rows, this method has no effect and b is
// false.
```

getArray

2.0

```
Array getArray(int columnIndex) throws SQLException
Array getArray(String columnName) throws SQLException
```

Gets the value of the designated column as an Array object.

RETURNS:
the value of column *columnIndex* (or *columnName*) as an Array object in the Java programming language. If the value is SQL NULL, getArray will return null.

EXAMPLE:
```
Array lengths = rs.getArray(5);
```
or
```
Array lengths = rs.getArray("Lengths");
```

getAsciiStream

```
java.io.InputStream getAsciiStream(int columnIndex) throws SQLException
java.io.InputStream getAsciiStream(String columnName) throws
                                                    SQLException
```

Retrieves a column value as a stream of ASCII characters that can be read in chunks from the stream. This method is particularly suitable for retrieving large LONGVARCHAR values. The JDBC driver will do any necessary conversion from the database format into ASCII.

Note that all the data in the returned stream must be read prior to getting the value of any other column. The next call to a getter method implicitly closes the stream.

RETURNS:
an input stream in the Java programming language that delivers the value of *columnIndex* (or *columnName*) as a stream of one-byte ASCII characters. If the value is SQL NULL, then the return value is null.

EXAMPLE:
```
java.io.InputStream in = rs.getAsciiStream(2);
```
or
```
java.io.InputStream in = rs.getAsciiStream("Comments");
```

getBigDecimal   DEPRECATED

```
java.math.BigDecimal getBigDecimal(int columnIndex, int scale)
                                            throws SQLException
java.math.BigDecimal getBigDecimal(String columnName, int scale)
                                            throws SQLException
```

Gets the value of the designated column as a java.math.BigDecimal object with *scale* digits to the right of the decimal point.

NOTE: Both of these methods are deprecated in favor of the 2.0 versions of getBigDecimal, which do not take a scale as a parameter and return a java.math.BigDecimal object with full precision.

PARAMETERS:
scale   the number of digits to the right of the decimal point

RETURNS:
the value of column *columnIndex* (or *columnName*) as a java.math.BigDecimal object or null if the value is SQL NULL

EXAMPLE:
```
java.math.BigDecimal num = rs.getBigDecimal(1, 8);
// retrieves a BigDecimal with 8 digits after the decimal point
// from column 1 of the ResultSet rs
```
or

```
java.math.BigDecimal num = rs.getBigDecimal("Number", 2);
// retrieves a BigDecimal with 2 digits after the decimal point
// from column "Number" of the ResultSet rs
```

getBigDecimal

```
java.math.BigDecimal getBigDecimal(int columnIndex) throws SQLException
java.math.BigDecimal getBigDecimal(String columnName)
                                                     throws SQLException
```

Gets the value of the designated column as a `java.math.BigDecimal` object with full precision.

RETURNS:
the value of column *columnIndex* (or *columnName*) as a `java.math.BigDecimal` object with full precision or `null` if the value is SQL NULL

EXAMPLE:
```
java.math.BigDecimal num = rs.getBigDecimal(1);
// retrieves a BigDecimal from column 1 of the ResultSet rs
```
or
```
java.math.BigDecimal num = rs.getBigDecimal("Number");
// retrieves a BigDecimal from column "Number" of the ResultSet rs
```

getBinaryStream

```
java.io.InputStream getBinaryStream(int columnIndex) throws
                                                     SQLException
java.io.InputStream getBinaryStream(String columnName) throws
                                                     SQLException
```

Retrieves a column value as a stream of uninterpreted bytes that can later be read in chunks from the stream. This method is particularly suitable for retrieving large LONGVARBINARY values.

Note that all the data in the returned stream must be read prior to getting the value of any other column. The next call to a `getter` method implicitly closes the stream.

RETURNS:

a Java input stream that delivers the value of column *columnIndex* (or *column-Name*) as a stream of uninterpreted bytes. If the value is SQL NULL, then the result is null.

EXAMPLE:
```
java.io.InputStream in = rs.getBinaryStream(2);
```
or
```
java.io.InputStream in = rs.getBinaryStream("Data");
```

2.0 getBlob

```
Blob getBlob(int columnIndex) throws SQLException
Blob getBlob(String columnName) throws SQLException
```

Gets the SQL BLOB value stored in the designated column as a Blob object in the Java programming language.

RETURNS:

the value of column *columnIndex* (or *columnName*) as a Blob object. If the value is SQL NULL, getBlob will return null.

EXAMPLE:
```
Blob stats = rs.getBlob(4);
```
or
```
Blob stats = rs.getBlob("Measurements");
```

getBoolean

```
boolean getBoolean(int columnIndex) throws SQLException
boolean getBoolean(String columnName) throws SQLException
```

Gets the value of the designated column as a boolean.

RETURNS:

the value of column *columnIndex* (or *columnName*) as a boolean in the Java programming language. If the value is SQL NULL, getBoolean will return false.

EXAMPLE:
```
boolean bool = rs.getBoolean(5);
```
or

```
boolean bool = rs.getBoolean("Completed");
```

getByte

```
byte getByte(int columnIndex) throws SQLException
byte getByte(String columnName) throws SQLException
```

Gets the value of the designated column as a byte in the Java programming language.

RETURNS:
the value of column *columnIndex* (or *columnName*) as a byte or 0 if the value is SQL NULL

EXAMPLE:
```
byte b = rs.getByte(5);
```
or
```
byte b = rs.getByte("Completed");
```

getBytes

```
byte[] getBytes(int columnIndex) throws SQLException
byte[] getBytes(String columnName) throws SQLException
```

Gets the value of the designated column as an array of bytes in the Java programming language.

RETURNS:
the value of column *columnIndex* (or *columnName*) as a byte array or null if the value is SQL NULL. The bytes represent the raw values returned by the driver.

EXAMPLE:
```
byte[] b = rs.getBytes(1);
```
or
```
byte[] b = rs.getBytes("Code");
```

getCharacterStream

2.0

```
java.io.Reader getCharacterStream(int columnIndex) throws SQLException
```

```
java.io.Reader getCharacterStream(String columnName)
                                            throws SQLException
```

Gets the value stored in the designated column and returns it as a java.io.Reader object in the Java programming language.

RETURNS:
the value of column *columnIndex* (or *columnName*) as a java.io.Reader object. If the value is SQL NULL, getCharacterStream will return null.

EXAMPLE:
```
java.io.Reader reader = rs.getCharacterStream(4);
```
or
```
java.io.Reader reader = rs.getCharacterStream("Notes");
```

`2.0` getClob

```
clob getClob(int columnIndex) throws SQLException
clob getClob(String columnName) throws SQLException
```

Gets the SQL CLOB value stored in the designated column and returns it as a Clob object in the Java programming language.

RETURNS:
the value of column *columnIndex* (or *columnName*) as a Clob object. If the value is SQL NULL, getClob will return null.

EXAMPLE:
```
Clob summary = rs.getClob(4);
```
or
```
Clob summary = rs.getClob("Summary");
```

`2.0` getConcurrency

```
int getConcurrency() throws SQLException
```

Gets the concurrency type for this ResultSet object. The concurrency was set by the Statement object that produced this ResultSet object.

The possible concurrency types are the constants CONCUR_READ_ONLY and CONCUR_UPDATABLE.

RETURNS:

the concurrency type of this result set

EXAMPLE:

```
int type = rs.getConcurrency();
// type will be either ResultSet.CONCUR_READ_ONLY or
// ResultSet.CONCUR_UPDATABLE
```

SEE:

"Concurrency Types," on page 701

getCursorName

```
String getCursorName() throws SQLException
```

Retrieves the SQL name for the cursor associated with this ResultSet object. If the method Statement.setCursorName was called before the Statement object created this result set, getCursorName should always return the name specified in Statement.setCursorName. If a DBMS supports positioned update/delete, and if the method Statement.setCursorName has not been called to specify a cursor name, the JDBC driver or underlying DBMS must generate a cursor name when a SELECT . . . FOR UPDATE statement is executed.

In SQL, a result table is retrieved through a named cursor. The current row of a result set can be updated or deleted using a positioned update or positioned delete statement that references the cursor name. JDBC supports this SQL feature by providing the name of the SQL cursor used by a ResultSet. The current row of a ResultSet is also the current row of this SQL cursor. The cursor remains valid until the ResultSet object or its parent Statement object is closed. If the cursor's SELECT statement (the query that produced this ResultSet object) is not of the form "SELECT . . . FROM . . . WHERE . . . FOR UPDATE . . .", a positioned update or delete may fail.

If positioned update is not supported, an SQLException is thrown.

New methods added in the JDBC 2.0 core API make positioned updates and deletes much easier and make named cursors unnecessary. In result sets that are updatable, the ResultSet.updater methods perform positioned updates, and the ResultSet.deleteRow method performs positioned deletes.

RETURNS:

the SQL name of the cursor associated with this ResultSet object; null if this ResultSet object is read-only and its cursor name has not been specified with the `Statement.setCursorName` method

EXAMPLE:
```
String s = rs.getCursorName();
```

getDate

```
java.sql.Date getDate(int columnIndex) throws SQLException
java.sql.Date getDate(String columnName) throws SQLException
```

Retrieves the value of the designated column as a `java.sql.Date` object. When the database does not provide time zone information, the driver uses the default time zone (the time zone of the Virtual Machine running the application) to construct the `Date` object.

RETURNS:
the value of column *columnIndex* (or *columnName*) as a `java.sql.Date` object or `null` if the value is SQL `NULL`

EXAMPLE:
```
Date d = rs.getDate(1);
```
or
```
Date d = rs.getDate("Deadline");
```

2.0   getDate

```
java.sql.Date getDate(int columnIndex, java.util.Calendar cal)
                                              throws SQLException
```

```
java.sql.Date getDate(String columnName, java.util.Calendar cal)
                                              throws SQLException
```

Gets the value of the designated column as a `java.sql.Date` object, using *cal* to construct an appropriate millisecond value for the `Date` object, when the underlying database does not store time zone information.

PARAMETERS:
cal   the `Calendar` object the driver will use to construct the `Date` object

RETURNS:
the value of column *columnIndex* (or *columnName*) as a java.sql.Date object or null if the value is SQL NULL

EXAMPLE:
```
java.util.Calendar cal = java.util.Calendar.getInstance();
java.util.TimeZone tz = java.util.TimeZone.getTimeZone("JST");
// sets tz to Japan Standard Time
cal.setTimeZone(tz);
Date d = rs.getDate(1, cal);
```
or
```
Date d = rs.getDate("Deadline", cal)
// d is a millisecond value calculated for Japan Standard Time
```

getDouble

```
double getDouble(int columnIndex) throws SQLException
double getDouble(String columnName) throws SQLException
```

Gets the value of the designated column as a double.

RETURNS:
the value of column *columnIndex* (or *columnName*) as a double in the Java programming language; 0 if the value is SQL NULL

EXAMPLE:
```
double d = rs.getDouble(3);
```
or
```
double d = rs.getDouble("Square_Root");
```

getFetchDirection

2.0

```
int getFetchDirection() throws SQLException
```

Gets the direction suggested to the driver as the direction in which to fetch rows from the database. The possible fetch directions are FETCH_FORWARD, FETCH_REVERSE, and FETCH_UNKNOWN.

RETURNS:
the fetch direction for this result set

EXAMPLE:
```
int direction = rs.getFetchDirection();
```

SEE:
"Providing Performance Hints," on page 704

getFetchSize

```
int getFetchSize() throws SQLException
```

Gets the number of rows suggested to the driver as the number of rows to fetch from the database when more rows are needed for this `ResultSet` object.

RETURNS:
the fetch size for this result set

EXAMPLE:
```
int size = rs.getFetchSize();
```

SEE:
"Providing Performance Hints," on page 704

getFloat

```
float getFloat(int columnIndex) throws SQLException
float getFloat(String columnName) throws SQLException
```

Gets the value of the designated column as a `float`.

RETURNS:
the value of column *columnIndex* (or *columnName*) as a `float` in the Java programming language; 0 if the value is SQL NULL

EXAMPLE:
```
float f = rs.getFloat(2);
```
or
```
float f = rs.getFloat("Cost");
```

getInt

```
int getInt(int columnIndex) throws SQLException
int getInt(String columnName) throws SQLException
```

Gets the value of the designated column as an int.

RETURNS:
the value of column *columnIndex* (or *columnName*) as an int in the Java programming language; 0 if the value is SQL NULL

EXAMPLE:
```
int x = rs.getInt(1);
```
or
```
int x = rs.getInt("EmployeeID");
```

getLong

```
long getLong(int columnIndex) throws SQLException
long getLong(String columnName) throws SQLException
```

Retrieves the value of the designated column as a long.

RETURNS:
the value of column *columnIndex* (or *columnName*) as a long in the Java programming language; 0 if the value is SQL NULL

EXAMPLE:
```
long q = rs.getLong(4);
```
or
```
long q = rs.getLong("Time_in_Secs");
```

getMetaData

```
ResultSetMetaData getMetaData() throws SQLException
```

Retrieves a ResultSetMetaData object that contains the number, types, and properties of this ResultSet object's columns.

RETURNS:
a ResultSetMetaData object containing information about this ResultSet object's columns

EXAMPLE:
ResultSetMetaData rsmd = rs.getMetaData();

int count = rsmd.getColumnCount();

// count represents the number of columns in rs

SEE:
ResultSetMetaData

getObject

Object **getObject**(int *columnIndex*) throws SQLException

Object **getObject**(String *columnName*) throws SQLException

Gets the value of the column *columnIndex* (or *columnName*) as an Object in the Java programming language. Unless there is a custom mapping, the data type of the object returned by getObject will be the default Java Object type corresponding to the column's JDBC type. The table "JDBC Types Mapped to Java Object Types," on page 1089, shows the default Java Object types that getObject will return for each JDBC type.

This method may be used to retrieve any data type. It is especially useful when an application wants to be generic and thus needs to be able to read any data type. Also, it is the only method that can read abstract data types that are specific to a particular database.

If the value in the specified column is an SQL UDT and the type map associated with the connection has an entry for it, the driver will use the custom mapping instead of the standard mapping.

RETURNS:
the value of column *columnIndex* (or *columnName*) as a java.lang.Object or null if the value is SQL NULL

EXAMPLE:
Object info = rs.getObject(2);

or

Object info = rs.getObject("Info");

SEE:
the table "JDBC Types Mapped to Java Object Types," on page 1089

getObject

2.0

```
Object getObject(int columnIndex, java.util.Map map)
                                        throws SQLException
Object getObject(String columnName, java.util.Map map)
                                        throws SQLException
```

Gets the value of the column *columnIndex* (or *columnName*) as an Object in the Java programming language using *map* to map an SQL UDT value to a class in the Java programming language. If *map* does not contain an entry for the value in the specified column, the driver will use the standard mapping. This method is used when an application wants to override the type map associated with the connection. Note that when a type map is supplied, getObject never uses the type map associated with the connection.

PARAMETERS:

map   a java.util.Map object that contains the mapping from SQL type names to classes in the Java programming language

RETURNS:
the value of column *columnIndex* (or *columnName*) as a java.lang.Object; null if the value is SQL NULL

EXAMPLE:
```
Address addr = (Address)rs.getObject(3, map);
```
or
```
Address addr = (Address)rs.getObject("ADDRESS", map);
// addr is an instance of the class Address, the class to which the
// UDT retrieved from the third column of rs (the column named
// ADDRESS) is mapped
```

SEE:
"Creating a Custom Mapping," on page 896

getRef

2.0

```
Ref getRef(int columnIndex) throws SQLException
Ref getRef(String columnName) throws SQLException
```

Gets the SQL REF<*structured-type*> value stored in the designated column and returns it as a Ref object in the Java programming language.

RETURNS:
a Ref object that represents the SQL REF value in column *columnIndex* (or *col-umnName*). If the value is SQL NULL, getRef returns null.

EXAMPLE:
```
Ref emp = rs.getRef(4);
```
or
```
Ref emp = rs.getRef("EMPLOYEE");
```

SEE:
"Ref Overview," on page 679

getRow

`2.0`

```
int getRow() throws SQLException
```

Retrieves the number of the current row in this ResultSet object. The first row is number 1, the second is 2, and so on.

RETURNS:
the number of the current row; 0 if there is no current row

EXAMPLE:
```
int n = rs.getRow();
```

getShort

```
short getShort(int columnIndex) throws SQLException
short getShort(String columnName) throws SQLException
```

Gets the value of the designated column as a short.

RETURNS:
the value of column *columnIndex* (or *columnName*) as a short in the Java programming language; 0 if the value is SQL NULL

EXAMPLE:
```
short age = rs.getShort(3);
```
or
```
short age = rs.getShort("AGE");
```

getStatement

2.0

```
Statement getStatement() throws SQLException
```

Retrieves the Statement object that produced this ResultSet object. Some result sets, for example those that are the return value for a DatabaseMetaData method, are not produced by a query and therefore have no Statement object to return.

RETURNS:
the Statement object that produced this ResultSet object or null if the result set was produced some other way

EXAMPLE:
```
Statement st = rs.getStatement();
```

getString

```
String getString(int columnIndex) throws SQLException
String getString(String columnName) throws SQLException
```

Retrieves the value of the designated column as a String object. If the column value is the fixed-length type JDBC CHAR, the String object returned will have exactly the same value the JDBC CHAR value had in the database, including any padding added by the database.

RETURNS:
the value of column *columnIndex* (or *columnName*) as a java.lang.String object in the Java programming language or null if the value is SQL NULL

EXAMPLE:
```
String lastName = rs.getString(2);
```
or
```
String lastName = rs.getString("LAST_NAME");
```

getTime

```
java.sql.Time getTime(int columnIndex) throws SQLException
java.sql.Time getTime(String columnName) throws SQLException
```

Retrieves the value of the designated column as a java.sql.Time object. When the DBMS does not provide time zone information, the driver uses the default time zone (the time zone of the Virtual Machine running the application) to construct the Time object.

RETURNS:
the value of column *columnIndex* (or *columnName*) as a java.sql.Time object or null if the value is SQL NULL

EXAMPLE:
```
Time start = rs.getTime(3);

or

Time start = rs.getTime("Start_Time");
```

⌜2.0⌟   getTime

```
java.sql.Time getTime(int columnIndex, java.util.Calendar cal)
                                            throws SQLException
java.sql.Time getTime(String columnName, java.util.Calendar cal)
                                            throws SQLException
```

Retrieves the value of the designated column as a Time object, using *cal* to construct an appropriate millisecond value for the Time object when the underlying database does not store time zone information.

PARAMETERS:

cal   the Calendar object the driver will use to construct the Time object if the DBMS does not supply time zone information

RETURNS:
the value of column *columnIndex* (or *columnName*) as a java.sql.Time object; null if the value is SQL NULL

EXAMPLE:
```
java.util.Calendar cal = java.util.Calendar.getInstance();
java.util.TimeZone tz = java.util.TimeZone.getTimeZone("CTT");
// sets tz to China Taiwan Time
cal.setTimeZone(tz);
Time deadline = rs.getTime(1, cal);
or
```

```
Time deadline = rs.getTime("Deadline", cal)
// deadline is a millisecond value calculated for China Taiwan Time
```

getTimestamp

```
java.sql.Timestamp getTimestamp(int columnIndex) throws SQLException
java.sql.Timestamp getTimestamp(String columnName) throws SQLException
```

Retrieves the value of the designated column as a `Timestamp` object. When the DBMS does not provide a time zone, the driver uses the default time zone (the time zone of the Virtual Machine running the application) to construct the `Timestamp` object.

RETURNS:
the value of column *columnIndex* (or *columnName*) as a java.sql.Timestamp object; null if the value is SQL NULL

EXAMPLE:
```
Timestamp recd = rs.getTimestamp(3);
```
or
```
Timestamp recd = rs.getTimestamp("Received");
```

getTimestamp

`2.0`

```
java.sql.Timestamp getTimestamp(int columnIndex,
                    java.util.Calendar cal) throws SQLException
java.sql.Timestamp getTimestamp(String columnName,
                    java.util.Calendar cal) throws SQLException
```

Retrieves the value of the designated column as a `Timestamp` object, using *cal* to construct an appropriate millisecond value for the `Timestamp` object when the underlying database does not store time zone information.

PARAMETERS:

cal   the Calendar object the driver will use to construct the Timestamp object if the DBMS does not provide time zone information

RETURNS:
the value of column *columnIndex* (or *columnName*) as a java.sql.Timestamp object; null if the value is SQL NULL

EXAMPLE:
```
java.util.Calendar cal = java.util.Calendar.getInstance();
java.util.TimeZone tz = java.util.TimeZone.getTimeZone("ECT");
// sets tz to European Central Time
cal.setTimeZone(tz);
Timestamp start = rs.getTimestamp(3, cal);
```
or
```
Timestamp start = rs.getTimestamp("Start_Time", cal)
// start is a millisecond value calculated for European Central Time
```

getType

`int getType() throws SQLException`

Retrieves the type of this ResultSet object. The Statement object that produced this result set determined its type.

RETURNS:
one of the following ResultSet constants: TYPE_FORWARD_ONLY, TYPE_SCROLL_INSENSITIVE, or TYPE_SCROLL_SENSITIVE

EXAMPLE:
```
int type = rs.getType();
// type is ResultSet.TYPE_FORWARD_ONLY,
// ResultSet.TYPE_SCROLL_INSENSITIVE, or
// ResultSet.TYPE_SCROLL_SENSITIVE
```

SEE:
"Types of Result Sets," on page 700, for result set types

getUnicodeStream   DEPRECATED

```
java.io.InputStream getUnicodeStream(int columnIndex)
                                            throws SQLException
java.io.InputStream getUnicodeStream(String columnName)
                                            throws SQLException
```

Retrieves a column value as a stream of two-byte Unicode characters that can later be read in chunks from the stream. This method is particularly suitable for retrieving large LONGVARCHAR values. The JDBC driver will do any necessary conversion from the database format into Unicode. The first byte of a Unicode character is the high byte, with the second byte being the low byte.

All the data in the returned stream must be read prior to getting the value of any other column because the next call to a getter method implicitly closes the stream.

NOTE: This method has been deprecated. Use the method getCharacter-Stream instead.

RETURNS:
a Java input stream that delivers the database column value as a stream of two-byte Unicode characters. If the value is SQL NULL, getUnicodeStream returns null.

EXAMPLE:
```
java.io.InputStream in = rs.getUnicodeStream(2);
```
or
```
java.io.InputStream in = rs.getUnicodeStream("Comments_German");
```

getURL

java.net.URL **getURL**(int *columnIndex*) throws SQLException
java.net.URL **getURL**(String *columnName*) throws SQLException

Retrieves the value of the designated column as a java.net.URL object.

RETURNS:
the value of column *columnIndex* (or *columnName*) as a java.net.URL object; null if the value is SQL NULL

THROWS:
SQLException if the URL is malformed

EXAMPLE:
```
java.net.URL url = rs.getURL(3);
```
or
```
java.net.URL url = rs.getURL("URL");
```

getWarnings

SQLWarning **getWarnings**() throws SQLException

Gets the first SQLWarning that has been reported for this ResultSet object. Subsequent warnings, if there are any, are chained to the first warning. The warning chain is automatically cleared each time a new row is read.

NOTE: This warning chain covers only warnings caused by ResultSet methods. Any warning caused by Statement methods (such as CallableStatement.getter methods for reading OUT parameters) will be chained on the Statement object.

RETURNS:
the first SQLWarning or null if there are no warnings

EXAMPLE:
SQLWarning w = rs.getWarnings();

insertRow

2.0

void **insertRow**() throws SQLException

Inserts the contents of the insert row into this ResultSet object and also into the database. The cursor must be on the insert row when this method is called.

EXAMPLE:
rs.insertRow();

THROWS:
SQLException if (1) the method insertRow was called when the cursor was not on the insert row, (2) no value has been given to a column in the insert row that is non-nullable or that does not have a default value, or (3) the concurrency of this ResultSet object is CONCUR_READ_ONLY

SEE:
"Inserting Rows," on page 712

isAfterLast

2.0

```
boolean isAfterLast() throws SQLException
```

Determines whether the cursor is after the last row in this `ResultSet` object.

This method should be called only on `ResultSet` objects that are scrollable (type `TYPE_SCROLL_SENSITIVE` or `TYPE_SCROLL_INSENSITIVE`).

RETURNS:
`true` if the cursor is after the last row in this result set; `false` otherwise or if this result set contains no rows

THROWS:
`SQLException` if the type of this `ResultSet` object is `TYPE_FORWARD_ONLY`

EXAMPLE:
```
boolean b = rs.isAfterLast();
```

isBeforeFirst

2.0

```
boolean isBeforeFirst() throws SQLException
```

Determines whether the cursor is before the first row in this `ResultSet` object.

This method should be called only on `ResultSet` objects that are scrollable (type `TYPE_SCROLL_SENSITIVE` or `TYPE_SCROLL_INSENSITIVE`).

RETURNS:
`true` if the cursor is before the first row in this result set; `false` otherwise or if this result set contains no rows

THROWS:
`SQLException` if the type of this `ResultSet` object is `TYPE_FORWARD_ONLY`

EXAMPLE:
```
boolean b = rs.isBeforeFirst();
```

isFirst

2.0

```
boolean isFirst() throws SQLException
```

Determines whether the cursor is on the first row in this ResultSet object.

This method should be called only on ResultSet objects that are scrollable (type TYPE_SCROLL_SENSITIVE or TYPE_SCROLL_INSENSITIVE).

RETURNS:
true if the cursor is on the first row in this result set; false otherwise

THROWS:
SQLException if the type of this ResultSet object is TYPE_FORWARD_ONLY

EXAMPLE:
boolean b = rs.isFirst();

isLast
`2.0`

```
boolean isLast() throws SQLException
```

Determines whether the cursor is on the last row in this ResultSet object.

This method should be called only on ResultSet objects that are scrollable (type TYPE_SCROLL_SENSITIVE or TYPE_SCROLL_INSENSITIVE).

RETURNS:
true if the cursor is on the last row in this result set; false otherwise

THROWS:
SQLException if the type of this ResultSet object is TYPE_FORWARD_ONLY

EXAMPLE:
boolean b = rs.isLast();

last
`2.0`

```
boolean last() throws SQLException
```

Moves the cursor to the last row in this ResultSet object.

This method should be called only on ResultSet objects that are scrollable (type TYPE_SCROLL_SENSITIVE or TYPE_SCROLL_INSENSITIVE).

RETURNS:
true if the cursor is on a valid row in this result set; false otherwise or if there are no rows in this result set

THROWS:
SQLException if the type of this ResultSet object is TYPE_FORWARD_ONLY

EXAMPLE:
boolean b = rs.last();

moveToCurrentRow

2.0

void **moveToCurrentRow**() throws SQLException

Moves the cursor to the remembered cursor position in this ResultSet object, usually the current row.

This method should be called only when the cursor is on the insert row and has no effect if the cursor is not on the insert row.

This method throws an SQLException if it is called on a ResultSet object that is not updatable (is not concurrency type CONCUR_UPDATABLE).

THROWS:
SQLException if the concurrency type of this ResultSet object is CONCUR_READ_ONLY

EXAMPLE:
rs.moveToCurrentRow();

moveToInsertRow

2.0

void **moveToInsertRow**() throws SQLException

Moves the cursor to the insert row for this ResultSet object. While the cursor is on the insert row, the result set remembers what the current position was before the cursor moved to the insert row.

The insert row, a special row associated with an updatable result set, is essentially a buffer where a new row may be constructed by calling updater methods to set the value for each column in the row. After each call to the method moveToInsertRow, it is required that all of the columns in a result set be given a value, after which the method insertRow may be called to insert the row into the result set as well as into the database.

While the cursor is on the insert row, only certain methods may be called: the updater methods, the getter methods, insertRow, and cursor placement methods. An updater method must be called on a column before a getter method can be called on that column.

This method should be called only on ResultSet objects that are updatable (concurrency level CONCUR_UPDATABLE).

THROWS:
SQLException if the concurrency level of this ResultSet object is CONCUR_READ_ONLY

EXAMPLE:
rs.moveToInsertRow();

next

---

boolean **next**() throws SQLException

Initially moves the cursor to the first row of this ResultSet object, with subsequent calls moving the cursor to the second row, the third row, and so on. If a getter method is called before the first call to next, an exception will be thrown. An exception will also be thrown if a getter method is called after the method next returns false.

This method returns false when there are no more rows to read, which makes it possible to use it in a while loop.

If an input stream from the previous row is open, a call to the method next will implicitly close it.

The ResultSet object's warning chain is cleared when a new row is read; that is, the warning chain is cleared each time the method next is called.

RETURNS:
true if the move to the next row was successful; false if there are no more rows

EXAMPLE:
```
ResultSet rs = stmt.executeQuery("SELECT a, b, c FROM Table1");
while (rs.next()) {
    // retrieve data with getter methods as long as next()
    // returns true (there is a valid current row)
}
```

previous

2.0

```
boolean previous() throws SQLException
```

Moves the cursor to the previous row in this `ResultSet` object.

This method should be called only on `ResultSet` objects that are scrollable (type `TYPE_SCROLL_SENSITIVE` or `TYPE_SCROLL_INSENSITIVE`).

RETURNS:
`true` if the cursor is on a valid row in this result set; `false` otherwise

THROWS:
`SQLException` if the type of this `ResultSet` object is `TYPE_FORWARD_ONLY`

EXAMPLE:
```
// iterate through rs in reverse order
rs.afterLast();
while (rs.previous()) {
    rs.get. . .(2); // retrieve column values and do something
    . . .
}
```

refreshRow

2.0

```
void refreshRow() throws SQLException
```

Replaces the values in the current row of this `ResultSet` object with their current values in the database. This method provides an explicit way for an application to tell the driver to refetch a row or rows from the database.

If the fetch size is greater than one, the driver may refetch multiple rows at once. All values are refetched subject to the transaction isolation level and cursor sensitivity of the result set. If `refreshRow` is called after calling `updater` but before calling `updateRow`, then the updates made to the row are lost. In many cases, calling the method `refreshRow` will slow performance.

This method is not supported for `ResultSet` objects that are type `TYPE_FORWARD_ONLY`, and it does nothing for those that are type `TYPE_SCROLL_INSENSITIVE`.

THROWS:
`SQLException` if this method is called when the cursor is on the insert row or if the concurrency of this `ResultSet` object is `CONCUR_READ_ONLY`

EXAMPLE:
rs.refreshRow();

SEE:
"Refetching a Row," on page 720

2.0   **relative**

---

boolean **relative**(int *rows*) throws SQLException

Moves the cursor *rows* rows relative to the current row (the current cursor position) in this ResultSet object. The number or rows may be positive, negative, or 0.

If *rows* is positive, the cursor is moved forward (toward the end of the result set). If the cursor is less than the specified number or rows from the last row, the cursor is positioned after the last row.

If *rows* is negative, the cursor is moved backward (toward the beginning of the result set). If the cursor is less than *rows* rows from the first row, the cursor is positioned before the first row.

If *rows* is 0, the cursor's position does not change.

A call to the method relative(-1) is equivalent to a call to the method previous; similarly, a call to the method relative(1) is equivalent to calling the method next.

This method should be called only on ResultSet objects that are scrollable (type TYPE_SCROLL_SENSITIVE or TYPE_SCROLL_INSENSITIVE). If this method is called on a ResultSet object that is TYPE_FORWARD_ONLY, it throws an SQLException.

PARAMETERS:

rows   the number of rows to move the cursor, starting at the current row. If *rows* is positive, the cursor moves forward; if *rows* is negative, the cursor moves backward; if *rows* is 0, the cursor does not move.

RETURNS:
true if the cursor is on a row in this ResultSet object; false if it is before the first row or after the last row

THROWS:
SQLException if (1) there is no current row or (2) the type of this ResultSet object is TYPE_FORWARD_ONLY

```
boolean b = rs.relative(-5);
// If the current row is between 1 and 5 inclusive, b will be false,
// and the cursor will be before the first row of rs.
```

rowDeleted

2.0

```
boolean rowDeleted() throws SQLException
```

Determines whether the current row in this ResultSet object has been deleted. A deleted row may leave a visible "hole" (an empty row that serves as a placeholder for the deleted row) in the result set.

This method will always return false if this ResultSet object cannot detect deletions.

RETURNS:
true if both of the following are true: (1) the row has been deleted and (2) this ResultSet object can detect deletions; false otherwise

THROWS:
SQLException if the concurrency of this ResultSet object is CONCUR_READ_ONLY

EXAMPLE:
```
boolean b = rs.rowDeleted();
```

SEE:
DatabaseMetaData.deletesAreDetected
"Detecting Changes," on page 719

rowInserted

2.0

```
boolean rowInserted() throws SQLException
```

Determines whether the current row in this ResultSet object has been inserted. This method will always return false if this ResultSet object cannot detect visible insertions.

RETURNS:
true if both of the following are true: (1) the row has been inserted and (2) this ResultSet object can detect insertions; false otherwise

THROWS:
SQLException if the concurrency of this ResultSet object is CONCUR_READ_ONLY

EXAMPLE:
boolean b = rs.rowInserted();

SEE:
DatabaseMetaData.insertsAreDetected
"Detecting Changes," on page 719

2.0   rowUpdated

boolean **rowUpdated**() throws SQLException

Determines whether the current row in this ResultSet object has been updated. This method will always return false if this ResultSet object cannot detect updates.

RETURNS:
true if both of the following are true: (1) the row has been visibly updated by the owner or someone else and (2) this ResultSet object can detect updates; false otherwise

THROWS:
SQLException if the concurrency of this ResultSet object is CONCUR_READ_ONLY

EXAMPLE:
boolean b = rs.rowUpdated();

SEE:
DatabaseMetaData.updatesAreDetected
"Detecting Changes," on page 719

2.0   setFetchDirection

void **setFetchDirection**(int *direction*) throws SQLException

Gives the driver a hint as to the direction in which the rows of this ResultSet object should be processed. The initial value is set by the Statement object that produced the result set. This method may be used at any time to change the suggested fetch direction.

This method should be called only on ResultSet objects that are scrollable (type TYPE_SCROLL_SENSITIVE or TYPE_SCROLL_INSENSITIVE).

PARAMETERS:

direction	one of the ResultSet constants to suggest the direction in which rows should be processed: FETCH_FORWARD, FETCH_REVERSE, or FETCH_UNKNOWN

THROWS:
SQLException if the type of this ResultSet object is TYPE_FORWARD_ONLY

EXAMPLE:
```
boolean b = rs.setFetchDirection(ResultSet.FETCH_FORWARD);
```

SEE:
"Providing Performance Hints," on page 704

setFetchSize

2.0

```
void setFetchSize(int rows) throws SQLException
```

Gives the driver a hint as to the number of rows that should be fetched from the database when more rows are needed for this ResultSet object. If *rows* is 0, the JDBC driver ignores the value and is free to make its own best guess as to what the fetch size should be. The initial value is set by the Statement object that produced the result set. This method may be used at any time to change the suggested fetch size.

PARAMETERS:

rows	an int indicating the number of rows to fetch at a time. This number must be 0 or more and not exceed the number of rows set as a limit for this ResultSet object by the Statement object that produced it.

EXAMPLE:
```
boolean b = rs.setFetchSize(25);
```

SEE:
"Providing Performance Hints," on page 704

updateArray

3.0

```
void updateArray(int columnIndex, Array x) throws SQLException
void updateArray(String columnName, Array x) throws SQLException
```

Updates the designated column with *x*, the given `Array` object in the Java programming language.

This method may be called to update column values in the current row or the insert row. It does not, however, update values in the underlying database. Updating the database requires a call to the method `updateRow` if the cursor is on the current row or `insertRow` if the cursor is on the insert row.

PARAMETERS:

x   the new `Array` object to which the column value is to be set

EXAMPLE:
```
rs.updateArray(8, x);
```

or

```
rs.updateArray("Scores", x);
```

updateAsciiStream

```
void updateAsciiStream(int columnIndex, java.io.InputStream x,
                              int length) throws SQLException
void updateAsciiStream(String columnName, java.io.InputStream x,
                              int length) throws SQLException
```

Updates the designated column with *x*, a `java.io.InputStream` object that is *length* characters long. Note that the length of the new stream must be supplied because it is required by some DBMSs.

This method may be called to update column values in the current row or the insert row. It does not, however, update values in the underlying database. Updating the database requires a call to the method `updateRow` if the cursor is on the current row or `insertRow` if the cursor is on the insert row.

PARAMETERS:

x   the `java.io.InputStream` object to which the column value is to be set

length   the length of the stream *x* in one-byte ASCII characters

THROWS:
`SQLException` if the concurrency of this `ResultSet` object is `CONCUR_READ_ONLY`

EXAMPLE:
```
java.io.InputStream in = rs.updateAsciiStream(3, x, 4096);
```

or

```
java.io.InputStream in = rs.updateAsciiStream("Comments", x, 4096);
```

updateBigDecimal

2.0

```
void updateBigDecimal(int columnIndex, java.math.BigDecimal x)
                                            throws SQLException
void updateBigDecimal(String columnName, java.math.BigDecimal x)
                                            throws SQLException
```

Updates the designated column with *x*, a java.math.BigDecimal object.

This method may be called to update column values in the current row or the insert row. It does not, however, update values in the underlying database. Updating the database requires a call to the method updateRow if the cursor is on the current row or insertRow if the cursor is on the insert row.

PARAMETERS:

x   the new java.math.BigDecimal object to which the column value is to be set

THROWS:

SQLException if the concurrency of this ResultSet object is CONCUR_READ_ONLY

EXAMPLE:
```
rs.updateBigDecimal(2, x);
```
or
```
rs.updateBigDecimal("Results", x);
```

updateBinaryStream

2.0

```
void updateBinaryStream(int columnIndex, java.io.InputStream x,
                            int length) throws SQLException
void updateBinaryStream(String columnName, java.io.InputStream x,
                            int length) throws SQLException
```

Updates the designated column with *x*, a java.io.InputStream object that is *length* bytes long. Note that the length of the new stream must be supplied because it is required by some DBMSs.

This method may be called to update column values in the current row or the insert row. It does not, however, update values in the underlying database. Updating the database requires a call to the method updateRow if the cursor is on the current row or insertRow if the cursor is on the insert row.

PARAMETERS:

x   the `java.io.InputStream` object to which the column
                                      value is to be set

length   the length of the stream *x* in bytes

THROWS:

`SQLException` if the concurrency of this `ResultSet` object is CONCUR_READ_ONLY

EXAMPLE:

`java.io.InputStream in = rs.updateBinaryStream(4, x, 1024);`

or

`java.io.InputStream in = rs.updateBinaryStream("Data", x, 1024);`

---

updateBlob
3.0

`void updateBlob(int columnIndex, Blob x) throws SQLException`
`void updateBlob(String columnName, Blob x) throws SQLException`

Updates the designated column with *x*, the given `Blob` object in the Java
programming language.

This method may be called to update column values in the current row or
the insert row. It does not, however, update values in the underlying database.
Updating the database requires a call to the method `updateRow` if the cursor is
on the current row or `insertRow` if the cursor is on the insert row.

PARAMETERS:

x   the new `Blob` object to which the column value is to be
                                      set

EXAMPLE:

`rs.updateBlob(3, x);`

or

`rs.updateBlob("Bin_data", x);`

---

updateBoolean
2.0

`void updateBoolean(int columnIndex, boolean x) throws SQLException`
`void updateBoolean(String columnName, boolean x) throws SQLException`

Updates the designated column with *x*, a `boolean` value in the Java programming language.

This method may be called to update column values in the current row or the insert row. It does not, however, update values in the underlying database. Updating the database requires a call to the method updateRow if the cursor is on the current row or insertRow if the cursor is on the insert row.

PARAMETERS:

x   the new boolean value to which the column value is to be set

THROWS:

SQLException if the concurrency of this ResultSet object is CONCUR_READ_ONLY

EXAMPLE:
```
rs.updateBoolean(8, x);
```
or
```
rs.updateBoolean("Checked", x);
```

updateByte

2.0

```
void updateByte(int columnIndex, byte x) throws SQLException
void updateByte(String columnName, byte x) throws SQLException
```

Updates the designated column with *x*, a byte value in the Java programming language.

This method may be called to update column values in the current row or the insert row. It does not, however, update values in the underlying database. Updating the database requires a call to the method updateRow if the cursor is on the current row or insertRow if the cursor is on the insert row.

PARAMETERS:

x   the new byte value to which the column value is to be set

THROWS:

SQLException if the concurrency of this ResultSet object is CONCUR_READ_ONLY

EXAMPLE:
```
rs.updateByte(5, x);
```
or
```
rs.updateByte("On", x);
```

updateBytes

2.0

```
void updateBytes(int columnIndex, byte [] x) throws SQLException
void updateBytes(String columnName, byte [] x) throws SQLException
```

Updates the designated column with *x*, a byte array object in the Java programming language.

This method may be called to update column values in the current row or the insert row. It does not, however, update values in the underlying database. Updating the database requires a call to the method updateRow if the cursor is on the current row or insertRow if the cursor is on the insert row.

PARAMETERS:

x   the new byte array value to which the column value is to be set

THROWS:

SQLException if the concurrency of this ResultSet object is CONCUR_READ_ONLY

EXAMPLE:

```
rs.updateBytes(5, x);
```

or

```
rs.updateBytes("On", x);
```

updateCharacterStream

2.0

```
void updateCharacterStream(int columnIndex, java.io.Reader x,
                               int length) throws SQLException
void updateCharacterStream(String columnName, java.io.Reader x,
                               int length) throws SQLException
```

Updates the designated column with *x*, a java.io.Reader object that is *length* characters long. Note that the length of the new stream must be supplied because it is required by some DBMSs.

This method may be called to update column values in the current row or the insert row. It does not, however, update values in the underlying database. Updating the database requires a call to the method updateRow if the cursor is on the current row or insertRow if the cursor is on the insert row.

PARAMETERS:

x   the java.io.InputStream object to which the column value is to be set *length*   the length of the stream *x* in characters

THROWS:

SQLException if the concurrency of this ResultSet object is CONCUR_READ_ONLY

EXAMPLE:

```
rs.updateCharacterStream(2, x, 2048);
```

or

```
rs.updateCharacterStream("Summary", x, 2048);
```

updateClob

3.0

```
void updateClob(int columnIndex, Clob x) throws SQLException
void updateClob(String columnName, Clob x) throws SQLException
```

Updates the designated column with *x*, the given Clob object in the Java programming language.

This method may be called to update column values in the current row or the insert row. It does not, however, update values in the underlying database. Updating the database requires a call to the method updateRow if the cursor is on the current row or insertRow if the cursor is on the insert row.

PARAMETERS:

x   the new Clob object to which the column value is to be set

EXAMPLE:

```
rs.updateClob(1, x);
```

or

```
rs.updateClob("Char_data", x);
```

updateDate

2.0

```
void updateDate(int columnIndex, java.sql.Date x)
                                        throws SQLException
void updateDate(String columnName, java.sql.Date x)
                                        throws SQLException
```

Updates the designated column with *x*, a java.sql.Date object in the Java programming language. To calculate the millisecond value of the date, the driver will use the time zone of the Virtual Machine running the application if the DBMS does not provide time zone information.

This method may be called to update column values in the current row or the insert row. It does not, however, update values in the underlying database. Updating the database requires a call to the method updateRow (if the cursor is on the current row) or insertRow (if the cursor is on the insert row).

PARAMETERS:

x   the new java.sql.Date value to which the column value is to be set

THROWS:
SQLException if the concurrency of this ResultSet object is CONCUR_READ_ONLY

EXAMPLE:
```
rs.updateDate(5, x);
```
or
```
rs.updateDate("HIRE_DATE", x);
```

updateDouble

```
void updateDouble(int columnIndex, double x) throws SQLException
void updateDouble(String columnName, double x) throws SQLException
```

Updates the designated column with x, a double value in the Java programming language.

This method may be called to update column values in the current row or the insert row. It does not, however, update values in the underlying database. Updating the database requires a call to the method updateRow (if the cursor is on the current row) or insertRow (if the cursor is on the insert row).

PARAMETERS:

x   the new double value to which the column value is to be set

THROWS:
SQLException if the concurrency of this ResultSet object is CONCUR_READ_ONLY

EXAMPLE:
```
rs.updateDouble(7, x);
```
or
```
rs.updateDouble("MILLIMETERS", x);
```

updateFloat

2.0

```
void updateFloat(int columnIndex, float x) throws SQLException
void updateFloat(String columnName, float x) throws SQLException
```

Updates the designated column with *x*, a `float` value in the Java programming language.

This method may be called to update column values in the current row or the insert row. It does not, however, update values in the underlying database. Updating the database requires a call to the method `updateRow` (if the cursor is on the current row) or `insertRow` (if the cursor is on the insert row).

PARAMETERS:

x	the new `float` value to which the column value is to be set

THROWS:

`SQLException` if the concurrency of this `ResultSet` object is `CONCUR_READ_ONLY`

EXAMPLE:
```
rs.updateFloat(7, 903.49103f);
```
or
```
rs.updateFloat("AVERAGE", 76011.2f);
```

updateInt

2.0

```
void updateInt(int columnIndex, int x) throws SQLException
void updateInt(String columnName, int x) throws SQLException
```

Updates the designated column with *x*, an `int` value in the Java programming language.

This method may be called to update column values in the current row or the insert row. It does not, however, update values in the underlying database. Updating the database requires a call to the method `updateRow` (if the cursor is on the current row) or `insertRow` (if the cursor is on the insert row).

PARAMETERS:

x	the new `int` value to which the column value is to be set

THROWS:

`SQLException` if the concurrency of this `ResultSet` object is `CONCUR_READ_ONLY`

EXAMPLE:
```
rs.updateInt(7, x);
```
or
```
rs.updateInt("UNITS", x);
```

updateLong

```
void updateLong(int columnIndex, long x) throws SQLException
void updateLong(String columnName, long x) throws SQLException
```

Updates the designated column with *x*, a long value in the Java programming language.

This method may be called to update column values in the current row or the insert row. It does not, however, update values in the underlying database. Updating the database requires a call to the method updateRow (if the cursor is on the current row) or insertRow (if the cursor is on the insert row).

PARAMETERS:

x   the new long value to which the column value is to be set

THROWS:

SQLException if the concurrency of this ResultSet object is CONCUR_READ_ONLY

EXAMPLE:
```
rs.updateLong(7, x);
```
or
```
rs.updateLong("MILLISECONDS", x);
```

updateNull

```
void updateNull(int columnIndex) throws SQLException
void updateNull(String columnName) throws SQLException
```

Updates the designated nullable column with a null value in the Java programming language.

This method may be called to update column values in the current row or the insert row. It does not, however, update values in the underlying database. Updating the database requires a call to the method updateRow (if the cursor is on the current row) or insertRow (if the cursor is on the insert row).

THROWS:
SQLException if the concurrency of this ResultSet object is CONCUR_READ_ONLY

EXAMPLE:
```
rs.updateNull(3);
```
or
```
rs.updateNull("COMPLETION_DATE");
```

updateObject   `2.0`

```
void updateObject(int columnIndex, java.lang.Object x, int scale)
                                              throws SQLException
void updateObject(String columnName, java.lang.Object x, int scale)
                                              throws SQLException
```

Updates the designated column with *x*, a *java.lang.Object* value in the Java programming language. This version of the method getObject should be used for updating values that are JDBC DECIMAL or NUMERIC types.

This method may be called to update column values in the current row or the insert row. It does not, however, update values in the underlying database. Updating the database requires a call to the method updateRow (if the cursor is on the current row) or insertRow (if the cursor is on the insert row).

PARAMETERS:

x   the new java.lang.Object value to which the column value is to be set

scale   the number of digits after the decimal point. The scale applies only to the JDBC types java.sql.Types.DECIMAL and java.sql.Types.NUMERIC; for all other types, this value is ignored.

THROWS:
SQLException if the concurrency of this ResultSet object is CONCUR_READ_ONLY

EXAMPLE:
```
rs.updateObject(7, x, 4);
```
or
```
rs.updateObject("STATS", x, 4);
// If the object in column 7 (the column named STATS) is JDBC type
// DECIMAL or NUMERIC, it will have four digits after the decimal
// point
```

updateObject

```
void updateObject(int columnIndex, java.lang.Object x)
                                            throws SQLException
void updateObject(String columnName, java.lang.Object x)
                                            throws SQLException
```

Updates the designated column with *x*, a *java.lang.Object* value in the Java programming language.

This method may be called to update column values in the current row or the insert row. It does not, however, update values in the underlying database. Updating the database requires a call to the method updateRow (if the cursor is on the current row) or insertRow (if the cursor is on the insert row).

PARAMETERS:

x   the new java.lang.Object value to which the column value is to be set

THROWS:

SQLException if the concurrency of this ResultSet object is CONCUR_READ_ONLY

EXAMPLE:
```
rs.updateObject(7, x);
```
or
```
rs.updateObject("STATS", x);
```

updateRef

```
void updateRef(int columnIndex, Ref x) throws SQLException
void updateRef(String columnName, Ref x) throws SQLException
```

Updates the designated column with *x*, the given Ref object in the Java programming language.

This method may be called to update column values in the current row or the insert row. It does not, however, update values in the underlying database. Updating the database requires a call to the method updateRow if the cursor is on the current row or insertRow if the cursor is on the insert row.

PARAMETERS:

x   the new Ref object to which the column value is to be set

EXAMPLE:
```
rs.updateRef(3, x);
```
or
```
rs.updateRef("ADDRESS", x);
```

updateRow

2.0

```
void updateRow() throws SQLException
```

Updates the underlying database with the new contents of the current row.

This method is called after updater methods have been called to update column values. It must be called when the cursor is on the current row; an exception will be thrown if it is called when the cursor is on the insert row.

THROWS:
SQLException if this method is invoked while the cursor is on the insert row or if the concurrency of this ResultSet object is CONCUR_READ_ONLY

EXAMPLE:
```
rs.updateRow();
```

updateShort

2.0

```
void updateShort(int columnIndex, short x) throws SQLException
void updateShort(String columnName, short x) throws SQLException
```

Updates the designated column with x, a short value in the Java programming language.

This method may be called to update column values in the current row or the insert row. It does not, however, update values in the underlying database. Updating the database requires a call to the method updateRow (if the cursor is on the current row) or insertRow (if the cursor is on the insert row).

PARAMETERS:

x   the new short value to which the column value is to be set

THROWS:
SQLException if the concurrency of this ResultSet object is CONCUR_READ_ONLY

EXAMPLE:
rs.updateShort(5, x);

or

rs.updateShort("AGE", x);

updateString

void **updateString**(int *columnIndex*, String *x*) throws SQLException
void **updateString**(String *columnName*, String *x*) throws SQLException

Updates the designated column with *x*, a String object in the Java programming language.

This method may be called to update column values in the current row or the insert row. It does not, however, update values in the underlying database. Updating the database requires a call to the method updateRow (if the cursor is on the current row) or insertRow (if the cursor is on the insert row).

PARAMETERS:

x   the new String object to which the column value is to be set

THROWS:
SQLException if the concurrency of this ResultSet object is CONCUR_READ_ONLY

EXAMPLE:
rs.updateString(1, x);

or

rs.updateString("NAME", x);

updateTime

void **updateTime**(int *columnIndex*, java.sql.Time *x*)
                                                              throws SQLException
void **updateTime**(String *columnName*, java.sql.Time *x*)
                                                              throws SQLException

Updates the designated column with *x*, a java.sql.Time object. This method uses the time zone of the Virtual Machine running the application to calculate the time if the DBMS does not supply a time zone.

This method may be called to update column values in the current row or the insert row. It does not, however, update values in the underlying database. Updating the database requires a call to the method updateRow (if the cursor is on the current row) or insertRow (if the cursor is on the insert row).

PARAMETERS:

x   the new java.sql.Time value to which the column val-
                                     ue is to be set

THROWS:

SQLException if the concurrency of this ResultSet object is CONCUR_READ_ONLY

EXAMPLE:
```
rs.updateTime(3, x);
```
or
```
rs.updateTime("TIME", x);
```

updateTimestamp

2.0

```
void updateTimestamp(int columnIndex, java.sql.Timestamp x)
                                            throws SQLException
void updateTimestamp(String columnName, java.sql.Timestamp x)
                                            throws SQLException
```

Updates the designated column with x, a java.sql.Timestamp object. This method uses the time zone of the Virtual Machine running the application to calculate the timestamp if the DBMS does not supply a time zone.

This method may be called to update column values in the current row or the insert row. It does not, however, update values in the underlying database. Updating the database requires a call to the method updateRow (if the cursor is on the current row) or insertRow (if the cursor is on the insert row).

PARAMETERS:

x   the new java.sql.Timestamp value to which the col-
                                     umn value is to be set

THROWS:

SQLException if the concurrency of this ResultSet object is CONCUR_READ_ONLY

EXAMPLE:
```
rs.updateTimestamp(3, x);
```
or
```
rs.updateTimestamp("TIMESTAMP", x);
```

wasNull

```
boolean wasNull() throws SQLException
```

Checks to see if the last value read was SQL NULL or not. Note that a ResultSet.getter method should be called on a column before wasNull is called to determine if the value read was SQL NULL.

RETURNS:
true if the last value read was SQL NULL; false otherwise

EXAMPLE:
```
ResultSet rs = stmt.executeQuery("SELECT a, b, c FROM Table1");
while (rs.next()) {
    int x = rs.getInt(1);
    if (rs.wasNull()) {  // check to see if x was SQL NULL
        // do something if x was SQL NULL
    }else {
        // do something else if x was not SQL NULL
    }
    String s = rs.getString(2); // if s = null, it was SQL NULL
    Date d = rs.getDate(3); // if d = null, it was SQL NULL
}
```

27.4 ResultSet Fields

The fields defined in the interface ResultSet are constants used as both method parameters and method return values.

The constants CONCUR_READ_ONLY and CONCUR_UPDATABLE, which indicate the concurrency type of a result set, can be supplied as parameters when a Connection object creates a statement with the methods createStatement, prepareStatement, or prepareCall. These constants are the possible return values for the ResultSet method getConcurrency.

The ResultSet constants TYPE_FORWARD_ONLY, TYPE_SCROLL_INSENSITIVE, and TYPE_SCROLL_SENSITIVE designate the type of a result set. One of these constants can be supplied when a Connection object creates a statement with the methods createStatement, prepareStatement, or prepareCall. These constants are the possible return values for the ResultSet method getType.

The constants FETCH_FORWARD, FETCH_REVERSE, and FETCH_UNKNOWN are used as hints to the driver and indicate the direction in which it is suggested that rows be fetched from the database. A `Statement` object calls the method `setFetchDirection`, supplying it with one of these constants, to set the default hint for `ResultSet` objects that its queries produce. A `ResultSet` object can, at any time, call the method `setFetchDirection`, supplying it with one of these constants, to change its fetch direction. These constants are the possible return values for the `getFetchDirection` method in both the `Statement` and `ResultSet` interfaces.

CLOSE_CURSORS_AT_COMMIT

`public static final int CLOSE_CURSORS_AT_COMMIT = 2`

Specifies that the `ResultSet` object is to be closed after the transaction in which it was created is committed.

SEE:
"Result Set Holdability," on page 702

CONCUR_READ_ONLY

`public static final int CONCUR_READ_ONLY = 1007`

Specifies that a `ResultSet` object cannot be updated and offers the highest possible level of concurrency.

SEE:
"Concurrency Types," on page 701

CONCUR_UPDATABLE

`public static final int CONCUR_UPDATABLE = 1008`

Specifies that a `ResultSet` object can be updated and offers a limited level of concurrency.

SEE:
"Concurrency Types," on page 701

FETCH_FORWARD

```
public static final int FETCH_FORWARD = 1000
```

Specifies that a hint to the driver be to fetch rows from the database in a forward direction (from top to bottom) when a ResultSet object needs more rows.

SEE:
"Providing Performance Hints," on page 704

FETCH_REVERSE

```
public static final int FETCH_REVERSE = 1001
```

Specifies that a hint to the driver be to fetch rows from the database in a reverse direction (from bottom to top) when a ResultSet object needs more rows.

SEE:
"Providing Performance Hints," on page 704

FETCH_UNKNOWN

```
public static final int FETCH_UNKNOWN = 1002
```

Specifies that the direction in which the driver should fetch rows from the database is unknown.

SEE:
"Providing Performance Hints," on page 704

HOLD_CURSORS_OVER_COMMIT

```
public static final int HOLD_CURSORS_OVER_COMMIT = 1
```

Specifies that the ResultSet object is to be kept open after the transaction in which it was created is committed.

SEE:
"Result Set Holdability," on page 702

TYPE_FORWARD_ONLY

`public static final int TYPE_FORWARD_ONLY = 1003`

Specifies that the `ResultSet` object is not scrollable; results must be retrieved from the top row down, and a row cannot be visited more than once.

SEE:
"Creating Different Types of Result Sets," on page 705
"Visibility of Changes Made by Others," on page 716

TYPE_SCROLL_INSENSITIVE

`public static final int TYPE_SCROLL_INSENSITIVE = 1004`

Specifies that the `ResultSet` object is scrollable and generally not sensitive to changes made while it is open.

SEE:
"Creating Different Types of Result Sets," on page 705
"Visibility of Changes Made by Others," on page 716

TYPE_SCROLL_SENSITIVE

`public static final int TYPE_SCROLL_SENSITIVE = 1005`

Specifies that the `ResultSet` object is scrollable and sensitive to changes made while it is open.

SEE:
"Creating Different Types of Result Sets," on page 705
"Visibility of Changes Made by Others," on page 716

CHAPTER **28**

ResultSetMetaData

28.1 `ResultSetMetaData` Overview

THE interface `ResultSetMetaData` provides information about the types and properties of the columns in a `ResultSet` object. Because the `RowSet` interface extends the `ResultSet` interface, a `ResultSetMetaData` object also provides information about a `RowSet` object's columns.

The information about a `ResultSet` object's columns that is contained in a `ResultSetMetaData` object is accessed by calling various `ResultSetMetaData` methods. Each method retrieves a particular piece of information about the `ResultSet` object's columns. The variables defined in `ResultSetMetaData` are constants that are the possible return values for the method `isNullable`.

28.1.1 Creating a `ResultSetMetaData` Object

The following code fragment, where *stmt* is a `Statement` object, illustrates creating a `ResultSetMetaData` object:

```
ResultSet rs = stmt.executeQuery("SELECT a, b, c FROM Table1");
ResultSetMetaData rsmd = rs.getMetaData();
```

The variable *rsmd* contains a `ResultSetMetaData` object that can be used for invoking `ResultSetMetaData` methods in order to get information about the `ResultSet` object *rs*.

28.1.2   Using `ResultSetMetaData`

Using the `ResultSetMetaData` object *rsmd* just created, the following method prints out the JDBC type and database name of that type for each column in the `ResultSet` object *rs*.

```
public static void printColumnTypes() throws SQLException {
    int numberOfColumns = rsmd.getColumnCount();
    for (int i=1; i <= numberOfColumns; i++) {
        int jdbcType = rsmd.getColumnType(i);
        String name = rsmd.getColumnTypeName(i);
        System.out.print("Column " + i + " is JDBC type " + jdbcType);
        System.out.println(", which is DBMS type " + name);
    }
}
```

The output for this code fragment might look something like the following:

```
➥ Column 1 is JDBC type 12, which is DBMS type VARCHAR
➥ Column 2 is JDBC type 4, which is DBMS type INTEGER
➥ Column 3 is JDBC type 8, which is DBMS type DOUBLE PRECISION
```

The number of columns should be three because the SELECT statement that created the result set *rs* specified three column names (*a*, *b*, and *c*). So, in this case, it is not really necessary to invoke the method `getColumnCount`. However, by doing so, the method `printColumnTypes` is more general purpose because it can be used when the number of columns is not known at compile time. If, for example, the user did not already know the number of columns in `Table1` and the query that produced the `ResultSet` *rs* was SELECT * FROM TABLE1, invoking the method `get-ColumnCount` would be necessary to determine the number of columns.

The `ResultSetMetaData` interface is especially useful in the case where the method `Statement.execute` has been used to execute an SQL statement for which the number and kind of results are not known at compile time. In such a case, a programmer could, for example, use `ResultSetMetaData` methods to ascertain which getter methods in the `ResultSet` interface to use for retrieving data. "Getting Column Type Information," on page 199, has sample code that illustrates getting the JDBC type of a result set column. When the JDBC type is known, Table 50.6, "Conversions by `ResultSet` getter Methods," on page 1092, can be used to determine which getter method to use.

If a query is executed by a `RowSetEvent`, `PreparedStatement`, or `CallableStatement` object, the method `PreparedStatement.getMetaData` may be called to get information about the result set that the query will return. The advantage of using `PreparedStatement.getMetaData` instead of `ResultSet.getMetaData` is that the method can be invoked before the query is executed. See "Using `ResultSetMetaData` Features," on page 206, for an explanation and example. Note, however, that calling the method `PreparedStatement.getMetaData` may be expensive for the driver to implement if the DBMS does not support this feature.

28.2 `ResultSetMetaData` Interface Definition

```
package java.sql;
public interface ResultSetMetaData {
    int getColumnCount() throws SQLException;
    boolean isAutoIncrement(int column) throws SQLException;
    boolean isCaseSensitive(int column) throws SQLException;
    boolean isCurrency(int column) throws SQLException;
    int isNullable(int column) throws SQLException;
    boolean isSigned(int column) throws SQLException;
    boolean isSearchable(int column) throws SQLException;
    int getColumnDisplaySize(int column) throws SQLException;
    String getColumnLabel(int column) throws SQLException;
    String getColumnName(int column) throws SQLException;
    String getColumnClassName(int column) throws SQLException;
    String getSchemaName(int column) throws SQLException;
    int getPrecision(int column) throws SQLException;
    int getScale(int column) throws SQLException;
    String getTableName(int column) throws SQLException;
    String getCatalogName(int column) throws SQLException;
    int getColumnType(int column) throws SQLException;
    String getColumnTypeName(int column) throws SQLException;
    boolean isReadOnly(int column) throws SQLException;
```

```
boolean isWritable(int column) throws SQLException;
boolean isDefinitelyWritable(int column) throws SQLException;


//-------------------------------------------------------------------
//         Possible return values for the method isNullable:
//-------------------------------------------------------------------


    int columnNoNulls         = 0;
    int columnNullable        = 1;
    int columnNullableUnknown = 2;
}
```

28.3 ResultSetMetaData Methods

getCatalogName

```
String getCatalogName(int column) throws SQLException
```

Gets the catalog name for the table from which column *column* of this
ResultSet was derived.

Because this feature is not widely supported, the return value for many
DBMSs will be an empty string.

PARAMETERS:

column   1 is the first column, 2 the second, and so on

RETURNS:

a String object representing the catalog name or "" if not applicable

EXAMPLE:

```
String s = rsmd.getCatalogName(1);
```

getColumnClassName

```
String getColumnClassName(int column) throws SQLException
```

     Gets the fully qualified name of the Java class to which a value in column *column* will be mapped. For example, the class name for `int` is `java.lang.Integer`, and the class name for a user-defined type with a custom mapping is the Java class that implements `SQLData`. If there is a custom mapping, when the method `ResultSet.getObject` is called to retrieve a value from column *column*, it will manufacture an instance of this class or one of its subclasses.

PARAMETERS:
column   1 is the first column, 2 the second, and so on

RETURNS:
a `String` object representing the fully qualified name of the Java class to which a value in the designated column will be mapped

EXAMPLE:
```
String s = rsmd.getColumnClassName(5);
```

getColumnCount

```
int getColumnCount() throws SQLException
```

     Gets the number of columns in the `ResultSet` object for which this `ResultSetMetaData` object stores information.

RETURNS:
an `int` indicating the number of columns in the `ResultSet` object

EXAMPLE:
```
ResultSetMetaData rsmd = rs.getMetaData();
int n = rsmd.getColumnCount();
// n contains the number of columns in the ResultSet object rs
```

getColumnDisplaySize

```
int getColumnDisplaySize(int column) throws SQLException
```

Gets the normal maximum width in characters for column *column*.

PARAMETERS:
column   1 is the first column, 2 the second, and so on.

RETURNS:
an `int` indicating the maximum width in characters

EXAMPLE:
`int n = rsmd.getColumnDisplaySize(1);`

getColumnLabel

`String getColumnLabel(int column) throws SQLException`

Gets the suggested column title for column *column,* to be used in print-outs and displays.

PARAMETERS:
column   1 is the first column, 2 the second, and so on

RETURNS:
a `String` object representing the suggested column title for use in printouts and displays

EXAMPLE:
`String s = rsmd.getColumnLabel(2);`

getColumnName

`String getColumnName(int column) throws SQLException`

Gets the name of column *column*.

PARAMETERS:
column   1 is the first column, 2 the second, and so on

RETURNS:
a `String` object representing the column name

EXAMPLE:
```
String s = rsmd.getColumnName(4);
```

getColumnType

```
int getColumnType(int column) throws SQLException
```

Gets the JDBC type (from the class java.sql.Types) for the value stored in column *column*. If the column type is one of the SQL99 data types, this method returns the corresponding new type code added to the JDBC 2.0 core API. The STRUCT and DISTINCT type codes are always returned for structured and distinct types, regardless of whether the value will be mapped according to the standard mapping or be custom mapped.

PARAMETERS:

column   1 is the first column, 2 the second, and so on

RETURNS:

an int (a constant defined in the class java.sql.Types) indicating the JDBC type of values in the designated column

EXAMPLE:
```
int n = rsmd.getColumnType(1);
// if the first column is a JDBC VARCHAR, n will be 12, which is the
// int value assigned to VARCHAR in the class java.sql.Types
```

SEE:
```
java.sql.Types
```

getColumnTypeName

```
String getColumnTypeName(int column) throws SQLException
```

Gets the type name used by this particular data source for the value stored in column *column*. If the type code for the type of value stored in column *column* is STRUCT, DISTINCT, or JAVA_OBJECT, this method returns a fully qualified SQL type name.

PARAMETERS:

column   1 is the first column, 2 the second, and so on

RETURNS:

a `String` object representing the type name used by the database. For SQL99 data types, this method returns the following:

Column Type	Column Type Name
JAVA_OBJECT	the SQL name of the Java type
DISTINCT	the SQL name of the distinct type
STRUCT	the SQL name of the structured type
ARRAY	data source-dependent type name
BLOB	data source-dependent type name
CLOB	data source-dependent type name
REF	data source-dependent type name

EXAMPLE:

```
String s = rsmd.getColumnTypeName(2);
```

getPrecision

```
int getPrecision(int column) throws SQLException
```

For number types, `getPrecision` gets the number of decimal digits in column *column*. For character types, it gets the maximum length in characters for column *column*. For binary types, it gets the maximum length in bytes for column *column*.

PARAMETERS:

column   1 is the first column, 2 the second, and so on

RETURNS:

an `int` indicating the number of decimal digits for number types, the maximum number of characters for character types, or the maximum number of bytes for binary types

EXAMPLE:

```
int n = rsmd.getPrecision(1);
```

getScale

```
int getScale(int column) throws SQLException
```

Gets the number of digits to the right of the decimal point for values in column *column*.

PARAMETERS:
column   1 is the first column, 2 the second, and so on

RETURNS:
an `int` indicating the number of digits to the right of the decimal point

EXAMPLE:
```
int n = rsmd.getScale(5);
```

getSchemaName

```
String getSchemaName(int column) throws SQLException
```

Gets the schema name for the table from which column *column* of this `ResultSet` was derived.

Because this feature is not widely supported, the return value for many DBMSs will be an empty string.

PARAMETERS:
column   1 is the first column, 2 the second, and so on

RETURNS:
a `String` object representing the schema name or "" if not applicable

EXAMPLE:
```
String s = rsmd.getSchemaName(1);
```

getTableName

```
String getTableName(int column) throws SQLException
```

Gets the name of the table from which column *column* of this `ResultSet` was derived, or "" if there is none (for example, for a join).

Because this feature is not widely supported, the return value for many DBMSs will be an empty string.

PARAMETERS:

column   1 is the first column, 2 the second, and so on

RETURNS:

a `String` object representing the table name or "" if not applicable

EXAMPLE:

```
String s = rsmd.getTableName(3);
```

isAutoIncrement

```
boolean isAutoIncrement(int column) throws SQLException
```

Checks whether column *column* is automatically numbered, which makes it read-only.

PARAMETERS:

column   1 is the first column, 2 the second, and so on

RETURNS:

true if so; `false` otherwise

EXAMPLE:

```
boolean b = rsmd.isAutoIncrement(3);
```

isCaseSensitive

```
boolean isCaseSensitive(int column) throws SQLException
```

Checks whether column *column* is case sensitive.

PARAMETERS:

column   1 is the first column, 2 the second, and so on

RETURNS:

true if so; `false` otherwise

EXAMPLE:

```
boolean b = rsmd.isCaseSensitive(1);
```

isCurrency

```
boolean isCurrency(int column) throws SQLException
```

Checks whether column *column* is a cash value.

PARAMETERS:
column   1 is the first column, 2 the second, and so on

RETURNS:
true if so; false otherwise

EXAMPLE:
```
boolean b = rsmd.isCurrency(3);
```

isDefinitelyWritable

```
boolean isDefinitelyWritable(int column) throws SQLException
```

Checks whether a write on column *column* will definitely succeed.

PARAMETERS:
column   1 is the first column, 2 the second, and so on

RETURNS:
true if so; false otherwise

EXAMPLE:
```
boolean b = rsmd.isDefinitelyWritable(2);
```

isNullable

```
int isNullable(int column) throws SQLException
```

Checks whether a NULL can be stored in column *column*.

PARAMETERS:
column   1 is the first column, 2 the second, and so on

RETURNS:
one of the constants defined in ResultSetMetaData. Possible values are:

columnNoNulls	column does not allow Null values
columnNullable	column allows NULL values
columnNullableUnknown	nullability is unknown

EXAMPLE:
```
boolean b = rsmd.isNullable(2);
```

SEE:
```
ResultSetMetaData.columnNoNulls
ResultSetMetaData.columnNullable
ResultSetMetaData.columnNullableUnknown
```

isReadOnly

```
boolean isReadOnly(int column) throws SQLException
```

Checks whether column *column* is definitely not writable.

PARAMETERS:

column   1 is the first column, 2 the second, and so on

RETURNS:
true if so; false otherwise

EXAMPLE:
```
boolean b = rsmd.isReadOnly(3);
```

isSearchable

```
boolean isSearchable(int column) throws SQLException
```

Checks whether the value stored in column *column* can be used in a WHERE clause.

PARAMETERS:

column   1 is the first column, 2 the second, and so on

RETURNS:
true if so; false otherwise

EXAMPLE:
```
boolean b = rsmd.isSearchable(1);
```

isSigned

```
boolean isSigned(int column) throws SQLException
```

Checks whether the value stored in column *column* is a signed number.

PARAMETERS:
column   1 is the first column, 2 the second, and so on

RETURNS:
true if so; false otherwise

EXAMPLE:
```
boolean b = rsmd.isSigned(3);
```

isWritable

```
boolean isWritable(int column) throws SQLException
```

Checks whether it is possible for a write on column *column* to succeed.

PARAMETERS:
column   1 is the first column, 2 the second, and so on

RETURNS:
true if so; false otherwise

EXAMPLE:
```
boolean b = rsmd.isWritable(2);
```

28.4 ResultSetMetaData Fields

columnNoNulls

```
public final static int columnNoNulls = 0
```

A possible return value for the method isNullable.
Indicates that this column does not allow NULL values.

columnNullable

```
public final static int columnNullable = 1
```
> A possible return value for the method isNullable.
> Indicates that this column allows NULL values.

columnNullableUnknown

```
public final static int columnNullableUnknown = 2
```
> A possible return value for the method isNullable.
> Indicates that the nullability of this column is unknown.

CHAPTER 29

RowSet

29.1 RowSet Overview

A RowSet object is a container for tabular data, encapsulating a set of zero or more rows that have been retrieved from a data source. In a basic implementation of the RowSet interface, the rows are retrieved from a JDBC data source, but a rowset may be customized so that its data can also be from a spreadsheet, a flat file, or any other data source with a tabular format. A RowSet object extends the ResultSet interface, which means that it can be scrollable, can be updatable, and can do anything a ResultSet object can do. The features of a RowSet object, which are summarized in this introductory section, will be explained in detail in later sections.

A RowSet object differs from a ResultSet object in that it is a JavaBeans component. Thus, it has a set of JavaBeans properties and follows the JavaBeans event model. A RowSet object's properties allow it to establish its own database connection and to execute its own query in order to fill itself with data. A rowset may be *disconnected*, that is, function without maintaining an open connection to a data source the whole time it is in use. In addition, a rowset can be serialized, which means that it can be sent to a remote object over a network.

In general, the JDBC API can be divided into two categories, the RowSet portion and the driver portion. RowSet and its supporting interfaces are intended to be implemented using the rest of the JDBC API. In other words, a class that implements the RowSet interface is a layer of software that is said to execute "on top" of a JDBC driver. Unlike other JDBC objects, a RowSet object contains within itself the means to operate without a driver and without being connected to a data source.

When J2SE version 1.5 is released, there will be a third category. In addition to the RowSet API and the driver, there will be five standard implementations of the RowSet interface. These implementations provide a set of interfaces that extend the basic RowSet interface. By building on these interfaces, developers can be sure that their implementations follow the JDBC API in their event handling, cursor manipulation, and other operations. The standard implementations are discussed more fully in "Standard Implementations," on page 808.

The RowSet interface provides a basic set of methods common to all rowsets, which this section describes. A later section presents an example implementation that adds more specialized capabilities. All RowSet objects are JavaBeans components; therefore, the RowSet interface has methods for adding and removing an event listener, and it has get/set methods for all of its properties. Most of these properties support setting up a connection or executing a command. A rowset uses a connection with a data source in order to execute a query and produce a result set from which it will get its data. It may also use a connection to write modified data back to the data source. In addition, the RowSet interface has methods (one for each data type) for setting the values of input parameters, if any, in a RowSet object's command string.

Five other interfaces and one class work together with the RowSet interface behind the scenes. The class RowSetEvent and the interface RowSetListener support the JavaBeans event model. When a RowSet object's cursor moves or its data is modified, it will invoke the RowSetListener method corresponding to the event, providing it with a RowSetEvent object that identifies itself as the source of the event.

A component that wants to be notified of the events that occur in a RowSet object will implement the RowSetListener interface and be registered with the RowSet object. Such a component, called a *listener*, is typically a GUI (graphical user interface) component, such as a table or bar chart, that is displaying the RowSet object's data. Because a listener is notified every time an event occurs in the rowset, it can keep its cursor position and data consistent with that of the rowset.

The interfaces RowSetInternal, RowSetReader, and RowSetWriter support the rowset reader/writer facility. A *reader*, an instance of a class that implements the RowSetReader interface, reads data and inserts it into a rowset. A *writer*, an instance of a class that implements the RowSetWriter interface, writes modified data back to the data source from which a rowset's data was retrieved. A reader and writer, like listeners, are dynamically registered with a rowset.

A RowSet object that calls a reader or a writer must be an instance of a class that implements the RowSetInternal interface. This interface provides additional methods for a reader or writer to use to manipulate the rowset's internal state. For example, a rowset can keep track of its original values, and `RowSetInternal` methods allow the writer to see if the corresponding data in the data source has been changed by someone else. In addition, `RowSetInternal` methods make it possible to retrieve the input parameters that were set for a rowset's command string and to retrieve the connection that was passed to it, if there is one. Finally, `RowSetInternal` methods allow a reader to set a new `RowSetMetaData` object, which describes to the rowset the rows that the reader will insert into it.

Rowsets may be either *connected* or *disconnected*. A connected `RowSet` object maintains a connection to its data source the entire time it is in use, whereas a disconnected rowset is connected to its data source only while it is reading data from the data source or writing data to it. While the rowset is disconnected, it does not need a JDBC driver or the full implementation of the JDBC API. This makes it very lean and therefore an ideal container for sending a set of data to a thin client. The client can, if it chooses, make updates to the data and send the rowset back to the application server. On the server, the disconnected `RowSet` object uses its reader to make a connection to the data source and write data back to it. Exactly how this is done depends on how the reader is implemented. Typically, the reader delegates making a connection and reading/writing data to the JDBC driver.

29.1.1 The Event Model for Rowsets

The RowSet event model makes it possible for a Java object, or component, to be notified about events generated by a `RowSet` object. Setting up the notification mechanism involves both the component to be notified and the `RowSet` object itself. First, each component that wants to be notified of events must implement the `RowSetListener` interface. Then the `RowSet` object must register each component by adding it to its list of components that are to be notified of events. At this point, such a component is a *listener*, an instance of a class that implements the `RowSetListener` methods and is registered with a `RowSet` object.

Three kinds of events can occur in a `RowSet` object: its cursor can move, one of its rows can change (be inserted, deleted, or updated), or its entire contents can be changed. The `RowSetListener` methods `cursorMoved`, `rowChanged`, and `rowSetChanged` correspond to these events. When an event occurs, the rowset will create a `RowSetEvent` object that identifies itself as the source of the event. The appropriate `RowSetListener` method will be invoked on each listener, with the `RowSetEvent` object being passed to the method. This will inform all of the rowset's listeners about the event.

For example, if a pie chart component, *pieChart*, wants to display the data in the RowSet object *rset*, *pieChart* must implement the RowSetListener methods cursorMoved, rowChanged, and rowSetChanged. The implementations of these methods specify what *pieChart* will do in response to an event on *rset*. After implementing these methods, *pieChart* can be registered with *rset*. When *pieChart* is added as a listener to *rset*, it will be notified when an event occurs on *rset* by having the appropriate method invoked with a RowSetEvent object as its parameter. The listener *pieChart* can then update itself to reflect the current data and cursor position of *rset*. If *pieChart* does not need to reflect one of the events on *rset*, it can implement the RowSetListener method for that event so that it does nothing. For instance, if *pieChart* does not need to show the current cursor position in *rset*, it can have the method cursorMoved do nothing.

Any number of components may be listeners for a given RowSet object. If, for example, the bar graph component *barGraph* is also displaying the data in *rset*, it can become a listener by implementing the RowSetListener methods and then being registered with *rset*. The following lines of code register the two components *pieChart* and *barGraph* as listeners with *rset*.

```
rset.addRowSetListener(pieChart);
rset.addRowSetListener(barGraph);
```

Removing a listener is done in a similar fashion with the method RowSet.removeListener.

```
rset.removeRowSetListener(pieChart);
rset.removeRowSetListener(barGraph);
```

The code for setting up the listeners for a rowset is often generated by a tool, which means that an applications programmer only needs to specify a rowset and the components that are to be notified when an event occurs on that rowset. After the listeners are set up, the processing of an event is done largely behind the scenes. For example, if an application updates a row in *rset*, *rset* will internally create a RowSetEvent object and pass it to the rowChanged methods implemented by *pieChart* and *barGraph*. The listeners will know where the event occurred because the RowSetEvent object passed to rowChanged is initialized with *rset*, the RowSet object that is the source of the event. The components *pieChart* and *barGraph* will update their displays of the row according to their own implementations of the RowSetListener.rowChanged method.

In the following code fragment, *pieChart* and *barGraph* are registered as listeners with the RowSet object *rset*. After *rset* fills itself with new data by calling the method execute, event notification takes place behind the scenes. (The method execute will be explained in detail in the section "Executing a Command," on page 805.) As the first step in the event notification process, the RowSetEvent object *rsetEvent* is created and initialized with *rset*. Next the *pieChart* and *barGraph* versions of the method rowSetChanged are called with *rsetEvent* as their arguments. This tells *pieChart* and *barGraph* that all the data in *rset* has changed, and each listener will carry out its own implementation of the method rowSetChanged.

```
rset.addRowSetListener(pieChart);
rset.addRowSetListener(barGraph);
. . .
rset.execute();

// The following methods will be invoked behind the scenes:
    RowSetEvent rsetEvent = new RowSetEvent(this);
    pieChart.rowSetChanged(rsetEvent);
    barGraph.rowSetChanged(rsetEvent);
```

29.1.2 Properties for a Rowset

The RowSet interface provides a set of JavaBeans properties so that a RowSet instance can be configured to connect to a data source and retrieve a set of rows. Some properties may not be required, depending on particular implementations. For example, either a URL or a data source name is required for establishing a connection, so if one property is set, the other one is optional. If both are set, the one set more recently is used. If data for a rowset is being retrieved from a non-SQL data source that does not support commands, such as a spreadsheet, the command property does not need to be set. Setting some properties is optional if the default is already the desired property. For example, escape processing is on by default, so an application does not need to set escape processing unless it wants to disable it. (Escape processing is explained in "SQL Escape Syntax in Statements," on page 958.)

The following list gives the get and set methods defined on the RowSet interface for retrieving and setting a RowSet object's properties. The two exceptions are the methods `getConcurrency` and `getType`, which are inherited from the `Result-Set` interface rather than being defined in the `RowSet` interface.

```
getCommand                      setCommand
ResultSet.getConcurrency        setConcurrency
getDataSourceName               setDataSourceName
getEscapeProcessing             setEscapeProcessing
getMaxFieldSize                 setMaxFieldSize
getMaxRows                      setMaxRows
getPassword                     setPassword
getQueryTimeout                 setQueryTimeout
getTransactionIsolation         setTransactionIsolation
ResultSet.getType               setType
getTypeMap                      setTypeMap
getUrl                          setUrl
getUsername                     setUsername
```

In addition, the standard JDBC `RowSet` implementations have various properties that are specific to them.

The following code fragment, in which *rset* is a `RowSet` object, sets properties that are typically required for establishing a connection with a data source.

```
rset.setDataSourceName("jdbc/logicalDataSourceName");
rset.setUsername("fernanda");
rset.setPassword("secret");
```

Note that `jdbc/logicalDataSourceName` is the name that has been registered with a JNDI (Java Naming and Directory Interface) naming service. When an application gives the naming service the logical name, it will return the `DataSource` object that has been bound to the logical name. "Using JNDI," on page 568, explains using `DataSource` objects and the JNDI API. Using a `DataSource` object instead of hardcoding connection information makes code more portable and makes maintaining it much easier. If the host machine or port number of a data source changes, for example, only the properties of the `DataSource` object entered in the JNDI naming service need to be updated, not every application that gets a connection to that data source.

A `RowSet` object also has methods for setting properties that affect command execution. For example, as a sampling of these methods, the following code fragment sets twenty seconds as the longest a driver will wait for a statement to execute, sets 1024 as the largest number of rows *rset* may contain, and specifies that *rset* will be allowed to read only data from committed transactions.

```
rset.setQueryTimeout(20);
rset.setMaxRows(1024);
rset.setTransactionIsolation(
                    Connection.TRANSACTION_READ_COMMITTED);
```

The type and concurrency may also be set for a RowSet object, as shown in the following lines of code.

```
rset.setType(ResultSet.TYPE_SCROLL_INSENSITIVE);
rset.setConcurrency(ResultSet.CONCUR_UPDATABLE);
```

The first line sets *rset* to be scrollable but not sensitive to the updates made while it is open. A RowSet object that maintains a continuously open connection with a data source may be TYPE_SCROLL_SENSITIVE, but one that does not is incapable of being sensitive to changes made by other objects or transactions. The second line of code sets *rset* to be updatable, meaning that it can modify its data.

Note that a RowSet object may be scrollable even if it uses a driver that does not support scrollable result sets. In fact, a rowset may often be used in place of a regular result set as a way of getting a scrollable result set. This is discussed in more detail in the section "Traversing a RowSet Object," on page 804.

An application fills a RowSet instance with data by executing the RowSet object's command string. This string must be a query that, when executed, will produce a result set from which the RowSet object will get its data. The method setCommand sets the given argument as the command that will be executed when the method execute is invoked. For example, the following line of code sets the command string to a query that selects the name and salary from every row in the table EMPLOYEES.

```
rset.setCommand("SELECT NAME, SALARY FROM EMPLOYEES");
```

With the preceding command string set, after *rset* invokes its execute method, it will contain exactly the same data as the result set that the query produces (one row for each row in the table EMPLOYEES, with each row containing a name and a salary).

29.1.3 Setting Parameters for the Command String

The example in the previous section uses a command that has no placeholders for parameters, but the command property may also be set with a query that takes input parameters. Note that the parameters must be input parameters and not output parameters. Values for input parameters can then be set at run time, which, for example, allows an application to be interactive and accept user input.

The RowSet interface, like the PreparedStatement interface, has setter methods for setting the value of input parameters. There is a setter method for each data type, including the SQL99 data types. The following code fragment sets the command string and then sets its two input parameters with values. Assuming that the column DEPT stores values of type VARCHAR, the method setString is used to set both parameters because that is the appropriate method for setting VARCHAR values.

```
rset.setCommand(
    "SELECT NAME, SALARY FROM EMPLOYEES WHERE DEPT = ? OR DEPT = ?");
rset.setString(1, "SALES");
rset.setString(2, "MARKETING");
```

After this command is executed, *rset* will contain the names and salaries of the employees in the sales and marketing departments.

Any parameters in a RowSet object's command string must be set with values before the command is executed. When a rowset is disconnected, the parameters that have been set are used by the reader's readData method, which is invoked internally by the method execute. A rowset stores these parameter values in an internal array, and the readData method retrieves them with a call to the rowset's RowSetInternal.getParams method. See "Reading Data for a Disconnected Rowset," on page 882, for a more complete description of the readData method.

29.1.4 Traversing a RowSet Object

The javax.sql.RowSet interface extends the java.sql.ResultSet interface, so moving the cursor in a scrollable RowSet object is exactly the same as moving a cursor in a scrollable ResultSet object. A RowSet object inherits all of the ResultSet methods, so it is really a result set with added features that allow it to function as a JavaBeans component. Most components that use instances of RowSet are likely to treat them as ResultSet objects.

Even though the methods for moving a RowSet object's cursor are identical to those of a ResultSet object from the user's point of view, a RowSet object's implementation of these methods is different. A RowSet object needs to let the listeners registered with it know about each movement of its cursor. Consequently, the cursor movement methods for a RowSet object are implemented to trigger the internal event notification process. For example, when the method next is called, its implementation will create a RowSetEvent object and call each listener's cursor-Moved method, supplying the RowSetEvent object as the parameter. The listener uses the RowSetEvent object to find out in which RowSet object the cursor has moved and then invokes its implementation of the method cursorMoved. The implementation could do nothing, or it could, for example, call the method ResultSet.getRow to get the cursor's current position and update the listener's display of that row's data.

To demonstrate that cursor movements are the same in RowSet and ResultSet, the following code fragment iterates forward through the RowSet object *rset* and prints out the two values retrieved from each row.

```
rset.beforeFirst();
while (rset.next()) {
    System.out.println(rset.getString(1) + " " + rset.getFloat(2));
}
```

Other cursor movements are also identical to those in the ResultSet interface. See "Cursor Movement Examples," on page 693, for more examples of how to move a result set's, and therefore a rowset's, cursor.

29.1.5 Executing a Command

The RowSet interface provides the method execute, which is invoked to fill a RowSet object with data. There can be many variations in the implementation of this method, and subtypes may define additional methods for populating themselves with data. The execute method makes use of rowset properties and will throw an SQLException if the necessary properties have not been set. Standard properties have been defined; however, additional properties depend on each particular RowSet implementation, so developers should check the documentation for the implementation they are using.

A disconnected rowset may optionally support the reader/writer facility by supplying methods for registering a reader (an object that implements the RowSet-Reader interface) and a writer (an object that implements the RowSetWriter interface). Such a rowset must also implement the RowSetInternal interface to make additional access to its internal state available to the reader and writer. With its reader/writer framework in place, a rowset's execute method is able to delegate tasks to its reader and writer components.

With the addition of the standard `RowSet` implementations, developers will find it much easier to implement the reader/writer facilities. They will be able to leverage the reader/writer facilities that are already included in these standard implementations by simply incorporating them into their own implementations.

In a typical implementation, a disconnected rowset's `execute` method will invoke the reader's `readData` method to accomplish the job of reading new data into the rowset. Generally, after clearing the rowset of its current contents, the `readData` method will get the properties it needs and establish a connection with the data source. If there are any parameters to be set, `readData` retrieves them from the rowset and sets them appropriately in the rowset's command string. Then the `readData` method executes the command string to produce a result set. Finally, `readData` populates the rowset with the data from the result set.

The reader's `readData` method may also be implemented to set the rowset's metadata. One of the many possible implementations is to have the `readData` method create a `RowSetMetaData` object and set it with information about the columns in the data source that is about to be read. The `readData` method next sets the new `RowSetMetaData` object to be the one associated with the rowset. The rowset can then use the `RowSetMetaData` object to see the format for the data that will be read into it.

When the rowset's command string is executed, all of a rowset's listeners need to be notified so that they can take the appropriate action. The `execute` method will invoke the `rowSetChanged` method on each listener, supplying `rowSetChanged` with a newly created `RowSetEvent` object that identifies the `RowSet` object in which the event occurred. The notification of listeners is also invisible to the application programmer using a rowset.

One more task for the `execute` method is that of setting the "original" values maintained by the rowset. These are the values, returned by the method `RowSetInternal.getOriginal`, that the writer will use the next time changes are written to the data source backing the rowset. The writer may compare these values with the ones in the data source to determine whether a value that is being modified in the rowset has also been modified in the data source from which the rowset got its data. If the rowset's original values (pre-modification values) and the underlying data source's values are not the same, someone else has already made changes to the data source. Therefore, if the rowset changes a value, it will cause a conflict. If the values are the same, however, there is no conflict, and the writer may decide to write the new rowset values to the data source.

If the writer does write new values to the underlying data source, the `execute` method will reset the original values to be the values currently in the rowset. Then the next time execute is called, which changes all of the values in the rowset, the writer can retrieve the original values to compare with those in the underlying data source to see if there is a conflict.

In summary, when an application invokes the execute method, many operations take place behind the scenes. When the rowset is disconnected, the following take place: the contents of the rowset are replaced with new data, any listeners using the rowset's data are notified, the rowset's metadata is updated, and the rowset's original values are reset to the current data values. For a connected rowset, the execute method generally just populates the rowset with new data and notifies the listeners of the event.

29.1.6 Using a RowSet Object's Metadata

A RowSet object maintains a set of metadata about the columns it contains. Being derived from ResultSet, a RowSet object's metadata can be retrieved with Result-SetMetaData methods in the same way that a ResultSet object's metadata can. For instance, the following code fragment creates a ResultSetMetaData object for the RowSet object *rset* and finds out how many columns *rset* contains.

```
ResultSetMetaData rsetmd = rset.getMetaData();
int columnCount = rsetmd.getColumnCount();
```

The variable *rsetmd* contains information about the columns in the RowSet *rset*. Any of the ResultSetMetaData methods can be invoked on *rsetmd* to retrieve the information that *rsetmd* contains. See "Using ResultSetMetadata," starting on page 784, for more information and for examples of retrieving result set metadata information.

The interface RowSetMetaData defines set methods corresponding to each of the get methods defined in ResultSetMetaData (except that there are no methods for setting the class name for a column or for setting whether the column is read-only, possibly writable, or definitely writable). The RowSetMetaData.set methods are called by a reader after it has read new data into a rowset and created a new RowSetMetaData object for describing the new data's columns. The following code shows what a reader might do behind the scenes. It creates the new RowSetMeta-Data object *rowsetmd* for the RowSet object *rowset*, sets the information for the columns, and finally calls the RowSetInternal method setMetaData to set *rowsetmd* as the metadata for *rowset*.

```
rowset.execute();
// ... as part of its implementation, execute calls readData
reader.readData((RowSetInternal)this);

// ... as part of the implementation of readData, the reader for
// the rowset would do something like the following to update the
// metadata for the rowset
RowSetMetaData rowsetmd = new ...; // create an instance of a class
// that implements RowSetMetaData
rowsetmd.setColumnCount(3);
rowsetmd.setColumnType(1, Types.INTEGER);
rowsetmd.setColumnType(2, Types.VARCHAR);
rowsetmd.setColumnType(3, Types.BLOB);
// ... set other column information
rowset.setMetaData(rowsetmd);
```

29.2   Standard Implementations

The Java platform will include five standard implementations of the RowSet interface with the release of the J2SE, version 1.5. These implementations are being provided as an aid for those who want to write their own implementations. The RowSet
interface may be implemented in any number of ways to serve any number of different purposes, and anyone may implement it. The expectation is, however, that
RowSet implementations will be written mostly by driver vendors who may include
their implementations as part of their JDBC products.

The standard implementations consist of two parts, the interfaces and the reference implementations. The interfaces are in the javax.sql.rowset package; the
implementations are in the com.sun.rowset package. They are being developed
with input from experts in the database field through the Java Community Process
as JSR 114. The goal is to standardize key rowset functionality so that developers
can leverage it in their own implementations. The standard RowSet implementations are:

- JdbcRowSet
- CachedRowSet
- WebRowSet
- FilteredRowSet
- JoinRowSet

This section discusses each implementation in turn. As of this writing, the implementations are not final, but the general information presented here is highly unlikely to change.

29.2.1 Overview of the `JdbcRowSet` Implementation

The standard implementation of the `JdbcRowSet` interface is the basic `RowSet` implementation. Other more complex implementations start with the same features, so its implementation of the basic features can be used as a foundation upon which to build.

A `JdbcRowSetImpl` object (an instance of the standard implementation of the `JdbcRowSet` interface) is, like all rowsets, a container for a set of rows. The source of these rows is always a `ResultSet` object because a `JdbcRowSetImpl` object is a connected `RowSet` object. In other words, it always maintains a connection with a DBMS via a JDBC driver. Note that other implementations may use any tabular data, such as a flat file or a spreadsheet, as their source of data if their reader and writer facilities are appropriately implemented.

A `JdbcRowSetImpl` object has many uses. Probably the most common use is to make a `ResultSet` object scrollable and thereby make better use of legacy drivers that do not support scrolling. A `JdbcRowSetImpl` object's rows of data (and those in any `RowSet` object) are identical to those in the `ResultSet` object that is the result of executing the rowset's command. Therefore, if the rowset is scrollable, it is the equivalent of having a scrollable `ResultSet` object.

Another common use is to make the driver or a `ResultSet` object a JavaBeans component. Like all `RowSet` objects, a `JdbcRowSetImpl` object is a JavaBeans component. By being continuously connected to a driver, it serves as a wrapper for the driver, which effectively makes the driver a JavaBeans component. This means that a driver presented as a `JdbcRowSetImpl` object can be one of the Beans that a tool makes available for composing an application. Being continuously connected also means that a `JdbcRowSetImpl` object is able to serve as a wrapper for its `ResultSet` object. It can take calls invoked on it and, in turn, call them on its `ResultSet` object. As a consequence, the `ResultSet` object can be, for example, a component in a GUI application that uses Swing technology.

The following code fragment illustrates creating a `JdbcRowSetImpl` object, setting its properties, and executing the command string in its `command` property. The `JdbcRowSet` interface provides a default constructor, but being a JavaBeans component, a `JdbcRowSetImpl` object will probably most often be created by a visual JavaBeans development tool.

```
JdbcRowSetImpl jrs = new JdbcRowSetImpl();
jrs.setCommand("SELECT * FROM TITLES);
jrs.setURL("jdbc:myDriver:myAttribute");
jrs.setUsername("cervantes");
jrs.setPassword("sancho");
jrs.execute();
```

At this point, *jrs* contains all of the data in the table TITLES.

From this point on, the code can simply use ResultSet methods because it is effectively operating on a ResultSet object. It can navigate the rows in *jrs*, retrieve column values, update column values, insert new rows, and so on. For example, the next two lines of code go to the second row and retrieve the value in the first column using ResultSet methods.

```
jrs.absolute(2);
String title = jrs.getString(1);
```

29.2.2   Overview of the CachedRowSet Implementation

An instance of the standard CachedRowSet interface implementation (a com.sun.rowset.CachedRowSetImpl object) provides a container for a set of rows that is being cached outside of a data source. It is disconnected, serializable, updatable, and scrollable. Because a CachedRowSetImpl object caches its own data, it does not need to maintain an open connection with a data source and is disconnected from its data source except when it is reading or writing data. Because it stores its rows in memory, a CachedRowSetImpl object is not appropriate for storing extremely large data sets. A CachedRowSetImpl object can populate itself with data, and because it is updatable, it can also modify its data. As with all RowSet objects, in addition to getting data in, it can get data out, propagating its modifications back to the underlying data source.

As stated previously, the specification of the standard CachedRowSet interface and its implementation are not yet final, so the material presented here should be regarded as illustrative rather than definitive. However, the likelihood is that it will bear a very close resemblance to the final specification.

29.2.3   Uses for a CachedRowSet Object

Being disconnected and serializable, a CachedRowSet object is especially well suited for use with a thin client. Other implementations of a rowset may stay connected to a data source while they are in use and require the presence of a JDBC driver, thereby needing more resources.

One of the major uses envisioned for a `CachedRowSetImpl` instance is to pass tabular data between different components of a distributed application. It will probably be used extensively in EnterpriseJavaBeans™ (EJB™) components running in an application server. The server can use the JDBC API to retrieve a set of rows from a database and then use a `CachedRowSetImpl` object to send the data over the network to, for example, a thin client running in a web browser.

Another use for a `CachedRowSetImpl` object is to provide scrolling and updating capabilities to a `ResultSet` object that does not itself have this functionality. For example, as with a `JdbcRowSetImpl` object, an application can create a `CachedRowSetImpl` object initialized with the data from a `ResultSet` object and then operate on the rowset instead of the result set. With the rowset set to be scrollable and updatable, the application can move the cursor, make updates, and then propagate the updates back to the data source.

The following code fragment populates the `CachedRowSetImpl` object *crset* with the data from the `ResultSet` object *rs*.

```
ResultSet rs = stmt.executeQuery("SELECT * FROM AUTHORS");
CachedRowSetImpl crset = new CachedRowSetImpl();
crset.populate(rs);
```

Once the rowset is populated, an application can pass it across the network to be manipulated by distributed components, or it can operate on *crset* instead of *rs* to gain scrollability or updatability.

The `CachedRowSet` interface uses some of the basic API from the `JdbcRowSet` interface and adds additional methods for the additional functionality it needs. For example, it needs a way to connect to a data source and read data from it or write data to it. The reader and writer facilities, based on the `RowSetReader` and `RowSetWriter` interfaces, provide these capabilities.

An implementation of the `RowSetWriter` interface supplies a mechanism for updating the data source with any changes it has made while it was disconnected, thus making the modified data persistent. This can get complicated if there is a conflict, that is, if another user has already modified the same data in the data source.

Two different ways of synchronizing the data have been implemented to allow for using higher and lower levels of concurrency. Using a pessimistic concurrency model limits other users in their access to the data, which means that conflicts are much less likely or can be avoided altogether. An optimistic concurrency model assumes that there will be few conflicts and allows a greater level of access to other users. Both approaches are implemented as part of the RowSet Implementations specification, and a CachedRowSetImpl object can plug in the one that better serves its needs. Third parties can write other implementations, and a rowset may plug those in as well.

The implementation of the CachedRowSet interface can be used as a basis for implementing other disconnected rowsets. For example, the implementations of the WebRowSet, FilteredRowSet, and JoinRowSet interfaces are all based on the implementation of the CachedRowSet interface. Therefore, the following discussion of the CachedRowSet interface goes into some detail about the methods it defines and what they do. The sections on the other disconnected rowset implementations discuss the capabilities they have beyond those of the CachedRowSet implementation.

29.2.4 Creating a CachedRowSetImpl Object

Any RowSet object is a JavaBeans component, so developers will often create them using a visual JavaBeans development tool while they are assembling an application. It is also possible for an application to create an instance at run time, using a public constructor provided by a class that implements the RowSet interface. For example, the interface CachedRowSet defines a public default constructor, so an instance of CachedRowSetImpl can be created with the following line of code.

```
CachedRowSetImpl crset = new CachedRowSetImpl();
```

The variable *crset* contains a CachedRowSetImpl object that is a container for a set of data. The newly created CachedRowSetImpl object will have the following defaults:

- Its escape processing is on.
- Its type map is empty.
- Its command string is null.
- It has a default reader and writer registered with it.
- It is scrollable and updatable.

RowSet methods can be used to set new values for any of these properties.

29.2.5 Populating a CachedRowSet Object

Although a `CachedRowSet` object can contain data that was retrieved from a data source such as a file or spreadsheet, it will probably get its data primarily from a `ResultSet` object via a JDBC driver. The `CachedRowSet` interface adds two methods for populating a `CachedRowSet` object with data from a `ResultSet` object. It adds a second version of the method `execute`, which takes a connection as a parameter, and it adds the method `populate`, which takes a `ResultSet` object as a parameter.

The version of `execute` inherited from the `RowSet` interface has to establish a connection behind the scenes before it can execute the rowset's command string. The version of `execute` defined in the `CachedRowSet` interface is passed a `Connection` object, so it does not need to establish its own connection. The method `populate` does not need to establish its own connection or execute a query because it is passed the `ResultSet` object from which it will get its data. Thus, the method `populate` does not require that the properties affecting a connection be set before it is called, nor does it require that the command string be set. The following code fragment shows how the method `populate` might be used.

```
ResultSet rs = stmt.executeQuery(
                        "SELECT NAME, SALARY FROM EMPLOYEES");
CachedRowSetImpl crset = new CachedRowSetImpl();
crset.populate(rs);
```

The new `CachedRowSetImpl` object *crset* contains the same data that the `ResultSet` object *rs* contains, but unlike *rs*, *crset* caches its data in memory. This means that after the method `populate` returns, *crset* will not maintain a connection with the data source from which *rs* got its data and to which *rs* remains connected.

The implementation details of the method `populate` may vary, of course, but because it is passed a `ResultSet` object, `populate` is in some ways quite different from the method `execute`. As stated previously, the `populate` method does not need to establish a connection. Nor does it use a reader because it can get its data directly from the given result set. By using `ResultSetMetaData` methods, it can get information about the format of the result set so that it is able to use the getter methods in the `ResultSet` interface to retrieve the result set's data.

The methods `execute` and `populate` do have some similarities. The main similarity is that both methods change the contents of the entire rowset. As a consequence, they both cause the following: notification of listeners, setting the original values equal to the current rowset values, and updating the rowset's metadata information.

The following code fragments give examples of using the two versions of the method execute. Both versions execute a query, so both require that a command string be set. When no connection has been passed to the method execute, the appropriate connection properties must be set before it can be called. The execute method will call the rowset's reader, which will use the necessary properties to establish a connection with the data source. Once the connection is established, the reader can call the method executeQuery to execute the rowset's command string and get a result set from which to retrieve data.

```
CachedRowSetImpl crset1 = new CachedRowSetImpl();
crset1.setCommand("SELECT NAME, SALARY FROM EMPLOYEES");
crset1.setDataSourceName("jdbc/myDataSource");
crset1.setUsername("paz");
crset1.setPassword("p38c3");
crset1.setTransactionIsolation(
                        Connection.TRANSACTION_READ_COMMITTED);
crset1.execute();
```

In the next example, the Connection object *con* is passed to the method execute. The CachedRowSet object *crset2* will use *con* for executing the command string instead of having to establish a new connection.

```
CachedRowSetImple crset2 = new CachedRowSetImpl();
crset2.setCommand("SELECT NAME, SALARY FROM EMPLOYEES");
crset2.execute(con);
```

Both *crset1* and *crset2* were connected to the data source while the command string was executed and while the resulting data was read and inserted into it. After the method execute returns, neither will maintain a connection with the data source.

29.2.6 Accessing Data

A CachedRowSet object, like all rowsets, uses the getter methods inherited from the ResultSet interface to access its data. Because a CachedRowSetImpl object is implemented so that it is always scrollable, it can also use the ResultSet methods for moving the cursor. For example, the following code fragment moves the cursor to the last row of the CachedRowSet object *crset* and then retrieves the String value in the first column of that row.

```
crset.last();
String note = crset.getString(1);
```

A `CachedRowSetImpl` object is implemented such that it always has type `ResultSet.TYPE_SCROLL_INSENSITIVE`, so in addition to being scrollable, a `CachedRowSet` object is always insensitive to changes made by others. This makes sense because a `CachedRowSet` object is mostly disconnected. While it is disconnected, it has no way of seeing the changes that others might make to the underlying data source from which it got its data.

29.2.7 Modifying Data

As shown in the previous section, a `CachedRowSetImpl` object can have its entire contents changed with its `execute` and `populate` methods. It can have one row at a time modified with the `ResultSet` updater methods and the methods `insertRow` and `deleteRow`.

An updater method modifies the value in the specified column in the current row, assigning it the value of its second parameter. An updater method changes only the value in the rowset, which is cached in memory; it does not affect the value in the underlying data source. Also, it does not affect the value that the rowset keeps track of as the original value.

When an application has made all its updates to a row, it calls the method `updateRow`. In a `CachedRowSetImpl` implementation, this method signals that the updates for the current row are complete, but, like the updater methods, it does not affect the values in the underlying data source. The `updateRow` method likewise does not affect the values stored as original values. After calling the `updateRow` method on all the rows being updated, an application needs to call the `CachedRowSet` method `acceptChanges`. This method invokes a writer component internally to propagate changes to the data source backing the rowset, and for each column value that was changed, it sets the original value to the current value.

Once it has called `updateRow`, an application may no longer call the method `cancelRowUpdates` to undo updates to the current row. If it has not yet invoked the method `acceptChanges`, however, it can call the method `restoreOriginal`, which undoes the updates to all rows by replacing the current values in the rowset with the original values. The `restoreOriginal` method does not need to interact with the underlying data source.

The following code fragment updates the first two rows in the `CachedRowSetImpl` object *crset*.

```
crset.execute();
// crset is initialized with its original and current values

crset.first();
crset.updateString(1, "Jane Austen");
crset.updateFloat(2, 150000f);
crset.updateRow();
// the current value of the first row has been updated

crset.relative(1);
crset.updateString(1, "Toni Morrison");
crset.updateFloat(2, 120000f);
crset.updateRow();
// the current value of the second row has been updated

crset.acceptChanges();
// the original value has been set to the current value and the
// database has been updated
```

29.2.8 Customizing Readers and Writers

Any class that implements the RowSet interface can take advantage of the ability to customize the retrieval and updating of data that the rowset framework provides. This applies especially to rowsets that are disconnected, such as CachedRowSetImpl objects, because they require the services of the SyncProvider SPI (service provider interface) to obtain a reader/writer facility.

The CachedRowSet interface defines the methods setReader and setWriter for assigning a reader and writer to a rowset, and it also defines a getReader and a getWriter method for retrieving a rowset's reader and writer. A rowset's reader and writer, which are usually set up at design time, operate completely behind the scenes, performing any number of tasks that can be customized to provide additional functionality.

The RowSetReader interface has one public method, readData, which can be customized in various ways. For example, a reader can be implemented so that it reads data straight from a file or from some other non-SQL data source rather than from a database using a JDBC driver. Such a reader might use the method RowSet.insertRow to insert new rows into the rowset. When invoked by a reader, this method could also be implemented so that it updates the original values stored by the rowset.

The RowSetWriter interface has one public method, writeData, which writes data that has been modified back to the underlying data source. This method can likewise be customized in a variety of ways. The writer establishes a connection with the data source, just as the reader did. How the writer decides whether or not to write data when there is a conflict depends on the implementation. If the writer uses an optimistic concurrency algorithm, it will check the data source to see that it has not been changed by others before updating it. If there is a conflict (some data in the underlying data source has changed), the writer may decide not to write the new data. The RowSetInternal methods getOriginal and getOriginalRow supply the values that existed before the current modifications, so the writer can compare them with the values read from the data source to see if the data source has been modified. Operations performed by a rowset's reader and writer all take place internally and are transparent to the programmer using a rowset.

A CachedRowSetImpl object that has been configured with a custom reader and/or writer can be made available as a normal JavaBeans component. This means that developers writing applications do not have to worry about customizing readers and writers and can concentrate on the more important aspects of using rowsets effectively.

29.2.9 Other Methods

The CachedRowSet interface defines a number of other methods. For example, it defines two versions of the method toCollection. Sometimes it is more convenient to work with a rowset's data as elements in a collection, which these methods make possible by converting a rowset's data into a Java collection. Other CachedRowSet methods create a copy of the rowset. CachedRowSet.clone and CachedRowSet.createCopy create an exact copy of the rowset that is independent from the original. By contrast, the CachedRowSet.createShared method creates a rowset that shares its state with the original rowset. In other words, both the new and the original rowset share the same physical, in-memory copy of their original and current values. If an updater method is called on one shared rowset, the update affects the other rowset as well. In effect, the createShared method creates multiple cursors over a single set of rows.

In summary, an implementation of the CachedRowSet interface, being disconnected and able to operate without a driver, is designed to work especially well with a thin client for passing data in a distributed application or for making a result set scrollable and updatable. Many other RowSet implementations can be designed for other purposes.

29.2.10 WebRowSet Implementation

The WebRowSet interface extends the CachedRowSet interface and therefore has all of the same capabilities. What it adds is the ability to read and write a rowset in XML format. A WebRowSetImpl object uses a WebRowSetXmlReader object to read a rowset in XML format and a WebRowSetXmlWriter object to write a rowset in XML format. The XML version contains a WebRowSetImpl object's metadata as well as its data.

A WebRowSetImpl object is designed to work well in a distributed client/server application. It is similar to a CachedRowSet implementation in that both connect a thin client to an application server. Thus, they are both good for providing data to a thin client. The difference is that they use different protocols for talking to the middle tier, where the application server resides. A CachedRowSetImpl object uses RMI/IIOP (Remote Method Invocation/Internet Interoperability Protocol) for talking with the middle tier and for sending rowsets. A WebRowSetImpl object uses HTTP/XML (Hypertext Transfer Protocol/eXtensible Markup Language) to communicate with the middle tier, so that, for example, Web clients can talk to Java servlets that provide data access.

XML has become more and more important for Web services because of the portability of data it provides. If two parties have the XML schema for a WebRowSetImpl object, they can use it to exchange rowsets in a common format even though they may store their data internally in entirely different formats. This makes a WebRowSetImpl object a powerful tool for data exchange.

Because the Java platform provides portability of code and XML provides portability of data, they are the ideal combination for Web services. Technologies like Java™ API for XML-based RPC, SOAP with Attachments API for Java™, Java™ Architecture for XML Binding, and Java™ API for XML Registries make developing Web services easier and easier. Plus the infrastructure that the J2EE platform provides saves developers from having to program their own "plumbing" for the management of distributed transactions, connection pooling, and security. Being able to use a WebRowSetImpl object for sending data adds even more to the value of using the Java platform for Web services.

The following code fragment is a simple example that creates the WebRowSetImpl object *wrs*, populates it with the data of the ResultSet object *rs*, and then updates a column value. The final two lines output *wrs* in XML format.

```
WebRowSetImpl wrs = new WebRowSetImpl();
wrs.populate(rs);

//perform updates
```

```
wrs.absolute(2)
wrs.updateString(1, "newString");

FileWriter fWriter = new FileWriter("/share/net/output.xml");
wrs.writeXml(fWriter);
```

The machine that receives the XML output will do something similar to the following to read it. Once *wrs* has read in the data and metadata in *fReader*, the code operates on it just as it would on any other WebRowSetImpl object.

```
WebRowSetImpl wrs = new WebRowsetImpl();

FileReader fReader = new FileReader("/share/net/output.xml");
wrs.readXml(fReader);

wrs.absolute(2);
String str = wrs.getString(1);
```

29.2.11 FilteredRowSet Implementation

A FilteredRowSetImpl object, an extension of a CachedRowSetImpl object, lets a programmer use a filtered subset of data from a rowset. For example, suppose a FilteredRowSetImpl object contains a fairly large set of rows. A programmer who wants to perform operations on only a subset of those rows can specify a range of values, and the FilteredRowSetImpl object will return only values in that range. This filtering is done by the method next, which is implemented to skip any rows that do not fall within the specified range. Without this capability, the programmer would have to make a connection to the data source, get a ResultSet object with the selected rows, and populate a rowset with those rows. Because establishing a connection is very expensive, far outweighing the cost of the memory needed to store a FilteredRowSetImpl object, the ability to get a selected set of rows without making a new connection can improve performance significantly.

Suppose you have a FilteredRowSetImpl object *frs* that contains all of the employees in Company XYZ. You have figured the average salary for the company, including everyone in the average. Now you want to get information about only the employees whose names range from Aaronson to Lee. The following code fragment causes *frs* to make available only the rows where the values in the column NAMES are in the range of Aaronson to Lee.

In the following code fragment, the FilteredRowSet object *frs* is populated with data from the ResultSet object *rs*. Then the code creates a Range object, specifying that the last names Aaronson through Lee, which are in the column NAME, make up the range of names that the method next can return.

```
FilteredRowSet frs = new FilteredRowSet();
frs.populate(rs);

Range names = new Range("Aaronson", "Lee", findColumn("NAME"));
frs.setFilter(names);

while (frs.next()) {
    String name = frs.getString("NAME");
    . . . // add each name to a mailing list
    // only names from "Aaronson" to "Lee" will be returned
}
```

29.2.12 JoinRowSet Implementation

A JoinRowSetImpl object lets a programmer combine data from two different RowSet objects. This can be especially valuable when related data is stored in different data sources. Any RowSet implementation can participate in a join, but it is typically two CachedRowSetImpl objects that are joined. With all of the relevant data combined into one JoinRowSetImpl object, an application can process the data just as it would for any other kind of RowSet object.

The following code fragment demonstrates how the data from two Cached-RowSetImpl objects is joined into one JoinRowSetImpl object. In this scenario, data from the table EMPLOYEES is joined with data from the table BONUS_PLAN, thereby giving information about each employee and his or her bonus plan all in one rowset. In both of the original rowsets, the first column is the employee identification number, so that is the column used to match the data from one table with the other. After the join, each row in the JoinRowSetImpl object will contain the columns from both rowsets that pertain to the same employee ID.

The first line of code creates the JoinRowSetImpl object *jrs*. Next, all the columns from the table EMPLOYEES are used to populate the new CachedRowSetImpl object *emp1*, the first column of *emp1* is set as the match column, and *emp1* is added to *jrs*. Then, in similar fashion, all the columns from the table BONUS_PLAN are used to populate the CachedRowSetImpl object *bonus*, the first column of *bonus* is set as the match column, and *bonus* is added to *jrs*. In both *emp1* and *bonus*, the first column is EMPLOYEE_ID, which is the primary key. It is the column both rowsets have in common, and it can be used to match the information from *emp1* about an employee with the information in *bonus* about the same employee. The last lines of code navigate *jrs* and retrieve a column value.

```
JoinRowSetImpl jrs = new JoinRowSetImpl();

ResultSet rs1 = stmt.executeQuery("SELECT * FROM EMPLOYEES");
CachedRowSetImpl emp1 = new CachedRowSetImpl();
emp1.populate(rs1);
emp1.setMatchColumn(1); // The first column is EMPLOYEE_ID
jrs.addRowSet(emp1);

ResultSet rs2 = stmt.executeQuery("SELECT * FROM BONUS_PLAN");
CachedRowSetImpl bonus = new CachedRowSetImpl();
bonus.populate(rs2);
bonus.setMatchColumn(1); // The first column is EMPLOYEE_ID
jrs.addRowSet(bonus);

    // The jrs instance now joins the two rowsets. The application
    // can browse the combined data as if it were browsing one single
    // RowSet object.

jrs.first();
int employeeID = jrs.getInt(1);
String employeeName = jrs.getString(2);
```

29.3 RowSet Interface Definition

```
package javax.sql;
public abstract interface RowSet extends java.sql.ResultSet {

    //================================================================
    //           Methods for JavaBeans event model
    //================================================================

    void addRowSetListener(RowSetListener listener);
```

```
void removeRowSetListener(RowSetListener listener);


//================================================================
// Methods to get/set JavaBeans properties for making a connection
//================================================================

java.lang.String getDataSourceName();
void setDataSourceName(java.lang.String name) throws SQLException;
java.lang.String getURL() throws SQLException;
void setURL(java.lang.String url) throws SQLException;
java.lang.String getPassword();
void setPassword(java.lang.String password) throws SQLException;
java.lang.String getUsername();
void setUsername(java.lang.String name) throws SQLException;
int getTransactionIsolation();
void setTransactionIsolation(int level) throws SQLException;
int getTypeMap() throws SQLException;
void setTypeMap(java.util.Map map) throws SQLException;


//================================================================
//    Methods to execute a statement and to get/set JavaBeans
//               properties for executing a statement
//================================================================

void execute() throws SQLException;
java.lang.String getCommand();
void setCommand(java.lang.String command) throws SQLException;
int getMaxFieldSize() throws SQLException;
void setMaxFieldSize(int max) throws SQLException;
int getMaxRows() throws SQLException;
void setMaxRows(int max) throws SQLException;
boolean getEscapeProcessing() throws SQLException;
void setEscapeProcessing(boolean enable) throws SQLException;
boolean isReadOnly() throws SQLException;
void setReadOnly(boolean value) throws SQLException;
int getQueryTimeout() throws SQLException;
void setQueryTimeout(int seconds) throws SQLException;
```

```
//===============================================================
//          Methods for setting type and concurrency
//===============================================================

void setConcurrency(int concurrency) throws SQLException;
void setType(int type) throws SQLException;


//===============================================================
//          Methods for setting input parameters
//===============================================================

void clearParameters() throws SQLException;
void setNull(int parameterIndex, int jdbcType) throws SQLException;
void setNull(int parameterIndex, int jdbcType, String typeName)
                                            throws SQLException;
void setBoolean(int parameterIndex, boolean x) throws SQLException;
void setByte(int parameterIndex, byte x) throws SQLException;
void setShort(int parameterIndex, short x) throws SQLException;
void setInt(int parameterIndex, int x) throws SQLException;
void setLong(int parameterIndex, long x) throws SQLException;
void setFloat(int parameterIndex, float x) throws SQLException;
void setDouble(int parameterIndex, double x) throws SQLException;
void setBigDecimal(int parameterIndex, java.math.BigDecimal x)
                                            throws SQLException;
void setString(int parameterIndex, String x) throws SQLException;
void setBytes(int parameterIndex, byte x[]) throws SQLException;
void setDate(int parameterIndex, java.sql.Date x) throws
                                            SQLException;
void setDate(int parameterIndex, java.sql.Date x,
                java.util.Calendar cal) throws SQLException;
void setTime(int parameterIndex, java.sql.Time x)
                                            throws SQLException;
void setTime(int parameterIndex, java.sql.Time x,
                java.util.Calendar cal) throws SQLException;
void setTimestamp(int parameterIndex, java.sql.Timestamp x)
                                            throws SQLException;
void setTimestamp(int parameterIndex, java.sql.Timestamp x,
                java.util.Calendar cal) throws SQLException;
```

```
    void setAsciiStream(int parameterIndex, java.io.InputStream x, int
                                        length) throws SQLException;
    void setBinaryStream(int parameterIndex, java.io.InputStream x, int
                                        length) throws SQLException;
    void setArray(int parameterIndex, Array x) throws SQLException;
    void setBlob(int parameterIndex, Blob x) throws SQLException;
    void setCharacterStream(int parameterIndex, java.io.Reader reader,
                                    int length) throws SQLException;
    void setClob(int parameterIndex, Clob x) throws SQLException;
    void setRef(int parameterIndex, Ref x) throws SQLException;
    void setObject(int parameterIndex, Object x, int targetJdbcType,
                                    int scale) throws SQLException;
    void setObject(int parameterIndex, Object x, int targetJdbcType)
                                            throws SQLException;
    void setObject(int parameterIndex, Object x) throws SQLException;
}
```

29.4 RowSet Methods

The RowSet interface inherits the following methods from java.sql.ResultSet.
Methods with more than one version are listed only once, and deprecated methods
are not listed.

JDBC 2.0 API:

absolute	afterLast	beforeFirst
cancelRowUpdates	clearWarnings	close
deleteRow	findColumn	first
getArray	getAsciiStream	getBigDecimal
getBinaryStream	getBlob	getBoolean
getByte	getBytes	getCharacterStream
getClob	getConcurrency	getCursorName
getDate	getDouble	getFetchDirection
getFetchSize	getFloat	getInt
getLong	getMetaData	getObject
getRef	getRow	getShort
getStatement	getString	getTime

getTimestamp	getType	getWarnings
insertRow	isAfterLast	isBeforeFirst
isFirst	isLast	last
moveToCurrentRow	moveToInsertRow	next
previous	refreshRow	relative
rowDeleted	rowInserted	rowUpdated
setFetchDirection	setFetchSize	updateAsciiStream
updateBigDecimal	updateBinaryStream	updateBoolean
updateByte	updateBytes	updateCharacterStream
updateDate	updateDouble	updateFloat
updateInt	updateLong	updateNull
updateObject	updateRow	updateShort
updateString	updateTime	updateTimestamp
wasNull		

JDBC 3.0 API

:

getURL	updateArray	updateBlob
updateClob	updateRef	

The following methods are defined in the interface `javax.sql.RowSet`:

addRowSetListener

void **addRowSetListener**(RowSetListener *listener*)

Registers *listener* as an object that will be notified of events affecting this RowSet object.

PARAMETERS:

listener   a RowSetListener object implemented by a component that wants to be notified when a significant event occurs in the life of this RowSet object

EXAMPLE:
```
RowSetListener listener =
                      new MySwingComponent.createRowSetListener();
rset.addRowSetListener(listener);
```

clearParameters

```
void clearParameters() throws SQLException
```

Clears the values set for this RowSet object's input parameters and releases the resources used by those values.

In general, parameter values remain in force for repeated use. Setting a new parameter value will automatically clear its previous value. In some cases, however, it is useful to immediately release the resources used by the current parameter values by calling the method clearParameters.

EXAMPLE:
```
rset.clearParameters();
```

execute

```
void execute() throws SQLException
```

Replaces this RowSet object's current contents with new data, typically by executing the rowset's command string. When a JDBC driver is used to execute the command string, this method creates both a Connection object for reading data and a Statement object for executing the command. The following properties may be used in setting up the connection: url or data source name, user name, password, transaction isolation, and type map. The following properties may be used in creating the statement: command, read only, maximum field size, maximum rows, escape processing, and query timeout. This method will throw an SQLException if the necessary properties have not been set.

If this method is successful, it discards this RowSet object's current data and disregards any outstanding updates. It also resets this RowSet object's metadata when it replaces the existing data.

THROWS:
`java.sql.SQLException` if (1) the properties needed to establish a connection and execute the command string have not been set, or (2) this method is invoked recursively (for example, if the reader called by this method invokes the method `execute`)

EXAMPLE:
`rset.execute();`

SEE:
"Executing a Command," on page 805

getCommand

`java.lang.String` **getCommand**()

Retrieves this `RowSet` object's command property, which is the command that can be executed to fill this `RowSet` object with data. The default value of the command property is `null`. This property is usually set before the method `execute` is called, but it may not be needed if the data source is something other than a JDBC data source.

RETURNS:
the command that will be executed when the method `execute` is called to replace this `RowSet` object's current contents; `null` if the data source is a file, spreadsheet, or other non-SQL data source

EXAMPLE:
`String command = rset.getCommand();`

getDataSourceName

`java.lang.String` **getDataSourceName**()

Retrieves this `RowSet` object's data source name property, which is usually the JNDI name of a JDBC data source. This is the logical name for the data source that was registered with a JNDI naming service. When this logical name is supplied to the `javax.naming.Context.lookup` method, `lookup` returns a `DataSource` object that can be used to get a connection to the data source. The method `execute` will connect to this data source, and, typically, it will execute this `RowSet` object's command string to fill it with data.

The user should set either the data source name or the url property before calling the method `execute`; `execute` will use the property that was specified most recently to create a connection. If neither property has been set, `execute` will throw an `SQLException`.

RETURNS:
the logical name for a data source that was bound to a `DataSource` object using a JNDI naming service

EXAMPLE:
```
String logicalName = rset.getDataSourceName();
```

SEE:
"Connecting to a Data Source," on page 570

getEscapeProcessing

```
boolean getEscapeProcessing() throws SQLException
```

Checks whether this `RowSet` object's escape processing is enabled. If it is enabled, the driver will scan for any escape syntax and do escape substitution before sending the escaped statement to the database. When escape processing is disabled, the driver will ignore escaped statements. The default is for escape processing to be enabled.

RETURNS:
`true` if escape processing is enabled; `false` otherwise

EXAMPLE:
```
boolean enabled = rset.getEscapeProcessing();
```

SEE:
"SQL Escape Syntax in Statements," on page 958

getMaxFieldSize

```
int getMaxFieldSize() throws SQLException
```

Retrieves the maximum number of bytes that may be returned from a column that stores BINARY, VARBINARY, LONGVARBINARY, CHAR, VARCHAR, or LONG-VARCHAR values. The limit does not apply to column values of other data types. If the limit is exceeded, the excess data is silently discarded.

RETURNS:
an int indicating the current maximum number of bytes for a column value; 0 indicates that the number of bytes is unlimited

EXAMPLE:
```
int limit = rset.getMaxFieldSize();
```

getMaxRows

```
int getMaxRows() throws SQLException
```

Retrieves the maximum number of rows that this RowSet object can contain. If the limit is exceeded, the excess rows are silently dropped.

RETURNS:
an int indicating the current maximum number of rows that a RowSet object can contain; 0 indicates that the number of rows is unlimited

EXAMPLE:
```
int limit = rset.getMaxRows();
```

getPassword

```
String getPassword()
```

Retrieves the password used to create a connection between this RowSet object and a database. The password property is typically set at run time before the method execute is called. This property is not usually part of the serialized state of a RowSet object.

RETURNS:
the password used to create a database connection

EXAMPLE:
```
String password = rset.getPassword();
```

getQueryTimeout

```
int getQueryTimeout() throws SQLException
```

Retrieves the maximum number of seconds that this `RowSet` object will wait for a statement to execute. If the time limit is exceeded, this `RowSet` object will throw an `SQLException`.

RETURNS:
an `int` indicating the current maximum number of seconds that this `RowSet` object will wait for a statement to be executed; 0 means that there is no time limit

EXAMPLE:
```
int limit = rset.getQueryTimeout();
```

 ## getTransactionIsolation

`int getTransactionIsolation()`

Retrieves the transaction isolation level for the connection between this `RowSet` object and a data source when a JDBC driver is used to read or write data. Transaction isolation levels are the constants defined in the `Connection` interface.

RETURNS:
one of the constants defined in the `Connection` interface, indicating the current transaction isolation level

EXAMPLE:
```
int level = rset.getTransactionIsolation();
```

SEE:
"Connection Fields," on page 428, for definitions of the different levels
"Transaction Isolation Levels," on page 393, for further explanation

 ## getTypeMap

`java.util.Map getTypeMap() throws SQLException`

Retrieves the type map associated with this `RowSet` object. This type map serves the same function as a type map associated with a connection. It will be used when appropriate for the custom mapping of user-defined data types that are retrieved with the method `ResultSet.getObject`, stored with the method `ResultSet.setObject`, or set with the method `RowSet.setObject`. Until the application puts entries in the type map, it will be empty.

RETURNS:
the `java.util.Map` object currently associated with this `RowSet` object

EXAMPLE:
`java.util.Map map = rset.getTypeMap();`

SEE:
"Creating a Custom Mapping," on page 896

getUrl

`String getUrl() throws SQLException`

Retrieves the URL used to create a JDBC connection. The default value is
`null`.

RETURNS:
the URL used to create a JDBC connection

EXAMPLE:
`String url = rset.getURL();`

SEE:
"JDBC URLs," on page 387

getUsername

`String getUsername()`

Retrieves the user name used to create a connection between this `RowSet`
object and a database. The user name property is set at run time before the
method `execute` is called. This property is not usually part of the serialized
state of a `RowSet` object.

RETURNS:
the user name used to create a database connection

EXAMPLE:
`String name = rset.getUsername();`

isReadOnly

```
boolean isReadOnly() throws SQLException
```

Checks whether this RowSet object is read-only or updatable.

Attempts to update a read-only RowSet object will cause an SQLException to be thrown.

RETURNS:
true if this RowSet object is read-only; false if it can be updated

EXAMPLE:
```
boolean readOnly = rset.isReadOnly();
```

removeRowSetListener

```
void removeRowSetListener(RowSetListener listener)
```

Deregisters *listener* so that it will no longer be notified of events affecting this RowSet object.

PARAMETERS:

listener   a RowSetListener object registered with this RowSet object

EXAMPLE:
```
rset.removeRowSetListener(listener);
```

setArray

```
void setArray(int parameterIndex, java.sql.Array x) throws SQLException
```

Sets parameter number *parameterIndex* to *x*, an Array object in the Java programming language. A JDBC driver converts this to a JDBC ARRAY value when it sends it to the database.

PARAMETERS:

parameterIndex   1 indicates the first parameter, 2 the second, and so on

x   the Array value, representing an SQL ARRAY value, to be set as a parameter

EXAMPLE:
```
rset.setArray(3, addresses);
// sets the third parameter to the Array object addresses
```

setAsciiStream

```
void setAsciiStream(int parameterIndex, java.io.InputStream fin,
                                    int length) throws SQLException
```

Sets the parameter in position *parameterIndex* to the input stream object *fin*, from which *length* bytes will be read and sent to the database.

This is useful when a very large ASCII value is input to a LONGVARCHAR parameter. JDBC will read the data from the stream as needed until it reaches end-of-file. A JDBC driver will do any necessary conversion from ASCII to the database CHAR format.

NOTE: This stream object can be either a standard stream object in the Java programming language or the programmer's own subclass that implements the standard interface.

PARAMETERS:

parameterIndex	1 indicates the first parameter, 2 the second, and so on
fin	the java.io.InputStream object that contains the input data in ASCII format
length	the number of bytes to be read from the stream and sent to the database. Note that if the stream contains more or fewer bytes than are specified in *length*, an exception is thrown.

EXAMPLE:
```
rset.setAsciiStream(3, fin, 4096);
// sets the third parameter to the input stream fin;
// 4096 bytes will be read
```

An alternate example:

```
rset.setAsciiStream(1, (new StringBufferInputStream(text)),
                                        text.length());
// uses text.length() to be sure the length is accurate
```

setBigDecimal

```
void setBigDecimal(int parameterIndex, java.math.BigDecimal n)
                                              throws SQLException
```

Sets parameter number *parameterIndex* to *n*. A JDBC driver converts this to a JDBC NUMERIC value when it sends it to the database.

PARAMETERS:

parameterIndex	1 is the first parameter, 2 is the second, and so on
n	an instance of the class java.math.BigDecimal to which the parameter will be set

EXAMPLE:
```
java.math.BigDecimal n = new java.math.BigDecimal(982359.434987);
pstmt.setBigDecimal(2, n); // sets second parameter to 982359.434987
```

setBinaryStream

```
void setBinaryStream(int parameterIndex, java.io.InputStream fin,
                            int length) throws SQLException
```

Sets the parameter in position *parameterIndex* to the input stream object *fin*, from which *length* bytes will be read and sent to the database.

This is useful when a very large binary value is input to a LONGVARBINARY parameter. A JDBC driver will read the data from the stream as needed until it reaches end-of-file.

NOTE: This stream object can be either a standard stream object in the Java programming language or the programmer's own subclass that implements the standard interface.

PARAMETERS:

parameterIndex	1 indicates the first parameter, 2 the second, and so on
fin	the java.io.InputStream object that contains the input data in binary form
length	the number of bytes to be read from the stream and sent to the database. Note that if the stream contains more or less bytes than are specified in *length*, an exception is thrown.

EXAMPLE:
```
rset.setBinaryStream(2, fin, 10000);
// sets the second parameter to the input stream fin;
// 10000 bytes will be read
```

setBlob

```
void setBlob(int parameterIndex, java.sql.Blob x) throws SQLException
```

Sets parameter number *parameterIndex* to *x*, a Blob object in the Java programming language. A JDBC driver converts this to a JDBC BLOB value when it sends it to the database.

PARAMETERS:

parameterIndex	1 indicates the first parameter, 2 the second, and so on
x	the Blob value to be set as a parameter

EXAMPLE:
```
rset.setBlob(1, sightings);
// sets the third parameter to the Blob object sightings
```

setBoolean

```
void setBoolean(int parameterIndex, boolean b) throws SQLException
```

Sets parameter number *parameterIndex* to *b*, a Java boolean value. A JDBC driver converts this to a JDBC BIT or BOOLEAN value when it sends it to the database.

PARAMETERS:

parameterIndex	1 indicates the first parameter, 2 the second, and so on
b	the parameter value—either true or false

EXAMPLE:
```
rset.setBoolean(3, false); // sets the third parameter to false
```

setByte

```
void setByte(int parameterIndex, byte x) throws SQLException
```

Sets parameter number *parameterIndex* to *x*, a Java byte value. A JDBC driver converts this to a JDBC `TINYINT` value when it sends it to the database.

PARAMETERS:

parameterIndex   1 indicates the first parameter, 2 the second, and so on

x   the parameter value to be set

EXAMPLE:
```
rset.setByte(2, 31); // sets the second parameter to 31
```

setBytes

```
void setBytes(int parameterIndex, byte x[]) throws SQLException
```

Sets parameter number *parameterIndex* to *x[]*, a Java array of bytes. A JDBC driver converts this to a JDBC `VARBINARY` or `LONGVARBINARY` value (depending on the argument's size relative to the driver's limits on `VARBINARY` values) when it sends it to the database.

PARAMETERS:

parameterIndex   1 is the first parameter, 2 is the second, and so on

x   a Java array of bytes.

EXAMPLE:
```
byte x[] = {1, 2, 3, 4, 5};
pstmt.setBytes(1, x); // sets the first parameter to the array x
```

setCharacterStream

```
void setCharacterStream(int parameterIndex, java.io.Reader reader,
                        int length) throws SQLException
```

Sets the parameter in position *parameterIndex* to the `Reader` stream object *reader*, from which *length* bytes will be read and sent to the database.

This is useful when a very large Unicode value is input to a `LONGVARCHAR` parameter. A JDBC driver will read the data from the stream as needed until it reaches end-of-file and will do any necessary conversion from Unicode to the database `char` format.

NOTE: This stream object can be either a standard stream object in the Java programming language or the programmer's own subclass that implements the standard interface.

PARAMETERS:

parameterIndex	1 indicates the first parameter, 2 the second, and so on
reader	the java.io.Reader object that contains the input data in Unicode form
length	the number of characters to be read from the stream and sent to the database. Note that if the stream contains more or less characters than are specified in *length*, an exception is thrown.

EXAMPLE:
```
rset.setCharacterStream(2, reader, 10000);
// sets the second parameter to the Reader stream reader;
// 10000 bytes will be read from reader
```

setClob

void **setClob**(int *parameterIndex*, java.sql.Clob *x*) throws SQLException

Sets parameter number *parameterIndex* to *x*, a Clob object in the Java programming language. A JDBC driver converts this to a JDBC CLOB value when it sends it to the database.

PARAMETERS:

parameterIndex	1 indicates the first parameter, 2 the second, and so on
x	the Clob value to be set as a parameter

EXAMPLE:
```
rset.setClob(2, comments);
// sets the second parameter to the Clob object comments
```

setCommand

void **setCommand**(java.lang.String *cmd*) throws SQLException

Sets the command property for this RowSet object. This property is optional when a rowset is produced by a data source that does not support commands, such as a spreadsheet.

PARAMETERS:

cmd	a command string; may be null

EXAMPLE:
```
rset.setCommand("SELECT LAST_NAME, FIRST_NAME FROM EMPLOYEES");
// sets the command for getting data from a relational database
```

setConcurrency

```
void setConcurrency(int concurrency) throws SQLException
```

Sets the concurrency mode for this RowSet object to *concurrency*.

PARAMETERS:

concurrency   either java.sql.ResultSet.CONCUR_READ_ONLY or
                        java.sql.ResultSet.CONCUR_UPDATABLE

EXAMPLE:
```
rset.setConcurrency(java.sql.ResultSet.CONCUR_UPDATABLE);
// makes rset updatable
```

SEE:
"Concurrency Types," on page 701

setDataSourceName

```
void setDataSourceName(java.lang.String name) throws SQLException
```

Sets the data source name property for this RowSet object to *name*. This is the logical name for a data source that is registered with a JNDI naming service.

PARAMETERS:

name   the JNDI name that identifies a data source

EXAMPLE:
```
rset.setDataSourceName("myDataSourceName");
```

setDate

```
void setDate(int parameterIndex, java.sql.Date x) throws SQLException
```

Sets parameter number *parameterIndex* to *x*. A JDBC driver converts this to a JDBC DATE value when it sends it to the database, using the default Calendar to calculate it.

PARAMETERS:

parameterIndex	1 is the first parameter, 2 is the second, and so on
x	a java.sql.Date object

EXAMPLE:
```
Date x = new Date(83592840159L);
rset.setDate(1, x);
```

SEE:
"Creating a Date Object," on page 590, for information about creating a Date object

setDate

```
void setDate(int parameterIndex, java.sql.Date x,
                    java.util.Calendar cal) throws SQLException
```

Sets parameter number *parameterIndex* to *x*, using *cal* to calculate the date. The driver uses the given Calendar object to construct a JDBC DATE value, which the driver then sends to the database. With a Calendar object, the date can be calculated taking into account a custom time zone. When no Calendar object is specified, the time zone of the Virtual Machine running the application is used.

PARAMETERS:

parameterIndex	1 is the first parameter, 2 is the second, and so on
x	a java.sql.Date object
cal	the Calendar object the driver will use to construct the date

EXAMPLE:
```
Date x = new Date(23593450569987987L);
rset.setDate(1, x, cal);
```

SEE:
"Advanced Features," on page 592, for information about dates and time zones

setDouble

```
void setDouble(int parameterIndex, double x) throws SQLException
```

Sets parameter number *parameterIndex* to *x*. A JDBC driver converts this to a JDBC DOUBLE value when it sends it to the database.

PARAMETERS:

parameterIndex   1 is the first parameter, 2 is the second, and so on

x   the double value to which the parameter will be set

EXAMPLE:
```
rset.setDouble(1, 3958325.89);
// sets first parameter to 3958325.89
```

setEscapeProcessing

```
void getEscapeProcessing(boolean enable) throws SQLException
```

Sets this RowSet object's escape processing to *enable*. If escape processing is enabled, a JDBC driver will scan for any escape syntax and do escape substitution before sending the escaped statement to the database. When escape processing is disabled, the driver will ignore escaped statements. Until this method is used to disable escape processing, it will be enabled. The most common reason for disabling escape processing is to increase performance.

PARAMETERS:

enable   true to enable escape processing; false to disable it

EXAMPLE:
```
rset.setEscapeProcessing(false); // turns off escape processing
```

SEE:
"SQL Escape Syntax in Statements," on page 958

setFloat

```
void setFloat(int parameterIndex, float x) throws SQLException
```

Sets parameter number *parameterIndex* to *x*. A JDBC driver converts this to a JDBC REAL value when it sends it to the database.

PARAMETERS:

parameterIndex	1 is the first parameter, 2 is the second, and so on
x	the `float` value to which the parameter will be set

EXAMPLE:

```
rset.setFloat(2, 18.0f); // sets second parameter to 18.0f
```

setInt

```
void setInt(int parameterIndex, int x) throws SQLException
```

Sets parameter number *parameterIndex* to *x*. A JDBC driver converts this to a JDBC `INTEGER` value when it sends it to the database.

PARAMETERS:

parameterIndex	1 is the first parameter, 2 is the second, and so on
x	the `int` value to which the parameter will be set

EXAMPLE:

```
rset.setInt(2, 18); // sets second parameter to 18
```

setLong

```
void setLong(int parameterIndex, long x) throws SQLException
```

Sets parameter number *parameterIndex* to *x*. A JDBC driver converts this to a JDBC `BIGINT` value when it sends it to the database.

PARAMETERS:

parameterIndex	1 is the first parameter, 2 is the second, and so on
x	the `long` value to which the parameter will be set

EXAMPLE:

```
rset.setLong(2, 18000000000L);
// sets second parameter to 18000000000
```

setMaxFieldSize

```
void setMaxFieldSize(int max) throws SQLException
```

Sets the maximum number of bytes of data that can be returned for a column value that has a data type of BINARY, VARBINARY, LONGVARBINARY, CHAR, VARCHAR, or LONGVARCHAR. If the limit is exceeded, the excess data is silently discarded. For maximum portability, the limit should be greater than 256.

PARAMETERS:

max   the new maximum column size in bytes; 0 means that there is no limit

EXAMPLE:
```
rset.setMaxFieldSize(1024);
```

setMaxRows

```
void setMaxRows(int max) throws SQLException
```

Sets the maximum number of rows that this RowSet object may contain. If the limit is exceeded, the excess rows are silently dropped.

PARAMETERS:

max   the new maximum number of rows; 0 means that there is no limit

EXAMPLE:
```
rset.setMaxRows(2048);
```

setNull

```
void setNull(int parameterIndex, int jdbcType) throws SQLException
```

Sets parameter number *parameterIndex* to JDBC NULL (the generic SQL NULL defined in java.sql.Types). Note that the JDBC type of the parameter to be set to JDBC NULL must be specified.

PARAMETERS:

parameterIndex   1 is the first parameter, 2 is the second, and so on

jdbcType   a JDBC type code defined by java.sql.Types, which is the JDBC type of the parameter to be set to JDBC NULL

EXAMPLE:
```
rset.setNull(2, java.sql.Types.INTEGER);
// sets the second parameter, whose type is JDBC INTEGER, to JDBC
// NULL
```

SEE:
```
java.sql.Types
```

setNull

```
void setNull(int parameterIndex, int jdbcType, String typeName)
                                               throws SQLException
```

Sets parameter number *parameterIndex* to JDBC NULL (the generic SQL NULL defined in java.sql.Types). This version of setNull should be used to set parameters that are REF or user-defined types. User-defined types include STRUCT, DISTINCT, JAVA_OBJECT, and named array types.

Note that the JDBC type of the parameter to be set to SQL NULL must be specified. To be portable, an application must give the JDBC type code and the fully qualified SQL type name when setting a REF or user-defined parameter to SQL NULL. Although this method is intended for setting parameters whose type is REF or a user-defined type, it can be used to set a parameter of any JDBC type to NULL. If the parameter to be set does not have a user-defined or REF type, a JDBC driver ignores the *typeName* parameter. If a JDBC driver does not need the type code and type name information, it may ignore both *jdbcType* and *typeName*.

PARAMETERS:

parameterIndex	1 is the first parameter, 2 is the second, and so on
jdbcType	a JDBC type code defined by java.sql.Types; if not REF, STRUCT, DISTINCT, or JAVA_OBJECT, a JDBC driver will ignore the parameter *typeName*
typeName	the fully qualified name of the parameter being set. If *jdbcType* is REF, *typeName* should be the fully qualified name of the structured type that the REF parameter identifies. If *jdbcType* is not REF, STRUCT, DISTINCT, or JAVA_OBJECT, a JDBC driver will ignore this parameter.

EXAMPLE:
```
rset.setNull(1, java.sql.Types.REF, "schemaName.DOG");
// sets the first parameter, a JDBC REF value that references the
```

```
// SQL structured type schemaName.DOG, to SQL NULL
```

SEE:
java.sql.Types

setObject

void **setObject**(int *parameterIndex*, Object *x*) throws SQLException

Sets parameter number *parameterIndex* to *x*. A JDBC driver converts *x* using the standard mapping of Java Object types to JDBC types before sending it to the database. This standard mapping is shown in the table "Java Object Types Mapped to JDBC Types," on page 1090.

Note that this method may be used to pass database-specific abstract data types by using a driver-specific Java data type. If *x* is an instance of a class that implements the interface SQLData, this RowSet object should call *x*'s writeSQL method to write *x* to the SQL data stream. If *x* is an instance of a class that implements Ref, Blob, Clob, Struct, or Array, this method should convert *x* to its corresponding SQL type using the standard mapping for Java Object types. In case of an ambiguity, for example, if *x* is an instance of a class implementing more than one of those interfaces, an exception should be thrown.

PARAMETERS:

parameterIndex	1 is the first parameter, 2 is the second, and so on
x	an instance of a Java Object containing the input parameter value

THROWS:
SQLException if the given object is an instance of a class that implements more than one of the following interfaces: SQLData, Ref, Blob, Clob, Struct, or Array

EXAMPLE:
```
Object x = new Integer(1234);
rset.setObject(1, x);
// sets the first parameter to 1234 and converts it to a JDBC INTEGER
// before sending it to the database
```

SEE:
"Using setObject," on page 651, for how to use the method setObject

setObject

```
void setObject(int parameterIndex, Object x, int targetJdbcType,
                              int scale) throws SQLException
```

Sets parameter number *parameterIndex* to *x*. A JDBC driver converts *x* to *targetJdbcType* before sending it to the database. If *targetJdbcType* is NUMERIC or DECIMAL, *scale* indicates the number of digits to the right of the decimal point; for all other data types, *scale* is ignored.

This form of the method setObject should be used when the target JDBC type is DECIMAL or NUMERIC.

Note that the setter methods for specific types convert their arguments to the JDBC type that is the default mapping for that particular type. Methods other than setObject do not, however, perform any general data type conversions. A setObject method can take any type (in the form of a generic Object object) and convert it to the specified JDBC type before sending it to the database. In order to be objects, values for built-in types need to be expressed in their java.lang equivalents. For example, an int needs to be an instance of class Integer.

This method may be used to pass database-specific abstract data types by using a driver-specified Java type for *x* and using java.sql.Types.OTHER for *targetJdbcType*.

PARAMETERS:

parameterIndex	1 is the first parameter, 2 is the second, and so on
x	an instance of a Java Object containing the input parameter value
targetJdbcType	an integer constant representing the JDBC type (as defined in java.sql.Types) to be sent to the database. The *scale* argument may further qualify this type.
scale	the number of digits to the right of the decimal point. This applies only to java.sql.Types.DECIMAL and java.sql.Types.NUMERIC types. For all other types, this value will be ignored.

EXAMPLE:
```
Object x = new Integer(1234);
rset.setObject(1, x, java.sql.Types.DECIMAL, 5);
// sets first parameter to 1234.00000 after converting it to a JDBC
// DECIMAL
```

SEE:

java.sql.Types

"Using setObject," on page 651, for how to use the method setObject

setObject

```
void setObject(int parameterIndex, Object x, int targetJdbcType)
                                              throws SQLException
```

Sets parameter number *parameterIndex* to *x* and assumes a scale of zero. A JDBC driver converts *x* to *targetJdbcType* before sending it to the database.

Note that the setter methods for specific types convert their arguments to the JDBC type that is the default mapping for that particular type. Methods other than setObject do not, however, perform any general data type conversions. A setObject method can take any type (in the form of a generic Object object) and convert it to the specified JDBC type before sending it to the database. In order to be objects, values for built-in types need to be expressed in their java.lang class equivalents. For example, an int needs to be an instance of class Integer.

This method may be used to pass database-specific abstract data types by using a driver-specified Java type for *x* and using java.sql.Types.OTHER for *targetJdbcType*.

PARAMETERS:

parameterIndex	1 is the first parameter, 2 is the second, and so on
x	an instance of a Java Object containing the input parameter value
targetJdbcType	an integer constant representing the JDBC type (as defined in java.sql.Types) to be sent to the database

EXAMPLE:

```
Object x = new Integer(1234);
rset.setObject(1, x, java.sql.Types.VARCHAR);
// sets first parameter to 1234 and converts it to JDBC type VARCHAR
```

SEE:

java.sql.Types

"Using setObject," on page 651, for how to use the method setObject

setPassword

```
void setPassword(java.lang.String password) throws SQLException
```

Sets the password property for this RowSet object to *password*. This property, which is typically set at run time before calling the method execute, is the password used to create a database connection. It is not usually part of the serialized state of a RowSet object.

PARAMETERS:

password   the user's password for connecting to a data source

EXAMPLE:
```
rset.setPassword("mysecret");
```

setQueryTimeout

```
void setQueryTimeout(int limit) throws SQLException
```

Sets the maximum number of seconds that this RowSet object will wait for a command to be executed to *limit*. If the limit is exceeded, the rowset will throw an SQLException.

PARAMETERS:

limit   the maximum number of seconds the rowset should wait for a query to execute

EXAMPLE:
```
rset.setQueryTimeout(30);
```

setReadOnly

```
void setReadOnly(boolean value) throws SQLException
```

Sets whether this RowSet object is read-only or updatable.

PARAMETERS:

value   true to set to read-only; false to set to updatable

EXAMPLE:
```
rset.setReadOnly(false); // sets rset to be updatable
```

setRef

```
void setRef(int parameterIndex, java.sql.Ref x) throws SQLException
```

Sets parameter number *parameterIndex* to *x*, a Ref object in the Java programming language. A JDBC driver converts this to a JDBC REF(structured-type) value when it sends it to the database.

PARAMETERS:

parameterIndex	1 indicates the first parameter, 2 the second, and so on
x	the Ref value, which represents data of an SQL REF type, to be set as a parameter

EXAMPLE:
```
rset.setRef(1, ref);
// sets the first parameter to the Ref object ref
```

setShort

```
void setShort(int parameterIndex, short x) throws SQLException
```

Sets parameter number *parameterIndex* to *x*. A JDBC driver converts this to a JDBC SMALLINT value when it sends it to the database.

PARAMETERS:

parameterIndex	1 is the first parameter, 2 is the second, and so on
x	the short value to which the parameter will be set

EXAMPLE:
```
rset.setShort(2, 8); // sets second parameter to 8
```

setString

```
void setString(int parameterIndex, java.lang.String x)
                                        throws SQLException
```

Sets parameter number *parameterIndex* to *x*. A JDBC driver converts this to a JDBC VARCHAR or LONGVARCHAR value (depending on the argument's size relative to the driver's limits on VARCHARs) when it sends it to the database.

PARAMETERS:

parameterIndex	1 is the first parameter, 2 is the second, and so on
x	the String object in the Java programming language to which the parameter will be set

EXAMPLE:
```
String x = "Happy days are here again";
rset.setString(2, x);
// sets second parameter to "Happy days are here again"
```

setTime

```
void setTime(int parameterIndex, java.sql.Time x) throws SQLException
```

Sets parameter number *parameterIndex* to *x*. A JDBC driver converts this to a JDBC TIME value when it sends it to the database, using the default Calendar to calculate it.

PARAMETERS:

parameterIndex	1 is the first parameter, 2 is the second, and so on
x	the java.sql.Time object to which the parameter will be set

EXAMPLE:
```
Time newRecord = new Time(345693456739L);
rset.setTime(2, newRecord); // sets second parameter to 17:57:36
```

SEE:
java.sql.Time

setTime

```
void setTime(int parameterIndex, java.sql.Time x,
                  java.util.Calendar cal) throws SQLException
```

Sets parameter number *parameterIndex* to *x*. A JDBC driver uses the given Calendar object to construct a JDBC TIME value, which the driver then sends to the database. With a Calendar object, the time can be calculated taking into account a custom time zone. If no Calendar object is specified, the rowset uses the default time zone.

PARAMETERS:

parameterIndex	1 is the first parameter, 2 is the second, and so on
x	the java.sql.Time object to which the parameter will be set
cal	the Calendar object the driver will use to calculate the time

EXAMPLE:
```
Time arrival = new Time(23502938562358L);
rset.setTime(2, arrival, cal);
```

setTimestamp

```
void setTimestamp(int parameterIndex, java.sql.Timestamp x)
                                              throws SQLException
```

Sets parameter number *parameterIndex* to *x*. A JDBC driver converts this to a JDBC TIMESTAMP value when it sends it to the database, using the default Calendar to calculate it.

PARAMETERS:

parameterIndex	1 is the first parameter, 2 is the second, and so on
x	a java.sql.Timestamp object

EXAMPLE:
```
Timestamp endOfEra = new Timestamp(25035912512350392L);
rset.setTimestamp(1, endOfEra);
// sets the first parameter to 795326-06-26 15:19:10.392
```

SEE:
java.sql.Timestamp

setTimestamp

```
void setTimestamp(int parameterIndex, java.sql.Timestamp x,
                     java.util.Calendar cal) throws SQLException
```

Sets parameter number *parameterIndex* to *x*. A JDBC driver uses the given `Calendar` object to construct a JDBC `TIMESTAMP` value, which the driver then sends to the database. With a `Calendar` object, the timestamp can be calculated taking into account a custom time zone. If no `Calendar` object is specified, the default time zone is used instead.

PARAMETERS:

parameterIndex	1 is the first parameter, 2 is the second, and so on
x	the `java.sql.Timestamp` object to which the parameter will be set
cal	the `Calendar` object the driver will use to construct the `TIMESTAMP` object

EXAMPLE:
```
Timestamp eruption2 = new Timestamp(-293458165L);
rset.setTimestamp(2, eruption2, cal);
```

setTransactionIsolation

```
void setTransactionIsolation(int level) throws SQLException
```

Sets the transaction isolation level for connections established by this RowSet object to *level*.

PARAMETERS:

level	one of the transaction isolation levels defined in the interface *java.sql.Connection*

EXAMPLE:
```
rset.setTransactionIsolation(
            java.sql.Connection.TRANSACTION_READ_COMMITTED);
// no reads will be allowed for data in a transaction that has not
// been committed
```

SEE:
"Connection Fields," on page 428, for definitions of the different levels
"Transaction Isolation Levels," on page 393, for further explanation

setType

```
void setType(int type) throws SQLException
```

Sets the type for this RowSet object to *type*.

PARAMETERS:

type   one of the following java.sql.ResultSet constants:
                            TYPE_FORWARD_ONLY, TYPE_SCROLL_INSENSITIVE, or
                            TYPE_SCROLL_SENSITIVE

EXAMPLE:
rset.setType(ResultSet.TYPE_SCROLL_INSENSITIVE);
// sets rset to be scrollable and insensitive to changes made while
// it is open

SEE:
"Types of Result Sets," on page 700

setTypeMap

void **setTypeMap**(java.util.Map *map*) throws SQLException

Replaces the current type map for this RowSet object with *map*. If a UDT has an entry in *map*, *map* will be used for custom mapping the UDT when no type map is supplied.

PARAMETERS:

map   a java.util.Map object that will replace the current
                            type map

EXAMPLE:
java.util.Map map = new java.util.Hashtable();
map.put("SchemaName.UDTName", Class.forName("javaClassName"));
rset.setTypeMap(map);
// creates a new type map, puts in an entry, and sets it as the new
// type map for rset

SEE:
"Creating a Custom Mapping," on page 896

setUrl

void **setUrl**(String *url*) throws SQLException

Sets the URL property for this RowSet object to *url*. This property is optional if the data source name property has been set.

When this RowSet object is reading or writing data, it will internally establish a connection using either the URL or the data source name, whichever was specified most recently. If a JDBC URL is used, a JDBC driver that accepts that URL must have been loaded by the application before the rowset attempts to make a connection.

PARAMETERS:

url   the URL that will be used for establishing a connection
                              with a data source; may be null

EXAMPLE:
`rset.setURL("jdbc:dcenaming:employees");`

SEE:
"JDBC URLs," on page 387

setUsername

`void setUsername(String name) throws SQLException`

Sets the user name property for this RowSet object to *name*. This property is used internally to establish a connection with a data source and is set at run time before the method execute is called. The user name property is not usually part of the serialized state of a RowSet object.

PARAMETERS:

name   the user name needed to establish a connection with a
                              data source

EXAMPLE:
`rset.setUsername("angelica");`

29.5 RowSet Fields

The RowSet interface inherits the following fields from java.sql.ResultSet:

JDBC 2.0 API:

CONCUR_READ_ONLY	FETCH_FORWARD	TYPE_FORWARD_ONLY
CONCUR_UPDATABLE	FETCH_REVERSE	TYPE_SCROLL_INSENSITIVE
	FETCH_UNKNOWN	TYPE_SCROLL_SENSITIVE

JDBC 3.0 API:

HOLD_CURSORS_OVER_COMMIT
CLOSE_CURSORS_AT_COMMIT

CHAPTER **30**

RowSetEvent

30.1 RowSetEvent Overview

A RowSetEvent object is used to notify a listener component that an event has occurred in a particular RowSet object. A RowSetEvent object is initialized with the RowSet object, called the *source*, in which the event occurred; thus, it simply identifies the source of an event. When an event occurs in a RowSet object, the RowSet object creates a RowSetEvent instance and sends it to each component that has been registered with it as a *listener* (a component that has implemented the RowSetListener interface). Each rowset listener must have implemented the three methods in the RowSetListener interface, one for each kind of event that can occur to a rowset. The source of the event will invoke the listener method corresponding to the event and supply it with the RowSetEvent object it has created.

30.1.1 RowSet Events

An event for a RowSet object is one of the following:

- its cursor is moved

- one of its rows is inserted, updated, or deleted

- the entire rowset is populated with new data

The RowSetListener interface defines a method corresponding to each of these types of changes. When a RowSet object invokes one of these methods and passes it a RowSetEvent object, the method tells the listener the nature of the event, and the RowSetEvent object identifies the rowset that is the source of the event. See "The Event Model for Rowsets" on page 799, for more information.

855

30.1.2   Creating a RowSetEvent Object

The RowSetEvent class defines only one constructor and no methods or fields. This constructor takes one argument, the RowSet object that is the source of the events about which a component wants to be notified. The following code fragment creates a RowSetEvent object for the RowSet instance denoted by *this*.

```
RowSetEvent event = new RowSetEvent(this);
```

The variable *event*, a RowSetEvent object, has its source field initialized to *this*. Because a change occurred in *this*, it created *event* behind the scenes and will pass it to the appropriate listener method that it will invoke on all of the listeners registered with it.

A listener that receives the RowSetEvent object *event* as the argument to a method notifying it of an event, can find out which RowSet object is the source of the event by calling the following line of code.

```
RowSet source = event.getSource();
```

The value of *source* is the RowSet object with which *event* was initialized, in this case, *this*. Note that the RowSetEvent class defines a constructor but no methods. Instead it uses methods inherited from the class java.util.EventObject. As a result, there is no formal explanation of the method getSource in this chapter.

30.2   RowSetEvent Interface Definition

```
package javax.sql;
public class RowSetEvent extends java.util.EventObject {
    RowSetEvent(RowSet source);
}
```

30.3 RowSetEvent Constructor

RowSetEvent

```
public RowSetEvent(RowSet source)
```

Constructs a new RowSetEvent object initialized with *source*. When an event occurs in *source*, *source* will create a RowSetEvent object internally as part of the JavaBeans event model. This RowSetEvent object will be sent to all components registered as listeners with *source*.

PARAMETERS:

source   the RowSet object that is the source of the event (the rowset in which the event occurred)

EXAMPLE:
Application code:

```
myRowSet.execute();
// myRowSet is filled with the data generated by executing the
// current command string for myRowSet
```

Possible code in the implementation of the method execute:

```
RowSetEvent event = new RowSetEvent(this);
// the method execute creates event, initializing it with a
// reference to this RowSet object
listener.rowSetChanged(event);
// the method execute passes event to the method rowSetChanged
```

30.4 RowSetEvent Methods

The RowSetEvent class does not define any methods, but it inherits the following methods from the class java.util.EventObject:

```
getSource              toString
```

CHAPTER 31

RowSetInternal

31.1 RowSetInternal Overview

THE RowSetInternal interface provides a RowSet object with additional methods that let a reader or writer access and modify the internal state of the rowset. This interface is part of the reader/writer facility that works behind the scenes and is invisible to most users. It is implemented by disconnected RowSet objects that support the reader/writer facility. (Disconnected rowsets are those that do not maintain a connection with their data sources.) Rowsets are not required to support the reader/writer facility.

A RowSetInternal object (a RowSet object that implements the RowSetInternal interface) can be passed to the RowSetReader.readData or RowSetWriter.writeData methods, which can then in turn invoke the rowset's RowSetInternal methods. These RowSetInternal methods, which allow the reader and writer to get information about the rowset's internal state and to change it when necessary, are used for capabilities beyond those already provided in the RowSet interface.

31.2 RowSetInternal Interface Definition

```
package javax.sql;
public abstract interface RowSetInternal {
    java.sql.Connection getConnection() throws java.sql.SQLException;
    java.sql.ResultSet getOriginal() throws java.sql.SQLException;
    java.sql.ResultSet getOriginalRow() throws java.sql.SQLException;
    java.sql.Object[] getParams() throws java.sql.SQLException;
```

```
        void setMetaData(RowSetMetaData md) throws java.sql.SQLException;
}
```

31.3 RowSetInternal Methods

getConnection

java.sql.Connection **getConnection**() throws java.sql.SQLException

Retrieves the Connection object that was passed to this RowSet object if there is one. This method is invoked by a RowSetReader.readData or RowSet-Writer.writeData method that has been passed a reference to this RowSetInternal object. The readData and writeData method call RowSetInternal.getConnection as part of their implementations for obtaining a connection to a data source. If this method returns a Connection object, they will use it; if no Connection was passed to the rowset, the reader or writer will establish one, getting the necessary information from the rowset's properties if necessary.

RETURNS:
the Connection object that was passed to the rowset; null if no Connection object was passed

EXAMPLE:
```
// caller is an instance of a RowSet class that implements the
// RowSetInternal interface and has a reader and writer registered
// with it
java.sql.Connection con = caller.getConnection();
// con contains either the connection that was passed to caller or
// null if caller was not passed a connection
```

getOriginal

java.sql.ResultSet **getOriginal**() throws java.sql.SQLException

Retrieves a ResultSet object that contains the original value of this RowSet object. Only rows contained in this result set are said to have an original value. After a method such as execute fills a rowset with data, it will enter that data as the rowset's original value. Before a writer propagates data to the data source backing the rowset, it may call this method to get the original value of the rowset. One of the possible implementations for a writer is that only if the data in the data source matches the original value returned by this method will the writer go ahead and update the data source.

The `ResultSet` object that this method returns will have its cursor positioned before the first row.

RETURNS:
a `ResultSet` object containing this `RowSet` object's original value, which includes all of the rows in the rowset

EXAMPLE:
```
// caller is an instance of a RowSet class that implements
// the RowSetInternal interface
ResultSet originalRowSet = caller.getOriginal();
// originalRowSet contains the original rows in caller
```

getOriginalRow

`java.sql.ResultSet` **getOriginalRow**`() throws java.sql.SQLException`

Retrieves a `ResultSet` object that contains the original value of this `RowSet` object's current row only. If the current row has no original value, this method returns an empty result set. If there is no current row, this method throws an `SQLException`.

This method is provided to make it possible for a writer to use an optimistic concurrency algorithm for determining whether to write data back to the rowset's underlying data source. A writer that uses this algorithm will invoke `getOriginalRow` in order to compare the values it returns with the values in the data source backing this `RowSet` object. If the values are not the same, meaning that someone else has modified the data source, the writer may decide not write new data to it.

The `ResultSet` object that this method returns will have its cursor positioned before the first row.

RETURNS:
a `ResultSet` object containing the original value of the current row of this `RowSet` object

THROWS:
`SQLException` when the cursor for this `RowSet` object is not on a row

EXAMPLE:
```
// caller is an instance of a RowSet class that implements
// the RowSetInternal interface
ResultSet originalRow = caller.getOriginalRow();
// originalRow contains the original value for the current row in
// caller
```

getParams

```
java.lang.Object[] getParams() throws java.sql.SQLException
```

Retrieves the parameters that were set for this rowset's command string. The parameters are returned as an array of java.lang.Object objects.

RETURNS:
an array of java.lang.Object objects containing the parameters set on this RowSet object

EXAMPLE:
```
// caller is an instance of a RowSet class that implements
// the RowSetInternal interface
java.lang.Object[] params = caller.getParams();
// params contains the parameters set on caller's current command
```

setMetaData

```
void setMetaData(RowSetMetaData md) throws java.sql.SQLException
```

Sets the RowSetMetaData object for this rowset to *md*. This method is called by a reader. The reader reads data and creates a RowSetMetaData object to describe it. The reader initializes the new RowSetMetaData object using the set methods provided by the RowSetMetaData interface. The reader invokes the setMetaData method in order to tell this RowSet object what a row that the reader will insert into it looks like.

PARAMETERS:

md   the RowSetMetaData object describing the row(s) that
                                  this RowSet object's reader will insert into it

EXAMPLE:
```
// the reader for the RowSet object rset has read data from a file and
```

```
// creates a metadata object to describe the columns for the data
// that the reader will insert into rset
RowSetMetaData md = new ...;
// creates an instance of a class that implements RowSetMetaData
md.setColumnCount(4);
md.setColumnName("PRICE");
... // set other values for md
rset.setMetaData(md);
```

CHAPTER 32

RowSetListener

32.1 RowSetListener Overview

A RowSetListener object, called a *listener*, is an instance of a class that wants to be notified whenever an event occurs on a RowSet object. Typically, such a class is a graphical user interface component that displays the data contained in the RowSet object. A RowSet object, being a JavaBeans component, follows the standard Java-Beans event model.

A component becomes a listener by implementing the RowSetListener interface and by having a RowSet object register it as a listener. Each method in the RowSetListener interface corresponds to one of the events that can occur on a RowSet object, and a listener's implementation prescribes how that listener will handle the event. When an event occurs, a RowSet object will invoke the appropriate listener method and pass it a newly created instance of RowSetEvent. The method tells the listener the nature of the event, and the RowSetEvent object tells it the source of the event.

The RowSetListener interface has three methods for handling rowset events. The method cursorMoved is called when a rowset's cursor has moved to a new position. The method rowChanged is called when one row in the rowset has changed. This method applies when an existing row is updated or deleted or when a new row is inserted. Finally, the rowSetChanged method is called when the contents of the entire rowset have changed. This event occurs when the method execute, defined in the RowSet interface, executes a command to fill a rowset with data. Because concrete implementations of the RowSetListener interface may define their own additional methods for filling a rowset with data, those methods would also trigger a rowset to invoke the rowSetChanged method. For example, the method `CachedRowSet.populate` reads new data to populate a rowset, so it would call the method `rowSetChanged`.

The following list shows the `RowSetListener` methods and the `RowSet` methods that trigger them.

Method	Triggered by
cursorMoved	any of the methods inherited from the `ResultSet` interface that move the cursor (this does not include `moveToInsertRow` and `moveToCurrentRow`)
rowChanged	`updateRow`, `insertRow`, and `deleteRow`
rowSetChanged	execute; methods in subtypes, such as `populate` in `CachedRowSet`

32.1.1   Registering and Deregistering a Listener

The `RowSet` object that is the source of the event handles the registering and deregistering of listeners. Assuming that the variable *barChart* references a JavaBeans component for a bar chart, the following line of code registers *barChart* as a listener with the `RowSet` object *rset*.

```
rset.addRowSetListener(barChart);
```

Any number of components may be registered as listeners with a `RowSet` object. If *graph* references a component for a Cartesian graph, and *pieChart* references a component for a pie chart, the following lines of code register them with *rset*.

```
rset.addRowSetListener(graph);
rset.addRowSetListener(pieChart);
```

Whenever *rset* changes, it will notify every component that has been registered with it, which in this case would be *barChart*, *graph*, and *pieChart*.

When a component should no longer be notified of changes in a `RowSet` object, it can be deregistered. The following line of code deregisters the bar chart component, meaning that *rset* will no longer notify it of changes.

```
rset.removeRowSetListener(barChart);
```

32.1.2 Using RowSetListener Methods

When a RowSet event occurs, the RowSet object invokes each listener's corresponding method, passing it a RowSetEvent object that tells the listener which RowSet object changed. Each listener will have implemented the three RowSetListener methods in a way that is appropriate for that particular component.

For example, if an application moves a RowSet object's cursor, that rowset will invoke the cursorMoved method on all of its listeners. In the following code fragment, an application moves the cursor of the RowSet object *rset* to the tenth row by calling the method absolute(10). The rowset *rset* has implemented the method absolute to invoke the method cursorMoved on the components registered with it as listeners, so cursorMoved is invoked on *barChart*, *graph*, and *pieChart*, the components that *rset* has registered as listeners.

In the application code:

```
rset.absolute(10);
```

Behind the scenes, as part of the implementation of the method absolute:

```
RowSetEvent event = new RowSetEvent(rset);
barChart.cursorMoved(event);
graph.cursorMoved(event);
pieChart.cursorMoved(event);
```

The listeners now know that the cursor in *rset* has been moved. They do not know, however, where the cursor moved. They can call the method ResultSet.getRow to find out its current position and update their displays, or do whatever else their implementations of cursorMoved specify. If an event does not affect a listener, for example, if a listener does not reflect the cursor in its display, it can define cursorMoved to do nothing.

The situation is similar with the other two events that can occur in a RowSet object. When a row has changed (has been inserted, updated, or deleted), the rowset will invoke the RowSetListener.rowChanged method; when the entire rowset has changed, the rowset will invoke the method RowSetListener.rowSetChanged. For example, the following code fragment shows what the RowSet object *rset* would do after its entire contents had been replaced.

In application code:

```
rset.execute();
```

Internally, as part of its implementation of the method execute, *rset* notifies all of its listeners:

```
RowSetEvent event = new RowSetEvent(rset);
barChart.rowSetChanged(event);
graph.rowSetChanged(event);
pieChart.rowSetChanged(event);
```

32.2   `RowSetListener` Interface Definition

```
package javax.sql;
public abstract interface RowSetListener extends
                                    java.util.EventListener {
    void CursorMoved(RowSetEvent event);
    void rowChanged(RowSetEvent event);
    void rowSetChanged(RowSetEvent event);
}
```

32.3   `RowSetListener` Methods

cursorMoved

```
void cursorMoved(RowSetEvent event)
```

Notifies this `RowSetListener` object that the position of the cursor in `event.getSource()` has moved.

PARAMETERS:

event   a RowSetEvent object specifying the RowSet object to which the event occurred

EXAMPLE:
```
barGraph.cursorMoved(event);
// the cursor in event.getSource() has moved, and barGraph will carry
// out its implementation of cursorMoved
```

rowChanged

void **rowChanged**(RowSetEvent *event*)

Notifies this RowSetListener object that a row in event.getSource() has changed.

PARAMETERS:

event   a RowSetEvent object specifying the RowSet object to which the event occurred

EXAMPLE:
```
barGraph.rowChanged(event);
// one or more values in a row in event.getSource() has changed, and
// barGraph will carry out its implementation of rowChanged
```

rowSetChanged

void **rowSetChanged**(RowSetEvent *event*)

Notifies this RowSetListener object that all the data in event.get-Source() has changed.

PARAMETERS:

event   a RowSetEvent object specifying the RowSet object to which the event occurred

EXAMPLE:
```
barGraph.rowSetChanged(event);
// all the values in event.getSource() have changed, and barGraph
// will carry out its implementation of rowSetChanged
```

CHAPTER 33

RowSetMetaData

33.1 RowSetMetaData Overview

A RowSetMetaData object contains information about the columns in a RowSet object. It inherits methods for retrieving information about columns from the ResultSetMetaData interface, and it provides additional methods for setting column information when the RowSet object on which it is based is populated or repopulated with a set of values.

Whenever the RowSet method execute is invoked, the RowSet object's current command string (a query) will be executed, and the rowset will be filled with the results of the query. As part of its implementation, the execute method will set or reset the metadata for the newly populated RowSet object. If the RowSet object is an instance of a class that has implemented the RowSetInternal interface, the method execute will call on the reader, which in turn invokes the method RowSetInternal.setMetaData and supplies it with the RowSetMetaData object to be set. (See the explanation of the RowSetInternal.setMetaData method on page 862 for more information about what the reader does.)

In general, for each ResultSetMetaData method that retrieves column information, the RowSetMetaData interface provides a method to set that information. For example, the ResultSetMetaData method getColumnCount returns the number of columns in a ResultSet object. The RowSetMetaData interface defines the method setColumnCount to set the number of columns in a RowSet object.

There are four ResultSetMetaData methods that do not have a counterpart in the RowSetMetaData interface because they are not needed or do not apply. The method RowSetMetaData.setColumnClassName is not needed for a rowset because the value returned by the method ResultSetMetaData.getColumnClassName is determined by the column type and the type map. RowSetMetaData methods for the `ResultSetMetaData` methods `isReadOnly`, `isWritable`, and `isDefinitely-Writable` do not apply because all of a rowset's columns will be either writable or read only, depending on whether the rowset is updatable or not.

The section "Using a `ResultSetMetaData`," starting on page 784, shows how to retrieve column information. The chapter "MetaData Tutorial" also has a section on using a `ResultSetMetaData` object, starting on page 194.

33.2   RowSetMetaData Interface Definition

```
package javax.sql;
public abstract interface RowSetMetaData
                              extends java.sql.ResultSetMetaData {
    void setColumnCount(int columnCount) throws SQLException;
    void setAutoIncrement(int column, boolean property)
                                                    throws SQLException;
    void setCaseSensitive(int column, boolean property)
                                                    throws SQLException;
    void setCurrency(int column, boolean property) throws SQLException;
    void setNullable(int column, int property) throws SQLException;
    void setSigned(int column, boolean property) throws SQLException;
    void setSearchable(int column, boolean property)
                                                    throws SQLException;
    void setColumnDisplaySize(int column, int size) throws SQLException;
    void setColumnLabel(int column, String label) throws SQLException;
    void setColumnName(int column, String name) throws SQLException;
    void setSchemaName(int column, String name) throws SQLException;
    void setPrecision(int column, int precision) throws SQLException;
    void setScale(int column, int scale) throws SQLException;
    void setTableName(int column, String name) throws SQLException;
    void setCatalogName(int column, String name) throws SQLException;
    void setColumnType(int column, int jdbcType) throws SQLException;
    void setColumnTypeName(int column, String name) throws SQLException;
}
```

33.3 RowSetMetaData Methods

The following methods are inherited from `java.sql.ResultSetMetaData`:

getCatalogName	getColumnClassName	getColumnCount
getColumnDisplaySize	getColumnLabel	getColumnName
getColumnType	getColumnTypeName	getPrecision
getScale	getSchemaName	getTableName
isAutoIncrement	isCaseSensitive	isCurrency
isDefinitelyWritable	isNullable	isReadOnly
isSearchable	isSigned	isWritable

The following methods are defined in the interface `javax.sql.RowSetMetaData`:

setAutoIncrement

void **setAutoIncrement**(int *column*, boolean *property*) throws SQLException

> Sets the auto-increment mode for column *column* to *property*. If *property* is `true`, the designated column will be numbered automatically and will thus be read-only in most cases.

PARAMETERS:

column	1 is the first column, 2 the second, and so on
property	`true` to specify that the column is automatically numbered; `false` to specify that it is not

EXAMPLE:
```
rsmd.setAutoIncrement(3, true);
// the third column will be automatically numbered
```

setCaseSensitive

void **setCaseSensitive**(int *column*, boolean *property*) throws SQLException

> Sets whether column *column* is case sensitive to *property*.

PARAMETERS:

column   1 is the first column, 2 the second, and so on

property   true to specify that the column is case sensitive; false
                         to specify that it is not

EXAMPLE:
```
rsmd.setCaseSensitive(1, false);
// sets the first column to be case insensitive
```

setCatalogName

```
void setCatalogName(int column, String catalogName) throws SQLException
```

Sets the catalog name for the table from which column *column* of this
RowSet object was derived to *catalogName*.

PARAMETERS:

column   1 is the first column, 2 the second, and so on

catalogName   the name of the catalog for the designated column's
                         table; "" if there is no catalog name for the table

EXAMPLE:
```
rsmd.setCatalogName(2, "catalogName");
```

setColumnCount

```
void setColumnCount(int columnCount) throws SQLException
```

Sets the number of columns contained in this RowSet object to *column-
Count*.

PARAMETERS:

columnCount   an int indicating the number of columns in this RowSet
                         object

EXAMPLE:
```
rsmd.setColumnCount(5); sets the column count for this rowset to 5
```

setColumnDisplaySize

```
void setColumnDisplaySize(int column, int size) throws SQLException
```

Sets the normal maximum width in characters for column *column* to *size*.

PARAMETERS:

column   1 is the first column, 2 the second, and so on

size   the normal maximum number or characters allowed in
                        the designated column

EXAMPLE:
```
rsmd.setColumnDisplaySize(3, 256);
// no more than 256 characters will normally be allowed in column 3
```

setColumnLabel

```
void setColumnLabel(int column, String label) throws SQLException
```

Sets the suggested column title for column *column,* to be used in printouts
and displays, to *label*.

PARAMETERS:

column   1 is the first column, 2 the second, and so on

label   the name suggested as the title for the designated col-
                        umn in printouts and displays, if any

EXAMPLE:
```
rsmd.setColumnLabel(2, "ID_NUMBER");
```

setColumnName

```
void setColumnName(int column, String name) throws SQLException
```

Sets the name of column *column* to *name*.

PARAMETERS:

column   1 is the first column, 2 the second, and so on

name   the name for the designated column

EXAMPLE:
```
rsmd.setColumnName(4, "DEPT");
```

setColumnType

void **setColumnType**(int *column*, int *jdbcType*) throws SQLException

       Sets the JDBC type (from the class java.sql.Types) for the value stored in column *column* to *jdbcType*.

PARAMETERS:

column	1 is the first column, 2 the second, and so on
jdbcType	a type code from the class java.sql.Types

EXAMPLE:
rsmd.getColumnType(2, Types.VARCHAR);
// the data type for values in the second column of this rowset is
// JDBC VARCHAR

SEE:
java.sql.Types

setColumnTypeName

void **setColumnTypeName**(int *column*, String *name*) throws SQLException

       Sets the type name used by this particular data source for the data type stored in column *column* to *name*.

PARAMETERS:

column	1 is the first column, 2 the second, and so on
name	the type name used by the data source for the data type stored in the designated column

EXAMPLE:
rsmd.setColumnTypeName(2, "IMAGE");
// the type name used by this data source for the data type stored in
// column 2 is set to IMAGE

setCurrency

void **setCurrency**(int *column*, boolean *property*) throws SQLException

       Sets whether column *column* stores cash values to *property*.

PARAMETERS:

column   1 is the first column, 2 the second, and so on

property   true to indicate that the designated column stores cash
                        values; false to indicate that it does not

EXAMPLE:
```
rsmd.setCurrency(3, false);
// the third column does not store cash values
```

setNullable

```
void setNullable(int column, int property) throws SQLException
```

Sets whether a NULL value can be stored in column *column* to *property*.

PARAMETERS:

column   1 is the first column, 2 the second, and so on

property   one of the constants defined in ResultSetMetaData.
                        Possible values are columnNoNulls (column does not
                        allow Null values), columnNullable (column allows
                        NULL values), or columnNullableUnknown (nullability
                        is unknown).

EXAMPLE:
```
rsmd.setNullable(1, java.sql.ResultSet.columnNoNulls);
// NULL values are not allowed in the first column of this rowset
```

SEE:
```
    ResultSetMetaData.columnNoNulls
    ResultSetMetaData.columnNullable
    ResultSetMetaData.columnNullableUnknown
```

setPrecision

```
void setPrecision(int column, int precision) throws SQLException
```

For number types, sets the number of decimal digits in column *column* to
precision. For character types, this method sets the maximum length in characters for column *column* to *precision*. For binary types, it sets the maximum
length in bytes for column *column* to *precision*.

PARAMETERS:

column	1 is the first column, 2 the second, and so on
precision	for number types, the number of decimal digits in a column; for character types, the maximum number of characters in a column; for binary types, the maximum number of bytes in a column

EXAMPLE:
```
rsmd.setPrecision(1, 20); // column 1 stores DECIMAL values; the
// values stored in the first column may have no more than twenty
// digits, including those to the right of the decimal point

rsmd.setPrecision(2, 256); // column 2 stores VARCHAR values; the
// maximum length for values in the second column is 256 characters

rsmd.setPrecision(3, 1024); // column 3 stores VARBINARY values; the
// maximum length for values in the third column is 1024 bytes
```

setScale

```
void setScale(int column, int scale) throws SQLException
```

Sets the number of digits to the right of the decimal point for values in column *column*.

PARAMETERS:

column	1 is the first column, 2 the second, and so on
precision	an int indicating the number of digits to the right of the decimal point

EXAMPLE:
```
rsmd.getScale(4, 5);
// values in the fourth column will have five digits to the right of
// the decimal point
```

setSchemaName

```
void setSchemaName(int column, String name) throws SQLException
```

Sets the schema name for the table from which column *column* of this

ResultSet was derived to *name*.

PARAMETERS:

column	1 is the first column, 2 the second, and so on
name	the name of the schema for the designated column's table; "" if there is no schema name

EXAMPLE:
```
rsmd.setSchemaName(1, "schemaName");
```

setSearchable

```
void setSearchable(int column, boolean property) throws SQLException
```

Sets whether the value stored in column *column* can be used in a WHERE clause to *property*.

PARAMETERS:

column	1 is the first column, 2 the second, and so on
property	true to specify that the column can be used in a WHERE clause; false to specify that it cannot

EXAMPLE:
```
rsmd.setSearchable(1, true);
// the value in the first column can be used in a WHERE clause
```

setSigned

```
void setSigned(int column, boolean property) throws SQLException
```

Sets whether the value stored in column *column* is a signed number to *property*.

PARAMETERS:

column	1 is the first column, 2 the second, and so on
property	true to specify that the value in the designated column is signed; false to specify that it is not

EXAMPLE:
```
rsmd.setSigned(3, false);
// values stored in the third column are not signed
```

setTableName

void **setTableName**(int *column*, String *name*) throws SQLException

> Sets the name of the table from which column *column* of this ResultSet was derived to *name*. If there is no table name (for example, when there is a join), *name* should be the empty string.

PARAMETERS:

column	1 is the first column, 2 the second, and so on
name	the name of the designated column's table; "" if there is no table name

EXAMPLE:
rsmd.setTableName(3, "EMPLOYEES");

33.4 RowSetMetaData Fields

The javax.sql.RowSetMetaData interface inherits the following fields from the java.sql.ResultSetMetaData interface:

```
ResultSet.columnNoNulls
ResultSet.columnNullable
ResultSet.columnNullableUnknown
```

CHAPTER 34

RowSetReader

34.1 RowSetReader Overview

A RowSetReader object, called a *reader*, produces a new set of rows for a RowSet object. The RowSetReader interface is part of a rowset framework for reading and writing data that goes on behind the scenes and is generally invisible to the user. At design time, an application initializes a RowSet object, which is a JavaBeans component, with its reader and writer components. Anyone may implement a rowset, a reader, and a writer, but generally a reader implementation will be provided by a vendor as part of its rowset product. Therefore, an application programmer seldom needs to bother with the inner workings of a reader. Programmers who are not implementing a reader may choose to skip the rest of this chapter.

34.1.1 The Reader/Writer Framework

The reader/writer framework is used with a disconnected RowSet object, that is, one that does not maintain a connection with its data source. A RowSet object that maintains a connection with its data source does not need a reader because it can retrieve data directly, and it does not need a writer because the data source will be updated directly when the methods ResultSet.insertRow, ResultSet.deleteRow, and ResultSet.updateRow are called. The reader/writer facility is extensible, allowing a developer to customize the way data is retrieved from its data source or sent back to it. The javax.sql package does not currently provide any implementations for this facility, but the specification for the JDBC 2.0 Optional Package API provides some partial examples, including example code illustrating one of the many possible ways to implement the `RowSetReader` interface. The specification is available from the following URL:

```
http://java.sun.com/products/jdbc
```

Each `RowSet` object is created with a default reader, which will typically be the reader implementation supplied as part of a rowset product sold by a third party. A `RowSet` object can be implemented so that it is possible to use a different reader, or the default reader can be extended to include new functionality.

34.1.2   Reading Data for a Disconnected Rowset

The `RowSetReader` interface provides one method, `readData`, which reads the data that will populate a disconnected rowset. When an application calls a `RowSet` object's `execute` method, `execute` will, in turn, call the reader's `readData` method. The implementation of the `readData` method may include several operations, some of them depending on how the `RowSet` object being populated has been implemented. A disconnected rowset generally uses the `readData` method to establish a connection in order to read the data with which it will populate the rowset. The reader's `readData` method uses the rowset's properties to set up the connection. The rowset receiving the data will have implemented the `RowSetInternal` interface, so `RowSetInternal` methods are available, when necessary, for getting the parameters that were set on the rowset. A reader that is reading a `ResultSet` object may also use the result set's metadata to get information about the format of the data being read.

Many different reader implementations are possible. For example, a reader can be implemented to read data directly from a regular file instead of from a JDBC result set, thus providing access to non-SQL data. In such an implementation, the `readData` method could use the `RowSet.insertRow` method to insert new rows into the rowset. When it is invoked by a reader, `insertRow` updates both the original value stored by the rowset and the current row of the rowset. A reader implemented to read data from files might also use the `RowSetMetaData` interface to tell the rowset about the format of the data that will be inserted into it.

As stated previously, `RowSetReader` and `RowSetWriter` objects are components of the reader/writer facility and must be registered with a `RowSet` object. It is also possible for a writer to be implemented such that a reader is registered with it. After the reader has read data and inserted it into the rowset, the rowset may call this writer to write the modified data back to the rowset's underlying data source.

Another possibility is to implement the reader and writer as one component, in which case only the one component is actually registered with the rowset.

Note that when a reader invokes RowSet methods, it does so internally; no event is generated and no listeners are notified.

34.2 RowSetReader Interface Definition

```
package javax.sql;
public abstract interface RowSetReader {
    void readData(RowSetInternal caller)
                                    throws java.sql.SQLException;
}
```

34.3 RowSetReader Methods

readData

void **readData**(RowSetInternal *caller*) throws java.sql.SQLException

Reads a set of rows that will be the new contents of *caller*. This method is invoked internally when *caller*'s RowSet.execute method is invoked by the application.

In general, this RowSetReader object may implement its readData method to call any of *caller*'s methods in order to read a set of rows and add them to *caller*. The method readData calls either the method RowSet.insertRow or a custom method to add rows to *caller*. If it is necessary to establish a connection with the data source before reading data, the method readData will call the RowSet methods that set up a connection. The only RowSet method that *caller* cannot invoke is execute, which will throw an SQLException if it is called recursively.

When the readData method invokes a RowSet method, it does not generate an event, so RowSetListener methods such as rowSetChanged are not called.

PARAMETERS:

caller   a RowSet object that has implemented the interface RowSetInternal and also implemented its RowSet.execute method (or a custom method) so that it calls a RowSetReader object's readData method

EXAMPLE:
```
// reader is an instance of a class that implements RowSetReader and
// is registered with the calling RowSet object
reader.readData((RowSetInternal)this);
// the calling rowset passes the readData method a reference to
// itself
```

CHAPTER 35

RowSetWriter

35.1 RowSetWriter Overview

A RowSetWriter object, called a *writer*, writes modified data back to a RowSet object's underlying data source. A writer is part of the reader/writer facility that, behind the scenes, reads and writes data for a rowset. At design time, an application initializes a RowSet object, which is a JavaBeans component, with its reader and writer components. Anyone may implement a rowset, a reader, and a writer, but generally a writer implementation will be provided by a vendor as part of its rowset product. Therefore, an application programmer seldom needs to bother with the inner workings of a writer. Programmers who are not implementing a writer may choose to skip the rest of this chapter.

A RowSet object that is detached from its data source may be modified, and it should have the ability to propagate those modifications back to its data source. In other words, when a RowSet object's data has been changed, it should be able to call its writer's writeData method internally to write the new data to its underlying data source.

Readers and writers can only be called by a RowSet object that supports the reader/writer facility. This support consists of having a reader and writer registered with it and also of implementing the interface RowSetInternal. The RowSetInternal interface gives a rowset the ability to provide additional access to its internal state, and the writer will need that access in order to do its job. A rowset that supports the reader/writer facility is passed to the reader's readData method as part of the implementation of a method such as execute. After the readData method has done its job, the rowset may modify some or all of its new data. If the rowset wants data that has changed to be written back to its underlying data source, the writer's writeData method will be invoked. For example, in a

CachedRowSet implementation, the method acceptChanges can be called to make modifications take effect in the rowset. This method can also call the writer's writeData method to propagate the changes to the data source backing the rowset.

The writeData method, the writer's only public method, may be implemented in various ways. Whatever the implementation, the writeData method must generally perform certain tasks as part of the process of writing data to the data source. It is possible for a reader to be registered with a writer at design time, which allows the two to work together.

If a writer needs to update the data source, it will most often have to establish a connection with the data source. If the rowset was passed a connection, the writer can simply use it. If not, the writer will make its own connection, generally using the rowset's properties.

The writeData method may be implemented so that before writing data to the data source, it checks that the data source has not been changed by anyone else. If the writer uses an optimistic concurrency algorithm, it may not write new data to the data source if there is a conflict, that is, if the data source has been changed by someone else. The calling rowset stores its original data as well as its new data, so after the rowset's data has changed, the writer can invoke the rowset's RowSetInternal methods getOriginalRow or getOriginal to get the rowset's original values (the values immediately before the change). The writer compares these "original" values with the values in the data source. Depending on its implementation, the writer may write the new data to the data source if the rowset's original values and the values in the data source match.

In another implementation alternative, a reader/writer pair can invoke stored procedures to read/write data.

35.2 **RowSetWriter** Interface Definition

```
package javax.sql;
public abstract interface RowSetWriter {
    boolean writeData(RowSetInternal caller)
                                    throws java.sql.SQLException;
}
```

35.3 RowSetWriter Methods

writeData

```
boolean writeData(RowSetInternal caller) throws java.sql.SQLException
```

Writes data to the data source that is backing *caller*. This method is called internally by a public *caller* method.

PARAMETERS:

caller   a RowSet object that has implemented the interface
                            RowSetInternal and has registered this RowSetWriter
                            object as its writer

RETURNS:

true if the row was written successfully; false if there was a conflict that prevented writing the row, such as the row in the data source having been changed

EXAMPLE:

```
// employeeRowSet is an instance of a RowSet class that implements
// RowSetInternal. writer is an instance of a class that
// implements RowSetWriter and is registered with employeeRowSet.
boolean successful = writer.writeData(employeeRowSet);
// successful will be true if the data read into employeeRowSet was
// successfully written to the data source backing employeeRowSet
```

CHAPTER 36

Savepoint ⬚ 3.0

36.1 Savepoint Overview

THE Savepoint interface, one of the features added in the JDBC 3.0 API, gives a developer more control over transactions. A transaction may contain multiple actions, and when the transaction is committed, all of the actions in it take effect. If the transaction is rolled back, none of the actions in it take effect. (See the section "Transactions," on page 392, for a more complete discussion of transactions.) The whole point of a transaction is that some changes to data may depend on other changes, so no change within a transaction becomes permanent unless all of them do.

A Savepoint object provides a way to mark an intermediate point within a transaction, thus making it possible to roll back the transaction to that point instead of rolling back the entire transaction. In other words, if the method rollback is supplied with a Savepoint object, everything in the transaction up to the savepoint will be saved, and everything after the savepoint will be undone.

The Connection interface handles transactions; therefore, the methods for creating, using, and removing Savepoint objects are Connection methods, just as rollback and commit are. Methods involving Savepoint objects work only if a driver/database supports them, which can be ascertained by calling the DatabaseMetaData method supportsSavepoints.

36.1.1 Creating a Savepoint Object

The method Connection.setSavepoint creates and sets a Savepoint object, as is shown in the following line of code, where *con* is a Connection object.

```
Savepoint save1 = con.setSavepoint("SAVEPOINT_1");
```

The `Savepoint` object *save1* has the name `"SAVEPOINT_1"` because that is the `String` object that was passed to the method `setSavepoint`. If no argument is supplied to the method `setSavepoint`, the new `Savepoint` object will automatically be assigned an identification number. See "Retrieving a `Savepoint` Object Identifier," on page 891, for how to retrieve a `Savepoint` object.

It is possible to create multiple savepoints in a transaction. This is done by calling the method `Connection.setSavepoint` for each savepoint to be set.

36.1.2 Using a Savepoint Object

A `Savepoint` object is used by passing it to the method `Connection.rollback`. For example, the next line of code rolls back the transaction containing the `Savepoint` object *save1* to the point where *save1* was created.

```
con.rollback(save1);
```

The following code fragment demonstrates setting a `Savepoint` object in a transaction, rolling the transaction back to that `Savepoint` object, and then committing the part of the transaction that precedes the `Savepoint` object.

```
Statement stmt = con.createStatement();
int rows = stmt.executeUpdate("INSERT INTO AUTHORS VALUES " +
        "(LAST_NAME, FIRST_NAME, HOME) 'TOLSTOY', 'LEO', 'RUSSIA'");
Savepoint save1 = con.setSavepoint("SAVEPOINT_1");

int rows = stmt.executeUpdate("INSERT INTO AUTHORS VALUES " +
        "(LAST_NAME, FIRST_NAME, HOME) 'MELVOY', 'HAROLD', 'FOOLAND'");
...
con.rollback(save1);
...
con.commit();
```

Because *save1* was passed to the method `rollback`, only the part of the transaction that precedes the creation of *save1* has been committed, which means that Leo Tolstoy was added to the table AUTHORS but Harold Melvoy was not.

36.1.3 Removing Savepoint Objects

A programmer may remove a particular `Savepoint` object by supplying it as the argument to the `Connection` method `releaseSavepoint`. The following line of code, in which *con* is a `Connection` object, removes the `Savepoint` object *save1*.

```
con.releaseSavepoint(save1);
```

Generally, however, a programmer does not need to worry about removing `Savepoint` objects because most of them are removed automatically. For example, all savepoints in a transaction are removed automatically when the transaction is committed. When an entire transaction is rolled back, all savepoints in it are likewise removed automatically. And, if a transaction is rolled back to a savepoint, any savepoints that were set after it are automatically removed.

There is a cost to maintaining a savepoint, however. Therefore, `Savepoint` objects should be set prudently, and they should always be removed when they are no longer needed. If there is any doubt about whether a `Savepoint` object has been removed, calling the `Connection` method `releaseSavepoint` is a good idea.

Once a `Savepoint` object has been removed, either automatically or with the method `releaseSavepoint`, it is no longer valid and cannot be used. Attempting to use an invalid `Savepoint` object by supplying it to the method `rollback` will cause an `SQLException` to be thrown.

36.1.4 Retrieving a Savepoint Object Identifier

The `Savepoint` interface defines only two methods, both of which retrieve a `Savepoint` object's identifier. These identifiers are not used by the JDBC API directly; rather, they are retrievable in case they are needed in a SQL command. Which of the two methods to use depends on how the `Savepoint` object was created.

- `getSavepointName`—the method to use when a `String` argument was supplied to the `Connection.setSavepoint` method that created the `Savepoint` object. The `setSavepoint` method sets the given `String` object as the new `Savepoint` object's name, which can be retrieved with the `Savepoint.getSavepointName` method. This method throws an `SQLException` object if it is called on a `Savepoint` object that was created without a name.

```
Savepoint save1 = con.setSavepoint("SAVEPOINT_1");
. . .
String name = save1.getSavepointName();
```

- getSavepointId—the method to use when no argument was supplied to the Connection.setSavepoint method that created the Savepoint object. In this case, a numeric identifier is automatically generated for the new Savepoint object. Numeric identifiers are retrieved with the Savepoint method getSavepointId. This method throws an SQLException object if it is called on a Savepoint object that does not have a numeric identifier.

```
Savepoint save2 = con.setSavepoint();
. . .
int idNumber = save2.getSavepointId();
```

36.2   Savepoint Interface Definition

```
package java.sql;
public interface Savepoint {
    int getSavepointId() throws SQLException;
    String getSavepointName() throws SQLException;
}
```

36.3   Savepoint Methods

getSavepointId

```
int getSavepointId() throws SQLException
```

Retrieves the numeric identifier that was automatically generated when this Savepoint object was created.

RETURNS:
an int indicating the numeric identifier the database assigned to this Savepoint object

THROWS:
SQLException if called on a Savepoint object that does not have a numeric identifier

EXAMPLE:
```
int numericId = savepoint1.getSavepointId();
```

getSavepointName

`String `**`getSavepointName`**`() throws SQLException`

Retrieves the name for this `Savepoint` object. The name is the `String` object that was passed to the `Connection` method `setSavepoint` when this `Savepoint` object was created.

RETURNS:
a `String` object indicating the name identifier for this `Savepoint` object, which is the name that was supplied when this `Savepoint` object was created

THROWS:
`SQLException` if called on a `Savepoint` object that does not have a `String` identifier

EXAMPLE:
`int nameId = savepoint2.getSavepointName();`

CHAPTER **37**

SQLData 2.0

37.1 **SQLData** Overview

THE SQLData interface is a special interface used only for the custom mapping of SQL user-defined types (UDTs), namely SQL structured types and distinct types. A custom mapping maps a UDT to a class in the Java programming language, and that class must implement the interface SQLData. There is a great deal of freedom allowed in how the class implements SQLData, but generally each attribute of a UDT is mapped to a field in the class.

An application programmer will probably never use this interface directly. For example, when an application calls a getObject method to retrieve a UDT with a custom mapping, the driver automatically uses the custom mapping rather than the standard mapping. (The standard mapping for an SQL structured type is a Struct object; for a distinct type, the standard mapping is that of the underlying type.) To accomplish a custom mapping, the driver creates an instance of the class that implements SQLData and calls the appropriate SQLData methods internally. These operations are completely transparent to the programmer.

Although it is possible that an application programmer might have occasion to write a class implementing the SQLData interface, it is expected that a tool will normally generate this class. A tool will probably query the programmer for the names of the UDT, the class, and the fields and then use them to write a class that implements SQLData. Besides supplying answers to a tool's queries, the only other thing that a programmer has to do to set up a custom mapping is to put an entry in a type map, which will be explained in the next section.

A key concept underlying the SQLData interface is that it presents a uniform standard to the driver writer while also allowing a great deal of freedom to the application programmer. For driver writers, the SQLData interface is the standard for reading and writing an SQL UDT, and this uniformity makes it possible for custom mappings to be portable across drivers.

Application programmers, on the other hand, have a great deal of freedom, which allows them to map SQL UDTs appropriately for different kinds of applications. First, there is complete freedom in the choice of the class name and field names. A programmer may base them on the SQL UDT names, or he/she may opt to use names that are more meaningful in a particular context. Second, the programmer controls the data types of the fields to which the attributes of an SQL UDT will be mapped. For example, an attribute that is a JDBC INTEGER could be mapped to a field that is a different numeric type or even a data type such as String. Third, programmers may augment the class to which a UDT is mapped (the class implementing the SQLData interface for that UDT) by adding their own fields and methods that implement domain-specific functionality. Fourth, the programmer has the option of generating JavaBeans components as the classes to which SQL UDTs will be mapped.

This freedom on the application writer's side includes having many different custom mappings for the same UDT. One approach is to have separate mappings, each with its own class implementing SQLData. In this case, entries can be put in separate type maps and the appropriate type map passed to a method to supersede the mapping in the connection's type map. In another approach, a single UDT can be mapped to a graph of multiple Java objects, with the attributes being divided up among the various Java objects. This requires that the readSQL method be customized so that it constructs multiple Java objects and then distributes the SQL attributes into fields of those objects.

Those who want to understand what is happening behind the scenes in a custom mapping should read all of this chapter, but it is quite possible to use a custom mapping without knowing everything about what the driver is doing internally. Accordingly, general application programmers may opt to read through the next section and to skip the rest of this chapter. Those who decide not to read about the internal workings of the SQLData interface will also want to skip the chapters on the two supporting interfaces, SQLInput and SQLOutput.

37.1.1   Creating a Custom Mapping

Creating a custom mapping for an SQL UDT involves defining the UDT, writing a class that implements the SQLData interface, and putting an entry in a type map. This section describes these three steps.

1. Defining a UDT in SQL

The following example defines the structured type DOG in SQL.

```
CREATE TYPE DOG
(
    BREED VARCHAR(50),
    NAME VARCHAR(50),
    WEIGHT NUMERIC
);
```

DOG is now a new data type in the schema in which it was defined. It can be used just as any of the predefined data types can be used.

See "Creating an SQL Structured Type," on page 999, for more information on creating an SQL structured type. Note that the syntax can vary from one DBMS to another.

2. Writing a class in the Java programming language that implements the SQLData interface

Probably the most important part of a custom mapping is the implementation of the SQLData interface. As said previously, it is expected that tools will provide the implementations for the methods in SQLData, so the programmer who wants to create a custom mapping for a UDT would not normally implement them by hand. A tool will probably ask the user to supply the following:

- the SQL name of the UDT to be mapped. This is the name used in the CREATE TYPE statement in which the UDT was defined.

- the name of the class in the Java programming language to which the UDT is being mapped. This name may be any valid class name.

- the names of the fields to which the attributes of the UDT will be mapped. These names may be any valid names the programmer chooses.

With this information, the tool can generate a class that is a mapping of the UDT from SQL to the Java programming language.

The following definition of the class Dog shows how a tool might implement SQLData so that it maps the SQL UDT DOG.

```
public class Dog implements SQLData {
    public String breed;
    public String name;
    public float weight;

    private String sql_type;
    public String getSQLTypeName() {
        return sql_type;
    }

    public void readSQL(SQLInput stream, String type)
                                        throws SQLException {
        sql_type = type;
        breed = stream.readString();
        name = stream.readString();
        weight = stream.readFloat();
    }

    public void writeSQL(SQLOutput stream) throws SQLException {
        stream.writeString(breed);
        stream.writeString(name);
        stream.writeFloat(weight);
    }
}
```

In this mapping, the attributes of the structured type DOG became fields of the class Dog, using the standard mapping from JDBC types to types in the Java programming language (shown in the table "JDBC Types Mapped to Java Types," on page 1087). Note that the structured type DOG has three attributes, whereas the class Dog has four: A private field, sql_type, was added. This field is a String object that holds the SQL type name of the structured type, which is the name used in the SQL CREATE TYPE statement when the UDT was created. After declaring its fields, the rest of the class Dog implements the three methods in SQLData.

• getSQLTypeName

This method simply returns the value of the field sql_type, which is the type name passed to the method readSQL. When the method setObject is invoked, this method will be called by the JDBC driver to determine the SQL type of the object to be mapped.

- `readSQL`

    This is the method that actually does the mapping from the SQL type `DOG` to the Java class `Dog`. First, it assigns the parameter passed to it, which specifies the type, to the field `sql_type`. The driver will have created an `SQLInput` object for this instance of `DOG` and put the attribute values for `DOG` into this stream in the proper order. The method `readSQL` calls the appropriate `SQLInput` reader methods in turn to read the value at the head of the given input stream and assign it to a field in `Dog`. The types of the values in the input stream correspond to the types read by the reader methods because they are both based on the order in which attributes for the structured type were defined. For the structured type `DOG`, the attribute order is `BREED`, `NAME`, and `WEIGHT`. An appropriate reader method must be used because a reader method converts the value it reads to the data type in its name. For example, the method `readString` converts the values for `BREED` and `NAME` to `String` objects, while `getFloat` converts the value for `WEIGHT` to a `float`.

- `writeSQL`

    This method maps the class `Dog` back to the SQL structured type `DOG` by writing the value for each field (except `sql_type`) to the given output stream. As with the method `readSQL`, the fields must be written in order, and the appropriate writer method from the interface `SQLOutput` must be used. Before calling the method `writeSQL`, the driver will have created an instance of `SQLOutput` that expects values to be written to it in the same order in which they were read from the `SQLInput` object.

    Note that the data type specified in writer methods (`writeString`, `writeInt`, and so on) is a type in the Java programming language, just as the data type specified in reader methods is. The driver will convert the value written to the stream to an SQL type before returning it to the database. The table "Java Types Mapped to JDBC Types," on page 1088, shows the standard mapping used in this conversion.

3. Putting an entry in a type map

A type map entry, an entry added to a `java.util.Map` object, contains the name of the UDT and the `Class` object of the class to which it is mapped. The following code fragment is an example of adding an entry to the type map associated with the Connection object *con*. It retrieves the connection's type map and inserts an entry containing the SQL structured type DOG and the Class object for the class Dog.

```
java.util.Map map = con.getTypeMap();
map.put("SCHEMA_NAME.DOG", Dog.class);
con.setTypeMap(map);
```

The variable *map*, which now contains the new entry, is the type map that a method will use for custom mapping a UDT. The connection's type map can be thought of as the default type map because that is the one a method will use when no Map object is specified.

If an application wants to override an entry in the connection's type map, it will pass a type map containing the desired mapping to the appropriate method. If necessary, the application will create a new Map object and add an entry to it before passing it to the method, as shown in the following code fragment.

```
java.util.Map newMap = new java.util.HashMap();
newMap.put("SCHEMA_NAME.DOG", Dog.class);
ResultSet myRS = myArray.getResultSet(newMap);
```

The following getter methods can take a Map object as a parameter:

- ResultSet.getObject
- CallableStatement.getObject
- Array.getArray
- Array.getResultSet
- Struct.getAttributes

In a type map entry, the Class object given must be for a class that implements the SQLData interface. It is an error if the class in a type map entry does not implement the interface SQLData.

Note that the existence of a type map does not guarantee a custom mapping. If there is no entry for the particular SQL UDT on which a method is operating, the driver will use the standard mapping.

37.1.2 Retrieving a Custom-mapped Object

This section describes what the driver does behind the scenes when a method has been invoked to retrieve an SQL UDT with a custom mapping.

First, the driver looks in the appropriate type map to get the name of the class to which the UDT is being mapped. If a type map has been passed to the method, it uses that; otherwise, it uses the connection's type map.

Second, the driver creates an instance of the class to which the UDT is mapped by calling the method `Class.newInstance`.

Third, if a type map has been passed to the method, the driver creates an input stream and initializes it with the type map. If no type map was supplied to the method, the driver initializes the input stream with the connection's type map.

Fourth, using the SQL definition for the UDT, the driver gets the attribute values and inserts them in order into the newly created input stream. The `SQLInput` object, with its type map and attribute values in place, is now ready to have the values read from it.

Fifth, the driver calls the `SQLData.readSQL` method that was defined in the class to which the UDT is being mapped. This method in turn calls the `SQLInput` reader methods in its implementation to read the database value at the head of the input stream, which it then assigns to the corresponding field in the class. If the first attribute value in the input stream is a JDBC `VARCHAR`, the first reader method called in the implementation of `readSQL` will be `readString`. If the second value is a JDBC `INTEGER`, the second method called by `readSQL` will be `readInt`, and so on. When all of the attribute values have been read and assigned to their respective fields, the retrieval and mapping of the UDT is complete.

The following code fragment uses the class `Dog`, defined in the previous section, to illustrate how the attribute values of the SQL UDT `DOG` might be mapped to an instance of `Dog`. First, an instance of `DOG` is selected from the table `PETS`. The method `getObject` is then used to retrieve this instance from the first column of the `ResultSet` object *rs*. In this case, the custom mapping entry is in the `java.util.Map` object *map*, which is supplied as the second argument to the method `getObject`.

Here is what the application says:

```
String query = "SELECT DOG FROM PETS WHERE OWNER_ID = 3528";
ResultSet rs = stmt.executeQuery(query);
rs.next();
Dog myDog = (Dog)rs.getObject(1, map);
```

Here is what the driver typically does behind the scenes when the method `getObject` is retrieving an SQL UDT with a custom mapping:

```
// 1. checks map and sees that DOG is being mapped to Dog
// 2. the driver retrieves the Class object for Dog from map and

//    creates an instance of Dog

SQLData sd = (SQLData)classObject.newInstance();

// 3. creates an SQLInput stream and initializes it with map
// 4. puts attribute values for DOG in the input stream
// 5. calls SQLData method readSQL on sd, supplying it with:
//       (1) the SQLInput stream it created and
//       (2) the SQL name it found in map

sd.readSQL(inputStream, "SCHEMA_NAME.DOG");

// 6. sd.readSQL calls the reader methods in its implementation

this.sql_type = "SCHEMA_NAME.DOG";
this.breed = inputStream.readString();
this.name = inputStream.readString();
this.weight = inputStream.readFloat();
```

The variable *myDog*, the instance of Dog in the application code, now contains the attribute values that are in the object retrieved from the column DOG in the table PETS. The field sql_type is assigned the SQL type name supplied to the method readSQL by the driver, so its value need not be read from the input stream. The field breed has been assigned the value for BREED because the driver put that value at the head of inputStream. The name field is assigned the value for NAME, the second value in the stream, and weight is assigned the value for WEIGHT, the last value in the stream.

37.1.3 Storing an Object with a Custom Mapping

A UDT with a custom mapping can be stored by passing it as a parameter to the method PreparedStatement.setObject. When the parameter passed to setObject is an instance of a class that implements SQLData (which means that it is a custom mapping of a UDT), the driver will create an output stream (an instance of SQLOutput) to which the SQLData instance will be written. The SQLData instance will have been created previously, for example, when the value was read from the DBMS.

This instance implements the method writeSQL with writer methods from the interface SQLOutput, similar to the way it implemented the method readSQL with reader methods from the interface SQLInput.

The method writeSQL takes one parameter, which is the output stream, created by the driver, to which it will write values. The values must be written in the order expected by the output stream, which is the same order in which the values were read from the input stream. The following code fragment, in which *con* is a valid Connection object, illustrates what an application might contain and what the driver would do internally.

Here is what the application says:

```
PreparedStatement pstmt = con.prepareStatement(
                "UPDATE PETS SET DOG = ? WHERE OWNER_ID = ?");
pstmt.setObject(1, myDog);
pstmt.setObject(2, 3582);
pstmt.executeUpdate();
```

Here is what the driver typically does behind the scenes when an instance of a class that implements SQLData is supplied as an argument to the method setObject:

```
// 1. calls the SQLData method getSQLTypeName on sd (the SQLData
//    object from the previous code example) to find out what to
//    expect

String sqlTypeName = sd.getSQLTypeName();

// 2. creates an SQLOutput stream (in this case, os) because myDog
//    is an instance of the class Dog, which implements SQLData

// 3. calls the SQLData method writeSQL on sd, supplying it with os

sd.writeSQL(os);

// 4. sd.writeSQL calls the SQLOuput writer methods in its
//    implementation
```

```
os.writeString(breed);
os.writeString(name);
os.writeFloat(weight);
```

To summarize storing a UDT with a custom mapping, when `setObject` is called with an object that implements `SQLData`, the driver creates an `SQLOutput` object and passes it to the `SQLData` method `writeSQL`. The method `writeSQL`, in turn, calls the appropriate writer methods to write the instance of `SQLData` to an output stream going to the driver, and ultimately back to the database.

37.2 SQLData Interface Definition

```
package java.sql;
public interface SQLData {
    public String getSQLTypeName() throws SQLException;
    public void readSQL(SQLInput stream, String typeName)
                                                throws SQLException;
    public void writeSQL(SQLOutput stream) throws SQLException;
}
```

37.3 SQLData Methods

getSQLTypeName

`String getSQLTypeName() throws SQLException`

Retrieves the fully qualified name of the SQL user-defined type that this object represents. This method is invoked by the JDBC driver and would not normally be used by the general programmer.

RETURNS:
the fully qualified name of the SQL user-defined type that this object represents

EXAMPLE:
`String type = mySQLData.getSQLTypeName();`

readSQL

```
void readSQL(SQLInput stream, String typeName)
                                    throws SQLException
```

Populates this object with data it reads from *stream*. This method must be implemented according to the following protocol:

1. Call the appropriate reader method from the interface SQLInput to read each of the attributes of the SQL type from *stream.*

   • For a distinct type, read a single attribute.

   • For a structured type, read each attribute in the order in which it appears in the SQL CREATE TYPE statement that created the structured type.

2. Assign the data to appropriate fields or elements (of this or other objects).

The JDBC driver initializes *stream* with the connection's type map before calling this method. The reader methods that are called will use this type map if the given *typeName* appears in an entry in the type map. Otherwise, the reader methods will map a structured type to an instance of java.sql.Struct and will map a distinct type to the standard mapping for the underlying type.

PARAMETERS:

stream	an input stream that is an instance of the interface SQLInput, from which SQL data will be read
typeName	the fully qualified SQL type name of the user-defined type being read from the data stream

writeSQL

```
void writeSQL(SQLOutput stream) throws SQLException
```

Writes this object to *stream*. The implementation of this method must call the appropriate writer method (from the interface SQLOutput) for writing each of the attributes of the SQL type to *stream.*

• For a distinct type, write a single attribute.

• For a structured type, write a value for each attribute of the SQL type in the order in which the attribute appears in the definition of the type.

PARAMETERS:

stream   an output stream that is an instance of the interface `SQLOutput`, to which SQL data will be written

CHAPTER 38

SQLException

38.1 SQLException Overview

THE class SQLException is used to signal unsuccessful or incomplete execution of SQL statements. Generally, when a method throws an SQLException object, it means that there was an error accessing a database. The SQLException class is derived from the more general class java.lang.Exception, which is in turn derived from Throwable. Methods that are defined with throws SQLException, which includes almost every method in the JDBC API, throw an instance of SQLException when an error occurs. Note that, as mentioned in Chapter 1, "Introduction," to avoid saying the same thing for almost every method, method explanations do not give the reason for throwing an SQLException unless the reason is something other than a problem accessing data. Thus, when there is no THROWS entry in a method explanation, the reason for throwing an SQLException is a data access error.

Warnings are handled by a separate warning mechanism that attaches a warning to the object that issued the SQL request. The class SQLWarning, which inherits from SQLException, represents a warning in the Java programming language. See "SQLWarning," on page 945, for information on warnings.

38.1.1 What an SQLException Object Contains

Each SQLException object contains the following kinds of information:

- a description of the error. This is a String object, which is used as the Java Exception message. It can be retrieved by calling the method getMessage, which is inherited from Throwable.

- an "SQLState" string identifying the exception. Its value depends on the underlying data source. Both X/Open and SQL99 define SQLState values and the conditions in which they should be set.

An application retrieves the SQLState string by calling the method SQLException.getSQLState. An application can call the DatabaseMetaData method getSQLStateType to see whether the SQLState returned by the data source is X/Open or SQL99.

- an error code identifying the error that caused the SQLException object to be thrown. This is an integer that is specific to each vendor. Normally this will be the actual error code returned by the underlying database, and its value is implementation-specific.

  An application can retrieve the error code by calling the SQLException method getErrorCode.

- a reference to the next SQLException object (a "chained" exception).

  An application calls the SQLException method getNextException on the exception that was thrown to retrieve the next exception if there is one. When there are multiple errors, the SQLException object that is retrieved with the method getNextException will contain a reference to the next exception, and so on. When there are no more exceptions, the method getNextException returns null, so it works well in a while or do while statement.

The class SQLException defines four constructors for creating instances of SQLException, plus three methods for retrieving information and one method for setting the next exception.

Three exceptions inherit from SQLException. The exception BatchUpdateException provides information about the commands in a batch that did not execute successfully. The other two are warnings. The exception SQLWarning provides warnings about database access; the exception DataTruncation provides warnings about data being truncated.

38.1.2 Retrieving SQLException Information

Information is retrieved from an SQLException object by getting each of its components. The method getMessage (inherited from java.lang.Exception, which in turn inherited it from java.lang.Throwable) returns the description of the exception. Three methods defined in SQLException get the other components: getSQL-State gets the SQLState value, getErrorCode gets the exception code used by the database vendor, and getNextException retrieves the exception chained to this one.

The following code fragment, the catch block of a try/catch construction, illustrates getting the components of the first SQLException object and then getting any subsequent ones that are chained to it.

```
catch (SQLException ex) {
    // If an SQLException was generated, catch it and display the
    // error information. It is possible for there to be multiple
    // error objects chained together.
    System.out.println ("\n--- SQLException caught---\n");
    do {
        System.out.println("SQLState: " + ex.getSQLState());
        System.out.println("Message:  " + ex.getMessage());
        System.out.println("Vendor code:   " + ex.getErrorCode());
        ex.printStackTrace(System.out);
        System.out.println("");
        ex = ex.getNextException();
    } while (ex != null)
}
```

38.1.3 What an SQLException Means

When an SQLException is thrown, it does not always mean that the method that caused it to be thrown was not executed. Thus a programmer should not make any assumptions about the state of a transaction based on exceptions. The safest course is to call the method rollback when there is any doubt and then to start again.

38.2 SQLException Class Definition

```
package java.sql;
public class SQLException extends java.lang.Exception {
    public SQLException(String reason, String SQLState, int vendorCode);
    public SQLException(String reason, String SQLState);
    public SQLException(String reason);
    public SQLException();
    public String getSQLState();
    public int getErrorCode();
    public SQLException getNextException();
    public synchronized void setNextException(SQLException ex);
}
```

38.3 SQLException Constructors

SQLException

public **SQLException**(String *reason*, String *SQLState*, int *vendorCode*)

Constructs a fully specified SQLException object.

PARAMETERS:

reason	a String object describing the exception
SQLState	a String object containing an Open Group code identifying the exception
vendorCode	an int indicating an exception code for a particular database vendor

RETURNS:
an SQLException object initialized with *reason*, *SQLState*, and *vendorCode*

EXAMPLE:
```
throw new SQLException(
                "Operation invalid at this time", "S1011", 59);
```

SQLException

public **SQLException**(String *reason*, String *SQLState*)

Constructs an SQLException object initialized with *reason* and *SQLState*. The vendor code is set to 0.

PARAMETERS:

reason	a String object describing the exception
SQLState	a String object containing an Open Group code identifying the exception

RETURNS:
an SQLException object initialized with *reason*, *SQLState*, and 0 for the vendor code

EXAMPLE:
throw new SQLException("No suitable driver", "08001");

SQLException

public **SQLException**(String *reason*)

Constructs an SQLException object initialized with *reason*. SQL state is set to null, and vendor code is set to 0.

PARAMETERS:

reason	a String object describing the exception

RETURNS:
an SQLException object initialized with *reason*, null for the SQL state, and 0 for the vendor code

EXAMPLE:
throw new SQLException("Unable to load JdbcOdbc.dll");

SQLException

public **SQLException**()

Constructs a SQLException object with reason and SQL state set to null, and vendor code set to 0.

RETURNS:
an SQLException object initialized with null for the error message, null for the
SQL state, and 0 for the vendor code

EXAMPLE:
```
throw new SQLException();
```

38.4   SQLException Methods

The following methods are inherited from the class java.lang.Exception, which
inherited them from the class java.lang.Throwable:

```
fillInStackTrace
getMessage
printStackTrace
toString
```

The following methods are defined in java.sql.SQLException:

getSQLState

```
public String getSQLState();
```

Gets the SQL state for this SQLException object.

RETURNS:
a String object giving the SQL state

EXAMPLE:
```
SQLException ex = new SQLException(
                    "Operation invalid at this time", "S1011", 59);
String s = ex.getSQLState(); // s = S1011
```

getErrorCode

```
public int getErrorCode()
```

Gets the vendor-specific error code for this SQLException object.

RETURNS:
an int indicating the error code used by the vendor of this database

EXAMPLE:
```
SQLException ex = new SQLException(
                    "Operation invalid at this time", "S1011", 59);
int n = ex.getErrorCode(); // n = 59
```

getNextException

```
public SQLException getNextException()
```

Gets the next SQLException object chained to this one.

RETURNS:
the next SQLException object or null if there are no more

EXAMPLE:
```
while(ex.getNextException() != null) {
    // print exceptions
}
```

setNextException

```
public synchronized void setNextException(SQLException next)
```

Sets *next* as the next element in the chain of exceptions. This method is normally used only by driver or tool writers.

PARAMETERS:

next   an SQLException object that will become the new end of the exception chain

EXAMPLE:
```
SQLException next = new SQLException("No suitable driver", "08001");
ex.setNextException(next);
```

CHAPTER 39

SQLInput

39.1 SQLInput Overview

THE SQLInput interface provides an input stream that contains a stream of values that represent an instance of an SQL structured or distinct type. Working with the interfaces SQLOutput and SQLData, SQLInput supports the custom mapping of SQL99 user-defined types (UDTs).

All of the methods in SQLInput except wasNull read the value at the head of the stream and return it as a type in the Java programming language. For example, the method readInt reads the value at the head of the input stream and returns it as an int; readByte reads the value at the head of the stream and returns it as a byte, and so on. In this book, these methods are referred to generically as read methods.

The method wasNull is called after a value is read (using one of the SQLInput.read methods) to determine whether the last value read was SQL NULL. If so, wasNull returns true.

39.1.1 Creating an SQLInput Object

A programmer never creates an SQLInput object directly. The driver creates one behind the scenes when both of the following are true:

- An application calls one of the methods that can perform custom mapping: ResultSet.getObject, CallableStatement.getObject, Array.getArray, Array.getResultSet, Struct.getAttributes

- There is a type map that contains an entry for the UDT being retrieved.

The type map may be the one associated with the connection, or it may be one that the application supplies to one of the methods than can do custom mapping.

The driver initializes the newly created SQLInput instance with the type map supplied as an argument or with the type map associated with the connection. When the driver calls the method SQLData.readSQL, the new input stream will use the type map to find out which implementation of SQLData to use. The stream then invokes the read methods defined in the SQLData object's implementation of the readSQL method.

In the following code fragment, the method getObject is given a type map, so the driver will create an SQLInput instance and initialize it with *myTypeMap*:

```
Dog dog = (Dog)rs.getObject(2, myTypeMap);
```

The value being retrieved from the second column of the current row of the result set *rs* is the SQL99 structured type DOG, which was defined in "Creating a Custom Mapping," on page 896. It has three attributes, each of which needs to be converted to a value in the Java programming language. To accomplish this, the driver creates an instance of SQLData that represents the structured type DOG. In the example, this instance of SQLData is an instance of the class Dog, which implements SQLData. (The class Dog is also defined in "Creating a Custom Mapping," on page 896.) The class implementing the SQLData method readSQL defines an appropriate SQLInput.read method to read each of the attribute values in DOG. When the driver invokes the method SQLData.readSQL, it in turn invokes its reader methods.

39.1.2 Using reader Methods

It is important that the reader methods be called in the proper order so that they will be reading the correct data type from the input stream. The order is determined by the definition of the structured type, taking into account attributes in types from which the structured type inherits and types that are embedded in it. (See "Ordering of Attributes," on page 1005, for an explanation of the ordering of attributes.) This ordering determines the order in which attribute values appear in an SQLInput instance and also the order in which an SQLOutput instance expects the values to be written. This same ordering is used in the implementation of the method readSQL, and that is why each reader method called is the correct method for reading the next attribute value.

The data type in the reader methods is the data type in the Java programming language to which the next attribute in the input stream will be converted. For example, for the method readBigDecimal, the next attribute in the input stream should be a NUMERIC or DECIMAL value, which will be returned to the application as a BigDecimal object. The table "JDBC Types Mapped to Java Types," on page 1087, shows the standard type mappings used by the reader methods.

39.2 SQLInput Interface Definition

```
package java.sql;
public interface SQLInput {
```
`2.0`   `boolean wasNull() throws SQLException;`

```
//============================================================
// Methods for reading the next attribute in the input stream:
//============================================================
```

`2.0`   `String readString() throws SQLException;`
`2.0`   `boolean readBoolean() throws SQLException;`
`2.0`   `byte readByte() throws SQLException;`
`2.0`   `short readShort() throws SQLException;`
`2.0`   `int readInt() throws SQLException;`
`2.0`   `long readLong() throws SQLException;`
`2.0`   `float readFloat() throws SQLException;`
`2.0`   `double readDouble() throws SQLException;`
`2.0`   `java.math.BigDecimal readBigDecimal() throws SQLException;`
`2.0`   `byte[] readBytes() throws SQLException;`
`2.0`   `java.sql.Date readDate() throws SQLException;`
`2.0`   `java.sql.Time readTime() throws SQLException;`
`2.0`   `java.sql.Timestamp readTimestamp() throws SQLException;`
`2.0`   `java.io.InputStream readAsciiStream() throws SQLException;`
`2.0`   `java.io.InputStream readBinaryStream() throws SQLException;`
`2.0`   `Reader readCharacterStream() throws SQLException;`
`3.0`   `java.net.URL readURL() throws SQLException;`

```
//============================================================
// Methods for reading the next SQL99 attribute in the input stream:
//============================================================
```

```
2.0    Object readObject() throws SQLException;

2.0    Blob readBlob() throws SQLException;
2.0    Clob readClob() throws SQLException;

2.0    Array readArray() throws SQLException;
2.0    Ref readRef() throws SQLException;
}
```

39.3   SQLInput Methods

readArray
`2.0`

```
Array readArray() throws SQLException
```

Reads the next attribute in this stream and returns it as an `Array` object in the Java programming language.

RETURNS:
the next attribute as an `Array` object or `null` if the value read is SQL `NULL`

EXAMPLE:
```
Array a = in.readArray();
// a contains the value that was at the head of the input stream in
```

readAsciiStream
`2.0`

```
java.io.InputStream readAsciiStream() throws SQLException
```

Reads the next attribute in this stream and returns it as an `InputStream` object in the Java programming language containing ASCII characters.

RETURNS:
the next attribute as a stream of ASCII characters; `null` if the value read is SQL NULL

EXAMPLE:
```
java.io.InputStream input = in.readAsciiStream();
```

```
// input contains the value that was at the head of the input stream
// in
```

readBigDecimal

`java.math.BigDecimal` **readBigDecimal**`() throws SQLException`

Reads the next attribute in this stream and returns it as a `BigDecimal` object in the Java programming language.

RETURNS:
the next attribute as a `BigDecimal` object or `null` if the value read is SQL NULL

EXAMPLE:
```
java.math.BigDecimal n = in.readBigDecimal();
// n contains the value that was at the head of the input stream in
```

readBinaryStream

`java.io.InputStream` **readBinaryStream**`() throws SQLException`

Reads the next attribute in this stream and returns it as an `InputStream` object in the Java programming language that contains a stream of uninterpreted bytes.

RETURNS:
the next attribute as an `InputStream` object or `null` if the value read is SQL NULL

EXAMPLE:
```
java.io.InputStream input = in.readBinaryStream();
// input contains the value that was at the head of the input stream
// in, as a stream of uninterpreted bytes
```

readBlob

`Blob` **readBlob**`() throws SQLException`

Reads the next attribute in this stream and returns it as a `Blob` object in the

Java programming language.

RETURNS:
the next attribute as a Blob object or null if the value read is SQL NULL

EXAMPLE:
```
Blob blob = in.readBlob();
// blob contains the value that was at the head of the input stream
// in
```

readBoolean

```
boolean readBoolean() throws SQLException
```

Reads the next attribute in this stream and returns it as a boolean in the Java programming language.

RETURNS:
the next attribute as a boolean; false if the value read is SQL NULL

EXAMPLE:
```
boolean b = in.readBoolean();
// b contains the value that was at the head of the input stream in
```

readByte

```
byte readByte() throws SQLException
```

Reads the next attribute in this stream and returns it as a byte in the Java programming language.

RETURNS:
the next attribute as a byte; 0 if the value read is SQL NULL

EXAMPLE:
```
byte x = in.readByte();
// x contains the value that was at the head of the input stream in
```

readBytes

```
byte [] readBytes() throws SQLException
```

Reads the next attribute in this stream and returns it as a byte array in the Java programming language.

RETURNS:
the next attribute as a byte array; null if the value read is SQL NULL

EXAMPLE:
```
byte [] bytes = in.readBytes();
// bytes contains the value that was at the head of the input stream
// in
```

readCharacterStream

2.0

```
Reader readCharacterStream() throws SQLException
```

Reads the next attribute in this stream and returns it as a Reader object in the Java programming language. A Reader object contains a stream of Unicode characters.

RETURNS:
the next attribute as a Reader object; null if the value read is SQL NULL

EXAMPLE:
```
Reader r = in.readCharacterStream();
// r contains the value that was at the head of the input stream in
```

readClob

2.0

```
Clob readClob() throws SQLException
```

Reads the next attribute in this stream and returns it as a Clob object in the Java programming language.

RETURNS:
the next attribute as a Clob object; null if the value read is SQL NULL

EXAMPLE:
```
Clob clob = in.readClob();
// clob contains the value that was at the head of the input stream
// in
```

readDate

`2.0`

Date **readDate**() throws SQLException

Reads the next attribute in this stream and returns it as a `java.sql.Date` object in the Java programming language. This method uses the default Calendar object for calculating the date; the custom mapping facility does not support the use of a non-default Calendar object in the JDBC 2.0 API.

RETURNS:
the next attribute as a Date object; null if the value read is SQL NULL

EXAMPLE:
```
java.sql.Date d = in.readDate();
// d contains the value that was at the head of the input stream in
```

readDouble

`2.0`

double **readDouble**() throws SQLException

Reads the next attribute in this stream and returns it as a `double` in the Java programming language.

RETURNS:
the next attribute as a double; 0 if the value read is SQL NULL

EXAMPLE:
```
double d = in.readDouble();
// d contains the value that was at the head of the input stream in
```

readFloat

`2.0`

float **readFloat**() throws SQLException

Reads the next attribute in this stream and returns it as a `float` in the Java programming language.

RETURNS:
the next attribute as a float; 0 if the value read is SQL NULL

EXAMPLE:
```
float f = in.readFloat();
```

```
// f contains the value that was at the head of the input stream in
```

readInt

`int readInt() throws SQLException`

Reads the next attribute in this stream and returns it as an int in the Java programming language.

RETURNS:
the next attribute as an int; 0 if the value read is SQL NULL

EXAMPLE:
```
int n = in.readInt();
// n contains the value that was at the head of the input stream in
```

readLong

`long readLong() throws SQLException`

Reads the next attribute in this stream and returns it as a long in the Java programming language.

RETURNS:
the next attribute as a long; 0 if the value read is SQL NULL

EXAMPLE:
```
long n = in.readLong();
// n contains the value that was at the head of the input stream in
```

readObject

`Object readObject() throws SQLException`

Reads the next attribute in this stream and returns it as an Object object in the Java programming language. The actual type of the object returned is determined by the standard type mapping and any customizations present in this stream's type map. (A type map is registered with the stream by the JDBC driver before the stream is passed to the method SQLData.readSQL.)

If the datum at the head of the stream is an SQL structured or distinct type with a custom mapping, the driver (1) determines the SQL type of the datum, (2) constructs an object of the appropriate class (a class that implements SQL-Data), and (3) calls the method SQLData.readSQL on that object. The method readSQL, in turn, calls the SQLInput reader methods that appear in its implementation. The instance of Object returned by getObject should be narrowed to the appropriate type.

RETURNS:
the next attribute as an Object object; null if the value read is SQL NULL

EXAMPLE:
```
Object x = in.readObject();
// x contains the value that was at the head of the input stream in
Struct struct = (Struct)in.readObject();
// struct contains the structured type that was at the head of the
// input stream in. The Object read was narrowed to a Struct object.
```

readRef

`2.0`

Ref **readRef**() throws SQLException

Reads the next attribute in this stream and returns it as a Ref object in the Java programming language.

RETURNS:
the next attribute as a Ref object; null if the value read is SQL NULL

EXAMPLE:
```
Ref ref = in.readRef();
// ref contains the value that was at the head of the input stream in
// as a Ref object
```

readShort

`2.0`

short **readShort**() throws SQLException

Reads the next attribute in this stream and returns it as a short in the Java programming language.

RETURNS:
the next attribute as a short; 0 if the value read is SQL NULL

EXAMPLE:
```
short n = in.readShort();
// n contains the value that was at the head of the input stream in
```

readString

`String readString() throws SQLException`

Reads the next attribute in this stream and returns it as a String object in the Java programming language.

RETURNS:
the next attribute as a String object; null if the value read is SQL NULL

EXAMPLE:
```
String s = in.readString();
// s is a String containing the value that was at the head of the
// input stream in
```

readTime

`java.sql.Time readTime() throws SQLException`

Reads the next attribute in this stream and returns it as a java.sql.Time object in the Java programming language. This method uses the default Calendar object for calculating a time; the custom mapping facility does not support the use of a non-default Calendar object in the JDBC 2.0 API.

RETURNS:
the next attribute as a java.sql.Time object; null if the value read is SQL NULL

EXAMPLE:
```
Time t = in.readTime();
// t is a Time object containing the value that was at the head of
// the input stream in
```

readTimestamp

`java.sql.Timestamp readTimestamp() throws SQLException`

Reads the next attribute in this stream and returns it as a `Timestamp` object in the Java programming language. This method uses the default `Calendar` object for calculating a timestamp; the custom mapping facility does not support the use of a non-default `Calendar` object in the JDBC 2.0 API.

RETURNS:
the next attribute as a `java.sql.Timestamp` object; `null` if the value read is SQL NULL

EXAMPLE:
```
java.sql.Timestamp ts = in.readTimestamp();
// ts contains the value that was at the head of the input stream in
// as a Timestamp object
```

readURL

`java.net.URL readURL() throws SQLException`

Reads the next attribute in this stream and returns it as a `java.net.URL` object in the Java programming language.

RETURNS:
the next attribute, which should be a DATALINK value, as a `java.net.URL` object; `null` if the value read is SQL NULL

EXAMPLE:
```
java.net.URL url = in.readURL();
// url is a URL object containing the value that was at the head of
// the input stream in
```

wasNull

`boolean wasNull() throws SQLException`

Determines whether the last value read was SQL NULL.

RETURNS:

true if the value read most recently was SQL NULL; `false` otherwise

EXAMPLE:

```
String s = in.readString();
boolean b = in.wasNull();
// if the SQL value read by readString is SQL NULL, b is true and
// s is null

int number = in.readInt();
boolean b = in.wasNull();
// b should be false because the mapping of an int cannot be null
```

CHAPTER 40

SQLOutput

40.1 SQLOutput Overview

THE SQLOutput interface represents an output stream to which a user-defined type (UDT) with a custom mapping can be written. All of the methods in SQLOutput are write methods for writing the various data types to the output stream. For example, writeDouble writes a double in the Java programming language back to the database as a JDBC DOUBLE; writeString writes a String back to the database as a CHAR, VARCHAR, or LONGVARCHAR. The driver will convert the value to the correct database-specific type.

Note that the general database programmer will never create an instance of this interface directly. SQLData objects use the SQLOutput interface internally, and driver writers are the ones who implement this interface. Drivers that support the custom mapping facility create an instance of SQLOutput and call its methods behind the scenes when a custom-mapped UDT is being written back to the database.

The interface SQLOutput is used for the custom mapping of both distinct and structured types. For a distinct type, what gets written to the SQLOutput object is its one value, which can be thought of as its single attribute; for a structured type, the values for each of the attributes of an instance get written to the SQLOutput object.

The SQLOutput interface is used in conjunction with the interfaces SQLInput and SQLData to support the custom mapping of SQL99 UDTs. In order to be custom mapped, an SQL UDT must have a corresponding class written in the Java programming language, and that class must implement the interface SQLData. The SQLData interface includes the methods readSQL and writeSQL, which call read and write methods to accomplish the actual mapping. The readSQL method calls appropriate `SQLInput.read` methods to map the attributes of a UDT instance as they are read into an application. The `writeSQL` method calls the appropriate `SQLOutput.write` methods to write the attributes of the UDT instance back to the database. Attribute values are read in from the input stream and written out to the output stream in the same order in which the attributes were defined in the SQL definition of the UDT.

The `SQLOutput.write` methods write the specified value to the output stream created for a particular UDT instance. For example, `writeClob` writes a `Clob` object to the output stream created for it, `writeInt` writes an `int`, and so on. The writer methods take a type in the Java programming language, and before returning it to the database, the driver converts this type to a JDBC type using the standard type conversions shown in "JDBC Types Mapped to Java Types," on page 1087. So, for example, the method `writeClob` writes a `java.sql.Clob` object, and the driver returns an SQL `CLOB` value to the database. If the database uses its own form of SQL `CLOB`, the driver will make the necessary conversions before returning the value to the database. Thus, the effect of the methods in the interface `SQLOutput` is to convert an object in the Java programming language back to the SQL form used by the database.

An application programmer never creates an `SQLOutput` object or calls its writer methods directly. The driver creates an `SQLOutput` object behind the scenes when an application invokes the method `PreparedStatement.setObject` and passes it an argument that is a UDT that has a custom mapping (that is, supplies it with an instance of a class that implements `SQLData`). The driver checks the SQL definition of the structured type and creates an `SQLOutput` object that expects values whose data types correspond to the data types of the attributes in the structured type definition. After creating the `SQLOutput` object, the driver then calls the `SQLData` method `writeSQL`, which has been implemented to call the writer methods of the appropriate type for writing this `SQLData` object.

In the following line of code, the method `setObject` is given an instance of the class `Dog`, which is mapped to the SQL structured type `DOG`. Because the method `setObject` has been called and been given an argument that requires a custom mapping, the driver will create an `SQLOutput` instance for it behind the scenes.

```
pstmt.setObject(1, myDog);
```

The argument *myDog* is an instance of the class Dog, which implements the interface SQLData. (Both DOG and Dog are defined in "Creating a Custom Mapping," on page 896.) The class Dog maps the three attributes of the SQL structured type DOG to fields in the Java programming language. The SQLData method writeSQL is implemented so that it calls the appropriate write methods for writing the fields of Dog back to the database via the output stream SQLOutput. Here is what writeSQL looks like for the class Dog:

```
public void writeSQL(SQLOutput stream) throws SQLException {
    stream.writeString(breed);
    stream.writeString(name);
    stream.writeFloat(weight);
}
```

It is important that the write methods be called in the proper order so that they will be writing the correct data type. Attributes are written to the stream in the order in which they are defined in the structured type, in this case, DOG. (See "Ordering of Attributes," on page 1005, for a complete explanation of the ordering of attributes.) This ordering determines the order in which attribute values appear in an SQLInput stream and also the order in which an SQLOutput stream expects the values to be written.

See "Storing an Object with a Custom Mapping," on page 902, for an example of application code for storing a UDT and what the driver does behind the scenes.

40.2 SQLOutput Interface Definition

```
package java.sql;
public interface SQLOutput {

    //============================================================
    // Methods for writing the next UDT value to the output stream:
    //============================================================

    void writeString(Srting str) throws SQLException;
    void writeBoolean(boolean b) throws SQLException;
    void writeByte(byte x) throws SQLException;
    void writeShort(short n) throws SQLException;
    void writeInt(int n) throws SQLException;
    void writeLong(long n) throws SQLException;
```

`2.0`   void **writeFloat**(float n) throws SQLException;

`2.0`   void **writeDouble**(double n) throws SQLException;
`2.0`   void **writeBigDecimal**(java.math.BigDecimal n) throws SQLException;
`2.0`   void **writeBytes**(byte [] b) throws SQLException;
`2.0`   void **writeDate**(java.sql.Date d) throws SQLException;
`2.0`   void **writeTime**(java.sql.Time t) throws SQLException;
`2.0`   void **writeTimestamp**(java.sql.Timestamp ts) throws SQLException;
`2.0`   void **writeAsciiStream**(InputStream in) throws SQLException;
`2.0`   void **writeBinaryStream**(InputStream in) throws SQLException;
`2.0`   void **writeCharacterStream**(Reader r) throws SQLException;


```
        //==========================================================
        // Methods for writing the next SQL99 value in
        // the output stream to the database:
        //==========================================================
```

`2.0`   void **writeObject**(SQLData x) throws SQLException;
`2.0`   void **writeRef**(Ref ref) throws SQLException;
`2.0`   void **writeBlob**(Blob blob) throws SQLException;
`2.0`   void **writeClob**(Clob clob) throws SQLException;
`2.0`   void **writeStruct**(Struct struct) throws SQLException;
`2.0`   void **writeArray**(Array array) throws SQLException;
`3.0`   void **writeURL**(java.net.URL url) throws SQLException;
    }

40.3 SQLOutput Methods

`2.0`   ### writeArray

void **writeArray**(Array *array*) throws SQLException

Writes *array* to this output stream; the driver will convert *array* to a JDBC ARRAY before returning it to the database.

PARAMETERS:

array   the Array object, representing a JDBC ARRAY

EXAMPLE:
```
out.writeArray(a);
```

writeAsciiStream

`2.0`

```
void writeAsciiStream(InputStream in) throws SQLException
```

Writes the stream of ASCII characters in *in* to this output stream; the driver will do any necessary conversion from ASCII to the CHAR format of the database.

PARAMETERS:

in   the InputStream object to be written to the database

EXAMPLE:
```
out.writeAsciiStream(in);
```

writeBigDecimal

`2.0`

```
void writeBigDecimal(java.math.BigDecimal x) throws SQLException
```

Writes *x* to this output stream; the driver will convert *x* to a JDBC NUMERIC before returning it to the database.

PARAMETERS:

x   the java.math.BigDecimal object to be written

EXAMPLE:
```
out.writeBigDecimal(x);
```

writeBinaryStream

`2.0`

```
void writeBinaryStream(InputStream in) throws SQLException
```

Writes *in* to this output stream.

PARAMETERS:

in   the InputStream object containing a stream of uninter-
                        preted bytes to be written to the database

EXAMPLE:
```
out.writeBinaryStream(in);
```


`2.0`   ## writeBlob

void **writeBlob**(Blob *blob*) throws SQLException

Writes *blob* to this output stream; the driver will convert *blob* to a JDBC BLOB before returning it to the database.

PARAMETERS:

blob   the Blob object to be written to the database

EXAMPLE:
```
out.writeBlob(blob);
```


`2.0`   ## writeBoolean

void **writeBoolean**(boolean *b*) throws SQLException

Writes *b* to this output stream; the driver will convert *b* to a JDBC BIT or BOOLEAN before returning it to the database.

PARAMETERS:

b   the boolean object to be written

EXAMPLE:
```
out.writeBoolean(b);
```


`2.0`   ## writeByte

void **writeByte**(byte *x*) throws SQLException

Writes *x* to this output stream. The driver converts *x* to a JDBC TINYINT value when it sends it to the database.

PARAMETERS:

x   the byte object to be written

EXAMPLE:
```
out.writeByte(x);
```

writeBytes

```
void writeBytes(byte [] x) throws SQLException
```

Writes *x* to this output stream. The driver will convert *x* to a JDBC VARBI-NARY or LONGVARBINARY value (depending on the argument's size relative to the driver's limits on VARBINARY values) before sending it to the database.

PARAMETERS:

x   the byte array to be written

EXAMPLE:
```
out.writeBytes(x);
```

writeCharacterStream

```
void writeCharacterStream(Reader r) throws SQLException
```

Writes *r* to this output stream. The JDBC driver will do any necessary conversion from Unicode to the database CHAR format.

PARAMETERS:

r   the Reader object containing a stream of Unicode characters to be written to the database

EXAMPLE:
```
out.writeCharacterStream();
```

writeClob

```
void writeClob(Clob clob) throws SQLException
```

Writes *clob* to this output stream; the driver will convert *clob* to a JDBC CLOB before returning it to the database.

PARAMETERS:

clob   the Clob object to be written

EXAMPLE:
```
out.writeClob();
```

writeDate

```
void writeDate(java.sql.Date date) throws SQLException
```

Writes *date* to this output stream; the driver will convert *date* to a JDBC DATE value before returning it to the database.

PARAMETERS:

date   the java.sql.Date object to be written

EXAMPLE:
```
out.writeDate(date);
```

 writeDouble

```
void writeDouble(double d) throws SQLException
```

Writes *d* to this output stream; the driver will convert *d* to a JDBC DOUBLE before returning it to the database.

PARAMETERS:

d   the double object to be written

EXAMPLE:
```
out.writeDouble(132509728355.0594);
```

 writeFloat

```
void writeFloat(float f) throws SQLException
```

Writes *f* to this output stream; the driver will convert *f* to a JDBC REAL before returning it to the database.

PARAMETERS:

f   the float value to be written

EXAMPLE:
```
out.writeFloat(0.384f);
```

writeInt

`2.0`

```
void writeInt(int i) throws SQLException
```

Writes *i* to this output stream; the driver will convert *i* to a JDBC INTE-GER before returning it to the database.

PARAMETERS:

i   the int to be written

EXAMPLE:
```
out.writeInt(64);
```

writeLong

`2.0`

```
void writeLong(long x) throws SQLException
```

Writes *x* to this output stream; the driver will convert *x* to a JDBC BIGINT before returning it to the database.

PARAMETERS:

x   the long to be written

EXAMPLE:
```
out.writeLong(3059673383L);
```

writeObject

`2.0`

```
void writeObject(SQLData x) throws SQLException
```

Writes the data in *x* to this output stream. If *x* is null, an SQL NULL is returned to the database. Otherwise, writeObject calls the SQLData method x.writeSQL, which in turn calls its writer methods. Each writer method is called in order, one for each attribute of a UDT.

This method is used only for UDTs that have a custom mapping (and thus are mapped to a class that implements the interface SQLData). If there is no custom mapping, writeStruct must be used for a structured type; for a distinct type, the writer method appropriate for its base type must be used.

PARAMETERS:

x   an instance of a class that implements `SQLData`. This instance contains the data for a distinct or structured type that is to be written to the database.

EXAMPLE:
```
out.writeObject(x);
```

writeRef

> 2.0

```
Ref writeRef(Ref ref) throws SQLException
```

Writes *ref* to this output stream; the driver will convert *ref* to a JDBC `REF(structured typeName)` before returning it to the database.

PARAMETERS:
ref   the `Ref` object to be written

EXAMPLE:
```
out.writeRef(ref);
```

writeShort

> 2.0

```
void writeShort(short n) throws SQLException
```

Writes *n* to this output stream; the driver will convert *n* to a JDBC `SMALL-INT` before returning it to the database.

PARAMETERS:
n   the short to be written

EXAMPLE:
```
out.writeShort(512);
```

writeString

> 2.0

```
void writeString(String s) throws SQLException
```

Writes *s* to this output stream; the driver will convert *s* to a JDBC `VAR-CHAR` or `LONGVARCHAR` (depending on the argument's size relative to the driver's limits on VARCHARs) before returning it to the database.

PARAMETERS:

s   the String object to be written

EXAMPLE:
```
out.writeString(s);
```

writeStruct

`2.0`

```
void writeStruct(Struct struct) throws SQLException
```

Writes *struct* to this output stream; the driver will convert it to an SQL structured type before returning it to the database. This method is used for writing Struct objects that were mapped to the Java programming language using the standard (default) mappings. For writing custom-mapped UDTs, the method `writeObject` should be used.

PARAMETERS:

struct   the Struct object to be written to the database

EXAMPLE:
```
out.writeStruct(struct);
```

writeTime

`2.0`

```
void writeTime(java.sql.Time t) throws SQLException
```

Writes *t* to this output stream; the driver converts *t* to a JDBC TIME value before returning it to the database.

PARAMETERS:

t   the java.sql.Time object to be written

EXAMPLE:
```
out.writeTime(t);
```

writeTimestamp

`2.0`

```
void writeTimestamp(java.sql.Timestamp ts) throws SQLException
```

Writes *ts* to this output stream; the driver converts *ts* to a JDBC TIME-STAMP value before returning it to the database.

PARAMETERS:

ts   the `java.sql.Timestamp` object to be written

EXAMPLE:
```
out.writeTimeStamp(ts);
```

writeURL

```
void writeURL(java.net.URL url) throws SQLException
```

Writes *url* to this output stream; the driver converts *url* to a JDBC DATALINK value before returning it to the database.

PARAMETERS:

url   the `java.net.URL` object to be written

EXAMPLE:
```
out.writeURL(url);
```

CHAPTER **41**

SQLPermission

41.1 SQLPermission Overview

THE SQLPermission class, which extends the BasicPermission class, is part of the security mechanism for applets. Its purpose is to grant permission for code running in an applet to set a logging stream. If such code calls the method DriverManager.setLogWriter, the SecurityManager object will check to see if there is an SQLPermission object. If not, the method setLogWriter throws a java.lang.SecurityException object.

When the DriverManager facility is used to establish a connection with a data source, the logging stream may contain information such as user names and passwords, SQL statements, and SQL data. In the context of an applet, others may get access to the content of the logging stream, which means that there is no real security for information that is logged. For this reason, a programmer writing code that will run in an applet must actively create an SQLPermission object giving permission for a logging stream to be set. Programmers should realize that this is a dangerous permission to grant.

Note that this potential security problem does not apply when code is running anywhere other than in an applet or when a connection is established using a DataSource object. In other words, calling the method DataSource.setLogWriter does not require that there be an SQLPermission object because there is no potential security problem.

An SQLPermission object is what is called a named permission. This means that it has a name but has no actions list (a list that specifies the actions that a permission allows). For example, the String object listing the actions for a FilePermission object might be "read, write". With a named permission such as SQLPermission, the SecurityManager object checks to see if the permission exists, and if so, the permission it names is granted. For example, the only name that is allowed for an SQLPermission object is *setLog*, and if a SQLPermission object exists, the SecurityManager object will allow a logging stream to be set. With named permissions, you either have the permission or you don't.

41.1.1   Creating an **SQLPermission** Object

Programmers never create an SQLPermission object using the constructors directly. Instead, they use policytool, which is implemented to use an SQLPermission constructor to create an SQLPermission object.

There are two constructors, one that takes a permission target name, and one that takes both a name and a list of actions. Currently, the only target name that can be used is *setLog*. The *actions* parameter does not apply to SQLPermission objects, so it is set to null.

2.0   41.2   **SQLPermission** Class Definition

```
package java.sql;
public final class SQLPermission extends BasicPermission{
    SQLPermission(String name);
    SQLPermission(String name, String actions);
}
```

41.3   **SQLPermission** Constructors

The following constructors are defined in the java.sql.SQLPermission interface:

2.0   **SQLPermission**

public **SQLPermission**(String *name*)

Constructs an SQLPermission object initialized with *name*.

PARAMETERS:

name   a `String` object indicating the symbolic name of this `SQLPermission` object; currently the only name allowed is *setLog*

RETURNS:

an `SQLPermission` object initialized with the given name, which must be *setLog*

SQLPermission

2.0

```
public SQLPermission(String name, String actions)
```

Constructs an `SQLPermission` object initialized with *name*.

PARAMETERS:

name   a `String` object indicating the symbolic name of this `SQLPermission` object; currently the only name allowed is *setLog*

actions   a `String` object indicating the actions for this `SQLPermission` object; currently there are no actions for an `SQLPermission` object, so this parameter must be `null`

RETURNS:

an `SQLPermission` object initialized with the given name, which must be *setLog*, and a `null` actions string

CHAPTER 42

SQLWarning

42.1 SQLWarning Overview

THE class SQLWarning provides information about database warnings. Warnings are silently chained to the object whose method caused the warning to be reported. Connection methods, Statement methods (including PreparedStatement and CallableStatement methods), and ResultSet methods may all cause warnings to be reported on the calling object. For example, a Connection object *con* would have a warning reported on it if a call to the method *con*.getConnection caused a database access warning. If a subsequent call to a method, for example, *con*.setTransactionIsolation, caused a warning, it would be chained to the first warning reported on *con*.

The Connection, Statement, and ResultSet interfaces have their own versions of the method getWarnings to retrieve the first SQLWarning object reported. Any subsequent warnings are retrieved by calling SQLWarning.getNexttWarning on the SQLWarning object just returned. Note that although the SQLWarning class is derived from SQLException, a SQLWarning object is not thrown when a warning has occurred. An application must explicitly call the method getWarnings to retrieve the first warning and getNextWarning to retrieve any subsequent warnings.

Executing a Statement object flushes warnings from the previous Statement object. In the case of a ResultSet object, warnings are removed when the cursor position changes. This keeps warnings from building up and consequently avoids forcing the user to clear warnings manually after each execution or cursor movement.

42.1.1 What an `SQLWarning` Object Contains

Each `SQLWarning` object contains the following kinds of information:

- a description of the warning. This is a `String` object that explains the warning.

- an "SQLState" string identifying the warning. Its value depends on the underlying data source. Both X/Open and SQL99 define SQLState values and the conditions in which they should be set.
  An application can call the `DatabaseMetaData` method `getSQLStateType` to see whether the SQLState returned by the data source is X/Open or SQL99.

- an error code. This is an integer that is specific to each vendor. Normally this will be the actual error code returned by the underlying database.

- a chain to the next `SQLWarning` object. This can be used if there is more than one warning.

The `SQLWarning` class defines four constructors for creating instances of `SQLWarning` plus two methods for getting and setting the next warning.

42.1.2 Retrieving `SQLWarning` Information

Information is retrieved from an `SQLWarning` object by getting each of its components. The method `getMessage` (inherited from `SQLException`, which inherited it from `java.lang.Exception`, which in turn inherited it from `java.lang.Throwable`) returns the description of the warning. Methods defined in `SQLException` retrieve two other components: `getSQLState` gets the SQLState value, and `getErrorCode` gets the warning code used by the database vendor. The method `getNextWarning`, defined in `SQLWarning`, retrieves the warning chained to this one.

The following code fragment defines a method that checks for and displays warnings. The `while` loop illustrates getting the components of the first `SQLWarning` object and then getting any subsequent ones that are chained to it:

```
private static void printWarnings (SQLWarning w) throws
                                      SQLException {
    // If an SQLWarning object was given, display the warning. It
    // is possible for there to be multiple warning objects chained
    // together.
```

```
    if (w != null {
        System.out.println("\n--- Warning---\n");
        do {
            System.out.println("SQLState: " + w.getSQLState());
            System.out.println("Message:  " + w.getMessage());
            System.out.println("Vendor:   " + w.getErrorCode());
            System.out.println("");
            w = w.getNextWarning();
        } while (w != null)
    }
}
```

42.2 SQLWarning Class Definition

```
package java.sql;
public class SQLWarning extends java.sql.SQLException {
    public SQLWarning(String reason, String SQLState, int vendorCode);
    public SQLWarning(String reason, String SQLState);
    public SQLWarning(String reason);
    public SQLWarning();
    public SQLWarning getNextWarning();
    public void setNextWarning(SQLWarning nextw);
}
```

42.3 SQLWarning Constructors

SQLWarning

public **SQLWarning**(String *reason*, String *SQLState*, int *vendorCode*)

Constructs a fully specified SQLWarning object.

PARAMETERS:

reason	a String object describing the warning
SQLState	a String object containing an Open Group code identifying the warning
vendorCode	an int indicating a warning code for a particular database vendor

RETURNS:

an SQLWarning object initialized with *reason*, *SQLState*, and *vendorCode*

EXAMPLE:

```
SQLWarning w = new SQLWarning(
        "Attempt to revoke privilege not successful",  "01006", 5);
// w contains an SQLWarning object initialized with the message,
// "Attempt to revoke privilege not successful", the SQL state
// "01006", and the vendor code 5
```

SQLWarning

```
public SQLWarning(String reason, String SQLState)
```

Constructs an SQLWarning object initialized with *reason* and *SQLState,* and with the vendor code set to 0.

PARAMETERS:

reason	a String object describing the warning
SQLState	a String object containing an Open Group code identifying the warning

RETURNS:

an SQLWarning object initialized with *reason*, *SQLState*, and 0 for the vendor code

EXAMPLE:

```
SQLWarning w = new SQLWarning(
   "An error occurred during the requested disconnection", "01002");
```

SQLWarning

```
public SQLWarning(String reason)
```

Constructs an SQLWarning object initialized with *reason*. The SQL state is set to null, and the vendor code is set to 0.

PARAMETERS:

reason   a String object describing the warning

RETURNS:

an SQLWarning object initialized with *reason*, null for the SQL state, and 0 for the vendor code

EXAMPLE:
```
SQLWarning w = new SQLWarning(
                    "Null value eliminated in set function");
```

SQLWarning

```
public SQLWarning()
```

Constructs an SQLWarning object with the description and SQL state set to null. The vendor code is set to 0.

RETURNS:

an SQLWarning object initialized with null for the error message, null for the SQL state, and 0 for the vendor code

EXAMPLE:
```
SQLWarning w = new SQLWarning();
```

42.4 SQLWarning Methods

The following methods are inherited from the class java.lang.Exception, which inherited them from the class java.lang.Throwable:

```
fillInStackTrace
getMessage
printStackTrace
toString
```

The following methods are inherited from the class `java.sql.SQLException`:

    getSQLState
    getErrorCode

The following methods are defined in the class `java.sql.SQLWarning`:

getNextWarning

```
public SQLWarning getNextWarning()
```

> Gets the next `SQLWarning` object chained to this one.

RETURNS:
the next `SQLWarning` object or `null` if there are no more warnings

EXAMPLE:
```
while(w.getNextWarning() != null) {
    // print warnings
}
```

setNextWarning

```
public void setNextWarning(SQLWarning nextw)
```

> Adds an `SQLWarning` object to the end of the chain.

PARAMETERS:

nextw   an `SQLWarning` object that will become the next warn-
                            ing in the warning chain

EXAMPLE:
```
SQLWarning nextw = new SQLWarning(
                        "Null value eliminated in set function");
w.setNextWarning(nextw);
```

CHAPTER 43

Statement

43.1 Statement Overview

A Statement object is used to send SQL statements to a database. There are actually three kinds of Statement objects, all of which act as containers for executing SQL statements on a given connection: Statement; PreparedStatement, which inherits from Statement; and CallableStatement, which inherits from PreparedStatement. They are specialized for sending particular types of SQL statements: A Statement object is used to execute a simple SQL statement with no parameters, a PreparedStatement object is used to execute a precompiled SQL statement with or without IN parameters, and a CallableStatement object is used to execute a call to a database stored procedure.

The Statement interface provides basic methods for executing statements and retrieving results. The PreparedStatement interface adds methods for setting IN parameters; the CallableStatement interface adds methods for retrieving OUT and INOUT parameters. The JDBC 3.0 API added methods to the CallableStatement interface for setting parameter by name.

NOTE: IN parameters are values passed to a method or stored procedure as input for that method or stored procedure. OUT parameters, as used in the context of the JDBC API, are value placeholders that are passed to a stored procedure. When the stored procedure executes, it returns the results via the OUT parameters. INOUT parameters are parameters passed to a stored procedure that serve two purposes. They provide input to the stored procedure and also a means for the stored procedure to return output. In Chapter 9, "CallableStatement," see "IN Parameters," on page 324; "OUT Parameters," on page 326; and "INOUT Parameters," on page 329, for more information.

43.1.1   Creating Statement Objects

Once a connection to a particular database is established, that connection can be used to send SQL statements. A Statement object is created with the Connection method createStatement, as in the following code fragment:

```
Connection con = DriverManager.getConnection(url, "sunny", "");
Statement stmt = con.createStatement();
```

The SQL statement that will be sent to the database is supplied as the argument to one of the execute methods on a Statement object. This is demonstrated in the following example, which uses the method executeQuery:

```
ResultSet rs = stmt.executeQuery("SELECT a, b, c FROM Table2");
```

The variable *rs* references a result set that cannot be updated and in which the cursor can move only forward, which is the default behavior for ResultSet objects. The JDBC 2.0 core API added a new version of the method Connection.createStatement that makes it possible to create Statement objects that produce result sets that are scrollable, updatable, or both. See "Creating Different Types of Result Sets," on page 705, for an explanation and example.

A new feature introduced in the JDBC 3.0 API is the ability to create statements (Statement, PreparedStatement, and CallableStatement objects) that will produce ResultSet objects that are not closed when a transaction is committed. This ability of a ResultSet object to remain open across commits is called *result set holdability*. Creating statements that produce ResultSet objects with holdable cursors is explained with examples in "Result Set Holdability," on page 702.

43.1.2   Executing Statements Using Statement Objects

The Statement interface provides three different methods for executing SQL statements: executeQuery, executeUpdate, and execute. The correct method to use is determined by what the SQL statement produces.

The method `executeQuery` is designed for statements that produce a single result set, such as `SELECT` statements.

The method `executeUpdate` is used to execute `INSERT`, `UPDATE`, or `DELETE` statements and also SQL DDL (Data Definition Language) statements such as `CREATE TABLE`, `DROP TABLE`, and `ALTER TABLE`. The effect of an `INSERT`, `UPDATE`, or `DELETE` statement is a modification of one or more columns in zero or more rows in a table. The return value of `executeUpdate` is an integer (referred to as the update count) that indicates the number of rows that were affected. For statements such as `CREATE TABLE` or `DROP TABLE`, which do not operate on individual rows, the return value of `executeUpdate` is always zero.

The method `execute` is used to execute statements that may return more than one result set, more than one update count, or a combination of the two. Because it is an advanced feature, it is explained in its own section later in this overview.

All of the methods for executing statements close the calling `Statement` object's current result set if there is one open. This means that any processing of the current `ResultSet` object needs to be completed before a `Statement` object is re-executed. For example, in the following code fragment, the `ResultSet` object *rs* that contains all the column values from `TABLE1` will be closed when the last line of code is executed, which produces the `ResultSet` object *rs* containing all the columns from `TABLE2`.

```
Statement stmt = con.createStatement();
ResultSet rs = stmt.executeQuery("SELECT * FROM TABLE1");
... // process data in rs
rs = stmt.executeQuery("SELECT * FROM TABLE2");
```

Note that the `PreparedStatement` interface, which inherits all of the methods in the `Statement` interface, has its own versions of the methods `executeQuery`, `executeUpdate` and `execute`. `Statement` objects do not themselves contain an SQL statement; therefore, one must be provided as the argument to the `State-ment.execute` methods. `PreparedStatement` objects, on the other hand, already contain a precompiled SQL statement and consequently do not supply an SQL statement as a parameter to these methods. `CallableStatement` objects inherit the `PreparedStatement` forms of these methods. Supplying a `String` parameter to the `PreparedStatement` or `CallableStatement` versions of these methods will cause an `SQLException` to be thrown.

43.1.3 Statement Completion

When a connection is in auto-commit mode, the statements being executed within it are committed or rolled back when they are completed. A statement is considered complete when it has been executed and all its results have been returned. For the method `executeQuery`, which returns one result set, the statement is completed when all the rows of the `ResultSet` object have been retrieved. Thus, the method `commit` will not be called automatically until all the rows have been returned. The situation is different for the method `executeUpdate` because, in this case, a statement is completed when it is executed. Consequently, the statement is committed as soon as it is executed. The situation is different still for the method `execute`. In this case, a statement is not complete until all of the result sets or update counts it generated have been retrieved.

Some DBMSs treat each statement in a stored procedure as a separate statement; others treat the entire procedure as one compound statement. This difference becomes important when auto-commit is enabled because it affects when the method `commit` is called. In the first case, each statement is individually committed; in the second, all are committed together.

43.1.4 Retrieving Automatically Generated Keys

Many DBMSs automatically generate a unique key field when a new row is inserted into a table. Implementations vary from vendor to vendor, but generally this key is a value that can serve as the primary key for the row that was inserted. In some DBMSs, the generated key is stored in a special column that is included in the CRE-ATE TABLE statement, so it is visible to the user. In other DBMSs, this special column is created internally and is not visible to users.

Methods and constants added in the JDBC 3.0 API make it possible to retrieve these keys, which is a two-step process. The first step is to alert the driver that it should make automatically generated keys available for retrieval. The second step is to access the generated keys by calling the `Statement` method `getGenerated-Keys`. The rest of this section explains these two steps more fully.

1. **Step One:** Tell the driver that it should make keys that the DBMS generates automatically available for retrieval. The driver is notified when an SQL statement is sent to the DBMS, which for `Statement` objects is when the statement is executed. For `PreparedStatement` and `CallableStatement` objects, on the other hand, the driver is notified when these statements are created.

Three new versions of the method `executeUpdate` and three new versions of the method `execute` signal the driver about making automatically generated keys available. These methods take two parameters, the first being, in all cases, an SQL `INSERT` statement. The second parameter falls into two categories. In the first category, a constant is supplied to indicate that all generated keys should be retrievable (`Statement.RETURN_GENERATED_KEYS`) or that no keys need to be made retrievable (`Statement.NO_GENERATED_KEYS`). For example, the following lines of code tell the driver to return all keys that the DBMS creates for the `INSERT` statement contained in *sql*.

```
String sql = "INSERT INTO ANIMALS VALUES ('Dog', 'Poodle', 'Omni')";
int count = stmt.executeUpdate(sql,
                        Statement.RETURN_GENERATED_KEYS);
```

The second category specifies the particular key columns that should be made retrievable. In this case, the parameter is an array whose elements are either the indexes or the names of the columns to be made available. The following code fragment tells the driver to make the automatically generated key in the first column available for retrieval.

```
String sql = "INSERT INTO ANIMALS VALUES ('Dog', 'Poodle', 'Omni')";
int [] colIndexes = {1};
int count = stmt.executeUpdate(sql, colIndexes);
```

The `Statement` method `execute` can also be used for notifying the driver about making generated keys retrievable. For example, the following lines of code alert the driver that it should make the key in column `ID` available.

```
String sql = "INSERT INTO ANIMALS VALUES ('Dog', 'Poodle', 'Omni')";
String [] colNames = {"ID"};
boolean b = stmt.execute(sql, colNames);
```

Note that unlike the methods `executeUpdate` and `executeQuery`, the method `execute` returns `true` or `false`. An application must call additional methods to retrieve an update count or `ResultSet` object. See "Executing Special Kinds of Statements," on page 965, for a detailed explanation of how to use the method `execute`.

For `PreparedStatement` objects, the SQL statement is sent to the DBMS to be precompiled when the `PreparedStatement` object is created. Thus, the driver is notified about making automatically generated keys retrievable via the `Connection.prepareStatement` methods. For example, the following line of code creates the `PreparedStatement` object *pstmt* with the SQL statement in *sql* and, in addition, tells the driver to make all keys that the DBMS generates for the inserted row available for retrieval.

```
PreparedStatement pstmt = con.prepareStatement(sql,
                    Statement.RETURN_GENERATED_KEYS);
```

The following lines of code demonstrate telling the driver for which particular columns it should make generated keys available. In this case, the array indicating the columns contains column names instead of column indexes.

```
String [] columnNames = {"KEY"};
PreparedStatement pstmt = con.prepareStatement(sql, columnNames);
```

2. **Step Two:** After the driver has been notified about making automatically generated keys available for retrieval, the keys can be retrieved by calling the `Statement` method `getGeneratedKeys`. This method returns a `ResultSet` object, with each row being a generated key. If there are no automatically generated keys, the `ResultSet` object will be empty.

The following code fragment creates a `Statement` object and signals the driver that it should be able to return any keys that are automatically generated as a result of executing the statement. The example then retrieves the keys that were generated and prints them out. If there are no generated keys, the printout says that there are none.

```
String sql = "INSERT INTO AUTHORS (LAST, FIRST, HOME) VALUES " +
                    "('PARKER', 'DOROTHY', 'USA')";

int rows = stmt.executeUpdate(sql,
                            Statement.RETURN_GENERATED_KEYS);

ResultSet rs = stmt.getGeneratedKeys();
if (rs.next()) {
    ResultSetMetaData rsmd = rs.getMetaData();
    int colCount = rsmd.getColumnCount();
    do {
        for (int i = 1; i <= colCount; i++) {
            String key = rs.getString(i);
```

```
            System.out.println("key " + i + " is " + key);
        }
    }
    while (rs.next();)
}
else {
    System.out.println("There are no generated keys.");
}
```

Instead of telling the driver to make all automatically generated keys available, the following code fragment tells the driver to make particular columns retrievable. It uses an array of column indexes (in this case, an array with one element) to indicate which columns with an automatically generated key should be made available for retrieval.

```
String sql = "INSERT INTO AUTHORS (LAST, FIRST, HOME) VALUES " +
                        "('PARKER', 'DOROTHY', 'USA')";
int [] keyColumn = {1};
int rows = stmt.executeUpdate(sql, keyColumn);
```

The following code fragment shows supplying an array of column names to indicate which ResultSet columns to make available. In this case, the driver is told to make the automatically generated key in the column AUTHOR_ID retrievable.

```
String sql = "INSERT INTO AUTHORS (LAST, FIRST, HOME) VALUES " +
                        "('PARKER', 'DOROTHY', 'USA')";
String [] keyColumn = {"AUTHOR_ID"};
int rows = stmt.executeUpdate(sql, keyColumn);
```

43.1.5 Closing Statements

Statement objects will be closed automatically by the Java garbage collector. Nevertheless, it is recommended as good programming practice that they be closed explicitly when they are no longer needed. This frees DBMS resources immediately and helps avoid potential memory problems. Also, the garbage collector may not release all internal resources, thus causing memory leaks. See "Freeing DBMS Resources," on page 395, for more information.

When an application closes a Connection object, all of the Statement objects that were created using that Connection object are also closed. In addition, all of the `ResultSet` objects produced by a `Statement` object are closed when the `Statement` object is closed. Nevertheless, it is good programming practice to close a `ResultSet` object explicitly when it is no longer needed. Likewise, it is good practice to close a `Statement` object explicitly when it is no longer needed. This is even more important given that the implementations of some DBMs have quirks that make it safer to close all `ResultSet`, `Statement`, and `Connection` objects explicitly. So besides not using resources needlessly, closing objects explicitly may avoid memory leaks in some DBMS implementations.

43.1.6 SQL Escape Syntax in Statements

`Statement` objects may contain SQL statements that use SQL escape syntax. Escape syntax signals the driver that the code within it should be handled differently. When escape processing is turned on, which is the default, the driver will scan for any escape syntax and translate it into code that the particular database understands. This makes escape syntax DBMS-independent and allows a programmer to use features that might not otherwise be available. But the main advantage to using escape syntax is that it makes an application portable across databases.

If escape processing has been disabled, it can be enabled as shown in the following line of code.

```
Statement.setEscapeProcessing(true);
```

A `RowSet` object enables escape processing with the following line of code.

```
RowSet.setEscapeProcessing(true).
```

A `Statement` object or `RowSet` object can disable the processing of escape syntax by supplying `false` to the method `setEscapeProcessing`.

An escape clause is demarcated by curly braces and a key word that indicates the kind of escape clause.

```
{keyword . . . parameters . . . }
```

The following keywords are used to identify escape clauses:

- **escape**   for LIKE escape characters

The percent sign (%) and underscore (_) characters work like wild cards in SQL LIKE clauses (% matches zero or more characters, and _ matches exactly one character). In order to interpret them literally, they can be preceded by a backslash (\), which is a special escape character in strings. One can specify which character to use as the escape character by including the following syntax at the end of a query:

```
{escape 'escape-character'}
```

For example, the following query, using the backslash character as an escape character, finds identifier names that begin with an underbar. Note that the Java compiler will not recognize the backslash as a character unless it is preceded by a backslash.

```
stmt.executeQuery("SELECT name FROM Identifiers
                   WHERE Id LIKE '\\_%' {escape '\\'}");
```

- **fn**   for scalar functions

  Almost all DBMSs have numeric, string, time, date, system, and conversion functions on scalar values. One of these functions can be used by putting it in escape syntax with the keyword fn followed by the name of the desired function and its arguments. For example, the following code calls the function concat with two arguments to be concatenated:

```
{fn concat("Hot", "Java")};
```

The following syntax gets the name of the current database user:

```
{fn user()};
```

Scalar functions may be supported by different DBMSs with slightly different syntax, and they may not be supported by all drivers. Various DatabaseMetaData methods will list the functions that are supported. For example, the method getNumericFunctions returns a comma-separated list of the Open Group CLI names of numeric functions, the method getStringFunctions returns string functions, and so on.

The driver will either map the escaped function call into the appropriate syntax or implement the function directly itself. Refer to "Support Scalar Functions," starting on page 1104, for a list of the scalar functions a driver is expected to support. A driver is required to implement these functions only if the DBMS supports them, however.

- **d, t,** and **ts**   for date and time literals

    DBMSs differ in the syntax they use for date, time, and timestamp literals. The JDBC API supports ISO standard format for the syntax of these literals, using an escape clause that the driver must translate to the DBMS representation. For example, a date is specified in a JDBC SQL statement with the following syntax:

    ```
    {d 'yyyy-mm-dd'}
    ```

    In this syntax, yyyy is the year, mm is the month, and dd is the day. The driver will replace the escape clause with the equivalent DBMS-specific representation. For example, the driver might replace {d 1999-02-28} with '28-FEB-99' if that is the appropriate format for the underlying database.

    There are analogous escape clauses for TIME and TIMESTAMP:

    ```
    {t 'hh:mm:ss'}
    {ts 'yyyy-mm-dd hh:mm:ss.f . . .'}
    ```

    The fractional seconds (.f . . .) portion of the TIMESTAMP can be omitted.

- **call** or **? = call**   for stored procedures

    If a database supports stored procedures, they can be invoked from JDBC with the syntax shown below. Note that the square brackets ([ ]) indicate that what is between them is optional, and they are not part of the syntax.

    ```
    {call procedure_name[(?, ?, . . .)]}
    ```

    or, where a procedure returns a result parameter:

    ```
    {? = call procedure_name[(?, ?, . . .)]}
    ```

    Input arguments may be either literals or parameters. See the section

"Numbering of Parameters," on page 328, for more information.

One can call the method `DatabaseMetaData.supportsStoredProcedures` to see if the database supports stored procedures.

- **oj** for outer joins

  The syntax for an outer join is:

  ```
  {oj outer-join}
  ```

  In this syntax, `outer-join` has the form

  ```
  table {LEFT|RIGHT|FULL} OUTER JOIN {table | outer-join}
                                    ON search-condition
  ```

  (Note that curly braces ({}) in the preceding line indicate that one of the items between them must be used; they are not part of the syntax.) The following `SELECT` statement uses the escape syntax for an outer join.

  ```
  Statement stmt = con.createStatement("SELECT * FROM {oj TABLE1
            LEFT OUTER JOIN TABLE2 ON DEPT_NO = 003420930}");
  ```

  Outer joins are an advanced feature and are not supported by all DBMSs; consult an SQL grammar reference publication for an explanation of them. JDBC provides three `DatabaseMetaData` methods for determining the kinds of outer joins a driver supports: `supportsOuterJoins`, `supportsFullOuterJoins`, and `supportsLimitedOuterJoins`.

The method `Statement.setEscapeProcessing` turns escape processing on or off, with the default being on. A programmer might turn it off to cut down on processing time when performance is paramount, but it would normally be turned on. It should be noted that the method `setEscapeProcessing` does not work for `PreparedStatement` objects because the statement may have already been sent to the database before it can be called. See "`PreparedStatement` Overview," on page 647, for an explanation of precompilation.

43.1.7 Sending Batch Updates

2.0

The batch update facility introduced in the JDBC 2.0 core API allows a `Statement` object to submit multiple update commands together as a single unit, or batch, to the underlying DBMS. This ability to submit multiple updates as a batch rather than having to send each update individually can improve performance greatly in some situations.

The following code fragment demonstrates how to send a batch update to a database. In this example, a new row is inserted into three different tables in order to add a new employee to a company database. The code fragment starts by turning off the Connection object *con*'s auto-commit mode in order to allow multiple statements to be sent together as a transaction. After creating the Statement object *stmt*, it adds three SQL INSERT INTO commands to the batch with the method addBatch and then sends the batch to the database with the method executeBatch. The code looks like this:

```
Statement stmt = con.createStatement();
con.setAutoCommit(false);

stmt.addBatch("INSERT INTO employees VALUES (1000, 'Joe Jones')");
stmt.addBatch("INSERT INTO departments VALUES (260, 'Shoe')");
stmt.addBatch("INSERT INTO emp_dept VALUES (1000, '260')");

int [] updateCounts = stmt.executeBatch();
```

Because the connection's auto-commit mode is disabled, the application is free to decide whether or not to commit the transaction if an error occurs or if some of the commands in the batch fail to execute. For example, the application may not commit the changes if any of the insertions fail, thereby avoiding the situation where employee information exists in some tables but not in others.

In the JDBC 2.0 core API, a Statement object is created with an associated list of commands. This list is empty to begin with; commands are added to the list with the Statement method addBatch. The commands added to the list must all return only a simple update count. If, for example, one of the commands is a query (a SELECT statement), which will return a result set, the method executeBatch will throw a BatchUpdateException. A Statement object's list of commands can be emptied by calling the method clearBatch.

In the preceding example, the method executeBatch submits the list of commands associated with *stmt* to the underlying DBMS for execution. The DBMS executes each command in the order in which it was added to the batch and returns an update count for each command in the batch, also in order. If one of the commands does not return an update count, its return value cannot be added to the array of update counts that the method executeBatch returns, so the method executeBatch will throw a BatchUpdateException object. This exception keeps track of the update counts for the commands that executed successfully before the error occurred, and the order of these update counts likewise follows the order of the commands in the batch.

In the following code fragment, an application uses a try/catch block, and if a BatchUpdateException is thrown, it retrieves the exception's array of update counts to discover which commands in a batch update executed successfully before the BatchUpdateException object was thrown.

```
try {
    stmt.addBatch("INSERT INTO employees VALUES (" +
                                        "1000, 'Joe Jones')");
    stmt.addBatch("INSERT INTO departments VALUES (260, 'Shoe')");
    stmt.addBatch("INSERT INTO emp_dept VALUES (1000, '260')");

    int [] updateCounts = stmt.executeBatch();

} catch(BatchUpdateException b) {
    System.err.println("Update counts of successful commands: ");
    int [] updateCounts = b.getUpdateCounts();
    for (int i = 0; i < updateCounts.length; i ++) {
        System.err.print(updateCounts[i] + "  ");
    }
    System.err.println("");
}
```

If a printout was generated and looked similar to the following, the first two commands succeeded and the third one failed.

```
➥ Update counts of successful commands:
➥ 1  1
➥
```

JDBC drivers are not required to support batch updates, so a particular driver might not implement the methods addBatch, clearBatch, and executeBatch. Normally a programmer knows whether a driver that he/she is working with supports batch updates, but if an application wants to check, it can call the `DatabaseMeta-Data` method `supportsBatchUpdates`. In the following code fragment, a batch update is used only if the driver supports batch updates; otherwise, each update is sent as a separate statement. The connection's auto-commit mode is disabled so that, in either case, all the updates are included in one transaction.

```
con.setAutoCommit(false);
if(dbmd.supportsBatchUpdates) {
    stmt.addBatch("INSERT INTO . . .");
    stmt.addBatch("DELETE . . .");
    stmt.addBatch("INSERT INTO . . .");
    . . .
    stmt.executeBatch();
} else {
    System.err.print("Driver does not support batch updates; ");
    System.err.println("sending updates in separate statements.");
    stmt.executeUpdate("INSERT INTO . . .");
    stmt.executeUpdate("DELETE . . .");
    stmt.executeUpdate("INSERT INTO . . .");
    . . .
}
con.commit();
```

3.0

Drivers that support batch updates may or may not continue to process the commands in a batch after a `BatchUpdateException` is thrown. Although this behavior is optional, it must be consistent for a particular DBMS. Thus, if a driver keeps processing commands in a batch after an error occurs, it must do so for all batches.

The JDBC 3.0 API added two constants that can be used by a `BatchUpdateException` object when a driver continues to process statements after a `BatchUpdateException` has been thrown. These constants, defined in the `Statement` interface, occur only in the array returned by a `BatchUpdateException` object. These constants indicate the following for commands processed after one of the commands in a batch has failed:

- **Statement.SUCCESS_NO_INFO**—the command was processed successfully, but there in no information available

- **Statement.EXECUTE_FAILED**—the command was not processed successfully

See the method explanation of BatchUpdateException.getUpdateCounts, on page 307, for more details about what can happen after a command in a batch update fails. Note that if a driver continues to process commands after a failure, the array returned by the method getUpdateCounts will contain an element for every command in the batch. If the driver does not continue processing after a failure, the array will contain only elements for the commands that succeeded before the failure.

43.1.8 Giving Performance Hints

2.0

The Statement interface contains two methods for giving performance hints to the driver: setFetchDirection and setFetchSize. These methods are also available in the ResultSet interface and do exactly the same thing. The difference is that the Statement methods set the default for all of the ResultSet objects produced by a particular Statement object, whereas the ResultSet methods can be called any time during the life of the ResultSet object to change the fetch direction or the fetch size. See the section "Providing Performance Hints," on page 704, for a full discussion of these methods.

Both the Statement and ResultSet interfaces have the corresponding get methods: getFetchDirection and getFetchSize. If Statement.getFetchDirection is called before a fetch direction has been set, the value returned is implementation-specific, that is, it is up to the driver. The same is true for the method Statement.getFetchSize.

43.1.9 Executing Special Kinds of Statements

The execute method should be used only when it is possible that a statement may return more than one ResultSet object, more than one update count, or a combination of ResultSet objects and update counts. These multiple results are possible when certain stored procedures are being executed or when an unknown SQL string (that is, a string unknown to the application programmer at compile time) is being executed dynamically. For example, a user might execute a stored procedure (using a CallableStatement object—see Chapter 9, "CallableStatement," starting on page 321), and that stored procedure could perform an update, then a select, then an update, then a select, and so on. In more typical situations, someone using a stored procedure already knows what it returns.

Because the method execute handles the cases that are out of the ordinary, it is no surprise that retrieving its results requires some special handling. The main point to remember is that the method execute does not return a ResultSet object or an update count. Rather, it returns a boolean indicating what kind of result it produced: true for a ResultSet object and false for an int (indicating an update count). An application has to call additional methods to retrieve the result itself.

This means that the method execute cannot simply be substituted for the methods executeQuery or executeUpdate. An application uses the method executeQuery when it is known that the statement being executed returns a ResultSet object. Likewise, it uses the method executeUpdate when the result is known to be an update count. An application uses the method execute only when the result may be either one or when there may be multiple results.

RIGHT:
```
ResultSet rs = stmt.executeQuery("SELECT * FROM TABLE Q");
```

WRONG:
```
ResultSet rs = stmt.execute("SELECT * FROM TABLE Q");
```

The following line shows the correct form for the method execute.

RIGHT:
```
boolean b = stmt.execute("SELECT * FROM TABLE Q");
```

If the method execute returns true, an application must call the method getResultSet to obtain the ResultSet object. Then it can retrieve values from the ResultSet object using the ResultSet getter methods. If the return value for execute is false, an application needs to call the method getUpdateCount.

Once the first result has been retrieved, the next step is to see if there is another result, which is done by calling the method getMoreResults. Similar to the method execute, getMoreResults returns a boolean: true if the next result is a ResultSet object and false if it is an int. The difference is that if getMoreResults returns false, the int indicates either an update count or no more results. So, once again, the application must call additional methods.

For instance, suppose it is known that a procedure returns two result sets. After using the method `execute` to execute the procedure, an application calls the method `getResultSet` to get the first result set and then the appropriate `ResultSet.getter` methods to retrieve values from it. To get the second result set, the application needs to call `getMoreResults` (which should return `true`) and then `getResultSet` a second time. If, on the other hand, it is known that a procedure returns two update counts, the method `getUpdateCount` is called first, followed by a call to `getMore-Results` and then a second call to `getUpdateCount`.

Those cases where the kind and number of results is unknown are more complicated. As stated earlier, the method `execute` returns `true` if the result is a result set and `false` if it is an `int`. When the method `execute` returns `false`, this means that the result is an update count or that the statement executed was a DDL command like `CREATE  TABLE` or `DROP  TABLE`. The first thing to do after calling the method `execute` is to call either `getResultSet` to get what might be the first of two or more `ResultSet` objects or `getUpdateCount` to get what might be the first of two or more update counts, depending on whether `execute` returned `true` or `false`.

When the result of an SQL statement is not a result set, the method `getResultSet` returns `null`. This can mean either that the result is an update count or that there are no more results. The only way to find out what the `null` really means in this case is to call the method `getUpdateCount`, which will return an `int`. This `int` will be the number of rows affected by the calling statement or -1 to indicate either that the result is a result set or that there are no more results. If the method `getResultSet` has already returned `null`, which means that the result is not a `ResultSet` object, then a return value of -1 has to mean that there are no more results. In other words, there are no results (or no more results) when the following is true:

```
((stmt.getResultSet() == null) && (stmt.getUpdateCount() == -1))
```

After an application has called the method `getResultSet` and processed the `ResultSet` object that was returned, it needs to call the method `getMoreResults` to see if there is another result set or update count. If `getMoreResults` returns `true`, then the application needs to call `getResultSet` again to retrieve the next result set. As already stated, if `getResultSet` returns `null`, the application has to call `getUpdateCount` to find out whether `null` means that the result is an update count or that there are no more results.

When `getMoreResults` returns `false`, it means either that the SQL statement returned an update count or that there are no more results. So an application needs to call the method getUpdateCount to find out which is the case. In this situation, there are no more results when the following is true:

```
((stmt.getMoreResults() == false) && (stmt.getUpdateCount() == -1))
```

The following code demonstrates one of the many ways an application can make sure that it has accessed all the result sets and update counts generated by a call to the method execute. Rather than going through the process of discovering that there are no more results, this code checks for the case when there *are* more results. It keeps iterating through the do/while block as long as there is another result. This approach is based on the fact that there is at least one more result when the following is true:

```
((stmt.getMoreResults() == true) || (stmt.getUpdateCount() != -1))

boolean results = stmt.execute(sqlStatement);
int rsnum = 0;                  // Number of ResultSet objects processed
int rowsAffected = 0;
do {
    if(results) {               // result is a ResultSet object
        ResultSet rs = stmt.getResultSet();
        System.out.println("\n\nDisplaying ResultSet: " + rsnum);
        dispResultSet(rs); // Processes and displays the result set
        rsnum++;
        rs.close();
    }
    else {                          // result is an int
        rowsAffected = stmt.getUpdateCount();
        if (rowsAffected >= 0) {    // update or DDL statement
            System.out.println(rowsAffected + " rows affected.");
        }
    }
    results = stmt.getMoreResults();
}
while (results || rowsAffected != -1);
```

The following code fragment uses a different approach to make sure that all results are retrieved. In this approach, the method getUpdateCount is called first to determine whether the result is (1) an update count, (2) a DDL command or an update with no rows affected, or (3) a result set or no more results.

```
stmt.execute(sqlStringWithUnknownResults);
while (true) {
    int rowCount = stmt.getUpdateCount();
    if (rowCount > 0) {                  // this is an update count
        System.out.println("Rows changed = " + rowCount);
        stmt.getMoreResults();
        continue;
    }
    if (rowCount == 0) {                  // DDL command or 0 updates
        System.out.println(
                "No rows changed or statement was DDL command");
        stmt.getMoreResults();
        continue;
    }

    // if we have gotten this far, we have either a result set
    // or no more results

    ResultSet rs = stmt.getResultSet();
    if (rs != null) {
        // use metadata to get info about result set columns
        while (rs.next()) {
        // process results
        }
        stmt.getMoreResults();
        continue;
    }
    break; // there are no more results
}
```

It is possible for the method getMoreResults to return multiple ResultSet objects. The JDBC 3.0 API added the feature of being able to keep these Result-Set objects open. The default behavior is for a call to getMoreResults to close any ResultSet object previously returned by the method getResultSet. With the addition of three constants that can be supplied to a new version of getMoreResults, an application can specify whether or not to close the ResultSet objects. The new

`Statement` constants that can be supplied to `getMoreResults` indicate the following:

- `Statement.CLOSE_CURRENT_RESULT`—Close the current `ResultSet` object when the next `ResultSet` object is returned.

- `Statement.KEEP_CURRENT_RESULT`—Keep the current `ResultSet` object open when the next `ResultSet` object is returned.

- `Statement.CLOSE_ALL_RESULTS`—Close any `ResultSet` objects that have been kept open when the next `ResultSet` object or update count is returned.

The following code fragment gets a result set and keeps it open while it gets more results. This is done by passing the constant `Statement.KEEP_CURRENT_RESULT` to the method `getMoreResults`. The code then tests to see if the result is a `ResultSet` object. If so, the code now has two `ResultSet` objects open at the same time. The final line of code closes both `ResultSet` objects by passing the constant `Statement.CLOSE_ALL_RESULTS` to the method `getMoreResults`.

```
ResultSet rs1 = cstmt.getResultSet();
rs1.next());
    ...

boolean retval = cstmt.getMoreResults(
                            Statement.KEEP_CURRENT_RESULT);
if (retval == true) {
    ResultSet rs2 = cstmt.getResultSet();
    rs2.next();
    ...
    rs1.next();
}

retval = cstmt.getMoreResults(Statement.CLOSE_ALL_RESULTS);
    ...
```

43.2 Statement Interface Definition

```
public interface Statement {
    ResultSet executeQuery(String sql) throws SQLException;
    int executeUpdate(String sql) throws SQLException;
    void close() throws SQLException;
    SQLWarning getWarnings() throws SQLException;
    void clearWarnings() throws SQLException;
    int getMaxFieldSize() throws SQLException;
    void setMaxFieldSize(int max) throws SQLException;
    int getMaxRows() throws SQLException;
    void setMaxRows(int max) throws SQLException;
    void setEscapeProcessing(boolean enable) throws SQLException;
    int getQueryTimeout() throws SQLException;
    void setQueryTimeout(int seconds) throws SQLException;


    //================================================================
    //                  Methods for batch updates
    //================================================================

    void addBatch(String sql) throws SQLException
    void clearBatch() throws SQLException
    int [] executeBatch() throws SQLException


    //================================================================
    //          JDBC 2.0 core getter and setter methods
    //================================================================

    Connection getConnection() throws SQLException
    int getResultSetConcurrency() throws SQLException
    int getResultSetType() throws SQLException
    int getFetchDirection() throws SQLException
    void setFetchDirection(int direction) throws SQLException
    int getFetchSize() throws SQLException
    void setFetchSize(int rows) throws SQLException


    //================================================================
    //                      Advanced 1.0 features
    //================================================================
```

```
void cancel() throws SQLException;
void setCursorName(String name) throws SQLException;
boolean execute(String sql) throws SQLException;
ResultSet getResultSet() throws SQLException;
int getUpdateCount() throws SQLException;
boolean getMoreResults() throws SQLException;


//===============================================================
//                     JDBC 3.0 methods
//===============================================================
```

3.0 `boolean getMoreResults(int current) throws SQLException;`
3.0 `ResultSet getGeneratedKeys() throws SQLException;`
3.0 `int executeUpdate (String sql, int autoGenerateddKeys)`
`                                        throws SQLException;`
3.0 `int executeUpdate (String sql, int [] columnIndexes)`
`                                        throws SQLException;`
3.0 `int executeUpdate (String sql, String [] columnNames)`
`                                        throws SQLException;`
3.0 `int execute (String sql, int autoGeneratedKeys)`
`                                        throws SQLException;`
3.0 `int execute (String sql, int [] columnIndexes)`
`                                        throws SQLException;`
3.0 `int execute (String sql, String [] columnNames)`
`                                        throws SQLException;`
3.0 `int getResultSetHoldability () throws SQLException;`

```
//===============================================================
//                     JDBC 3.0 constants
//===============================================================
```

3.0 `static final int CLOSE_CURRENT_RESULT = 1;`
3.0 `static final int KEEP_CURRENT_RESULT = 2;`
3.0 `static final int CLOSE_ALL_RESULTS = 3;`
3.0 `static final int SUCCESS_NO_INFO = -2;`
3.0 `static final int EXECUTE_FAILED = -3;`
3.0 `static final int RETURN_GENERATED_KEYS = 1;`
3.0 `static final int NO_GENERATED_KEYS = 2:`
`}`

43.3 Statement Methods

addBatch

2.0

```
void addBatch(String sql) throws SQLException
```

Adds *sql* to this Statement object's current list of commands. A driver is not required to implement this method; therefore, it should not be used unless a call to the DatabaseMetaData method supportsBatchUpdates returns true.

PARAMETERS:

sql   an SQL statement that returns an update count, typically an INSERT or UPDATE command

EXAMPLE:
```
stmt.addBatch("INSERT INTO Table1 VALUES(1039, 0)");
```

THROWS:
SQLException if the driver does not support batch statements

SEE:
"Sending Batch Updates," on page 961

cancel

```
void cancel() throws SQLException
```

This method can be used by one thread to cancel a statement that is being executed by another thread if the driver and DBMS both support aborting an SQL statement.

EXAMPLE:
```
stmt.cancel(); // called from another thread to cancel stmt
```

clearBatch

2.0

```
void clearBatch() throws SQLException
```

Empties this Statement object's current list of commands. This method can be called to reset a batch if the application decides not to submit a batch of commands that has been constructed for a statement.

A driver is not required to implement this method; therefore, it should not be used unless a call to the `DatabaseMetaData` method `supportsBatchUpdates` returns `true`.

EXAMPLE:
```
stmt.clearBatch();
```

THROWS:
`SQLException` if the driver does not support batch statements

SEE:
"Sending Batch Updates," on page 961

clearWarnings

```
void clearWarnings() throws SQLException
```

Clears the warnings reported for this `Statement` object. After a call to the method `clearWarnings`, a call to the method `getWarnings` will return `null` until a new warning is reported.

EXAMPLE:
```
stmt.clearWarnings();
```

close

```
void close() throws SQLException
```

Releases a `Statement` object's database and JDBC resources immediately instead of waiting for this to happen when the `Statement` object is closed automatically during garbage collection.

It is recommended that `Statement` objects be closed explicitly when they are no longer needed, thereby freeing DBMS resources as soon as possible.

EXAMPLE:
```
stmt.close();
```

execute

```
boolean execute(String sql) throws SQLException
```

Executes *sql*, an SQL statement that may return one or more result sets, one or more update counts, or any combination of result sets and update counts. It also closes the calling `Statement` object's current `ResultSet` if an open one exists.

In some rare situations, a single SQL statement may return multiple result sets and/or update counts. The method execute should be used instead of executeQuery or executeUpdate in such situations. This might be the case when one is executing a stored procedure that one knows may return multiple results. Execute might also be used when one is dynamically executing an unknown SQL string. Normally, however, one would use either the method executeQuery or executeUpdate.

A call to the method execute executes an SQL statement and returns `true` if the first result is a result set; it returns `false` if the first result is an update count. One needs to call either the method getResultSet or getUpdateCount to actually retrieve the result and then the method getMoreResults to move to any subsequent result(s).

PARAMETERS:

sql   any SQL statement

RETURNS:

true if the first result is a `ResultSet` or false if it is an integer

EXAMPLE:

```
boolean b = stmt.execute(sqlStatementWithUnknownResults);
```

SEE:

"Executing Special Kinds of Statements," on page 965

execute

`3.0`

```
boolean execute(String sql, int autoGeneratedKeys) throws SQLException
```

Executes *sql*, an SQL statement that may return multiple results, and signals the driver that if the database creates any auto-generated keys, they should be made available for retrieval. If *sql* is not an INSERT statement, the driver will ignore the flag *autoGeneratedKeys*.

It may happen, though rarely, that a single SQL statement returns one or more result sets, one or more update counts, or a combination of result sets and update counts. An application needs to take this into account only if (1) a stored procedure is being executed and it is known that it might return multiple results or (2) an unknown SQL statement is being executed dynamically. The method execute should be used instead of executeQuery or executeUpdate in such situations.

A call to the method execute executes an SQL statement and returns true if the first result is a result set; it returns false if the first result is an update count. One needs to call either the method getResultSet or getUpdateCount to actually retrieve the result and then the method getMoreResults to move to any subsequent result(s).

PARAMETERS:

sql	any SQL statement
autoGeneratedKeys	a constant telling the driver whether it should make auto-generated keys available for retrieval; must be one of the following constants: Statement.RETURN_GENERATED_KEYS or Statement.NO_GENERATED_KEYS

RETURNS:
true if the first result is a ResultSet object; false the first result is an integer

THROWS:
SQLException if the second parameter is not either Statement.RETURN_GENERATED_KEYS or Statement.NO_GENERATED_KEYS

EXAMPLE:
```
boolean b = stmt.execute(sqlStatementWithUnknownResults,
                         Statement.RETURN_GENERATED_KEYS);
```

SEE:
"Executing Special Kinds of Statements," on page 965

3.0   execute

```
boolean execute(String sql, int [] columnIndexes) throws SQLException
```

Executes *sql*, an SQL statement that may return multiple results, and signals the driver that it should make available the auto-generated keys in the column(s) indicated in *columnIndexes*. The driver will ignore *columnIndexes* if *sql* is not an INSERT statement.

It may happen, though rarely, that a single SQL statement returns one or more result sets, one or more update counts, or a combination of result sets and update counts. An application needs to take this into account only if (1) a stored procedure is being executed and it is known whether it might return multiple results or (2) an unknown SQL statement is being executed dynamically. The method execute should be used instead of executeQuery or executeUpdate in such situations. In all other cases, the methods executeQuery or executeUpdate are more appropriate.

A call to the method execute executes an SQL statement and returns true if the first result is a result set; it returns false if the first result is an update count. One needs to call either the method getResultSet or getUpdateCount to actually retrieve the result and then the method getMoreResults to move to any subsequent result(s).

PARAMETERS:

sql	any SQL statement
columnIndexes	an int array telling the driver the column indexes of the auto-generated keys in the inserted row that it should make available for retrieval

RETURNS:
true if the first result is a ResultSet object; false if the first result is an integer

THROWS:
SQLException if the second parameter is not an int array

EXAMPLE:
```
int [] columnIndexes = {1, 2};
boolean b = stmt.execute(sqlStatement, columnIndexes);
```

SEE:
"Executing Special Kinds of Statements," on page 965

execute

3.0

```
boolean execute(String sql, String [] columnNames) throws SQLException
```

Executes *sql*, an SQL statement that may return multiple results, and signals the driver that it should make available the auto-generated keys in the column(s) indicated in *columnNames*. The driver will ignore *columnNames* if *sql* is not an INSERT statement.

It may happen, though rarely, that a single SQL statement returns one or more result sets, one or more update counts, or a combination of result sets and update counts. An application needs to take this into account only if (1) a stored procedure is being executed and it is known whether it might return multiple results or (2) an unknown SQL statement is being executed dynamically. The method execute should be used instead of executeQuery or executeUpdate in such situations. In all other cases, the methods executeQuery or executeUpdate are more appropriate.

A call to the method execute executes an SQL statement and returns true if the first result is a result set; it returns false if the first result is an update count. One needs to call either the method getResultSet or getUpdateCount to actually retrieve the result and then the method getMoreResults to move to any subsequent result(s).

PARAMETERS:

sql	any SQL statement
columnNames	a String array telling the driver the column names of the auto-generated keys in the inserted row

RETURNS:
true if the first result is a ResultSet object; false if the first result is an integer

THROWS:
SQLException if the second parameter is not a String array

EXAMPLE:
```
String [] columnNames = {"ID"};
boolean b = stmt.execute(sqlStatement, columnNames);
```

SEE:
"Executing Special Kinds of Statements," on page 965

executeBatch

```
int [] executeBatch() throws SQLException, BatchUpdateException
```

Submits this Statement object's list of commands to the database for execution as a unit. A driver is not required to implement this method; therefore, it should not be used unless a call to the DatabaseMetaData method supportsBatchUpdates returns true.

RETURNS:

an array containing update counts that correspond to the commands that executed successfully. An update count of –2 indicates that the command was successful but that the number of rows affected is unknown.

THROWS:

`SQLException` if the driver does not support batch statements; `BatchUpdateException` if one of the commands returns something other than an update count

EXAMPLE:
```
int [] updateCounts = stmt.executeBatch();
// If there are three commands in the batch and they executed
// successfully, updateCounts should contain three int values
// indicating the number of rows affected by each update
```

SEE:
"Sending Batch Updates," on page 961

executeQuery

```
ResultSet executeQuery(String sql) throws SQLException
```

Executes *sql*, an SQL statement that returns a single result set, and closes this `Statement` object's current `ResultSet` if an open one exists.

PARAMETERS:

sql	typically an SQL `SELECT` statement. It must produce one `ResultSet` object only.

RETURNS:

a `ResultSet` object representing the table of data (result set) produced by *sql*. It may return an empty `ResultSet` object but never returns `null`.

THROWS:

`SQLException` if an error occurs in processing the SQL query or if the specified argument is a statement that generates a row count instead of a result set

EXAMPLE:
```
ResultSet rs = stmt.executeQuery("SELECT a, b, c FROM Table1");
```

executeUpdate

```
int executeUpdate(String sql) throws SQLException
```

Executes an SQL INSERT, UPDATE, or DELETE statement that does not have parameter placeholders and closes the calling Statement object's current ResultSet if an open one exists.

This method may also be used to execute SQL DDL statements (CREATE TABLE, DROP TABLE, CREATE INDEX, DROP INDEX, and so on).

This method may not be used to return a ResultSet object; if the parameter supplied is an SQL SELECT statement, this method will throw an SQLException.

PARAMETERS:

sql   an SQL INSERT, UPDATE, or DELETE statement or a DDL
                                       statement

RETURNS:

an int indicating the number of rows affected by an INSERT, UPDATE or DELETE statement; 0 if no rows were affected or the statement executed was a DDL statement

THROWS:

SQLException if the specified argument is a statement that generates a result set

EXAMPLE:

```
Statement stmt = con.createStatement();
int x = stmt.executeUpdate("UPDATE Table2 SET m = 8 WHERE q = true");
    // x will be 0 or more, indicating the number of rows affected
int x = stmt.executeUpdate("DROP TABLE Table2");
    // x will be 0
```

3.0   **executeUpdate**

```
int executeUpdate(String sql, int autoGeneratedKeys)
                                                 throws SQLException
```

Executes *sql* and, by means of *autoGeneratedKeys*, tells the driver whether it should make all automatically generated keys available for retrieval. If *sql* is not an INSERT statement, the driver ignores *autoGenerated-Keys*.

This method may not be used to return a ResultSet object; if the parameter supplied is an SQL SELECT statement, this method will throw an SQLException.

PARAMETERS:

sql   an SQL INSERT, UPDATE, or DELETE statement, or a DDL statement

autoGeneratedKeys   an int indicating whether the driver should make auto-generated keys available for retrieval; must be either Statement.RETURN_GENERATED_KEYS or Statement.NO_GENERATED_KEYS

RETURNS:

an int indicating the number of rows affected by an INSERT, UPDATE, or DELETE statement; 0 if no rows were affected or the statement executed was a DDL statement

THROWS:

SQLException if the specified SQL statement generates a result set or the second parameter is not either Statement.RETURN_GENERATED_KEYS or Statement.NO_GENERATED_KEYS

EXAMPLE:

```
Statement stmt = con.createStatement();
int x = stmt.executeUpdate("INSERT INTO AUTHORS VALUES ('Barth', " +
        "'John', 'Letters'", Statement.RETURN_GENERATED_KEYS);
    // x will be 0 or more, indicating the number of rows affected,
    // and the driver is alerted to make all the keys generated for
    // this insertion available for retrieval
```

executeUpdate   `3.0`

```
int executeUpdate(String sql, int [] columnIndexes) throws SQLException
```

Executes *sql* and tells the driver to make the automatically generated keys in the column(s) indicated in *columnIndexes* available for retrieval. If *sql* is not an INSERT statement, the driver ignores *columnIndexes*.

This method may not be used to return a ResultSet object; if the parameter supplied is an SQL SELECT statement, this method will throw an SQLException.

PARAMETERS:

sql   an SQL INSERT, UPDATE, or DELETE statement or a DDL statement

columnIndexes   an int array indicating the indexes of the column val-
                           ues (keys) that the driver should make available for re-
                           trieval

RETURNS:
an int indicating the number of rows affected by an INSERT, UPDATE, or DELETE
statement; 0 if no rows were affected or the statement executed was a DDL
statement

THROWS:
SQLException if the specified SQL statement generates a result set or the second parameter is not an int array

EXAMPLE:
```
int [] columnIndexes = {1};
Statement stmt = con.createStatement();
int x = stmt.executeUpdate("INSERT INTO AUTHORS VALUES ('Barth', " +
        "'John', 'Letters'", columnIndexes);
    // x will be 0 or more, indicating the number of rows affected,
    // and the driver is alerted to make the key in the first column
    // available for retrieval
```

[3.0]   **executeUpdate**

```
int executeUpdate(String sql, String [] columnNames)
                                        throws SQLException
```

Executes *sql* and tells the driver to make the automatically generated keys
in the column(s) indicated in *columnNames* available for retrieval. If *sql* is not
an INSERT statement, the driver ignores *columnNames*.
    This method may not be used to return a ResultSet object; if the parame-
ter supplied is an SQL SELECT statement, this method will throw an SQLException.

PARAMETERS:
sql   an SQL INSERT, UPDATE, or DELETE statement, or a DDL
                           statement
columnNames   a String array indicating the names of the column(s)
                           containing keys that the driver should make available
                           for retrieval

RETURNS:
an int indicating the number of rows affected by an INSERT, UPDATE, or DELETE statement; 0 if no rows were affected or the statement executed was a DDL statement

THROWS:
SQLException if the specified SQL statement generates a result set or the second parameter is not a String array

EXAMPLE:
```
int [] columnNames = {"AUTHOR_ID"};
Statement stmt = con.createStatement();
int x = stmt.executeUpdate("INSERT INTO AUTHORS VALUES ('Barth', " +
            "'John', 'Letters'", columnNames);
    // x will be 0 or more, indicating the number of rows affected,
    // and the driver is alerted to make the key in the column
    // AUTHOR_ID available for retrieval
```

getConnection

2.0

```
Connection getConnection() throws SQLException
```

Retrieves the Connection object that produced this Statement object.

RETURNS:
the Connection object on which the method createStatement was called to produce this Statement object

EXAMPLE:
```
Connection con = stmt.getConnection();
```

getFetchDirection

2.0

```
int getFetchDirection() throws SQLException
```

Retrieves the fetch direction this Statement object set as a performance hint to the driver. The int returned will be one of the following constants from the ResultSet interface: FETCH_FORWARD, FETCH_REVERSE, or FETCH_UNKNOWN.

If this Statement object has not called the method setFetchDirection, the return value of getFetchDirection is determined by the driver.

RETURNS:
the fetch direction set by this `Statement` object with a call to the method `set-FetchDirection`. If no fetch direction has been set, the return value is implementation-specific.

EXAMPLE:
```
int direction = stmt.getFetchDirection();
```

2.0   getFetchSize

```
int getFetchSize() throws SQLException
```

Retrieves the fetch size this `Statement` object set as a performance hint to the driver. The fetch size is the recommended number of rows for the driver to fetch from the database when a result set needs more rows. The driver is free to ignore this performance hint.

If this `Statement` object has not called the method `setFetchSize`, the return value of `getFetchSize` is determined by the driver.

RETURNS:
the fetch size set by this `Statement` object with a call to the method `setFetchSize`. If no fetch size has been set, the return value is implementation-specific.

EXAMPLE:
```
int size = stmt.getFetchSize();
```

3.0   getGeneratedKeys

```
ResultSet getGeneratedKeys() throws SQLException
```

Retrieves the keys the DBMS generated automatically as a result of executing this `Statement` object. If no keys were generated, this method returns an empty `ResultSet` object.

RETURNS:
a `ResultSet` object in which each row is a key the DBMS generated automatically as a result of the execution of this `Statement` object

EXAMPLE:
```
ResultSet keys = stmt.getGeneratedKeys();
```

getMaxFieldSize

```
int getMaxFieldSize() throws SQLException
```

Retrieves the maximum number of bytes that a result set column may contain. The maximum field size is set to limit the size of data that can be returned for any result set column value. It applies only to fields of type BINARY, VARBINARY, LONGVARBINARY, CHAR, VARCHAR, and LONGVARCHAR. If the limit is exceeded, the excess data is silently discarded.

For maximum portability, the maximum field size should be greater than 256. By default there is no limit.

RETURNS:
an int representing the current maximum number of bytes that a ResultSet column may contain. Zero means that there is no limit.

EXAMPLE:
```
int x = stmt.getMaxFieldSize();
```

getMaxRows

```
int getMaxRows() throws SQLException
```

Retrieves the maximum number of rows that a ResultSet object may contain. If the limit is exceeded, the excess rows are silently dropped. By default there is no limit.

RETURNS:
an int representing the current maximum number of rows that a ResultSet object may contain. Zero means that there is no limit.

EXAMPLE:
```
int x = stmt.getMaxRows();
```

getMoreResults

```
boolean getMoreResults() throws SQLException
```

Moves to a Statement object's next result and implicitly closes any current ResultSet object (obtained by calling the method getResultSet). The method getMoreResults is used after a Statement has been executed with a call to the method execute and the method getResultSet or getUpdateCount has been called.

RETURNS:
true if the next result is a ResultSet object; false if it is an integer (indicating that it is an update count or there are no more results). There are no more results when the following is true:

```
((getMoreResults() == false) && (getUpdateCount() == -1))
```

EXAMPLE:
boolean b = stmt.getMoreResults();

SEE:
the methods execute and getResultSet
"Executing Special Kinds of Statements," on page 965

3.0   getMoreResults

---

boolean **getMoreResults**(int *current*) throws SQLException

Moves to this Statement object's next result and deals with any current ResultSet object (obtained by calling the method getResultSet) according to the instructions in the flag *current*. The method getMoreResults is used after a Statement has been executed with a call to the method execute and after the method getResultSet or getUpdateCount has been called.

PARAMETERS:

current   a constant indicating what should happen to current ResultSet objects obtained by calling the method getResultSet; must be one of the following:
Statement.CLOSE_CURRENT_RESULT
Statement.KEEP_CURRENT_RESULT
Statement.CLOSE_ALL_RESULTS

RETURNS:
true if the next result is a ResultSet object; false if it is an integer (indicating that it is an update count or there are no more results). There are no more results when the following is true:

```
((getMoreResults() == false) && (getUpdateCount() == -1))
```

EXAMPLE:
```
boolean b = stmt.getMoreResults(Statement.KEEP_CURRENT_RESULT);
// Moves to the next result and keeps any current ResultSet object
// open
```

SEE:
the methods execute and getResultSet
"Executing Special Kinds of Statements," on page 965

getQueryTimeout

```
int getQueryTimeout() throws SQLException
```

Retrieves the number of seconds the driver will wait for a Statement object to execute. If the limit is exceeded, an SQLException is thrown. By default there is no limit.

RETURNS:
the current query timeout limit in seconds. Zero means that there is no time limit.

EXAMPLE:
```
int x = stmt.getQueryTimeout();
```

getResultSet

```
ResultSet getResultSet() throws SQLException
```

Returns a ResultSet object that was produced by a call to the method execute. When the execute method has been used to execute a statement, the method getResultSet must be called to actually retrieve the result. It should be called only once per result.

RETURNS:
the current result as a ResultSet object; null if the result is an integer (indicating that the result is an update count or there are no more results)

EXAMPLE:
```
ResultSet rs = stmt.getResultSet();
```

SEE:
execute()

"Executing Special Kinds of Statements," on page 965

`2.0`   ## getResultSetConcurrency

int **getResultSetConcurrency**() throws SQLException

Retrieves the concurrency mode for the ResultSet objects generated from queries that this Statement object executes.

RETURNS:
one of the following constants, indicating whether the ResultSet objects generated from this Statement object are read only or updatable:

ResultSet.CONCUR_READ_ONLY
ResultSet.CONCUR_UPDATABLE

EXAMPLE:
int concurrency = stmt.getResultSetConcurrency();

`3.0`   ## getResultSetHoldability

int **getResultSetHoldability**() throws SQLException

Retrieves the holdability mode for the ResultSet objects generated from queries that this Statement object executes.

RETURNS:
one of the following constants:

ResultSet.HOLD_CURSORS_OVER_COMMIT
ResutlSet.CLOSE_CURSORS_AT_COMMIT

EXAMPLE:
int holdability = stmt.getResultSetHoldability();

getResultSetType

`int getResultSetType() throws SQLException`

Retrieves the type of the ResultSet objects generated from queries that this Statement object executes.

RETURNS:
one of TYPE_FORWARD_ONLY, TYPE_SCROLL_INSENSITIVE, or TYPE_SCROLL_SENSITIVE, indicating whether the ResultSet objects generated from this Statement object are forward only (not scrollable), scrollable and insensitive to changes, or scrollable and sensitive to changes

EXAMPLE:
`int type = stmt.getResultSetType();`

getUpdateCount

`int getUpdateCount() throws SQLException`

This method should be called only after a call to execute or getMoreResults, and it should be called only once per result.

If the method getUpdateCount returns an integer greater than zero, the integer represents the number of rows affected by a statement modifying a table. Zero indicates either that no rows were affected or that the SQL statement was a DDL command such as CREATE TABLE or DROP TABLE. A return value of -1 means that the result is a ResultSet object or that there are no more results.

The only way to be certain about whether a return value of -1 indicates a result set is to call the method getResultSet. It will return a ResultSet object if there is one, and null otherwise. In other words, there are no more results under the following conditions:

`((stmt.getUpdateCount() == -1) && (stmt.getResultSet() == null))`

Another approach is to call the method getMoreResults before calling getUpdateCount. If one has called getMoreResults and determined that the result is not a result set (the return value is false), the method getUpdate-Count can be called to determine whether the result is an update count or there are no more results. In this case, there are no more results when the following is true:

```
((stmt.getMoreResults() == false) && (stmt.getUpdateCount() == -1))
```

RETURNS:
(1) an int greater than 0 representing the number of rows affected by an update operation, (2) 0 if no rows were affected or the operation was a DDL command, or (3) –1 if the result is a ResultSet object or there are no more results

EXAMPLE:
NOTE: For the purposes of this example, suppose that the argument *sqlStatementWithUnknownResult* is a string that has been returned from a procedure call and that the user does not know what it will return.

```
boolean b = stmt.execute(sqlStatementWithUnknownResult);
if (!b) {                       // result is not a ResultSet object
    int rowCount = stmt.getUpdateCount();
    if (rowCount > 0) {
        System.out.println("Number of rows updated = " + rowCount);
    } else if (rowCount == 0) {
        System.out.println("DDL command or no rows updated");
    } else {                              // rowCount == -1
        System.out.println("There are no results");
    }
}
```

SEE:
Statement.execute
"Executing Special Kinds of Statements," on page 965

getWarnings

```
SQLWarning getWarnings() throws SQLException
```

Returns the first warning reported by calls on this Statement object. Subsequent warnings, if there are any, are chained to this first warning. A call to this method does not clear warnings.

The methods execute, executeQuery, and executeUpdate will clear a Statement object's warning chain. In other words, a Statement object's warning chain is automatically cleared each time it is (re)executed.

Warnings that are reported while a `ResultSet` object is being read will be chained on that `ResultSet` object rather than on the `Statement` object that generated the result set.

RETURNS:
the first `SQLWarning` or `null` if there are no warnings

EXAMPLE:
```
SQLWarning w = stmt.getWarnings();
// w = null if there are no warnings; methods inherited from
// SQLException will retrieve the message, SQLState, and vendor code
// contained in w
```

SEE:
`SQLWarning.getNextWarning`

setCursorName

```
void setCursorName(String name) throws SQLException
```

Sets to *name* the SQL cursor name that will be used by subsequent `State-ment` execute methods. This name can then be used in SQL positioned update and positioned delete statements to identify the current row in the `ResultSet` object generated by this `Statement` object. If the database does not support positioned updates or positioned deletes, this method does nothing.

Note that, by definition, positioned updates and positioned deletes must be executed by a different `Statement` object than the one that generated the `ResultSet` object being used for positioning. Also note that the cursor's `SELECT` statement should be of the form:

```
SELECT FOR UPDATE ... FROM ... WHERE ...
```

If the `SELECT` statement does not follow this form, the cursor may not have the proper isolation level to support updates.

The cursor name is used only in an SQL `UPDATE` statement. The following example, in which `cursor1` is a cursor name, shows the form:

```
UPDATE ... WHERE CURRENT OF cursor1
```

Note also that setting a cursor name with this method prior to creating a result set does not necessarily mean that the result set is updatable.

New methods added in the JDBC 2.0 core API make positioned updates and deletes much easier and make named cursors unnecessary. In result sets that are updatable, the `ResultSet` updater methods perform positioned updates, and the `ResultSet.deleteRow` method performs positioned deletes.

PARAMETERS:

name   the new cursor name, which must be unique within a connection

EXAMPLE:
```
stmt.setCursorName("cursor1");
// the cursor associated with the next result set produced by this
// Statement object will be named cursor1
```

SEE:
```
ResultSet.getCursorName
ResultSet.updater methods
```

setEscapeProcessing

```
void setEscapeProcessing(boolean enable) throws SQLException
```

Sets the `Statement` object's escape scanning mode to *enable*. When *enable* is `true` (the default), the driver will scan for any escape syntax and do escape substitution before sending the escaped SQL statement to the database. When *enable* is `false`, the driver will ignore escaped SQL statements.

Note that this does not work for `PreparedStatement` objects because they may have already been sent to the database for precompilation before being called.

PARAMETERS:

enable   either `true` to enable escape scanning or `false` to disable it

EXAMPLE:
```
stmt.setEscapeProcessing(false); // disables escape scanning
```

2.0 ## setFetchDirection

```
void setFetchDirection(int direction) throws SQLException
```

Sets *direction* as the fetch direction that is this Statement object's hint to the database for improving performance. The driver is free to ignore this hint. This fetch direction will be the default for ResultSet objects produced by this Statement object.

If this method is not called, the return value of getFetchDirection is determined by the driver.

PARAMETERS:

direction   the fetch direction given as a performance hint to the driver; one of the ResultSet constants FETCH_FORWARD, FETCH_REVERSE, or FETCH_UNKNOWN

RETURNS:

the fetch direction set by this Statement object with a call to the method set-FetchDirection. If no fetch direction has been set, the return value is implementation-specific.

EXAMPLE:
stmt.setFetchDirection(ResultSet.FETCH_REVERSE);

SEE:
"Giving Performance Hints," on page 965

setFetchSize

2.0

void **setFetchSize**(int *rows*) throws SQLException

Sets *rows* as the fetch size that is this Statement object's hint to the driver for improving performance. The driver is free to ignore this hint. This fetch size will be the default for ResultSet objects produced by this Statement object.

If this method is not called, the return value of getFetchSize is determined by the driver.

PARAMETERS:

size   the number of rows to fetch from the database when a result set needs more rows

EXAMPLE:
stmt.setFetchSize(25);

SEE:
"Giving Performance Hints," on page 965

setMaxFieldSize

void **setMaxFieldSize**(int *max*) throws SQLException

Sets the maximum size for a column in a result set to *max* bytes.

This method sets the limit for the size of data (in bytes) that can be returned for any column value. The limit applies only to fields of type BINARY, VARBINARY, LONGVARBINARY, CHAR, VARCHAR, and LONGVARCHAR. If the limit is exceeded, the excess data is silently discarded. By default there is no limit.

For maximum portability, the maximum field size should be set to a value greater than 256.

PARAMETERS:

max   the new maximum column size limit in bytes; zero
                        means that there is no limit to the size of a column

EXAMPLE:
stmt.setMaxFieldSize(1024);

setMaxRows

void **setMaxRows**(int *max*) throws SQLException

Sets the limit for the maximum number of rows in a ResultSet object to *max*. If the limit is exceeded, the excess rows are silently dropped. By default there is no limit.

PARAMETERS:

max   the new maximum number of rows; zero means that
                        there is no limit

EXAMPLE:
stmt.setMaxRows(256);

setQueryTimeout

void **setQueryTimeout**(int *seconds*) throws SQLException

Sets to *seconds* the time limit for the number of seconds a driver will wait for a Statement object to be executed. By default there is no limit.

PARAMETERS:

seconds   the new query timeout limit in seconds; zero means that there is no limit

EXAMPLE:
```
stmt.setQueryTimeout(10);
```

43.4 Statement Fields

The following fields are defined in the Statement interface.

CLOSE_ALL_RESULTS

```
public static final int CLOSE_ALL_RESULTS
```

    The constant indicating that all open ResultSet objects should be closed. This constant is a possible parameter value for the method getMoreResults.

CLOSE_CURRENT_RESULT

```
public static final int CLOSE_CURRENT_RESULT
```

    The constant indicating that the current ResultSet object should be closed. This constant is a possible parameter value for the method getMoreResults.

EXECUTE_FAILED

```
public static final int EXECUTE_FAILED
```

    The constant indicating that an error occurred while executing a batch update statement. This constant is a possible value in the array returned by the method BatchUpdateException.getUpdateCounts.

KEEP_CURRENT_RESULT

`public static final int KEEP_CURRENT_RESULT`

The constant indicating that the current `ResultSet` object should be kept open. This constant is a possible parameter value for the method `getMoreResults`.

NO_GENERATED_KEYS

`public static final int NO_GENERATED_KEYS`

The constant telling the driver that no automatically generated keys need to be made available for retrieval. This constant is a possible parameter for the methods `execute` and `executeUpdate`.

RETURN_GENERATED_KEYS

`public static final int RETURN_GENERATED_KEYS`

The constant telling the driver that all keys the DBMS generated automatically for this `INSERT` statement need to be made available for retrieval. This constant is a possible parameter for the methods `execute` and `executeUpdate`.

SUCCESS_NO_INFO

`public static final int SUCCESS_NO_INFO`

The constant indicating that a batch statement executed successfully but that no count of the number of rows it affected is available. This constant is a possible value in the array returned by the method `BatchUpdateException.getUpdateCounts`.

CHAPTER 44

Struct 2.0

44.1 Struct Overview

THE Struct interface represents the standard mapping of an SQL structured type. An SQL structured type is a new type defined by a user that contains one or more attributes. These attributes may be any SQL data type, including other structured types. An instance of an SQL structured type is mapped to a Struct object, which contains the values for the instance's attributes. The values in a Struct object must appear in the same order in which the attributes appear in the SQL definition of the structured type.

An SQL structured type can be used as a column value in a table, and it is manipulated the same way built-in types are. Because it is logically an object type, a structured type is accessed with a getObject method, either ResultSet.getObject or CallableStatement.getObject. Similarly, a structured type is stored in a database with the method PreparedStatement.setObject.

The Struct interface provides three methods: one for getting the SQL type name of the structured object it maps and two for retrieving the structured type's attribute values in the form of an array of Object in the Java programming language.

44.1.1 Custom Mapping

In addition to the standard mapping, the SQL user-defined types (SQL structured types and DISTINCT types) can be custom mapped. In a custom mapping, an SQL user-defined type is mapped to a class in the Java programming language.

A custom mapping is declared via an entry in a java.util.Map object that names the SQL structured type (or distinct type) and the Class object that maps it.

This custom mapping entry can be in the type map associated with a connection, or it can be in a Map object that is passed to one of the methods that can do custom mapping. If an instance of a structured type has a custom mapping, the driver will map it to the class indicated in the type map instead of to a Struct object. The ResultSet.getObject and CallableStatement.getObject methods are the only getter methods that can take a type map as a parameter, so the fact that a Struct instance can be retrieved only with a getObject method ensures that an application gets a custom mapping if there is one.

Eight methods in the ARRAY interface, four versions of Array.getArray and four versions of Array.getResultSet, may do custom mapping when they materialize an SQL ARRAY value's data on the client. When the base type of an SQL ARRAY is an SQL structured type that has a custom mapping, the Array.getArray methods conceptually call ResultSet.getObject on each element in turn to map it to a class in the Java programming language. The result is an array of Java classes, with each class mapping a structured type. The Array.getResultSet methods likewise map each element that is an SQL structured type to a class in the Java programming language, but the result is a ResultSet object with each row being a class.

Two methods in the Struct interface may do custom mapping of an SQL structured type when they produce an array in the Java programming language containing the structured type's attributes. Both versions of the method getAttributes will map an attribute to a field in a Java class if there is an appropriate entry in the type map being used.

The reason for using a custom mapping is that it is often easier to deal with a custom mapping than with the standard mapping. The standard mapping, a Struct object, contains the values for the instance's attributes but does not contain any explanatory names for these values. For example, for a structured type DOG, a particular instance might have the values "Poodle" for the attribute BREED, "Jacques" for the attribute NAME, and 35.0 for the attribute WEIGHT. The Struct object for this instance of DOG will contain the values "Poodle", "Jacques", and 35.0. With a custom mapping to a class in the Java programming language, the three values would be easier to recognize and keep track of because they would be values for fields rather than just unassociated data. In a custom mapping, the programmer is free to name the fields almost anything, and fields with meaningful names can make it much easier to keep track of data. See Chapter 37 on the SQLData interface, especially the section "Creating a Custom Mapping," on page 896, for an explanation of what is involved in a custom mapping.

44.1.2 Creating an SQL Structured Type

Being a user-defined type, a structured type must be defined in SQL and used in a table before an instance of it can be mapped to a `Struct` object. This section demonstrates how to define a structured type in SQL.

The SQL command for creating a user-defined type is, appropriately, CREATE TYPE, and the word following the command is the SQL name for the new type. An ordered, comma-separated list within parentheses gives the name and type for each attribute. The following example contains SQL definitions for three new structured types, RESIDENCE, FULLNAME, and PERSON. (Note that different DBMSs may vary in their syntax. For example, some DBMSs use the command CREATE TYPE <TYPE_NAME> AS OBJECT to create a structured type.)

```
CREATE TYPE RESIDENCE
(
    DOOR NUMERIC(6),
    STREET VARCHAR(100),
    CITY VARCHAR(50),
    OCCUPANT REF(PERSON)
);

CREATE TYPE FULLNAME
(
    FIRST VARCHAR(50),
    LAST VARCHAR(50)
);

CREATE TYPE PERSON
(
    NAME FULLNAME,
    HEIGHT NUMERIC,
    WEIGHT NUMERIC,
    HOME REF(RESIDENCE)
);
```

After being defined, RESIDENCE, PERSON, and FULLNAME are new data types that can be used as column types in a database table and as attribute types in an SQL structured type definition.

The preceding SQL type definitions illustrate two features of structured types:

1. They may contain other structured types. For example, the structured type FULLNAME is embedded in the structured type PERSON, serving as the type for the attribute NAME.

2. They may contain references to other structured types. For example, in the structured type RESIDENCE, the attribute OCCUPANT is a REF(PERSON). And, in the type PERSON, the attribute HOME is a REF(RESIDENCE).

Using a reference to a structured type can sometimes be more convenient or more efficient than using the structured type itself, particularly when the structured type is large. If the proper table has been set up, each time an instance of a structured type is created, the DBMS will automatically create a unique identifier for that instance. This identifier is a REF value that references the instance, and it can be used as an attribute value or as a column value in place of the structured type instance. (For a more complete explanation of the type REF, see Chapter 26, "Ref," starting on page 679.) The next section explains the table that associates an instance of a structured type with its REF value.

44.1.3   Storing Instances of a Structured Type

Instances of a structured type cannot be referenced unless a special kind of table has been created specifically to store the instances of that structured type. Each row of the table represents an instance of the structured type and conceptually consists of one column for each attribute of the structured type instance and one for the value that uniquely identifies the instance (an SQL REF value). The REF values in such a table are not only unique but also may never be reused to identify a different value.

The SQL command for creating this special type of table specifies the table name, the structured type whose instances will be stored in the table, and the name and type for the column that contains the unique identifiers. The syntax your database uses may vary, but the general form of the command looks like this:

```
CREATE TABLE <table name> OF <structured type> (
>       REF IS (<ref-column-name>) SYSTEM GENERATED)
```

The column OID stores the unique, persistent REF values, and the definition of it must include the phrase SYSTEM GENERATED. When an instance of the structured type is created (inserted into the table as shown in the next section), the DBMS will automatically generate a unique REF value for that instance and store it in the OID column. When an application wants to use one of these identifiers as a reference to a structured type instance, it retrieves the appropriate REF value from the OID column with a SELECT statement. An example is given later in this section. Note that in the example, OID is the name for the column that stores REF values, but the column may be given any name.

The following two table definitions create tables for instances of the structured types RESIDENCE and PERSON, defined earlier in this chapter. The following SQL statement creates the table HOMES, which will store instances of the structured type RESIDENCE:

```
CREATE TABLE HOMES OF RESIDENCE (REF IS OID SYSTEM GENERATED);
```

The following SQL statement creates the table PEOPLE, which will store instances of the structured type PERSON:

```
CREATE TABLE PEOPLE OF PERSON (REF IS OID SYSTEM GENERATED);
```

In order to populate such a table, instances of the structured type are created with an INSERT INTO statement. This statement adds a row to the table, with that row holding the attribute values for an instance of the structured type. The INSERT INTO statement includes the attribute names in parentheses followed by a comma-separated list, also in parentheses, of the attribute values for this particular instance. For example, the following SQL statement inserts values for the first three attributes of PERSON into the table PEOPLE, and the order of the attributes is the same as that in the definition of PERSON. (A value for the attribute HOME, the fourth attribute of PERSON, will be added later in an update statement. It cannot be added now because it depends on a value in the table HOMES, which does not yet contain any values.)

```
INSERT INTO PEOPLE (NAME, HEIGHT, WEIGHT) VALUES
(
    FULLNAME('DAFFY', 'DUCK'),
    4,
    58,
);
```

Since FULLNAME is a structured type, the statement supplies the values for its attributes in order. When FULLNAME was defined, the DBMS defined a constructor for it behind the scenes, so the effect of FULLNAME('DAFFY', 'DUCK') is to create an instance of FULLNAME with the attribute FIRST being DAFFY and the attribute LAST being DUCK. As will be seen in a later example, an attribute of an attribute can be accessed with TABLE_NAME.ATTRIBUTE_NAME.ATTRIBUTE_NAME. In this example, PEOPLE.NAME.FIRST accesses DAFFY.

The next example inserts the attribute values for an instance of RESIDENCE into the table HOMES. The fourth attribute, OCCUPANT, is a reference to an instance of the structured type PERSON. Because the REF objects that identify instances of PERSON are stored in the special table PEOPLE, a SELECT statement is used to retrieve the REF value from PEOPLE. This statement selects the value in column OID of the table PEOPLE from the row where the value in NAME.FIRST is DAFFY.

```
INSERT INTO HOMES (DOOR, STREET, CITY, OCCUPANT) VALUES
(
    1032
    'CARTOON LANE',
    'LOS ANGELES',
    (SELECT OID FROM PEOPLE P WHERE P.NAME.FIRST = 'DAFFY')
);
```

The following SQL statement supplies a value for the attribute HOME (the attribute of PERSON not supplied previously) in the table PEOPLE.

```
UPDATE PEOPLE SET HOME = (SELECT OID FROM HOMES H WHERE
    H.OCCUPANT->NAME.FIRST = 'DAFFY') WHERE
    NAME.FIRST = 'DAFFY'
```

As in the previous SQL statement, a SELECT statement is used to get the REF value that will be used as an attribute value. The final effect of this statement is that in the table PEOPLE, the attribute HOME (which is a reference to RESIDENCE) will be set with a value from the column OID in the table HOMES. The condition for determining the correct row for the column involves a REF value in the attribute OCCUPANT. The value accessed through the REF value in OCCUPANT is itself a structured type, FULLNAME, which has two attributes, FIRST and LAST. The same condition, that FIRST be equal to DAFFY, applies both to (1) what value is to be assigned and (2) which instance of PERSON is to be assigned the new value.

SQL uses some special operators for accessing references and attributes within attributes: the dereference operator (->) and the dot operator (.). In the preceding example, the value of the attribute OCCUPANT is a reference to the structured type PERSON, so the dereference operator was used to get the value of NAME.

```
SELECT OID FROM HOMES H WHERE H.OCCUPANT->NAME.FIRST = 'DAFFY'
```

Since the value in NAME is type FULLNAME, the dot operator was used to get the value of its attribute FIRST.

44.1.4 Creating a **Struct** Object

Once a structured type has been defined and used as a column value, it can be mapped to a Struct object in the Java programming language. The following code fragment illustrates creating a Struct object, where *stmt* is a Statement object and the values in the column SWIMMERS are instances of the structured type PERSON.

```
ResultSet rs = stmt.executeQuery("SELECT SWIMMERS FROM ATHLETES");
rs.next();
Struct swimmer = (Struct)rs.getObject("SWIMMERS");
```

Note that since the method getObject returns an Object, which is the superclass of all objects in the Java programming language, the object it returns needs to be converted (narrowed) to type Struct.

The variable *swimmer* now represents the instance of the structured type PERSON stored in column SWIMMERS in the current row of *rs*. Unlike instances of the interfaces Blob, Clob, Array, and Ref, which do not materialize the contents of the types they designate, instances of the interface Struct *do* materialize the contents of the structured types they represent. In other words, the Struct object *swimmer* contains the actual NAME, HEIGHT, and WEIGHT values for this instance of PERSON.

The number of attributes in an SQL structured type is usually relatively small; thus, it makes sense for a Struct object to contain the attribute values it maps. This is in contrast to the SQL types whose values may be very large, such as BLOB, CLOB, and ARRAY, making it more efficient to have their mappings contain locators rather than the actual data. But, as illustrated in the preceding example, SQL does provide a way to have a pointer to a structured type in the form of a REF object. As shown in preceding SQL definitions, a structured type can be defined such that one or more attributes are references to other structured types. For example, in the structured type RESIDENCE, the attribute OCCUPANT is a reference to the structured type PERSON. OCCUPANT could have contained an instance of the type PERSON directly, but since it has several attributes, REF(PERSON) was used instead. Conversely, in the definition of the structured type PERSON, the type for the attribute NAME is FULLNAME, itself a structured type. NAME could alternatively have been of type REF(FULLNAME), but since FULLNAME has only two attributes, it was used directly instead of using a reference to it. An SQL REF object is mapped to an instance of the interface Ref in the Java programming language. As noted previously, there is more information about the Ref interface in Chapter 26, starting on page 997.

Struct instances are most often created from a result set column value, but they can also be created from an output parameter returned by a stored procedure. The following code fragment illustrates retrieving the first output parameter of the CallableStatement object *cstmt*:

```
Struct book = (Struct)cstmt.getObject(1);
```

The variable *book* now contains the attribute values for the structured type object that the stored procedure called by *cstmt* returned as the first output parameter. The two getAttributes methods of Struct can now be called on *book* (or on *swimmer* from the previous example) to get an array of the attribute values.

In a driver implementation that is JDBC Compliant, a Struct instance such as *swimmer* or *book* will remain valid as long as an application maintains a reference to it. Being a normal object in the Java programming language, a Struct object does not maintain a database connection internally.

44.1.5 Mapping SQL Inheritance

Not all DBMSs support inheritance, but for those that do, structured types defined in SQL may inherit from other structured types and may form an inheritance hierarchy. For example, the following SQL commands define two structured types, PERSON and STUDENT, with STUDENT inheriting from PERSON.

```
CREATE TYPE PERSON (
        LAST_NAME VARCHAR(40), FIRST_NAME VARCHAR(40), BIRTH DATE);

CREATE TYPE STUDENT EXTENDS PERSON (GPA NUMERIC(4,2));
```

As with inheritance in the Java programming language, the derived type STUDENT includes the attributes LAST_NAME, FIRST_NAME, and BIRTH from PERSON as well as the attribute GPA.

The definition for the type GRAD_STUDENT, which inherits from STUDENT, might look like this:

```
CREATE TYPE GRAD_STUDENT EXTENDS STUDENT (MAJOR VARCHAR(40));
```

The type `GRAD_STUDENT` includes the attributes in `STUDENT` plus the additional attribute it defines, `MAJOR`.

44.1.6 Ordering of Attributes

The order in which attributes are listed in the SQL definition of a structured type is a matter of personal preference. Once the attributes have been listed in an SQL definition, however, the order cannot be changed because it determines the following:

- the order of the attribute values in the array returned by the method `getAttributes`

- for structured types with a custom mapping:

  - the order of the reader methods in the implementation of the method `SQLData.readSQL` in the class mapping the structured type (which is also the order of the attribute values in an `SQLInput` input stream)

  - the order of the writer methods in the implementation of the method `SQLData.writeSQL` in the class mapping the structured type (which is also the order of the attribute values expected by an `SQLOutput` output stream)

The order in which attributes are defined can become complicated if one structured type inherits from another or if an attribute is an embedded structured type or a reference. For this reason, the following rules govern the ordering of attributes:

1. The order of attribute values is determined by the order in which the attributes are defined in the original SQL definition of the structured type.

2. Attributes are ordered in a "depth-first" traversal of the structured types. In other words, if a structured type is embedded within another structured type, all of the attribute values of the embedded type are ordered before going on to the next attribute.

3. If there is an inheritance hierarchy, the attributes defined in a super type always precede those in a sub type. Thus, the attributes defined at the topmost level precede all attributes defined in derived structured types, and the attributes defined in the most derived sub type come last.

Based on the structured types defined in the preceding example to illustrate an inheritance hierarchy, the following SQL statement creates a table and inserts two rows into it. The first column, ID, holds an identification number; the second column, GRAD, holds an instance of the structured type GRAD_STUDENT. Note that the INSERT INTO command that supplies values for an instance of a structured type is very similar to the INSERT INTO command that populates a table, just as the commands CREATE TYPE and CREATE TABLE are very similar.

```
CREATE TABLE GRAD_STUDENTS
(
    ID DOUBLE,
    GRAD GRAD_STUDENT
);

INSERT INTO GRAD_STUDENTS VALUES
(
    8359037,
    'LEE', 'JIANG', '04-MAR-56', 03.85, 'MATH'
);

INSERT INTO GRAD_STUDENTS VALUES
(
    8359038,
    'ALVAREZ', 'JOSE', '24-JAN-59', 03.25, 'BIOLOGY'
);
```

In the following code fragment, the variable *grad* is a Struct object that contains the attribute values for the instance of GRAD_STUDENT in the row of *rs* where the column ID contains 8359037. Calling the method getAttributes on *struct* produces an array of the attribute values, and the for loop prints out the values.

```
ResultSet rs = stmt.executeQuery(
            "SELECT GRAD FROM GRAD_STUDENTS WHERE ID = 8359037");
rs.next();
Struct grad = (Struct)rs.getObject("GRAD");
Object [] grads = grad.getAttributes();
```

```
for (int i = 0; i < grads.length; i++) {
    Object obj = grads[i];
    System.out.println("Attribute " + (i+1) + " is " + obj);
}
```

The output from this code fragment might look like the following:

- ➥ Attribute 1 is LEE
- ➥ Attribute 2 is JIANG
- ➥ Attribute 3 is 04-MAR-56
- ➥ Attribute 4 is 03.85
- ➥ Attribute 5 is MATH

44.1.7 Storing a Struct Object

An instance of the interface Struct may be stored in a database by passing it as an input parameter to a prepared statement. Note that for a Struct object, the method to use is setObject.

The following code fragment demonstrates creating the Struct object *dog*, which designates the SQL structured type instance stored in the fourth column of the ResultSet object *rs*, and then passing it as a parameter to the PreparedStatement object *pstmt*.

```
Struct dog = (Struct)rs.getObject(4);
PreparedStatement pstmt = con.prepareStatement(
                "UPDATE PETS SET PET = ? WHERE OWNER_ID = 0385");
pstmt.setObject(1, dog);
```

In the table PETS, the column PET in the row where column OWNER_ID is 0385 now stores the SQL99 structured type that *dog* represents.

44.2 Struct Interface Definition

2.0

```
package java.sql;
public interface Struct {
    String getSQLTypeName() throws SQLException;
    Object [] getAttributes() throws SQLException;
    Object [] getAttributes(java.util.Map map) throws SQLException;
}
```

44.3 Struct Methods

`2.0` **getAttributes**

Object [] **getAttributes**() throws SQLException

Creates an array containing the ordered values of the attributes in the SQL structured type mapped by this Struct object. This method uses the type map associated with the connection for the custom mapping of attribute values. If the connection's type map does not have an entry for a structured type, the standard mapping is used.

Conceptually, this method calls the ResultSet method getObject on each attribute of the structured type in the order in which the attributes were defined. If an attribute is a structured type or a distinct type and it has an entry in the connection's type map, it will be custom mapped to the class indicated in the connection's type map. The result of each invocation of getObject is appended to an array of type Object.

RETURNS:
an array in the Java programming language that contains the ordered attribute values of the SQL structured type represented by this object

EXAMPLE:
```
Struct spider = (Struct)rs.getObject(3);
// spider contains the SQL structured type stored in the third column
// of the current row of the ResultSet object rs
Object [] spider_attr = spider.getAttributes();
// spider_attr is an array containing the mapped attribute values of
// the SQL structured type represented by spider
```

`2.0` **getAttributes**

Object [] **getAttributes**(java.util.Map *map*) throws SQLException

Creates an array containing the ordered values of the attributes in the SQL structured type mapped by this Struct object. This method uses the Map object *map* for the custom mapping of attribute values. If the given type map does not have an entry for the SQL structured type, the standard mapping is used.

Conceptually, this method calls the `ResultSet` method `getObject` on each attribute of the structured type in the order in which the attributes were defined. If an attribute is a structured type or a distinct type and it has an entry in *map*, it will be custom mapped to the class indicated in *map*. The result of each invocation of `getObject` is appended to an array of type `Object`.

PARAMETERS:

map   the `Map` object that contains the mapping of SQL type
                             names to classes in the Java programming language

RETURNS:

an array in the Java programming language that contains the ordered attributes of the SQL structured type represented by this object

EXAMPLE:
```
Struct arana = (Struct)rs.getObject("PERSON");
// arana is a mapping of the SQL structured type stored in the column
// PERSON in the current row of the ResultSet object rs
Object [] attributes = arana.getAttributes(personMap);
// attributes contains the mapped attribute values of the SQL
// structured type represented by arana. Attribute values were
// mapped using personMap where appropriate.
```

getSQLTypeName   2.0

```
String getSQLTypeName() throws SQLException
```

Retrieves the fully qualified SQL type name for the structured type that this object represents. This is the name used in a `CREATE TABLE` statement to specify a column of this type.

RETURNS:

the SQL type name of the SQL structured type for which this `Struct` object is the standard mapping in the Java programming language

EXAMPLE:
```
Struct struct = (Struct)rs.getObject(3);
String typeName = struct.getTypeName();
// struct represents the SQL structured type stored in column 3 of
// the current row of the ResultSet object rs. typeName contains the
// fully qualified SQL name of the structured type that struct
// represents.
```

Time

45.1 Time Overview

THE class java.sql.Time represents a JDBC TIME value. The class java.util.Date cannot be used because it contains both date and time information, and the type JDBC TIME contains only time information. To remedy this, java.sql.Time acts as a thin wrapper around java.util.Date, using only the time part. Whenever a Time object is retrieved from the database, the driver will normalize the date component (set the date component to January 1, 1970) before returning it to an application. An application that creates a java.sq.Time object should first create a java.util.Calendar object and explicitly set its date fields to January 1, 1970. (An application can compare two Time objects meaningfully only if the Date components of both have been normalized.) Then the application can convert the Calendar object to its milliseconds equivalent and supply that value to the java.sql.Time constructor. This process is demonstrated in the next section.

The JDBC Time class adds methods for formatting and parsing so that the JDBC escape syntax for time values can be used. See "SQL Escape Syntax in Statements," on page 958, for more information about using JDBC escape syntax.

45.1.1 Creating a Time Object

There are two ways to create a Time object: (1) by using the constructor or (2) by creating one from a string using the method valueOf.

1. Using the constructor to create a Time object

   The following code sample uses a Calendar object, which is the recommended way to create a Time object.

```java
import java.sql.*;
import java.util.*;

public class CreateTime {
    public static void main(String [] args) {

        Calendar cal = Calendar.getInstance();
        cal.set(Calendar.YEAR, 1970);
        cal.set(Calendar.MONTH, Calendar.JANUARY);
        cal.set(Calendar.DATE, 1);
        cal.set(Calendar.HOUR_OF_DAY, 16);
        cal.set(Calendar.MINUTE, 30);
        cal.set(Calendar.SECOND, 0);
        cal.set(Calendar.MILLISECOND, 0);

        long millis = cal.getTime().getTime();
        java.sql.Time t = new java.sql.Time(millis);

        System.out.println("millis = " + millis);
        System.out.println("Time t = " + t);
    }
}
```

Running this code produces output similar to this:

```
➥ millis = 88200377
➥ Time t = 16:30:00
```

The variable *t* now contains a Time object that represents the time 4:30 p.m.

The preceding example illustrates the following features:

- The example sets the date to January 1, 1970 because that is the zero epoch, the date from which all dates are calculated in the Java programming language.

- The field HOUR_OF_DAY, used in the example, has a 24-hour clock; the field HOUR, which is an alternate, uses a 12-hour clock and requires that you also set the AM_PM field to either Calendar.AM (which is 0) or Calendar.PM (which is 1).
- The call cal.getTime().getTime() returns a milliseconds value. The first invocation of getTime converts the Calendar instance *cal* to a java.util.Date object, and the next call to the getTime method converts the Date object to its milliseconds value.

Note that it is a good idea to append L to the number supplied to the Time constructor. This identifies the number as a long, so the compiler will not interpret it as an int and reject numbers that are out of range for an int.

2. Using the method valueOf to convert a string to a Time object

```
Time tm = Time.valueOf("16:30:00");
```

The variable *tm* contains a Time object representing 4:30 p.m.

45.1.2 Deprecated Methods

Even though a java.sql.Time object includes the date components inherited from java.util.Date, they should never be accessed. The exception java.lang.IllegalArgumentException will be thrown if a java.sql.Time object invokes any of the methods that get or set date components. In the JDBC 2.0 API, the following java.sql.Time methods, inherited from java.util.Date, are deprecated:

```
getYear
getMonth
getDay
getDate
setYear
setMonth
setDate
```

45.1.3 Retrieving a Time Object

A Time object is retrieved using either the method ResultSet.getTime or CallableStatement.getTime. As an example, the following code fragment, in which *stmt* is a Statement object, uses ResultSet.getTime to retrieve the time for the course whose identification number is 0831.

```
ResultSet rs = stmt.executeQuery(
        "SELECT TIME FROM SCHEDULE WHERE COURSE_NO = 0831");
rs.next();
java.sql.Time time = rs.getTime("TIME");
```

45.1.4 Advanced Features

The number of milliseconds in a java.sql.Time object always takes into account a time zone, which, of course, affects the time in a particular place. In the examples up to this point, the driver has used the default time zone, the time zone of the Java virtual machine running an application. The JDBC 2.0 core API added new versions of the getTime methods to the ResultSet and CallableStatement interfaces that take a java.util.Calendar object, in which time zone information can be stored with an appropriate instance of the TimeZone class.

When a getTime method is called, the driver converts a JDBC TIME instance, which is generally a string, to a java.sql.Time object, which is a milliseconds value. In order to calculate the milliseconds, the driver takes into account the time zone, information a DBMS may or may not store. If a DBMS does provide time zone information, the driver will always use that and ignore a Calendar object that may have been passed to it. Otherwise, because a Time object itself has no way to keep track of time zone information, the driver relies on a java.util.Calendar object to get this information. If no Calendar object is supplied, the driver will use the default Calendar, whose time zone is that of the Java virtual machine that is running the application. For greater portability, an application should supply a Calendar object to a getTime method. This ensures that time zone information is always available, if not from the DBMS, then from the Calendar object.

The following code fragment illustrates using a Calendar object to retrieve a time that is accurate for Central Standard Time.

```
ResultSet rs = stmt.executeQuery(
                "SELECT CLOSE FROM HOURS WHERE STORE_ID = 0034");
java.util.Calendar cal = java.util.Calendar.getInstance();
java.util.TimeZone tz = java.util.TimeZone.getTimeZone("CST");

cal.setTimeZone(tz);
```

```
rs.next();
Time close = rs.getTime("CLOSE", cal);
```

After creating an instance of `Calendar`, the code gets the time zone for Central Standard Time and assigns it to a `TimeZone` object. Then it sets the `Calendar` instance with that `TimeZone` object and passes it to the method `getTime`. The variable *close* contains a `Time` object that has been calculated for Central Standard Time.

45.2 Time Class Definition

```
package java.sql;
public class Time extends java.util.Date {
    public Time(int hour, int minute, int second); DEPRECATED
    public Time(long milliseconds);
    public void setTime(long time);
    public static Time valueOf(String s);
    public String toString();
}
```

45.3 Time Constructors

Time   **DEPRECATED**
_____

```
public Time(int hour, int minute, int second)
```

Constructs a `java.sql.Time` object initialized with *hour*, *minute*, and *second* to represent a time value that can be used as a JDBC `TIME` value.

Since `java.sql.Time` is a subclass of `java.util.Date`, it inherits the date components of `java.util.Date`. However, these date components are not accessible from a `java.sql.Time` object and trying to access them will cause an exception to be thrown.

This method has been deprecated; in its place, use the constructor that takes a long.

PARAMETERS:

hour	a Java int from 0 to 23
minute	a Java int from 0 to 59
second	a Java int from 0 to 59

RETURNS:
a java.sql.Time object representing a JDBC TIME value

EXAMPLE:
```
Time t = new Time(15, 45, 0); // t represents 3:45 p.m. exactly
```

Time

```
public Time(long milliseconds)
```

Constructs a java.sql.Time object from *milliseconds*, a milliseconds time value, to represent a value that can be used as a JDBC TIME value. The milliseconds parameter value should be obtained from a java.util.Calendar object with its time component set to the desired time and its date component set to January 1, 1970. Date components are not accessible from a java.sql.Time object, and an attempt to access them will throw an SQLException.

PARAMETERS:

milliseconds	a long representing the number of milliseconds since January 1, 1970, 00:00:00 GMT; a negative number means the number of milliseconds before January 1, 1970, 00:00:00 GMT

RETURNS:
a java.sql.Time object representing a JDBC TIME value

EXAMPLE:
```
Calendar cal = Calendar.getInstance();
cal.set(Calendar.YEAR, 1970);
cal.set(Calendar.MONTH, Calendar.JANUARY);
cal.set(Calendar.DATE, 1);
cal.set(Calendar.HOUR_OF_DAY, 16);
cal.set(Calendar.MINUTE, 30);
cal.set(Calendar.SECOND, 0);
```

```
cal.set(Calendar.MILLISECOND, 0);

long millis = cal.getTime().getTime();
java.sql.Time t = new java.sql.Time(millis);
// millis = 88200000 and t = 16:30:00, or 4:30 p.m.
```

45.4 Time Methods

setTime

```
public void setTime(long time)
```

Sets this Time object to *time*, which represents the milliseconds since January 1, 1970. This method overrides the setTime method in the class java.util.Time.

PARAMETERS:

time   a long indicating the number of milliseconds since January 1, 1970; a negative number indicates the number of milliseconds before January 1, 1970

EXAMPLE:

```
import java.sql.*;
import java.util.*;

public class SetTime {
    public static void main(String [] args) {

        java.sql.Time tm = java.sql.Time.valueOf("18:30:00");
        System.out.println("Time tm = " + tm);
        //tm represents 18:30:00, or 6:30 p.m.
        Calendar cal = Calendar.getInstance();
        cal.set(Calendar.YEAR, 1970);
        cal.set(Calendar.MONTH, Calendar.JANUARY);
        cal.set(Calendar.DATE, 1);
        cal.set(Calendar.HOUR, 3);
        cal.set(Calendar.AM_PM, Calendar.AM);
```

```
cal.set(Calendar.MINUTE, 5);
cal.set(Calendar.SECOND, 20);
cal.set(Calendar.MILLISECOND, 0);

long millis = cal.getTime().getTime();
tm.setTime(millis);
// millis = 39920000 and tm = 3:05:20 a.m.
```

OVERRIDES:
java.util.Date.setTime

toString

public String **toString**()

Formats this Time object as a String object with the format hh:mm:ss. The driver uses the default time zone to calculate the time; therefore, this method should not be used with times in other time zones.

RETURNS:
a String object with the format "hh:mm:ss"

EXAMPLE:
java.sql.Time tm = java.sql.Time(95400000L);
String s = tm.toString();
// s = 18:30:00

OVERRIDES:
java.util.Date.toString

valueOf

public static Time **valueOf**(String s)

Converts s, a formatted string, to a Time object. The driver uses the default time zone to calculate the number of milliseconds in the newly created Time object; therefore, this method should not be used with times in other time zones.

PARAMETERS:

s a `String` object in the format "hh:mm:ss", where hh is hours, mm is minutes, and ss is seconds

RETURNS:

a `Time` object representing the hours, minutes, and seconds specified in the given `String` object

EXAMPLE:

```
String s = new String("15:45:00");
java.sql.Time t = java.sql.Time.valueOf(s);
// t represents 3:45 p.m.
```

OVERRIDES:

`java.util.Date.valueOf`

Timestamp

46.1 `Timestamp` Overview

THE class `java.sql.Timestamp` represents a JDBC TIMESTAMP value in the Java programming language. A JDBC TIMESTAMP value has date and time information and also a field for nanoseconds. (A nanosecond is a billionth of a second.) The class `java.util.Date` cannot be used as a JDBC TIMESTAMP value because, although it contains both date and time information, it does not contain nanoseconds. To remedy this, `java.sql.Timestamp` extends `java.util.Date`, adding a field for nanoseconds. In other words, `java.sql.Timestamp` is a thin wrapper around `java.util.Date` and consists of two parts: One part is a `java.util.Date`, and the other part is a separate field for nanoseconds.

The `java.sql.Timestamp` class adds methods for formatting and parsing so that the JDBC escape syntax for timestamp values can be used. See "SQL Escape Syntax in Statements," starting on page 958. It also adds methods for getting and setting the nanoseconds field and for comparing two `Timestamp` objects.

46.1.1 Creating a `Timestamp` Object

There are two ways to create a `Timestamp` object, one using the constructor and one using the method `valueOf`.

1. Using the constructor to create a `Timestamp` object

    The following code sample uses a `Calendar` object, which is the recommended way to create a `Timestamp` object.

```
import java.sql.*;
import java.util.*;

public class CreateTimestamp {
    public static void main(String [] args) {

    Calendar cal = Calendar.getInstance();

    cal.set(Calendar.YEAR, 2000);
    cal.set(Calendar.MONTH, Calendar.JANUARY);
    cal.set(Calendar.DATE, 1);
    cal.set(Calendar.HOUR_OF_DAY, 11);
    cal.set(Calendar.MINUTE, 45);
    cal.set(Calendar.SECOND, 30);
    cal.set(Calendar.MILLISECOND, 0);

    long millis = cal.getTime().getTime();
    System.out.println("milliseconds in millis = " + millis);
    java.sql.Timestamp ts = new java.sql.Timestamp(millis);
    System.out.println("Timestamp ts before setting nanos = " + ts);

    ts.setNanos(500);
    System.out.println("Timestamp ts with nanos set = " + ts);
    }
}
```

Running this code will produce output similar to the following:

- ➥ milliseconds in millis = 946755930000
- ➥ Timestamp ts before setting nanos = 2000-01-01 11:45:30.0
- ➥ Timestamp ts with nanos set = 2000-01-01 11:45:30.0000005

The variable *ts* now contains a Timestamp object that represents January 1, 2000, at 11:45:30 a.m. plus five hundred billionths of a second.

The preceding example illustrates the following features:

- The example sets all fields for the desired date and time. The method `Cal-endar.instanceOf` returns a `Calendar` object whose fields are set with the current date and time of the Java virtual machine running the application. If a field is not explicitly set, it will retain its original value, which is probably not what is wanted.
- The field `HOUR_OF_DAY`, used in the example, has a 24-hour clock; the field `HOUR`, which is an alternate, uses a 12-hour clock and requires that you also set the `AM_PM` field to either `Calendar.AM (0)` or `Calendar.PM (1)`.
- The call `cal.getTime().getTime()` returns a milliseconds value. The first invocation of `getTime` converts the `Calendar` instance *cal* to an instance of `java.util.Date`, and the next call to the `getTime` method converts the `Date` object to its milliseconds value.

Note that it is a good idea to append `L` to the number supplied to the `Time-stamp` constructor. This identifies the number as a `long`, so the compiler will not interpret it as an `int` and reject numbers that are out of range for an `int`.

To create a `Timestamp` object for the current time and date, the following line of code can be used.

```
java.sql.Timestamp ts =
                java.sql.Timestamp(System.currentTimeMillis());
```

2. Using the method `valueOf` to convert a string to a `Timestamp` object

```
Timestamp ts = Timestamp.valueOf("2003-05-31 18:30:00.9");
```

The variable *ts* contains a `Timestamp` object representing May 31, 2003 at 6:30 p.m. plus nine-tenths of a second (900 milliseconds).

46.1.2   Retrieving a `Timestamp` Object

A `Timestamp` object is retrieved using one of the `getTimestamp` methods. The method `ResultSet.getTimestamp` retrieves a `Timestamp` object from a result set, and the `CallableStatement.getTimestamp` method retrieves a `Timestamp` object from an `OUT` or `INOUT` parameter of a stored procedure. For example, the following code fragment, in which *stmt* is a `Statement` object, uses `ResultSet.getTimestamp` to retrieve the timestamp telling when order number 0023592 was received.

```
ResultSet rs = stmt.executeQuery(
        "SELECT TIME_RECD FROM ORDERS WHERE ORDER_NO = 0023592");
rs.next();
java.sql.Timestamp ts = rs.getTimestamp("TIME_RECD");
```

46.1.3 Advanced Features

The number of milliseconds in a `java.sql.Timestamp` object always takes into account a time zone, which, of course, affects the time and may affect the date in a particular place. In the examples up to this point, the driver has used the default time zone, the time zone of the Java virtual machine running an application. The JDBC 2.0 core API adds new versions of the `getTimestamp` methods to the `ResultSet` and `CallableStatement` interfaces that take a `java.util.Calendar` object, in which time zone information can be stored with an appropriate instance of the `TimeZone` class.

When a `getTimestamp` method is called, the driver converts a JDBC TIME-STAMP instance, which is generally a string, to a `java.sql.Timestamp` object, which is a milliseconds value. In order to calculate the milliseconds, the driver takes into account the time zone, information a DBMS may or may not store. Because a `Timestamp` object itself has no way to keep track of time zone information, the driver relies on a `java.util.Calendar` object to get this information. If no `Calendar` object is supplied, the driver will use the default `Calendar`, whose time zone is that of the Java virtual machine that is running the application. If the DBMS does provide time zone information, the driver will simply use that and ignore a `Calendar` object that may have been passed to it. Therefore, to be portable, an application should supply a `Calendar` object to a `getTimestamp` method, thereby not relying on the DBMS to supply a time zone but still being able to use the time zone supplied by a DBMS when one is available.

For example, the following code fragment illustrates using a `Calendar` object to retrieve a timestamp that is accurate for Central Standard Time.

```
ResultSet rs = stmt.executeQuery(
    "SELECT COMPLETED FROM ORDERS WHERE ORDER_NO = 0029581");
```

```
java.util.Calendar cal = java.util.Calendar.getInstance();
java.util.TimeZone tz = java.util.TimeZone.getTimeZone("CST");
cal.setTimeZone(tz);
rs.next();
Timestamp completed = rs.getTimestamp("COMPLETED", cal);
```

After creating an instance of Calendar, the code gets the time zone for Central Standard Time and assigns it to a TimeZone object. Then it sets the Calendar instance with that TimeZone object and passes it to the method getTimestamp. The variable *completed* contains a Timestamp object that has been calculated for Central Standard Time.

46.2 Timestamp Class Definition

```
package java.sql;
public class Timestamp extends java.util.Date {
    public Timestamp(int year, int month, int day, int hour, int minute,
                        int second, int nano); (DEPRECATED)
    public Timestamp(long milliseconds);
    public static Timestamp valueOf(String s);
    public String toString();
    public int getNanos();
    public void setNanos(int n);
    public boolean equals(Timestamp ts);
    public boolean before(Timestamp ts);
    public boolean after(Timestamp ts);
}
```

46.3 Timestamp Constructors

Timestamp   **DEPRECATED**
_____

```
public Timestamp (int year, int month, int day, int hour, int minute,
                                            int second, int nano)
```

Constructs a `java.sql.Timestamp` object initialized with *year*, *month*, *day*, *hour*, *minute*, *second*, and *nano* to represent a timestamp value that can be used as a JDBC `TIMESTAMP` value.

This constructor has been deprecated; instead, use the constructor that takes a `long` value.

PARAMETERS:

year	an `int` calculated by subtracting 1900 from the year
month	an `int` from 0 to 11 (0 is January; 11 is December)
day	an `int` from 1 to 31, representing the day of the month
hour	an `int` from 0 to 23, representing hours
minute	an `int` from 0 to 59, representing minutes
second	an `int` from 0 to 59, representing seconds
nano	an `int` from 0 to 999,999,999, representing nanoseconds

RETURNS:
a `java.sql.Timestamp` object representing a timestamp

EXAMPLE:
```
Timestamp ts = new Timestamp(100, 0, 1, 15, 45, 0, 999999999);
// ts represents one nanosecond before 3:45:01 p.m. on January 1,
// 2000
```

Timestamp

```
public Timestamp (long milliseconds)
```

Constructs a `java.sql.Timestamp` object from *milliseconds*, a milliseconds time value. The integral seconds are stored in the underlying `java.util.Date` value; the fractional seconds are stored in the `nanos` field of the `Timestamp` object. The milliseconds parameter value should be obtained from a `java.util.Calendar` object with its date and time components set to those desired.

PARAMETERS:

milliseconds	a `long` representing milliseconds since January 1, 1970 00:00:00 GMT; a negative value represents milliseconds before January 1, 1970 00:00:00 GMT

RETURNS:
a `java.sql.Timestamp` object representing a JDBC `TIMESTAMP` value

EXAMPLE:

```
import java.sql.*;
import java.util.*;

public class TSExample {
    public static void main(String [] args) {
    Calendar cal = Calendar.getInstance();
    cal.set(Calendar.YEAR, 1900);
    cal.set(Calendar.MONTH, Calendar.OCTOBER);
    cal.set(Calendar.DATE, 31);
    cal.set(Calendar.HOUR_OF_DAY, 11);
    cal.set(Calendar.MINUTE, 45);
    cal.set(Calendar.SECOND, 30);
    cal.set(Calendar.MILLISECOND, 0);

    long millis = cal.getTime().getTime();
    java.sql.Timestamp ts = new java.sql.Timestamp(millis);
    ts.setNanos(100);
    }
}
// milliseconds in millis = -2182738470000
// Timestamp ts before setting nanos = 1900-10-31 11:45:30.0
// Timestamp ts with nanos set = 1900-10-31 11:45:30.0000001
```

46.4 Timestamp Methods

after

```
public boolean after(Timestamp ts)
```

Tests to see if this Timestamp object is later than *ts*.

PARAMETERS:

ts   the Timestamp object with which to compare this Time-
                                stamp object

RETURNS:
true if this Timestamp object is later than the given Timestamp object; false if they are equal or this Timestamp object is earlier than the given Timestamp object

EXAMPLE:
```
Timestamp ts = new Timestamp(0986325098723L);
Timestamp ts2 = new Timestamp(0986325098723L);
boolean b = ts2.after(ts); // b = false
```

OVERRIDES:
java.util.Date.after to include the fractional seconds component of a Timestamp object

before

```
public boolean before(Timestamp ts)
```

Tests to see if this Timestamp object is before *ts*.

PARAMETERS:

ts   the Timestamp object with which to compare this Timestamp object

RETURNS:
true if this Timestamp object is before the given Timestamp object; false if they are equal or this Timestamp object is after the given Timestamp object

EXAMPLE:
```
Timestamp ts1 = new Timestamp(13509862305986123L);
Timestamp ts2 = new Timestamp(235098623059861239L);
boolean b = ts2.before(ts1); // b = false
```

OVERRIDES:
java.util.Date.before to include the fractional seconds component of a Timestamp object

equals

```
public boolean equals(Timestamp ts)
```

Tests to see if this Timestamp object is equal to *ts*.

PARAMETERS:

ts   the `Timestamp` object with which to compare this Time-
                                stamp object

RETURNS:
true if the two `Timestamp` objects are equal; `false` otherwise

EXAMPLE:
```
Timestamp ts1 = new Timestamp(235098761203521398571L);
Timestamp ts2 = new Timestamp(235098761203521398571L);
boolean b = ts2.equals(ts); // b = true
```

OVERRIDES:
`java.util.Date.equals` to include the fractional seconds component of a
`Timestamp` object

getNanos

```
public int getNanos()
```

Retrieves the number of nanoseconds stored in the `nanos` field of this
`Timestamp` object.

RETURNS:
an `int` indicating the number of nanoseconds stored in this `Timestamp` object

EXAMPLE:
```
Timestamp ts = new Timestamp(986151600000L);
int n = ts.getNanos();
// n = 0; ts = 2001-04-01 12:00:00.0
```

setNanos

```
public void setNanos(int n)
```

Sets the `nanos` field of this `Timestamp` object to *n*.

PARAMETERS:

n   the new fractional seconds component

EXAMPLE:
```
Timestamp ts = new Timestamp(1009326600000L);
ts.setNanos(5000);
```

```
int n = ts.getNanos();
// n = 5000
// ts before setting nanos = 2001-12-25 16:30:00.0
// ts after setting nanos = 2001-12-25 16:30:00.000005
```

toString

`public String` **`toString`**`()`

Formats this `Timestamp` object as a `String` object with the format yyyy-mm-dd hh:mm:ss.f . . . . The driver uses the default time zone in its conversion of the milliseconds value to a `String` object; therefore, this method should not be used with timestamps in other time zones.

RETURNS:
a `String` object with the format "yyyy-mm-dd hh:mm:ss.f . . ."

EXAMPLE:
```
Timestamp ts = new Timestamp(960642600000L);
String s = ts.toString(); // s is "2000-06-10 06:10:00.0"
```

OVERRIDES:
`java.util.Date.toString` to include a nanoseconds component

valueOf

`public static Timestamp` **`valueOf`**`(String s)`

Converts *s*, a formatted `String` object, to a `Timestamp` object. Note that this is a static method, so it operates on `java.sql.Timestamp`, not instances of `java.sql.Timestamp`. The driver uses the default time zone in its conversion of a `String` object to a `Timestamp` object; therefore, this method should not be used with timestamps in other time zones.

PARAMETERS:

s   a `String` object in the format "yyyy-mm-dd hh:mm:ss.f
                             . . .", where yyyy is year, mm is month, dd is day, hh
                             is hours, mm is minutes, ss is seconds, and f is a frac-
                             tion of a second

RETURNS:

a newly created `Timestamp` object representing the year, month, day, hours, minutes, seconds, and nanoseconds specified in the `String` object *s*

EXAMPLE:
```
Timestamp ts1 = java.sql.Timestamp.valueOf(
                                    "1492-10-12 18:30:00.0");
ts1.setNanos(500);
Calendar cal = Calendar.getInstance();
cal.set(Calendar.YEAR, 1492);
cal.set(Calendar.MONTH, Calendar.OCTOBER);
cal.set(Calendar.DATE, 12);
cal.set(Calendar.HOUR, 6);
cal.set(Calendar.AM_PM, Calendar.PM);
cal.set(Calendar.MINUTE, 30);
cal.set(Calendar.SECOND, 0);
cal.set(Calendar.MILLISECOND, 0);
long millis = cal.getTime().getTime();
Timestamp ts2 = new java.sql.Timestamp(millis);
ts2.setNanos(500);
boolean b = ts1.equals(ts2);
// b = true
```

OVERRIDES:

`java.util.Date.valueOf` to include a nanoseconds component

CHAPTER 47

Types

47.1 Overview of Class Types

THE class Types is simply a list of constants that are used to identify generic SQL data types. These generic SQL type identifiers are called JDBC types, which distinguishes them from database-specific SQL types. See the overview section of "Mapping SQL and Java Types," starting on page 1065, for a discussion of JDBC types and local DBMS types.

The class Types is never instantiated.

47.1.1 Using the Constants in Class Types

The constants defined in the class Types are used in various ways. They can be arguments supplied to methods or values returned in ResultSet objects.

For instance, one of the constants in java.sql.Types must be supplied as the second argument to the method CallableStatement.registerOutParameter. This method will register the specified OUT parameter with the given JDBC type. The value that the database assigns to this parameter must have the same JDBC type that is registered to this parameter. For example, if *cstmt* is a CallableStatement object, the following code registers the second parameter of its stored procedure as a JDBC SMALLINT. The value that the database assigns to the second output parameter will have a JDBC type of SMALLINT.

```
cstmt.registerOutParameter(2, Types.SMALLINT);
```

Note that in the definition of Types, SMALLINT is assigned the value 5, which is an int. Either SMALLINT or 5 can be used as the argument to a method, but it is generally considered good programming practice to use the name, which makes the meaning clear.

The method `DatabaseMetaData.supportsConvert` provides another example of using the constants in `Types` as method arguments. In this case, the two arguments represent the JDBC types to convert to and to convert from.

Another use of a `Types` constant is as a column value in the `ResultSet` object returned by a `DatabaseMetaData` method. For example, each row in the `ResultSet` object returned by the method `getTypeInfo` contains a `Types` constant and a description of that type as supported by a particular database.

47.1.2   Using the Constant OTHER

The constant `java.sql.Types.OTHER` indicates that the data type is not one of the standard JDBC types, but rather an SQL type used only by this particular database. If an output parameter is registered with a JDBC type of `java.sql.Types.OTHER`, the value assigned to it gets mapped to a Java object, which can be accessed using the `CallableStatement.getObject` method.

This constant is one component of JDBC's support for dynamic database access. See "Dynamic Data Access," on page 1084.

47.1.3   JDBC Types Added in the JDBC 2.0 Core API

The JDBC 2.0 core API added seven JDBC types to the class `Types`, and the JDBC 3.0 API added two more, which are covered in the next section. These types, added to the JDBC API to reflect the new types in the SQL99 specification, are also known as SQL99 types.

- JAVA_OBJECT
- ARRAY
- BLOB
- CLOB
- DISTINCT
- REF
- STRUCT

The JDBC type JAVA_OBJECT denotes an object type in the Java programming language. Along with SQL structured types and distinct types, JAVA_OBJECT is one of the user-defined types (UDTs) in SQL.

As is true of all type codes, JAVA_OBJECT is used mainly as a return value for methods that return metadata information. For example, it can be the value for the column DATA_TYPE in the ResultSet objects returned by the following methods in the DatabaseMetaData interface: getTypeInfo, getUDTs, getColumns, getBestRow-Identifier, getProcedureColumns, and getVersionColumns. JAVA_OBJECT can also be used as a method parameter, as shown in the following example:

```
int [] types = {Types.JAVA_OBJECT};
ResultSet rs = dbmd.getUDTs("catalogName", "schemaName",
                                              "%", types);
```

The six other new type codes represent SQL99 data types that can be used the same way other data types are used, that is, as column types in a database table or as attribute types in an SQL structured type.

47.1.4 JDBC Data Types Added in the JDBC 3.0 API

3.0

Two JDBC type codes were added to the Types class in the JDBC 3.0 API:

- BOOLEAN

- DATALINK

The BOOLEAN type code maps to a Java boolean, as you would expect. Previously, the Java boolean type was mapped to a JDBC BIT. The DATALINK type code represents data that is not stored in a database table and maps to a java.net.URL object. For more information on these type codes, see "JDBC Types Added in the JDBC 3.0 API," on page 1078.

47.2 Types Class Definition

The class Types defines constants that are used to identify generic SQL types. The actual type constant values for JDBC 1.0 API data types are equivalent to those in the Open Group CLI. The SQL99 data types, mapped in the JDBC 2.0 core API, are not included in the Open Group CLI.

Since the class definition already contains complete information about its fields, they are not listed again in a separate "Fields" section.

```
package java.sql;
public class Types {
    public final static int BIT           = -7;
    public final static int TINYINT       = -6;
    public final static int SMALLINT      = 5;
    public final static int INTEGER       = 4;
    public final static int BIGINT        = -5;

    public final static int FLOAT         = 6;
    public final static int REAL          = 7;
    public final static int DOUBLE        = 8;

    public final static int NUMERIC       = 2;
    public final static int DECIMAL       = 3;

    public final static int CHAR          = 1;
    public final static int VARCHAR       = 12;
    public final static int LONGVARCHAR   = -1;

    public final static int DATE          = 91;
    public final static int TIME          = 92;
    public final static int TIMESTAMP     = 93;

    public final static int BINARY        = -2;
    public final static int VARBINARY     = -3;
    public final static int LONGVARBINARY = -4;

    public final static int NULL          = 0;

    public final static int OTHER         = 1111;

    public final static int JAVA_OBJECT   = 2000;
    public final static int DISTINCT      = 2001;
    public final static int STRUCT        = 2002;

    public final static int ARRAY         = 2003;
    public final static int BLOB          = 2004;
```

```
     2.0    public final static int CLOB          = 2005;

     2.0    public final static int REF           = 2006;

     3.0    public final static int DATALINK      = 70;
     3.0    public final static int BOOLEAN       = 16;
          }
```

CHAPTER **48**

XAConnection

48.1 XAConnection Overview

AN XAConnection object is a PooledConnection object that can be used in a distributed transaction. It represents a physical database connection and is used by a middle-tier server to create a Connection object that can be returned to an application. Being an interface that extends PooledConnection, XAConnection inherits all of the PooledConnection methods, and it adds one method of its own: getXAResource. The XAResource object returned by this method is what makes it possible for the XAConnection to participate in distributed transactions.

Distributed transactions, in which commands are sent to more than one DBMS server, are especially important for Enterprise JavaBeans (EJB) components. Because one component may call a method in another component in the context of a distributed transaction, it is easier to combine EJB components into an application if all of the components can participate in distributed transactions. The section "Distributed Transactions and EJB," on page 1050, explains more about the importance of distributed transactions in EJB components.

48.1.1 Application Code in Distributed Transactions

A distributed transaction has very little effect on application code because all of the transaction management is done by the distributed transaction infrastructure. This infrastructure includes an application server, a transaction manager, and a JDBC driver. The only impact on code is that an application cannot invoke a method that would affect the boundaries of a transaction while the connection is in the scope of a distributed transaction. Specifically, an application cannot call the methods Connection.commit and Connection.rollback because they would interfere with the infrastructure's management of the distributed transaction. Both methods throw an SQLException when they are called in the scope of a distributed transaction. The only other restriction is that a Connection object cannot have Connection.setAuto-Commit(true) called on it. This enables auto-commit mode, meaning that the method Connection.commit will be called automatically after each statement is executed. Because auto-commit mode conflicts with the work done by the transaction manager, enabling auto-commit mode will also throw an SQLException. This explains why a Connection object produced by an XAConnection object has its auto-commit mode disabled by default.

Note that these restrictions apply only to Connection objects produced by an XAConnection object and only if the Connection objects are used in the scope of a distributed transaction. For example, suppose that the transaction attribute for an EJB component specifies that the component must be used in the scope of a transaction. Suppose also that a method in that component is invoked, which initiates several actions, including a query to one DBMS and an update to another DBMS. When the method is invoked, the transaction manager will start a distributed transaction and associate it with the actions on each connection used in the EJB component. When the connections are closed, the transaction manager will get a vote from the DBMS servers involved as to whether to commit their part of the transaction. If all votes are for committing, the transaction manager will commit all branches of the distributed transaction. If not, the transaction manager will roll back the actions on all branches. If the EJB component itself contained code that committed or rolled back its part of the distributed transaction, that would conflict with the global management of the distributed transaction.

In summary, all that application programmers really need to know about distributed transactions is that they should not call the Connection methods commit, rollback, or setAutoCommit(true) in the scope of a distributed transaction. Therefore, the information in the rest of this chapter is mainly for the benefit of server and driver developers; others may choose not to read about the details of distributed transactions.

48.1.2 Distributed Transaction Requirements

Distributed transactions are managed by a middle-tier application server such as an Enterprise JavaBeans (EJB) server that works with an external transaction manager and also with a JDBC driver. These three parts of the middle-tier infrastructure provide the "plumbing" that makes distributed transactions possible. More specifically, this infrastructure includes the following:

- A transaction manager

- A driver that implements the JDBC 2.0 API, including the Optional Package interfaces XADataSource and XAConnection

- An application server that provides
    - A connection pooling module (not required but almost always included to improve performance)
    - A DataSource class that is implemented to interact with the distributed transaction infrastructure

The first element of a distributed transaction infrastructure is a transaction manager, which may be an implementation of the Java Transaction API. The transaction manager controls transaction boundaries and the two-phase commit process. It starts and ends the association of an XAConnection object with a distributed transaction and keeps track of which resource managers (DBMS servers) are participating in a distributed transaction. A transaction manager gets a vote from each resource manager on whether or not to commit. Only if all resource managers vote to commit will the transaction manager commit the transaction; otherwise, it will abort the transaction by rolling it back.

Another element of a distributed transaction infrastructure is a JDBC driver that supports the JDBC 2.0 API. In particular, the driver must include classes implementing the XADataSource and XAConnection interfaces. The XADataSource interface is similar to the DataSource interface except that it creates XAConnection objects instead of Connection objects. What is distinctive about an XAConnection object, which is derived from PooledConnection, is that it can be used to obtain an XAResource object. The transaction manager uses this XAResource object to begin and end the XAConnection object's association with a distributed transaction.

A third part of a distributed transaction infrastructure is generally a connection pooling module. The XAConnection interface is derived from the PooledConnection interface, which means that a connection that participates in a distributed transaction has the capability to be from a pool of connections managed by the connection pooling module. For more information on connection pooling, see Chapter 24, "PooledConnection."

Another requirement for distributed transactions is a DataSource class that is implemented to interact with the distributed transaction infrastructure. It should work with the connection pooling module, the transaction manager, and the JDBC 2.0 driver to provide connection pooling and distributed transaction functionality to the application. The DataSource implementation should reference an XAData-Source object, which is the factory that produces XAConnection objects. When an EJB server provides a DataSource implementation that supports distributed transactions, it is possible to deploy an EJB component (an enterprise Bean) that uses the JDBC API on that EJB server. The enterprise Bean will be portable to other EJB servers if they also implement the DataSource interface so that it interacts with a distributed transaction infrastructure.

To work with distributed transactions, the DataSource.getConnection method should be implemented to return a Connection object created by an XAConnection object. When the method DataSource.getConnection is called in the scope of a distributed transaction, the middle-tier server should check to see if an XAConnection object is available in the connection pool. If so, it is used to create the Connection object to return to the application. If not, the XADataSource object is used to create a new XAConnection object by calling the XAData-Source.getXAConnection method. The newly created XAConnection object can then be used to create the Connection object that DataSource.getConnection will return.

In order for the XAConnection object to participate in connection pooling, the component managing the connection pool needs to be registered with it. This assures that the connection pool module will be notified when the connection is closed or an error occurs. Also, in order for the XAConnection object to participate in distributed transactions, the method XAConnection.getXAResource needs to be called on it. This produces a javax.transaction.xa.XAResource object that the transaction manager uses to manage the connection's participation in a distributed transaction.

48.1.3 Creating an XAConnection Object

A particular vendor's implementation of a DataSource object determines when an XAConnection object is created. Generally, a new one is created when an application calls the method DataSource.getConnection and there is no XAConnection object available in the connection pool. To create a new XAConnection object, the first thing a middle-tier server will do is to retrieve an XADataSource object from the JNDI naming service with which it is registered.

```
Context ctx = new InitialContext();
XADataSource xads = (XADataSource)ctx.lookup("jdbc/xa/AuthorsDB");
```

The server uses the Java Naming and Directory Interface (JNDI) API to obtain a Context object, *ctx*, on which it can call the method lookup to retrieve an XADataSource object. As part of its deployment, a system administrator or other person registered the XADataSource object with a JNDI naming service. At that time the deployer supplied jdbc/xa/AuthorsDB as the logical name to be bound to it. The deployer also set properties on the XADataSource object so that it references a particular data source. When the server supplies jdbc/xa/AuthorsDB, the method lookup returns the XADataSource object that was bound to that logical name. The object returned needs to be cast to the narrower data type XADataSource before it is assigned to the variable *xads*. The variable *xads* can be used to create connections to the data source it represents. The server needs to retrieve *xads* only once because it can use *xads* over and over again to create new XAConnection objects.

The following line of code provides the method getXAConnection with a user name and password to get a connection to the data source that *xads* represents.

```
XAConnection xacon = xads.getXAConnection("charlie", "extra8");
```

The variable *xacon* is a physical connection to the data source that *xads* represents. So that the connection pooling module will be notified when *xacon* is closed or has an exception thrown, it needs to be registered with *xacon* as a listener. The following line of code, in which *listener* is the server's connection pooling module, registers *listener* as a listener for *xacon*.

```
xacon.addConnectionEventListener(listener);
```

If the Connection objects that *xacon* creates are to participate in distributed transactions, *xacon* also needs to obtain an XAResource object. What an XAResource object does is discussed in the next section.

48.1.4 What an XAResource Object Does

The XAResource interface is the mapping in the Java programming language of the industry standard Open Group XA interface. A transaction manager uses an XAResource object to control the distributed transactions associated with an XAConnection object.

The middle-tier server calls the XAConnection.getXAResource method on an XAConnection object. In response, the driver creates an XAResource object and returns it to the middle-tier server. If `getXAResource` is called on the `XAConnection` object again, the driver will return the same `XAResource` object it returned previously, so there is only one `XAResource` object for any one `XAConnection` object. The middle-tier server passes the `XAResource` object to the transaction manager, which uses it to control the transaction on the `XAConnection`. The following line of code, in which *xacon* is an `XAConnection` object, would be called by the middle-tier server.

```
javax.transaction.xa.XAResource resource = xacon.getXAResource();
```

The variable *resource* represents an instance of `XAResource` that is associated with *xacon*. The transaction manager will use *resource* to manage *xacon*. For example, the transaction manager would call the following code fragment, which associates and dissociates actions performed on *xacon* with the distributed transaction identified by the `Xid` object *xid*.

```
javax.transaction.xa.XAResource resource = xacon.getXAResource();
resource.start(xid, javax.transaction.xa.TMNOFLAGS);
// ... distributed transaction code
resource.end(xid, javax.transaction.xa.TMSUCCESS);
```

The call to the method `start` tells the resource manager that subsequent operations on *xacon* are part of the distributed transaction identified by *xid*. The call to the method end tells the resource manager that operations on *xacon* are no longer part of *xid*. The second argument to the method `start` is a flag indicating that the operations on *xacon* are not joining an existing branch of the transaction or resuming a suspended branch. The second argument to the method end is a flag indicating why the association of *xid* with *xacon* is being discontinued. The other two possibilities are `javax.transaction.xa.XAResource.TMFAIL` and `javax.transaction.xa.XAResource.TMSUSPEND`.

Note that the transaction manager never operates on an `XAConnection` object directly; it operates only on the `XAResource` object associated with it. The same `XAResource` object is associated with a particular `XAConnection` object for as long as the `XAConnection` object exists. For example, after the commands in a transaction branch have been sent to the DBMS server, the transaction manager dissociates the `XAConnection` object from the transaction by calling the method `XAResource.end`. If the `XAConnection` object is going to be used for another distributed transaction, the middle-tier server may call the `XAConnection` method getXAResource again. Instead of creating a new instance of XAResource, however, the driver will return the same instance of XAResource that it returned previously.

48.1.5   How the Two-phase Commit Protocol Works

Committing a distributed transaction involves two steps, or phases, that take place after the method XAResource.end has been called. At this point, all the commands on each connection have been executed but not yet committed, and the connections are no longer associated with the distributed transaction. In the first phase, the transaction manager will ask each DBMS server, or resource manager, whether it wants to commit its branch of the transaction. This phase is started by calling the method XAResource.prepare for each resource manager. If the middle-tier server initiated the distributed transaction, it calls the method XAResource.prepare; if a remote process is controlling the distributed transaction, that entity invokes XAResource.prepare.

The XAResource object used must be an object associated with the underlying resource manager, but it does not necessarily have to be the same one that was directly involved in the transaction. What matters is that the XAResource object be associated with the correct resource manager, not that it be associated with the connection that sent the commands to the resource manager. Because it can be assumed that all connections created by a particular DataSource object are connections to the same data source, it can also be assumed that any XAResource objects associated with connections from that DataSource object refer to the same data source.

After the resource managers have voted, the second phase of the two-phased commit process begins. If all of the resource managers involved in the distributed transaction vote to commit, the transaction manager will call the method XAResource.commit for each resource manager. If one or more resource managers vote not to commit, the transaction manager will instead call the method XAResource.rollback for each resource manager. As was the case with the method prepare, the XAResource object on which the method commit is called must be associated with the proper resource manager. It does not, however, have to be the same XAResource object involved in the transaction, and it does not even have to be the same one on which XAResource.prepare was called.

48.1.6 Using an XAResource Object to Commit

DBMS server A	DBMS server B
dsA	dsB1, dsB2
xaconA1	xaconB1
xaconA2	xaconB2_1
	xaconB2_2
xaresA1	xaresB1
xaresA2	xaresB2_1
	xaresB2_2

By way of example, suppose that a distributed transaction sends commands to two DBMS servers, A and B in the preceding table. Also suppose that a Data-Source object *dsA* represents A and that DataSource objects *dsB1* and *dsB2* both represent B. *dsA* manufactures the XAConnection objects *xaconA1* and *xaconA2*; *dsB1* manufactures the XAConnection *xaconB1*; *dsB2* manufactures *xaconB2_1* and *xaconB2_2*. Finally, each XAConnection object retrieves an XAResource object: *xaconA1* gets *xaresA1*, *xaconA2* gets *xaresA2*, *xaconB1* gets *xaresB1*, and so on. In the table, all of the objects with A in their names are associated with the server A, and all the objects with B in their names are associated with the server B.

The use of XAResource objects in the following code sample illustrates that the only requirement for the XAResource object used to prepare or commit a branch of a distributed transaction is that it be associated with the proper resource manager. The *xid* argument used for the methods prepare, commit, and rollback identifies the transaction; the second argument to the method commit is false to indicate that *xid* is following a two-phase commit protocol rather than a one-phase commit protocol.

The following code fragment gets votes from resource managers A and B on whether to commit their branches of the transaction. Because they both agree to commit, their transaction results are committed.

```
xaresA2.prepare(xid);// gets A's vote on whether to commit
xaresB1.prepare(xid);// gets B's vote
// ... A and B both vote to commit
xaresA2.commit(xid, false); // commits results on A
xaresB2_2.commit(xid, false); // commits results on B
```

The following code fragment polls resource managers A and B, but because they do not both agree to commit, their transaction results are rolled back.

```
xaresA1.prepare(xid);// gets A's vote on whether to commit
xaresB2_2.prepare(xid);// gets B's vote
// ... A votes to commit but B does not
xaresA2.rollback(xid); // restores original values
xaresB2_1.rollback(xid); // restores original values
```

48.1.7 The XAResource Interface

The following is the XAResource interface. Any thread in an application server process may call a method on the XAResource interface.

```
public interface XAResource {
    void commit(XID xid, boolean onePhase) throws XAException;
    void end(XID xid, int flags) throws XAException;
    void forget(XID xid) throws XAException;
    void prepare(XID xid) throws XAException;
    Xid[] recover(int flag) throws XAException;
    void rollback(XID xid) throws XAException;
    void start(XID xid, int flags) throws XAException;
    boolean isSameRM(XAResource xares) throws XAException;
    int getTransactionTimeout() throws XAException;
    boolean setTransactionTimeout(int seconds) throws XAException;
}
```

The XAResource interface, part of the Java Transaction API (JTA), is defined in the specification for JTA. Developers should consult this document for a more detailed description and the most current information. It is available from the following URL:

```
http://java.sun.com/products/jta
```

48.1.8 Steps in a Distributed Transaction

This section puts together the entire sequence for a distributed transaction. It assumes a network with the following three-tier architecture:

1. First tier—a client, such as a web browser

2. Second tier—includes a middle-tier application server, such as an EJB server, that implements connection pooling and distributed transactions

3. Third tier—two or more DBMS servers

This list simply puts together in sequential order the operations in a distributed transaction. The actions listed in the following sequence are explained in more detail in this chapter or in other chapters as follows:

- Getting a `Connection` object—see "DataSource," "ConnectionPoolData-Source," "XADataSource"

- Connection pooling—see "PooledConnection"

- Event notification—see "ConnectionEventListener"

- `XAResource` and the two-phase commit process—see "XAConnection"

The following list outlines the steps in a distributed transaction.

CLIENT SUCH AS A WEB BROWSER
Client Request

1. A remote client makes a request, which goes to the middle-tier server. If work is already being done in the scope of a distributed transaction, the request includes an `Xid` object that identifies a distributed transaction. If not, the middle-tier server begins a distributed transaction, which produces an `Xid` object. The remote request is passed to the application code.

MIDDLE-TIER SERVER, SUCH AS AN EJB APPLICATION SERVER
Application Code to Get a Connection

2. The application obtains the initial JNDI context and calls the method `Context.lookup` to retrieve a `DataSource` object from a JNDI service provider.

3. The JNDI naming service returns a `DataSource` object to the application.

4. The application calls the method `DataSource.getConnection`.

Getting an XAConnection

5. The middle tier invokes the method `lookup` on the connection pool, looking for an `XAConnection` object that can be reused.

6. If an `XAConnection` object is available, it is returned, and the connection-pool module updates its internal data structure. If there are none available, an `XADataSource` object is used to create a new `XAConnection` object to return to the middle tier.

7. The connection pooling module registers itself as a `ConnectionEventListener` with the `XAConnection` object.

Getting an XAResource Object and Associating the XAConnection Object with a Distributed Transaction

8. The middle-tier server calls the method `XAConnection.getXAResource`.

9. The JDBC driver returns an `XAResource` object to the middle-tier server.

10. The middle-tier server passes the `XAResource` object to the transaction manager.

11. The transaction manager calls `XAResource.start(xid, javax.transaction.xa.TMNOFLAGS)`.

Getting a Connection to Return

12. The middle-tier server calls the method `XAConnection.getConnection`.

13. The JDBC driver creates a `Connection` object that is conceptually a handle for the `XAConnection` object on which `getConnection` was called and returns it to the middle-tier server.

14. The connection pool module returns the `Connection` object to the application.

Application Code

15. The application uses the `Connection` object to send statements to the data source but may not enable auto-commit mode or call the `Connection` methods `commit` or `rollback`.

16. When the application is finished using the `Connection` object, it calls the method `Connection.close`.

Recycling the Connection

17. The `Connection` object delegates the application's invocation of the method `close` to the underlying `XAConnection` object.

18. The `XAConnection` object notifies its listeners that the method `close` has been called on it.

19. The middle-tier server receives the event notification and notifies the transaction manager that the application is finished using the `XAConnection` object.

20. The connection pooling module updates its internal data structure so that the `XAConnection` object can be reused.

Committing the Transaction

21. The transaction manager calls `XAResource.end(xid, javax.transaction.xa.XAResource.TMSUCCESS)`.

22. The transaction manager calls `XAresource.prepare(xid)` on each resource manager to begin the two-phase commit process.

23. If all resource managers vote to commit, the transaction manager calls `XAResource.commit(xid, false)`. If not, the transaction manager calls `XAResource.rollback(xid)`.

48.1.9   Distributed Transactions and EJB

The Enterprise JavaBeans framework provides the infrastructure, or "plumbing," that makes it possible to compose portable distributed applications by putting together EJB components, called enterprise Beans. Whereas JavaBeans components, typically used to create graphical user interfaces for a web browser, are reusable components for the client, Enterprise JavaBeans components are reusable components for the server. An application programmer can write an enterprise Bean that does a particular task or set of tasks, and, if it is implemented properly, it can be combined with other enterprise Beans and run on an EJB server. The EJB infrastructure takes care of handling the knotty issues such as security and transaction management, leaving the application programmer free to concentrate on writing better applications.

The JDBC API is well suited to working in component-based transactional applications and is an integral part of the EJB framework. In fact, its support for distributed transactions is an essential part of the EJB distributed transaction architecture. In particular, the `XADataSource` and `XAConnection` interfaces provide a `Connection` object that can be used in a distributed transaction. Also, the `Connection` interface provides the constants used to set the transaction isolation level for a connection in a distributed transaction. These and the `DataSource` API work with a JDBC driver and EJB server to make distributed transactions something that an application programmer does not need to worry about.

The vendor providing an EJB component will declare the component's transactional behavior using one of the transaction attributes defined in the EJB API. This behavior is specified at deployment time and may not be changed later. The following list describes the possible transaction attributes for an EJB component (enterprise Bean). An enterprise Bean's container manages its distributed transactions unless its transaction attribute is `TX_BEAN_MANAGED`, in which case an enterprise Bean manages its own distributed transactions.

These are the transaction attributes for EJB components:

- `TX_NOT_SUPPORTED`
  This EJB component does not support distributed transactions, so the container must not invoke the enterprise Bean's method in the scope of a distributed transaction.

- `TX_BEAN_MANAGED`
  This EJB component manages transaction boundaries itself by using the `javax.transaction.CurrrentTransaction` interface.

- `TX_REQUIRED`
  This EJB component requires that a method be executed in a distributed transaction; it may be the transaction associated with the entity calling the enterprise Bean's method or a new global transaction created by the container.

- `TX_REQUIRES_NEW`
  This EJB component requires that a method be executed only in the scope of a new distributed transaction. When one of the enterprise Bean's methods is invoked, the container must create a new global transaction for it and

commit the new transaction when the enterprise Bean's method has completed.

- TX_SUPPORTS

  This EJB component supports the execution of a method in a distributed transaction. If the entity calling the enterprise Bean's method is associated with a global transaction, the execution of the enterprise Bean's method will be associated with the caller's transaction; otherwise, the container executes the enterprise Bean's method without a transaction.

- TX_MANDATORY

  This EJB component requires that the client invoke a method within the scope of a distributed transaction; the execution of the enterprise Bean's method will be associated with the caller's transaction.

For example, consider the case where the transaction attribute for an EJB component is TX_REQUIRES_NEW. This means that when a method in the component is invoked, the transaction manager must start a new transaction. This new transaction will be associated with the actions on any connections created by the component. When all of the connections associated with the transaction have been closed, the transaction manager will handle committing or rolling back the transaction.

As explained in "Application Code in Distributed Transactions," on page 1039, the only change to JDBC application code made necessary because a transaction is distributed is that the application cannot affect the boundaries of the transaction. In other words, in a distributed transaction, the application cannot call the methods commit or rollback, and it cannot enable auto-commit mode. This applies equally in an EJB component, regardless of the transaction attribute declared for it.

An EJB implementation should know whether or not it is operating in the context of a distributed transaction and should use the JDBC API accordingly. In fact, an EJB component with the transaction attribute of TX_BEAN_MANAGED manages its own transaction boundaries and is therefore able to use the same connection in a local transaction, a distributed transaction, or both. It is free to use the methods commit, rollback, and setAutoCommit on any of these connections; the difference is that the behavior of the methods varies depending on whether the scope of the transaction is local or distributed.

48.2   XAConnection Interface Definition

```
package javax.sql;
public abstract interface XAConnection extends PooledConnection {
    public javax.transaction.xa.XAResource getXAResource()
                                    throws java.sql.SQLException;
}
```

48.3   XAConnection Methods

The following methods are inherited from the `javax.sql.PooledConnection` interface:

```
addConnectionEventListener        close        getConnection
removeConnectionEventListener
```

The following method is defined in the interface XAConnection:

getXAResource

```
javax.transaction.xa.XAResource getXAResource()
                                    throws java.sql.SQLException
```

  Retrieves an XAResource object that can be used to enlist this XAConnection object in a distributed transaction. A middle-tier server calls this method.

RETURNS:
an XAResource object

EXAMPLE:
```
// XAcon is an XAConnection object
javax.transaction.xa.XAResource xares = XAcon.getXAResource();
```

XADataSource

49.1 XADataSource Overview

AN XADataSource object creates XAConnection objects, connections derived from PooledConnection that can be used for distributed transactions. An application that uses distributed transactions will need to be run using a JDBC driver that supports the XADataSource and XAConnection interfaces.

A local transaction is a sequence of one or more commands sent to a single database that are either all committed or all rolled back as a single unit. If a transaction is committed, all of the changes resulting from it are made permanent; if the transaction is rolled back, the database is returned to the state it was in before the transaction began. In a distributed transaction, commands are distributed; that is, they are sent via two or more connections to one or more database servers. The commands sent to each DBMS server, or resource manager, constitute a branch of the transaction. In order for a distributed transaction to be committed, all resource managers must vote to commit. If even one of the resource managers does not agree to commit, the transaction manager will roll back the results of command execution on all of the transaction branches.

The XADataSource interface is much like the DataSource and Connection-PoolDataSource interfaces. All three have the same basic functionality, serving as factories for connections. Objects of each type also maintain a set of properties that identify the data source to which they manufacture connections. The difference is that they create different kinds of connections. A DataSource object creates a Connection object that represents a physical connection to a data source. A ConnectionPoolDataSource object creates a PooledConnection object that represents a reusable physical connection to a data source. An XADataSource object creates an XAConnection object that represents a reusable physical connection to a data source that can be used in a distributed transaction.

Only Connection objects can be returned by the DataSource.getConnection method. This means that in order for a middle-tier server to support connection pooling, this method must be implemented so that it can return a Connection object produced by a PooledConnection object. And, as part of the support for distributed transactions, the DataSource.getConnection method must also be able to return a Connection object produced by an XAConnection object.

The Connection objects created by PooledConnection objects and XAConnection objects are handles for the underlying physical connections they represent. In order to include distributed transactions, an application needs to get a Connection object that was produced by an XAConnection object. However, the application itself does not have to do anything other than call the method DataSource.get-Connection.

Management of connection pooling and distributed transactions is done in the middle tier, which resides between the client and the database server(s). In a typical configuration that supports distributed transactions, a server such as an EJB server includes a DataSource class that has been implemented to interact with the connection pooling manager and the transaction manager in the middle tier. A driver, which also operates in the middle tier, will include implementations of the XADataSource and XAConnection interfaces.

49.1.1   Obtaining an XADataSource Object

As with DataSource objects and ConnectionPoolDataSource objects, a system administrator or someone acting in that capacity will register an XADataSource object with a JNDI service provider at deployment time. The following code fragment illustrates code that might be used by a tool or application to register an XADataSource object with a JNDI service provider. First it creates the XADataSource object *xads* and sets its properties. Next it registers *xads* with a JNDI naming service, binding *xads* with the logical name that an application will use; a system property specifies the naming service. Note that the following code is system-level code, so most developers will not use the XADataSource interface directly.

```
XADataSource vendorXADataSource = new XADataSource();
vendorXADataSource.setServerName("shakespeare");
vendorXADataSource.setDatabaseName("XYZ6.2");
```

```
vendorXADataSource.setDescription("XYZ database for Authors");

Context ctx = new InitialContext();
ctx.bind("jdbc/xa/AuthorsDB", vendorXADataSource);
```

An application does not operate directly on an XADataSource object such as *vendorXADataSource*; instead, it operates on a DataSource object that references an XADataSource object. As explained in the DataSource chapter, a system administrator or other person who sets the properties for an XADataSource object will also create a DataSource object and set its dataSourceName property to the logical name that is bound to the XADataSource object. In this case, the logical name is jdbc/xa/AuthorsDB. The system administrator will also bind the DataSource object to the logical name jdbc/AuthorsDB, which is the name an application will use to retrieve a DataSource object it can use to get a connection to the Authors database. The following code fragment shows the code that a tool used by the system administrator would generate.

```
DataSource ds = new DataSource();
ds.setDataSourceName("jdbc/xa/AuthorsDB");
ds.setDescription("Authors database");
// ...
Context ctx = newInitialContext();
ctx.bind("jdbc/AuthorsDB", ds);
```

With the preceding DataSource and XADataSource objects registered with a JNDI naming service, the following code fragment retrieves a DataSource object and uses it to get a connection to the Authors database.

```
Context ctx = new InitialContext();
DataSource ds = (DataSource)ctx.lookup("jdbc/AuthorsDB");
Connection con = ds.getConnection("merlin", "magic");
```

What is special about the Connection object *con* is that it can be used in a distributed transaction. This is true because *con* is a handle for a physical connection that was created by an XAConnection object. In this case, *con* is a handle to a physical connection to the Authors database, which was produced by the XAConnection object that *ds* references. As with all connections produced by XAConnection objects, *con* has its auto-commit mode disabled, which keeps it from interfering with the transaction manager's management of distributed transaction boundaries.

If the DataSource implementation being used includes connection pooling, as is usually the case to improve performance, *con* will participate in connection pooling as well as be able to participate in a distributed transaction. When this is the case, the DataSource.getConnection method will be implemented so that it checks to see if there is a usable XAConnection object being pooled. If there is, that object will be used to create the Connection object to return to the application. When there is no XAConnection object available, a new one needs to be created in the middle tier, as is done in the following code fragment. This code first creates the XADataSource object *xads*. Then it uses *xads* to create the XAConnection *xacon*. Finally, the code uses *xacon* to create the Connection object that will be returned to the application. So the following middle-tier code was triggered by an application that invoked the getConnection method on the DataSource object *ds*.

```
XADataSource xads = (XADataSource)ctx.lookup("jdbc/xa/AuthorsDB");
XAConnection xacon = xads.getXAConnection("merlin", "magic");
Connection con = xacon.getConnection();
```

The XAConnection object *xacon* is a physical connection to the Authors database. The Connection object *con*, a handle for *xacon*, will be returned to the application. As stated before, because it was produced by an XAConnection object, *con* can be used in a distributed transaction, and it has its auto-commit mode disabled by default.

49.1.2 XADataSource Objects and Resource Managers

An XADataSource object represents a database, and it will produce XAConnection objects that are physical connections to the DBMS server for that database. In the context of the JDBC API and distributed transactions, the DBMS server is known as a *resource manager* (RM).

In a distributed transaction, commands are sent via connections that were produced by XAConnection objects. Commands generally go to two or more resource managers, and the command(s) sent to one resource manager typically constitute a transaction branch. Therefore, an application server needs to keep track of which XADataSource object refers to which resource manager. The application server can count on the fact that all of the XAConnection objects produced by one XADataSource object are connections to the same resource manager. But unless it has special knowledge, it cannot know for sure whether two different XADataSource objects represent the same resource manager or different ones. As a consequence, when different XADataSource objects are part of the same distributed transaction and the application server does not know whether they refer to different underlying resource managers, it should assign the XADataSource objects to different transaction branches.

49.2 **XADataSource** Interface Definition

```
package javax.sql;
public abstract interface XADataSource {
    public javax.sql.XAConnection getXAConnection()
                                    throws java.sql.SQLException;
    public javax.sql.XAConnection getXAConnection(java.lang.String
        user, java.lang.String password) throws java.sql.SQLException;
    public void setLoginTimeout(int seconds);
                                    throws java.sql.SQLException;
    public int getLoginTimeout() throws java.sql.SQLException;
    public void setLogWriter(java.io.PrintWriter out)
                                    throws java.sql.SQLException;
    public java.io.PrintWriter getLogWriter()
                                    throws java.sql.SQLException;
}
```

49.3 **XADataSource** Methods

NOTE: A vendor's implementation of an XADataSource object must include methods for getting and setting all of an XADataSource object's properties in addition to the public methods listed in this section.

getLoginTimeout

```
public int getLoginTimeout() throws java.sql.SQLException
```

Retrieves the maximum number of seconds that this XADataSource object can wait while attempting to connect to the data source it represents. A value of zero means that the timeout is the default system timeout, if there is one; otherwise, zero means that there is no timeout.

The default is for a newly created XADataSource object to have a login timeout of zero.

RETURNS:
an int representing the maximum number of seconds that this XADataSource object can wait to connect to a database

EXAMPLE:
```
int limit = ds.getLoginTimeout();
// ds is an XADataSource object
```

getLogWriter

```
public java.io.PrintWriter getLogWriter()
                                    throws java.sql.SQLException
```

Retrieves the character output stream to which all logging and tracing messages will be printed for the data source that this XADataSource object represents. This includes messages printed by the methods of this XADataSource object and also messages printed by methods of other objects manufactured by this XADataSource object.

RETURNS:
the log writer for this XADataSource object; null if the log writer has been disabled

EXAMPLE:
```
java.io.PrintWriter logWriter = ds.getLogWriter();
// ds is an XADataSource object
```

getXAConnection

```
XAConnection getXAConnection() throws java.sql.SQLException
```

Attempts to establish a connection to the data source that this XAData-Source object represents. This method is called as part of a middle-tier server's implementation of connection pooling in a distributed transaction. When an application requests a connection with the DataSource.getConnection method in such an implementation, the connection returned by Data-Source.getConnection will be a handle for the XAConnection object returned by this method.

RETURNS:
an XAConnection object that is a physical connection to the data source that this XADataSource object represents

EXAMPLE:
```
// jdbc/xa/CoffeesDB has been registered with a JNDI naming service
XADataSource xads = (XADataSource)ctx.lookup("jdbc/xa/CoffeesDB");
XAConnection xacon = xads.getXAConnection();
```

getXAConnection

```
XAConnection getXAConnection(java.lang.String user,
              java.lang.String password) throws java.sql.SQLException
```

Attempts to establish a connection to the data source that this XADataSource object represents. This method is called as part of a middle-tier server's implementation of connection pooling in a distributed transaction. When an application requests a connection with the DataSource.getConnection method in such an implementation, the connection returned by Data-Source.getConnection will be a handle for the XAConnection object returned by this method.

PARAMETERS:

user	the data source user on whose behalf the connection is being made
password	the user's password

RETURNS:
an XAConnection object that is a connection to the data source that this XADataSource object represents

EXAMPLE:
```
// jdbc/xa/CoffeesDB has been registered with a JNDI naming service
XADataSource ds = (XADataSource)ctx.lookup("jdbc/xa/CoffeesDB");
XAConnection xacon = ds.getXAConnection("archibald", "jdbc4all");
```

setLoginTimeout

```
public void setLoginTimeout(int seconds)
                                    throws java.sql.SQLException
```

Sets the maximum number of seconds that this XADataSource object can wait for a connection to be established to *seconds*. A value of zero specifies that the timeout is the default system timeout if there is one; otherwise, zero specifies that there is no timeout.

The default login timeout for a newly created XADataSource object is zero.

PARAMETERS:

seconds   the maximum number of seconds that this XADataSource object can wait for a connection to be established; 0 to set the timeout to the default system timeout, if there is one, or else 0 to specify no timeout limit

EXAMPLE:
```
ds.setLoginTimeout(30);
// sets the timeout limit for ds, an XADataSource object, to 30
// seconds

ds.setLoginTimeout(0);
// sets the timeout limit for ds to the default system timeout; if
// there is no system default, sets the timeout to have no limit
```

setLogWriter

```
public void setLogWriter(java.io.PrintWriter out)
                                    throws java.sql.SQLException
```

Sets the character output stream to which all logging and tracing messages for this XADataSource object will be printed to *out*. The messages that will be printed to *out* include those printed by the methods of this XADataSource object and also messages printed by methods of other objects manufactured by this XADataSource object.

PARAMETERS:

out   the `java.io.PrintWriter` object to which logging and tracing messages will be sent; `null` to disable logging and tracing

EXAMPLE:

```
ds.setLogWriter(out);
// logging and tracing messages for ds, an XADataSource object, and
// any objects manufactured by ds will be printed to out

ds.setLogWriter(null);
// no logging or tracing messages will be printed
```

Mapping SQL and Java Types

50.1 Mapping Overview

BECAUSE data types in SQL and data types in the Java programming language are not identical, there needs to be some mechanism for transferring data between an application using Java types and a database using SQL types. (Note that the phrase "Java types," as used in this book, stands for "types in the Java programming language.")

In order to transfer data between a database and an application written in the Java programming language, the JDBC API provides three main sets of methods:

1. Methods on the `ResultSet` interface for retrieving SQL `SELECT` results as Java types (getter methods) and for updating column values (updater methods)

2. Methods on the `PreparedStatement` interface for sending Java types as SQL statement parameters (setter methods)

3. Methods on the `CallableStatement` interface for retrieving SQL `OUT` parameters as Java types (getter methods) and for sending Java types as `IN` parameters for named parameters (setter methods)

In addition, when custom mapping is being done, methods on the `SQLInput` interface read SQL types and convert them to Java types (reader methods). Similarly, methods on the `SQLOutput` interface write Java types to the database as SQL types (writer methods).

This section brings together information about data types affecting various classes and interfaces and puts all the tables showing the mappings between SQL types and Java types in one place for easy reference. It also describes each of the generic SQL data types, including the SQL99 types.

50.2   Mapping SQL Types to Java Types

Unfortunately, there are significant variations between the SQL types supported by different database products. Even when different databases support SQL types with the same semantics, they may give those types different names. For example, most of the major databases support an SQL data type for large binary values, but Oracle calls this type LONG RAW, Sybase calls it IMAGE, Informix calls it BYTE, and DB2 calls it LONG VARCHAR FOR BIT DATA.

Fortunately, programmers will normally not need to concern themselves with the actual SQL type names used by a target database. Most of the time they will be programming against existing database tables, and they need not concern themselves with the exact SQL type names that were used to create these tables.

The JDBC API defines a set of generic SQL type identifiers in the class java.sql.Types. These types have been designed to represent the most commonly used SQL types. In programming with the JDBC API, programmers will normally be able to use these JDBC types to reference generic SQL types without having to be concerned about the exact SQL type name used by the target database. These JDBC types are fully described in the next section.

The one major place where programmers may need to use SQL type names is in the SQL CREATE TABLE statement when they are creating a new database table. In this case programmers must take care to use SQL type names that are supported by their target databases. The table "JDBC Types Mapped to Database-specific SQL Types," on page 1093, provides some suggestions for suitable SQL type names to be used for JDBC types for some of the major databases. We recommend that you consult your database documentation if you need exact definitions of the behavior of the various SQL types on a particular database.

If you want to be able to write portable JDBC programs that can create tables on a variety of different databases, you have two main choices. First, you can restrict yourself to using only very widely accepted SQL type names such as INTEGER, NUMERIC, or VARCHAR, which are likely to work for all databases. Or second, you can use the java.sql.DatabaseMetaData.getTypeInfo method to discover which SQL types are actually supported by a given database and select a database-specific SQL type name that matches a given JDBC type. This is what was done in the sample code application CreateNewTable.java. See "Getting Information about DBMS Data Types," on page 214, for an explanation of how to use the method DatabaseMetaData.getTypeInfo, and refer to "Sample Code 17 and 18," on page 233, to see how the program CreateNewTable.java used the results of the method `getTypeInfo` to build a `CREATE TABLE` statement that can be used for any JDBC Compliant driver and DBMS.

The JDBC specification defines a standard mapping from the JDBC database types to Java types. For example, a JDBC `INTEGER` is normally mapped to a Java `int`. This supports a simple interface for reading and writing JDBC values as simple Java types.

The Java types do not need to be exactly isomorphic to the JDBC types; they just need to be able to represent them with enough type information to correctly store and retrieve parameters and recover results from SQL statements. For example, a Java `String` object does not precisely match any of the JDBC `CHAR` types, but it gives enough type information to represent `CHAR`, `VARCHAR`, or `LONGVARCHAR` successfully.

50.3 Basic JDBC Types

This section describes the JDBC data types supported by the JDBC API. It also explains how they are related to standard SQL types and to types in the Java programming language. JDBC data types introduced in the JDBC 2.0 core API are described in "Advanced JDBC Data Types," on page 1075. New types added in the JDBC 3.0 API are described in "JDBC Types Added in the JDBC 3.0 API," on page 1078.

50.3.1 CHAR, VARCHAR, and LONGVARCHAR

The JDBC types `CHAR`, `VARCHAR`, and `LONGVARCHAR` are closely related. `CHAR` represents a small, fixed-length character string; `VARCHAR` represents a small, variable-length character string; and `LONGVARCHAR` represents a large, variable-length character string.

The SQL `CHAR` type corresponding to JDBC `CHAR` is defined in SQL92 and is supported by all the major databases. It takes a parameter that specifies the string length. Thus `CHAR(12)` defines a 12-character string. All the major databases support `CHAR` lengths up to at least 254 characters.

The SQL `VARCHAR` type corresponding to JDBC `VARCHAR` is defined in SQL92 and is supported by all the major databases. It takes a parameter that specifies the maximum length of the string. Thus `VARCHAR(12)` defines a string whose length may be up to 12 characters. All the major databases support `VARCHAR` lengths up to 254 characters. When a string value is assigned to a `VARCHAR` variable, the database remembers the length of the assigned string and, on a SELECT, it will return the exact original string.

Unfortunately, there is no consistent SQL mapping for the JDBC LONGVARCHAR type. All the major databases support some kind of very large variable-length string supporting up to at least a gigabyte of data, but the SQL type names vary. See the table "JDBC Types Mapped to Database-specific SQL Types," on page 1093, for some examples.

Java programmers do not need to distinguish among the three types of JDBC strings, CHAR, VARCHAR, and LONGVARCHAR. Each can be expressed as a Java String, and it is possible to read and write an SQL statement correctly without knowing the exact data type that was expected.

CHAR, VARCHAR, and LONGVARCHAR could have been mapped to either String or char[], but String is more appropriate for normal use. Also, the String class makes conversions between String and char[] easy: There is a method for converting a String object to a char[] and also a constructor for turning a char[] into a String object.

One issue that had to be addressed is how to handle fixed-length SQL strings of type CHAR(n). The answer is that JDBC drivers (or the DBMS) perform appropriate padding with spaces. Thus, when a CHAR(n) field is retrieved from the database, the driver will convert it to a Java String object of length n, which may include some padding spaces at the end. Conversely, when a String object is sent to a CHAR(n) field, the driver and/or the database will add any necessary padding spaces to the end of the string to bring it up to length n.

The method ResultSet.getString, which allocates and returns a new String object, is recommended for retrieving data from CHAR, VARCHAR, and LONGVARCHAR fields. This is suitable for retrieving normal data, but can be unwieldy if the JDBC type LONGVARCHAR is being used to store multi-megabyte strings. To handle this case, two methods in the ResultSet interface allow programmers to retrieve a LONGVARCHAR value as a Java input stream from which they can subsequently read data in whatever size chunks they prefer. These methods are getAsciiStream and getCharacterStream, which deliver the data stored in a LONGVARCHAR column as a stream of ASCII or Unicode characters. Note that the method getUnicodeStream has been deprecated.

See page 1075 for information about the SQL99 CLOB data type, which provides an alternate means of representing large amounts of character data.

50.3.2 BINARY, VARBINARY, and LONGVARBINARY

The JDBC types BINARY, VARBINARY, and LONGVARBINARY are closely related. BINARY represents a small, fixed-length binary value; VARBINARY represents a small, variable-length binary value; and LONGVARBINARY represents a large, variable-length binary value.

Unfortunately, the use of these various BINARY types has not been standardized, and support varies considerably among the major databases.

The SQL BINARY type corresponding to JDBC BINARY is a nonstandard SQL extension and is only implemented on some databases. It takes a parameter that specifies the number of binary bytes. Thus BINARY(12) defines a 12-byte binary type. Typically, BINARY values are limited to 254 bytes.

The SQL VARBINARY type corresponding to JDBC VARBINARY is a nonstandard SQL extension and is only implemented on some databases. It takes a parameter that specifies the maximum number of binary bytes. Thus VARBINARY(12) defines a binary type whose length may be up to 12 bytes. Typically, VARBINARY values are limited to 254 bytes. When a binary value is assigned to a VARBINARY variable, the database remembers the length of the assigned value and, on a SELECT, it will return the exact original value.

Regrettably, there is no consistent SQL type name corresponding to the JDBC LONGVARBINARY type. All the major databases support some kind of very large variable length binary type supporting up to at least a gigabyte of data, but the SQL type names vary. See the table "JDBC Types Mapped to Database-specific SQL Types," on page 1093, for some examples.

BINARY, VARBINARY, and LONGVARBINARY can all be expressed identically as byte arrays in the Java programming language. Since it is possible to read and write SQL statements correctly without knowing the exact BINARY data type that was expected, there is no need for programmers writing code in the Java programming language to distinguish among them.

The method recommended for retrieving BINARY and VARBINARY values is ResultSet.getBytes. If a column of type JDBC LONGVARBINARY stores a byte array that is many megabytes long, however, the method getBinaryStream is recommended. Similar to the situation with LONGVARCHAR, this method allows a programmer to retrieve a LONGVARBINARY value as a Java input stream that can be read later in smaller chunks.

See page 1075 for information about the SQL99 BLOB data type, which provides an alternate means of representing large amounts of binary data.

50.3.3 BIT

The JDBC type BIT represents a single bit value that can be zero or one.

SQL92 defines an SQL BIT type. However, unlike the JDBC BIT type, this SQL92 BIT type can be used as a parameterized type to define a fixed-length binary string. Fortunately, SQL92 also permits the use of the simple non-parameterized BIT type to represent a single binary digit, and this usage corresponds to the JDBC BIT type. Unfortunately, the SQL92 BIT type is only required in "full" SQL92 and is currently supported by only a subset of the major databases. Portable code may therefore prefer to use the JDBC SMALLINT type, which is widely supported.

The recommended Java mapping for the JDBC BIT type is as a Java boolean.

50.3.4 TINYINT

The JDBC type TINYINT represents an 8-bit integer value between 0 and 255 that may be signed or unsigned.

The corresponding SQL type, TINYINT, is currently supported by only a subset of the major databases. Portable code may therefore prefer to use the JDBC SMALLINT type, which is widely supported.

The recommended Java mapping for the JDBC TINYINT type is as either a Java byte or a Java short. The 8-bit Java byte type represents a signed value from -128 to 127, so it may not always be appropriate for larger TINYINT values, whereas the 16-bit Java short will always be able to hold all TINYINT values.

50.3.5 SMALLINT

The JDBC type SMALLINT represents a 16-bit signed integer value between −32768 and 32767.

The corresponding SQL type, SMALLINT, is defined in SQL92 and is supported by all the major databases. The SQL92 standard leaves the precision of SMALLINT up to the implementation, but, in practice, all the major databases support at least 16 bits.

The recommended Java mapping for the JDBC SMALLINT type is as a Java short.

50.3.6 INTEGER

The JDBC type INTEGER represents a 32-bit signed integer value ranging between −2147483648 and 2147483647.

The corresponding SQL type, INTEGER, is defined in SQL92 and is widely supported by all the major databases. The SQ92 standard leaves the precision of INTEGER up to the implementation, but, in practice, all the major databases support at least 32 bits.

The recommended Java mapping for the INTEGER type is as a Java int.

50.3.7 BIGINT

The JDBC type BIGINT represents a 64-bit signed integer value between –9223372036854775808 and 9223372036854775807.

The corresponding SQL type BIGINT is a nonstandard extension to SQL. In practice, the SQL BIGINT type is not yet implemented by any of the major databases, and we recommend that its use be avoided in code that is intended to be portable.

The recommended Java mapping for the BIGINT type is as a Java long.

50.3.8 REAL

The JDBC type REAL represents a "single precision" floating-point number that supports seven digits of mantissa.

The corresponding SQL type REAL is defined in SQL92 and is widely, though not universally, supported by the major databases. The SQL92 standard leaves the precision of REAL up to the implementation, but, in practice, all the major databases supporting REAL support a mantissa precision of at least seven digits.

The recommended Java mapping for the REAL type is as a Java float.

50.3.9 DOUBLE

The JDBC type DOUBLE represents a "double precision" floating-point number that supports 15 digits of mantissa.

The corresponding SQL type is DOUBLE PRECISION, which is defined in SQL92 and is widely supported by the major databases. The SQL92 standard leaves the precision of DOUBLE PRECISION up to the implementation, but, in practice, all the major databases supporting DOUBLE PRECISION support a mantissa precision of at least 15 digits.

The recommended Java mapping for the DOUBLE type is as a Java double.

50.3.10 FLOAT

The JDBC type FLOAT is basically equivalent to the JDBC type DOUBLE. We provided both FLOAT and DOUBLE in a possibly misguided attempt at consistency with previous database APIs. FLOAT represents a "double precision" floating-point number that supports 15 digits of mantissa.

The corresponding SQL type FLOAT is defined in SQL92. The SQL92 standard leaves the precision of FLOAT up to the implementation, but, in practice, all the major databases supporting FLOAT support a mantissa precision of at least 15 digits.

The recommended Java mapping for the FLOAT type is as a Java double. However, because of the potential confusion between the double precision SQL FLOAT and the single precision Java float, we recommend that JDBC programmers should normally use the JDBC DOUBLE type in preference to FLOAT.

50.3.11 DECIMAL and NUMERIC

The JDBC types DECIMAL and NUMERIC are very similar. They both represent fixed-precision decimal values.

The corresponding SQL types DECIMAL and NUMERIC are defined in SQL92 and are very widely implemented. These SQL types take precision and scale parameters. The precision is the total number of decimal digits supported, and the scale is the number of decimal digits after the decimal point. For most DBMSs, the scale is less than or equal to the precision. So, for example, the value "12.345" has a precision of 5 and a scale of 3, and the value ".11" has a precision of 2 and a scale of 2. JDBC requires that all DECIMAL and NUMERIC types support both a precision and a scale of at least 15.

The sole distinction between DECIMAL and NUMERIC is that the SQL92 specification requires that NUMERIC types be represented with exactly the specified precision, whereas for DECIMAL types, it allows an implementation to add additional precision beyond that specified when the type was created. Thus, a column created with type NUMERIC(12,4) will always be represented with exactly 12 digits, whereas a column created with type DECIMAL(12,4) might be represented by some larger number of digits.

The recommended Java mapping for the DECIMAL and NUMERIC types is java.math.BigDecimal. The java.math.BigDecimal type provides math operations to allow BigDecimal types to be added, subtracted, multiplied, and divided with other BigDecimal types, with integer types, and with floating-point types.

The method recommended for retrieving `DECIMAL` and `NUMERIC` values is `ResultSet.getBigDecimal`. JDBC also allows access to these SQL types as simple `Strings` or arrays of `char`. Thus, Java programmers can use `getString` to receive a `DECIMAL` or `NUMERIC` result. However, this makes the common case where `DECIMAL` or `NUMERIC` are used for currency values rather awkward, since it means that application writers have to perform math on strings. It is also possible to retrieve these SQL types as any of the Java numeric types.

50.3.12 DATE, TIME, and TIMESTAMP

There are three JDBC types relating to time:

- The JDBC `DATE` type represents a date consisting of day, month, and year. The corresponding SQL `DATE` type is defined in SQL92, but it is implemented by only a subset of the major databases. Some databases offer alternative SQL types that support similar semantics.

- The JDBC `TIME` type represents a time consisting of hours, minutes, and seconds. The corresponding SQL `TIME` type is defined in SQL92, but it is implemented by only a subset of the major databases. As with `DATE`, some databases offer alternative SQL types that support similar semantics.

- The JDBC `TIMESTAMP` type represents `DATE` plus `TIME` plus a nanosecond field. The corresponding SQL `TIMESTAMP` type is defined in SQL92, but it is implemented by only a very small number of databases.

Because the standard Java class `java.util.Date` does not match any of these three JDBC date/time types exactly (it includes both `DATE` and `TIME` information but has no nanoseconds), JDBC defines three subclasses of `java.util.Date` to correspond to the SQL types. They are:

- `java.sql.Date` for SQL `DATE` information. The hour, minute, second, and millisecond fields of the `java.util.Date` base class should be set to zero. If the number of milliseconds supplied to the `java.sql.Date` constructor is negative, the driver will compute the date as the number of milliseconds before January 1, 1970. Otherwise, the date is computed as the specified number of milliseconds after January 1, 1970.

- `java.sql.Time` for SQL `TIME` information. The year, month, and day fields of the `java.util.Date` base class are set to 1970, January, and 1. This is the "zero" date in the Java epoch.

- `java.sql.Timestamp` for SQL `TIMESTAMP` information. This class extends `java.util.Date` by adding a `nanoseconds` field.

All three of the JDBC time-related classes are subclasses of `java.util.Date`, and, as such, they can be used where a `java.util.Date` is expected. For example, internationalization methods take a `java.util.Date` object as an argument, so they can be passed instances of any of the JDBC time-related classes.

A JDBC `Timestamp` object has its parent's date and time components and also a separate nanoseconds component. If a `java.sql.Timestamp` object is used where a `java.util.Date` object is expected, the nanoseconds component is lost. However, since a `java.util.Date` object is stored with a precision of one millisecond, it is possible to maintain this degree of precision when converting a `java.sql.Timestamp` object to a `java.util.Date` object. This is done by converting the nanoseconds in the nanoseconds component to whole milliseconds (by dividing the number of nanoseconds by 1,000,000) and then adding the result to the `java.util.Date` object. Up to 999,999 nanoseconds may be lost in this conversion, but the resulting `java.util.Date` object will be accurate to within one millisecond.

The following code fragment is an example of converting a `java.sql.Timestamp` object to a `java.util.Date` object that is accurate to within one millisecond.

```
Timestamp t = new Timestamp(98724573287540L);
java.util.Date d;
d = new java.util.Date(t.getTime() + (t.getNanos() / 1000000));
```

2.0   Methods added in the JDBC 2.0 core API make it possible for the driver to take a specified time zone into account when it is calculating a date, time, or timestamp. The time zone information is included in a `java.util.Calendar` object that is passed to new versions of the methods for getting and setting `Date`, `Time`, and `Timestamp` values. When no time zone is specified, the driver uses the time zone of the virtual machine running the application when it calculates a date, time, or timestamp.

50.4   Advanced JDBC Data Types

The ISO (International Organization for Standardization) and IEC (the International Electrotechnical Commission) have defined new data types that are commonly referred to as SQL99 types. Of these new SQL99 data types, BLOB, CLOB, ARRAY, and REF are predefined types, whereas the SQL structured type and the DISTINCT type are user-defined types (UDTs). These new types, with the exception of DISTINCT, are mapped to interfaces that were introduced in the JDBC 2.0 core API. This section describes each data type briefly; more complete information on each type can be found in the reference chapter for the corresponding interface. There is a chapter on the DISTINCT data type, but because DISTINCT types are mapped to a built-in type, there is no separate interface for it.

The new data types in the JDBC 2.0 core API represent a significant expansion in the types of data that can be used in a relational database. In general, they are more like objects; in fact, two of the new data types (STRUCT and DISTINCT) are UDTs that can optionally be custom mapped to classes in the Java programming language. A third UDT (JAVA_OBJECT) is itself an instance of a class defined in the Java programming language. Despite their advanced nature, all of the new data types introduced in the JDBC 2.0 core API can be used as conveniently as the data types in the JDBC 1.0 API. For example, they can be used as column values in database tables, and they can be retrieved and stored using the appropriate getter and setter methods.

50.4.1   BLOB

The JDBC type BLOB represents an SQL99 BLOB (Binary Large Object).

A JDBC BLOB value is mapped to an instance of the Blob interface in the Java programming language. If a driver follows the standard implementation, a Blob object logically points to the BLOB value on the server rather than containing its binary data, greatly improving efficiency. The Blob interface provides methods for materializing the BLOB data on the client when that is desired. Chapter 8, "Blob," starting on page 309, gives complete information about the Blob interface.

50.4.2   CLOB

The JDBC type CLOB represents the SQL99 type CLOB (Character Large Object).

A JDBC CLOB value is mapped to an instance of the Clob interface in the Java programming language. If a driver follows the standard implementation, a Clob object logically points to the CLOB value on the server rather than containing its character data, greatly improving efficiency. Two of the methods on the Clob interface materialize the data of a CLOB object on the client.

Chapter 10, "Clob," starting on page 373, gives complete information about the Clob interface.

50.4.3   ARRAY

The JDBC type ARRAY represents the SQL99 type ARRAY.

An ARRAY value is mapped to an instance of the Array interface in the Java programming language. If a driver follows the standard implementation, an Array object logically points to an ARRAY value on the server rather than containing the elements of the ARRAY object, which can greatly increase efficiency. The Array interface contains methods for materializing the elements of the ARRAY object on the client in the form of either an array or a ResultSet object.

Chapter 6, "Array," starting on page 283, gives more information about the Array interface.

50.4.4   DISTINCT

The JDBC type DISTINCT represents the SQL99 type DISTINCT.

The standard mapping for a DISTINCT type is to the Java type to which the base type of a DISTINCT object would be mapped. For example, a DISTINCT type based on a CHAR would be mapped to a String object, and a DISTINCT type based on an SQL INTEGER would be mapped to an int. Chapter 19, "Distinct," starting on page 599, shows how to create and use a DISTINCT type value.

The DISTINCT type may optionally have a custom mapping to a class in the Java programming language. A custom mapping consists of a class that implements the interface SQLData and an entry in a java.util.Map object. See "Custom Mapping," on page 1083, for more about custom mapping.

50.4.5   STRUCT

The JDBC type STRUCT represents the SQL99 structured type. An SQL structured type, which is defined by a user with a CREATE TYPE statement, consists of one or more attributes. These attributes may be any SQL data type, built-in or user-defined.

The standard mapping for the SQL type STRUCT is to a Struct object in the Java programming language. A Struct object contains a value for each attribute of the STRUCT value it represents. See Chapter 44, "Struct," starting on page 997, for more information about the Struct interface.

A STRUCT value may optionally be custom mapped to a class in the Java programming language, and each attribute in the STRUCT may be mapped to a field in the class. A custom mapping consists of a class that implements the interface SQL-Data and an entry in a java.util.Map object. See "Custom Mapping," on page 1083, for more about custom mapping.

50.4.6   REF

The JDBC type REF represents an SQL99 type REF<structured type>. An SQL REF references (logically points to) an instance of an SQL structured type, which the REF persistently and uniquely identifies. In the Java programming language, the interface Ref represents an SQL REF.

If an application wants to point to an instance of an SQL structured type in the database rather than having its attribute values materialized on the client, it can use the type REF<structured type>, a reference to that SQL structured type.

A REF value is a unique identifier created specifically for a particular instance of an SQL structured type. It is persistently stored with the instance it references in a special table on the server. An application can select the REF value from its special table and use it in place of the structured type instance it identifies.

For more information on the interface Ref and its special table, see Chapter 26, "Ref," starting on page 679.

50.4.7   JAVA_OBJECT

The JDBC type JAVA_OBJECT makes it easier to use objects in the Java programming language as values in a database. JAVA_OBJECT is simply a type code for an instance of a class defined in the Java programming language that is stored as a database object. The type JAVA_OBJECT is used by a database whose type system has been extended so that it can store Java objects directly. The JAVA_OBJECT value may be stored as a serialized Java object, or it may be stored in some vendor-specific format.

The type JAVA_OBJECT is one of the possible values for the column DATA_TYPE in the ResultSet objects returned by various DatabaseMetaData methods, including getTypeInfo, getColumns, and getUDTs. The method getUDTs will return information about the Java objects contained in a particular schema when it is given the appropriate parameters. Having this information available facilitates using a Java class as a database type.

For DBMSs that support them, values of type JAVA_OBJECT are stored in a database table using the method PreparedStatement.setObject. They are retrieved with the methods ResultSet.getObject or CallableStatement.getObject and updated with the ResultSet.updateObject method.

For example, assuming that instances of the class Engineer are stored in the column ENGINEERS in the table PERSONNEL, the following code fragment, in which *stmt* is a Statement object, prints out the names of all of the engineers.

```
ResultSet rs = stmt.executeQuery("SELECT ENGINEERS FROM PERSONNEL");
while (rs.next()) {
    Engineer eng = (Engineer)rs.getObject("ENGINEERS");
    System.out.println(eng.lastName + ", " + eng.firstName);
}
```

After the query returns the ResultSet object *rs*, which contains all of the instances of Engineer, the code retrieves each instance in turn with the method getObject. The value returned by getObject is an Object type, so it must be narrowed to the more specific type Engineer before being assigned to the variable *eng*.

50.5   JDBC Types Added in the JDBC 3.0 API

The JDBC types DATALINK and BOOLEAN were added to the class Types in the JDBC 3.0 API.

50.5.1   BOOLEAN

Before the BOOLEAN type code was added, a Java boolean mapped to a JDBC BIT. This worked because a bit can be either 0 or 1 (on or off), corresponding to true and false. However, it is more natural to have the Java boolean type mapped to the JDBC BOOLEAN type code, which has the values true and false.

50.5.2   DATALINK

The DATALINK type code is used to represent a file that is stored somewhere other than in a database but that is managed by the database. The method for accessing such an external file is getURL, which returns a java.net.URL object. For example, the following code fragment, in which *rs* is a ResultSet object, retrieves a

DATALINK value as a java.net.URL object. This URL object can then be used to manipulate the data it contains.

```
java.net.URL url = rs.getURL(3);
```

The following code fragment demonstrates how a reference to external data can be stored as a column value in a table when the DBMS supports storing such values.

```
java.net.URL url = "http://www.marvelsgalore.com/info/marvel4.html"
String sql = "UPDATE INFO SET DATA = ? WHERE CLASS = ?";

PreparedStatement pstmt = con.prepareStatement(sql);
pstmt.setURL(1, url);
pstmt.setInt(2, 2010);
```

Several interfaces have methods for dealing with DATALINK values:

- ResultSet – getURL, getObject
- CallableStatement – getURL, getObject, setURL
- PreparedStatement – setURL, setObject, updateURL
- SQLInput – readURL, readObject
- SQLOutput – writeURL, writeObject

In some cases, the type of URL returned by the methods getURL and getObject may not be supported by the Java platform. In such a case, the method getString may be used to retrieve the URL. Similarly, if the type of URL to be set is not supported by the Java platform, the method setString may be used in place of setURL or setObject. Further, in the SQLInput interface, the method readObject may be used in place of readURL, and in the SQLOutput interface, writeObject may be used in place of writeURL

For DBMSs that support storing external data, the DATALINK type code can also be a return value for the DatabaseMetaData methods that return a ResultSet object containing the column DATA_TYPE. Such methods include getTypeInfo, getUDTs, getAttributes, getColumns, and so on.

50.6   Examples of Mapping

In any situation where a program written in the Java programming language retrieves data from a database, there has to be some form of mapping and data conversion. In most cases, programmers using the JDBC API will be programming with knowledge of their target database's schema. In other words, they know, for example, what tables the database contains and the data type for each column in those tables. They can therefore use the strongly typed access methods in the interfaces `ResultSet`, `PreparedStatement`, and `CallableStatement`. This section presents three different scenarios, describing the data mapping and conversion required in each case.

50.6.1   Simple SQL Statement

In the most common case, a user executes a simple SQL statement and gets back a `ResultSet` object with the results. Each value returned by the database and stored in a `ResultSet` column will have a JDBC data type. A call to a getter method in the `ResultSet` interface will retrieve that value as a Java data type. For example, if a `ResultSet` column contains a JDBC `FLOAT` value, the method `getDouble` will retrieve that value as a Java `double`.

The table "Conversions by `ResultSet` getter Methods," on page 1092, shows which getter methods may be used to retrieve which JDBC types. (A user who does not know the type of a `ResultSet` column can get that information by calling the method `ResultSet.getMetaData` and then calling the method `ResultSetMetaData.getColumnType`.)

50.6.2   1079

SQL Statement with IN Parameters
In another possible scenario, the user sends an SQL query that takes input parameters. In this case, the user calls the setter methods in the `PreparedStatement` interface to assign a value to each input parameter. For example, `PreparedStatement.setLong(1,  2345678)` will assign the value `2345678` to the first parameter as a Java `long`. The driver will convert `2345678` to a JDBC `BIGINT` in order to send it to the database. Which JDBC type the driver sends to the database is determined by the standard mapping from Java types to JDBC types, shown in the table "Java Types Mapped to JDBC Types," on page 1088.

50.6.3 SQL Statement with INOUT Parameters

In yet another scenario, a user wants to call a stored procedure, assign values to its INOUT parameters, retrieve values from a ResultSet object, and retrieve values from the parameters. This case is rather uncommon and more complicated than most, but it gives a good illustration of mapping and data conversion.

In this scenario, the first thing to do is to assign values to the INOUT parameters using PreparedStatement setter methods. In addition, because the parameters will also be used for output, the programmer must register each parameter with the JDBC type of the value that the database will return to it. Registering OUT parameters is done with the method CallableStatement.registerOutParameter, which takes one of the JDBC types defined in the class Types. A programmer retrieves the values stored in the output parameters with CallableStatement getter methods.

The data type used for CallableStatement getter methods must map to the JDBC type registered for that parameter. For example, if the database is expected to return an output value whose type is JDBC REAL, the parameter should have been registered as java.sql.Types.REAL. Then, to retrieve the JDBC REAL value, the method CallableStatement.getFloat should be called (the mapping from JDBC types to Java types is shown in the table "JDBC Types Mapped to Java Types," on page 1087). The method getFloat will return the value stored in the output parameter after converting it from a JDBC REAL to a Java float. To accommodate various databases and make an application more portable, it is recommended that values be retrieved from ResultSet objects before values are retrieved from output parameters.

The following code demonstrates calling a stored procedure named getTest-Data, which has two parameters that are both INOUT parameters and which also returns a normal JDBC ResultSet. First the Connection object *con* creates the CallableStatement object *cstmt*. Then, the method setByte sets the first parameter to 25 as a Java byte. The driver will convert 25 to a JDBC TINYINT and send it to the database. The method setBigDecimal sets the second parameter with an input value of 83.75. The driver will convert this Java BigDecimal object to a JDBC NUMERIC value. Next, the two parameters are registered as OUT parameters, the first parameter as a JDBC TINYINT and the second parameter as a JDBC NUMERIC with two digits after the decimal point. After *cstmt* is executed, the values are retrieved from the ResultSet object using ResultSet getter methods. The method getString gets the value in the first column as a Java String object, get-

Int gets the value in the second column as a Java `int`, and the second `getInt` retrieves the value in the third column as a Java `int`.

Then, `CallableStatement` getter methods retrieve the values stored in the output parameters. The method `getByte` retrieves the JDBC `TINYINT` as a Java `byte`, and `getBigDecimal` retrieves the JDBC `NUMERIC` as a Java `BigDecimal` object with two digits after the decimal point. Note that when a parameter is both an input and an output parameter, the setter method uses the same Java type as the getter method (as in `setByte` and `getByte`). The `registerOutParameter` method registers it to the JDBC type that is mapped from the Java type. (A Java byte maps to a JDBC `TINYINT`, as shown in the table "Java Types Mapped to JDBC Types," on page 1088.)

```
CallableStatement cstmt = con.prepareCall(
                            "{call getTestData(?, ?)}");
cstmt.setByte(1, 25);
cstmt.setBigDecimal(2, 83.75);
// register the first parameter as a JDBC TINYINT and the second
// as a JDBC NUMERIC with two digits after the decimal point
cstmt.registerOutParameter(1, java.sql.Types.TINYINT);
cstmt.registerOutParameter(2, java.sql.Types.NUMERIC, 2);
ResultSet rs = cstmt.executeQuery();
// retrieve and print values in result set
while (rs.next()) {
    String name = rs.getString(1);
    int score = rs.getInt(2);
    int percentile = rs.getInt(3);
    System.out.print("name = " + name + ", score = " + score);

    System.out.println(", percentile = " + percentile);
}
// retrieve values in output parameters
byte x = cstmt.getByte(1);
java.math.BigDecimal n = cstmt.getBigDecimal(2);
```

To generalize, the data type in `CallableStatement` getter and setter methods is a Java type. For setter methods, the driver converts the Java type to a JDBC type before sending it to the database (using the standard mappings shown in the table "Java Types Mapped to JDBC Types," on page 1088). For getter methods, the driver converts the JDBC type returned by the database to a Java type (using the standard mappings shown in the table "JDBC Types Mapped to Java Types," on page 1087) before returning it to the getter method.

The method `registerOutParameter` always takes a JDBC type as an argument, and the method `setObject` may take a JDBC type as an argument.

Note that if a JDBC type is supplied in its optional third argument, the method `setObject` will cause an explicit conversion of the parameter value from a Java type to the JDBC type specified. If no target JDBC type is supplied to `setObject`, the parameter value will be converted to the JDBC type that is the standard mapping from the Java `Object` type (as shown in the table "Java Object Types Mapped to JDBC Types," on page 1090). The driver will perform the explicit or implicit conversion before sending the parameter to the database.

50.7 Custom Mapping

2.0

The SQL99 user-defined types (UDTs), structured types and `DISTINCT` types, can be custom mapped to classes in the Java programming language. If a custom mapping has been set up, the driver will use that mapping instead of the standard mapping when it converts a UDT from a JDBC type to a Java type or vice versa.

UDTs are retrieved from the database with the methods `ResultSet.getObject` and `CallableStatement.getObject`; UDTs are sent back to the database with the method `PreparedStatement.setObject`. When an application calls a `getObject` method to retrieve a UDT, the driver will check to see if the type map associated with the connection has an entry for the UDT. If it does, the driver will use that type map to custom map the UDT; if there is no matching entry, the driver will use the standard mapping.

Almost all custom mapping is done using the connection's type map. It is possible, however, to have the driver use a different type map. The methods for which a custom mapping is possible have two versions, one that takes a type map and one that does not. The usual situation is not to supply a type map, in which case the driver uses the connection's type map by default. When a type map is supplied to a method, it supersedes the connection's type map, and the driver will use it instead of the type map associated with the connection to map a UDT. If the type map supplied has no entry for the UDT, the driver will use the standard mapping.

The `setObject` method does not take a type map as a parameter, so it operates a little differently. If `setObject` is passed an instance of a class that implements the `SQLData` interface, that is, an object that was custom mapped when it was retrieved, the driver will already have set up the mechanism for mapping it. The driver will convert the class instance, mapping the UDT back to its SQL type before sending it to the database. If the parameter to be set by the method `setObject` has not been custom mapped, the driver will use the standard mapping to convert it before sending it to the database.

The fact that only the methods `getObject` and `setObject` can be used to retrieve or store SQL structured types ensures that a custom mapping will be used if there is one. Four methods in the `Array` interface may be passed a type map so that if the `ARRAY` elements are UDTs, they can be custom mapped when the elements are materialized on the client. The `Struct` method `getAttributes` also has a version that takes a type map, which is used to custom map an SQL structured type's attributes before bringing them over to the client. For more detailed information on custom mapping, see Chapter 37, "SQLData," starting on page 895.

50.8 Dynamic Data Access

In most cases, the user wants to access results or parameters whose data types are known at compile time. However, some applications, such as generic browsers or query tools, are compiled with no knowledge of the database schema they will access. For this reason, JDBC provides support for fully dynamically typed data access in addition to static data type access.

Three methods facilitate accessing values whose data types are not known at compile time:

- `ResultSet.getObject`

- `PreparedStatement.setObject`

- `CallableStatement.getObject`

If, for example, an application wants to be able to accept a variety of types as results in a `ResultSet` object, it can use the method `ResultSet.getObject`.

The methods `ResultSet.getObject` and `CallableStatement.getObject` retrieve a value as a Java `Object`. Since `Object` is the base class for all Java objects, an instance of any Java class can be retrieved as an instance of `Object`. However, the following Java types are built-in "primitive" types and are therefore not instances of the class `Object`: `boolean`, `char`, `byte`, `short`, `int`, `long`, `float`, and `double`. As a result, these types cannot be retrieved by `getObject` methods. However, each of these primitive types has a corresponding class that serves as a wrapper. Instances of these classes are objects, which means that they can be retrieved with the methods `ResultSet.getOb-ject` and `CallableStatement.getObject`. The table "JDBC Types Mapped to Java Object Types," on page 1089, shows the mapping from a JDBC type to a Java `Object` type. This table differs from the standard mapping from JDBC type to Java type in that each primitive Java type is replaced by its wrapper class, except that JDBC `TINYINT` and JDBC `SMALLINT` are mapped to the Java class `Integer`.

50.9   Storing Java Objects in a Database

`2.0`

Additions to the JDBC 2.0 core API make it easier to store Java objects in a database. The `PreparedStatement.setObject` method in the JDBC 1.0 API has always provided some support for persistent storage of objects defined in the Java programming language. With the new data type `JAVA_OBJECT`, in conjunction with the new method `DatabaseMetaData.getUDTs`, it is now easier to keep track of the Java objects stored in a database.

The JDBC 3.0 API added the JDBC type `DATALINK`, which allows a DBMS to control objects stored outside of the database.

`3.0`

50.10 Tables for Type Mapping

This section contains the following tables relating to the mapping of JDBC and Java data types:

Table 50.1—JDBC Types Mapped to Java Types

Table 50.1 shows the conceptual correspondence between JDBC types and Java types. A programmer should write code with this mapping in mind. For example, if a value in the database is a `SMALLINT`, a `short` should be the data type used in a JDBC application.

All **CallableStatement** getter methods except for `getObject` use this mapping. The `getObject` methods for both the `CallableStatement` and `ResultSet` interfaces use the mapping in the table "JDBC Types Mapped to Java Object Types," on page 1089.

Table 50.2—Java Types Mapped to JDBC Types

Table 50.2 shows the mapping a driver should use for the **ResultSet** updater methods and for IN parameters. **PreparedStatement** setter methods and **RowSet** setter methods use this table for mapping an IN parameter, which is a Java type, to the JDBC type that will be sent to the database. Note that the setObject methods for these two interfaces use the mapping shown in "Java Object Types Mapped to JDBC Types," on page 1090.

Table 50.3—JDBC Types Mapped to Java Object Types

ResultSet.getObject and CallableStatement.getObject use the mapping shown in Table 50.3 for standard mappings.

Table 50.4—Java Object Types Mapped to JDBC Types

PreparedStatement.setObject and RowSet.setObject use the mapping shown in Table 50.4 when no parameter specifying a target JDBC type is provided.

Table 50.5—Conversions by setObject from Java Object Types to JDBC Types

Table 50.5 shows which JDBC types may be specified as the target JDBC type to the methods PreparedStatement.setObject and RowSet.setObject.

Table 50.6—Type Conversions Supported by ResultSet getter Methods

Table 50.6 shows which JDBC types may be returned by **ResultSet** setter methods. A bold **X** indicates the method recommended for retrieving a JDBC type. A plain x indicates for which JDBC types it is possible to use a getter method.

This table also shows the conversions used by the **SQLInput** reader methods, except that they use only the recommended conversions.

Table 50.7—JDBC Types Mapped to Database-specific SQL Types

Table 50.7 shows the names used by individual databases for their data types that most closely correspond to the JDBC types.

50.10.1 JDBC Types Mapped to Java Types

Table 50.1: JDBC Types Mapped to Java Types

JDBC Type	Java Type
CHAR	String
VARCHAR	String
LONGVARCHAR	String
NUMERIC	java.math.BigDecimal
DECIMAL	java.math.BigDecimal
BIT	boolean
BOOLEAN	boolean
TINYINT	byte
SMALLINT	short
INTEGER	int
BIGINT	long
REAL	float
FLOAT	double
DOUBLE	double
BINARY	byte[]
VARBINARY	byte[]
LONGVARBINARY	byte[]
DATE	java.sql.Date
TIME	java.sql.Time
TIMESTAMP	java.sql.Timestamp
CLOB	Clob
BLOB	Blob
ARRAY	Array
DISTINCT	mapping of underlying type
STRUCT	Struct
REF	Ref
DATALINK	java.net.URL
JAVA_OBJECT	underlying Java class

Table 50.1 has two purposes. First, it illustrates the general correspondence between types in the Java programming language and the SQL types. Second, it shows the mapping used by getter methods in the CallableStatement interface and reader methods in the SQLInput interface.

50.10.2 Java Types Mapped to JDBC Types

Table 50.2: Standard Mapping from Java Types to JDBC Types

Java Type	JDBC Type
String	CHAR, VARCHAR, or LONGVARCHAR
java.math.BigDecimal	NUMERIC
boolean	BIT or BOOLEAN
byte	TINYINT
short	SMALLINT
int	INTEGER
long	BIGINT
float	REAL
double	DOUBLE
byte[]	BINARY, VARBINARY, or LONGVARBINARY
java.sql.Date	DATE
java.sql.Time	TIME
java.sql.Timestamp	TIMESTAMP
Clob	CLOB
Blob	BLOB
Array	ARRAY
Struct	STRUCT
Ref	REF
java.net.URL	DATALINK
Java class	JAVA_OBJECT

Table 50.2 shows the conversions used for IN parameters before they are sent to the DBMS, used by the PreparedStatement setter and RowSet setter methods. These same conversions are also used by ResultSet updater methods and SQLOutput writer methods. (Note that the PreparedStatement.setObject and RowSet.setObject methods use the mapping in Table 50.4.)

The mapping for String will normally be VARCHAR but will turn into LONGVARCHAR if the given value exceeds the driver's limit on VARCHAR values. The same is true for byte[], which may be mapped to either VARBINARY or LONGVARBINARY values, depending on the driver's limit on VARBINARY values. In most cases, the choice between CHAR and VARCHAR is not significant. In any case, drivers will just make the right choice. The same is true for the choice between BINARY and VARBINARY.

50.10.3 JDBC Types Mapped to Java Object Types

Table 50.3: Mapping from JDBC Types to Java Object Types

JDBC Type	Java Object Type
CHAR	String
VARCHAR	String
LONGVARCHAR	String
NUMERIC	java.math.BigDecimal
DECIMAL	java.math.BigDecimal
BIT	Boolean
BOOLEAN	Boolean
TINYINT	Integer
SMALLINT	Integer
INTEGER	Integer
BIGINT	Long
REAL	Float
FLOAT	Double
DOUBLE	Double
BINARY	byte[]
VARBINARY	byte[]
LONGVARBINARY	byte[]
DATE	java.sql.Date
TIME	java.sql.Time
TIMESTAMP	java.sql.Timestamp
DISTINCT	Object type of underlying type
CLOB	Clob
BLOB	Blob
ARRAY	Array
STRUCT	Struct or SQLData
REF	Ref
DATALINK	java.net.URL
JAVA_OBJECT	underlying Java class

Table 50.3 shows the mapping from JDBC types to Java object types that is used by the ResultSet.getObject and CallableStatement.getObject methods.

50.10.4 Java Object Types Mapped to JDBC Types

Table 50.4: Mapping from Java Object Types to JDBC Types

Java Object Type	JDBC Type
String	CHAR, VARCHAR, or LONGVARCHAR
java.math.BigDecimal	NUMERIC
Boolean	BIT or BOOLEAN
Integer	INTEGER
Long	BIGINT
Float	REAL
Double	DOUBLE
byte[]	BINARY, VARBINARY, or LONGVARBINARY
java.sql.Date	DATE
java.sql.Time	TIME
java.sql.Timestamp	TIMESTAMP
Clob	CLOB
Blob	BLOB
Array	ARRAY
Struct	STRUCT
Ref	REF
java.net.URL	DATALINK
Java class	JAVA_OBJECT

These are the mappings used by the `PreparedStatement.setObject` method when no parameter specifying a target JDBC type is given. (The JDBC types that may be specified to the `PreparedStatement.setObject` method are shown in Table 50.5.)

Note that the mapping for `String` will normally be VARCHAR but will turn into LONGVARCHAR if the given value exceeds the driver's limit on VARCHAR values. The case is similar for `byte[]`, which will be VARBINARY or LONGVARBINARY, depending on the driver's limit for VARBINARY values.

50.10.5 Conversions by `setObject`

Table 50.5: Conversions Performed by `setObject` Between Java Object Types and Target JDBC Types

	TINYINT	SMALLINT	INTEGER	BIGINT	REAL	FLOAT	DOUBLE	DECIMAL	NUMERIC	BIT	BOOLEAN	CHAR	VARCHAR	LONGVARCHAR	BINARY	VARBINARY	LONGVARBINARY	DATE	TIME	TIMESTAMP	ARRAY	BLOB	CLOB	STRUCT	REF	DATALINK	JAVA_OBJECT
String	X	X	X	X	X	X	X	X	X	X	X	X	X	X	X	X	X	X	X	X							
java.math.BigDecimal	X	X	X	X	X	X	X	X	X	X	X	X	X	X													
Boolean	X	X	X	X	X	X	X	X	X	X	X	X	X	X													
Integer	X	X	X	X	X	X	X	X	X	X	X	X	X	X													
Long	X	X	X	X	X	X	X	X	X	X	X	X	X	X													
Float	X	X	X	X	X	X	X	X	X	X	X	X	X	X													
Double	X	X	X	X	X	X	X	X	X	X	X	X	X	X													
byte[]															X	X	X										
java.sql.Date												X	X	X				X		X							
java.sql.Time												X	X	X					X								
java.sql.Timestamp												X	X	X				X	X	X							
Array																					X						
Blob																						X					
Clob																							X				
Struct																								X			
Ref																									X		
java.net.URL																										X	
Java class																											X

In Table 50.5, an "x" means that the given Java object type may be converted to the given JDBC type. This table shows the possible values for the parameter specifying a target JDBC type that is passed to the method `PreparedStatement.setObject` or `RowSet.setObject`. Note that some conversions may fail at run time if the value presented is invalid.

50.10.6 Conversions by `ResultSet` getter Methods

Table 50.6: Use of getter Methods to Retrieve JDBC Data Types

Method	TINYINT	SMALLINT	INTEGER	BIGINT	REAL	FLOAT	DOUBLE	DECIMAL	NUMERIC	BIT	BOOLEAN	CHAR	VARCHAR	LONGVARCHAR	BINARY	VARBINARY	LONGVARBINARY	DATE	TIME	TIMESTAMP	CLOB	BLOB	ARRAY	REF	DATALINK	STRUCT	JAVA_OBJECT
getByte	**X**	x	x	x	x	x	x	x	x	x	x	x	x	x													
getShort	x	**X**	x	x	x	x	x	x	x	x	x	x	x	x													
getInt	x	x	**X**	x	x	x	x	x	x	x	x	x	x	x													
getLong	x	x	x	**X**	x	x	x	x	x	x	x	x	x	x													
getFloat	x	x	x	x	**X**	x	x	x	x	x	x	x	x	x													
getDouble	x	x	x	x	x	**X**	**X**	x	x	x	x	x	x	x													
getBigDecimal	x	x	x	x	x	x	x	**X**	**X**	x	x	x	x	x													
getBoolean	x	x	x	x	x	x	x	x	x	**X**	**X**	x	x	x													
getString	x	x	x	x	x	x	x	x	x	x	x	**X**	**X**	x	x	x	x	x	x	x					x		
getBytes															**X**	**X**	x										
getDate												x	x	x				**X**		x							
getTime												x	x	x					**X**	x							
getTimestamp												x	x	x				x	x	**X**							
getAsciiStream												x	x	**X**	x	x	x										
getBinaryStream															x	x	**X**										
getCharacterStream												x	x	**X**	x	x	x										
getClob																					**X**						
getBlob																						**X**					
getArray																							**X**				
getRef																								**X**			
getURL																									**X**		
getObject	x	x	x	x	x	x	x	x	x	x	x	x	x	x	x	x	x	x	x	x	x	x	x	x	x	**X**	**X**

In Table 50.6, a small "x" means that the method *can* retrieve the JDBC type. A large, bold "**X**" means that the method is *recommended* for retrieving the JDBC type. `SQLInput` reader methods support only the recommended conversions.

50.10.7 JDBC Types Mapped to Database-specific SQL Types

There is considerable variation among the different SQL types supported by the different databases. Table 50.7 shows the database-specific SQL types that best match the JDBC types for various major databases. The presence of a database-specific type name indicates that the given type can be used to achieve the semantics of the corresponding JDBC type, although the database-specific type may also provide additional semantics.

Notes and lamentations:

- Some databases provide extra precision for some integral and floating-point types.

- Some databases provide a DATE or DATETIME type that can be used to contain either a DATE or a TIME or both.

- VARCHAR and VARCHAR2 are currently synonyms in Oracle9i.

- For LONGVARCHAR, DB2 also supports CLOB(n) with a limit of 2 gigabytes.

- For LONGVARBINARY, DB2 also supports BLOB(n) with a limit of 2 gigabytes.

- Handling of BINARY, VARBINARY, and LONGVARBINARY literals in SQL statements varies widely among databases. We recommend using Prepared-Statement.setBytes to set values in a portable way.

- Handling of DATE, TIME, and TIMESTAMP literals in SQL statements varies widely among databases. We recommend using the JDBC SQL escape syntax for dates and times (see "SQL Escape Syntax in Statements," on page 958) to set Date, Time, and Timestamp values in a portable way.

- ASE 12.5 supports JAVA_OBJECT as a column type. However, the column is declared as type OBJECT. Objects bound to this column must be serializable or externalizable.

Table 50.7: JDBC Types Mapped to Database-specific SQL Types

JDBC Type Name	Oracle 9i	Sybase ASE 12.5	MySQL 4.0	IBM DB2 Universal V8.1 (Unix, NT)	Microsoft SQL Server 2000	Microsoft Access XP	Sybase SQL Anywhere 8.0
BIT	NUMBER(1, 0)	BIT	SMALLINT	SMALLINT	BIT	BIT	BIT
TINYINT	NUMBER(3, 0)	TINYINT	SMALLINT	SMALLINT	TINYINT	BYTE	TINYINT
SMALLINT	SMALLINT, NUMBER(5, 0)	SMALLINT	SMALLINT	SMALLINT	SMALLINT	SMALLINT	SMALLINT
INTEGER	INTEGER, NUMBER(10, 0)	INTEGER	INTEGER, SERIAL	INTEGER	INT	INTEGER, COUNTER	INTEGER
BIGINT	NUMBER		INT8, SERIAL8	BIGINT	BIGINT		BIGINT
REAL	REAL, NUMBER	REAL	REAL	REAL	REAL	REAL	REAL
FLOAT	FLOAT, NUMBER	FLOAT	FLOAT	FLOAT	FLOAT		FLOAT
DOUBLE	DOUBLE PRECISION, NUMBER	DOUBLE PRECISION	DOUBLE PRECISION	FLOAT	DOUBLE PRECISION	DOUBLE	DOUBLE PRECISION
NUMERIC(p,s)	NUMERIC(p,s), NUMBER(p,s)	NUMERIC(p,s)	NUMERIC(p,s)	NUMERIC(p,s)	NUMERIC(p,s)	CURRENCY	NUMERIC(p,s)
DECIMAL(p,s)	DECIMAL(p,s), NUMBER(p,s)	DECIMAL(p,s), MONEY	DECIMAL(p,s)	DECIMAL(p,s)	DECIMAL(p,s), MONEY		DECIMAL(p,s)
CHAR(n)	CHAR(n) n <= 2000	CHAR(n) n <= 16384	CHAR(n) n <= 32767	CHAR(n) n <= 254	CHAR(n), n <= 8000 NCHAR(n) n <= 4000	CHAR(n) n <= 255	CHAR(n) n <= 32,767
VARCHAR(n)	VARCHAR2(n) n <= 4000	VARCHAR(n) n <= 16384	VARCHAR(n) n <= 255	VARCHAR(n) n <= 32672	VARCHAR(n), n <= 8000 NVARCHAR(n) n <= 4000	VARCHAR(n) n <= 255	VARCHAR(n) n <= 32,767
LONGVAR-CHAR	LONG limit is 2 Gigabytes	TEXT limit is 2 Gigabytes	TEXT limit is 2 Gigabytes	LONG VARCHAR limit is 32,700 bytes	TEXT, NTEXT limit is 2 Gigabytes	LONGCHAR limit is 2.0 Gigabytes	LONG VARCHAR limit is 2 Gigabytes
BINARY(n)	RAW	BINARY(n) n <= 16384	BYTE	CHAR(n) FOR BIT DATA n < = 254	BINARY(n) n <= 8000	BINARY(n) n <= 255	BINARY n <= 32,767
VARBINARY	RAW(n) n <= 2000	VARBINARY(n) n <= 16384	BYTE	VARCHAR(n) FOR BIT DATA n <= 4000	VARBINARY(n) n <= 8000	VARBINARY(n) n <= 255	VARBINARY(n) n <= 32767
LONGVAR-BINARY	LONG RAW limit is 2 Gigabytes	IMAGE limit is 2 Gigabytes	BYTE limit is 2 Gigabytes	LONG VARCHAR FOR BIT DATA limit is 32,700 bytes	IMAGE limit is 2 Gigabytes	LONGBINARY limit is 1.0 Gigabytes	LONGVARBINARY limit is 2 Gigabytes
DATE	DATE		DATE	DATE			DATE

Table 50.7: JDBC Types Mapped to Database-specific SQL Types

JDBC Type Name	Oracle 9i	Sybase ASE 12.5	MySQL 4.0	IBM DB2 Universal V8.1 (Unix, NT)	Microsoft SQL Server 2000	Microsoft Access XP	Sybase SQL Anywhere 8.0
TIME	DATE		DATETIME HOUR TO SECOND	TIME			TIME
TIMESTAMP	TIMESTAMP	DATETIME, SMALL-DATETIME	DATETIME YEAR TO FRACTION(5)	TIMESTAMP	DATETIME	DATETIME	TIMESTAMP
CLOB	CLOB		CLOB	CLOB(n) n <= 2,147,483,647 bytes			
BLOB	BLOB, BFILE		BLOB	BLOB(n) n <= 2,147,483,647 bytes			
ARRAY	VARRAY, Nested Table		LIST, SET, MULTISET				
STRUCT	OBJECT		ROW				
DISTINCT			DISTINCT				
REF	REF		REF				
JAVA_OBJECT	OBJECT						

APPENDIX **A**

For Driver Writers

THIS appendix contains information aimed at driver developers; in addition, it can be of interest to application developers, who often find it illuminating to see what is required in a driver implementation.

As far as possible, there should be a standard JDBC API that works in a uniform way across all databases. To this end, the JDBC 3.0 Specification imposes some requirements that apply to all drivers. However, it is unavoidable that different databases support different SQL features and provide different semantics for some operations. Consequently, the JDBC specification allows some variations in particular situations.

Appendix A outlines requirements and allowed variations, addresses some implementation issues, and lists security responsibilities of drivers.

A.1 Requirements for All Drivers

This section covers the requirements for standard implementations of drivers that are based on JDBC technology ("JDBC drivers"). In general, a JDBC driver is not required to support a feature that its DBMS does not support.

A.1.1 Guidelines

The following guidelines apply to implementations of the JDBC 1.0 API, the JDBC 2.0 API, and the JDBC 3.0 API.

- A JDBC API implementation is required to support the SQL command DROP TABLE as specified by SQL 92 Transitional Level. See "Support Extensions to SQL92 Entry Level," on page 1102 for details.

- Drivers must support escape syntax. The section "Support Extensions to SQL92 Entry Level," on page 1102 gives more information. Escape syntax is described in "SQL Escape Syntax in Statements," on page 958.

- Drivers must support transactions.

- Drivers should provide access to every feature implemented by the underlying data source, including features that extend the JDBC API. When a feature is not supported, the corresponding methods throw an SQLException. The intent is for applications using the JDBC API to have access to the same feature set as native applications.

- If a DatabaseMetaData method indicates that a given feature is supported, it must be supported via standard syntax and semantics as described in the relevant specifications. This may require the driver to provide the mapping to the data source's native API or SQL dialect if it differs from the standard.

- If a feature is supported, all of the relevant metadata methods must be implemented. For example, if a JDBC API implementation supports the RowSet interface, it must also implement the RowSetMetaData interface.

- If a feature is not supported, the corresponding DatabaseMetaData method must say so. Attempting to access the unsupported feature causes an SQLException to be thrown.

A.1.2   Implement Methods in the Interfaces

All of the methods in the interfaces contained in the JDBC 1.0 API must be implemented so that they support at least ANSI SQL92 Entry Level and X/Open SQL CLI. Methods in the JDBC 2.0 API and JDBC 3.0 API must be implemented to support ANSI SQL92 Entry Level, the relevant sections of ANSI SQL99, and X/Open SQL CLI.

Beyond this base level, which is always required, a driver does not have to support a feature if the DBMS for which it is written does not support that feature. For example, if a DBMS does not support SQL99 data types, implementing the interfaces that support the new types (Array, Blob, Clob, Ref, SQLData, SQLInput, SQLOutput, and Struct) is optional. Or, if a DBMS does not support an Optional Package feature, such as connection pooling, the interfaces that support connection pooling (`ConnectionEvent`, `ConnectionEventListener`, `ConnectionPool-DataSource`, `PooledConnection`) are optional. If an individual method supports a feature that a DBMS does not include, that method may be implemented to throw an `SQLException`.

Metadata interfaces should be fully implemented. The purpose of the `DatabaseMetaData` interface is to tell users what a DBMS does and does not support, so every method should be implemented. The `ResultSetMetaData` and `ParameterMetaData` interfaces should likewise always be fully implemented. A driver vendor that supplies a `javax.sql.RowSet` implementation should also supply a full implementation of the `javax.sql.RowSetMetaData` interface.

Note that the interfaces in the JDBC Optional Package API, contained within the `javax.sql` package, are an integral part of the JDBC 3.0 API, and a JDBC driver should implement them on the same basis as the core JDBC API. The `RowSet` interface and the interfaces that support it, however, are not included in the following lists because they are implemented on top of the JDBC API and thus are not part of a driver's implementation.

JDBC drivers that support distributed transactions must support the `XAConnection` and `XADataSource` interfaces.

A.2   Requirements for JDBC 1.0 API Compliance

To be compliant with the JDBC 1.0 API, a driver implementation must do the following:

- Adhere to the preceding guidelines and requirements

- Fully implement the following interfaces:

  - `java.sql.Driver`
  - `java.sql.DatabaseMetaData`—except for methods introduced in the JDBC 2.0 API or JDBC 3.0 API

  - `java.sql.ResultSetMetaData`—except for methods introduced in the JDBC 2.0 API or JDBC 3.0 API

- Include the following required interfaces:

  - `java.sql.CallableStatement`
  - `java.sql.Connection`
  - `java.sql.PreparedStatement`
  - `java.sql.ResultSet`
  - `java.sql.Statement`

A.3   Requirements for JDBC 2.0 API Compliance

To be compliant with the JDBC 2.0 API, a driver implementation must do the following:

- Comply with the JDBC 1.0 API requirements

- Fully implement the DatabaseMetaData interface, including the following methods added in the JDBC 2.0 API:

  - deletesAreDetected
  - getConnection
  - getUDTs
  - insertsAreDetected
  - othersDeletesAreVisible
  - othersInsertsAreVisible
  - othersUpdatesAreVisible
  - ownDeletesAreVisible
  - ownInsertsAreVisible
  - ownUpdatesAreVisible
  - supportsBatchUpdates
  - supportsResultSetConcurrency
  - supportsResultSetType
  - updatesAreDetected

- Implement the following additional ResultSetMetaData methods:

  - getColumnClassName
  - getColumnType
  - getColumnTypeName

A.4   Requirements for JDBC 3.0 API Compliance

To be compliant with the JDBC 3.0 API, a driver implementation must do the following:

- Comply with the JDBC 2.0 API requirements

- Include the following required interfaces:

  - java.sql.ParameterMetaData
  - java.sql.Savepoint

- Fully implement the DatabaseMetaData interface, including the following methods added in the JDBC 3.0 API:

- `supportsSavepoints`
- `supportsNamedParameters`
- `supportsMultipleOpenResults`
- `supportsGetGeneratedKeys`
- `getSuperTypes`
- `getSuperTables`
- `getAttributes`
- `getResultSetHoldability`
- `supportsResultSetHoldability`
- `getSQLStateType`
- `getDatabaseMajorVersion`
- `getDatabaseMinorVersion`
- `getJDBCmajorVersion`
- `getJDBCMinorVersion`

A.5   API That Is Already Implemented

The following classes and exceptions are already fully implemented in the JDBC 3.0 API:

- `java.sql.BatchUpdateException`
- `java.sql.DataTruncation`
- `java.sql.Date`
- `java.sql.DriverManager`
- `java.sql.DriverPropertyInfo`
- `java.sql.SQLException`
- `java.sql.SQLPermission`
- `java.sql.SQLWarning`
- `java.sql.Time`
- `java.sql.Timestamp`
- `java.sql.Types`
- `javax.sql.ConnectionEvent`
- `javax.sql.RowSetEvent`

A.6   Additional Requirements

In addition to satisfying the requirements already listed, a JDBC driver must also comply with the requirements presented in the following sections.

A.6.1   Implement a Static Initializer

Every `Driver` class should contain a special static block, sometimes referred to as a static initializer, that is used when the `Driver` class is loaded using the `DriverManager` facility. This static initializer does two things when the `Driver` class is loaded:

1. It creates an instance of itself.

2. It registers the newly created instance by calling the method `DriverManager.registerDriver`.

This static initializer is demonstrated in the following code fragment.

```
public class MyDriver implements java.sql.Driver {
    static {
        java.sql.DriverManager.registerDriver(new MyDriver());
    }
     . . .
}
```

When the `Driver` class is implemented to do these two things, a user can load and register a JDBC driver with the `DriverManager` simply by calling the method `Class.forName` with the `Driver` class name as the argument. See the section "Loading and Registering a Driver," on page 604, for more information.

Note that the static initializer applies only to drivers that are loaded using the `DriverManager` class. Drivers loaded via the `DataSource` API should *not* automatically register with the `DriverManager`, and their implementations should *not* contain the static initializer. The `DriverManager` and `DriverPropertyInfo` classes and the `Driver` interface may be deprecated in the future.

A.6.2   Support Extensions to SQL92 Entry Level

Certain SQL features beyond SQL92 Entry Level are widely supported and are desirable to include as part of the JDBC compliance definition so that applications can depend on the portability of these features. However, SQL92 Transitional Level, the next higher level of SQL compliance defined by ANSI, is not widely supported. Even where Transitional Level semantics are supported, the syntax is often different across DBMSs.

Therefore, JDBC defines two kinds of extensions to SQL92 Entry Level that must be supported by a JDBC Compliant driver:

- Selective Transitional Level syntax and semantics. Currently the only feature at this level that is required for JDBC compliance is the command DROP TABLE. Because some popular databases currently do not fully support the DROP TABLE options CASCADE and RESTRICT, this requirement has been relaxed so that support for these options is no longer required. The behavior of the DROP TABLE command is implementation-defined when views or integrity constraints reference a table that is being dropped.

- An escape syntax that supports the Selective Transitional Level semantics. A driver should scan for and translate this escape syntax into DBMS-specific syntax. Note that these escapes need only be supported where the underlying database supports the corresponding Transitional Level semantics. Where appropriate, an escape syntax must be included for stored procedures, time and date literals, scalar functions, LIKE escape characters, and outer joins. These escapes are described in the section "SQL Escape Syntax in Statements," on page 958.

The JDBC API supports the same DBMS-independent escape syntax as ODBC for stored procedures, scalar functions, dates, times, and outer joins. By mapping this escape syntax into DBMS-specific syntax, a driver allows portability of application programs that require these features.

This ODBC-compatible escape syntax is, in general, *not* the same as has been adopted by ANSI in SQL92 Transitional Level for the same functionality. In cases where all of the desired DBMSs support the standard SQL92 syntax, the user is encouraged to use that syntax instead of these escapes. When enough DBMSs support the more advanced SQL92 syntax and semantics, these escapes should no longer be necessary. In the meantime, however, JDBC drivers should support them.

A.6.3   Support Scalar Functions

Support for scalar functions needs some extra explanation. JDBC supports numeric, string, time, date, system, and conversion functions on scalar values. For those who want more detail than is provided in the section "SQL Escape Syntax in Statements," on page 958, the X/Open Group CLI specification provides more information on the semantics of the scalar functions. The functions supported are listed below for reference.

If a DBMS supports a scalar function, the driver should also. Because scalar functions are supported by different DBMSs with slightly different syntax, it is the driver's job either to map them into the appropriate syntax or to implement the functions directly in the driver.

A user should be able to find out which functions are supported by calling metadata methods. For example, the method `DatabaseMetaData.getNumericFunctions` should return a comma-separated list of the Open Group CLI names of the numeric functions supported. Similarly, the method `DatabaseMetaData.getStringFunctions` should return a list of string functions supported, and so on.

The scalar functions are listed by category:

NUMERIC FUNCTIONS

Function Name	**Function Returns**
ABS(number)	Absolute value of number
ACOS(float)	Arccosine, in radians, of float
ASIN(float)	Arcsine, in radians, of float
ATAN(float)	Arctangent, in radians, of float
ATAN2(float1, float2)	Arctangent, in radians, of float2 / float1
CEILING(number)	Smallest integer >= number
COS(float)	Cosine of float radians
COT(float)	Cotangent of float radians
DEGREES(number)	Degrees in number radians
EXP(float)	Exponential function of float
FLOOR(number)	Largest integer <= number
LOG(float)	Base e logarithm of float
LOG10(float)	Base 10 logarithm of float
MOD(integer1, integer2)	Remainder for integer1 / integer2
PI()	The constant pi
POWER(number, power)	number raised to (integer) power
RADIANS(number)	Radians in number degrees
RAND(integer)	Random floating point for seed integer
ROUND(number, places)	number rounded to places places

SIGN(number)	−1 to indicate number is < 0; 0 to indicate number is = 0; 1 to indicate number is > 0
SIN(float)	Sine of float radians
SQRT(float)	Square root of float
TAN(float)	Tangent of float radians
TRUNCATE(number, places)	number truncated to places places

STRING FUNCTIONS

Function Name	**Function Returns**
ASCII(string)	Integer representing the ASCII code value of the leftmost character in string
CHAR(code)	Character with ASCII code value code, where code is between 0 and 255
CONCAT(string1, string2)	Character string formed by appending string2 to string1; if a string is null, the result is DBMS-dependent
DIFFERENCE(string1, string2)	Integer indicating the difference between the values returned by the function SOUNDEX for string1 and string2
INSERT(string1, start, length, string2)	A character string formed by deleting length characters from string1 beginning at start, and inserting string2 into string1 at start
LCASE(string)	Converts all uppercase characters in string to lowercase
LEFT(string, count)	The count leftmost characters from string
LENGTH(string)	Number of characters in string, excluding trailing blanks
LOCATE(string1, string2[, start])	Position in string2 of the first occurrence of string1, searching from the beginning of string2; if start is specified, the search begins from position start. 0 is returned if string2 does not contain string1. Position 1 is the first character in string2.
LTRIM(string)	Characters of string with leading blank spaces removed
REPEAT(string, count)	A character string formed by repeating string count times
REPLACE(string1, string2, string3)	Replaces all occurrences of string2 in string1 with string3
RIGHT(string, count)	The count rightmost characters in string
RTRIM(string)	The characters of string with no trailing blanks

SOUNDEX(string)	A character string, which is data source-dependent, representing the sound of the words in string; this could be a four-digit SOUNDEX code, a phonetic representation of each word, etc.
SPACE(count)	A character string consisting of count spaces
SUBSTRING(string, start, length)	A character string formed by extracting length characters from string beginning at start
UCASE(string)	Converts all lowercase characters in string to uppercase

TIME and DATE FUNCTIONS

Function Name	**Function Returns**
CURDATE()	The current date as a date value
CURTIME()	The current local time as a time value
DAYNAME(date)	A character string representing the day component of date; the name for the day is specific to the data source
DAYOFMONTH(date)	An integer from 1 to 31 representing the day of the month in date
DAYOFWEEK(date)	An integer from 1 to 7 representing the day of the week in date; 1 represents Sunday
DAYOFYEAR(date)	An integer from 1 to 366 representing the day of the year in date
HOUR(time)	An integer from 0 to 23 representing the hour component of time
MINUTE(time)	An integer from 0 to 59 representing the minute component of time
MONTH(date)	An integer from 1 to 12 representing the month component of date
MONTHNAME(date)	A character string representing the month component of date; the name for the month is specific to the data source
NOW()	A timestamp value representing the current date and time
QUARTER(date)	An integer from 1 to 4 representing the quarter in date; 1 represents January 1 through March 31
SECOND(time)	An integer from 0 to 59 representing the second component of time
TIMESTAMPADD(interval,	A timestamp calculated by adding count num-

count, timestamp)	ber of interval(s) to timestamp; interval may be one of the following: SQL_TSI_FRAC_SECOND, SQL_TSI_SECOND, SQL_TSI_MINUTE, SQL_TSI_HOUR, SQL_TSI_DAY, SQL_TSI_WEEK, SQL_TSI_MONTH, SQL_TSI_QUARTER, or SQL_TSI_YEAR
TIMESTAMPDIFF(interval, timestamp1, timestamp2)	An integer representing the number of interval(s) by which timestamp2 is greater than timestamp1; interval may be one of the following: SQL_TSI_FRAC_SECOND, SQL_TSI_SECOND, SQL_TSI_MINUTE, SQL_TSI_HOUR, SQL_TSI_DAY, SQL_TSI_WEEK, SQL_TSI_MONTH, SQL_TSI_QUARTER, or SQL_TSI_YEAR
WEEK(date)	An integer from 1 to 53 representing the week of the year in date
YEAR(date)	An integer representing the year component of date

SYSTEM FUNCTIONS

Function Name	**Function Returns**
DATABASE()	Name of the database
IFNULL(expression, value)	value if expression is null; expression if expression is not null
USER()	User name in the DBMS

CONVERSION FUNCTIONS

Function Name	**Function Returns**
CONVERT(value, SQLtype)	value converted to SQLtype where SQLtype may be one of the following SQL types: BIGINT, BINARY, BIT, CHAR, DATE, DECIMAL, DOUBLE, FLOAT, INTEGER, LONGVARBINARY, LONGVARCHAR, REAL, SMALLINT, TIME, TIMESTAMP, TINYINT, VARBINARY, or VARCHAR

A.6.4   Provide Locks for Positioned Updates and Deletes

The JDBC 3.0 core API provides various methods for positioning a result set cursor, thereby making it easy to update or delete a particular row in a result set. The JDBC 1.0 API, however, provides only simple cursor support, which makes positioned updates and deletes a little more complicated.

When a query is executed with the method executeQuery, the result is a ResultSet object with a cursor pointing above the first row. This cursor will remain valid until the ResultSet object or its parent Statement object (the query that generated the result set) is closed. If a driver does not support the new cursor positioning methods, an application must get the name of the cursor associated with the current ResultSet object by calling the method ResultSet.getCursor-Name. This cursor name can then be used in positioned update or positioned delete statements.

Not all DBMSs support positioned updates and positioned deletes. An application can use the methods DatabaseMetaData.supportsPositionedUpdate and DatabaseMetaData.supportsPositionedDelete to determine whether a particular connection supports them. Since many DBMSs do not support "for update" in a SELECT statement (as in SELECT FOR UPDATE), drivers for these DBMSs will have to scan for this phrase and implement the intended semantics. The purpose of this syntax is to signal that the result set generated from a query will be used in a positioned update or positioned delete.

3.0   In addition, the JDBC 3.0 API allows an application to specify the holdability of a ResultSet object, which allows ResultSet objects that have been created during a transaction to be maintained beyond the life cycle of a committed transaction. Maintaining ResultSet objects beyond a commit means that a JDBC driver must take into account additional locking responsibilities.

When positioned updates and deletes are supported, the DBMS/driver must ensure that rows selected are properly locked so that positioned updates do not result in update anomalies or other concurrency problems.

A.6.5   Support Multithreading

All operations on java.sql and javax.sql objects are required to be multithread safe. They must be able to cope correctly with having several threads simultaneously calling the same object. In other words, a statement execution in one thread should not block an execution in another thread. In particular, JDBC drivers should operate correctly when used from multiple threads.

An example of a specific use of multithreading is the way a long-running statement can be cancelled. This is done by using one thread to execute the statement and a second one to cancel it with the method Statement.cancel.

Even though it is expected that in practice most JDBC objects will be accessed in a single-threaded way, there needs to be support for multithreading.

Some database APIs, such as ODBC, provide mechanisms for allowing SQL statements to execute asynchronously. This allows an application to start up a database operation in the background and then handle other work (such as managing a user interface) while waiting for the operation to complete.

Because the Java programming language provides a multithreaded environment, there seems to be no real need to provide support for asynchronous statement execution. Programmers can easily create a separate thread if they wish to execute statements asynchronously with respect to their main thread.

Some drivers may allow more concurrent execution than others, but developers should be able to assume fully concurrent execution. If the driver requires some form of synchronization, then the driver should provide it. In this situation, the only difference visible to the developer should be that applications run with reduced concurrency.

For example, two Statement objects on the same connection can be executed concurrently, and their ResultSet objects can be processed concurrently (from the perspective of the developer). Some drivers will provide this full concurrency. Others may execute one statement and wait until it completes before sending the next one.

A.6.6   Throw Exceptions for Truncated Input Parameters

If input parameters are truncated, a DataTruncation exception should be thrown. See Chapter 17, "DataTruncation," starting on page 581, for general information about data truncation warnings and exceptions.

A.6.7   Use Default Behaviors for SQL99 Data Types

To be JDBC Compliant, a driver written for a DBMS that supports SQL99 data types must implement the default behaviors for SQL99 data types. The JDBC 3.0 API specifies the default behaviors for SQL99 data types in two general areas: (1) their lifetime and (2) whether they are implemented using locators.

1. The lifetime of an instance of an SQL99 data type

   - Blob, Clob, and Array instances are valid for the duration of the transaction in which they were created.

   - Ref instances remain valid while the session, or connection on which they were created, is open.

- `Struct` instances are valid as long as an application retains a reference to them.

2. Whether an instance uses a locator or materializes its data on the client. A locator, a temporary object residing on the client, is a logical pointer to a column value on the server. For example, a `LOCATOR(CLOB)` designates a `CLOB` instance stored as a column value. Operations on the `LOCATOR(CLOB)` affect the `CLOB` value on the server.

   - `Blob`, `Clob`, and `Array` instances are implemented as locators; that is, they are logical pointers to values on the server and *do not* materialize their data on the client.
     The semantics of updates made to `LOB` objects are implementation-defined. In some implementations, the changes are made to a copy of the `LOB`, while in others the changes are made directly to the `LOB` in the database column. Implementations that make changes to a copy of the `LOB` must issue an additional update statement to update the `LOB` stored in the DBMS. The method `locatorsUpdateCopy` in the `DatabaseMetaData` interface should return `true` if the underlying DBMS updates a copy of the `LOB` and `false` if it updates the `LOB` directly.

   - `Ref` instances map an SQL data type that is already a logical pointer to a structured type; therefore, they do not materialize the structured type's data and also do not need to be implemented as locators.

   - `Struct` instances *do* materialize the data of the structured types they represent. A JDBC driver should materialize the attribute values of a structured type on the client before returning a reference to the `Struct` instance to an application.

Though not to be done casually, it is possible for a driver to override the defaults. For example, the duration of a `Blob` instance could be changed to be the session in which it was created instead of the transaction in which it was created. Or, the implementation of a `Struct` instance could be changed to use a locator. Any such changes should be considered carefully, weighing the advantages of the new behavior against the disadvantage of making the implementation nonstandard, and therefore nonportable. The JDBC 3.0 API does not specify how to override the defaults.

A.7   Permitted Variants

Because of the variation in database functionality and syntax, JDBC allows some variation in driver implementations. The actual SQL used by one database may vary from that used by other databases. For example, different databases provide different support for outer joins. Also, the syntax for a number of SQL features may vary between databases.

The `java.sql.DatabaseMetaData` interface provides a number of methods with which a user can determine exactly which SQL features are supported by a particular database. It is the responsibility of the driver writer to be sure that the `DatabaseMetaData` methods return accurate information about what the DBMS does and does not support.

A.7.1   When Functionality Is Not Supported

Some variation is allowed for drivers written for databases that do not support certain functionality. For example, some databases do not support OUT parameters with stored procedures. In this case, the `CallableStatement` methods that deal with OUT parameters (`registerOutParameter` and the various getter methods) would not apply, and they may be written so that when they are called, they throw an `SQLException`.

A.7.2   Variation in Fundamental Properties

Variation is also permitted in some fundamental properties, such as transaction isolation levels. The default properties of the current database and the range of properties it supports can be obtained by calling `DatabaseMetaData` methods.

A.7.3   Adding Functionality

Database vendors who wish to expose additional functionality that is supported by their databases may create subclasses of existing JDBC classes and provide additional methods in the new subclasses. For example, the SQL99 type `NVAR` and `NVAR-CHAR` could be added by the Foobah corporation, which might define a new Java type `foobah.sql.FooBahType` that extends the class `java.sql.Types`.

A.8   Security Responsibilities of Drivers

Because JDBC drivers may be used in a variety of different situations, it is important that driver writers follow certain simple security rules to prevent applets from making illegal database connections.

These rules are unnecessary if a driver is downloaded as an applet because the standard security manager will prevent an applet driver from making illegal connections. However, JDBC driver writers should bear in mind that if their drivers are "successful," then users may start installing them as trusted parts of the Java environment and must make sure that they are not abused by visiting applets. We therefore urge all JDBC driver writers to follow the basic security rules.

These rules apply at connection open time. This is the point when the driver and the virtual machine should check that the current caller is really allowed to connect to a given database. After a connection is opened, no additional checks are necessary.

Only native code drivers need to verify database access prior to connecting. Pure Java drivers can rely on the security manager.

The sections that follow discuss the basic security measures that drivers need to address.

A.8.1   Check Shared TCP Connections

If a JDBC driver attempts to open a TCP connection, then the open will be automatically checked by the Java security manager. The security manager will check to see if there is an applet on the current call stack and, if so, will restrict the open to whatever set of machines that applet is allowed to call. So, normally a JDBC driver can leave TCP open checks up to the Java Virtual Machine.

However, if a JDBC driver wants to share a single TCP connection among several different database connections, then it becomes the driver's responsibility to make sure that each of its callers is really allowed to talk to the target database. For example, if a TCP connection is opened to the machine foobah for applet A, this does not mean that applet B should automatically be allowed to share that connection. Applet B may have no right whatsoever to access machine foobah.

Therefore, before allowing someone to reuse an existing TCP connection, the JDBC driver should check with the security manager that the current caller is allowed to connect to that machine. This can be done with the following code fragment:

```
SecurityManager security = System.getSecurityManager();
if (security != null) {
    security.checkConnect(hostName, portNumber);
}
```

The `SecurityManager.checkConnect` method will throw a `java.lang.SecurityException` if the connection is not permitted.

A.8.2 Check All Local File Access

If a JDBC driver needs to access any local data on the current machine, then it must ensure that its caller is allowed to open the target files. The following code fragment illustrates this:

```
SecurityManager security = System.getSecurityManager();
if (security != null) {
    security.checkRead(fileName);
}
```

The `Security.checkRead` method will throw a `java.lang.SecurityException` if the current caller is an applet that is not allowed to access the given file.

As with TCP connections, the driver need only be concerned with these security issues if file resources are shared among multiple calling threads and the driver is running as trusted code.

A.8.3 Assume the Worst

Some drivers may use native methods to bridge to lower-level database libraries. In these cases, it may be difficult to determine what files or network connections will be opened by the lower-level libraries.

In these circumstances the driver must make worst-case security assumptions and deny all database access to downloaded applets unless the driver is completely confident that the intended access is innocuous.

For example, a JDBC–ODBC bridge might check the meaning of ODBC data source names and allow an applet to use only those ODBC data source names that reference databases on machines to which the applet is allowed to open connections. But for some ODBC data source names, the driver may be unable to determine the host name of the target database and must therefore deny downloaded applets access to these data sources.

In order to determine whether the current caller is a trusted application or applet (and can therefore be allowed arbitrary database access), the JDBC driver can check to see if the caller is allowed to write an arbitrary file:

```
SecurityManager security = System.getSecurityManager();
if (security != null) {
    security.checkWrite("foobah");
}
```

A.9   Use `SQLException` for Exceptions

As just stated, if a DBMS does not support certain functionality, a method may be implemented so that it throws an `SQLException`.

There are cases where a Java `RunTimeException` and an `SQLException` might overlap. For example, if a method expects an argument to be a `java.sql.Types` constant and something else is supplied, the exception thrown could be an `IllegalArgumentException` or an `SQLException`. In such cases, it is recommended that the `SQLException` be thrown because that gives JDBC more consistent control over errors.

A.10   Implementation Suggestions

A.10.1   Prefetch Rows

JDBC provides methods for retrieving individual columns within individual rows, one field at a time. It does not at present provide the means for prefetching rows in larger chunks. However, in order to reduce the number of interactions with the target database, it is recommended that drivers normally prefetch rows in suitable chunks.

[2.0] Methods added in the JDBC 2.0 core API set the number of rows to be fetched, but a driver may ignore this number, especially if it conflicts with optimizations on the part of the DBMS and/or driver. Similarly, drivers may also ignore the fetch direction indicated by new methods in the JDBC 3.0 core API.

A.10.2   Provide "Finalize" Methods

Users are advised to call the method `close` on `Statement` and `Connection` objects when they are done with them. However, some users will forget, and some code may get killed before it can close these objects. Therefore, if JDBC drivers have state associated with JDBC objects that need to be cleared up explicitly, they should provide `finalize` methods to take care of them. The garbage collector will call these `finalize` methods when the objects are found to be garbage, and this will give the driver a chance to close (or otherwise clean up) the objects. Note, however, that there is no guarantee that the garbage collector will ever run. If that is the case, the finalizers will not be called.

Driver writers should look carefully at the semantics used for finalization in Java. A good source of information on this is *The Java™ Language Specification*, by James Gosling, Bill Joy, and Guy Steele. Some care is required to ensure that the finalization process occurs in the correct order regardless of the order in which the garbage collector deals with a driver's objects.

A.10.3 Avoid Implementation-dependent States

Some databases have restrictions that result in hidden dependencies between JDBC objects. For instance, two `Statement` objects may be open, but while the `ResultSet` object of one is in use, the other `Statement` object cannot be executed. This implies that an implementation-defined `Statement` state exists that is controlled via another `Statement` object.

The JDBC API does not define such states, and, if at all possible, JDBC implementations should not introduce them. They hinder portability, and implementations containing them are not fully JDBC Compliant.

A.11 Connection and Statement Pooling Implementations

Obtaining a connection to a data source is one of the more expensive operations in a database application. Therefore, a mechanism for pooling connections so that they can be reused can offer substantial gains in performance. The JDBC API provides one class (`ConnectionEvent`) and three interfaces (`ConnectionEventListener`, `ConnectionPoolDataSource`, and `PooledConnection`) to be used in the implementation of connection pooling.

This API determines some general guidelines for how connection pooling should work, but it does not address the details of how connection pooling is implemented. Moreover, the JDBC 3.0 specification does not define where it is to be implemented, leaving a great deal of freedom to implementers. Typically, an application server will implement the management of both connection pooling and distributed transactions. Driver vendors typically implement the DataSource and ConnectionPoolDataSource interfaces so that they work with a J2EE application server's implementation of connection pooling. If a JDBC driver includes its own implementation of connection pool management, it should also provide a means by which an application can turn off the driver's implementation. This way, an application can choose to use the application server's implementation, thus preventing two pools from being established.

Similarly, reusing a PreparedStatement object can enhance performance, especially when the prepared statement is large and is used many times. A driver and DBMS may expend a great deal of energy precompiling a statement and preparing a strategy for executing it, so doing this once for a statement instead of multiple times is much more efficient. Statements may be pooled when the connection used to create them is pooled. The JDBC 3.0 specification adds some properties to ConnectionPoolDataSource that can be used to set up the initial size of the statement pool, the minimum number of statements to be maintained in the pool, and so on. These properties are set in an implementation and are not part of the API exposed to application developers. From an application devveloper's point of view, then, there is no new API for statement pooling.

Implementations of connection pooling and statement pooling must be completely transparent to the user. The one exception is that the driver should make it possible to turn off the driver's implementation of connection pooling in order to use the application server's implementation. An application creates, uses, and closes a connection in exactly the same way it always does, regardless of whether or not the connection is being pooled. Likewise, an application creates a new PreparedStatement object each time it uses one. The only difference is that if a programmer knows that connection pooling is in effect, he/she might make better use of prepared statements. In general, though, the only way an application should know that connection pooling or statement pooling is being done is through the improvement in performance.

A.12 JDBC Test Suite

Driver vendors can test whether their drivers are compatible with the J2EE platform by using the JDBC test suites. There are two versions:

- JDBC Test Suite 1.2.1: tests for conformance with the JDBC 2.0 API
- JDBC Test Suite 1.3.1: tests for conformance with the JDBC 3.0 API

These test suites cover the driver functionality tested by the J2EE compatibility tests. They are free and may be downloaded from

```
http://java.sun.com/products/jdbc/download.html#jdbctestsuite
```

Documentation for how to install and run the test suites is available at

```
http://java.sun.com/products/jdbc/jdbctestsuite-1_3_1.html
```

Passing the test suite indicates that a driver is compatible with other products that conform to the J2EE specification, but it does not mean that a driver can be labelled as J2EE compatible. For that to happen, the driver must be tested by an outside testing organization and be certified as compatible. Complete instructions on how to have a driver certified are available at

```
http://java.sun.com/products/jdbc/certification.html
```

The JDBC web pages maintain a database of JDBC drivers, which users can search to find drivers that satisfy their requirements. Search criteria include the type of driver, which versions of the JDBC Specification are supported, and which drivers have been certified to be compatible with the J2EE platform. The database is maintained at

```
http://java.sun.com/products/jdbc/drivers.html
```

Drivers may have themselves listed in the database by filling out the submission form at

```
http://java.sun.com/products/jdbc/add_driver.html
```

A.13 Connectors

A developer writing applications for the J2EE platform will almost always want to use the JDBC API to access one or more DBMSs. It therefore is in the interest of driver vendors to make it easy to connect a JDBC driver to a J2EE application server.

A.13.1 J2EE Connector Architecture

The J2EE Connector Architecture 1.0 Specification and the J2EE Connector Architecture 1.5 Specification provide a framework that makes it possible to connect a J2EE application server with external resources, such as a DBMS, in a pluggable way. The software that accomplishes this is called a *resource adapter*, or alternatively, a *connector*.

The heart of the connector architecture is a set of contracts. A driver implementation that satisfies these contracts will be able to plug in to any J2EE application server that also satisfies these contracts. The Service Provider Interface (SPI) contracts define what the J2EE server and a resource adapter must implement in the following areas:

- Transaction management

- Connection pool management

- Security

The following interfaces describe services that are equivalent to those in the server contracts:

- `DataSource`
- `ConnectionPoolDataSource`
- `XADataSource`

The `DataSource` and `ConnectionPoolDataSource` interfaces describe services that are equivalent to the server contracts dealing with connection pooling. The `XADataSource` interface describes services that are equivalent to the server contracts dealing with distributed transactions. The JDBC API does not have any API that corresponds to the security contracts because authentication always consists of the user name and password.

Driver vendors have various options for supplying JDBC drivers that use the Connector system contracts. The options are:

- Write a set of classes that wrap a JDBC driver and implement the Connector system contracts. Constructing these wrappers is fairly straightforward and should allow vendors to provide resource adapters quickly enough so that they are available when application server vendors have implemented the Connector contracts.

- Implement the Connector system contracts natively. This approach avoids the overhead of wrapper classes, but the implementation effort may be more involved and time-consuming. This alternative is a more long-term option.

- Use the JDBC Connector implementation. Information for downloading the JDBC Connector is at

```
http://java.sun.com/products/jdbc/related.html
```

The JDBC 3.0 Specification, Section 19.3, gives instructions for packaging a JDBC driver in Connector resource archive (RAR) file format. The download includes these RAR files plus documentation explaining how the JDBC Connector works and how to deploy it. Vendors will find that using the SPI RAR files is very easy because they do not need to change any code in their driver implementations.

The JDBC Connector download includes common client interface (CCI) RAR files as well as SPI RAR files, but they are included more to show what the CCI approach looks like than anything else. Driver vendors will more likely use the SPI RAR files because they make it possible for users to use the JDBC API just as they have always done. The overview document in the JDBC Connector download gives more complete information.

Summary of Changes

THIS appendix covers the changes that the JDBC API has undergone since its inception. It shows what is new in the JDBC 3.0 API and also includes earlier changes and some of the design considerations that played a role in these changes. It is hoped that readers will better understand how the JDBC API has developed by being aware of the some of the issues addressed in the past.

The overall goal of the JDBC 3.0 specification is twofold:

- to "round-out" the API by filling in areas of missing functionality

- to combine all of the previous JDBC core API specifications and the JDBC Optional Package specification into one comprehensive specification

The result is that the JDBC 3.0 API includes both the core API and the JDBC Optional Package API. The core API consists of all the classes, interfaces, and exceptions in the java.sql package. In other words, it includes all of the JDBC API in earlier releases plus all of the changes and additions listed in this appendix. The JDBC Optional Package API consists of all the classes and interfaces in the javax.sql package.

An important change is that the JDBC 2.0 Optional Package no longer needs to be downloaded separately. Starting with J2SE version 1.4, the complete JDBC 3.0 API is bundled as part of the J2SE download. Among other things, this makes it more convenient to use a DataSource object, which is part of the javax.sql package, to obtain a connection to a database. With a DataSource object being the preferred way to obtain a connection (as opposed to using the DriverManager facility), it makes sense to include all of the JDBC API in the J2SE platform.

The rest of this appendix presents a complete listing of what has changed in the JDBC API. Changes are presented in reverse chronological order, discussing the new features of the JDBC 3.0 API first. This is followed by a detailed look at JDBC 2.0 core API changes, which is in turn followed by a summary and listing of the JDBC Optional Package. The last part covers earlier historical changes.

The following list gives the order in which topics are covered:

- Summary of the new features in the JDBC 3.0 API

- Complete listing of all of the new JDBC 3.0 interfaces, methods, and fields

- Summary of features new in the JDBC 2.0 core API

- Complete listing of new methods and fields in the JDBC 2.0 core API

- Complete listing of methods and constructors deprecated in the JDBC 2.0 API

- Summary of the JDBC Optional Package features

- Complete listing of the methods and constructors in the JDBC Optional Package interfaces and classes

- Summary of changes made in JDBC API versions 1.1 and 1.2

- Early design decisions

B.1   Overview of JDBC 3.0 API Changes

The JDBC 3.0 API introduced two new interfaces and added new methods and fields to several existing interfaces.

Applications that use earlier versions of the JDBC API can be run using the Java 2 platform with no problem, in keeping with the goal of backward compatibility. (See section B.9.1 on page 1156 for the special case of what is needed for applications that use `java.lang.Bignum` instead of `java.math.BigDecimal`.) However, an application that takes advantage of the new 3.0 features can only be run with a driver that implements those features.

The new features in the JDBC 3.0 API can be divided into two broad categories: (1) support for new functionality and (2) extended support for SQL99 data types.

1. Support for new functionality

   - Savepoint support

   - Reuse of prepared statements by connection pools

- Connection pool configuration
- Retrieval of parameter metadata
- Retrieval of auto-generated keys
- Ability to have multiple open `ResultSet` objects
- Passing parameters to `CallableStatement` objects using the parameter name
- Holdable cursor support

2. Extended support for advanced data types

- Addition of `BOOLEAN` and `DATALINK` data types
- Ability to make internal updates to `Blob` and `Clob` objects
- Additional metadata for retrieving SQL type hierarchies.

In addition, the JDBC 3.0 Specification spells out the relationship between the JDBC SPI (Service Provider Interface) and the Connector architecture. See "Connectors," on page 1117, for more information.

B.2   Summary of New Functionality

3.0

The JDBC 3.0 core API adds important new functionality. The following sections briefly explain each new area of functionality and summarize the supporting API.

B.2.1   Savepoint Support

A savepoint sets a point within a transaction and provides the ability to roll back a transaction to that point instead of having to roll back the entire transaction. This gives a developer finer-grained control over what happens in a transaction.

The new `Savepoint` interface represents a savepoint and provides methods for retrieving the name of a `Savepoint` object. New methods in the `Connection` interface allow an application to create and release `Savepoint` objects.

The following interfaces have been added or modified to supply this functionality:

`Savepoint`
- methods for retrieving the name of a `Savepoint` object

`Connection`

- methods for setting and releasing a savepoint
- a version of the `rollback` method that takes a `Savepoint` object. This method undoes all the changes in the current transaction that follow the given `Savepoint` object.

`DatabaseMetaData`

- a method to determine whether the JDBC driver supports savepoints

B.2.2   Connection Pooling and Reusing Prepared Statements

Connection pooling provides the ability to recycle connections to a database rather than having to create a new physical connection each time an application calls the method `DataSource.getConnection`. The fact that a connection is being pooled is completely transparent to the application, which uses the connection the same way it always does.

When connection pooling is being done, it is also possible to pool a `PreparedStatement` object so that it can be reused. The JDBC 3.0 API provides a set of properties for the `ConnectionPoolDataSource` interface, which are set by an implementation of the interface. These properties determine the size of the pool and various other aspects of the pool of statements. These properties are not exposed to the user, and statement pooling, like connection pooling, is handled completely behind the scenes.

The only impact of connection and statement pooling on an application is the possibility of improved performance. No API regarding statement pooling was added except for one `DatabaseMetaData` method.

`DatabaseMetaData`

- method indicating whether the DBMS and driver support statement pooling

B.2.3   Retrieval of Parameter Metadata

The ability to retrieve parameter metadata from a given `PreparedStatement` object allows an application to determine the number of parameters and their characteristics.

`ParameterMetaData`

- methods to retrieve parameter count and parameter type

- method to retrieve the parameter mode—IN, OUT, INOUT—and constants to indicate each possible mode

- methods to retrieve information about a parameters that is a number—its scale, its precision, and whether it can be a signed number

- various methods to retrieve other information about a parameter, including whether it can be `null`

PreparedStatement

- method to create a `ParameterMetaData` object

B.2.4 Automatically Generated Keys

Some DBMSs automatically generate a unique key for a row when it is inserted into a table. Later this key can be retrieved and used to identify the row.

Statement

- a method to retrieve automatically generated keys

- additional parameters for the methods `executeUpdate` and `execute` that signal the driver to make automatically generated keys available for retrieval

DatabaseMetaData

- a method to determine whether the driver supports retrieving automatically generated keys

B.2.5 Ability to Have Multiple Open ResultSet Objects

When the method `execute` is called on a stored procedure, it may return multiple results, consisting of one or more update counts, one or more `ResultSet` objects, or both. Previously, a `ResultSet` object was closed when a new one was returned. With a new version of the method `getMoreResults`, an application can specify whether any currently open `ResultSet` objects should be closed or left open when a new `ResultSet` object is retrieved. Thus, it is now possible to have multiple `ResultSet` objects open at the same time.

Statement

- the method `getMoreResults(int)`, in which the parameter indicates whether to keep the current `ResultSet` object open when another one is retrieved with the method `getMoreResults`

- a set of three constants used to indicate what should happen to current results when new results are retrieved. These constants are used as the parameter for the method `getMoreResults`.

B.2.6   Holdable Cursor Support

Typically, `ResultSet` objects (cursors) are closed when the transaction in which they were created is committed. An application can specify that `ResultSet` objects remain open by using methods and constants added to the JDBC 3.0 API.

Connection

- methods to create `Statement`, `PreparedStatement`, and `CallableStatement` objects that will produce `ResultSet` objects with holdable cursors
- methods to get and set the holdability of `ResultSet` objects produced by statements created using the connection

ResultSet

- constants to indicate whether `ResultSet` objects should be closed or kept open after the method `commit` is called

DatabaseMetaData

- a method returning the default holdability of `ResultSet` objects returned by the DBMS

B.2.7   New Updating Capabilities

Various new methods add updating capabilities.

Blob

- methods for modifying the contents of `Blob` objects

Clob

- methods for modifying the contents of `Clob` objects

ResultSet

- methods for updating `Array`, `Blob`, `Clob`, and `Ref` objects

B.2.8   New Data Types

The JDBC 3.0 API added two new SQL99 data types and also added methods for retrieving, reading, writing, and setting a `java.net.URL` object (the mapping of an SQL `DATALINK` value to the Java programming language).

Types
- BOOLEAN
- DATALINK

ResultSet
- methods for retrieving a URL object

CallableStatement
- methods for retrieving a URL object
- methods for setting a URL object

PreparedStatement
- methods for setting a URL object

SQLInput
- method for reading a URL object

SQLOutput
- method for writing a URL object

B.3   Complete List of JDBC 3.0 API Changes

The following section give a complete listing of all of the API added in the JDBC 3.0 API. New interfaces are listed first in alphabetical order; interfaces with new methods or fields are listed next in alphabetical order.

B.3.1   New Interfaces

Two new interfaces were added to the JDBC 3.0 API. The following lists include each interface's methods followed by its fields.

ParameterMetaData
```
getParameterClassName(int param)
getParameterCount()
getParameterMode(int param)
```

```
getParameterType(int param)
getParameterTypeName(int param)
getPrecision(int param)
getScale(int param)
isNullable(int param)
isSigned(int param)

parameterModeIn
parameterModeInOut
parameterModeUnknown
parameterNoNulls
parameterNullable
parameterNullableUnknown
```

Savepoint

```
getSavepointId()
getSavepointName()
```

B.3.2 New Methods and Fields

The following API changes in the JDBC 3.0 are methods and fields added to existing interfaces.

Blob

```
setBinaryStream(long pos)
setBytes(long pos, byte[] bytes)
setBytes(long pos, byte[] bytes, int offset, int len)
truncate(long len)
```

Clob

```
setAsciiStream(long pos)
setCharacterStream(long pos)
setString(long pos, String str)
setString(long pos, String str, int offset, int len)
truncate(long len)
```

CallableStatement

```
getArray(String parameterName)
getBigDecimal(String parameterName)
getBlob(String parameterName)
getBoolean(String parameterName)
getByte(String parameterName)
getBytes(String parameterName)
getClob(String parameterName)
getDate(String parameterName)
getDate(String parameterName, Calendar cal)
getDouble(String parameterName)
```

```
getFloat(String parameterName)
getInt(String parameterName)
getLong(String parameterName)
getObject(String parameterName)
getObject(String parameterName, java.util.Map map)
getRef(String parameterName)
getShort(String parameterName)
getString(String parameterName)
getTime(String parameterName)
getTime(String parameterName. Calendar cal)
getTimestamp(String parameterName)
getTimestamp(String parameterName. Calendar cal)
getURL(int parameterIndex)
getURL(String parameterName)
registerOutParameter(String parameterName, int sqlType)
registerOutParameter(String parameterName, int sqlType, int
    scale)
registerOutParameter(String parameterName, int sqlType, String
    typeName)
setAsciiStream(String parameterName, java.io.InputStream x, int
    length)
setBinaryStream(String parameterName, java.io.InputStream x,
    int length)
setBigDecimal(String parameterName, BigDecimal x)
setBoolean(String parameterName, boolean x)
setByte(String parameterName, byte x)
setBytes(String parameterName byte [] x)
setCharacterStream(String parameterName, java.io.Reader reader,
    int length)
setDate(String parameterName, java.sql.Date x)
setDate(String parameterName, java.sql.Date x, Calendar cal)
setDouble(String parameterName, double x)
setFloat(String parameterName, float x)
setInt(String parameterName, int x)
setLong(String parameterName, long x)
setNull(String parameterName, int sqlType)
setNull(String parameterName, int sqlType, String typeName)
setObject(String parameterName, Object x)
setObject(String parameterName, Object x, int targetSqlType)
setObject(String parameterName, Object x, int targetSqlType,
    int scale)
setShort(String parameterName, short x)
setString(String parameterName, String x)
setTime(String parameterName, java.sql.Time x)
setTime(String parameterName. java.sql.Time x, Calendar cal)
setTimestamp(String parameterName, java.sql.Timestamp x)
setTimestamp(String parameterName. java.sql.Timestamp x, Calen-
    dar cal)
setURL(int parameterIndex, java.net.URL x)
```

Connection

```
createStatement(int resultSetType, int resultSetConcurrency,
    int resultSetHoldability)
getHoldability()
prepareCall(String sql, int resultSetType, int resultSetConcur-
    rency, int resultSetHoldability)
prepareStatement(String sql, int autoGenerateddKeys)
prepareStatement(String sql, int [] columnIndexes)
prepareStatement(String sql, int resultSetType, int resultSet-
    Concurrency, int resultSetHoldability)
prepareStatement(String sql, String [] columnNames)
releaseSavepoint(Savepoint savepoint)
rollback(Savepoint savepoint)
setHoldability(int holdability)
setSavepoint()
setSavepoint(String name)
```

DatabaseMetaData

```
getAttributes(String catalog, String schemaPattern, String
    typeNamePattern, String attributeNamePattern)
getDatabaseMajorVersion()
getDatabaseMinorVersion()
getJDBCMajorVersion()
getJDBCMinorVersion()
getResultSetHoldability()
getSQLStateType()
getSuperTables(String catalog, String schemaPattern, String
    tableNamePattern)
getSuperTypes(String catalog, String schemaPattern, String
    typeNamePattern)
locatorsUpdateCopy()
supportsGetGeneratedKeys()
supportsMultipleOpenResults()
supportsNamedParameters()
supportsResultSetHoldability(int holdability)
supportsSavepoints()
supportsStatementPooling()

attributeNoNulls
attributeNullable
attributeNullableUnknown
sqlStateSQL99
sqlStateXOpen
```

PreparedStatement

```
getParameterMetaData()
setURL()
```

Ref

```
getObject()
getObject(java.util.Map map)
setObject(Object value)
```

ResultSet

```
getURL(int columnIndex)
getURL(String columnName)
updateArray(int columnIndex, Array x)
updateArray(String columnName, Array x)
updateBlob(int columnIndex, Blob x)
updateBlob(String columnName, Blob x)
updateClob(int columnIndex, Clob x)
updateClob(String columnName, Clob x)
updateRef(int columnIndex, Ref x)
updateRef(String columnName, Ref x)

CLOSE_CURSORS_AT_COMMIT
HOLD_CURSORS_OVER_COMMIT
```

SQLInput

```
readURL()
```

SQLOutput

```
writeURL(java.net.URL value)
```

Statement

```
execute(String sql, int autoGeneratedKeys)
execute(String sql, int [] columnIndexes)
execute(String sql, String [] columnNames)
executeUpdate(String sql, int autoGeneratedKeys)
executeUpdate(String sql, int [] columnIndexes)
executeUpdate(String sql, String [] columnNames)
getGeneratedKeys()
getMoreResults(int current)
getResultSetHoldability()

CLOSE_ALL_RESULTS
CLOSE_CURRENT_RESULT
EXECUTE_FAILED
KEEP_CURRENT_RESULT
NO_GENERATED_KEYS
RETURN_GENERATED_KEYS
SUCCESS_NO_INFO
```

Types

```
BOOLEAN
DATALINK
```

B.4   Overview of JDBC 2.0 Core API Changes

The JDBC 2.0 core API includes the JDBC 1.0 API and adds enhancements and new functionality to it. These additions put the Java programming language at the forefront of database computing, providing both universal data access and improved performance. The JDBC 2.1 core API, which in the terminology of this book is included in the JDBC 2.0 core API, adds two changes:

1. A driver may continue processing all commands in a batch after an exception is thrown. See page 307 and page 965 for details.

2. A driver no longer has to support the CASCADE and RESTRICT options of the SQL command DROP TABLE (see page 1103 for details).

Applications that use earlier versions of the JDBC API can be run using the Java 2 platform with no problem, in keeping with the goal of backward compatibility. (See section B.9.1 on page 1156 for the special case of what is needed for applications that use java.lang.Bignum instead of java.math.BigDecimal.) However, an application that takes advantage of 2.0 features must be run with a driver that implements those features.

The new features in the JDBC 2.0 core API fall into two broad categories: support for new functionality and support for the SQL99 data types.

1. Support for new functionality

   - scrollable result sets

   - batch updates

   - programmatic inserts, deletes, and updates

   - other

     • performance hints

     • character streams for streams of internationalized Unicode characters

- full precision for `java.math.BigDecimal` values
- support for time zones in `Date`, `Time`, and `Timestamp` values

2. Support for advanced data types

- new SQL data types (SQL99 data types)
- increased support for storing persistent objects in the Java programming language

In addition to making the retrieval, storage, and manipulation of data more convenient, the new features make JDBC applications more efficient. For example, batch updates can increase performance dramatically. The new interfaces `Blob`, `Clob`, and `Array` allow applications to operate on large amounts of data without having to materialize the data on the client, which can mean a significant savings in transfer time and the amount of memory needed. Also, new methods for setting the fetch size and fetch direction let a programmer fine tune an application for more efficient data retrieval and processing.

B.5   Summary of New Functionality

2.0

The JDBC 2.0 core API added important new functionality. The following sections briefly explain each new area of functionality and summarize the supporting API.

B.5.1   Scrollable Result Sets

Scrollable result sets provide the ability to move the cursor forward and backward to a specified position or to a position relative to the current position. The following interfaces have new methods that support scrollable result sets.

ResultSet

- methods for moving the cursor to a particular row or to a relative position (either forward or backward)
- methods for ascertaining the current position of the cursor
- constants indicating the scrollability of a result set

Connection

- new versions of the methods for creating `Statement`, `PreparedState-`

ment, and `CallableStatement` objects that make the result sets they produce scrollable

DatabaseMetaData

- method indicating whether the DBMS and driver support scrollable result sets

B.5.2 Batch Updates

The new batch update facility provides the ability to send multiple updates to the database to be executed as a batch rather than sending each update separately. The following interfaces add methods that support batch updates, and the exception `BatchUpdateException` is new.

Statement, PreparedStatement, and CallableStatement

- methods for adding update statements to a batch, clearing all update statements, and executing a batch. The driver may optionally continue processing the remaining commands in a batch after an error occurs.

DatabaseMetaData

- method indicating whether the DBMS and driver support batch updates

BatchUpdateException

- exception thrown when an error occurs in a batch update

B.5.3 Programmatic Updates

Programmatic updates provide the ability to make updates using the JDBC API rather than SQL statements. The following interfaces have new methods and constants that support programmatic updates.

ResultSet

- an updater method for updating each data type
- methods for inserting, deleting, or updating a row
- methods indicating whether a row was inserted, deleted, or updated
- method for cancelling a row update
- constants indicating the updatability of a result set

DatabaseMetaData
- methods indicating the visibility of changes to a result set
- methods indicating whether a result set detects inserts, deletes, or updates
- method indicating whether the DBMS and driver support updatable result sets

B.5.4 Other New Features

The JDBC 2.0 core API provides various other new features, which are summarized in the following list.

- Performance enhancements: New methods that allow a programmer to fine tune the retrieval of rows from the database. These methods provide the ability to specify (1) the number of result set rows fetched from the database when more rows are needed and (2) the direction in which rows are fetched from the database.

  - `ResultSet` methods for getting and setting the current fetch size and fetch direction
  - `Statement`, `PreparedStatement`, and `CallableStatement` methods for getting and setting the default fetch size and default fetch direction that result sets generated by executing a query will have when they are first created

- Character streams: New methods that allow character data to be retrieved or sent to the database as a stream of internationalized Unicode characters. These methods replace the deprecated `getUnicodeStream` and `setUnicodeStream` methods.

  - `ResultSet.getCharacterStream`
  - `CallableStatement.getCharacterStream`
  - `PreparedStatement.setCharacterStream`

- Full precision for `java.math.BigDecimal` values: New versions of the methods that retrieve a `java.math.BigDecimal` value with full precision. Unlike the deprecated versions they replace, these new versions do not take a specified precision.

- `ResultSet.getBigDecimal`
- `CallableStatement.getBigDecimal`

- Support for time zones: Methods with new versions that take a `Calendar` object as a parameter, which allows the driver to use a specified time zone rather than the default when calculating a value for a date, time, or timestamp

  - `ResultSet.getDate`
  - `ResultSet.getTime`
  - `ResultSet.getTimestamp`
  - `CallableStatement.getDate`
  - `CallableStatement.getTime`
  - `CallableStatement.getTimestamp`
  - `PreparedStatement.setDate`
  - `PreparedStatement.setTime`
  - `PreparedStatement.setTimestamp`

2.0

B.5.5   Support for Advanced Data Types

One of the major changes in the JDBC 2.0 core API is the addition of support for advanced data types, making it as easy to use them as it is to use simple data types. This support includes the ability to store, retrieve, and update even the new SQL data types that are essentially objects, blurring the distinction between object databases and relational databases. The next four sections ("What Are the SQL99 Data Types?," on page 1137, "Summary of Support for the SQL99 Data Types," on page 1138, "Mapping of the New SQL99 Types," on page 1139, and "SQL Locators," on page 1140) describe how the JDBC 2.0 core API provides support for these advanced data types.

In addition to being able to store objects defined in SQL as values in a database table, programmers writing Java applications can also store objects defined in the Java programming language as values in a database table. The section "Support for Storing Java Objects," on page 1140, describes this capability.

Note that a driver is not required to implement functionality that its DBMS does not support, so not all drivers necessarily implement the functionality described here. DatabaseMetaData methods such as getTypeInfo, getColumns, and getUDTs may be called to get information about which data types a driver supports.

B.5.6   What Are the SQL99 Data Types?

This section briefly describes the new SQL99 data types. Their mapping to types in the Java programming language is described in section B.5.8 on page 1139.

The SQL99 data types can be categorized as follows:

- New built-in types: Types for storing large objects. These are in addition to the standard built-in data types, such as CHAR, FLOAT, DATE, and so on.
  - BLOB (Binary Large Object)
  - CLOB (Character Large Object)

- Constructed types: Types based on a given base type
  - REF(*structured type*): A reference to the specified SQL structured type
  - ARRAY[n]: An array of n elements that are all one data type

- User-defined types (UDTs): New types created with the SQL command CREATE TYPE
  - Distinct type: A new type based on the representation of a single built-in type
  - Structured type: A new type containing multiple attributes, each of which may be either a built-in or a user-defined data type

- Locator types: Types that are logical pointers to data that resides on the database server
  - LOCATOR(<structured type>)
  - LOCATOR(array)
  - LOCATOR(blob)
  - LOCATOR(clob)

B.5.7   Summary of Support for the SQL99 Data Types

The JDBC 2.0 core API supports the new SQL99 data types by means of the following new interfaces, methods, and fields.

- New interfaces for the new data types. The SQL99 types are mapped by the following new JDBC 2.0 core API interfaces:

  - `java.sql.Array`
  - `java.sql.Blob`
  - `java.sql.Clob`
  - `java.sql.Ref`
  - `java.sql.Struct`

- New interfaces that support customizing the mapping of UDTs (SQL structured and distinct types) into classes in the Java programming language

  - `SQLData`
  - `SQLInput`
  - `SQLOutput`

- New methods added to existing interfaces in order to retrieve, store, and update the new SQL99 types

  - new getter methods in the `ResultSet` interface to retrieve SQL99 type column values from a result set
  - new getter methods in the `CallableStatement` interface to retrieve SQL99 type values in output parameters
  - new setter methods in the `PreparedStatement` interface to set a SQL99 type column value
  - new updater methods in the `ResultSet` interface to update values programmatically

- New methods in the `DatabaseMetaData` and `ResultSetMetaData` interfaces for getting metadata about the new data types

- New fields (constants) added to the class `java.sql.Types` to support the new data types and persistent storage

- DISTINCT
- STRUCT
- ARRAY
- BLOB
- CLOB
- REF
- JAVA_OBJECT

B.5.8   Mapping of the New SQL99 Types

The JDBC API does not try to replicate the SQL99 types exactly; rather, its goal is to map them to types in the Java programming language so that they retain their functionality and are convenient to use. For example, SQL99 has what are called *locator types*, which are used on a client to designate data that is stored on a database server. Locators can be very useful for working with data that is large because they allow the data to be manipulated without having to be materialized on the client machine. SQL99 includes locators for the types ARRAY, BLOB, CLOB and structured types. The JDBC API does not include locators for these types directly (and not at all for structured types) but rather provides interfaces that are implemented such that the driver and DBMS use the appropriate locators behind the scenes. The result is that a developer using the JDBC API to access an SQL ARRAY, BLOB, or CLOB value need not even be aware of locators. See section B.5.9 on page 1140 for more information about locators.

In the JDBC API, the following SQL99 types are mapped to interfaces in the Java programming language:

- ARRAY: Mapped to `java.sql.Array`
- BLOB: Mapped to `java.sql.Blob`
- CLOB: Mapped to `java.sql.Clob`
- REF: Mapped to `java.sql.Ref`
- An SQL structured type: Mapped to `java.sql.Struct`

Distinct types are not mapped to an interface because they are based on a single built-in type and thus can simply be mapped to the standard mapping for that built-in type. For example, the following is an SQL statement that creates the new type MONEY.

```
CREATE TYPE MONEY AS NUMERIC(10, 2)
```

This new UDT is based on the data type NUMERIC, which maps to java.math.Big-Decimal, so the type MONEY maps to java.math.BigDecimal. This means that a value of type MONEY would be retrieved with the method getBigDecimal, stored with the method setBigDecimal, and updated with the method updateBigDecimal. Chapter 19, "Distinct Types," on page 599, has more information and examples.

B.5.9   SQL Locators

An SQL LOCATOR is a logical pointer to data that resides on a database server. It typically refers to data that is too large to materialize on the client, such as images or audio. Locators exist only in a client environment, and their existence is transient. A standard implementation of the JDBC 2.0 API will use locators internally for instances of the Blob, Clob, and Array interfaces. This means that Blob, Clob, and Array objects contain a locator that points to the data on the server rather than containing the data itself. Programmers operating on Blob, Clob, and Array instances are actually operating on the database objects they represent. This ability to operate on large database objects without bringing their data to the client is a major plus in performance.

Note that the JDBC 2.0 API does not call for using the SQL LOCATOR(*<structured type>*). In a standard implementation, a Struct object contains the data of the structured type that it maps and is not implemented internally as a locator, as are Blob, Clob, and Array objects.

B.5.10 Support for Storing Java Objects

The JDBC API has always supported persistent storage of objects defined in the Java programming language through the methods getObject and setObject. But, of course, persistent storage of Java objects does not actually occur unless a DBMS also supports it. Up to this point, support was limited, but a new generation of DBMSs that recognize Java objects as a data type is emerging. In these DBMSs, termed Java relational DBMSs, an instance of a Java class can be stored as a column value in a database table.

The particular mechanism a DBMS uses to store objects defined in the Java programming language is left up to database vendors. One option is to store instances of Java classes as serialized Java objects, in which case references between objects can be treated according to the rules specified by Java object serialization. A DBMS is free, however, to use its own vendor-specific format.

New metadata methods in the JDBC 2.0 API make it easier for drivers to implement persistence for Java object types. These methods return descriptions of the Java objects that a data source contains, using the new type code `java.sql.Types.JAVA_OBJECT`. For example, the `DatabaseMetaData.getUDTs` method returns descriptions of the user-defined types, one of which is `JAVA_OBJECT`, that a specified schema contains.

In addition to making the retrieval, storage, and manipulation of data more convenient, the new features make JDBC applications more efficient. For example, batch updates can increase performance dramatically. The new interfaces `Blob`, `Clob`, and `Array` allow applications to operate on large amounts of data without having to materialize the data on the client, which can mean a significant savings in transfer time and the amount of memory needed. Also, new methods for setting the fetch size and fetch direction let a programmer fine tune an application for more efficient data retrieval and processing.

B.6   JDBC 2.0 Core API Changes

This section lists all of the new API in the JDBC 2.0 core API plus all of the deprecations.

- New methods and fields added to existing interfaces and classes are listed in section B.6.2 on page 1142.

- Deprecated methods and constructors, as well as the new methods and constructors to use in their place, are listed in section B.6.3 on page 1146.

- New interfaces, including their methods and fields, plus one new exception, are listed in section B.6.4 on page 1148.

B.6.1   What Did Not Change in the JDBC 2.0 API

First, here is the smallest list, a list of what did *not* change. As the brevity of this section suggests, very little in the `java.sql` package is unaffected by the new JDBC 2.0 core API. The existing exception classes had no modifications, but one exception class was added (listed in section B.6.4 on page 1148).

The classes `Date`, `Time`, and `Timestamp` were not changed substantively; their changes consist of the deprecation of constructors and of methods for accessing components that should not be accessed. Note, however, that `ResultSet` and `Call-ableStatement` methods for retrieving them have new versions that take a `java.util.Calendar` object that makes it possible to specify a time zone to use in computing a date, time, or timestamp. The `PreparedStatement` setter methods for storing `Date`, `Time`, and `Timestamp` objects likewise have new versions that take a `java.util.Calendar` object.

Exceptions with no changes:

```
java.sql.DataTruncation
java.sql.SQLException
java.sql.SQLWarning
```

Classes with no changes:

```
java.sql.DriverPropertyInfo
```

Interfaces with no changes:

```
java.sql.Driver
```

B.6.2   Additions to Existing Interfaces and Classes

This section lists all of the methods and fields that were added to existing interfaces and classes as part of the JDBC 2.0 core API. Deprecated methods and constructors are listed in section B.6.3 on page 1146.

CallableStatement
```
getArray(int parameterIndex)
getBigDecimal(int parameterIndex)
getBlob(int parameterIndex)
getClob(int parameterIndex)
getDate(int parameterIndex, Calendar cal)
getObject(int parameterIndex)
getRef(int parameterIndex)
getTime(int parameterIndex, java.util.Calendar cal)
```

```
getTimestamp(int parameterIndex, java.util.Calendar cal)
registerOutParameter(int paramIndex, int sqlType, String type-
    Name)
```

Connection

```
createStatement(int resultSetType, int resultSetConcurrency)
getTypeMap()
prepareCall(String sql, int resultSetType, int resultSetConcur-
    rency)
prepareStatement(String sql, int resultSetType, int resultSet-
    Concurrency)
setTypeMap(java.util.Map map)
```

DatabaseMetaData

```
deletesAreDetected(int type)
getConnection()
getUDTs(String catalog, String schemaPattern, String typeName-
    Pattern, int[] types)
insertsAreDetected(int type)
othersDeletesAreVisible (int type)
othersInsertsAreVisible (int type)
othersUpdatesAreVisible (int type)
ownDeletesAreVisible (int type)
ownInsertsAreVisible (int type)
ownUpdatesAreVisible (int type)
supportsBatchUpdates()
supportsResultSetConcurrency(int type, int concurrency)
supportsResultSetType(int type)
updatesAreDetected(int type)
```

The following DatabaseMetaData methods return result sets that may contain new type codes (from the class java.sql.Types) added in the JDBC 2.0 core API:

```
getColumns(String catalog, String schemaPattern, String table-
    NamePattern, String columnNamePattern)
getProcedureColumns(String catalog, String schemaPattern,
    String procedureNamePattern, String columnNamePattern)
getTypeInfo()
getVersionColumns(String catalog, String schema, String table)
getUDTs(String catalog, String schemaPattern, String typeName-
    Pattern, int[] types)
```

DriverManager

```
getLogWriter()
setLogWriter(PrintWriter out)
```

PreparedStatement

```
addBatch()
```

```
getMetaData()
setArray(int parameterIndex, Array x)
setBlob(int parameterIndex, Blob x)
setCharacterStream(int parameterIndex, Reader reader, int
    length)
setClob(int parameterIndex, Clob x)
setDate(int parameterIndex, Date x, java.util.Calendar cal)
setNull(int parameterIndex, int sqlType, String typeName)
setRef(int parameterIndex, Ref x)
setTime(int parameterIndex, Time x, java.util.Calendar cal)
setTimestamp(int parameterIndex, Timestamp x, java.util.Calen-
    dar cal)
```

ResultSet

```
absolute(int row)
afterLast()
beforeFirst()
cancelRowUpdates()
deleteRow()
first()
getArray(int columnIndex)
getArray(String columnName)
getBigDecimal(int columnIndex)
getBigDecimal(String columnName)
getBlob(int columnIndex)
getBlob(String columnName)
getCharacterStream(int columnIndex)
getCharacterStream(String columnName)
getClob(int columnIndex)
getClob(String columnName)
getConcurrency()
getDate(int columnIndex, java.util.Calendar cal)
getDate(String columnName, java.util.Calendar cal)
getFetchDirection()
getFetchSize()
getObject(int columnIndex, java.util.Map map)
getObject(String columnName, java.util.Map map)
getRef(int columnIndex)
getRef(String columnName)
getRow()
getStatement()
getTime(int columnIndex, java.util.Calendar cal)
getTime(String columnName, java.util.Calendar cal)
getTimestamp(int columnIndex, java.util.Calendar cal)
getTimestamp(String columnName, java.util.Calendar cal)
getType()
insertRow()
isAfterLast()
isBeforeFirst()
isFirst()
```

```
isLast()
last()
moveToCurrentRow()
moveToInsertRow()
previous()
refreshRow()
relative(int rows)
rowDeleted()
rowInserted()
rowUpdated()
setFetchDirection(int direction)
setFetchSize(int rows)
updateAsciiStream(int columnIndex, InputStream x, int length)
updateAsciiStream(String columnName, InputStream x, int length)
updateBigDecimal(int columnIndex, BigDecimal x)
updateBigDecimal(String columnName, BigDecimal x)
updateBinaryStream(int columnIndex, InputStream x, int length)
updateBinaryStream(String columnName, InputStream x, int
    length)
updateBoolean(int columnIndex, boolean x)
updateBoolean(String columnName, boolean x)
updateByte(int columnIndex, byte x)
updateByte(String columnName, byte x)
updateBytes(int columnIndex, byte[] x)
updateBytes(String columnName, byte[] x)
updateCharacterStream(int columnIndex, Reader x, int length)
updateCharacterStream(String columnName, Reader x, int length)
updateDate(int columnIndex, Date x)
updateDate(String columnName, Date x)
updateDouble(int columnIndex, double x)
updateDouble(String columnName, double x)
updateFloat(int columnIndex, float x)
updateFloat(String columnName, float x)
updateInt(int columnIndex, int x)
updateInt(String columnName, int x)
updateLong(int columnIndex, long x)
updateLong(String columnName, long x)
updateNull(int columnIndex)
updateNull(String columnName)
updateObject(int columnIndex, Object x)
updateObject(int columnIndex, Object x, int scale)
updateObject(String columnName, Object x)
updateObject(String columnName, Object x, int scale)
updateRow()
updateShort(int columnIndex, short x)
updateShort(String columnName, short x)
updateString(int columnIndex, String x)
updateString(String columnName, String x)
updateTime(int columnIndex, Time x)
updateTime(String columnName, Time x)
```

```
updateTimestamp(int columnIndex, Timestamp x)
updateTimestamp(String columnName, Timestamp x)

CONCUR_READ_ONLY
CONCUR_UPDATABLE
FETCH_FORWARD
FETCH_REVERSE
FETCH_UNKNOWN
TYPE_FORWARD_ONLY
TYPE_SCROLL_INSENSITIVE
TYPE_SCROLL_SENSITIVE
```

ResultSetMetaData

```
getColumnClassName(int column)
```

The following `ResultSetMetaData` methods may return (1) new type codes (from the class `java.sql.Types`) added in the JDBC 2.0 core API or (2) database-specific names for new data types:

```
getColumnType(int columnIndex)
getColumnTypeName(int columnIndex)
```

Statement

```
addBatch(String sql)
clearBatch()
executeBatch()
getConnection()
getFetchDirection()
getFetchSize()
getResultSetConcurrency()
getResultSetType()
setFetchDirection(int direction)
setFetchSize(int rows)
```

Types

```
ARRAY
BLOB
CLOB
DISTINCT
JAVA_OBJECT
REF
STRUCT
```

B.6.3   Deprecated Methods and Constructors

Some of the JDBC 1.0 methods and constructors have been deprecated as a result of changes in the JDK API. The following is a complete list of deprecations in the java.sql package released in the Java 2 platform. If there is a method or constructor to be used instead, it is indicated immediately below the deprecated method or constructor.

CallableStatement

```
getBigDecimal(int parameterIndex, int scale)
    USE INSTEAD: getBigDecimal(int parameterIndex)
```

Date

```
Date(int year, int month, int day)
    USE INSTEAD: Date(long milliseconds)
getHours()
getMinutes()
getSeconds()
setHours(int i)
setMinutes(int i)
setSeconds(int i)
```

DriverManager

```
getLogStream()
    USE INSTEAD: getLogWriter()
setLogStream(PrintStream out)
    USE INSTEAD: setLogWriter(PrintWriter out)
```

PreparedStatement

```
setUnicodeStream(int parameterIndex, InputStream x, int length)
    USE INSTEAD: setCharacterStream(int parameterIndex,
                                    Reader reader, int length)
```

ResultSet

```
getBigDecimal(int columnIndex, int scale)
    USE INSTEAD: getBigDecimal(int columnIndex)
getBigDecimal(String columnName, int scale)
    USE INSTEAD: getBigDecimal(String columnName)
getUnicodeStream(int columnIndex)
    USE INSTEAD: getCharacterStream(int columnIndex)
getUnicodeStream(String columnName)
    USE INSTEAD: getCharacterStream(String columnName)
```

Time

```
getDay()
getMonth()
getYear()
setDate(int i)
setMonth(int i)
setYear(int i)
Time(int hour, int minute, int second)
    USE INSTEAD: Time(long milliseconds)
```

Timestamp

```
Timestamp(int year, int month, int date, int hour, int minute,
                                             int second)
    USE INSTEAD: Timestamp(long milliseconds)
```

B.6.4   New Interfaces, Classes, and Exceptions

This section lists the interfaces, classes, and exceptions added as part of the JDBC 2.0 core API, including their methods, fields, and constructors.

Array

```
getArray()
getArray(long index, int count)
getArray(long index, int count, java.util.Map map)
getArray(java.util.Map map)
getBaseType()
getBaseTypeName()
getResultSet()
getResultSet(long index, int count)
getResultSet(long index, int count, java.util.Map map)
getResultSet(java.util.Map map)
```

BatchUpdateException

```
BatchUpdateException()
BatchUpdateException(int [] updateCounts)
BatchUpdateException(String reason, int [] updateCounts)
BatchUpdateException(String SQLState, String reason,
    int [] updateCounts)
BatchUpdateException(String SQLState, String reason,
    int vendorCode, int [] updateCounts)
getUpdateCounts()
```

Blob

```
getBinaryStream()
getBytes(long pos, int length)
length()
position(Blob pattern, long start)
position(byte[] pattern, long start)
```

Clob

```
getAsciiStream()
getCharacterStream()
getSubString(long pos, int length)
length()
position(Clob searchstr, long start)
position(String searchstr, long start)
```

Ref

getBaseTypeName()

SQLData

getSQLTypeName()
readSQL(SQLInput stream, String typeName)
writeSQL(SQLOutput stream)

SQLInput

readArray()
readAsciiStream()
readBigDecimal()
readBinaryStream()
readBlob()
readBoolean()
readByte()
readBytes()
readCharacterStream()
readClob()
readDate()
readDouble()
readFloat()
readInt()
readLong()
readObject()
readRef()
readShort()
readString()
readTime()
readTimestamp()
wasNull()

SQLOutput

writeArray(Array x)
writeAsciiStream(InputStream x)
writeBigDecimal(BigDecimal x)
writeBinaryStream(InputStream x)
writeBlob(Blob x)
writeBoolean(boolean x)
writeByte(byte x)
writeBytes(byte[] x)
writeCharacterStream(Reader x)
writeClob(Clob x)
writeDate(Date x)
writeDouble(double x)
writeFloat(float x)
writeInt(int x)
writeLong(long x)
writeObject(SQLData x)

```
writeRef(Ref x)
writeShort(short x)
writeString(String x)
writeStruct(Struct x)
writeTime(Time x)
writeTimestamp(Timestamp x)
```

Struct

```
getAttributes()
getAttributes(java.util.Map map)
getSQLTypeName()
```

B.7   JDBC Optional Package Features

The JDBC Optional Package API (the `javax.sql` package) is now part of the JDBC 3.0 API and is included in the J2SE platform download. It is also available separately from the following web site:

```
http://java.sun.com/products/jdbc/download.html
```

This package adds functionality that is especially important for enterprise applications. The JDBC Optional Package API makes it easier to build server-side applications using the Java platform by providing an open architecture that supports connection pooling and distributed transactions that span multiple DBMS servers. It also makes it possible to use JNDI (Java Naming and Directory Interface) to specify data sources. Finally, it adds rowsets, which support the Java-Beans component model.

The JDBC Optional Package API is compatible with other Optional Package APIs, which is why it can work with JNDI and the Java Transaction API (JTA). This compatibility allows for the easy addition of more specialized data access facilities in the future, such as online analytical processing (OLAP), data warehousing, heterogeneous database access, bulk loading, and so on.

The next four sections summarize the main areas of functionality in the JDBC Optional Package API.

B.7.1 JNDI

Using the JNDI API and the new `DataSource` interface, an application does not need to specify a driver name in its code to make a connection to a data source. It can specify a logical name that has been registered with a JNDI naming service and retrieve a `DataSource` object that will get a connection to the desired data source. This capability makes code more portable and much easier to maintain.

B.7.2 Connection Pooling

Connection pooling allows an application to (re)use database connections that have already been established instead of always having to create new connections. Because creating and destroying database connections is expensive, this feature is important for good performance, especially for server applications.

The JDBC 2.0 Optional Package API provides hooks that allow connection pooling to be implemented on top of the JDBC driver layer. This makes it possible to have a single cache of connections available for all of the JDBC drivers in use.

B.7.3 Support for Distributed Transactions

The JDBC 2.0 Optional Package API allows a JDBC driver to support the standard two-phase commit protocol defined in the Java Transaction API (JTA). This means that a transaction may be distributed over multiple servers, which lets developers write Enterprise JavaBeans components that are transactional across multiple DBMS servers.

B.7.4 Rowsets

`RowSet` objects are containers for tabular data that can be implemented on top of JDBC. Rowsets make it possible to pass rows of data across a network, so they are likely to be used extensively in distributed applications. Rowsets may be very lean by being disconnected from a data source, making it possible to display data on a thin client. They also make it possible to use scrolling when the underlying DBMS does not support scrollable result sets. A rowset is a JavaBeans component and consequently is easy to use in building an application, especially with a development tool.

Typically, a third party will provide a `RowSet` implementation, and the application programmer just uses it. The API for a `RowSet` implementation is generally very easy to use because most of a rowset's functionality is inherited from the

ResultSet interface. The more complicated aspects of a rowset take place internally and are invisible to the application programmer.

The J2SE platform, version 1.5 will include five standard implementations of the RowSet interface. These implementations were developed jointly with various industry leaders through the Java Community Process as JSR 114. For more information, see

```
http://jcp.org/en/introduction/overview
http://jcp.org/en/jsr/detail?id=114
```

The RowSet chapter devotes a section to each of the following implementations:

- JDBCRowSet
- CachedRowSet
- WebRowSet
- FilteredRowSet
- JoinRowSet

B.8   Complete List of Optional Package API

This section lists the classes and interfaces in the javax.sql package in bold type, with their methods and/or constructors listed beneath them. Only ConnectionEvent and RowSetEvent are classes; all the rest are interfaces.

ConnectionEvent

```
ConnectionEvent(PooledConnection con)
ConnectionEvent(PooledConnection con, java.sql.SQLException ex)
getSQLException()
```

ConnectionEventListener

```
connectionClosed(ConnectionEvent event)
connectionErrorOccurred(ConnectionEvent event)
```

ConnectionPoolDataSource

```
getLoginTimeout()
getLogWriter()
getPooledConnection()
getPooledConnection(java.lang.String user, java.lang.String
                                              password)
setLoginTimeout(int seconds)
```

```
    setLogWriter(java.io.PrintWriter out)
```

DataSource

```
    getConnection()
    getConnection(java.lang.String user, java.lang.String password)
    getLoginTimeout()
    getLogWriter()
    setLoginTimeout(int seconds)
    setLogWriter(java.io.PrintWriter out)
```

PooledConnection

```
    addConnectionEventListener(ConnectionEventListener listener)
    close()
    getConnection()
    removeConnectionEventListener(ConnectionEventListener listener)
```

RowSet

```
    addRowSetListener(RowSetListener listener)
    clearParameters()
    execute()
    getCommand()
    getDataSourceName()
    getEscapeProcessing()
    getMaxFieldSize()
    getMaxRows()
    getPassword()
    getQueryTimeout()
    getTransactionIsolation()
    getTypeMap()
    getUrl()
    getUsername()
    isReadOnly()
    removeRowSetListener(RowSetListener listener)
    setArray(int parameterIndex, java.sql.Array x)
    setAsciiStream(int parameterIndex, java.io.InputStream x)
    setBigDecimal(int parameterIndex, java.math.BigDecimal x)
    setBinaryStream(int parameterIndex, java.io.InputStream x)
    setBlob(int parameterIndex, java.sql.Blob x)
    setBoolean(int parameterIndex, boolean x)
    setByte(int parameterIndex, byte x)
    setBytes(int parameterIndex, byte[] x)
    setCharacterStream(int parameterIndex, java.io.Reader reader)
    setClob(int parameterIndex, java.sql.Clob x)
    setCommand(java.lang.String cmd)
    setConcurrency(int concurrency)
    setDataSourceName(java.lang.String name)
    setDate(int parameterIndex, java.sql.Date x)
    setDate(int parameterIndex, java.sql.Date x,
                                        java.util.Calendar cal)
    setDouble(int parameterIndex, double x)
```

```
setEscapeProcessing(boolean enable)
setFloat(int parameterIndex, float x)
setInt(int parameterIndex, int x)
setLong(int parameterIndex, long x)
setMaxFieldSize(int max)
setMaxRows(int max)
setNull(int parameterIndex, int jdbcType)
setNull(int parameterIndex, int jdbcType,
                              java.lang.String typeName)
setObject(int parameterIndex, java.lang.Object x)
setObject(int parameterIndex, java.lang.Object x,
                                   int targetSqlType)
setObject(int parameterIndex, java.lang.Object x,
                             int targetSqlType. int scale)
setPassword(java.lang.String password)
setQueryTimeout(int seconds)
setReadOnly(boolean value)
setRef(int parameterIndex, java.sql.Ref x)
setShort(int parameterIndex, short x)
setString(int parameterIndex, java.lang.String x)
setTime(int parameterIndex, java.sql.Time x)
setTime(int parameterIndex, java.sql.Time x,
                              java.util.Calendar cal)
setTimestamp(int parameterIndex, java.sql.Timestamp x)
setTimestamp(int parameterIndex, java.sql.Timestamp x,
                              java.util.Calendar cal)
setTransactionIsolation(int level)
setType(int type)
setTypeMap(java.util.Map map)
setUrl(java.lang.String url)
setUsername(java.lang.String name)
```

RowSetEvent

```
RowSetEvent(RowSet source)
```

RowSetInternal

```
getConnection()
getOriginal()
getOriginalRow()
getParams()
setMetaData(RowSetMetaData md)
```

RowSetListener

```
cursorMoved(RowSetEvent event)
rowChanged(RowSetEvent event)
rowSetChanged(RowSetEvent event)
```

RowSetMetaData

```
setAutoIncrement(int columnIndex, boolean property)
```

```
        setCaseSensitive(int columnIndex, boolean property)
        setCatalogName(int columnIndex, java.lang.String catalogName)
        setColumnCount(int columnCount)
        setColumnDisplaySize(int columnIndex, int size)
        setColumnLabel(int columnIndex, java.lang.String label)
        setColumnName(int columnIndex, java.lang.String columnName)
        setColumnType(int columnIndex, int sqlType)
        setColumnTypeName(int columnIndex, java.lang.String typeName)
        setCurrency(int columnIndex, boolean property)
        setNullable(int columnIndex, int property)
        setPrecision(int columnIndex, int precision)
        setScale(int columnIndex, int scale)
        setSchemaName(int columnIndex, java.lang.String schemaName)
        setSearchable(int columnIndex, boolean property)
        setSigned(int columnIndex, boolean property)
        setTableName(int columnIndex, java.lang.String tableName)
```

RowSetReader

```
        readData(RowSetInternal caller)
```

RowSetWriter

```
        writeData(RowSetInternal caller)
```

XAConnection

```
        getXAResource()
```

XADataSource

```
        getLoginTimeout()
        getLogWriter()
        getXAConnection()
        getXAConnection(java.lang.String username,
                                        java.lang.String password)
        setLoginTimeout(int seconds)
        setLogWriter(java.io.PrintWriter out)
```

B.9   Post JDBC 1.0 API Changes

Every effort was made not to change anything after the JDBC 1.0 specification was finalized, but two modifications became unavoidable. The first was made necessary by a change in the Java API; the second had repeatedly been requested by reviewers.

B.9.1   Numeric to Bignum to BigDecimal

The Java API for extended-precision fixed point numbers was changed in an effort to offer the best possible API. That change, however, necessitated some corresponding changes in the JDBC API.

Originally, the JDBC API provided the class `java.sql.Numeric` to handle extended-precision fixed-point numbers, so early specifications used that class. For example, the `ResultSet` and `CallableStatement` getter methods included `getNumeric`, and `PreparedStatement` included the method `setNumeric`.

The JDBC class `java.sql.Numeric` was incorporated into the Java programming language and became `java.lang.Bignum` with the result that `getNumeric` became `getBignum` and `setNumeric` became `setBignum`. The JDBC API version 1.1 used `java.lang.Bignum`; it is the JDBC API version that is compatible with version 1.0.2 of the JDK.

Subsequently, the facilities of `java.lang.Bignum` were divided up into the two classes, `java.math.BigDecimal` and `java.math.BigInteger`. The class `java.math.BigInteger` deals with the security-oriented integer operations, and since neither the JDBC API nor typical drivers or users reference this functionality, `java.math.BigInteger` does not need to appear in the JDBC API. The class `java.math.BigDecimal`, on the other hand, replaced those operations of `java.lang.Bignum` that the JDBC API does reference, so it was necessary for `java.math.BigDecimal` to replace `java.lang.Bignum` in the JDBC API. In the JDBC API version 1.2, `getBignum` became `getBigDecimal`, and `setBignum` became `setBigDecimal`. JDK versions 1.1 and later use `java.math.BigDecimal` and `java.math.BigInteger`, so the JDBC API version 1.2 must be used with them to be compatible. Note that the JDBC API version 1.2, part of the JDK1.1 release, does not need to be installed separately.

The JDBC 2.0 core API deprecates methods that specify a scale (the number of digits after the decimal point) for a `java.math.BigDecimal` value, thus no longer limiting its precision. All `java.math.BigDecimal` values should now be returned with full precision whenever possible.

B.9.2   AutoClose Mode Dropped

One of the basic design considerations for JDBC was that simple things be kept simple. Originally, a connection was set up so that in its default mode, statements and cursors would be automatically closed when the statement was committed, thus making it easier for the programmer and also ensuring that statements were properly closed without waiting for the garbage collector.

It became evident, however, that in one particular case, this strategy to keep simple things simple was making life measurably more difficult for sophisticated users. In order to keep a `PreparedStatement` object open so that it could be executed multiple times, `autoClose` mode had to be disabled. Unfortunately, the effects of disabling and then again enabling `autoClose` mode could sometimes get unduly complicated. Consequently, after much prodding from developers and with much reluctance, `autoClose` mode was eventually dropped.

B.10 Early Design Decisions

Although the basic goals of JDBC have remained constant, various API changes were made as the JDBC API was taking shape in its formative stages. This section recounts some early design decisions.

B.10.1 `ResultSet` getter Methods

In the earliest versions, the getter methods took no argument; they simply returned the next column value in left-to-right order. This seemed simpler, but it made the resulting example code difficult to read. It was frequently found necessary to count through the various getter calls in order to match them up with the columns specified in the `SELECT` statement. Using the column number as an argument to the getter methods greatly improved readability.

Then, several developers who were using early specifications requested that they be able to use the name of a column as the argument to the getter methods. This was problematic because it doubled the number of getter methods. Nevertheless, it is often more meaningful and more convenient to use a name rather than a column index, and it is less prone to error. In the final analysis, the ease of using column names won out.

The same arguments in favor of convenience, being more meaningful, and being less prone to error prevailed when the updater methods were added to the `ResultSet` interface in the 2.0 API. The result is that there are also two versions for each updater method.

B.10.2 `PreparedStatement` Methods for Setting Column Values

Initially, there was only one method for setting parameter values: `setParameter`. This method was overloaded with different argument types, and the argument type determined the type to which a parameter was being set. Reviewers found this confusing, particularly in cases where the mapping between SQL types and Java types is ambiguous. So, in the end, each type had its own setter method, as in `setByte`, `setBoolean`, and so on.

B.10.3 `CallableStatement.registerOutParameter` Method

The original designers did not want JDBC to require a `registerOutParameter` method. It was felt that drivers should be able to determine the OUT parameter types from the database metadata or from the setter calls made by the programmer instead of requiring this redundancy. However, the parameter type is required by at least one widely used DBMS before the setter calls are executed, and the performance impact of database metadata calls seemed an excessive penalty to pay for each stored procedure call. Feedback from early reviewers was so convincing that it was decided to require the use of the method `registerOutParameter`.

B.10.4 Support for Large OUT Parameters

Supporting OUT parameters that are very large was considered and eventually decided against. It would probably have consisted of allowing programmers to register `java.io.OutputStreams` into which the JDBC run.time could send the OUT parameter data when a statement executed. This seemed harder to explain than it was worth, given that there is already a mechanism for handling large results as part of a `ResultSet` object.

B.10.5 `isNull` versus `wasNull`

It was difficult to determine a good way of handling the type JDBC NULL. By JDBC 0.50 there was a `ResultSet.isNull` method that seemed fairly pleasant to use. The `isNull` method had the advantage that it could be called on any column to check for NULL before (or after) reading the column.

```
if(!ResultSet.isNull(3)) {
    count += ResultSet.getInt(3);
}
```

Unfortunately, harsh reality intervened, and it emerged that `isNull` could not be implemented reliably on all databases. Some databases have no separate means for determining whether a column is null other than by reading the column, and they would permit reading a given column only once. Reading the column value and "remembering" it for later use was considered, but this caused problems when data conversions were required.

A number of different solutions were examined, but the decision was reluctantly made to replace the `isNull` method with the `wasNull` method. The method `wasNull` merely reports whether the last value read from the given `ResultSet` or `CallableStatement` object was of type JDBC `NULL`.

B.10.6 Java Type Names or JDBC Type Names

Originally, the getter and setter methods used JDBC types. For example, there were `getChar` and `setSmallInt`. Since it is Java programmers who use JDBC, however, it seemed that the meaning of each method would be clearer if the methods used Java types instead. Consequently, `getChar` became `getString`, and `setSmallInt` became `setShort`. Using Java type names also avoids potential confusion in those cases where the local type names used by a DBMS differ from the generic JDBC type names.

B.11 Where to Send Suggestions

Comments and suggestions are appreciated and will be considered carefully. Suggestions for future JDBC directions should be sent to:

    jdbc@sun.com

Constructive suggestions with attention to specifics and implications are likely to receive the closest attention.

Glossary

The terms in this glossary are defined as they are used in connection with databases and JDBC technology. They may have different meanings in other contexts.

Absolute positioning The ability of a cursor to move to a specified row in a result set. The absolute position specified can be the first row, the last row, or the number of any row, such as row number five. The JDBC definition of absolute positioning is modeled on the Open Group (formerly X/Open) SQL CLI specification.

Access error An error caused by the inability to access data in a data source. An access error may be caused by many conditions, including the following: one user trying to access data that has been locked by another user; a user trying to access data without having the proper permissions; a user attempting to violate a key constraint, such as trying to insert a duplicate key; and so on. An access error causes an SQLException to be thrown, and it is the cause of the vast majority of exceptions thrown by methods in the JDBC API.

API Application Programming Interface. When applied to the Java programming language, this is a set of classes and interfaces that specify a particular functionality, for example, the JDBC API.

Applet A Java program that can be downloaded over the network and executed by a browser. Java applets can be contrasted to Java applications, which are loaded from a disk, as are programs in other programming languages.

Attribute A named component of a user-defined type (UDT); a member of an SQL structured type.

Base type In reference to an SQL ARRAY, the data type of the array elements. For example, an array of STRUCT values has a base type of STRUCT.

Batch update A set of multiple update operations submitted to a database as a single unit for processing all at once. In some cases, batch updates may improve performance dramatically.

BLOB Binary Large Object. A contiguous sequence of binary values that may be several megabytes or more in size.

Bytecodes An intermediate form of code in which executable Java programs are represented. This is higher level than machine code, so it runs on multiple platforms; but it is lower level than source code, so it is efficient to move around, execute, or compile into machine code. Calling javac on a .java file produces a .class file, which is the executable consisting of bytecodes. Bytecodes make Java applications portable to any machine using a Java Virtual Machine.

Catalog A name space mechanism for databases, used to keep people from tripping over each other. Database schemas are grouped into catalogs. Each catalog is a separate name space. Some DBMSs map catalog to "database."

Class The Java programming language's basic type mechanism, in which an object contains its data and behavior.

CLOB Character Large Object. A contiguous sequence of character values that may be several megabytes or more in size.

Commit An operation that causes all of the updates made during a transaction to be permanently written into the database, completing the transaction. If a transaction is explicitly or implicitly aborted (rolled back), it is incomplete and all changes made are backed out, as if the transaction never happened. In the JDBC API, the method Connection.commit commits a transaction.

Concurrency The ability of multiple users or programs to share the same database simultaneously. Transactions and locks are used to give each user or program a consistent view of the database. *See also* optimistic concurrency *and* pessimistic concurrency.

Connected A term used to describe a RowSet object that maintains an open database connection as long as it is in use.

Connection A session with a database opened by a JDBC application program, so called because it represents a connection between the program and a (usually remote) database. Only one transaction at a time can be associated with a connection.

Connection pooling A facility whereby physical connections to a data source can be stored and reused. Connection pooling improves performance because it saves the overhead of having to create a new connection every time a connection is requested.

Cursor A mechanism that references the current position in a result set. SQL defines a cursor mechanism that can be used through the JDBC API to do positioned updates and deletes; however, positioned updates and deletes are no longer necessary with the new JDBC 2.0 core API, in which `ResultSet` methods can move the cursor and update or delete a row.

Data source A repository for storing data. A data source can be anything from a local file to a large corporate database on a remote server.

Database A set of data that conforms to a particular schema. In the case of JDBC, the database is generally a set of tables. Often the term *database* is used loosely to refer to the software that stores the database (a DBMS).

Database system A shorter term for database management system (DBMS).

DBMS (DataBase Management System) Software used to manage databases. In a client/server environment, this software runs on a different machine than the database application program. A JDBC driver usually is designed to work with only one DBMS or middleware server.

DDL (Data Definition Language) A subset of SQL commands dealing with database objects. The most common DDL commands are `CREATE TABLE` and `DROP TABLE`.

Deadlock A condition that can occur when two or more users are all waiting for each other to give up locks. More advanced DBMSs do deadlock detection and abort one of the user transactions when this happens.

Dirty read A read of data that is possibly incorrect. A dirty read happens when Transaction A reads data from a database that has been modified by Transaction B, and that data has not yet been committed. If the change is rolled back instead of being committed, Transaction A will have read data that is no longer correct. To avoid dirty reads, one must specify a higher isolation level (possibly resulting in lower performance).

Disconnected A term used to describe a `RowSet` object that is connected to a data source only while it is executing a query or writing data back to the data source. Most of the time it is totally independent of a data source, and it can operate without a driver.

DISTINCT An SQL99 data type that is a user-defined type (UDT) based on an SQL built-in type. A `DISTINCT` type is a new data type, created with the SQL statement `CREATE TYPE` or `CREATE DISTINCT TYPE`. A `DISTINCT` type can be thought of as a structured type that has only one attribute; for a custom mapping, this single attribute is mapped to a field in a class in the Java programming language.

Distributed transaction A transaction in which commands are sent to more than one database server. Determining the boundaries of a distributed transaction and whether or not to commit the transaction is managed by a transaction manager in the middle tier of a distributed application. In an EJB application, the EJB container generally manages a distributed transaction.

Driver A JDBC driver is a Java (or partly Java) software component that implements the driver portion of the JDBC API, that is, all of the API in the `java.sql` and `javax.sql` packages except the rowset APIs. A driver can be loaded using the JDBC `DriverManager` class, or it can be accessed using a `DataSource` object.

Error An error is a problem that is not recoverable. A JDBC error causes an exception to be thrown.

Escape character/syntax Escape characters are special characters that JDBC drivers scan for in SQL strings before passing the SQL on to the underlying DBMS. They are used to delimit special DBMS-independent syntax that the driver must translate into DBMS-specific syntax, generally used where DBMSs are not standardized in the SQL they support.

Finalization An opportunity for an object that is no longer in use to clean up loose ends before the garbage collector deletes it. For example, a `Connection` object must ensure that the underlying DBMS connection is closed before going away.

Foreign key An attribute (or group of attributes) of a table that is used to refer to rows of another table (more precisely, to the primary key of another table). For example, an employee table may contain an attribute that is the employee's department number. The department number is used to look up the correct row of the department table.

Global transaction A transaction in which commands are sent to more than one DBMS server. A synonym for distributed transaction.

HTTP Hypertext Transfer Protocol. The standardized protocol used by browsers to get information for servers over the network.

Index A data structure on disc that allows rows of tables to be found quickly based on the values of one or more attributes. Multiple indexes can be defined on a table or a database, and the SQL processor will pick the best ones to use to execute a query. Without indexes, a DBMS would inefficiently look at every row of a table or tables in order to find the information requested by a query.

Also, the ordinal position of a column or parameter, whichc can be passed to a method to indicate the column or parameter to be acted upon.

Insert row A special row associated with a `ResultSet` object that is used as a staging area for creating the contents of a new row before inserting it into the `ResultSet` object itself.

Interface A data structure that defines methods without defining how they are implemented. Fields defined in an interface must be constants. An interface's methods are implemented by a class that implements the interface. A class can implement multiple interfaces.

Intranet Multiple local area networks (LANs) within one company or group.

Isolation level The level of care taken by a DBMS to keep data consistent. A programmer who uses a database with other concurrent users must choose a compromise between performance and a slightly inconsistent view of data because the other users may be updating data at the same time. Unless a programmer chooses the highest level of isolation (full serializability), his/her programs may see such anomalies as dirty reads or phantom reads.

J2EE The Java 2 Enterprise Edition, one of three Java platforms offered by Sun Microsystems. J2EE provides a server-side platform for heavy duty enterprise computing. EJB components work within a container that manages the "plumbing" for enterprise applications, including security, distributed transactions, and connection pooling.

J2ME The Java 2 Micro Edition, one of three Java platforms offered by Sun Microsystems. J2ME is a platform for thin clients such as smart cards, wireless telephones, PDAs (personal digital assistants), and other small devices.

J2SE The Java 2 Standard Edition, one of three Java platforms offered by Sun Microsystems. The J2SE platform is the core of Java technology, providing the essential compiler, tools, runtimes, and APIs for writing, deploying, and running applets and applications in the Java programming language.

JavaBeans component A reusable software component, typically a GUI object that resides on a client, that can be combined with other components in an application. A JavaBeans component follows certain protocols, which include `get`/`set` methods for properties and an event model with events and listeners. There are many visual development tools that make it easy to put together JavaBeans components to create an application. A `RowSet` object is a JavaBeans component.

JDBC 1.0 API The API (application programming interface) included in the JDK 1.1 release. The book *JDBC Database Access with Java*, the Java Series book by Graham, Cattell, and Fisher, includes only JDBC 1.0 API.

JDBC 2.0 API The JDBC API included in the Java 2 Platform (the `java.sql` package) plus the JDBC Optional Package API (the `javax.sql` package). All of the new API is listed in Appendix B.

JDBC 2.0 Core API The API included in the `java.sql` package. Methods and fields that are new in the JDBC 2.0 core API are indicated with an icon that has the number "2.0" in it. In this book, "JDBC 2.0 core API" is used generically and includes the JDBC 2.1 core API.

JDBC 2.0 Standard Extension API Former name for the JDBC 2.0 Optional Package API (the package `javax.sql`). Methods and fields that are part of the JDBC Optional Package API are indicated with an arrow icon that has the letters "javax" in it.

JDBC 3.0 API The complete JDBC API, which includes the `java.sql` package and the `javax.sql` package. New features and enhancements to existing features that were added to the JDBC 3.0 API are indicated with an icon that has the number "3.0" in it. The JDBC 3.0 API is bundled as part of the J2SE, starting with version 1.4.

JDK Java Development Kit. The software released by Sun Microsystems, Inc. to support the Java environment. The JDK includes the Java compiler and interpreter, and many Java libraries.

JNDI (Java Naming and Directory Interface) An API that provides naming and directory services. In regard to JDBC technology, the JNDI API is used by someone acting in the capacity of a system administrator to register a `Data-`

Source object with a JNDI service provider and associate that `DataSource` object with a logical data source name. An application can then use the JNDI API to retrieve the `DataSource` object and thereafter use normal JDBC calls to make a connection to the data source that the `DataSource` object represents.

Join The basic relational operator that allows data from more than one table to be combined. A join matches rows of two tables based on columns with common values. For example, the employee table may contain a column specifying the department number for each employee. The department number is also a column of the department table. Rows of the employee table can be matched up (joined) with the department table based on these values.

Lock A mechanism for keeping data consistent. Locks allow a database transaction to mark data it is using (for example, rows or tables) in order to exclude a concurrent user from performing certain operations on the same data. There are different kinds of locks; for example, an exclusive (write) lock disallows all other users, while a read lock allows other concurrent readers.

Materialize To physically copy data from the DBMS server to the client. Instances of the data types `Array`, `Blob`, and `Clob` contain a logical pointer to their underlying SQL99 data instead of the data itself. The interfaces `Array`, `Blob`, and `Clob` all have methods for materializing the data from the database values that they designate onto the client.

Metadata Data that describes the kind of functionality a DBMS provides (for example, whether it supports specific SQL features) and the types of data in the database (that is, the database schema).

Method A procedure associated with a class or interface, defining one of the legal operations on instances of the class or interface.

MIS Management Information Services. An MIS department is in charge of the corporate information on computers, such as inventory and payroll, and usually determines which computers (Windows, Solaris, Macintosh, and so on) are used by administrative personnel.

Multithreading Multithreading allows more than one concurrent thread of control within one address space (or Java Virtual Machine). This is useful, for example, when writing a service that responds to requests from multiple client programs on a network. The JDBC API supports multithreading.

Native code Code written in a language other than Java (usually C) and compiled to machine code. Mixing Java and native code in an application requires use of the JNI (Java™ Native Interface) to allow calls from Java to native code. It is generally good to avoid native code in applications because many of the benefits of the Java programming language (for example, machine independence and automatic installation over the network) are lost.

Network protocol The convention for encoding of data and commands over the network between a client and server. HTTP and FTP are protocols. Most DBMSs have a proprietary protocol they have evolved for communicating between clients and their database servers. Two-tier JDBC drivers can speak these protocols directly to the DBMS.

Non-repeatable read Data returned by an SQL query that would be different if the query were repeated within the same transaction. Non-repeatable reads can occur when other users are updating the same data you are reading. They can be avoided by specifying a higher isolation level, in exchange for some performance loss.

Null A data value that is unknown or unspecified. The Java programming language has a distinguished `null` object value, and SQL has a distinguished `NULL` value that represents the absence of an actual value.

ODBC Open Database Connection. An API defined by Microsoft, a derivative of the Open Group CLI API.

Open Group (Formerly X/Open) An international standards organization that promotes the development and production of open standards and that also provides certification for products that conform to open standards. It has defined a database Call-Level Interface (CLI) for C that allows SQL strings to be passed to a DBMS and results to be returned. The JDBC API is based on the Open Group CLI, but with different design goals. (It uses the Java programming language instead of C, focuses more on ease of use, uses object-orientation, and so on.)

Optimistic concurrency A concurrency control mechanism that assumes that there will be few conflicts among users who are accessing the same data in a database. This mechanism avoids using locks and checks to see if there was a conflict between two transactions after a modification is made. If there was a conflict, one of the transactions is aborted to maintain consistency. Optimistic concurrency allows a higher level of concurrency but may be less efficient if there are many conflicts. *See* pessimistic concurrency.

Pessimistic concurrency A concurrency control mechanism that assumes that there will be many conflicts among users who are accessing the same data in a database. This mechanism locks everything before it is touched, allowing only one user at a time to have access to a data item. Pessimistic concurrency limits access, and therefore performance, unnecessarily if there are, in fact, very few conflicts. *See* optimistic concurrency.

Phantom read A read by one user that fetches a tuple that has been inserted by another user's transaction. For example, one user's SELECT statement might select four rows from a table the first time it is executed and five rows the next time if a second user has, in the meantime, inserted a row that satisfies the first user's query.

Positioned update/delete A mechanism to update or delete the row at the current position through an SQL cursor.

Precision In SQL, the total number of digits in a numeric value. For example 243.24 has a precision of 5.

Prepared statement An SQL statement that has been compiled for efficiency. The SQL processor parses and analyzes the query, decides which indexes to use to fetch tuples, and produces an execution plan for the prepared statement.

Primary key An attribute or set of attributes that are unique among rows of a table. A table's primary key is used to refer to rows of the table. For example, an employee ID attribute uniquely identifies the rows (employees) in an employee table.

Protocol A convention for communication between programs. *See* network protocol.

Pseudo column A column that is not actually stored but that appears as an ordinary column in a table to the user or application program.

Pure Java An adjective referring to a program that is written entirely in Java, with no native code.

Query An SQL SELECT statement. Queries return result sets.

RDBMS Relational Database Management System. There is some debate in the database literature about what is truly "relational," but generally a DBMS that supports the SQL standard is considered relational.

Reader An instance of a class that implements the `RowSetReader` interface; part of the reader/writer facility for rowsets. A `RowSet` object may call a reader to read new data and insert it into the rowset.

Record A row of a table or a row of the result set returned by a query.

REF An SQL99 data type that is a reference to an instance of a particular SQL structured type. For example, a `REF(ADDRESS)` would be a reference to an instance of the structured type `ADDRESS`.

Referential integrity Correctness of foreign keys. A DBMS maintains referential integrity by ensuring that for every reference to a table, there exists a row in the referenced table. For example, if employee records refer to department records through a department ID attribute, there should be a valid department record for each employee.

Relation A table, the basic data structure of the relational model.

Relative positioning The ability of a cursor to move a specified number of rows from the current position in a result set. Supplying a positive number to the method `ResultSet.relative` moves the cursor forward the specified number of rows; supplying a negative number moves the cursor backward. The JDBC API definition of relative positioning is modeled on the Open Group SQL CLI specification.

Rollback Undoing the changes made by a transaction. This can be initiated in a JDBC application by explicitly calling the method `Connection.rollback`, and, in some cases, a rollback can be spontaneously generated by the DBMS due to an error or unresolvable deadlock between transactions.

Rowset A software component that implements the `RowSet` interface. The `RowSet` interface is part of the rowset API, which includes the `RowSetEvent` class and the following interfaces: `RowSet`, `RowSetEventListener`, `RowSetReader`, `RowSetWriter`, `RowSetInternal`, and `RowSetMetaData`. A rowset is a container for tabular data. It may be connected to a data source, or it may operate independently. Rowsets are used mainly to pass tabular data between components in distributed applications and to provide scrolling and updating capabilities to a `ResultSet` object when a driver does not provide them.

Runtime exception A Java exception that does not need to be explicitly declared in a method that throws it.

Savepoint A point that can be set within a transaction to mark the point to which a transaction may be rolled back.

Scalar value A single entry in a table, at the intersection of a row and column. Scalar functions operate on scalar values, as opposed to an aggregate of values.

Scale The number of decimal digits after the decimal point in numeric values. For example, the number 123.45678 has a scale of 5.

Schema A description of the tables in a database and their attributes. A schema name, which some DBMSs map to a user, is a way of qualifying a table name within a catalog.

Scrollable result set A result set in which the cursor can move backward (from last row to first row) through a result set as well as move forward (from first row to last row) through it. In addition, the cursor is capable of absolute positioning and relative positioning.

Server A machine providing services of some kind to client machines on the network. In a two-tier approach, a database server is called directly by JDBC drivers on client machines. In a three-tier approach, client programs make calls (through RMI, IIOP, HTTP, or some other protocol) to services on a separate machine, which in turn make JDBC calls to the database server.

SQL A standardized database language for defining database objects and manipulating data. The SQL statements used most frequently are those specifying queries and updates. ANSI X3H2 is the U.S. organization responsible for SQL; ISO is the corresponding international body.

SQL92 The version of SQL standardized by ANSI in 1992. Sometimes called SQL2.

SQL92 entry level A subset of full SQL92 specified by ANSI/ISO that is supported by nearly all major DBMSs today. This subset, unfortunately, is not complete enough to allow portability of nontrivial database applications; in particular, it does not specify a full set of standard data types. JDBC compliance requires entry-level SQL compliance and defines escape syntax and metadata routines for more advanced features.

SQL92 intermediate level A subset of full SQL92 specified by ANSI/ISO that contains more functionality than SQL92. Hopefully most DBMSs will support this soon.

SQL99 The next version of the ANSI SQL Standard. SQL99 follows SQL92 and includes new functionality and new data types. SQL99 is also referred to as SQL3.

SQLJ A set of standards that includes specifications for embedding SQL statements in methods in the Java programming language and specifications for calling Java static methods as SQL stored procedures and user-defined functions. For more information on SQLJ, see `http://www.sqlj.org`.

Static method A method that is associated with a class rather than operating on a specific instance of the class. A static method in the Java programming language may be installed as a stored procedure in DBMSs that conform to the SQLJ specification for stored procedures.

Stored procedure A mechanism for writing programming-language-style procedures with arguments and procedural code that are stored in and executed in the DBMS server. Stored procedures are called similar to the way methods are called.

Structured type A user-defined type that may have multiple attributes. The attributes may be any data type, and an attribute may even be a structured type itself. In a custom mapping, each attribute is mapped to a field in a class in the Java programming language.

Synchronized An attribute of a Java method that provides concurrency control among multiple threads sharing an object by locking the object during execution of the method.

Three-tier JDBC driver A driver that implements the JDBC API by making calls to a "middle-tier" server that translates the calls into DBMS-specific protocols and makes the calls to the DBMS server.

Transaction A sequence of SQL/JDBC calls that constitute an atomic unit of work: Either all of the commands in a transaction are committed as a unit, or all of the commands are rolled back as a unit. Transactions provide ACID properties: atomicity, consistency, integrity of data, and durability of database changes. *See* commit and rollback. A transaction in which commands are sent to more than one DBMS server is a distributed transaction. *See* destributed transaction.

Tuple A row of a table.

Two-tier JDBC driver A JDBC driver that translates JDBC calls directly into a DBMS vendor's on-the-wire protocol. Ideally, a two-tier driver is all-Java, but for the short term many include native code from existing client-side DBMS libraries.

UDT User-defined type. In reference to the JDBC API, there are two kinds of UDTs: an SQL DISTINCT type and an SQL structured type. A UDT is a new data type that a user defines with an SQL command, usually CREATE TYPE or CREATE TYPE AS. After it is defined, a UDT may be used as the data type for a column in a table.

Underlying type When used in relation to DISTINCT types, the data type on which a DISTINCT type is based. For example, if a DISTINCT type is defined to be a CHAR(10), the underlying type is CHAR.

Unicode A character encoding used in Java strings to support multiple language character sets.

URL Universal Resource Locator. First used on the World Wide Web to identify HTML documents. A specialized form of URL is used in JDBC technology to identify databases and drivers.

Warning An exceptional condition that does not interrupt execution of an application program, such as truncation of data values. The JDBC API provides getWarnings methods on various interfaces to obtain this information.

Writer An instance of a class that implements the RowSetWriter interface; part of the rowset reader/writer facility. When a disconnected rowset has been changed, it may call a writer to write the changes to the data source backing the rowset.

X/Open CLI X/Open Call Level Interface. *See* Open Group.

Index

NOTE: If a letter follows a page number:
T = Tutorial Section
tb = Table

A

aborting

See also errors; exceptions

transactions, with `rollback` method
(`Connection` interface) 76T

absolute method (`ResultSet` interface)

argument, positive or negative 120T

absolute positioning

definition, glossary 1161

effect of deleting rows on 718

example of 710

Abstract Window Toolkit

See `java.awt` package

acceptsURL method (`Driver` interface) 606

access

See also retrieving

conflicts,

avoiding with locks 75T

transaction isolation level as
mechanism for managing 393

data,

dynamic 1084

in a relational table 59T

dirty read avoidance 75T

restrictions, monitored by bytecode
verifier 36

rows, with `next` method 65T

specifiers, `protected` 30

transaction isolation level value 75T

two-tier model compared with three-tier
model 18

warnings, handling 84T

access error

definition, glossary 1161

defintion in context 7

active connection instance

required to create `Statement` objects 57T

addBatch method (`Statement` interface)
962, 973

**addConnectionEventListener method
(`PooledConnection` interface) 644**

adding

rows, INSERT use for 43

**addRowSetListener method (`RowSet`
interface) 825**

ADO API

JDBC comparison with 18

after method (`Timestamp` class) 1027

afterLast method (`ResultSet` interface)

method explanation 694

use with `ResultSet.previous` method
119T

**allProceduresAreCallable method
(`DatabaseMetaData` interface) 466**

**allTablesAreSelectable method
(`DatabaseMetaData` interface) 467**

ALTER TABLE

as DDL command, purpose 44

ANSI SQL92 Entry Level

as JDBC Compliant requirement 21

API (Application Programming Interface)

definition, glossary 1161

high-level, planned for JDBC 15

JDBC as Java, for executing SQL
statements 13

applets

See also URL (Uniform Resource
Locator)s

appletviewer use 102T

creating, from an application 99T

definition, glossary 1161

displaying the content of 101T

finalize methods, suggested for driver
implementations 1114

`java.applet` package handling of 35

security in 941

H

I

J

The Java™ Series

ISBN 0-201-63456-2 ISBN 0-201-70433-1 ISBN 0-201-31005-8 ISBN 0-201-79168-4 ISBN 0-201-70393-9 ISBN 0-201-48558-3

ISBN 0-201-74622-0 ISBN 0-201-75280-8 ISBN 0-201-76810-0 ISBN 0-201-31002-3 ISBN 0-201-31003-1 ISBN 0-201-48552-4

ISBN 0-201-71102-8 ISBN 0-201-70329-7 ISBN 0-201-30955-6 ISBN 0-201-31008-2 ISBN 0-201-78472-6 ISBN 0-201-78791-1

ISBN 0-201-31009-0 ISBN 0-201-70502-8 ISBN 0-201-32577-2 ISBN 0-201-43294-3 ISBN 0-201-91466-2 ISBN 0-321-19801-8

ISBN 0-201-74627-1 ISBN 0-201-70456-0 ISBN 0-201-77580-8 ISBN 0-201-78790-3 ISBN 0-201-71041-2

ISBN 0-201-77582-4 ISBN 0-201-43321-4 ISBN 0-201-43328-1 ISBN 0-201-70969-4 ISBN 0-321-17384-8

Visit http://www.awprofessional.com/javaseries for more information on these titles.

inform**IT**

YOUR GUIDE TO IT REFERENCE

Articles

Keep your edge with thousands of free articles, in-depth features, interviews, and IT reference recommendations – all written by experts you know and trust.

Online Books

Answers in an instant from **InformIT Online Book's** 600+ fully searchable on line books. For a limited time, you can get your first 14 days **free**.

POWERED BY
Safari®
TECH BOOKS ONLINE®

Catalog

Review online sample chapters, author biographies and customer rankings and choose exactly the right book from a selection of over 5,000 titles.